Alan S. Golub and
Judith Samson

SAMS Teach Yourself
WordPerfect® Office 2000 for Linux® in 24 Hours

SAMS

A Division of Macmillan USA
201 West 103rd St., Indianapolis, Indiana, 46290 USA

Sams Teach Yourself WordPerfect® Office 2000 for Linux® in 24 Hours

Copyright © 2000 by Sams Publishing

All rights reserved. No part of this book shall be reproduced, stored in a retrieval system, or transmitted by any means, electronic, mechanical, photocopying, recording, or otherwise, without written permission from the publisher. No patent liability is assumed with respect to the use of the information contained herein. Although every precaution has been taken in the preparation of this book, the publisher and authors assume no responsibility for errors or omissions. Nor is any liability assumed for damages resulting from the use of the information contained herein.

International Standard Book Number: 0-672-31911-X

Library of Congress Catalog Card Number: 00-102114

Printed in the United States of America

First Printing: August 2000

03 02 01 00   4 3 2 1

Trademarks

All terms mentioned in this book that are known to be trademarks or service marks have been appropriately capitalized. Sams Publishing cannot attest to the accuracy of this information. Use of a term in this book should not be regarded as affecting the validity of any trademark or service mark.

WordPerfect is a registered trademark of Corel Corporation.

Linux is a registered trademark of Linus Torvalds.

Warning and Disclaimer

Every effort has been made to make this book as complete and as accurate as possible, but no warranty or fitness is implied. The information provided is on an "as is" basis. The authors and the publisher shall have neither liability nor responsibility to any person or entity with respect to any loss or damages arising from the information contained in this book or from the use of programs accompanying it.

ACQUISITIONS EDITOR
Betsy Brown

DEVELOPMENT EDITOR
Laura N. Williams

MANAGING EDITOR
Charlotte Clapp

PROJECT EDITOR
Elizabeth Finney

COPY EDITOR
Bart Reed

INDEXER
Greg Pearson

PROOFREADER
Maryann Steinhart

TECHNICAL EDITOR
Kevin MacPherson

TEAM COORDINATOR
Amy Patton

INTERIOR DESIGNER
Gary Adair

COVER DESIGNER
Aren Howell

PRODUCTION
Tim Osborn
Gloria Schurick

Contents at a Glance

	Introduction	1

Part I Introducing WordPerfect Office 2000 for Linux — 7

Hour		
1	Exploring WordPerfect Office 2000 for Linux	9
2	Introducing the WordPerfect Office 2000 for Linux Environment	27
3	Common Tasks in WordPerfect Office 2000 for Linux	49

Part II Word Processing with WordPerfect 9 — 73

Hour		
4	WordPerfect 9 Basics	75
5	Formatting WordPerfect 9 Documents	93
6	The WordPerfect 9 Writer's Toolkit	111
7	Working with Tables and Columns	129
8	Creating and Working with Graphics in WordPerfect 9	147
9	Advanced WordPerfect 9 Techniques	169

Part III Creating Spreadsheets with Quattro Pro 9 — 191

Hour		
10	Quattro Pro 9 Basics	193
11	Creating Your First Spreadsheet	211
12	Updating and Printing Your Spreadsheet	231
13	Advanced Spreadsheet Design	251

Part IV Express Yourself with Corel Presentations 9 — 275

Hour		
14	Corel Presentations 9 Basics	277
15	Creating Your First Slideshow	297
16	Advanced Presentations	315

Part V Managing Your Life with CorelCENTRAL 9 — 335

Hour		
17	Getting Organized with CorelCENTRAL 9	337
18	Managing Contacts with CorelCENTRAL 9 Address Book	353

Part VI Creating Databases with Paradox 9 — **367**

Hour 19	Paradox 9 Database Basics	369
20	Creating Your First Database	385
21	Managing Paradox 9 Data	405
22	Advanced Paradox 9 Techniques	419

Part VII WordPerfect Office 2000 for Linux Web Tools — **437**

Hour 23	WordPerfect 9 and the Web	439
24	Web Integration in Other WordPerfect Office Applications	455

Appendixes — **469**

A	Introducing Corel Linux OS	471
B	Answers to Quiz Questions	479
	Index	501

Contents

Introduction	**1**
Part I Introducing WordPerfect Office 2000 for Linux	**7**
Hour 1 Exploring WordPerfect Office 2000 for Linux	**9**
The Excitement Behind Corel, Linux, and WordPerfect Office 2000	10
What's In The Box?	12
WordPerfect 9 at a Glance	12
Quattro Pro 9 at a Glance	13
Presentations 9 at a Glance	13
CorelCENTRAL 9 at a Glance	15
Paradox 9 at a Glance	15
Integration Among WordPerfect Office 2000 Applications	16
For Users of WordPerfect 8 for Linux	18
Out with the Bad, in with the Good!	20
For Users of WordPerfect Suite for Windows	22
Summary	23
Q&A	24
Workshop	25
Hour 2 Introducing the WordPerfect Office 2000 for Linux Environment	**27**
Installing WordPerfect Office 2000 for Linux	28
Starting and Quitting Applications	29
Launching Programs from the Corel Application Starter	29
Launching Applications Using the Run Command	30
Creating a Shortcut on the Desktop	32
Quitting Applications	33
Welcome to the WordPerfect Office 2000 Workspace	34
Working with Menus	34
WordPerfect Office 2000 Toolbars	36
The Context-Sensitive Property Bar	40
Using the Application Bar to Manage Your Workspace	41
Customizing the Application Bar	41
Finding Help When You Need It	41
Netscape Navigator Help	41
PerfectExpert Help	43
Summary	47
Q&A	47
Workshop	47
Quiz	48
Exercises	48

Hour 3	Common Tasks in WordPerfect Office 2000 for Linux	49
	Managing Files Within the Linux File System	50
	Creating a New Document	52
	Saving Your Documents	52
	What's in a Name?	52
	To Err Is Human, To Save Divine	53
	Opening an Existing Document	54
	Importing a File	55
	Working with Other Drives and Partitions	55
	Entering Text and Data	58
	Selecting Items with the Mouse and Keyboard	58
	Moving Things Around	59
	With Drag and Drop	59
	With Cut and Paste	60
	With Copy and Paste	61
	Undo and Redo	61
	Zoom	63
	Navigating with the Scrollbars	64
	Printing Documents	66
	Adding a Printer	67
	Print Settings	68
	Print Preview	70
	Summary	70
	Q&A	70
	Workshop	71
	Quiz	71
	Exercises	71

Part II Word Processing with WordPerfect 9   73

Hour 4	WordPerfect 9 Basics	75
	Introducing the WordPerfect 9 Workspace	76
	WordPerfect 9 Customization Tools: The View Menu and the Settings Dialog Box	76
	Changing the Document View	78
	Changing the Bar View	78
	Clicking and Typing with the Shadow Cursor	79
	Using the Show Paragraphs View	80
	Understanding Reveal Codes	81
	Using Reveal Codes	84
	Showing Hidden Text	84
	Customizing Menu Settings	85

Customizing File Settings	87
Customizing Toolbars	89
Summary	91
Q&A	91
Workshop	92
Quiz	92
Exercises	92

Hour 5 Formatting WordPerfect 9 Documents — 93

Working with Fonts in WordPerfect 9	94
Managing Fonts Using the Property Bar	94
Managing Fonts Using the Font Properties Dialog Box	96
Installing Fonts with BitStream FontTastic Font Installer	99
Formatting Paragraphs	100
Line Spacing in WordPerfect	100
Setting Tabs and Indents	101
Setting Page Margins	104
Setting Paragraph Justification	106
Creating and Working with Styles	107
Summary	109
Q&A	109
Workshop	110
Quiz	110
Exercises	110

Hour 6 The WordPerfect 9 Writer's Toolkit — 111

Correcting Text with WordPerfect 9's Spelling and Grammar Tools	112
Spelling Tools	112
Grammar Tools	115
Finding the Perfect Word with the WordPerfect Thesaurus	116
Inserting Special Text	117
Using Comments for Follow-up and Collaboration	119
Outlining a Document	121
Navigating Long Documents	123
Cruising with AutoScroll	124
The Browse Forward and Back Buttons	124
The QuickFind Buttons	125
Summary	125
Q&A	126
Workshop	126
Quiz	126
Exercises	127

Hour 7 Working with Tables and Columns 129

What's the Difference Between a Table and a Column? 130
Creating a Table 131
    The Table QuickCreate Button 131
    The Create Table Dialog Box 132
Mastering Cell Selection..132
Inputting Table Data 134
Performing Calculations in Tables 134
    QuickSumming Columns and Rows 134
Formatting Tables 136
Creating a Table Header 137
    Inserting Rows and Columns 138
    Deleting Rows, Columns, and Cell Contents 139
    Deleting Tables 139
Working with Columns..140
    Creating Columns 140
    Exploring the Columns Dialog Box 141
    Getting Around in Columns 142
    Formatting Columns 143
    Deleting Columns 143
Summary 144
Q&A 144
Workshop 144
    Quiz 144
    Exercises 145

Hour 8 Creating and Working with Graphics in WordPerfect 9 147

Inserting Graphics into a Document..148
    Inserting Graphics from the Scrapbook 149
    Managing Graphics within the Scrapbook 151
    Inserting Graphics from a File Location 154
Editing Graphics in WordPerfect 9..154
    Repositioning Graphics 157
    Editing with Image Tools 158
    Grouping and Layering Graphics 163
    Graphics Controls on the Property Bar 164
Summary 166
Q&A 166
Workshop 167
    Quiz 167
    Exercises 167

Hour 9 Advanced WordPerfect 9 Techniques   169

What Are Macros? 169
   Macros Provided by Corel..170
   Adding a Macro to the Toolbar 171
   Recording a New Macro 173
   Editing Macros 176
What Is a Merge? 177
   The First Step in Creating Merge Documents: Building the Data Source 177
   The Second Step: Creating the Form File......................................182
   Performing a Merge..186
   Performing an Envelope Merge..186
Summary 188
Q&A 189
Workshop 190
   Quiz 190
   Exercises 190

Part III Creating Spreadsheets with Quattro Pro 9   191

Hour 10 Quattro Pro 9 Basics   193

What Is a Spreadsheet?..194
   The Notebook Concept 194
   Spreadsheets Within a Notebook..195
   Working with Spreadsheet Data 196
Introducing the Quattro Pro 9 Workspace 198
   Columns, Rows, and Cell Addresses..200
   The Cell Selector 200
   The Sheet Tabs 201
   Using the Input Line 201
   The Quattro Pro Property and Application Bars: What's Different? 202
Customizing Quattro Pro 9 203
   Object View 203
   Show/Hide Formulas 203
   Changing Display Settings 203
   Understanding Format Options 204
Navigating Through Notebooks and Spreadsheets......................................204
   Activating Cells, Rows, Columns, and Blocks 204
   Quattro Pro 9 Keyboard Shortcuts 206
   Other Quattro Pro 9 Navigation Tools 206
Summary 208
Q&A 208
Workshop 208
   Quiz 209
   Exercises 209

Hour 11 Creating Your First Spreadsheet   211

Creating Simple Spreadsheets with Quattro Pro 9 212
    Step One: Identifying the Purpose of the Spreadsheet 212
    Step Two: Collecting Your Data 213
    Step Three: Plugging It In 213
    Step Four: Working with Formulas 216
    Step Five: Formatting Your Spreadsheet 225
Summary 228
Q&A 228
Workshop 229
    Quiz 229
    Exercises 230

Hour 12 Updating and Printing Your Spreadsheet   231

Updating Your Spreadsheet 232
Editing the Cells in a Spreadsheet 232
    Replacing the Contents of a Cell 233
    Deleting the Contents of a Cell 234
    Clearing a Cell of All Formatting 235
    Clearing Both Contents and Formatting 236
    Deleting Cells 237
    Inserting Cells 238
    Transposing Cell Contents 241
    Resizing Columns 241
Printing Your Work 242
    The Print Spreadsheet Dialog Box 242
    Print Preview 247
Summary 248
Q&A 248
Workshop 249
    Quiz 249
    Exercises 250

Hour 13 Advanced Spreadsheet Design   251

Overview of Advanced Formatting Techniques 251
    Working With PerfectExpert Projects 252
    Working in Styles 255
    Rolling Over with QuickFormat 258
    SpeedFormatting in a Single Bound 259
    Using Lines and Borders 261
    Working in Color 263
    Inserting Headers and Footers 264

Enhancing Your Spreadsheet with Charts	266
Creating a Chart	266
Positioning and Sizing Your Chart	270
Editing Charts	271
Summary	273
Q&A	273
Workshop	274
Quiz	274
Exercises	274

Part IV Express Yourself with Corel Presentations 9   275

Hour 14 Corel Presentations 9 Basics   277

What Is Presentations 9?	278
Starting Presentations	278
Exploring the Presentations 9 Environment	280
The Menus and Toolbars	281
The Drawing Window	281
PerfectExpert	282
Starting a Presentations Project	282
Slide Projects	283
Using the Master Gallery	284
Understanding Slide Layers	285
Slide Layer	285
Layout Layer	285
Background Layer	287
Slide Objects	287
Text Objects	287
Data Charts	288
Organizational Charts	289
Graphics	289
Slide Editing Views	290
Slide Outliner	290
Slide Editor	291
Slide Sorter	292
QuickPlay	292
Summary	294
Q&A	294
Workshop	295
Quiz	295
Exercises	295

Hour 15 Creating Your First Slideshow	**297**
Step One: Outlining Your Slideshow	298
Using the Slide Outliner	298
Choosing Titles, Subtitles, and Text	299
Adding and Deleting Slides	299
The Context-Sensitive PerfectExpert	300
Navigating the PerfectExpert Menus	301
Working with the Tools Palette	302
Step Two: Building Your Slides Using Slide Editor	302
Adding and Changing Text	303
Adding Graphics	303
Adding Speaker Notes and Audience Notes	304
Rearranging the Slides in Slide Sorter	305
Step Three: Adding Presentation Effects	306
Spicing Up Your Slideshow with Transitions	306
Controlling How the Slide Is Displayed with Display Sequence	307
Controlling Animation with SpeedKeys	307
Adding Sound to Your Slideshow	309
Step Four: Customizing and Playing the Slideshow	310
Customizing Slideshows	310
Packing It Up with Show on the Go	311
Publishing the Slideshow As an HTML File	312
Publishing the Slideshow in PDF Format	312
Saving Slideshows As Graphics	312
Summary	313
Q&A	313
Workshop	313
Quiz	313
Exercises	314
Hour 16 Advanced Presentations	**315**
Working with Data Charts	316
The Data Chart Gallery	317
Entering Data in Your Chart	318
Modifying the Layout	320
Keeping Things Crystal Clear with Titles, Legends, and Labels	321
Saving the Data Chart	322
Working with Organization Charts	323
Creating an Organization Chart	323
Incorporating Images into Your Presentations	325
Using Lines and Shapes	325
Using Colors, Patterns, and Textures	327

Applying Special Effects	328
Editing Images in Bitmap Editor	330
Cropping Images	330
Resizing, Rotating, and Skewing an Image	331
Summary	332
Q&A	333
Workshop	333
Quiz	333
Exercises	334

Part V Managing Your Life with CorelCENTRAL 9 — 335

Hour 17 Getting Organized with CorelCENTRAL 9 — 337

Working with CorelCENTRAL 9 Calendar	338
Scheduling Events	340
Repeating and All-Day Events	341
Editing and Deleting an Event	343
Using the Task Feature to Create a To-Do List	344
Adding Subtasks	345
Editing a Task	346
Locating Records in Your CorelCENTRAL 9 Calendar	346
Using Find to Search Your Calendar	347
Using Filters to Sort Your Event List	347
Linking Events and Tasks	348
Editing and Deleting Links	349
Summary	350
Q&A	350
Workshop	350
Quiz	350
Exercises	351

Hour 18 Managing Contacts with CorelCENTRAL 9 Address Book — 353

Working with the CorelCENTRAL 9 Address Book	354
Starting the CorelCENTRAL 9 Address Book	354
The CorelCENTRAL 9 Address Book Interface	355
Adding a New Address and Editing Addresses	356
Editing Address Information	357
Customizing Address Fields	357
Adding a New Address Book	358
Importing and Exporting Addresses	358
Using the Find Feature to Search Your Contacts	360
Using Filters to Sort Your Contacts	361
Summary	364
Q&A	364

Workshop	364
Quiz	365
Exercises	365

Part VI Creating Databases with Paradox 9   367

Hour 19 Paradox 9 Database Basics   369

What Is a Database?	370
Welcome to Paradox	372
Paradox 9 Database Objects	372
Exploring the Paradox 9 Interface	375
The Welcome Screen	375
The Paradox 9 Desktop	377
PerfectExpert	377
Project Viewer	378
Setting the Working Directory	378
Using the Private Directory	379
Setting Preferences	380
Setting Aliases	380
Summary	382
Q&A	382
Workshop	383
Quiz	383
Exercises	383

Hour 20 Creating Your First Database   385

Instant Databases with the Paradox 9 Experts	386
Working from Database Templates	386
Using the Paradox Experts	387
Building a Database from the Ground Up with Tables	388
Creating Tables the Easy Way with the Table Expert	388
Creating Tables from Scratch with the Field Roster	389
Field Types	390
Designating a Primary Key Field	391
Validity Checks	392
Creating a Picture	393
Editing Your Table	394
Creating a Secondary Index	395
Creating and Using Table Lookups	396
Setting Passwords	398
Ensuring Referential Integrity	399
The Visual Database Designer	400

Summary 401
Q&A 402
Workshop 402
    Quiz 402
    Exercises 402

Hour 21 Managing Paradox 9 Data   405

A Table with a View 406
    Using the Table View 406
    Navigating in Your Table 407
Adding and Deleting Data 408
Editing Data 409
    Using Field View and Persistent Field View 410
Inserting Memos and Graphics 410
Locating Data 412
    Using Wildcard Symbols 415
Sorting Data 415
Summary 417
Q&A 417
Workshop 417
    Quiz 417
    Exercises 418

Hour 22 Advanced Paradox 9 Techniques   419

Creating and Using Forms 420
    Quick Form 421
    Building Forms with the Form Expert 422
    Two-Table Forms 423
Fine-Tuning the Design of Your Forms in the Design Window 426
    Adding Design Objects in the Design Window 427
Delivering Your Form to End Users 429
    Viewing Data and Entering Data into the Form 429
    Printing the Form 430
Presenting Your Data in Reports 430
    Instant Reports with Quick Report 430
Retrieving Information with Queries 432
Summary 434
Q&A 434
Workshop 434
    Quiz 434
    Exercises 435

Part VII WordPerfect Office 2000 for Linux Web Tools   437

Hour 23 WordPerfect 9 and the Web   439

Introducing the WordPerfect 9 Internet Tools 440
    Formatting Existing Documents for the Web 441
    Using the Web Editor 442
Creating a Basic Web Page with WordPerfect 9 442
    Creating a New Web Document 443
    Setting the Properties for Your Web Page 443
    Working with Hyperlinks 446
    Adding Bookmarks 446
    Inserting Graphics in Your Web Page 447
    Inserting a Table in Your Web Page...448
    Creating a Form...449
    Publishing Documents to the Internet or an Intranet 450
Bringing the Web into Your WordPerfect Documents with SpeedLinks 451
Summary 452
Q&A 452
Workshop 452
    Quiz 453
    Exercises 453

Hour 24 Web Integration in Other WordPerfect Office Applications   455

Publishing Quattro Pro 9 Notebooks to HTML 456
    Working with Hyperlinks in Quattro Pro 9 Notebooks 457
Publishing Presentations 9 Slideshows to the Web with Internet Publisher 458
Publishing CorelCENTRAL 9 Calendars to HTML 462
Publishing Paradox 9 Databases to HTML 464
    The HTML Report Expert and HTML Table Expert 464
    Inserting Hyperlinks into a Paradox Database 466
    Importing HTML Tables and Spreadsheets into Paradox 9 Databases..........466
Summary 467
Q&A 467
Workshop 467
    Quiz 467
    Exercises 468

Appendixes   469

Appendix A Introducing Corel Linux OS   471

Starting Corel Linux and Logging In 472
Welcome to the Corel Linux Desktop 473
Introducing Corel Linux "Windows" 475

Customizing the Desktop from the Control Center 476
Finding Help when You Need It 477
System Updates for Corel Linux 477
Summary 478

Appendix B Answers to Quiz Questions   **479**

Answers for Hour 2 479
   Quiz 479
   Exercises 479
Answers for Hour 3 480
   Quiz 480
   Exercises 480
Answers for Hour 4 481
   Quiz 481
   Exercises 481
Answers for Hour 5 482
   Quiz 482
   Exercises 482
Answers for Hour 6 483
   Quiz 483
   Exercises 483
Answers for Hour 7 483
   Quiz 483
   Exercises 483
Answers for Hour 8 484
   Quiz 484
   Exercises 484
Answers for Hour 9 485
   Quiz 485
   Exercises 485
Answers for Hour 10 486
   Quiz 486
   Exercises 486
Answers for Hour 11 486
   Quiz 486
   Exercises 487
Answers for Hour 12 488
   Quiz 488
   Exercises 488
Answers for Hour 13 489
   Quiz 489
   Exercises 489

Answers for Hour 14 489
    Quiz 489
    Exercises 490
Answers for Hour 15 490
    Quiz 490
    Exercises 491
Answers for Hour 16 492
    Quiz 492
    Exercises 492
Answers for Hour 17 493
    Quiz 493
    Exercises 493
Answers for Hour 18 494
    Quiz 494
    Exercises 494
Answers for Hour 19 495
    Quiz 495
    Exercises 495
Answers for Hour 20 496
    Quiz 496
    Exercises 496
Answers for Hour 21 497
    Quiz 497
    Exercises 497
Answers for Hour 22 498
    Quiz 498
    Exercises 498
Answers for Hour 23 499
    Quiz 499
    Exercises 499
Answers for Hour 24 499
    Quiz 499
    Exercises 500

Index   **501**

About the Authors

Alan S. Golub is a partner in the Totowa, New Jersey, law firm of Dwyer, Kinburn, Hall & Golub. In addition to his full-time duties as a litigation partner, for the past four years he has served as the firm's System Administrator, overseeing a sophisticated computer network of machines running Linux, Mac OS, and several flavors of Windows. He has written numerous legal and technical articles for publication and currently writes the "Macs To Go" back-page column for *MacHome* magazine. Golub has been using WordPerfect since the days of DOS and has served as a beta tester in the development of WordPerfect Office 2000 for Linux.

Judith Samson is the author of *Sams Teach Yourself GNOME in 24 Hours* as well as a writer for *TechRepublic* and *Linux Application Developer*. She is pursuing graduate studies in mathematics and artificial intelligence at Eastern Michigan University. In her spare time she writes for the GNOME Documentation Project and dreams up evil Linux graphic applications. Send email to judith@samsonsource.com or visit http://www.samsonsource.com.

Dedication

To Jennifer, of course, whose love, encouragement, and support made this book possible. There's nothing like marrying your best friend....

And to our daughter, Emily, whose first lesson in life was one of patience, waiting for dad to finish this book.

—Alan Golub

To Alain

—Judith Samson

Acknowledgments

Writing a book about an entire office suite is more work than I ever imagined. Without the help of many people, projects like this would never get off the ground.

First, thanks go to the crackerjack editors at Macmillan—Elizabeth Finney, Laura Williams, Bart Reed, and Kevin MacPherson. I am truly honored to have worked with such a talented team—this book would have been only half as good without you. Special thanks to my acquisitions editor, Betsy Brown, who brought me into the Macmillan family—what a thrill to be given the chance to work with the best my first time out!

I applaud the ingenious folks at Corel for their commitment to the Linux platform and their top of the line, award-winning products. It was a pleasure serving on the beta team for WordPerfect Office 2000 for Linux, and I can't wait to see what you come up with next!

I am indebted to the law firm of Dwyer, Kinburn, Hall & Golub, where I am lucky enough to hang my hat every day. Special thanks to my partners, Terrence Dwyer, Daniel Kinburn, and Susan Hall, who understood the importance of this project and gave me room to run with it. I am blessed to be among you as a partner and a friend.

I would still be on page 250 without the help of my co-author, Judith Samson, who stepped in at the eleventh hour to save the day. A million thanks for your excellent contributions throughout, Judith. When can you autograph my copy of *Sams Teach Yourself GNOME in 24 Hours*?

A note of thanks to Paul F. Campano, Esq., who taught me a "couple-a-three" things about Quattro Pro 9. Paul laid the groundwork for the hours dedicated to Corel's awesome spreadsheet application and came up with the idea of incorporating *Fundamentally Yours, Inc.* into the material. Thanks for your time and talent, Paul!

Finally, a special acknowledgment to my wife, Jennifer, and my daughter, Emily. Your love makes me a better husband, father, lawyer, and writer, each and every day.

—Alan Golub

Thanks to Laura Williams, truly the world's best development editor; Betsy Brown, the amazing and resilient acquisitions editor; Elizabeth Finney for being a wonderful project editor; and Bart Reed for his copyediting. Thanks to Chip Maxwell at Corel for his cheerful emails and enthusiasm (not to mention software). Thanks also to everyone on the Corel WordPerfect 2000 for Linux newsgroups for your great questions and insights. Thanks to the Corel Corporation for creating such phenomenal applications. Special thanks to Alain for all the input on Web design and HTML coding for Hours 23 and 24, as well as doing far more than your share of housework!

—Judith Samson

Tell Us What You Think!

As the reader of this book, *you* are our most important critic and commentator. We value your opinion and want to know what we're doing right, what we could do better, what areas you'd like to see us publish in, and any other words of wisdom you're willing to pass our way.

Please note that I cannot help you with technical problems related to the topic of this book, and that due to the high volume of mail I receive, I might not be able to reply to every message.

When you write, please be sure to include this book's title and authors as well as your name and phone or fax number. I will carefully review your comments and share them with the authors and editors who worked on the book.

Fax:	317-581-4770
Email:	office_sams@mcp.com
Mail:	Mark Taber
	Associate Publisher
	Sams Publishing
	201 West 103rd Street
	Indianapolis, IN 46290 US

Introduction

Welcome to *Sams Teach Yourself WordPerfect Office 2000 for Linux in 24 Hours*!

Thanks so much for buying this book—writing it has been a true labor of love for me. I have been living with Linux as my primary operating system for several years now, and I've never been more excited about all that the platform has to offer. Today, with its ease of installation, compatibility with the majority of Intel-based PC hardware, and available technical support from a wide variety of vendors and a literal army of thousands of Linux users online, Linux is the hottest thing to happen to personal computing in years!

And it's only going to get better. With the release of WordPerfect Office 2000 for Linux, Corel has given the Linux community the gift of a world-class, full-featured office suite for Linux. With sophisticated word processing, spreadsheet, presentation, database, calendaring, contact management, and Internet tools, as well as unprecedented compatibility with office suites running on other platforms, Corel has single-handedly bridged the gap between hardcore Linux users and the rest of us. This book is the only guide you need to walk that bridge with confidence and see for yourself what all the Linux fuss is about.

Who Should Buy This Book

Writing a book about the most powerful application currently available for Linux is a tricky business. Unlike books about office suites for Windows, it's not necessarily fair to assume that the reader knows enough about Linux to follow along. Therefore, some basic coverage of the underlying operating system (OS) is probably time well spent.

On the other hand, most experienced Linux users have neither the time nor the tolerance to suffer through a brief history of Linux or an explanation of how it works and why it is in many ways just plain better than anything else out there. These readers understandably want to get straight to work and won't go for much extra chitchat.

I have therefore made every effort to cater to the broadest possible audience in writing, organizing, and presenting the material in this book. When I tell you that this is a book for Linux users of all levels, I mean it—whether you are just starting to explore the wonderful world of Linux or have been at it for years, this book contains what you need to know to quickly and easily use WordPerfect Office 2000 on the Linux platform.

For Beginners

Beginners who are still learning Linux, and even those just thinking about taking it for a spin, get a special bonus. Craftily hidden in the back of the book, you'll find one full hour of extra material to help get you started. In order to stick to the *24 Hour* game plan, I've cleverly called this extra hour an "appendix." Regardless of the name, what you're getting is a one-hour crash course on Linux basics.

In Appendix A, "Introducing Corel Linux OS," new users are treated to an introduction to the Corel Linux OS. If you've never worked with Linux, this walking tour of the Corel Linux interface will help ease your transition from other operating systems, such as Windows 9*x* and Mac OS.

Although there's no substitute for a volume dedicated exclusively to Linux, this bonus section covers the basic material you need to feel comfortable using WordPerfect Office 2000 for Linux for most of the tasks that you now perform on your current operating system of choice.

For Linux Pros

If you're already an old hand at Linux, you're primed to make a beeline for Hour 1's introduction to WordPerfect Office 2000.

Throughout the book, you'll find plenty of useful instructions for using WordPerfect Office 2000 to accomplish most of your everyday business and personal computing tasks. WordPerfect Office 2000 is a big, complicated suite of programs, tools, and resources that at first glance seems overwhelming. The good news is that your mastery of Linux gives you a terrific head start. With your Linux background, and this book as your guide, you'll be up and running with WordPerfect Office 2000 in no time!

Hardware Requirements

One of the amazing things about Linux is that it can run on just about any IBM-compatible computer out there. WordPerfect Office 2000, however, is a mammoth-sized program that demands a little more of your system's resources. Here are the minimum and recommended system requirements for installing WordPerfect Office 2000 (as with everything, however, a faster processor and more RAM can make WordPerfect Office 2000 fly):

- CPU—Any Intel Pentium or compatible processor (100MHz minimum; 200MHz Pentium II or better recommended)
- RAM—16MB minimum; 64MB or better recommended
- Free disk space—375MB minimum; 500MB recommended
- 3.5" floppy disk recommended

- CD-ROM drive
- A supported video card (2MB VRAM minimum; 4MB or better recommended)
- External serial port modem and supported printer recommended

Software

You'll need the latest stable release of the Linux kernel and a copy of WordPerfect Office 2000 for Linux.

As for choosing a Linux distribution, most of the screenshots in this book are based on Corel Linux OS, which is recommended, but not required. If you already have one of the other major distributions of Linux, such as Red Hat or Caldera OpenLinux, you should have no problems following along.

You're also encouraged to install the latest version of the KDE desktop environment, which is the default desktop installed with several major distributions, including Corel Linux OS, Mandrake 7, and Caldera OpenLinux 2.3. Although WordPerfect Office 2000 for Linux will work in the GNOME desktop environment, it will be easier to follow along if you switch to KDE while using this book.

Conventions Used in This Book

Like most computer books, this one relies on icons, symbols, and varied fonts to communicate important information.

The Command Line Interface

Although Linux sports an attractive graphical user interface (GUI) that allows you to point and click with your mouse to get things done, it also utilizes a command line interface that requires you to type in commands that tell your computer what to do. Although the point-and-click technique is fine for most users and most Linux tasks, many users love the power and flexibility of the command line interface and come to depend on it as a powerful tool for managing their Linux PCs.

In order to help you get the most out of your WordPerfect Office 2000 for Linux experience, this book covers certain relevant Linux commands that you'll need to know. Linux commands that you'll need to type into the command line appear throughout the book in a monospaced font, as follows, with the end of line of type signaling you to hit the Enter key:

```
cp /disks/c/My Documents/testmemo /asg/docs/memos
```

If this looks cryptic to you now, don't worry—it won't for long! All I've done here is copy the file `testmemo` from the Windows partition of my computer to a folder on my Linux partition. Although WordPerfect Office 2000 provides an easy point-and-click interface to accomplish the same thing (as you'll see in Hour 3, "Common Tasks in WordPerfect 2000 for Linux"), die-hard Linux-heads often prefer to use the command-line interface for many tasks. Because I aim to please, this book will show you how to do certain things the Linux way (that is, via the command line). Even if you decide that the command line isn't your cup of tea, knowing how it works will give you a greater appreciation and understanding of your Linux system.

Menu Commands

Sometimes there's just no substitute for the good ol' point-and-click approach, and that's where menu commands can be most helpful. When a task requires you to use a menu command, the command will simply list the menu items in the order they appear, separated by a comma. For example, instructions for executing the Print command from the File menu look like this: File, Print.

Shortcut Keys

Shortcut keys can be the fastest way to get something done. For example, instead of using the command line or a menu command to print an open document in WordPerfect Office 2000, you could simply hold down the Ctrl key, press the P key, and then simultaneously release both keys. Throughout the book, I indicate such keyboard shortcuts by listing the keys in the order in which they are to be pressed, separated by a plus (+) sign. Therefore, the print shortcut keys would appear as this: Ctrl+P. Remember that this means you must hold down the first key, press the second key, and then release both keys at the same time.

Notes, Tips, and Cautions

The following special elements set off different types of informantion. Their icons make them easily recognizable.

> Notes are designed to provide you with relevant information that's hopefully interesting, but not necessarily crucial, to your understanding of the topic at hand. If you're pressed for time to get through a lesson, feel free to skip the notes—you can always come back to them later.

I wouldn't be introducing you to the wonderful world of Linux without including Linux-specific tips to maximize your use of WordPerfect Office 2000. Whenever you see the Tip icon in the margins of this book, get ready for a pointer or two that will help you take advantage of features that are unique to the Linux version of WordPerfect Office 2000.

Cautions warn you about pitfalls. Although Linux has certainly come a long way, it is still a few notches below Windows and Mac OS on the user-friendly scale. Similarly, WordPerfect Office 2000 is a complex and sophisticated suite of programs that may be a little intimidating to the uninitiated. Combined, the two may cause even the most adventurous souls to give pause.

Fortunately, this book includes sections to highlight these rough areas, providing concentrated instruction to get you over these hurdles quickly and with confidence. Whenever you see the Caution icon, read it carefully to avoid common pitfalls that have plagued users in the past. Although you'll no doubt quickly get used to the WordPerfect Office 2000 for Linux way of doing things, a little bit of caution at this stage may save you a great deal of time and frustration down the road.

By now I'm sure you're ready to dive right into the main attraction, so let's do it! Hour 1, "Exploring WordPerfect Office 2000 for Linux," provides an overview of the massive tools Corel has crammed into WordPerfect Office 2000 for Linux and describes some of the many tasks they can help you accomplish.

Get ready to be wowed!

PART I

Introducing WordPerfect Office 2000 for Linux

Hour

1 Exploring WordPerfect Office 2000 for Linux

2 Introducing the WordPerfect Office 2000 for Linux Environment

3 Common Tasks in WordPerfect 2000 Office for Linux

Hour 1

Exploring WordPerfect Office 2000 for Linux

WordPerfect Office 2000 for Linux is the most eagerly anticipated software in the history of Linux—and I'm not just saying that to sell books. The truth is, one of the major obstacles to mainstream acceptance of Linux is the lack of popular commercial software for the platform. Users want to be able to buy off-the-shelf versions of the applications they know and love and aren't interested in settling for alternatives they've never heard of, much less used.

For instance, the GIMP is a marvelous image-manipulation program for Linux that does just about everything most consumers should ever need—but if it were called *Adobe Photoshop for Linux*, the GIMP (and Linux) would be running on a heck of a lot more machines.

Slowly but surely, this is changing. In the past year, we've seen Linux versions of some of the most popular software in the world, including everything from Quake II to the latest version of Netscape Communicator. Until now, however, the Linux community has sorely lacked a mainstream office suite comparable to those available for Microsoft Windows.

Enter Corel WordPerfect Office 2000 for Linux. This is not Corel's first foray into the world of Linux; the WordPerfect word processor has been available for Linux since version 7. It is, however, the first time that Corel has expanded its WordPerfect for Linux offering to include the full suite of business applications that Windows users have enjoyed for years. We're not just talking word processing anymore—we're talking spreadsheets, slideshow presentations, Web pages, databases, and more!

In this hour you will

- Discover the applications that comprise WordPerfect Office 2000 for Linux.
- Learn about the new and exciting features in WordPerfect Office 2000 for Linux.
- Examine how WordPerfect Office 2000 for Linux differs from prior versions of WordPerfect products for Linux and Windows.

The Excitement Behind Corel, Linux, and WordPerfect Office 2000

It's an exciting time to get acquainted with Linux. Thanks to Corel, for the first time, Linux users have a competitive, professional set of office tools at their disposal. In the past, Linux users demanding the power of a full-featured office suite had two choices: StarOffice and Applixware. Although both suites have their merits, neither has won over many Windows users, who are understandably reluctant to sacrifice a moment of productivity to experiment with office software they're not familiar with.

WordPerfect Office 2000 for Linux handily addresses this concern. Although the WordPerfect brand has lost ground to Microsoft Office in recent years, it's still one of the world's most popular and easy-to-use office suites. WordPerfect Office 2000 for Linux is an integrated set of software tools designed to help you create professional documents and projects. But ease of use is only part of the picture—WordPerfect Office 2000 is also the most versatile application ever unleashed on the Linux community. Whether you want to draft business letters that sport your company logo or create complex, multimedia slideshow presentations for the Web, you can get the job done quickly and easily with WordPerfect Office 2000 for Linux. There are few documents or formats that this powerhouse suite can't handle.

WordPerfect Office 2000 for Linux also plays nicely with documents created in other suites, regardless of the platform. So, if you currently use Microsoft Office, Lotus Smart Suite, or Corel WordPerfect on another platform, you can make the switch to WordPerfect Office 2000 for Linux without losing any of your work.

But there's even more to it. Corel is in the process of reinventing itself as a giant in the Linux community. Since 1998, the Linux press releases coming out of Corel's headquarters in Ottawa, Canada, have made clear that Linux has a tremendous role in the future of the company. Here are some highlights:

- Back in December 1998, Corel tested the Linux waters by making its WordPerfect 8 for Linux word processor available for users to download, free of charge, from the Internet. The public response was overwhelming, and by May 1999, there had been more than one million attempts to download the software.
- Taking its cue from the success of WordPerfect 8 for Linux, in March 1999, Corel announced plans to release its own distribution of Linux by the end of the year. Corel promised to greatly simplify the Linux installation process and the desktop interface, and to finally bring Linux to the masses. Corel also hinted that it was working on Linux versions of its flagship Windows products—WordPerfect Office 2000 and CorelDRAW 9.
- In November 1999, Corel made good on its promise with the release of the Corel Linux operating system (OS). Touting innovative features such as Corel Install Express (an intuitive, graphical approach to installing Linux), Corel Update (a utility for locating and installing software), and the Corel File Manager (a Windows Explorer–like utility for managing folders and files), the fledgling Linux OS debuted to rave reviews. Corel was instantly recognized as a rising star on the Linux scene and capitalized on this momentum with a series of announcements that solidified Corel's commitment to the platform.
- In early 2000, Corel announced several key partnerships that will play a role in increasing the functionality and flexibility of Corel Linux:
    - Corel announced that it would integrate GraphOn Bridges into its Linux desktop, which will allow Linux users to access and use Windows applications stored on another computer via any type of network connection.
    - Corel partnered up with Macromedia to license the Macromedia Flash Player as part of Corel Linux OS. The Macromedia deal makes Corel Linux the first distribution to bring Flash content to Linux.
- Also in early 2000, Corel previewed its much anticipated powerhouse suites for Linux: WordPerfect Office 2000 and CorelDRAW 9. Anticipation in the Linux community boomed, and perhaps more importantly, even the rest of the world couldn't help but take notice.

By the time you read this, Corel will no doubt have made many more announcements solidifying its position as a major player in the Linux community. At a time when Linux is making headline, technical, and financial news, Corel's whole-hearted embrace of Linux seems perfectly timed to propel the company straight to the top of the Linux food chain.

What's In The Box?

I'm glad you asked. WordPerfect Office 2000 for Linux is available in two versions: Standard and Deluxe. The Standard version includes a full version of the Corel Linux OS and four professional office applications: WordPerfect 9, Quattro Pro 9, Presentations 9, and CorelCENTRAL 9. The Deluxe version includes everything in the Standard version, plus Paradox 9, enhanced technical support, an entertainment pack, and an adorable bean-filled Linux penguin toy.

Regardless of which version you choose, WordPerfect Office 2000 for Linux comes with more exciting features than any other Linux application. This book covers the core applications included in the Deluxe version, including WordPerfect 9, Quattro Pro 9, Presentations 9, CorelCENTRAL 9, and Paradox 9.

Unfortunately, space constraints dictate that I omit coverage of the entertainment pack (and the bean-filled Linux penguin). After all, I've made a promise to get you up and running in just 24 hours!

Let's take a quick look at the applications covered in this book.

WordPerfect 9 at a Glance

At the heart of WordPerfect Office 2000 is version 9 of the WordPerfect word processor. WordPerfect has been around for many years and is justifiably relied upon by millions of users to handle all their document-creation tasks. If you're familiar with prior versions of WordPerfect for Windows, you'll be pleased to know that version 9 for Linux works in much the same way—the changes and improvements are more evolutionary than revolutionary. But the improvements will be instantly noticeable and appreciated—new features such as Real-Time Preview for fonts and text formatting and the new Auto-Scroll button for navigating your documents make it easier than ever to create and edit documents with WordPerfect.

Figure 1.1 shows the WordPerfect 9 workspace. The work in progress is a letter generated with the help of the WordPerfect PerfectExpert, one of many tools that make it easy to create beautiful documents in WordPerfect.

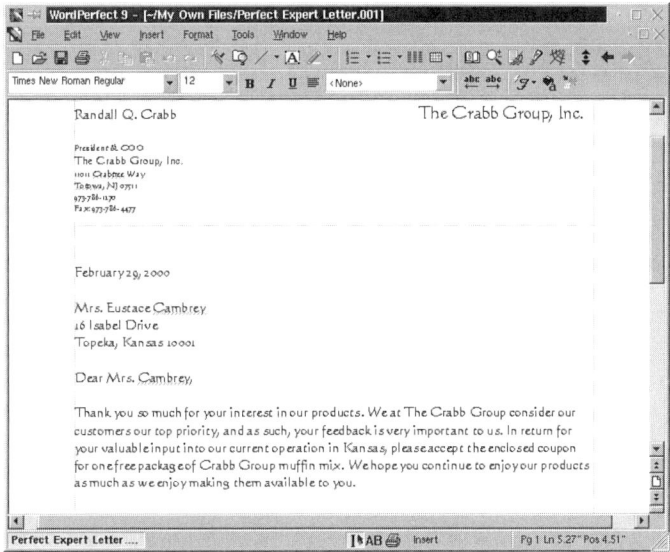

FIGURE 1.1
WordPerfect 9 looks and works similar to version 8.

Quattro Pro 9 at a Glance

Quattro Pro 9 for Linux does spreadsheets as well as any other program on the planet, including the wildly popular Microsoft Excel. You don't have to be a math wizard to appreciate the power and flexibility of Quattro Pro. If you have a project involving numbers and data of any kind, Quattro Pro can help you organize, present, and analyze the information in the form of tables, charts, and reports. Whether you need to keep track of your monthly business expenses or inventory your commemorative plate collection, Quattro Pro 9 can do the job quickly and easily.

Figure 1.2 shows the Quattro Pro 9 workspace. The work in progress is a timesheet created with a few simple mouse clicks from a PerfectExpert Project. A little help is a beautiful thing, and Corel has packed lots of help into Quattro Pro 9. This timesheet project includes sample data provided by Corel, which allows you to preview how the information and data in the timesheet will be processed and presented.

Presentations 9 at a Glance

These days, slideshow presentations are a standard means of conveying information at meetings, seminars, lectures, and even family reunions. Presentations 9 for Linux allows you to create multimedia slideshows, complete with sound clips, graphics, and animation, that can be played on any computer running Linux or Windows (even if Presentations 9 isn't installed on your playback PC). With dozens of tools for creating graphics and special effects, Presentations 9 will help you create compelling slideshows that effectively communicate your message to your audience.

FIGURE 1.2
Quattro Pro 9 includes PerfectExpert Projects that you can customize for your own use.

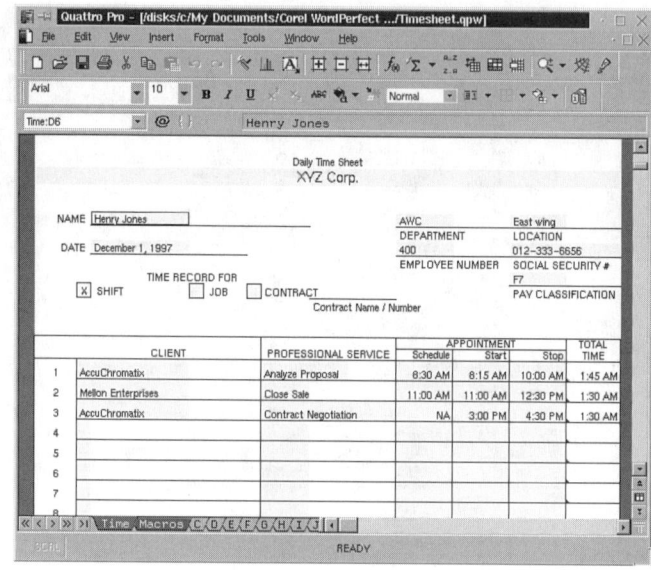

As shown in Figure 1.3, presenting your data in a Presentations 9 slideshow can add pizzazz to even the most boring information.

FIGURE 1.3
Presentations 9 helps you create slideshows and drawings for business and personal use.

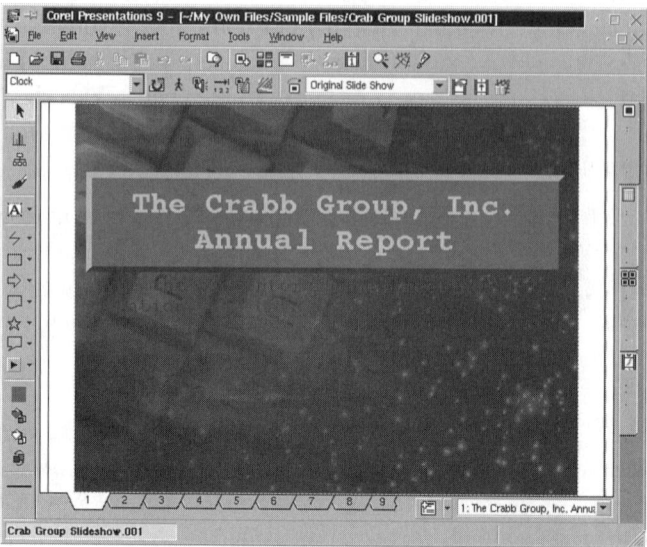

CorelCENTRAL 9 at a Glance

If you've had any experience with the WordPerfect 8 Suite for Windows, you probably know that CorelCENTRAL has always been criticized as the weak link in an otherwise fabulous suite. From its confusing interface to its clumsy integration with Netscape Navigator, CorelCENTRAL truly bombed as a Personal Information Manager (PIM).

Good news! CorelCENTRAL has been completely revamped in version 9 for Linux, with the emphasis on keeping the application exceptionally simple and lightning quick. As shown in Figure 1.4, CorelCENTRAL 9 for Linux helps you keep track of your appointments, contacts, task lists, and other personal information, and it does an excellent job of integrating this information with other applications in the suite. For example, contacts that appear in your CorelCENTRAL Address Book are accessible from WordPerfect, making it super easy to dash out letters and envelopes to the people you most need to stay in touch with.

FIGURE 1.4
CorelCENTRAL 9 makes it easy to keep track of your daily appointments and tasks.

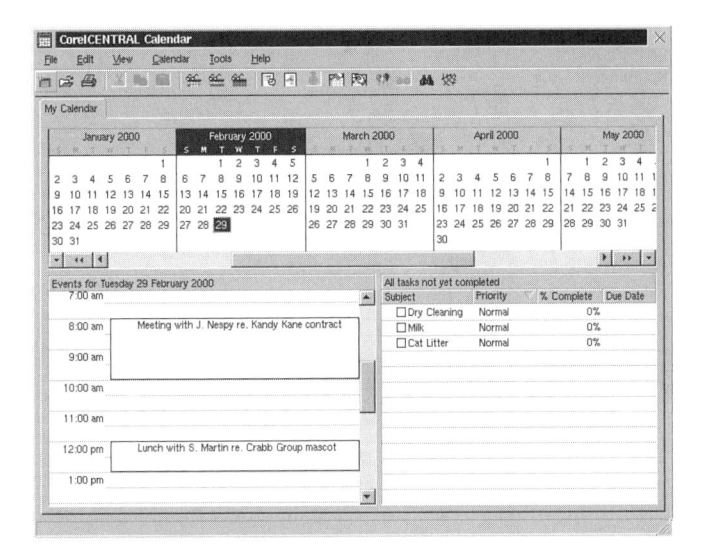

Paradox 9 at a Glance

Although Paradox 9 is included only with the Deluxe version, I'll nevertheless spend a good four hours introducing you to the wonderful world of Paradox 9 database creation and management. Like Quattro Pro, Paradox can help you record, organize, manage, and present any kind of data, including numbers, text, graphics, and even sound clips and animation. Why use Paradox when Quattro Pro will do? Good question. Simply put, Paradox goes much further than Quattro Pro, allowing you to define complex relationships that can be used to create more sophisticated means of recording, retrieving, and presenting your data. With Paradox, you can perform the following tasks:

- Design forms that make it simple for users to add new records to your database
- Restrict the types of data users are allowed to enter, such as dates, social security numbers, and geographic locations
- Create complex queries that allow users to retrieve only certain records from your database
- Design reports that effectively present your data in print or on the Web

Figure 1.5 shows a simple Paradox 9 database created to keep track of a music collection.

FIGURE 1.5
A well-designed Paradox 9 database makes it easy for users to access and modify the records stored in the database.

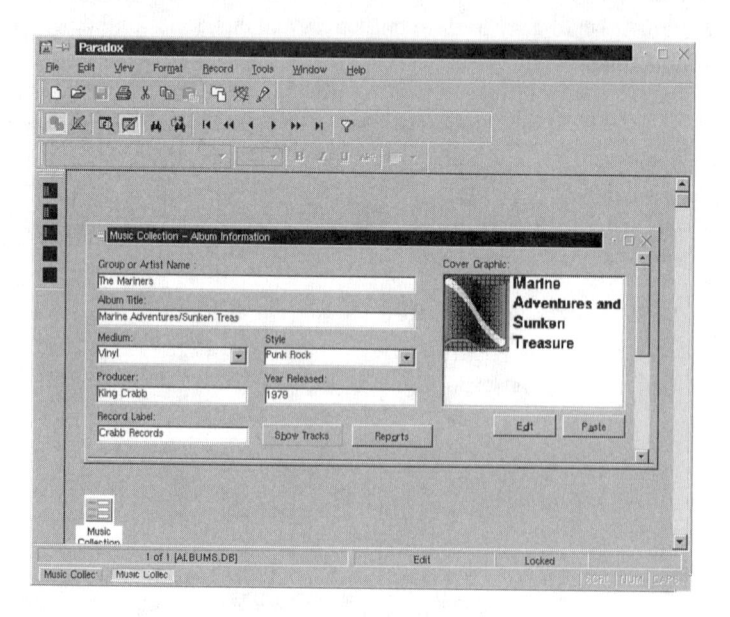

Integration Among WordPerfect Office 2000 Applications

When WordPerfect 7 Suite for Windows was released, it was widely recognized as a powerful set of applications capable of performing just about every type of office task imaginable. It was also criticized as a sprawling, almost random, patchwork of programs that weren't intended to work together. In a failed attempt to get a leg up on the competing Microsoft Office suite, Corel went overboard, cramming version 7 of its flagship

WordPerfect product with no less than 13 applications, only a few of which were truly designed to share information.

With WordPerfect 8 Suite for Windows, Corel wisely trimmed the fat. WordPerfect 8 boasted a new, mostly successful, attempt to "integrate" suite applications. The programs in the suite offered a more consistent interface in the menus and toolbars, and they were able to recognize and share each other's file formats right out of the box.

If WordPerfect 8 came up short, it was due to Corel's first effort to include its own PIM within the suite. With CorelCENTRAL 8, Corel attempted to meld calendar, contact manager, email, and task list functionality with the Internet via a Corel-customized version of Netscape Navigator. From the start, it was clear that Corel had bitten off more than it could chew. CorelCENTRAL was slow, buggy, and confusing. Even a slew of software patches from Corel could not overcome what many viewed as an unnecessarily difficult interface.

What a difference a version number makes! With version 9, the WordPerfect suite has been streamlined to perfection, with integration improvements across the board. Even the name of the new suite suggests Corel's focus on tighter integration: Instead of shipping as the *WordPerfect 9 Suite*, Corel's flagship product was delivered to retailers as *Corel WordPerfect Office 2000*.

Here's a sampling of the improved integration among the WordPerfect Office 2000 applications:

- With the limited exception of CorelCENTRAL, all WordPerfect Office 2000 for Linux applications feature a similar interface. From menus and toolbars, to the Application Bar and navigational scrollbars, the core applications of the suite work amazingly alike, even though they accomplish very different tasks. The bottom line is that it's easier than ever to apply knowledge of one application to any other application in the suite.

- When creating a letter in WordPerfect 9, you can automatically insert contact information from your Address Book in CorelCENTRAL 9.

- You can insert Paradox 9 databases and Quattro Pro 9 spreadsheets directly into your WordPerfect 9 documents, with all original formatting intact. If you subsequently need to change your database record or spreadsheet, no problem—by linking your WordPerfect 9 document to the original source, WordPerfect 9 can automatically update the imported database or spreadsheet, either on command or every time you open the document!

- All WordPerfect Office 2000 applications can import text from WordPerfect 9 documents.

- All WordPerfect Office 2000 applications feature one-click access to Corel's new Office Community Web site for tips, tricks, and freebies from Corel. From new PerfectExpert Projects, to free macros and clip art, Corel on the Web is a terrific source for maximizing your investment in WordPerfect Office 2000 for Linux.
- Macros, long a favorite timesaver for automating frequently performed tasks in WordPerfect, now have cross-application functionality in WordPerfect, Quattro Pro, and Presentations. For example, you can launch a WordPerfect macro from Presentations and drop the result into your slideshow. You can also create a macro in WordPerfect that executes a Quattro Pro formula and insert the result directly into your document.

Trying to explain all the "new" features in WordPerfect Office 2000 for Linux is no easy feat. The problem is that, until now, there has never been a WordPerfect "suite" for Linux. Does this mean that every feature is "new"? In a way, yes. But I'm willing to bet that most of you have some experience with WordPerfect, so brief mention of some of the latest and greatest features included in this new release is time well spent.

For Users of WordPerfect 8 for Linux

If you're already using WordPerfect 8 for Linux, you're in for a few surprises. Corel has seen fit to do away with certain features and functions that may take some getting used to.

Bye, Bye Program Manager

By now you're probably used to working with the Program Manager, shown in Figure 1.6. The Program Manager, also known as the *Program window*, was a powerful tool for managing documents and customizing WordPerfect 8 for Linux. Oddly enough, it was unique to the Linux version of WordPerfect 8—the Windows version had no such component.

FIGURE 1.6

The Program Manager, an integral part of WordPerfect 8 for Linux, is gone in WordPerfect 9.

In the spirit of encouraging users to try Linux, Corel has done everything possible to make WordPerfect Office 2000 for Linux look, work, and act exactly like the Windows version. Like it or not, one of the most noticeable results is that version 8's

Program Manager has fallen by the wayside and its functions have been incorporated directly into the menus available in every open WordPerfect Office 2000 document window.

For example, the most important function of the Program Manager was its Preferences menu, from which you launched the Preferences dialog box to customize WordPerfect 8's default settings. In WordPerfect 9, the same feature has been renamed *Settings* and is launched by clicking Tools, Settings from the menu. Figure 1.7 shows a side-by-side comparison of WordPerfect 8's Preferences dialog box and WordPerfect 9's Settings dialog box.

FIGURE 1.7
The Settings dialog box in WordPerfect 9 serves the same purpose as the Preferences dialog box in WordPerfect 8.

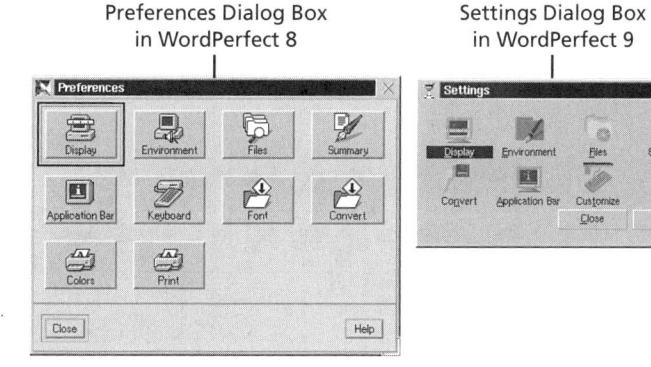

Personally, I think the elimination of the Program Manager is a good thing. Not only did it hog up precious screen real estate, but it made WordPerfect 8 unnecessarily confusing. Integrating the Program Manager's functions directly into WordPerfect 9's document windows not only brings the program more into line with the Windows version, it makes for a cleaner, more intuitive interface.

Ciao, WordPerfect Draw

Probably less noticeable to WordPerfect 8 for Linux users will be the elimination of WordPerfect Draw. Like the Program Manager, WordPerfect Draw was unique to the Linux version of WordPerfect 8. As shown in Figure 1.8, WordPerfect Draw was really a separate program that allowed users to create simple graphics to incorporate into WordPerfect documents.

Admittedly, WordPerfect Draw was a neat tool, the full features of which have not been incorporated in WordPerfect Office 2000 for Linux. Instead, the new suite includes enhanced Graphics toolbars that are available in WordPerfect 9 and Presentations 9, both shown in Figure 1.9.

FIGURE 1.8
WordPerfect Draw, a separate application included in WordPerfect 8 for Linux, has been eliminated in version 9.

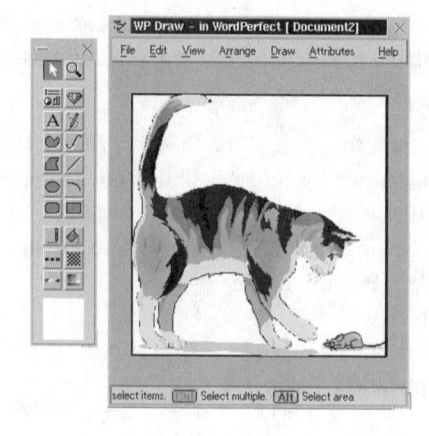

FIGURE 1.9
WordPerfect Office Suite includes enhanced Graphics toolbars.

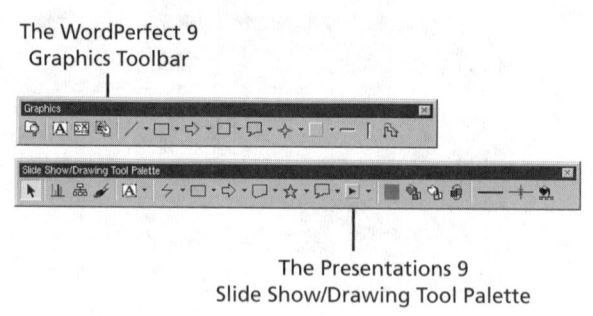

The WordPerfect 9 Graphics Toolbar

The Presentations 9 Slide Show/Drawing Tool Palette

Out with the Bad, in with the Good!

Remember, WordPerfect 8 for Linux was simply a word processor—WordPerfect Office 2000 for Linux is an entire suite of office applications! Sheer volume and utility alone are worth the price of upgrading to the latest release. Nevertheless, Corel has taken no chances and has packed its office suite with dozens of new and improved features that make WordPerfect Office 2000 the most powerful, user-friendly office suite to ever grace the Linux platform.

Here are some of the exciting new and improved features:

- Worried about the transition from Microsoft Office 97 for Windows to WordPerfect Office 2000 for Linux? Corel hasn't forgotten that it has lost ground to Microsoft in the battle of the office suites and has made a valiant attempt to bridge the gap by improving WordPerfect Office 2000's conversion and compatibility features. What this means is that all of your Microsoft Office documents needn't be trashed for you to make the leap to Linux and WordPerfect Office 2000—document conversions are smooth and perfect nearly every time, regardless of platform. What's more, Corel has generously provided users with the option of customizing WordPerfect 9 and Quattro Pro 9 for Linux to look like their respective Microsoft Office 97 counterparts, Word 97 and Excel 97. It doesn't get much easier, folks!

- There are several new ways to navigate through documents in WordPerfect Office 2000 for Linux. The most exciting is the AutoScroll feature, which allows you to scroll up and down the length of a document with the click of a button. Think of AutoScroll as the toolbar button equivalent to scrolling your documents with a wheel mouse. You'll take a closer look at AutoScroll in Hour 3, "Common Tasks in WordPerfect Office 2000 for Linux."

- The Forward and Back browse buttons are another new navigation feature. Working just like the navigation buttons in a Web browser, WordPerfect Office 2000's browse buttons track every move you make in an open document, providing point-and-click access to all the recent places you've been. As with Auto-Scroll, the new browse features are covered in Hour 3.

- Most office applications have long featured a print preview capability, allowing users to preview how their documents will look on the printed page without having to waste paper by printing out drafts in hard copy. Corel has raised the bar on this excellent feature by providing *editing* capabilities in Print Preview mode. That's right! No more switching in and out of Print Preview to get your document looking just so—now you can make your edits directly in print preview mode and view your changes on-the-fly! Print Preview is given its fair due in Hour 3.

- Related to better compatibility with Microsoft Office is the dramatic bump in size given to Quattro Pro 9 notebooks. In order to allow for instant conversions of large Microsoft Excel spreadsheets, Corel has increased the size of its Quattro Pro notebooks from 256 sheets to 18,278 sheets. Frankly, if you need a larger notebook, you're working too hard and should take time out to smell the roses.

- For good reason, Real-Time Preview is one of the most talked-about new features in the suite. Real-Time Preview works automatically to show you the effect of a contemplated formatting change before you commit to it. Whether you want to change a font style, size, or justification, Real-Time Preview gives you an instant gander at the consequences of your proposed change, without incorporating it into your document. You can learn more about Real-Time Preview in Hour 5, "Formatting WordPerfect 9 Documents."

- Recognizing the finite universe of frequently used functions in Quattro Pro 9 spreadsheets, Corel has wisely provided access to these functions from the toolbar in the form of SpeedFunctions. Functions such as @SUM and @AVG are now a mouse click away! You'll take a closer look at SpeedFunctions in Hour 11, "Creating Your First Spreadsheet."

- The new SpeedLinks feature allows you to instantly create hyperlinks in your documents. This happens automatically with entries beginning with www, ftp, http, or mailto—WordPerfect Office 2000 recognizes these prefixes as Internet or intranet destinations and converts them into hyperlinks from your document. You can build and customize SpeedLinks to automatically turn any word you choose into a hyperlink every time it's typed. You'll spend some more time with SpeedLinks in Hours 23, "WordPerfect 9 and the Web," and 24, "Web Integration in Other WordPerfect Office Applications."

- Paradox 9 features an improved interface that makes getting started with databases easier than ever. The new Welcome Expert greets you by default every time you fire up Paradox 9 and lets you choose the specific task you want to focus on for each session. Whether you want to build your database from scratch or rely on a PerfectExpert Project to get you started, the Paradox 9 Welcome Expert provides all the hand-holding you need. You'll explore all that the Welcome Expert has to offer in Hour 19, "Paradox 9 Database Basics."

For Users of WordPerfect Suite for Windows

If you already use any version of WordPerfect Office 2000 for Windows, there's good news and bad news. The good news is that almost every feature of WordPerfect Office 2000 for Linux is identical to its counterpart in the Windows version. Therefore, aside from getting up to speed on the Linux platform, you're already well equipped to switch over to WordPerfect Office 2000 for Linux.

The bad news is that there are several features of the suite for Windows that have been nixed from the Linux version. Here's what's missing:

- *Have you seen my DAD?* The Linux version doesn't incorporate the Desktop Application Director, better known in WordPerfect circles as *DAD*. Essentially, DAD was a utility for controlling WordPerfect launch icons in the taskbar of your Windows Desktop. With DAD engaged, clicking a WordPerfect icon in the taskbar would launch the appropriate application. Honestly, I was never much of a DAD fan—the DAD icons created too much clutter in the taskbar, making it difficult to quickly locate and launch applications. If the loss of DAD in the Linux version troubles you, rest assured there are other shortcuts to launching your WordPerfect applications in Linux. All of them are covered in Hour 2, "Introducing the WordPerfect Office 2000 for Linux Environment."

- *No reasonable facsimile.* These days, most office suites include a fax function that allows you to fax documents directly from your desktop. In WordPerfect Office 2000 for Windows, this was done by clicking File, Send To, Fax and then entering the relevant information when prompted. WordPerfect Office 2000 for Linux doesn't include this fax capability.

- *Exit XML.* For you Web gurus out there, WordPerfect Office 2000 for Linux drops the XML capabilities of the Windows version. XML stands for the *Extensible Markup Language*, which required some fairly sophisticated knowledge to use. Fear not, the Linux version includes more than enough tools to create simple Web pages without sophisticated knowledge of coding for the Web. You'll be up and running in no time after reading Hours 23 and 24.

- *What? No bonus applications?* Alas, there are several bonus applications in the Windows version that didn't make the cut for WordPerfect Office 2000 for Linux. Fans of WordPerfect Office 2000 for Windows may bemoan the absence of Corel Photo House and Corel Print Office from the Linux version. To be honest, I always viewed these applications as throwaways—minor programs that duplicated functions better performed by the core applications in the suite. If you prefer quality over quantity, you won't miss them!

- *Trellix.* You also don't get Trellix, a nifty Web document–creation tool that goes beyond WordPerfect Office 2000's native capabilities. As with the loss of XML capability, however, this is a relatively minor sacrifice for most users. WordPerfect Office 2000 for Linux has sufficient Web tools for folks who want to create simple pages to post to the Web.

- *Speech recognition.* By far the greatest loss in the Linux version is the absence of an integrated speech-recognition application. Most editions of the Windows version include Dragon NaturallySpeaking, one of the best consumer speech-recognition programs on the market. Dragon NaturallySpeaking allows you to dictate your documents into a microphone attached to your PC, and it translates your dictation into text that appears almost instantaneously on your computer screen. Users of WordPerfect Office 2000 for Linux, at least for the time being, will have to make due by entering text the old-fashioned way—by hand!

Summary

In this hour, you learned about the applications included in the Deluxe version of WordPerfect Office 2000 for Linux. From correspondence and memos, to timesheets, slideshows, and Web pages, WordPerfect Office 2000 for Linux is a powerful suite that can handle most of the documents you'll ever need to create.

Although Linux is gaining in popularity, most users are still wedded to Windows or Mac OS as their primary platform. To help ease your transition to Linux, you learned about Corel's commitment to the Linux platform. With its own Linux distribution and Linux versions of its flagship products, Corel is determined to bring Linux to the masses.

Finally, for those of you familiar with prior versions of WordPerfect, I provided a heads-up on major changes you can expect to see in the new office suite for Linux. I touched upon many of the new and improved features Corel has included in the suite, but this is only the beginning. All this and more will be covered in detail in the lessons that follow.

In the next hour, you'll explore the WordPerfect Office 2000 for Linux environment and nail down some basic tasks applicable to all applications within the suite.

Q&A

Q I've never used Linux before. Should I give it a try?

A It used to be that Linux users were limited to computer professionals or experienced home users with a sense of adventure and a penchant for tinkering. These days, however, Linux is easier than ever to install and use, making it a viable alternative platform for most users.

But you don't have to take my word for it—read as much as you can about the many advantages of Linux, how it works, and what it takes to get it up and running on your computer. I think you'll be pleasantly surprised at how popular Linux has become, and how many resources there are to help you along. Once you're satisfied that you'd like to give it a try, pick up one of the more popular Linux distributions available from Corel, Mandrake, or Red Hat. Although you'll have to pay anywhere from $29 to $90 for a boxed version of the software, you'll get plenty of extras for the money, including lots of instruction to help get you started and loads of extra software that you can use on your new Linux system.

You should also be aware that most Linux distributions come with tools that help you install Linux to coexist on a computer running Windows. At startup, you'll be given the choice of which operating system you want to use. With a "dual-boot" system running Windows and Linux, you can experiment with Linux without losing any of your Windows information and settings.

If you decide to give it a try, the good news is that WordPerfect Office 2000 for Linux looks and works almost exactly like the Windows version. In time, you may find yourself using Linux as your primary operating system.

Q **My clients all use Microsoft Office for Windows. Will I be able to share documents with them using WordPerfect Office 2000?**

A Yes. WordPerfect Office 2000 does an excellent job of converting all documents created in Microsoft Office. There may be some occasional formatting glitches, but they are insignificant and won't affect your ability to collaborate with users running Microsoft Office.

Workshop

If you haven't already done so, install WordPerfect Office 2000 for Linux. Corel has made the installation process extremely easy, no matter which distribution of Linux you're using. Simply navigate to the file named "setup" on your WordPerfect Office 2000 for Linux CD-ROM, double-click it, and follow the prompts to install your new software.

HOUR 2

Introducing the WordPerfect Office 2000 for Linux Environment

Hour 1, "Exploring WordPerfect Office 2000 for Linux," pointed out some of the differences between the Windows and Linux versions of WordPerfect Office 2000. These differences aside, Corel has gone far to ensure cross-platform compatibility. Not only do the different versions of WordPerfect Office 2000 look and work remarkably alike, they also share the same file format. This means that WordPerfect Office 2000 for Linux can seamlessly read and write to documents created in the Windows version, and vice versa.

If you're currently migrating to Linux from Windows or frequently collaborate with users who aren't willing to leave Windows behind, this cross-platform compatibility will go a long way toward easing your transition. You'll see what I mean in this hour's walking tour of the WordPerfect Office 2000 for Linux environment.

In this hour, you will

- Install WordPerfect Office 2000 for Linux.
- Launch WordPerfect Office 2000 for Linux applications for the first time.
- Create shortcut links on your desktop.
- Use common interface elements, such as menus, toolbars, the Property Bar, and the Application Bar.
- Learn how to get help when you need it, using Corel's built-in online help system.

Installing WordPerfect Office 2000 for Linux

Until recently, installing new software on a Linux PC was a complicated affair, requiring some advanced knowledge of the Linux file system and Linux commands. I'm thrilled to tell you that installing WordPerfect Office 2000 for Linux is flat-out the easiest software installation for Linux I've ever seen. It's so easy that we won't spend more than a minute on it, right here, right now.

I assume that you're already running Linux, and that you're familiar with how to access your CD-ROM drive. For those of you who are just getting started, you might want to review the general Linux information contained in the rest of this hour, Hour 3, "Common Tasks in WordPerfect Office 2000 for Linux," and Appendix A, "Introducing Corel Linux OS," before tackling the installation process. For everyone else, you'll have your software installed in no time.

To Do: Install WordPerfect Office 2000 for Linux

1. Fire up your Linux box and insert the WordPerfect Office 2000 for Linux software in your CD-ROM drive.
2. Access your CD-ROM drive and navigate to the Setup file.
3. Double-click the Setup file and follow the prompts to install WordPerfect Office 2000 for Linux.
4. Restart your system and you're ready to roll!

Those of you who have used Linux commands or the Red Hat Package Manager to install Linux software will appreciate the amazing simplicity Corel has brought to installing WordPerfect Office 2000 for Linux. As you'll see throughout the rest of this book, installing the software is just the beginning of the major advances that WordPerfect Office 2000 brings to the Linux platform.

> WordPerfect Office 2000 for Linux operates in the X Window System (also known as *X*), which launches by default in most modern Linux distributions. The X Window System provides the graphical user interface, or *GUI*, that most users expect when they think about personal computing. If, after logging in, you're staring at a black screen and a blinking prompt, you aren't working in X.
>
> Be careful! If this is a fresh installation of Linux, your video card is either not supported or not properly configured. If you try to launch X and your video card isn't properly set up, you run the risk of damaging your monitor.
>
> If you're sure that Linux has been properly installed and that your video card has been properly configured, you can usually launch X by typing the command **startx** and hitting Enter.

Starting and Quitting Applications

In Windows, applications are typically launched in three different ways:

- From the Start button's Program menu
- Using the Run command, which requires you to type in the path to the application
- From a desktop shortcut

Each of these methods has a direct counterpart on the Linux platform.

Launching Programs from the Corel Application Starter

If you like the Windows Start button, you'll feel right at home with the Corel Application Starter in Corel Linux. As shown in Figure 2.1, the Application Starter is located on the bottom-left corner of your screen, sitting on the KPanel (the equivalent of the Windows Taskbar).

FIGURE 2.1
You can launch WordPerfect Office 2000 applications from the Corel Application Starter.

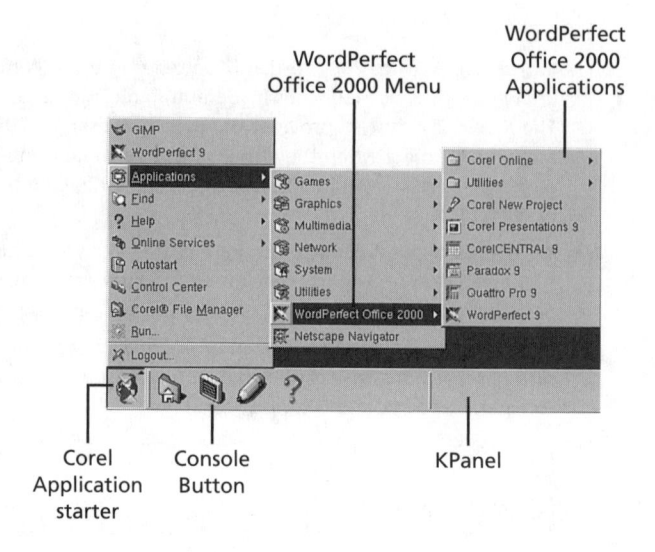

> If you're using another distribution of Linux, you obviously don't have the Corel Application Starter. Fear not—the distribution you're using has its own equivalent to the Windows Start button. What it's called depends on the desktop environment that came with your distribution. Most distributions use either the K Desktop Environment (KDE) or GNOME.
>
> In KDE, the Start button equivalent is called the K Menu, which is marked with a capital *K*. In GNOME, it's called the Main Menu, which is marked with a footprint. The K and Main Menus work the same way as the Corel Application Starter.

As shown in Figure 2.1, clicking the Application Starter displays several menus, including the Applications menu. Rest your cursor on the Applications menu to open a list of submenus and applications. One of the submenus is labeled WordPerfect Office 2000. Rest your cursor there to access the WordPerfect Office 2000 application icons.

Click once on any of these icons to launch an application.

Launching Applications Using the Run Command

In Windows, clicking Start, Run opens the Run command dialog box, which invites you to type in the path to an executable file that launches an application. For example, to launch Microsoft Word, you would click Start, Run and then type `C:\Program Files\Microsoft Office\Office\Winword.exe` in the space provided.

Introducing the WordPerfect Office 2000 for Linux Environment

The Linux Run command works the same way. Click Corel Application Starter, Run to open the Run command dialog box. Just as in Windows, in the space provided, you can type in or browse to the path for an application. In WordPerfect Office 2000 for Linux, Corel has made it even easier by creating single-word launch commands so that you don't have to search for the path to the applications in the suite.

As shown in Figure 2.2, to launch WordPerfect 9, open the Run dialog box, type **wordperfect** in the space provided, and then press Enter or click OK.

FIGURE 2.2
You can launch WordPerfect Office 2000 applications from the Run dialog box by typing a simple command.

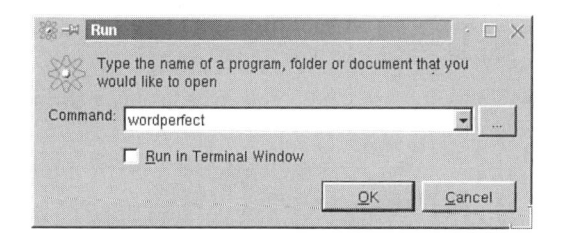

This trick will work with any application in the suite. Table 2.1 lists the launch commands for each application.

TABLE 2.1 Application Commands for WordPerfect Office 2000

If You Want to Launch This Application...	Type This Command...
WordPerfect 9	wordperfect
Quattro Pro 9	quattropro
Presentations 9	presentations
Paradox 9	paradox
CorelCENTRAL 9 Calendar	cccalendar
CorelCENTRAL 9 Address Book	ccaddressbook
CorelCENTRAL 9 Memos	ccmemos
Corel PerfectExpert	perfectexpert
Corel PerfectScript	perfectscript
FontTastic Font Installer	ftfi
Borland Database Administrator	bdeadmin

> You don't need to access the Run command dialog box to launch WordPerfect Office 2000 applications with the commands in Table 2.1. As experienced Linux users know, Linux commands are typically entered into the command line of a "shell," which understands each command and marches your system into responsive action.
>
> In Corel Linux, the shell window is called the *Console*, which can be launched from the KPanel on your desktop. In Figure 2.1, the Console button is the second button to the right of the Corel Application Starter—it looks like a computer monitor. Click the Console button to open the Console window. It may not look like much, but this window is the key to advanced Linux system administration.
>
> Give it a try! Launch the Console, type in any of the single-word commands listed in Table 2.1, and press Enter.

Creating a Shortcut on the Desktop

One of the most popular ways to launch an application in Windows is to create a shortcut on the desktop. You can do the same thing in Linux. In this section, you'll learn how by creating a desktop shortcut to launch the CorelCENTRAL 9 Calendar.

In Corel Linux, place your mouse pointer anywhere on the desktop and right-click once to display a floating menu of desktop tasks. Select New, Nickname to open the Nickname dialog box shown in Figure 2.3.

In the Nickname field, replace Untitled App with a name for your new shortcut. A good name for this shortcut would be My Calendar or CorelCENTRAL 9 Calendar.

Press the Tab key to jump down to the Target field. Remember the Linux commands covered in Table 2.1? Each command is a link to an executable file located somewhere on your computer, and the Target field is where you enter the location of the executable file for the application you want to run. Click the Browse button and navigate to the /usr/bin folder. This is where all the executable files for WordPerfect Office 2000 applications are stored. Find the file named cccalendar (just like the command in Table 2.1) and double-click it. You're automatically returned to the Nickname dialog box, with the path to CorelCENTRAL Calendar entered in the Target field.

Next, click the Change Icon button. Click the pull-down menu on the left and select the folder /usr/X11R6/share/icons. Navigate through the icons and double-click the one you want to use for your calendar. (Hint: To see the default icons designated by Corel, use the Corel Application Starter to navigate to the WordPerfect Office 2000 menu).

Exit the Nickname dialog box by clicking OK, and that's it! Your new shortcut will appear on the desktop.

FIGURE 2.3
Creating a desktop shortcut with the Nickname dialog box.

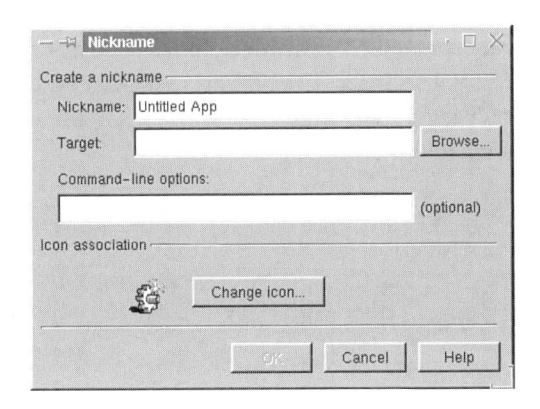

Quitting Applications

Quitting a WordPerfect Office 2000 application is the same as quitting applications in Windows:

- With your mouse, simply click the X in the upper-right corner of an open window.
- From the menu bar, select File, Exit.
- Press Alt+F4.

> I hate to mention it, but there might come a day when a WordPerfect Office 2000 application freezes on you. I've been using the final version of the software for most of this book, and I'm pleased to say that so far I haven't experienced a singe freeze. Somebody knock on wood, pronto.
>
> I'll keep my fingers crossed, but if you do experience a freeze while working in WordPerfect Office 2000, here's what you should do. Open a Console window and enter the command `killall -9 wine`. This forces all open WordPerfect Office 2000 applications to close, and you can restart your system and start again. If you don't close all your WordPerfect Office applications, your system might become sluggish and unstable, and it might not shut down properly.

Welcome to the WordPerfect Office 2000 Workspace

Let's dive right in and explore the WordPerfect Office 2000 environment. Figure 2.4 shows the WordPerfect 9 workspace. Even if you've never used Linux or WordPerfect before, as long as you've had some word processing experience on a personal computer, you should feel at home in this environment.

FIGURE 2.4
The WordPerfect 9 for Linux workspace should look very familiar.

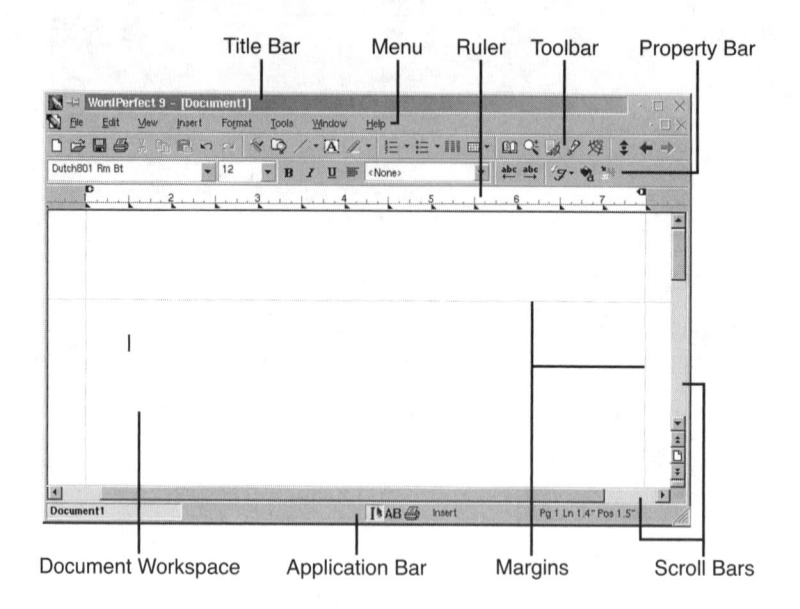

As you can see, Corel has made every effort to ease your transition to Linux from Windows—WordPerfect 9 for Linux looks and acts just like the Windows version. Let's run through the key interface elements shown in Figure 2.4.

Working with Menus

Most users are familiar with program menus. Located just under the title bar, menus contain drop-down lists of tasks you can perform with the click of a mouse button.

Figure 2.5 shows the menus for the key applications in WordPerfect Office 2000 for Linux. Note that the menus for WordPerfect 9, Quattro Pro 9, and Presentations 9 are identical. Even Paradox 9 and the CorelCENTRAL 9 Calendar share most of these menus, although they also include application-specific menus that the others lack. The common menus help create a consistent interface among all suite applications.

Introducing the WordPerfect Office 2000 for Linux Environment

FIGURE 2.5
Common menu headings reduce the learning curve from one application to another.

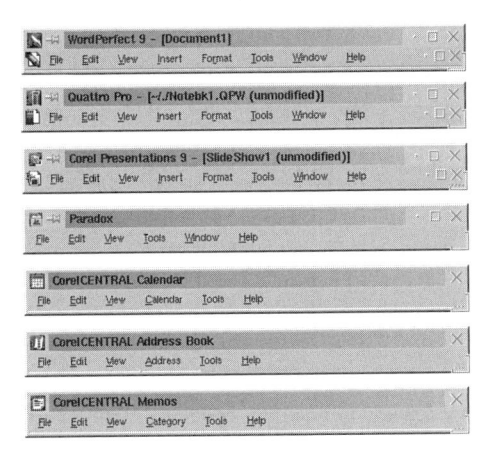

In order to view a menu, simply move your cursor to the menu you want to use, click once, and a list of items drops into view. To select an item from the menu, move your cursor to the item you want to select and click.

As shown in Figure 2.6, some of the items are followed by an ellipsis (...), some are followed by a small triangular arrow pointing right (▶), and some are flagged on the left by either a black dot (•) or a check mark (✓).

FIGURE 2.6
The Tools menu in WordPerfect 9.

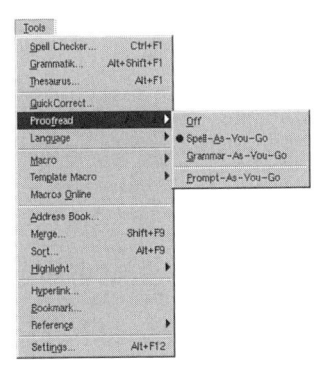

If you click once on a menu item that is followed by an ellipsis, a dialog box will open, prompting you to make further selections. If you rest your cursor on a menu item that's followed by an arrow, a submenu listing additional items pops out, in order for you to make another selection. Menu items flagged by a black dot or check mark tell you that the item is currently active. You can deactivate it by clicking a different item in the same menu or clicking the Off option that sometimes appears.

> Although the menus are similar from one application to another, they are not identical. For example, the items available in the Tools menu in WordPerfect will not be the same as those available in the Tools menu in Paradox. This makes sense—the applications within the suite serve different functions and can be expected to have their own respective sets of tools. By creating a common Tools menu heading in each application, Corel has simply provided users with a consistent interface to find the tools they need for each application.

> In Figure 2.6, some menu items have keyboard shortcuts listed on the far right. For example, the keyboard shortcut for the Spell Checker is Ctrl+F1. Keyboard shortcuts provide another way to perform the tasks listed in the menus. To open the Spell Checker, you can either click Tools, Spell Checker from the menu or just press the Ctrl+F1 keys. Keyboard shortcuts allow you to keep your hands on your keyboard—a real timesaver for you touch-typists out there.

WordPerfect Office 2000 Toolbars

Toolbars are another interface element that most users will recognize. Toolbars sit under the menus and contain buttons that allow you to perform basic tasks.

Common Toolbar Buttons

As with menus, the toolbars in WordPerfect Office 2000 are similar, with several buttons in common. With the exception of the CorelCENTRAL applications, there are nine toolbar buttons that appear in every application in the suite. These buttons, as well as a brief description of what they do, appear in Table 2.2.

TABLE 2.2 Common WordPerfect Office 2000 for Linux Toolbar Buttons

Toolbar Button	Description
New	Opens a new blank document
Open	Opens an existing document or project
Save	Saves an open document or project to the default file location
Print	Prints an open document or project
Cut	Deletes selected text from a document and saves it to the clipboard for pasting to another location

Toolbar Button	Description
Copy	Copies selected text from a document and saves it to the clipboard for pasting to another location
Paste	Pastes text from the clipboard to an open document or project
Web	Launches a Web browser to the Corel Web site
PerfectExpert	Launches the PerfectExpert, a source of online help accessible from every application in the suite

> If you can't remember what a toolbar button does, just hold your cursor over it to display a pop-up balloon that tells you the name of the button and its function.

Available Toolbars

Each application has a default toolbar displayed every time you launch the application. But there are many more toolbars than meets the eye. In WordPerfect 9 alone there are more than a dozen preconfigured toolbars at your disposal, each one designed to suit a specific set of tasks.

To get at the hidden toolbars, simply rest your mouse on an open toolbar (such as the Wordperfect 9 toolbar shown in Figure 2.7) and right-click to open the toolbar menu. Point and click to select the toolbar you want to use, and it appears under your current toolbar. You can open as many toolbars as you want, but remember that toolbars take up precious screen real estate—the more toolbars you open, the less room in which you have to work.

FIGURE 2.7
The WordPerfect 9 toolbar.

You can close a toolbar the same way you opened it. Access the toolbar menu and select the toolbar you want to close.

> I'd be remiss in failing to mention the Microsoft Word 97 toolbar available in WordPerfect 9. As you've no doubt guessed, this toolbar mimics the default toolbar in Microsoft's competing word processor. If you're migrating to WordPerfect from Word 97, you can select this toolbar to keep yourself on familiar ground.

Customizing Toolbars

You're not stuck with Corel's default toolbars. You can add or delete buttons from your toolbars, and you can even rearrange them until they're organized to suit the way you work.

To customize a toolbar, open the toolbar menu on the toolbar you want to edit. Click Edit to open the Toolbar Editor. Figure 2.8 shows the Toolbar Editor for the WordPerfect 9 toolbar.

FIGURE 2.8

The Toolbar Editor in WordPerfect 9.

With the Toolbar Editor open, there are two ways to edit a toolbar. If all you want to do is rearrange or remove toolbar buttons, you can do it directly on the toolbar. To remove a toolbar button, click and hold down your mouse pointer on the button you want to remove and then drag it off the toolbar. When you release your mouse, the button is gone! To rearrange a toolbar button, click and hold on it with your mouse, drag it to where you want it, and release the mouse. Your toolbar button is instantly relocated!

The other method of editing your toolbar comes into play when you want to add a toolbar button, which you'll have to do from the Toolbar Editor. As shown in Figure 2.8, the Toolbar Editor has a drop-down menu called Feature Categories. Many of the items in this drop-down menu match the regular menus in the suite, such as File, Edit, View, and so on. This is no accident—these items are organized in menu-like categories so that they are easy to search by task. For example, select the features category named File. In the Features box, just below the drop-down menu, you'll see a list of tasks relating to file management, such as opening, printing, and saving documents.

If you click one of these tasks, two things happen:

- An icon symbolizing the selected tasks appears below the Features box, with a description of the task and a keyboard shortcut, if any.
- The Add Button button in the upper-right corner of the Toolbar Editor is enabled.

If you click Add Button, your new toolbar button will immediately appear at the tail end of the toolbar. To move it elsewhere, just drag and drop it wherever you want —as long as the Toolbar Editor remains open, you can move it (or remove it) by dragging it with your mouse.

In order to make your toolbar edits final, you need to click the OK button on the Toolbar Editor. Until then, you can click the Cancel button, and any changes made during the editing session are wiped away.

> Be careful playing with the default toolbars provided by Corel—you might regret major changes to the organization of the toolbar buttons. You can, however, always restore the default toolbars settings. Simply open the toolbar menu and select Settings to open the Customize Settings window. In the Available Toolbars menu, select the toolbars you want to restore. Click the Reset button and click Yes when asked if you're sure you want to continue. Your toolbar is instantly restored to the default setting—no harm, no foul.

To Do: Create Your Own Toolbar

WordPerfect Office 2000 also makes it easy to create your own toolbars. To give it a try walk through the following steps:

1. Open the toolbar menu from any toolbar.
2. Click Settings to open the Customize Settings window shown in Figure 2.9.
3. Click the Create button, and you'll be prompted to name your new toolbar.

FIGURE 2.9

The Customize Settings window in WordPerfect 9.

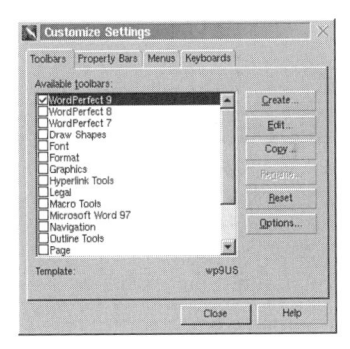

4. Name your toolbar something clever, such as My Toolbar, and click OK.

5. If you look at your open document or project, you'll see a blank toolbar appear. You'll also find yourself back in the Toolbar Editor, inviting you to add buttons to your new toolbar. Just as you used the Toolbar Editor to add buttons to Corel's default toolbars, you can use the Toolbar Editor to add buttons to your own toolbar.

The Context-Sensitive Property Bar

One of the neatest features in WordPerfect Office 2000 is the context-sensitive Property Bar, a special toolbar that changes by task. The Property Bar is available in all the suite applications except CorelCENTRAL.

Figure 2.10 shows the Property Bars for three different tasks in WordPerfect 9. The first is the default Property Bar, which assumes that you're writing and editing simple text. If you decide to insert a table into the same document, your Property Bar will automatically change to provide a different set of tools you're likely to need. Finally, if you insert a graphic into the same document, the Property Bar will morph yet again to display a powerful set of graphics tools.

FIGURE 2.10
WordPerfect 9 Property Bars.

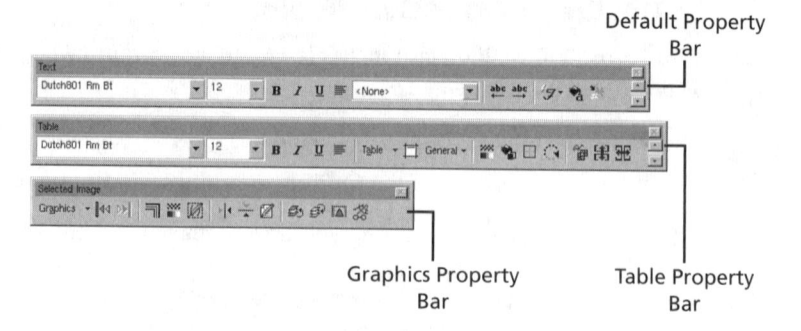

Default Property Bar

Graphics Property Bar

Table Property Bar

> Just like a toolbar, a Property Bar can be customized to suit your needs. Just right-click the Property Bar and select Edit to open the Property Bar Editor, which works just like the Toolbar Editor to help you add, remove, or rearrange the buttons on your Property Bar. Note that if you right-click the Property Bar and select Settings instead of Edit, you'll see a list of available Property Bars for the application you're working in.

Using the Application Bar to Manage Your Workspace

The Application Bar, available only in WordPerfect 9 and Quattro Pro 9, specializes in providing information about your workspace. As shown in Figure 2.11, the Application Bar tells you, among other things, which documents are open, whether you're in Insert or Typeover mode, and your exact cursor location.

FIGURE 2.11
The WordPerfect 9 Application Bar.

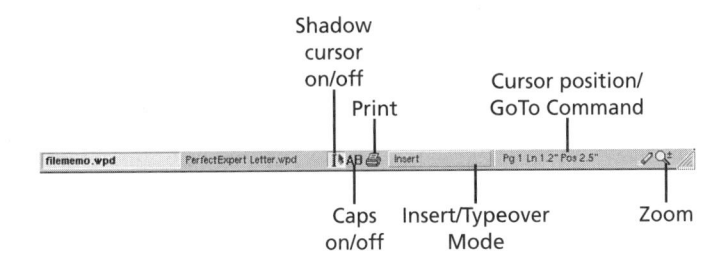

Customizing the Application Bar

As with most features in WordPerfect Office 2000, you can customize the Application Bar. Simply right-click the Application Bar and select Settings to open the Application Bar Settings dialog box. This list of all available Application Bar buttons makes it easy to turn buttons on or off using the check mark boxes that appear next to each item.

Finding Help When You Need It

Corel has packed more online help into WordPerfect Office 2000 for Linux than you're ever likely to use, and you can find it all on the Help menu available in each application. WordPerfect Office 2000 help comes in two forms:

- The online manual, searchable index, and Web-based support that you can access using Netscape Navigator
- Templates for frequently used documents and context-sensitive tips that you can access using the PerfectExpert

Netscape Navigator Help

The WordPerfect Office 2000 installation includes a copy of Netscape Communicator, a full-featured Web browser, email, and newsreader program. The Web browsing component, Netscape Navigator, is an integral part of WordPerfect Office 2000's online help system.

Help Topics

Click the Help menu of any suite application and select Help Topics. As shown in Figure 2.12, a Netscape Navigator window opens, providing help for the open application.

FIGURE 2.12

Help Topics for WordPerfect 9 in Netscape Navigator.

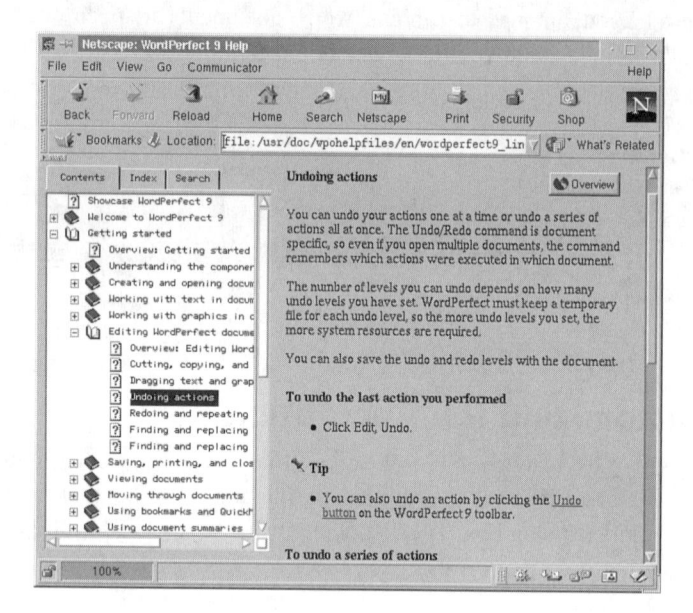

On the left side of the browser window is a separate frame with three tabs labeled Contents, Index, and Search. When you installed WordPerfect Office 2000, part of the installation included a massive database of help topics, tips, and tutorials. You can use the Content, Index, and Search tabs to access this database and find the help you need:

- The Contents tab is your gateway to an online manual of instructions and tips for each application. Brows through the table of contents listed beneath the Contents tab. As shown in Figure 2.12, if you click to select a heading from the table of contents, the relevant information appears to the right in the main browser window. Many of these manual pages have hyperlinks, providing one-click access to additional information.

- The Index tab is the Yellow Pages of WordPerfect Office 2000 help, providing access to an alphabetical list of items in the help database. For example, say you want to learn more about the Undo feature. Simply scroll down the index and click any listings that appear relevant. In this case, you would find the following listings: Undo Levels, Undo/Redo History, and Undoing Actions. If you clicked Undoing Actions, a smaller browser window would open with a list of more precise, potentially relevant topics, including one called Using Undo and Redo. Clicking that would display the relevant information in the main browser window.

- As its name suggests, the Search tab allows you to search the help database using keywords. To use the search feature, simply type a keyword in the space provided and click the Find button. In seconds, a list of relevant "hits" for your keyword will appear below the Find button, and you can hunt among them for the listing that best answers your question.

Corel on the Web

The Help menu also provides one-click access to support pages on Corel's Web site. As shown in Figure 2.13, items in the Corel Web Site submenu take you directly to Corel's Office Community, Technical Support, and Tips and Tricks Web pages. Here you'll find up-to-date support for WordPerfect Office 2000, including downloadable projects, clip art, macros, and advanced tips for using the applications in the suite.

FIGURE 2.13
Corel's Office Community on the Web.

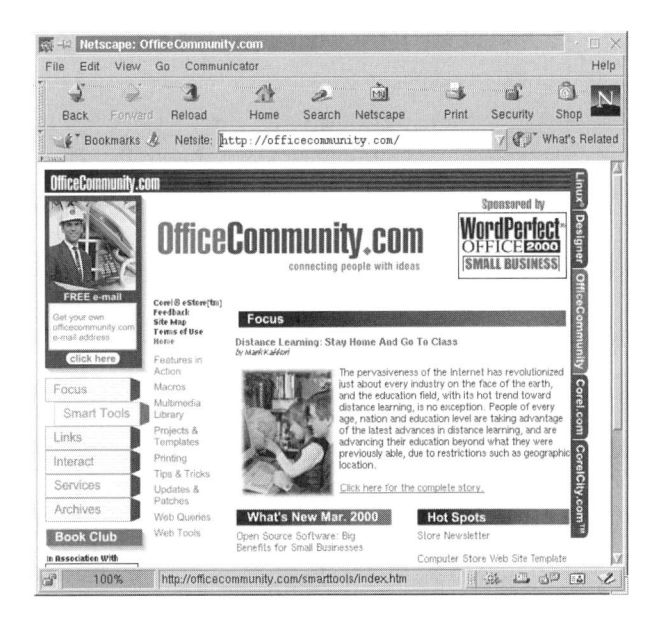

PerfectExpert Help

The second kind of help available comes by way of the PerfectExpert, the WordPerfect Office 2000 equivalent of the Microsoft Office Assistant. PerfectExpert guides you in two ways:

- By providing a seemingly endless array of templates, called *PerfectExpert Projects*, that you can use as a starting point in building your own documents
- By providing context-sensitive help through the PerfectExpert window

Working with PerfectExpert Projects

PerfectExpert Projects are customizable templates for documents that most users will want to create, such as letters, memos, fax cover sheets, expense reports, business cards, and even Happy Birthday banners. Corel has done a great job designing sophisticated and professional Projects that you'll be able to customize and use with very little effort.

To start a new PerfectExpert Project, you need to access the PerfectExpert Project dialog box. There are several different ways to do this:

- From the Corel Application Starter (or equivalent), click Applications, WordPerfect Office 2000, Corel New Project.
- In any open application (except CorelCENTRAL, which doesn't feature PerfectExpert Projects), click File, New From Project.
- In Presentations 9, the PerfectExpert dialog box greets you by default every time you launch the program.
- In Paradox 9, the new Welcome Expert greets you every time you launch the program. The Welcome Expert includes two buttons that launch Paradox 9's unique version of the PerfectExpert: Database Templates and Paradox Experts. These are covered in more detail in Hour 20, "Creating Your First Database."

Figure 2.14 shows the PerfectExpert dialog box. Notice the drop-down menu at the top of the dialog box. This menu allows you to select, by application, the type of Project you want to create.

FIGURE 2.14
The PerfectExpert dialog box.

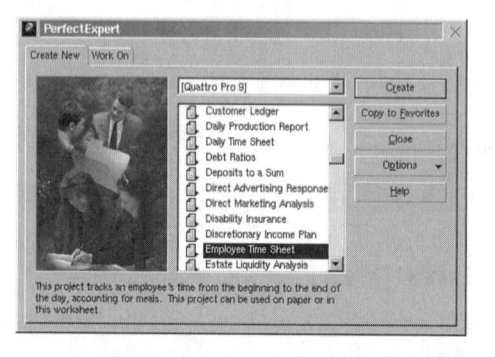

For example, Quattro Pro is the best application for creating employee timesheets. If you select Quattro Pro from the drop-down menu, the box below the menu will list all available Quattro Pro Projects. Navigate down this list to find the Daily Time Sheet Project. Double-click it, and the PerfectExpert automatically generates a "Perfect" timesheet from a template. You can now customize your timesheet to suit your needs.

Introducing the WordPerfect Office 2000 for Linux Environment 45

> In WordPerfect, Quattro Pro, and Presentations, you can also start a new Project from the PerfectExpert window by clicking the Start button and selecting New Project/Existing Document. The PerfectExpert window, shown in Figure 2.15, is covered in the next section.

The PerfectExpert Window

After you've created a new Project, the PerfectExpert stays with you to help you customize it. After creating a new document from a Project, the PerfectExpert window appears on the left side of the screen. The PerfectExpert window displays one-click access to functions that are relevant to whatever document or task you're working on.

For example, in Figure 2.15, after a cash receipt is created from a Quattro Pro PerfectExpert Project, the PerfectExpert window opens automatically on the left side of the screen, containing buttons with suggestions about what to do next with the new document.

FIGURE 2.15
The PerfectExpert window.

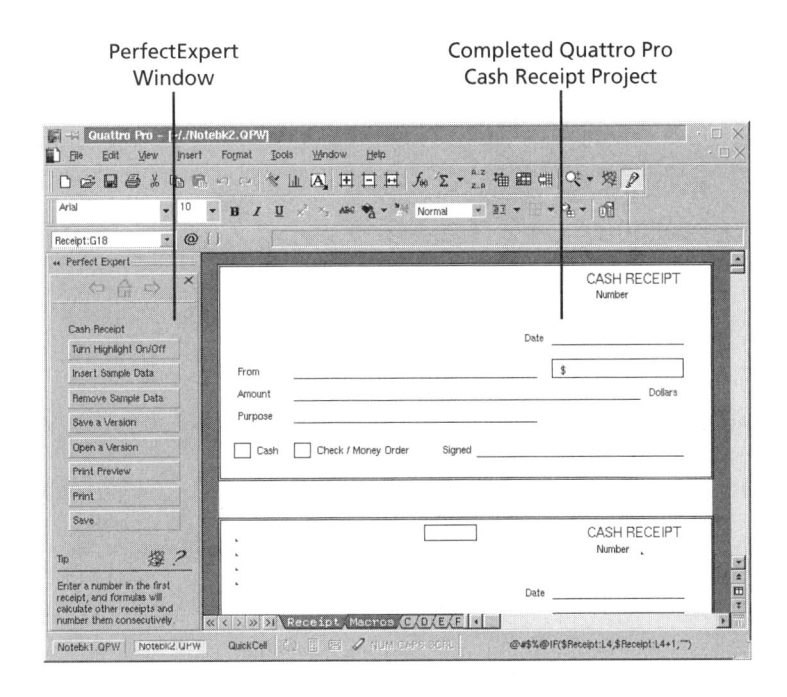

Part of the beauty of the PerfectExpert window is that, like the Property Bar, it is context-sensitive, meaning that it provides you with task-specific help based on the actual work you're performing. Figures 2.16 through 2.18 demonstrate how the PerfectExpert window adapts to help you, respectively, with graphics, tables, and documents prepared for the Internet.

FIGURE 2.16
The Selected Graphic PerfectExpert window.

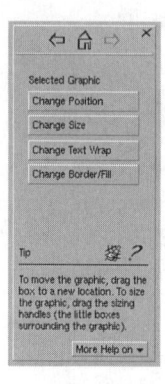

FIGURE 2.17
The Table PerfectExpert window.

FIGURE 2.18
The Internet Publisher PerfectExpert window.

You don't need to create a new Project to launch the PerfectExpert window. You can open it any time from the menu by clicking Help, Perfect Expert or by clicking the PerfectExpert toolbar button shown earlier in Table 2.2.

Summary

In Hour 2, we took a walking tour of the WordPerfect Office 2000 environment. Common elements such as menus, toolbars, and the Property Bar enhance WordPerfect Office 2000's function as an integrated suite of applications. We also covered several ways to launch WordPerfect Office 2000 applications and where to find built-in help when you need it.

The next hour will introduce you to common tasks you can quickly master and use in all applications in the suite.

Q&A

Q **The Application Bar doesn't do anything for me. Can I get rid of it?**

A Yes. There are two ways to hide the Application Bar. You can click the View menu and select Application Bar to turn it on or off. You can also right-click the Application Bar and select Hide Application Bar. To turn it on again, just select it from the View menu.

Q **Can I edit a desktop shortcut after I create it?**

A Yes. Simply right-click the shortcut you want to edit and select Properties to open the Properties dialog box. Click the Execute tab, from which you can edit the shortcut.

Q **How do I delete a desktop shortcut?**

A Just as in Windows, click the shortcut you want to delete and drag it to the trash icon that appears on your desktop. You can also right-click the shortcut, select Delete, and click Yes when asked if you're sure you want to continue.

Workshop

The Workshop contains quiz questions and exercises to help reinforce what you've learned in this hour. If you get stuck, the answers can be found in Appendix B, "Answers to Quiz Questions."

Quiz

1. What is the Corel Linux OS equivalent of the Start button in Microsoft Windows?
2. What is the Linux command to launch WordPerfect 9?
3. Which WordPerfect Office 2000 feature changes based on the task you're trying to perform?

Exercises

1. Create a desktop shortcut for Paradox 9.
2. From WordPerfect 9, jump to Corel's Office Community Web site to check for any new PerfectExpert Projects to download.
3. Create your own WordPerfect 9 toolbar containing buttons for the following tasks:
   - Close All Documents
   - Save As
   - Print Preview
   - Print Pages

HOUR 3

Common Tasks in WordPerfect Office 2000 for Linux

Hour 2, "Introducing the WordPerfect Office 2000 for Linux Environment," explored the common interface elements among WordPerfect Office 2000 for Linux applications. This hour takes it one step further by explaining how to perform tasks that are common to each application in the suite.

In this hour, you will

- Manage files on a Linux system.
- Use the keyboard and mouse to enter and edit text and other objects.
- Review basic methods of navigating through documents.
- Configure your printer and print documents in WordPerfect Office 2000.

Managing Files Within the Linux File System

Linux stores programs and files in a manner similar to other operating systems. Although there are some differences, the metaphor of your hard drive as a file cabinet holds true: Linux utilizes directories, or *folders*, in which all information (subfolders, files, applications, and the operating system) are stored.

Corel Linux includes several default directories, each of which contains specific types of files. Table 3.1 lists a few of the directories you'll come across.

TABLE 3.1 The Corel Linux File System

The System (/)	A single forward slash (/) is well known to Linux users as the *root* directory, in which all the directories and files contained in your Linux system reside. In Corel Linux, it is also known as *The System* directory, which is only accessible to the root, or *administrative*, user.
My Home or /home/*username*	For each user, Corel Linux sets up a home location where all subdirectories and files relating to the user are stored. All user home directories are filed in the /home directory of The System and take the form /home/*username*, where *username* stands for a user's login name. For example, a workstation user with the login name "emilyrose" would find her home location in the /home/emilyrose directory.
/home/*username*/ Documents	This is the equivalent of the My Documents directory in Windows. It's set up by default as a suggested place for all users to store their "stuff."
/bin	This is where Linux stores most basic system commands.
/usr/man	Linux incorporates an online help system known as the *manual pages* (or *man pages* for short). The man pages provide general information about user and system administration commands, among other things, and can be very helpful if you get stuck and need a quick refresher. The /usr/man directory is one place where the man pages are typically stored.

Table 3.1 is only a partial list of an incredibly complex file system. Although it's not important to memorize the typical Linux file system, understanding at least a piece of this universe will make it easier to navigate through your Linux system.

In Corel Linux, the directories listed in Table 3.1 can be accessed through the Corel File Manager, shown in Figure 3.1. You can access the Corel File Manager from the launch button on the Corel Panel. You can also click Corel Application Starter, Corel File Manager, or click the My Home icon on the desktop.

FIGURE 3.1
The Corel Linux File Manager.

> When you installed Linux, you were probably prompted to create a username for your workstation. My username on my Corel Linux workstation, for example, is asg618. Each time I boot into Linux, I have the option of logging in as root, with full access and permissions, or as asg618, with limited access and permissions. Unless you intend to perform administrative functions, it's best to do all your work under your username rather than as root. Root access opens doors to restricted system files. By doing your day-to-day work under your username, you reduce the risk of inadvertently altering or corrupting these protected files.

> If you ever get lost in the maze of the Corel Linux file system, use the Corel File Manager to regain your bearings. By default, the Corel File Manager opens to the home directory for the current user.

Creating a New Document

You have several ways to create a new document in any application in the suite (with the exception of CorelCENTRAL, which isn't in the business of creating documents):

- From the menu bar, select File, New.
- Use the keyboard shortcut Ctrl+N.
- From a PerfectExpert Project or template (which you can access from the menu bar by selecting File, New from Project).

Saving Your Documents

Once you've created something new, you'll need to save it to your hard drive. Saving a document can be broken down into two steps: naming the document and finding a place to store the document.

What's in a Name?

Naming conventions in Linux are different from those of other platforms. In order to start off on the right foot, keep these general rules in mind:

- Windows users, particularly those familiar with MS-DOS, are used to seeing the backward slash (\) in the syntax for file locations. The location for a Windows file might look like this:

  C:\Corel\MyDocs\testmemo

  In contrast, Linux syntax uses the forward slash (/), so the location for the same file on a Linux system might look like this:

  /home/asg618/Documents/testmemo

- In Linux, the general rule is that filenames are case sensitive. Therefore, testmemo and TESTmemo are recognized as two different documents. This can get confusing when you're looking at two documents that appear to have the same name, except for minor differences in capitalization. Linux fans usually avoid this confusion by consistently using lowercase letters for all directories and filenames.

  One of the improvements in WordPerfect Office 2000 for Linux is the abandonment of this admittedly annoying quirk. In all WordPerfect Office 2000 applications, if you try to save a file named TESTmemo to a directory that already contains a file named testmemo, the program will ask if you really want to replace an existing file.

  If you've already gotten used to the preferred Linux method of using all lowercase letters to name your files, you may want to stick with it so that your filenames are consistent throughout your Linux system. If you're new to Linux, you should be

aware of this naming convention to avoid confusion when working in applications other than WordPerfect Office 2000.
- With the exception of periods and underscores, you should stick to using letters and numbers when naming new documents. In fact, Linux will refuse to recognize most symbols if you try to include them in your filenames. For example, the file `little_red_riding_hood` is fine, but `three*little*pigs` just won't work.
- Linux filenames include suffix-like references called *extensions* that identify the format of the file. If you're familiar with Windows, you know that most Windows applications automatically assign an extension to the files they create. For example, a WordPerfect document saved to your Desktop bears the extension .WPD, which automatically tells Windows to use WordPerfect to open the file whenever it's accessed.

Good news! The extensions used to identify documents generated in WordPerfect Office 2000 for Windows are the same as those used in the Linux version. Therefore, regardless of which version of the office suite you use, the extensions shown in Table 3.2 are tacked onto the end of your document to link it with the application that was used to create it.

TABLE 3.2 WordPerfect Office 2000 File Formats

Extension	Application
.WPD	WordPerfect
.QPW	Quattro Pro
.SHW	Presentations Slide Show
.WPG	WordPerfect Graphic used for Presentations Drawings and WordPerfect Clipart
.DB	Paradox Database

To Err Is Human, To Save Divine

Now that you've created and given a name to your new document, the next step is to learn how to save the document to your hard drive. You have several ways to save your document in WordPerfect Office 2000:

- From the menu bar, click File, Save.
- Click the Save button on the default toolbar.
- Use the keyboard shortcut Ctrl+S.

No matter which method you use, the first time you try to save a new document, the Save File dialog box, shown in Figure 3.2, will open, prompting you to give your new document a name.

FIGURE 3.2
The WordPerfect 9 Save File dialog box.

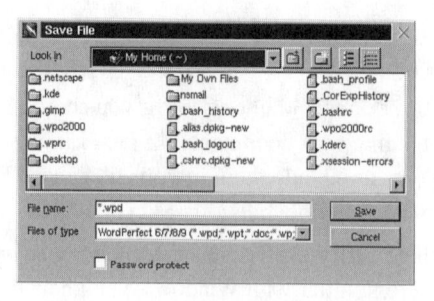

If you've ever saved a file on a computer, the Save File dialog is nothing new. It contains a pull-down menu for selecting a directory to store your file, a space for entering the name of the file, a drop-down menu that designates the file type, a Save button for committing the file to the chosen directory, and a Cancel button for backing out of the deal.

After navigating to the directory in which you want to store your file, enter a filename and hit Enter or click the Save button to save your file and get back to work.

> If you're just starting out with Corel Linux, I recommend saving all your files to the Documents directory. Once you're more familiar with the Linux filing system, you can create additional directories to manage your files to suit your needs.

To Do: Create a Document in WordPerfect 9

1. Launch WordPerfect 9 and type in some text in the open document window.
2. Select File, Save from the menu bar, or hit Ctrl+S to open the Save dialog box.
3. Use the "Look in:" pull-down menu to navigate to the Documents folder.
4. In the "File name:" box, type in **Firstdoc** and hit Enter or click the Save button to save your document.

Opening an Existing Document

After you've created one or more WordPerfect Office 2000 files and saved them to your hard drive, you have four different routes you can take to access them again:

- From the menu bar, click File, Open.
- Click the Open button on the default toolbar.
- Use the keyboard shortcut Ctrl+O.
- Open the Corel File Manager.

Each of these methods requires you to navigate to the location of the file you want to open. The first three methods launch the Open File dialog box shown in Figure 3.3.

FIGURE 3.3
The WordPerfect 9 Open File dialog box.

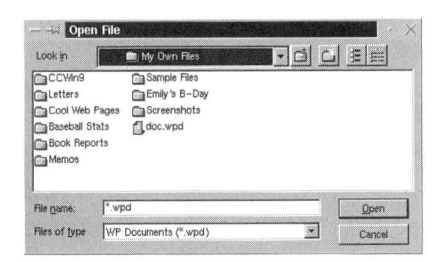

The last method, using the Corel File Manager, is the only method that does not require you to first launch a WordPerfect Office 2000 application. In the Corel File Manager window, just double-click the icon for the document you want to open, and Corel Linux will automatically fire up the application associated with the file.

Importing a File

To bring another file into an open WordPerfect Office 2000 document, position your cursor in the open document to pinpoint exactly where you want to insert the file. Select Insert, File from the menu bar to open the Insert File dialog box. Navigate to the file you want to insert and either double-click it or click the Open button to insert it directly into your open document.

Working with Other Drives and Partitions

Most modern Linux distributions, including Corel Linux, spare users the ordeal of entering commands to "mount" and "unmount" connected drives by automating these functions to work much like they do in Windows and Mac OS.

Accessing a Floppy Drive

In WordPerfect Office 2000, as long as a user has access to a floppy disk drive, saving to a floppy is a snap. Click File, Save As to open the Save As dialog box. The default Save As directory for each user is My Home, which appears in the pull-down menu at the top of the Save As dialog box. As shown in Figure 3.4, clicking the pull-down menu reveals a list of directories, including a floppy drive, to which you can save your document.

FIGURE 3.4
Accessing the floppy disk drive in the Save As dialog box.

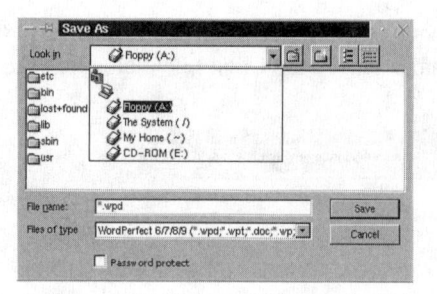

> If you don't see your floppy disk in the Save As pull-down menu, chances are your system administrator hasn't given you permission to access the drive. Contact your administrator to request access.
>
> If *you* are the system administrator but don't know what to do, fear not. Just follow these steps to provide users with access to their floppies (and any other access you want to provide):
>
> 1. In Corel Linux, log in as root.
> 2. From the Corel Application Starter, select Applications, System, User Manager to open the KDE User Manager, shown in Figure 3.5.
> 3. Locate the username you want to edit and double-click it to open the Edit User dialog box.
> 4. Click the Groups tab, which, as shown in Figure 3.6, displays the list of available and selected groups for the user. Make sure that "floppy" appears in the list of selected groups on the right side of the dialog box. If it doesn't, find it in the list of available groups on the left and either double-click it or use the right-pointing arrows in the center of the dialog box to move "floppy" into the selected groups column.
> 5. Click OK and exit the KDE User Manager. Select Yes when asked if you want to save your changes. The next time the user logs in, the floppy drive will appear in the pull-down menu in the Save As dialog box.

Common Tasks in WordPerfect Office 2000 for Linux

FIGURE 3.5
The KDE User Manager allows the system administrator to control the permissions for each user.

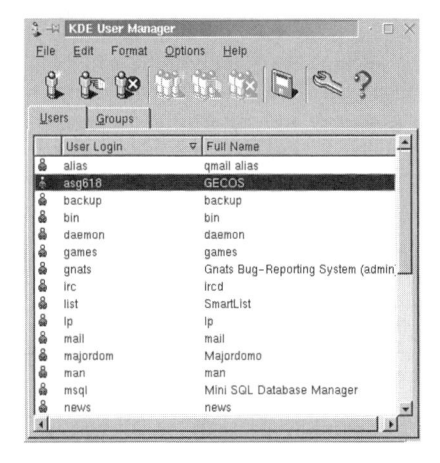

FIGURE 3.6
The Groups tab displays the file permissions for each user.

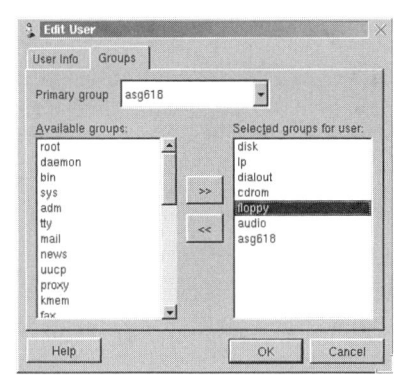

Accessing Your Windows Partition

If you plan to install Corel Linux on the same hard drive as an existing Windows partition, you'll be glad to know that accessing files stored on your Windows partition is as easy as knowing where to find them.

To Do: Access a Windows Partition

1. From the menu bar, select Open or Save As.
2. In the Open or Save As dialog box, use the pull-down menu to navigate to The System (/) directory. Double-click on the folder labeled `"disks,"` and then double-click the folder labeled `"c."`
3. Lo and behold, the contents of your Windows partition appear, and you can open or save to any folder located on your Windows system.

> If you plan to maintain a dual-boot machine running Microsoft Windows and any distribution of Linux, install Windows first. Most Linux distributions actually look for your Windows partition during the installation process in order to provide an easy means of accessing it from Linux. In contrast, if you install Linux first, Windows will try to reformat your hard drive when you install it, overwriting your existing Linux partition. Trust me on this one—if you must have Windows on you hard drive, take the easy road and install Windows first.

Entering Text and Data

I'm willing to bet that somehow, somewhere, you've entered text or other data on a personal computer. Regardless of platform or application, the entry of data on a PC is a task that doesn't see much in the way of innovation.

The general approach is the same for all WordPerfect Office 2000 applications:

1. Launch a WordPerfect Office 2000 application.
2. Start a new document or project.
3. In the open document window, use your mouse to select a location to begin data entry.
4. Left-click once when the mouse pointer lands on the place you want to begin typing. A blinking cursor appears wherever you've pointed, prompting you to begin entering data using the keyboard.
5. Type away!

That's all there is to entering text and data in WordPerfect Office 2000 documents. Play around with this a little, entering text in different applications to see how it works in each one.

Selecting Items with the Mouse and Keyboard

Coming up with the words, images, and data and getting them down on paper is the hard part. Selecting text and other items for editing and formatting in WordPerfect Office 2000 is the easy part, and you can do it all with the mouse, the keyboard, and sometimes both working together.

In order to work with any item in a WordPerfect Office 2000 file, you must first select it using one of the following methods:

- Left-click once on an object to select it.
- Double-click a word to select it for formatting or editing.
- Triple-click anywhere within a sentence to select the entire sentence. In WordPerfect, you can also select only the first sentence in a line by moving your cursor into the left margin of the sentence and clicking once.
- Quadruple-click to select an entire paragraph. In WordPerfect, you can also position your cursor in the left margin of the paragraph and double-click to select it.
- In WordPerfect, place your cursor anywhere in the word, sentence, or paragraph you want to edit. Move your cursor into the left margin and right-click. The pop-up menu gives you the choice of selecting the sentence, paragraph, page, or all, and it allows you to edit the page margins, add a comment or a sound clip, or create a subdocument.
- To select a block, place your cursor at the starting point of the block you want to select, left-click and, holding down the mouse button, drag the mouse to the end of the block. Release the mouse button and the selected block will be highlighted. If you want to mark another, noncontiguous block for editing at the same time, press and hold down the Ctrl key while selecting your blocks.
- An even cooler way to select a block is to place your cursor at either the start or end of the block you want to select. While holding down the Shift key, use the arrow keys to highlight everything you want to select.
- To select everything within an open document, press Ctrl+A.

Moving Things Around

The thrill of selecting items in your WordPerfect Office 2000 documents won't last very long—trust me on this one. The real excitement comes with the ability to move selected items around within your document. Whether working with a graphic, a word, or a selected block, you have several ways to delete, move, and copy items in your WordPerfect Office 2000 documents.

With Drag and Drop

Point and click to select a desired item or block, and, holding down the mouse button, drag the item with your mouse to the desired location. As shown in Figure 3.7, when you begin to drag the item, a four-pronged arrow appears, indicating that the application is ready to move the item in any direction you choose. As you move the four-pronged arrow to a new location, a blinking cursor follows your movement, indicating where the item will be inserted when you release the mouse button. When you've found the perfect spot, release the mouse button, and your item or block is automatically moved to the new location.

FIGURE 3.7
Dragging and dropping a block of text in WordPerfect 9.

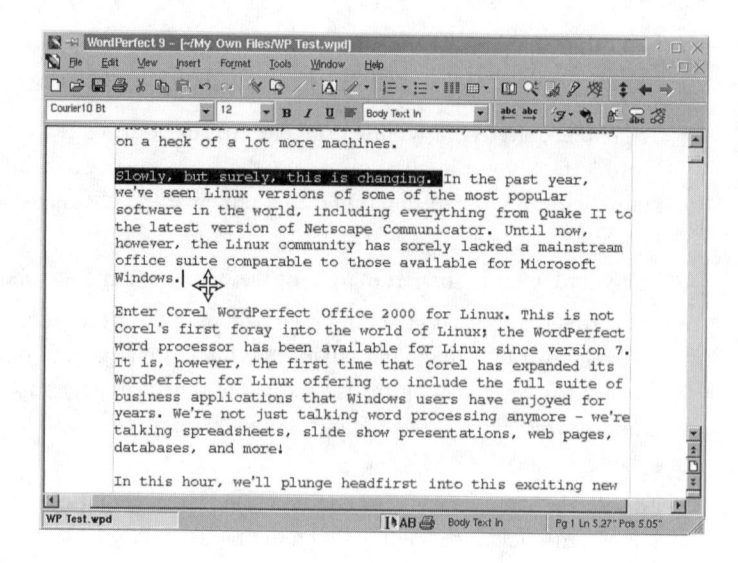

> If you have more than one open document, you can click and drag text or an object from one document to another with the Application Bar. As shown in Hour 2, the Application Bar displays a button for every open document in your application. To drag an item from one document to another, select the item in the first document, hold down the mouse button to drag it to the Application Bar, and hold it over the button for the document you want to drag it to. The receiving document springs open, and you can drag and position the item anywhere you like.

With Cut and Paste

Drag and drop is similar to using the mouse to cut an item from one location and paste it to another. But what if you only want to delete your selection or aren't quite sure where you want to move it to? In such a case, you can avail yourself of several other tools to help you cut or cut and paste an item.

Here are the methods you can use to delete a selected item:

- Press the Delete or Backspace key.
- Press Ctrl+X.
- Begin typing. This will replace the selected item with the new data you input.

Here are the methods you can use to cut and paste a selected item:

- Press Ctrl+X to cut the item. Move your mouse pointer to where you want to move the item and click once to activate the cursor at the new insertion point. Press Ctrl+V to paste the item to your new location.
- Use the toolbar buttons. With the item selected, click the Cut button. Move your mouse pointer to where you want to move the item and click once to activate the cursor at the new insertion point. Click the Paste button to paste the item to your new location.

> Be careful about how you delete selected items. When you cut an item using Ctrl+X or the Cut button on the toolbar, the item is stored on a virtual clipboard, which holds it until you paste it to a new location or post another item on the clipboard. Therefore, if you make a mistake in cutting a selected item from your document, you at least have a chance to restore it from the clipboard. Simply press Ctrl+Z, or select Edit, Undo from the menu bar, to undo the deletion. WordPerfect Office 2000's undo feature is covered in more detail later on in this hour.
>
> Note that if you delete the selected item by hitting the Delete or Backspace key or by typing over the selected item to replace it with new data, the undo option is not available because the item is not posted to the clipboard. Unfortunately, the deleted item is gone for good.

With Copy and Paste

You can also copy, rather than cut or delete, a selected item and paste it to a new location. With the item selected, press Ctrl+C or click the Copy button on the toolbar to copy the item. Move your mouse pointer to where you want to insert the copy and click once to activate the cursor at the new insertion point. Press Ctrl+V or click the Paste button on the toolbar to paste the copy to your new location.

Undo and Redo

Ever make a mistake in a document and wish there were an easy way to undo it? Have you deleted the wrong paragraph or pasted a block of text to the wrong location? Fear not, with WordPerfect Office 2000 for Linux, you can undo a mistake with the click of a button. If you change your mind again, you can even redo something you've undone.

Here's how it works. Every time you strike a key to edit a document, the action is recorded by the application you're working in. Whether you've changed the font in a paragraph of text or cut and copied an entire page from one location to another, you can undo or redo the action in several ways.

Here are the methods you can use to undo an action:

- Click the Undo button on the toolbar.
- Press Ctrl+Z.
- Select Edit, Undo from the menu bar.

Here are the methods you can use to redo an action:

- Click the Redo button on the toolbar.
- Press Ctrl+Shift+Z.
- Select Edit, Undo from the menu bar.

To undo or redo more than one action, simply repeat any of the aforementioned methods as many times as necessary.

WordPerfect 9 provides an additional Undo/Redo tool that isn't included in the other applications in the suite. As shown in Figure 3.8, the Undo/Redo History dialog box contains two columns listing all the actions WordPerfect 9 can undo or redo. This is extremely helpful if you've made several edits to a document before realizing your mistake and need to jump back several steps to correct it. Simply click all items you want to undo or redo and then click the appropriate Undo or Redo button in the dialog box for your changes to take effect.

The Options button in the Undo/Redo History dialog box allows you to set the number of Undo/Redo actions that WordPerfect 9 will record. You can configure Undo/Redo to record anywhere between 10 and 300 actions. Just click the Options button, select the number of actions to record, and click OK or hit Enter.

To Do: Undo and Redo Actions in WordPerfect

1. Begin typing in a new WordPerfect document. Type a full page of anything you want.
2. Drag and drop a sentence from one location to another.
3. Select a paragraph and delete it.
4. Cut and paste a word from the beginning of the document to the end.
5. When you have a full page, select Edit, Undo/Redo History from the menu bar to open the Undo/Redo History dialog box. Review the items in your Undo history and note the specificity with which WordPerfect explains the actions you took.
6. Undo four or more of your actions at once, then redo the last two of them.

FIGURE 3.8
WordPerfect 9's Undo/Redo History dialog box is an extra tool for correcting mistakes.

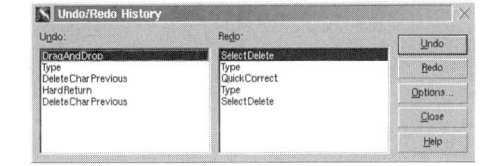

> The Undo/Redo feature doesn't work for file saves, which can lead to disastrous data loss if you're not careful. For example, say you're using WordPerfect 9 to write the great American novel, and you've just finished chapter one after months of hard work. You've saved your document as `chapter.01`, and you're ready to begin work on `chapter.02`. To save time, you open `chapter.01` to use as a template for `chapter.02`. Unfortunately, you forget to save the file as a new document, and you begin typing over your original text, saving your work as you go. Because you didn't change the filename, WordPerfect 9 will continue to save your work as `chapter.01`, writing over the original text. Because Undo/Redo doesn't record file saves, you cannot undo the saves that have erased all your hard work.

Zoom

The Zoom feature allows you to change the magnification of your document on the screen. You can zoom in to magnify your document by up to 400 percent, and you can zoom out to shrink it down to as little as 25 percent. Although Zoom has no impact on how your document looks on the printed page, it's a helpful tool that allows you to focus in on a specific element of a document or take a step back for a "big picture" view.

You can access the Zoom feature by clicking the Zoom button on the toolbar or by selecting View, Zoom from the menu bar. Whichever method you use, you're provided with several default Zoom levels to choose from. To select a custom Zoom level, click Other and enter any zoom level between 25 percent and 400 percent.

Figure 3.9 shows the Zoom button in action on the WordPerfect 9 toolbar. WordPerfect 9 also features Real-Time Preview Zoom, by which your document automatically resizes to the magnification level you point to with your cursor, giving you a chance to preview the Zoom level before making a final selection.

FIGURE 3.9
You can use Zoom to increase the magnification level of your onscreen view by up to 400 percent.

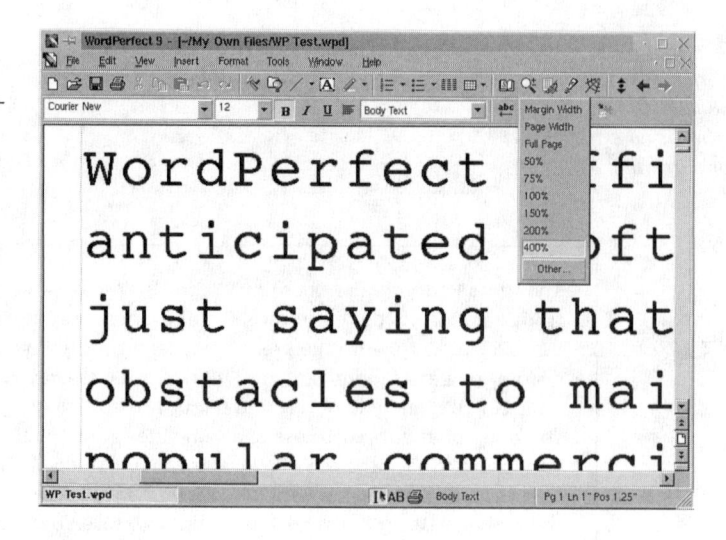

Navigating with the Scrollbars

Scrollbars are a familiar means of navigating through open windows in any window-based operating system. In WordPerfect Office 2000, scrollbars are an integral part of navigating through files and records created in WordPerfect, Quattro Pro, Paradox, and CorelCENTRAL (Presentations 9 has its own unique navigation tools, as will be shown in Hour 14, "Corel Presentations 9 Basics").

The basics of scrollbar navigation are the same regardless of the application. As shown in Figure 3.10, the vertical scrollbar at the far right of an open window and the horizontal scrollbar along the bottom of an open window can be used to "scroll" through your documents to view pages located offscreen.

FIGURE 3.10
WordPerfect Office 2000's scrollbars help you navigate vertically and horizontally through your open documents.

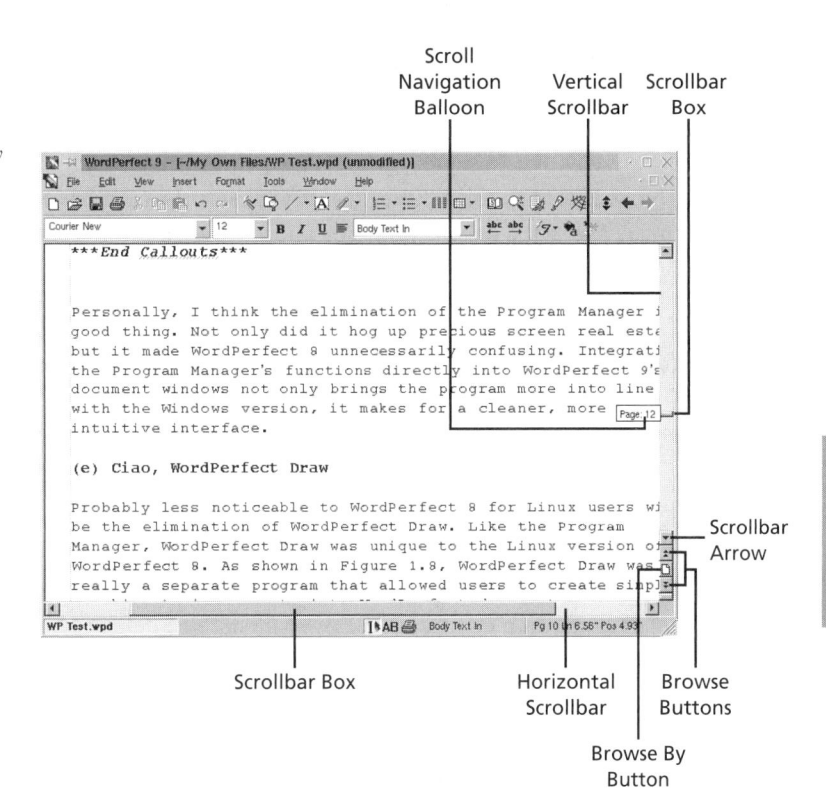

You have several ways to move through a document using the scrollbars:

- Use the scrollbar arrows to scroll the document up, down, left, or right.
- Point and click anywhere on a scrollbar. The direction your document will scroll depends on where you click in relation to the scroll box. For example, clicking in the vertical scrollbar at a point above the scroll box scrolls the document up, whereas clicking below the scroll box scrolls the document down.
- You can also click and drag a scrollbar box. This scrolling method provides the added benefit of letting you know where you are in the document as you scroll. For example, as shown in Figure 3.10, as you drag the vertical scrollbar box down in a WordPerfect 9 document, a scroll navigation balloon pops up telling you what page you've dragged the scroll box to. When you reach the page you want, simply let go of the mouse.

- Only WordPerfect 9 and Quattro Pro 9 make use of the Browse By button on the vertical scrollbar. The Browse By button works in conjunction with the browse buttons to let you jump from one element to another of the same type within the same document. For example, by default the Browse By button in WordPerfect 9 is set to browse by page. This means that if you click the up browse button, you scroll up one page in the document; if you click the down browse button, you scroll down one page. In WordPerfect 9, you can change the default setting for the Browse By button by clicking it. Each time you click it, it rolls over to the next setting in the following order: page, table, box, footnote, endnote, heading, edit position, and comment.

  The Browse By settings in Quattro Pro 9 are a little more complex, and they're covered in Hour 10, "Quattro Pro 9 Basics."

Printing Documents

As shown in Table 2.2 in Hour 2, to print documents from any open WordPerfect Office 2000 application, you can click the Print button in the default toolbar to open the Print dialog box. You can also open the Print dialog box by clicking File, Print on the menu bar or by pressing Ctrl+P.

Figure 3.11 shows the WordPerfect 9 Print dialog box, which is very similar to that of Presentations 9 and Paradox 9. In the case of Quattro Pro 9, the print dialog box is truly unique to address special issues related to printing spreadsheets. We'll take a closer look at printing from Quattro Pro 9 in Hour 12, "Updating and Printing Your Spreadsheet."

FIGURE 3.11
The WordPerfect 9 Print dialog box.

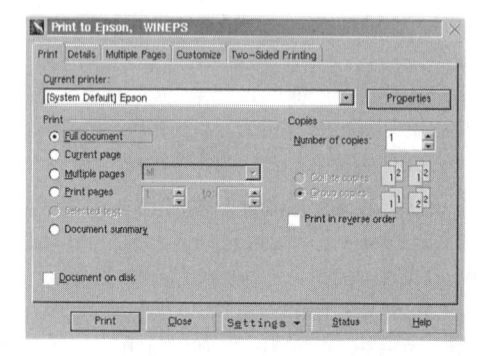

As shown in Figure 3.11, the title bar and the Current Printer menu list "Epson," the name given to the default printer used on my Linux system. It goes without saying that to print WordPerfect Office 2000 documents, you'll have to set up your own printer. Although this topic is somewhat beyond the scope of this book, let's spend a few minutes on the basics of printer configuration in Corel Linux.

Adding a Printer

To add a printer, single-click the printer icon on the Corel Linux OS Desktop. This opens the Print tab in the Corel Linux Control Center, as shown in Figure 3.12.

> Because adding a printer is an administrative task, if you're not logged in as root you won't have access to all the buttons in the Print tab. To gain limited root access to add or edit a printer setting, press the Modify button, enter the root user password at the prompt, and click OK. The buttons in the Print tab will become active, and you can continue the procedure for adding or editing your printer.

FIGURE 3.12
The Corel Linux Control Center print setup window.

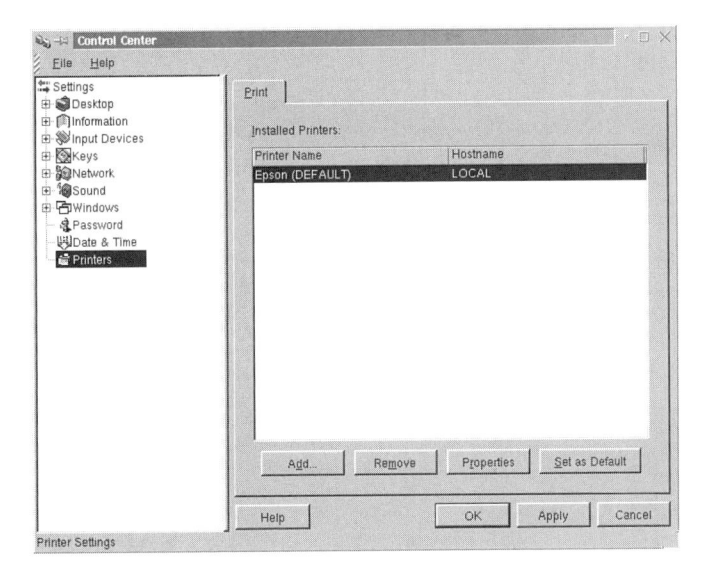

> The Corel Linux Control Center is command central for Corel Linux. Like the Control Panel in Windows, the Control Center can be used to take charge of many aspects of your Linux system, including monitor resolution, screensavers, sound, and peripherals. Although detailed coverage of the Control Center is way beyond the scope of this book, we touch on it again in Appendix A, "Introducing Corel Linux OS."

Click the Add button to launch the Kcmprint printer configuration utility. To keep things simple, let's assume your printer is attached to your computer, rather than a remote printer accessed on a network. Select Locally on My Computer and click Next. Give your printer a name. I call my printer by the name of its manufacturer (that is, Epson).

In the Device or Port pull-down menu, select the port that your printer is plugged into. Most printers are assigned to the lp0 or lp1 port. Try lp0 first—if it doesn't work, you can run printer setup again and select lp1. After selecting the printer port, click Next.

> To make sure you have the right printer port, boot into Windows and open the My Computer icon on the Desktop. Double-click the Printers folder to find your current printer. Right-click the printer and select Properties from the pop-up menu. In the Properties dialog box, click the Details tab for your current printer port setting. Write it down and use the information to properly configure the printer in Linux. If your printer still isn't working, it's either not properly configured or it's not supported. You'll want to consult with the manufacturer, and/or a good book dedicated to Linux, for alternative troubleshooting techniques.

Enter the make and model of your printer from the pull-down menus provided. Click Finish.

That's all there is to it. Your new printer appears in the Print tab of the Corel Linux Control Center. If you ever need to edit your printer, access the Print tab, select your printer, and use the Remove, Properties, or Set as Default keys to access and change your printer settings.

Print Settings

Take another look at Figure 3.11 and note the tabs along the top of the dialog box labeled Print, Details, Multiple Pages, Customize, and Two-Sided Printing. These tabs give you control over every aspect of a print job. Although only WordPerfect has all these print tabs, the print tabs for the other applications in the suite are all subsets of the WordPerfect set. Here's what they are and what they do:

- The Print tab lets you control which pages to print, the number of print copies, and whether to collate your copies or print them in reverse order. The Properties button next to the Current Printer menu gives you access to the Printer Properties dialog box, shown in Figure 3.13, which gives you even greater control over the hardware configuration for your printer.

FIGURE 3.13
The Printer Properties dialog box.

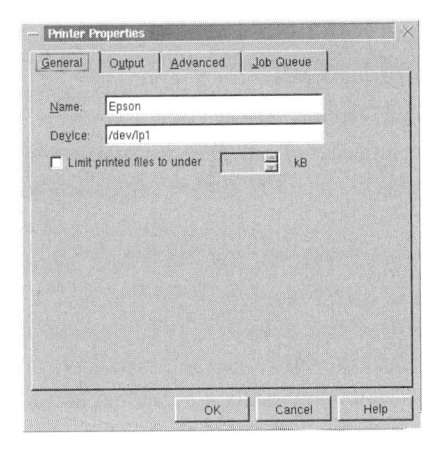

- The Details tab lets you select the default font for your files, print an existing document to another file, assign a fax driver to a current printer, print in color, print text only, and print all text as graphics.
- The Multiple Pages tab gives you even more control over the printing of a noncontiguous range of pages, chapters, or volumes. For example, entering **5-** would print from page 5 to the end of your document, whereas entering **-5** would print from the beginning of your document through page 5. Noncontiguous pages, such as pages 6–7, 11–15, and 19, could be printed by typing **6-7, 11-15, 19**. Click the Examples button at the bottom right of the Multiple Pages tab for additional help on using this syntax to print odd blocks of pages.
- The Customize tab caters to you creative souls out there by providing control over the size of your print output. If your printer supports it, you can print out posters, thumbnail sketches, or custom-size print jobs. The Output Page button opens the Page Setup dialog box, from which you can define the page dimensions and margins as well as whether to print in portrait or landscape format.
- The Two-Sided Printing tab works exactly as it sounds. Here, you can customize a print job to print on double-sided pages, which is perfect for creating booklets, brochures, or similar promotional material. You can also assign one edge of your document to serve as the binding edge, which clears text out of the way for a binding to fasten the pages together.

The Settings button at the bottom of the print dialog box allows you to control the options displayed on each of these print tabs. If you want to modify your print tabs, simply click the Settings button and select Named Setting to open the Named Setting dialog box. From here, you can use the check boxes to toggle on and off the items displayed in each print tab. Click the Restore button to restore your Named Settings dialog box to its default setting.

Print Preview

The Print Preview feature in WordPerfect Office 2000 saves countless trees by giving you a preview of how your document will look on the printed page, before you actually commit it to hard copy. You can access Print Preview by selecting File, Print Preview. Alternatively, there's a Print Preview button in the Print dialog box that opens whenever you try to print a document.

Summary

In this hour you learned many of the basic tasks that will serve you well in all WordPerfect Office 2000 for Linux applications, including how to create a new document, how to save a document, and how to open an existing document. To help you find a home for your documents, you also learned about the Corel Linux file system and how to access documents stored on floppy drives and a Windows partition.

You also learned many of the core skills required in the creation of documents, including how to enter text and data, how to navigate through your documents, and how to print documents.

You'll put these skills to good use as we move on to Hour 4, "WordPerfect 9 Basics."

Q&A

Q I want to jump right into a new PerfectExpert Project. Do I need to open a WordPerfect Office 2000 application to access the PerfectExpert?

A No. There are two ways to access the PerfectExpert without first opening a WordPerfect Office 2000 application: (1) from the Corel Application Starter, navigate to the WordPerfect Office 2000 menu and select Corel new Project; or (2) open a Console window and enter the command `perfectexpert`.

Q How do I change the password for a user in Corel Linux?

A Log in as root. From the Corel Application Starter, select Applications, System and launch the User Manager. In the Users tab, double-click the user whose password you want to change. This opens the Edit User dialog box. In the User Info tab, press the Set Password button. Enter the new password as prompted and click OK. Close out of the User Manager and click Yes when asked if you want to save your changes.

Q Can I cut and paste text from WordPerfect into any other WordPerfect Office 2000 application.

A Absolutely. In fact, with the limited exception of CorelCENTRAL (which doesn't do graphics), you can cut and paste text, graphics, data, symbols, and just about any other item from one application in the suite to another.

Workshop

The Workshop contains quiz questions and exercises to help reinforce what you've learned in this hour. If you get stuck, the answers to the quiz questions can be found in Appendix B, "Answers to Quiz Questions."

Quiz

1. In the Corel Linux File Manager, what is the name of the directory for the My Documents folder stored on a separate Windows partition running on the same PC?
2. How do you select a block of text using the arrow keys?
3. Identify the keyboard shortcuts for the following commands:

    Select all

    Undo

    Redo

    Open an existing document

    Save a document

    Print a document

Exercises

1. Log in as root and make sure your normal username has access to your PC's floppy drive.
2. Create a blank WordPerfect 9 document. Name it `Testing123` and save it to your Documents directory. Enter some text into your document and close WordPerfect 9. Using the Corel File Manager, find and open `Testing123`. Make some changes to the text you entered and save the new version as `321Testing`.
3. Configure your printer using the Corel Control Center and the Kcmprint utility. Give it a test run by printing out a copy of `Testing123`.

PART II
Word Processing with WordPerfect 9

Hour

4 WordPerfect 9 Basics

5 Formatting WordPerfect 9 Documents

6 The WordPerfect 9 Writer's Toolkit

7 Working with Tables and Columns

8 Creating and Working with Graphics in WordPerfect 9

9 Advanced WordPerfect 9 Techniques

HOUR 4

WordPerfect 9 Basics

WordPerfect is the one application in the suite that's probably familiar to most readers. If you haven't actually used a version of WordPerfect, I'm willing to bet you've used another word processor at some point along the road that brought you here. As such, this hour covering WordPerfect basics won't be an excruciating tutorial that assumes you've heretofore relied on longhand and a typewriter to generate documents. Instead, this hour focuses on helping you get the most out of the program by showing off certain unique aspects of the WordPerfect 9 interface, with tips on how to customize the interface along the way.

In this hour, you will

- Explore the WordPerfect 9 interface with an emphasis on unique features of WordPerfect 9, including the Shadow Cursor and Reveal Codes.
- Learn about WordPerfect views, including the Draft, Page, Two Pages, and Web Page views.
- Customize Corel's default settings so that WordPerfect 9 looks and works the way you want.

Introducing the WordPerfect 9 Workspace

In Hour 2, "Introducing the WordPerfect Office 2000 for Linux Environment," you learned several ways to launch WordPerfect Office 2000 applications. It's time to put that knowledge to good use by firing up WordPerfect 9.

Figure 4.1 shows the WordPerfect 9 program window, which should look very familiar. Common interface elements such as menus, toolbars, and the Property Bar were covered in Hour 2, and WordPerfect served as the model application for the review in Hour 3, "Common Tasks in WordPerfect Office 2000 for Linux."

FIGURE 4.1
The WordPerfect 9 workspace in Page view.

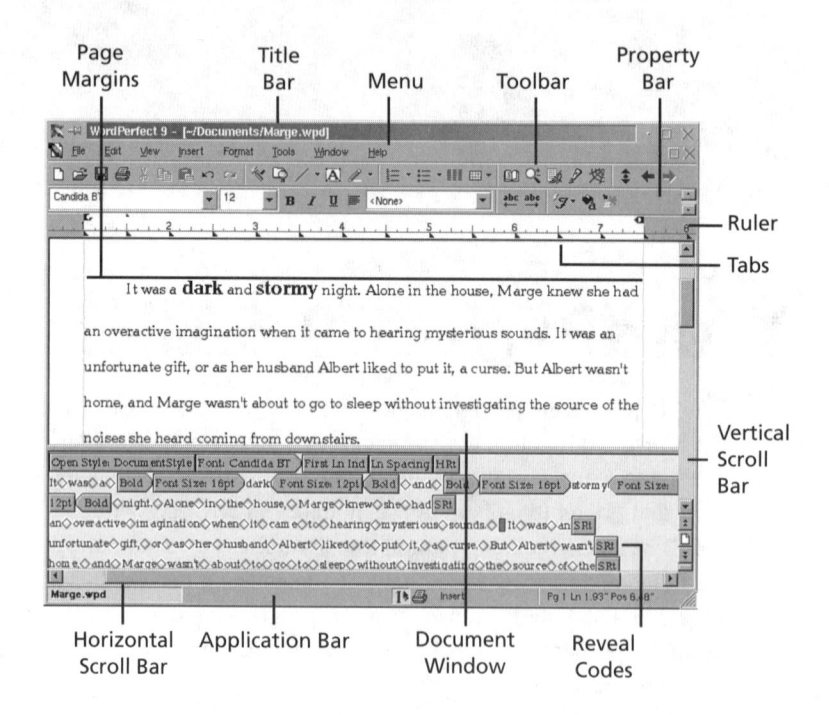

Although you're wading in familiar waters, there are many aspects of the WordPerfect 9 interface that haven't been touched upon. Learning what they are, and how to customize them, are what this hour is all about.

WordPerfect 9 Customization Tools: The View Menu and the Settings Dialog Box

This hour describes two main routes you can take to customize WordPerfect 9:

- You can control the WordPerfect 9 interface by making selections from the View menu shown in Figure 4.2.
- You can select Tools, Settings to open the Settings dialog box. As shown in Figure 4.3, the Settings dialog box is your gateway to changing WordPerfect 9's default settings in seven categories: Display, Environment, Files, Summary, Convert, Application Bar, and Customize.

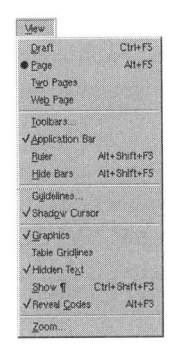

FIGURE 4.2
The WordPerfect 9 View menu.

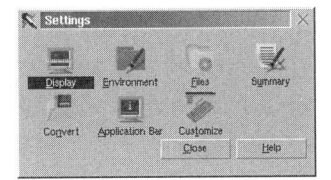

FIGURE 4.3
The WordPerfect 9 Settings dialog box.

Although there are other ways to control the WordPerfect 9 interface, the View menu and the Settings dialog box provide access to most of the customizable features of the program. This hour focuses on the most powerful and popular features you'll probably want to tinker with.

> As you work through this hour, you'll cover some of WordPerfect 9's most sophisticated formatting tools, including Reveal Codes and Hidden Text. Although these tools could have been covered in Hour 5, "Formatting WordPerfect 9 Documents," they're covered here because of your ability to customize them via the View menu and/or the Settings dialog box. Because WordPerfect 9 allows you to customize these and other formatting tools in ways that impact the WordPerfect 9 interface, there's bound to be some overlap in the hours dedicated to customization and formatting. My advice is to accept Hours 4 and 5 hand in hand. Collectively, these hours will provide you with expert control over not only the WordPerfect 9 interface but also the documents you create with it.

Changing the Document View

The View menu provides four different document views that affect how your documents are presented onscreen:

- *Draft view*. This view is for when you need to get your words down in a hurry and without distraction. In Draft view, WordPerfect hides top and bottom page margins, headers, footers, footnotes, and endnotes so that your text flows without interruption. Text, graphics, and the left and right margins are displayed as usual, and a thin black line indicates page breaks. Otherwise, your document looks like one continuous stream of text and/or graphics, which allows you to see more of your work onscreen at any given time.

- *Page view*. This view is the most popular view because, as shown previously in Figure 4.1, it simulates how your document will look in print. Page view restores everything that Draft view keeps hidden, including all page margins, headers and footers, and footnotes and endnotes. Seeing these elements onscreen has two advantages: You can monitor how your document will look when you print it, and you can edit certain elements, such as headers and footnotes, the same way you edit text in the body of your document. The only disadvantage to Page view is that showing all these elements takes up precious screen real estate, which means there's slightly less room onscreen for the body of your document.

- *Two Pages view*. This view takes a step back to provide you with a "big picture" view of two adjacent pages placed side by side. Two Pages view is perfect for sampling the layout of pages in a newsletter or other documents with facing pages, but it renders text too small for actual editing work.

- *Web Page view*. This view is used only to create Web pages in WordPerfect 9 or to preview how an existing document will look on the Web. We'll cover Web Page view in more detail in Hour 23, "WordPerfect 9 and the Web."

To change your view, simply select the desired view from the View menu.

Changing the Bar View

In Hour 2, you covered much of what you need to know about customizing the default bars (that is, toolbars, Property Bars, and the Application Bar) in WordPerfect Office 2000. However, the View menu provides additional options you may want to take advantage of:

- *Toolbars*. Opens the Toolbar dialog box from which you can toggle on or off all of WordPerfect 9's toolbars. The effect is the same as right-clicking a toolbar and using the pop-up menu to control which toolbars are displayed. If you prefer a dialog box interface or don't have a two-button mouse, the View, Toolbar option is for you.

- *Application Bar.* Toggles on and off the Application Bar at the bottom of your document window. Alternatively, you can eliminate the Application Bar by right-clicking it and selecting Hide Application Bar. To restore it, select View, Application Bar and you're back in business.
- *Ruler.* Toggles on and off the Ruler that sits beneath the Property Bar at the top of the document window. The Ruler is much more than a measurement guide in WordPerfect. You can use the Ruler to set tabs, page margins, and paragraph formatting.
- *Hide Bars.* This option is like dynamite for WordPerfect documents—it blows them up to full-screen size and blows away all menus, toolbars, scroll bars, the Ruler, the Property Bar, and the Application Bar. Hide Bars view is recommended only if you're comfortable doing all document creation and navigation with the keyboard. You can also use a scroll mouse to navigate documents in Hide Bars view. To exit Hide Bars view, press the Esc key.

> For those of you migrating from Microsoft Word 97/98/2000, WordPerfect's Hide Bars option is the equivalent of Word's Full Screen view option on the View menu.

> You can use keyboard shortcuts to trick Hide Bars into restoring the menu. You've probably noticed that one letter in each menu title, usually the initial letter, is underlined (for example, File, Edit, View, and so on). The underlined letter can be used with the Alt key to open the menu in which the underlined letter appears. In Hide Bars view, you can use any of these shortcut keys to access the menu. Once you've summoned a particular menu, the entire menu bar stays put and can be utilized in Hide Bars view.

Clicking and Typing with the Shadow Cursor

Not to be confused with the cursor prompt (the blinking vertical bar that marks the insertion point where text will appear when you type) or the mouse pointer (the white arrow you control with your mouse to operate WordPerfect Office applications), the Shadow Cursor is a unique feature that was first introduced in WordPerfect 8.

The Shadow Cursor tags along behind the mouse pointer to show you where the cursor prompt will appear if you click with your mouse. The beauty of the Shadow Cursor is that it allows you to click and type anywhere in the body of a document without having to press the Tab and Enter keys to get the cursor prompt to the desired location.

To Do: Use the Shadow Cursor

1. Open a new WordPerfect document, select the View menu, and make sure that Shadow Cursor is checked. Note the blinking cursor prompt in the upper-left corner of your document, patiently waiting for you to enter text.
2. Move your mouse pointer around in the open document and watch the Shadow Cursor follow the pointer wherever it goes. Move the pointer to the right side of the document window, down slightly from the top of the page. Keep your eye on the Shadow Cursor and click once to see the cursor prompt "jump" to the exact point indicated by the Shadow Cursor.
3. In the View menu, select Show ¶ to display tabs, spaces, and returns onscreen. As shown in Figure 4.4, when you use the Shadow Cursor to insert the cursor prompt in a blank section of your document, WordPerfect automatically inserts all the hard return and tab keystrokes needed to get your cursor prompt to the desired location.

FIGURE 4.4

When you use the Shadow Cursor to place the cursor prompt in the middle of a document, WordPerfect automatically enters the keystrokes needed to get you there.

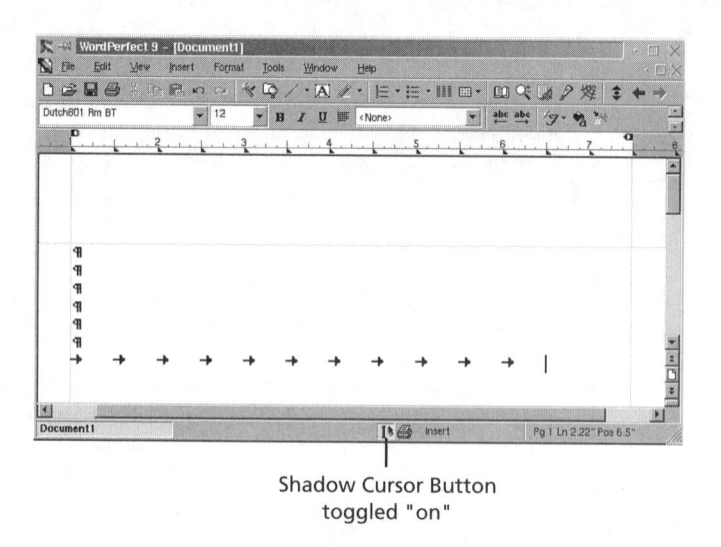

Shadow Cursor Button toggled "on"

If you find the Shadow Cursor distracting, you can turn it off by clicking the Shadow Cursor button on the Application bar, as shown in Figure 4.4. Alternatively, select View, Shadow Cursor from the menu to toggle the Shadow Cursor on and off.

Using the Show Paragraphs View

In experimenting with the Shadow Cursor, you had your first taste of the Show ¶ view available from the View menu. As shown in Figure 4.5, Show ¶ allows you to see certain nonprinting formatting symbols that are normally hidden from view, such as tabs, spaces, indents, and hard returns. Depending on the font size and zoom level you use in your documents, Show ¶ can be helpful because it displays your keystrokes onscreen, thus eliminating guesswork as to how you achieved certain formatting in your document.

FIGURE 4.5
Show ¶ displays hidden formatting codes such as tabs, spaces, indents, and hard returns.

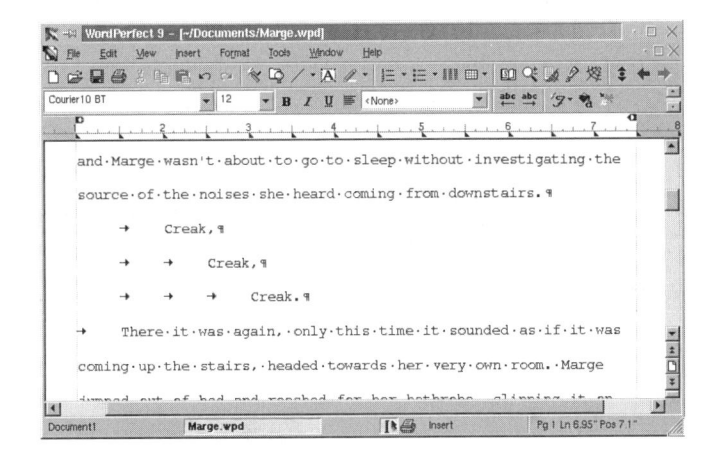

> To change the formatting symbols that Show ¶ displays, select Tools, Settings and choose Display from the Settings dialog box. Navigate to the Symbols tab and place a check next to each of the formatting symbols you want to keep in Show ¶ view. Your options include Space, Hard Return, Tab, Indent, Center, Flush Right, Soft Hyphen, Advance, and Center Page. Click OK and close out of the Settings dialog box to return to your document.

Understanding Reveal Codes

Have you ever run into a bizarre formatting glitch that you couldn't explain, much less fix? Perhaps a running header that you inserted on page 2 of an important letter suddenly appeared on page 1 and refused to leave. Maybe you were typing a signature line when your word processor automatically, and seemingly irreversibly, extended your line the across the entire page as soon as you hit Enter. If these or similar formatting glitches sound familiar, you were probably using some other word processor (no names, please) that didn't have Reveal Codes, one of the most powerful features of WordPerfect 9.

The Reveal Codes feature displays the underlying formatting codes that tell WordPerfect what to do with your text. For example, if you highlight a word and click the Bold button on the toolbar, WordPerfect places a secret code before the highlighted word that turns boldface type on and another code after the highlighted word that turns boldface type off. The result is that the highlighted word is displayed onscreen and in print in boldface type.

This behind-the-scenes format coding goes on every time you add, delete, or manipulate the text in an open WordPerfect document. Most of the time, WordPerfect allows you to remain blissfully ignorant of the coding it pours into your documents. There are times, however, when your ability to access these codes to better understand or control the formatting of a document is extremely useful. Here's how you do it: Select View, Reveal Codes from the menu bar or press Alt+F3. As shown in Figure 4.6, this opens up the Reveal Codes window at the bottom of your WordPerfect document.

FIGURE 4.6
The Reveal Codes window uncovers all the mysterious formatting codes you can control to make adjustments to your documents.

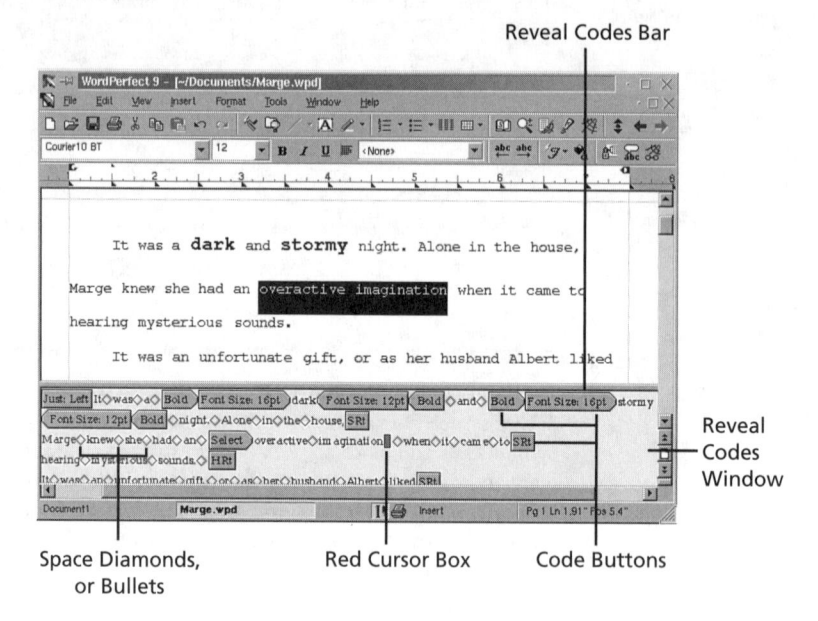

You can also open and close Reveal Codes by dragging the Reveal Codes bar shown in Figure 4.6. Using the Reveal Codes bar gives you the added flexibility of controlling the size of the Reveal Codes window to reveal as much, or as little, code as you need.

The Reveal Codes window shows the same text you see in your document without any formatting applied. Instead, text in Reveal Codes is surrounded by the following mysterious-looking shapes:

- *Space diamonds (or bullets).* No, these aren't diamonds from outer space. WordPerfect uses tiny diamonds as the code for spaces that appear between words in the Reveal Codes window. Every time you hit the space bar, another diamond appears in Reveal Codes. WordPerfect calls its space codes *bullets*, but they sure look like diamonds to me.

- *Red cursor box.* The red cursor box is the Reveal Codes version of the cursor prompt in your normal document window. If you move the cursor prompt to a new location in your document, the red cursor box jumps to the same location in Reveal Codes. If you move the red cursor box in Reveal Codes, the cursor prompt jumps to that location in your document window. There's no magic behind the cursor box being red—it's just easier to see amid the unformatted text and code swimming in the Reveal Codes window.

- *Code buttons.* These gray buttons in the Reveal Codes window signify actual formatting tasks performed in your document. You needn't memorize what the codes are and what they do. Although most of them are self-explanatory, if you're ever uncertain about a code button in your document, hold your mouse over the button and wait. In a few seconds, a pop-up window opens describing the function of the code. To give you a better sense of how codes work, Table 4.1 provides a description of how WordPerfect uses the codes shown in Figure 4.6.

TABLE 4.1 Sample Codes Used in Figure 4.6

Code Button	Description
Just: Left	Left justification. This justifies the text in your document to the left, meaning that all text that follows this code aligns to the left margin. You'll learn more about justification in Hour 5.
Bold	Boldface type. In Figure 4.6, the words *dark* and *stormy* appear in boldface. Note how WordPerfect handles the codes: Code buttons for bold appear both before and after each word that appears in boldface type. The first code button turns boldface on; the second turns it off. There are many other formatting codes in WordPerfect, such as italics and underlining, that work the same way. Codes that work in pairs to turn formatting on and off are sometimes called *Paired Codes*.
Font Size: 16pt	Font size. In this case, the code changes the font size to 16-point type.
Font Size: 12pt	Font size. In this case, the code changes the font size to 12-point type.
SRt	Soft return. When a line of text reaches the right margin, WordPerfect automatically sends it on to the next line by inserting this code for a soft return.
Select	Select. This one is self-explanatory, but notice how the select code appears just before the first word that's part of a block of highlighted text in the document window. Once your text is no longer highlighted, the select code disappears.
HRt	Hard return. When you hit Enter at the end of each paragraph, WordPerfect inserts a hard return code in Reveal Codes.

Using Reveal Codes

Understanding Reveal Codes and knowing what they do is fine, but how do you actually use Reveal Codes in your work?

The red cursor box and the code buttons are the key to using Reveal Codes to effectively control document formatting. You can use your mouse or the arrow keys to navigate the red cursor box through Reveal Codes to find and delete code buttons to eliminate formatting that appears in the document window. To delete a code button, place the red cursor box before the code button to be deleted and press Delete, or after the code button to be deleted and press Backspace. Better yet, you can click a code button and drag it out of the Reveal Codes window to delete it for good.

Note that when deleting Paired Code, such as boldface code buttons that appear on both sides of the affected text, you need only remove one member of the pair of code buttons. The matching code button will disappear automatically with the deletion of its partner.

To Do: Customize Reveal Codes

1. To customize Reveal Codes, select Tools, Settings from the menu bar.
2. In the Settings dialog box, click Display and navigate to the Reveal Codes tab. Uncheck the Use System Colors box and select text and background colors that'll be easier on your eyes. Do yourself another favor by clicking the Font button to change the font size and type to make Reveal Codes even easier to read.
3. The Reveal Codes tab also lets you set Reveal Codes text to wrap when it reaches the end of the Reveal Codes window, as opposed to the default wrapping at the end of a line in the document window. You can also choose whether to show spaces as diamonds (called *bullets* in the Reveal Codes tab) and whether to show codes in detail.
4. When you're through making your selections, click OK and close out of the Setting dialog box to see the changes in your newly customized Reveal Codes window.

Showing Hidden Text

Hidden Text is one of the coolest features of WordPerfect, yet it is seldom talked about or used. Hidden Text is like digital whiteout you can apply and remove as necessary to hide selected text from view. Hidden Text doesn't alter the size of your document—though invisible, your Hidden Text remains in place, ready to appear onscreen and in print at your command.

Here's how it works: Say you're the type of math teacher who likes to spring a pop quiz on the class every now and then. You can use WordPerfect 9's Hidden Text feature to type out all the quiz questions and answers, hide the answers while you print a quiz copy to give to your students, and then recall the answers to use as your answer key when you grade the quiz.

To set this up, type out your questions and answers just like any other WordPerfect document. To hide an answer, drag with your mouse to highlight the entire answer. Select Format, Font to open the Font Properties dialog box shown in Figure 4.7. In the column labeled Appearance, make sure that Hidden is checked. Do the same for all the quiz answers.

Click OK to return to your document. That's all there is to it. Now you can make your Hidden Text appear and disappear by toggling Hidden Text on and off from the View menu.

FIGURE 4.7

Setting Hidden Text in the Font Properties dialog box.

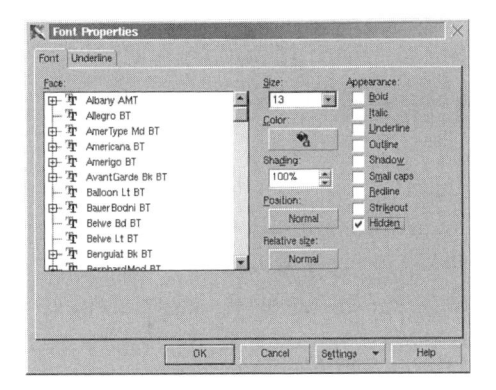

If you ever want to convert Hidden Text back to normal text, just reverse the procedure and deselect the Hidden check box in the Font Properties dialog box. Alternatively, you can open Reveal Codes, find the code button labeled Hidden, and delete it or drag it out of the Reveal Codes window.

Customizing Menu Settings

Figure 4.8 shows my File menu in WordPerfect 9. Aside from the standard point-and-click commands (Open, Save, Print, and so on), there's a lot going on here. At the far right are handy keyboard shortcut references to the commands on the menu. At the bottom, just above the Exit command, is one-click access to the nine documents I accessed most recently.

FIGURE 4.8
The WordPerfect 9 File menu.

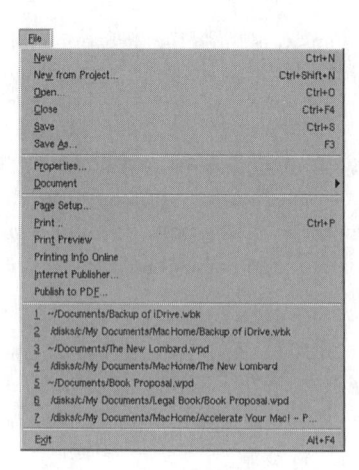

To Do: Customize Your Menu Settings

Unless you like your menus as clean as possible, keyboard shortcuts and access to recent documents are conveniences you're sure to appreciate. To turn these features on:

1. Select Tools, Settings from the menu to open the Settings dialog box.
2. Select Environment to open the Environment Settings dialog box. Then navigate to the Interface tab shown in Figure 4.9.
3. Under the Items to Display on Menus heading, select Last Opened Documents on the File Menu and Shortcut Keys. While you're at it, select QuickTips, which I'll explain in a moment.
4. Click OK and close out of the Settings dialog box to return to your document.

FIGURE 4.9
The Interface tab in the Environment Settings dialog box lets you configure certain menu features.

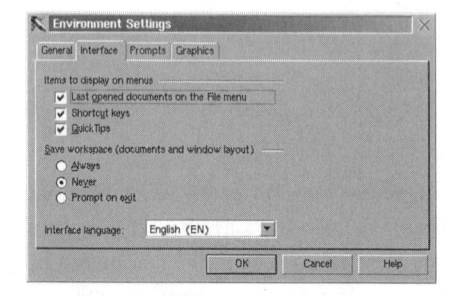

Test your new menu settings by selecting any menu. Keyboard shortcuts should appear on the far right for every command to which a shortcut has been assigned. You'll have to open a few documents to confirm that recently accessed documents are accessible from the File menu.

As for QuickTips, it really has no business under the Items to Display in Menu heading. QuickTips has nothing to do with menus, but you'll be glad to learn about it anyway. As shown in Figure 4.10, QuickTips are tiny balloons that pop open when you hold your mouse pointer over certain items, such as toolbar buttons and pull-down menus. QuickTips provide the name of the item and a brief description. If there's a keyboard shortcut for the item and you've selected Shortcut Keys (as shown in Figure 4.9), QuickTips will also show the shortcut.

FIGURE 4.10
The QuickTips feature displays the item name, description, and shortcut key.

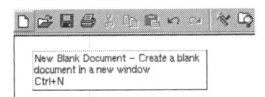

Customizing File Settings

In Hour 3, you learned about the Linux file system and how to save documents in WordPerfect Office 2000. After you've had some experience creating documents in WordPerfect 9 and have grown comfortable with the Linux file system, you may want to take charge of how and where WordPerfect 9 saves your documents.

You can customize the default WordPerfect 9 file settings by selecting Tools, Settings to open the Settings dialog box and clicking Files to open the Files Settings dialog box, shown in Figure 4.11.

FIGURE 4.11
The File Settings dialog box.

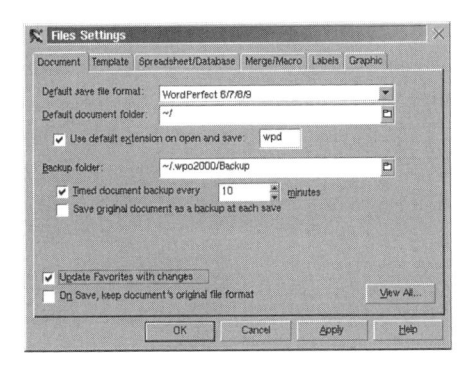

The File Settings dialog box presents tabs that lead to the settings for six different types of WordPerfect 9 files: Document, Template, Spreadsheet/Database, Merge/Macro, Labels, and Graphic. The file settings work in pretty much the same way regardless of file type, so this hour will focus only on customizing file settings under the Document tab.

Customizing the Default File Format

As shown previously in Figure 4.11, the first option presented under the Document tab is to configure the default file format. Just because you're working in WordPerfect 9 for Linux, WordPerfect doesn't insist that you save all your files in WordPerfect format. Using the drop-down menu next to the Default Save File Format heading, you can click to select a new default from more than 50 different file formats. Changing the default means that all new documents generated in WordPerfect 9 will be saved in the file format you've selected.

Modifying the default file format makes it easy to collaborate with friends, family, and coworkers who haven't yet discovered the wonder and glory of WordPerfect Office 2000. By changing your default file format to match what everyone else is using, their word processor of choice will be able to open documents you've created in WordPerfect 9.

> Here's some good news for WordPerfect fans trading up to version 9. As shown in Figure 4.11, the default WordPerfect 9 file format is listed as WordPerfect 6/7/8/9. This tells you that although version 9 boasts many exciting new features and enhancements, it is 100-percent compatible with documents created in WordPerfect 6, 7, and 8. WordPerfect 9 can read and write to documents generated in any of these prior versions, and vice versa.

Customizing the Default Document Folder

The next heading in Document tab of the File Settings dialog box is Default Document Folder. WordPerfect 9 designates each user's My Home folder as the default location for saving files. You can change the default by selecting the tiny folder icon at the edge of the white box next to the Default Document Folder heading. This opens the Choose a Directory dialog box shown in Figure 4.12, where I've selected /My Home/Documents as the new default file location for WordPerfect 9 documents.

FIGURE 4.12
The Choose a Directory dialog box lets you change the default location for saving WordPerfect files.

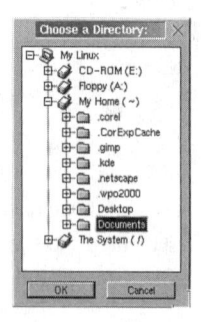

Customizing Backup Settings

WordPerfect 9 saves a backup copy of your works in progress every 10 minutes. The default directory for your backup files is /My Home/.wpo2000/Backup. Of course, you can change both the frequency and the file location of your backup saves.

Returning to the Document tab in the File Settings dialog box (shown previously in Figure 4.11), click the tiny folder icon on the end of the long white box next to the heading Backup Folder. As you did in selecting a default file folder, click the folder icon to open the Choose a Directory dialog box, from which you can select a new default location for backup saves.

Beneath the Backup Folder heading are additional tools to turn backup saves on and off and to control the frequency of backup saves. Frankly, there's little reason to mess with WordPerfect's defaults. Unless you're really short on hard drive space, I can't imagine disabling automatic backups. Setting automatic backups for every 10 minutes also makes sense—there's probably little you could do in 10 minutes that you couldn't re-create if you lost an open document due to a system crash.

Customizing Toolbars

You can exercise maximum control over your toolbars (and other items) by clicking Customize in the Settings dialog box shown previously in Figure 4.3. This opens the Customize Settings dialog box shown in Figure 4.13, which offers customization tabs labeled Toolbars, Property Bars, Menus, and Keyboards.

FIGURE 4.13
The Customize Settings dialog box opened to the Toolbars tab.

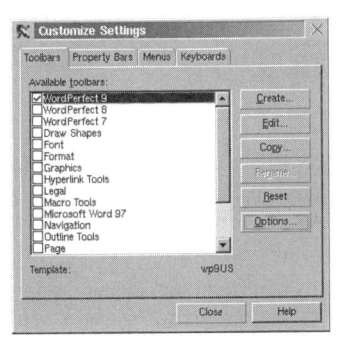

The Toolbars tab presents a list of all available toolbars in WordPerfect 9. Click to select the WordPerfect 9 toolbar and click the Options button to open the Toolbar Options dialog box, shown in Figure 4.14.

FIGURE 4.14

The Toolbar Options dialog box.

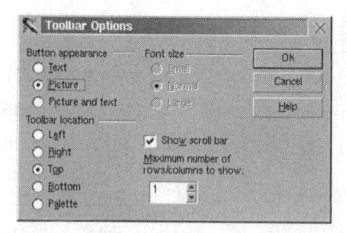

By default, every toolbar in WordPerfect 9 is configured to sit at the top of the document window. You can change this by making alternative selections under the Toolbar Location heading in the Toolbar Options dialog box. You can force your toolbar to be displayed on the left, right, or bottom of the document window, or you can turn it into a free-floating palette you can place anywhere onscreen.

You can also change the button settings for your toolbars to display text instead of, or as well as, the icon pictures that adorn toolbar buttons by default. To give you a sense of the fun you can have customizing your toolbars, Figure 4.15 shows the WordPerfect 9 toolbar configured as a standalone palette with picture buttons and scroll bars. Feel free to experiment with your own toolbar settings to find whatever's comfortable for you to work in.

FIGURE 4.15

The WordPerfect 9 toolbar configured as a palette with picture buttons and a scroll bar.

> By selecting the Property Bars tab in the Customize Settings dialog box, you can customize WordPerfect 9's Property Bars the same way you customized the toolbars. Simply select a Property Bar to configure, click the Options button, and make your changes.
>
> The Menu and Keyboard tabs don't include an Options button. Instead, use the Edit button to customize menu and keyboard settings. In the Menu tab, clicking Edit opens the Menu Editor; in the Keyboard tab, clicking Edit opens the Keyboard Shortcut dialog box.

Have fun playing around with as many settings as you like. If WordPerfect 9 is anything, it's eager to please, and you can practically make your new word processor work, look, and act however you want.

Summary

In this hour you learned how to customize the WordPerfect 9 interface to suit your work style. You studied the highlights of the two main routes to customizing WordPerfect 9: the View menu and the Settings dialog box. Along the way, you also learned more than a little about some of WordPerfect 9's powerful formatting tools, most notably Reveal Codes.

In the next hour, you'll learn much more about formatting documents in WordPerfect 9. From exploring new features such as Real-Time Preview to learning how to insert special text such as page numbers and symbols, you'll be formatting WordPerfect documents like a champ.

Q&A

Q Some of the keyboard shortcuts presented in this book don't seem to work. Am I doing something wrong?

A Not at all. Although the keyboard shortcuts presented in this book have been thoroughly tested, it is possible that one or more of them don't work on your Linux system. This is because certain keyboard shortcuts in WordPerfect Office 2000 conflict with keyboard shortcuts assigned by the system in certain distributions/configurations of Linux. If a keyboard shortcut isn't working for you, don't sweat it—wherever possible, this book provides you with alternative ways to perform the same task.

Q Is there a way to customize the Shadow Cursor?

A Of course! Select Tools, Settings or press Alt+F12 to open the Settings dialog box. Press the Display button to open the Display Settings dialog box and then navigate to the Document tab. The Color button lets you change the drab gray that coats the Shadow Cursor by default. The Shape button lets you change how the Shadow Cursor looks when it follows your mouse pointer into existing text. To take maximum advantage of the Shadow Cursor, select Spaces and Both, respectively, under the headings labeled Snap To and Active In. With these selections, the Shadow Cursor will let you insert a cursor prompt in any space on an open page, regardless of whether text already exists in that space. When you're through making your selections, click OK, then close out of the Settings dialog box to return to your document.

Workshop

The Workshop contains quiz questions and exercises to help reinforce what you've learned in this hour. If you get stuck, the answers can be found in Appendix B, "Answers to Quiz Questions."

Quiz

1. How do you use menus in Hide Bars view?
2. What is the keyboard shortcut to open the Settings dialog box?
3. What's the difference between the file format for documents created in WordPerfect 6 for Windows and WordPerfect 9 for Linux?

Exercises

1. Configure the WordPerfect 9 Graphics toolbar to appear on the left side of the document window.
2. Open Reveal Codes and configure the Reveal Codes window to share equal space onscreen with the document window.
3. Open WordPerfect 9 and type out the questions and answers to the quiz for Hour 3. Use the Hidden Text feature to hide the answers. Once you're sure Hidden Text worked, open Reveal Codes and delete the code for all your Hidden Text.

HOUR 5

Formatting WordPerfect 9 Documents

In Hour 4, "WordPerfect 9 Basics," you learned about Reveal Codes, one of WordPerfect's most powerful formatting tools. This hour introduces a treasure trove of additional WordPerfect 9 formatting tools, many of which you'll come to use on a daily basis.

In this hour, you will

- Take control of the face, size, and style of your fonts.
- Practice setting basic tabs and indents with the Ruler and the menu bar.
- Learn how to use WordPerfect styles to apply several formatting commands at once.

Working with Fonts in WordPerfect 9

Fonts are the key to determining how your text looks on paper and onscreen. WordPerfect 9 includes many font formatting and management tools to help you control three basic attributes of your fonts:

- *Font face*. The design of a font, such as Courier or Dutch, is known as the font's face. The Standard edition of WordPerfect Office 2000 for Linux comes with more than 100 font faces; the Deluxe edition comes with 1,000 font faces.
- *Font size*. Font size determines the size of a font in *points*. For example, business correspondence typically appears in 12-point type.
- *Font style*. Font *style* refers to formatting applied to a font. In WordPerfect 9 for Linux, font styles range from basic (including normal, underline, bold, and italic) to advanced (including shadow, small caps, redline, and strikeout).

Naturally, WordPerfect 9 provides more than one way to control font attributes—you can have your way with them with one-click ease on the Property Bar, or you can exercise greater control by using the Font Properties dialog box.

Managing Fonts Using the Property Bar

As shown in Figure 5.1, the first three items on the Property Bar are your keys to controlling, respectively, font face, font size, and font style.

FIGURE 5.1

The font controls on the WordPerfect 9 Property Bar include font face, font size, and font style.

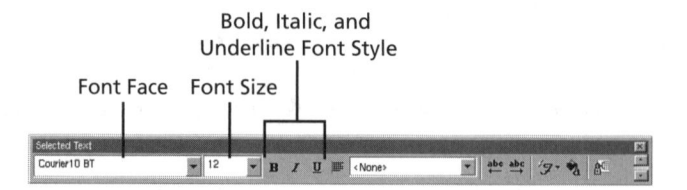

To change the font face from the Property Bar, select your text and click the font face drop-down box. As shown in Figure 5.2, a list of all installed font faces appears in alphabetical order, with the most recently used font faces at the top. As you move your cursor over each font face, Real-Time Preview shows how the new font will look applied to your text. To apply a new font face, click to select it from the font face drop-down box.

Formatting WordPerfect 9 Documents

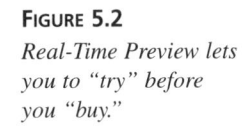

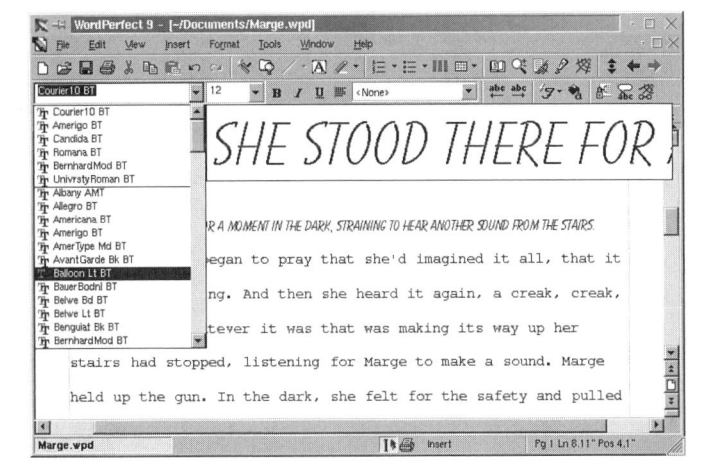

FIGURE 5.2
Real-Time Preview lets you to "try" before you "buy."

Next to the font face drop-down box is the font size drop-down box, which works the same way. Select your text, click the font size drop-down box, and move your mouse pointer down the list for a preview of different font sizes.

> If you know which font face or font size you want to apply, you can type it into the appropriate box on the Property Bar instead of scrolling through the drop-down lists.

To the right of the font size drop-down box are three buttons that provide one-click access to the most common font styles: bold, italic, and underline. To apply any of these, select your text and click a font style button to toggle it on/off. You can apply multiple font styles, in any combination, to your selection. When you are through applying the styles you need, click anywhere in your document to deactivate the selected text.

At the opposite end of the Property Bar is the Font Color button, shown in Figure 5.3. To change the font color, select text and click the Font Color button to open the drop-down color palette. Real-Time Preview works here, too, so you can hold your cursor over different colors in the palette to preview how they'll look applied to your text selection. When you find the perfect color, click it to apply it to your text.

FIGURE 5.3
The Font Color button opens a color palette that allows you to sample different colors in Real-Time Preview mode.

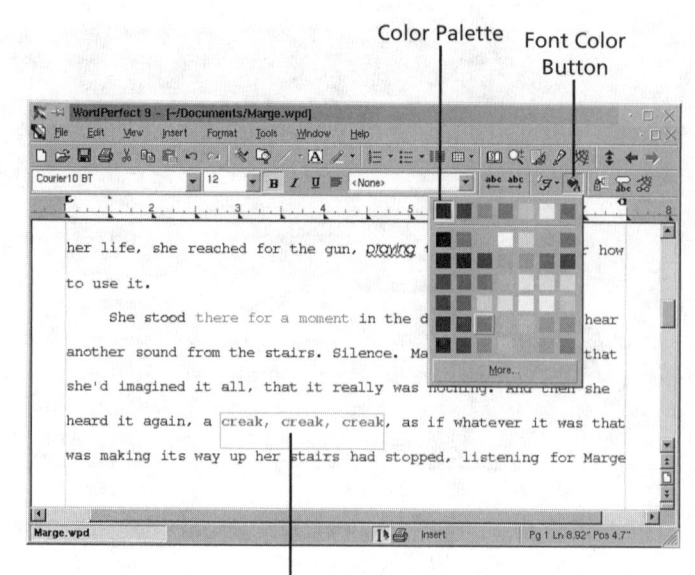

Color Palette
Font Color Button

Font Color Real-Time Preview applied to text

> Now that you've practiced changing font attributes, you'll truly appreciate the Property Bar's QuickFonts button. As shown in Figure 5.4, QuickFonts displays the 10 most recent combinations of font attributes applied to your text in a drop-down list. To apply a QuickFont, select your text, click the QuickFonts button, and select a QuickFont from the list. Note that clicking "Font" at the bottom of the QuickFonts list opens the Font Properties dialog box, which is covered in the next section.

FIGURE 5.4
QuickFonts remembers the last 10 font attribute settings used and allows you to reapply them with a single click.

Managing Fonts Using the Font Properties Dialog Box

You can exercise greater control over font attributes using the Font Properties dialog box, which you can access in four different ways:

- Right-click in a document and select Font from the pop-up menu.
- Select Format, Font from the menu bar.
- Use the keyboard shortcut F9.
- Click the QuickFonts button on the Property Bar and select Font.

As shown in Figure 5.5, the Font Properties dialog box opens to the Font tab, which contains several font attribute controls, including face, size, bold, italic, underline, and color. You've already learned how to manage each of these font attributes through the Property Bar, and it works almost exactly the same way through the Font Properties dialog box. Just select your text, access the Font Properties dialog box, select the font attributes you want to turn on (or deselect those you want to turn off), and click OK.

FIGURE 5.5
The Font Properties dialog box opened to the Font tab.

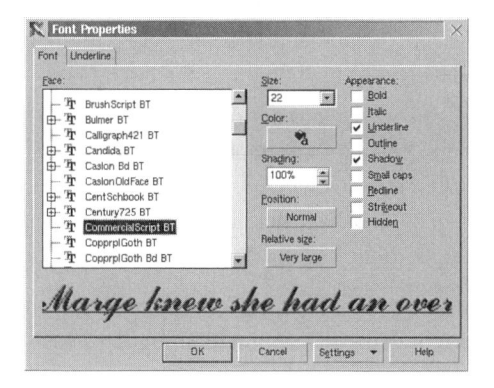

In addition to the font attributes already covered, the Font Properties dialog box opens the door to these additional controls:

- *Shading*. Shading allows you to control font color intensity within a range of 5 to 100 percent. For example, if you select red as your font color, you can experiment with different shades of red by changing the shading percentage. A 5-percent shade is a much lighter red than a 100-percent shade.
- *Position*. The Position button gives you three options for the placement of your text: Normal, Superscript, and Subscript. The Normal position is the default, in which your text rests comfortably on an imaginary *baseline*. Superscript elevates your text above the baseline, as in a footnote reference, whereas Subscript takes your text below the baseline. Figure 5.6 shows all three positions.

FIGURE 5.6
Subscript and Superscript shrink your text and place it, respectively, below and above the Normal baseline.

$_{subscript}$normal^{superscript}

- *Relative Size.* Using a range of sizes from Fine (60 percent) to Extra Large (200 percent), the Relative Size option allows you to change font sizes without having to mess with point type settings.
- *Additional appearance attributes.* In addition to the font attributes already covered, the Appearance section of the Font tab includes the settings Outline, Shadow, Small Caps, Redline, Strikeout, and Hidden. Play with these settings and note the results in the preview text at the bottom of the dialog box.
- *Default font settings.* The Settings button at the bottom of the Font Properties dialog box allows you to change the default font face and size for the current document or for all documents. To change the default font, select the font face and font size you want to use by default. Click the Settings button and select whether your new default will apply to the current document or to all documents. Then click OK.

The Font Properties dialog box also features the Underline tab shown in Figure 5.7. The Underline tab gives you more control over underlining than you're ever likely to need:

- *Apply To.* This allows you to control the scope of your underline, from underlining an entire text selection (All) to underlining only text and tabs (Text & Tabs). As shown in the preview at the bottom of the dialog box in Figure 5.7, selecting Text Only underlines text but not spaces.
- *Color.* By default, the Same As Text box is checked, making your underline the same color as the text it underscores. To change the underline color, uncheck the check box, click the Color button, and select a color from the pop-up color palette.
- *Line Style.* As shown in Figure 5.7, you've got a variety of line styles to choose from. Click any line style to preview it at the bottom of the dialog box.

When you're through making your selections from both the Font and Underline tabs, click OK to apply your changes and return to your document.

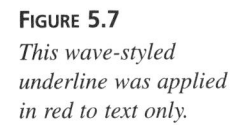

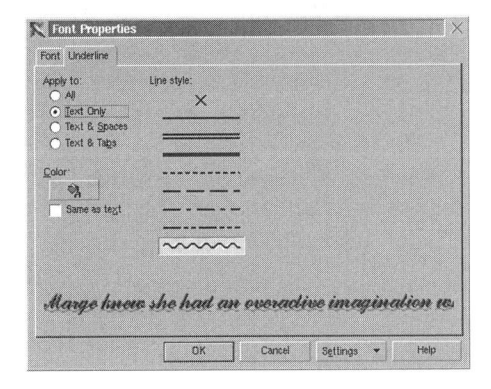

FIGURE 5.7
This wave-styled underline was applied in red to text only.

Installing Fonts with BitStream FontTastic Font Installer

WordPerfect Office 2000 for Linux includes the BitStream FontTastic Font Installer (FontTastic), which you can use to manage the fonts available in all applications in the suite. FontTastic allows you to add and delete fonts as well as to toggle fonts on and off.

To Do: Use FontTastic

1. Close all open WordPerfect Office 2000 for Linux applications and insert Disc Two of your WordPerfect Office 2000 for Linux software into your CD-ROM drive.

2. From the Corel Application Starter, select Applications, WordPerfect Office 2000, Utilities, FontTastic Font Installer. This launches the BitStream FontTastic Font Installer dialog box shown in Figure 5.8. (Note that if you're not logged in as root, you'll be prompted to enter the root password before proceeding.)

3. To add fonts, click Add to open the Select Fonts dialog box. In the Look In box, navigate to the `/mnt/amnt/cdrom1/Type1Fonts` directory to access a set of 24 folders, each labeled with a letter. Each folder contains fonts that begin with the letter of the folder.

4. Double-click the folder containing the font you want to add; then double-click the font to automatically add it to the FontTastic font menu.

> FontTastic can only install Type 1 fonts, a font technology developed for and primarily used on the Windows platform. When selecting a font to add, make sure it bears a T1 icon, which marks it as a Type 1 font. If you try to add any other kind of font, FontTastic will warn you that the selected font isn't recognized.

5. To delete a font, select it in the BitStream FontTastic Font Installer dialog box and click Delete.

6. You can also use FontTastic to toggle fonts on and off without adding or deleting them from your system. Turning off all fonts you don't use can speed up application performance. To turn a font on or off, select it in the BitStream FontTastic Font Installer dialog box and click the On/Off button, or you can just check/uncheck the on/off box to the left of the font name.

7. Click Close to exit FontTastic. The next time you open a WordPerfect Office 2000 application, your changes will be reflected in the list of fonts available from the Property Bar and the Font Properties dialog box.

FIGURE 5.8
The BitStream FontTastic Font Installer dialog box.

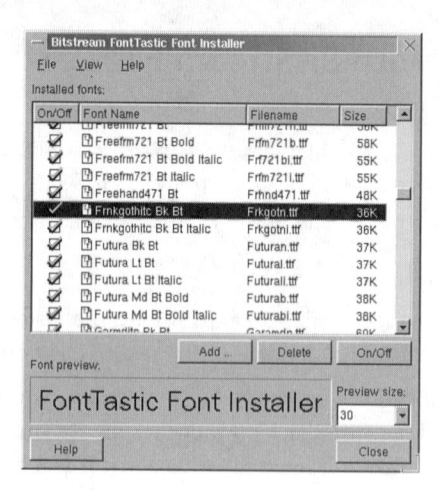

Formatting Paragraphs

It's a broad topic, and perhaps not an overly exciting one, but paragraph formatting is one of the most important skills to learn in WordPerfect 9. This section will cover basic but mandatory paragraph-formatting tasks that every user needs to know, including line spacing, tab and indent settings, and justification.

Line Spacing in WordPerfect

Changing line spacing is simple. Rest your cursor at the place in your document where you want the new line spacing to take effect. Select Format, Line, Spacing from the menu bar to open the Line Spacing dialog box, shown in Figure 5.9. Set the line spacing as desired in the Spacing box and click OK.

FIGURE 5.9
The Line Spacing dialog box.

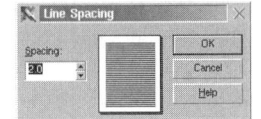

Although the procedure for changing line spacing is simple, it's important to understand what's going on behind the scenes. When you tell WordPerfect to change line spacing, WordPerfect inserts a line spacing code at the beginning of the paragraph (the insertion point) in which your cursor rests when the command is entered. The code changes the line spacing of all text that comes after the insertion point, with no impact on any text that comes before. In effect, the insertion point marks the place in your document where your new line spacing is turned "on." To turn it "off," you'll have to insert a new line spacing command in a subsequent paragraph.

If you're just starting a new document or want to change the line spacing throughout an existing document, you can rest your cursor at the beginning of the document and change your line spacing as described without a problem. If, however, you want to edit the line spacing for only one or a few paragraphs, select the paragraphs you want to change before making any line spacing changes. This tells WordPerfect to turn the new line spacing "on" at the beginning of the selection and "off" at the end of the selection. This way, no text before or after the selected text is affected.

Setting Tabs and Indents

Tabs are used to indent the first line of a paragraph. By default, WordPerfect inserts a tab at every half-inch interval from the left margin. The result is that every time you hit the Tab key, the first line of your paragraph moves one half-inch away from the left margin.

In contrast, indents are used to indent the first and all subsequent lines of a paragraph away from the left margin, the right margin, or both margins. Like tabs, indents rely on the tab settings to determine how far from the margins to move your text.

Because tabs and indents both rely on tab settings, you need to understand how tab settings work and how you can customize them to suit your needs. First, take a look at the default tab settings on the Ruler by pressing Alt+Shift+F3 or by selecting View, Ruler from the menu bar. As shown in Figure 5.10, the Ruler displays default tab settings as tiny triangles placed at half-inch intervals from the left margin to the right.

FIGURE 5.10

The Ruler is a powerful tool from which you can control tab, indent, and margin settings.

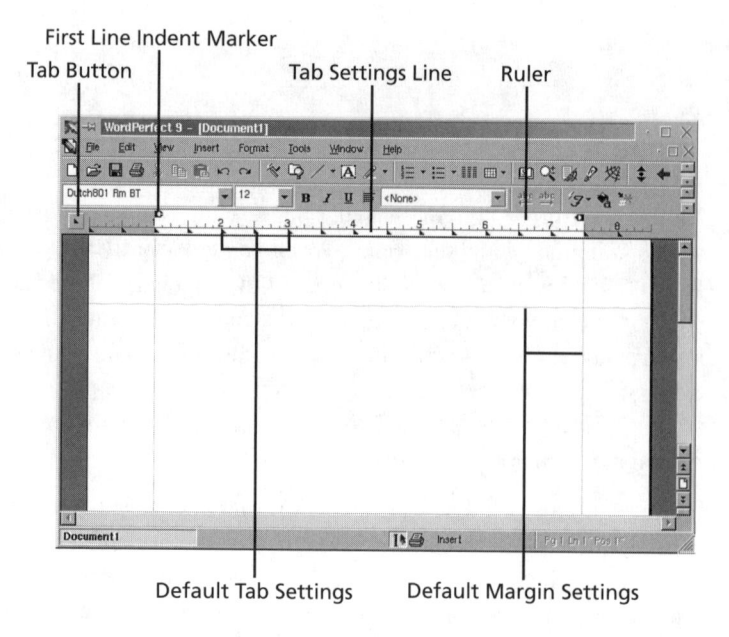

- First Line Indent Marker
- Tab Button
- Tab Settings Line
- Ruler
- Default Tab Settings
- Default Margin Settings

The easiest way to add a tab to a paragraph is to click in the paragraph and then click the tab settings line along the bottom of the Ruler at the insertion point for the new tab. A new tab will instantly appear in the Ruler. To delete a tab, simply click on the tab in the tab settings line and drag it off the Ruler.

> You can also control tab settings through the Tab Set dialog box shown in Figure 5.11. To use this method, click in the paragraph you want to modify and then access the Tab Set dialog box in one of the following ways:
>
> - Select Format, Line, Tab Set from the menu bar.
> - Right-click anywhere in the Ruler and select Tab Set from the pop-up menu.
> - Click the Tab button to the left of the Ruler and select Tab Set from the pop-up menu. (Note: If you don't see the Tab button next to your Ruler, use the Zoom button on the toolbar to decrease the zoom level to 75 percent.)
>
> When you're through setting your custom tabs in the Tab Set dialog box, click Set and Close to return to your document.

Formatting WordPerfect 9 Documents 103

FIGURE 5.11
You can also control tab settings through the Tab Set dialog box.

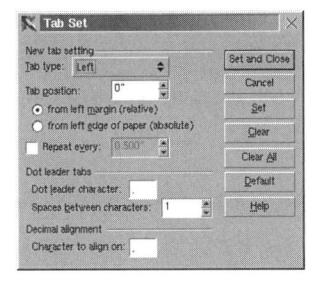

Using tabs is simple enough. Whenever you hit the Tab key, all text in the line to the right of your cursor moves right to the next tab stop. Remember that tabs only affect the line in which your cursor sits—all preceding and subsequent lines are unaffected.

To move all text within a paragraph to a tab stop, you'll have to use indents. There are three different kinds of indents you can use in WordPerfect:

- *Indent*. Moves all text within a paragraph or selection one tab stop to the right, away from the left margin.
- *Hanging indent*. Moves all but the first line of text within a paragraph or selection one tab stop to the right, away from the left margin.
- *Double indent*. Moves all text within a paragraph or selection one tab stop to the right, away from the left margin, and one tab stop to the left, away from the right margin.

Examples of all three types of indents are shown in Figure 5.12.

FIGURE 5.12
Unlike tabs, indents go beyond the first line of text to affect an entire paragraph or selection.

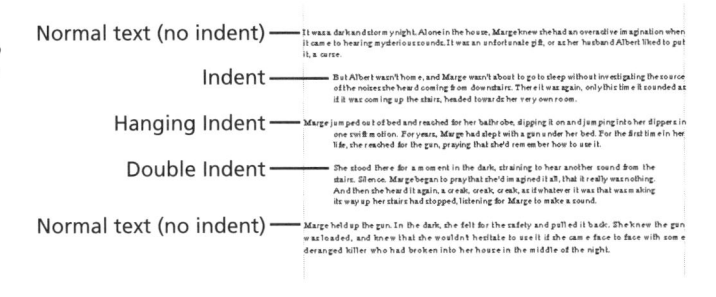

To apply indents to a paragraph or selection, place your cursor in the paragraph you want to indent, or select the text you want to indent, and use one of the following procedures:

- Select Format, Paragraph from the menu bar and then select Indent, Hanging Indent, or Double Indent.

- Use the keyboard shortcut F7 for an indent, Ctrl+F7 for a hanging indent, or Ctrl+Shift+F7 for a double indent.
- Right-click the toolbar and select the Format toolbar. As shown in Figure 5.13, the Format toolbar contains a separate button for each kind of indent.

FIGURE 5.13
The Indent buttons on WordPerfect 9's Format toolbar.

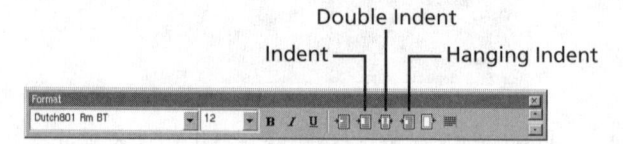

To Do: Set Tabs

1. Open a new WordPerfect document and use the Tab Set dialog box to clear the default tabs.
2. Set new tabs to begin one inch from the left margin and to repeat every inch.
3. Set and close your new tab settings and view them in the Ruler.
4. When you've confirmed that your changes worked, use the Tab Set dialog box to restore the default settings.

Setting Page Margins

You can change the margin settings of a document at any time. As with line spacing, WordPerfect 9 turns margin changes "on" and "off" by inserting codes. Therefore, if you click within a paragraph and change a margin, the change will be applied to your current paragraph and everything after. You'll have to change the margin again in a subsequent paragraph to turn your first change off. Of course, if you make a text selection before applying a margin change, the change is limited to the selected text.

To Do: Change Margin Settings

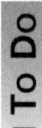

The easiest way to change margin settings is to physically drag the margin guides across the page. To change margin settings using this method:

1. Select View, Page from the menu bar to enter Page View.
2. To change the left or right margins, click within a paragraph or make a text selection.
3. Move your mouse pointer over the margin guide you want to move.
4. When your mouse pointer turns into a two-way arrow, click and drag the margin guide to its new location.

Formatting WordPerfect 9 Documents

▼ To change the top or bottom margin guides, follow the same steps with one exception—you don't need to click in a paragraph or make a text selection before dragging the margin guide. Instead, navigate to the page where you want the margin change to begin. Top and bottom margin changes are applied on a page-by-page basis and will be applied to
▲ your current page and everything after.

As shown in Figure 5.14, as you drag the margin guide, two things happen. First, the selected text moves with the margin guide, allowing a preview of your new setting. Second, a tiny window pops up displaying in inches the space between the edge of the page and the current position of the margin guide.

FIGURE 5.14
You can change margin settings by dragging a margin line across the page.

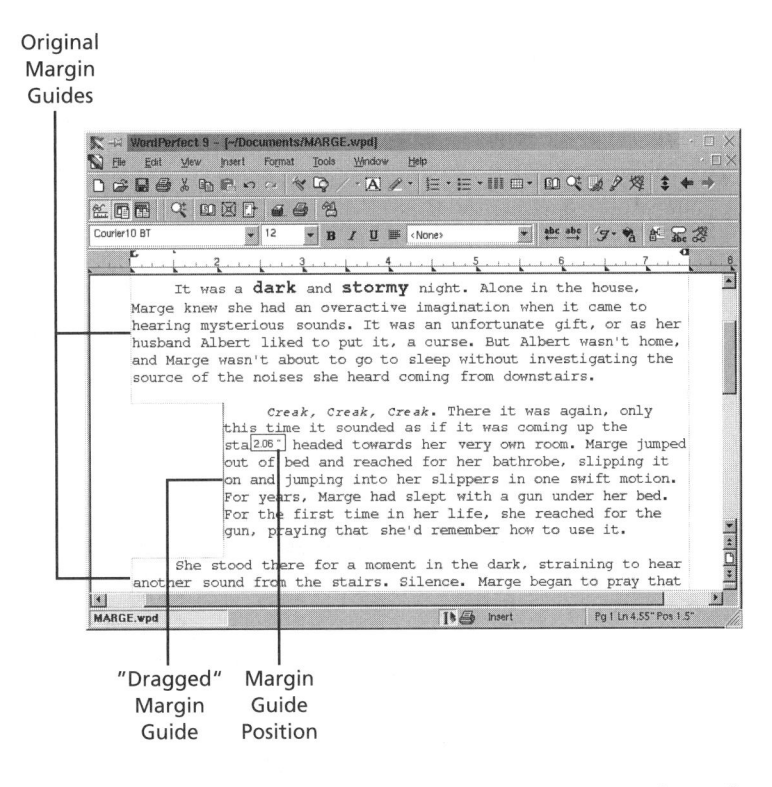

You can also change margin settings using the Margins/Layout tab in the Page Setup dialog box. To use this method, click in a paragraph or make a text selection and then do one of the following:

- Select Format, Margins from the menu bar.
- Press Ctrl+F8.
- Select File, Page Setup from the menu bar and navigate to the Margins/Layout tab.

- Right-click the toolbar and select the Format toolbar or the Print Preview toolbar. Both toolbars include a Page Margins button, shown in Figure 5.15. Note that the Print Preview toolbar also appears automatically when you select File, Print Preview from the menu bar.

FIGURE 5.15
The Page Margins button on the Format toolbar.

- If you want to apply your margin settings to the current paragraph and everything after, click in the document at the point where you want the new margin setting to start; then right-click in the left margin and select Margins from the pop-up menu.

Any one of the foregoing methods opens the Margins/Layout tab in the Page Setup dialog box (see Figure 5.16). From here, you can control your left, right, top, and bottom margins by entering the number of inches for each margin (that is, the number of inches between your text and the left, right, top, and bottom edges of the page).

> To apply the same margin setting to all four margins, enter your setting for the left margin and click Equal.

FIGURE 5.16
The Margins/Layout tab in the Page Setup dialog box.

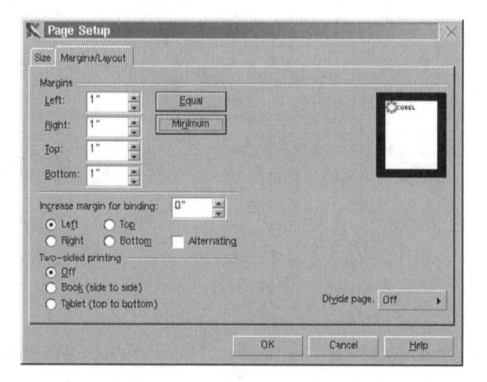

Setting Paragraph Justification

Justification refers to the alignment of your text between the left and right margins. As shown in Figure 5.17, the easiest way to control paragraph justification is from the Justification button on the Property Bar. When you click the Justification button, a drop-down menu gives you the five justification options shown in Table 5.1.

FIGURE 5.17
WordPerfect 9's Justification button provides five options for aligning your text in relation to the left and right margins.

TABLE 5.1 WordPerfect 9's Justification Options

Justification	Description/Demonstration
Left	Here's an example of left justification in which all text is aligned to the left margin, thus producing a jagged effect along the right margin.
Right	Here's an example of right justification in which all text is aligned to the right margin, thus producing a jagged effect along the left margin.
Center	Here's an example of center justification in which all text is aligned from the center of the page, thus producing a jagged effect along the left and right margins.
Full	Here's an example of full justification in which all text, except the last line of a paragraph, is aligned to the left and right margins. Although full justification eliminates the jagged effect along the margins, it can create awkward spacing between words.
All	Here's an example of all justification in which all text, including the last line of a paragraph, is aligned to the left and right margins. Like full justification, all justification eliminates the jagged effect along the margins, but it also creates awkward spacing between words.

By default, all text in WordPerfect 9 documents is justified left. You can change the justification by selecting some text, clicking the justification button on the toolbar, and selecting your justification preference from the drop-down menu. Before making your selection, note that as you wave your mouse pointer over the justification options, Real-Time Preview demonstrates how your text will look with the new justification setting.

Creating and Working with Styles

A *style* is a collection of formatting commands you can apply with just a few mouse clicks. For example, a single style can include settings for font face, font size, font style, indentation, and line spacing. If you had to enter each of these attributes separately, you'd be at it for awhile. However, a style can do it all in one fell swoop.

To apply your first style, open an existing WordPerfect 9 document and click any paragraph. From the Property Bar, click the Select Style drop-down box, as shown in Figure 5.18.

FIGURE 5.18

The Select Style drop-down box on the Property Bar.

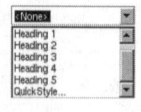

By default, the Select Style box offers seven options: None, Headings 1 through 5, and QuickStyle. Select Heading 1 and watch what happens to your text—the font face and size remain the same, but the font style changes to boldface, and the relative size of the font changes to *very large*. (Don't take my word for it. Select Format, Font from the menu bar and see for yourself in the Font Properties dialog box.)

To get rid of the Heading 1 style, you can either click Undo or click in the paragraph, click the Select Style drop-down box, and select None or another style to apply to the paragraph.

Naturally, WordPerfect 9 provides all the tools you need to create your own styles. The easiest way to do it is to take advantage of QuickStyles, the last option in the Select Style drop-down box. Say you've manually applied several formatting attributes to a paragraph of text and you want to preserve the settings by saving them as a style.

To Do: Use QuickStyle

1. Click in the paragraph whose formatting attributes you want to preserve as a style.
2. Click the Select Style drop-down box and select QuickStyle.
3. In the QuickStyle dialog box, type in a name for your style, and, if desired, a brief description. Since you want your style to include all the formatting contained in the paragraph, for Style Type select "Paragraph with automatic update." Click OK.

That's all there is to it! Your new style will appear in the Select Style drop-down box, and you can apply it to other paragraphs or text selections just as you'd apply any other style.

> You can exercise even greater control over styles by pressing Alt+F8 or selecting Format, Styles from the menu bar to access the Styles dialog box. The Styles dialog box provides a list, description, and preview of all styles, an Edit button to edit a selected style, and an Options button from which, among other things, you can delete a style you've created.

Summary

In this hour you explored WordPerfect 9's many text-formatting tools. Starting with a quick mastery of font attributes and paragraph formatting, you worked your way up to creating styles to apply many formatting commands at once.

In the next hour you'll discover the WordPerfect 9 Writer's Toolkit, consisting of dozens of tools that make any writing job a heck of a lot easier. From checking your spelling and grammar to creating outlines, WordPerfect 9's Writer's Toolkit is a must for everyone who puts words to page on a regular basis.

Q&A

Q How do I create an automatic first line indent?

A You can drag the first line indent marker (refer to Figure 5.10) to the desired location in the Ruler. Alternatively, select Format, Paragraph, Format from the menu bar. The Paragraph Format dialog box includes a First Line Indent box, where you can enter the size of your first line indent. Click OK to enter your change.

Q Does WordPerfect 9 have the equivalent of Microsoft Word's Format Painter to copy paragraph formatting?

A You bet, and it's called *QuickFormat*. Nestled between the Redo and Clipart buttons on the toolbar is the QuickFormat button (it looks like a paint roller with a lightening bolt). To copy formatting from one paragraph to another, click the paragraph with the formatting you want to copy and then click the QuickFormat button. In the QuickFormat dialog box, select Selected Characters to copy font attributes but no paragraph formatting, or you can select Headings to copy all formatting. Click OK and your mouse pointer turns into a paint roller, ready to apply your formatting to the next item you click. Click as many items as you like to apply the selected formatting; then click the QuickFormat button again to turn it off.

Workshop

The Workshop contains quiz questions and exercises to help reinforce what you've learned in this hour. If you get stuck, the answers can be found in Appendix B, "Answers to Quiz Questions."

Quiz

1. List three ways to open the Font Properties dialog box. Quick—for extra credit name a fourth!
2. What is the keyboard shortcut to open the Styles dialog box?
3. Which of the following moves text away from the right margin?
   a. Center justification
   b. Double indent
   c. Right justification
   d. Answers a and b
   e. Answers b and c

Exercises

1. Using FontTastic, turn off the Bard font. Open any WordPerfect Office 2000 application and confirm your change. Close the application and return to FontTastic to turn the Bard font back on.
2. Set up a double indent to move all text two inches away from the left and right margins.
3. Create a style named *Insanely Red* in Bard, underlined, boldfaced, 16-point type. Set the relative size to "very large" and set the font color to red with 75-percent shading.

Hour 6

The WordPerfect 9 Writer's Toolkit

WordPerfect 9 builds upon an already solid set of tools for writers. The built-in spelling, grammar, and thesaurus tools have been enhanced, and the new AutoScroll and Browse Forward/Backward buttons make it easier than ever to navigate through your documents. No matter what kind of writing you do, WordPerfect 9 provides a writer-friendly environment that's a real pleasure to work in.

In this hour you will

- Polish your prose with WordPerfect 9's spelling, grammar, and thesaurus tools.
- Insert special text, such as headers/footers, footnotes, and comments into your documents.
- Fly through your documents with new navigation tools, including the AutoScroll and Browse buttons.

Correcting Text with WordPerfect 9's Spelling and Grammar Tools

WordPerfect 9 features a bevy of spelling and grammar tools you can use to proofread your documents. These tools can be broken down into two categories: automatic tools that check your spelling and grammar as you work, and manual tools that check all or part of your document at your command.

Spelling Tools

There are four spelling tools at your disposal in WordPerfect 9: Spell-As-you-Go, Prompt-As-You-Go, QuickCorrect, and Spell Checker. The first three tools are automatic, and will suggest or make corrections to your text as you type. The last tool is manual and will run only at your command.

Figure 6.1 shows all three automatic tools in action at once.

FIGURE 6.1
Spell-As-You-Go, Prompt-As-You-Go, and QuickCorrect work automatically to check and correct your spelling as you type.

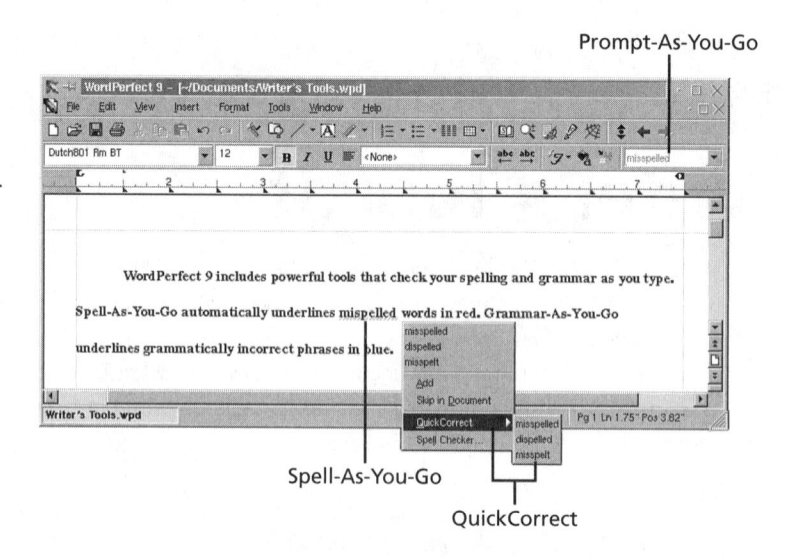

Here's how each automatic tool proofreads your documents on-the-fly:

- *Spell-As-You-Go*. Spell-As-You-Go proofreads your spelling as you type and marks misspelled words with a red underline. Right-click the misspelled word for a pop-up list of possible correct spellings. Select any alternative spelling from the pop-up list to insert your selection directly in your text. By default, Spell-As-You-Go is enabled when you install WordPerfect Office 2000. You can toggle it off by selecting Tools, Proofread, Off from the menu bar.

- *QuickCorrect*. QuickCorrect doesn't just watch out for spelling errors—it automatically corrects them based on a built-in list of frequently misspelled words and typographical errors. You can access this list by selecting Tools, QuickCorrect from the menu bar to open the QuickCorrect dialog box shown in Figure 6.2. The QuickCorrect list is divided into the Replace column, which lists dozens of misspelled or mistyped words, and the With column, which lists the QuickCorrect substitute for each word in the Replace column. You can add your own QuickCorrect items by typing the misspelled word in the Replace box, typing its substitute in the With box, and clicking the Add Entry button. Click OK to return to your document.

    To turn off QuickCorrect, uncheck the Replace Words As You Type box at the bottom of the QuickCorrect dialog box and click OK.

FIGURE 6.2

The QuickCorrect dialog box contains a list of frequently misspelled words and typographical errors.

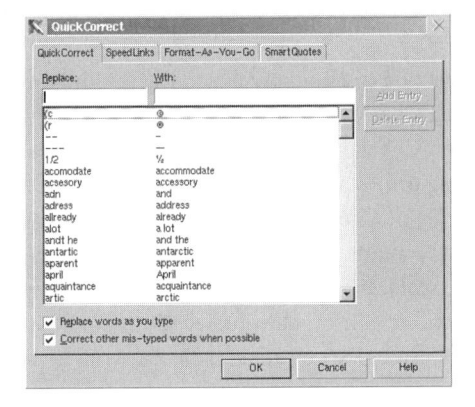

> The QuickCorrect dialog box has three additional tabs for controlling automatic formatting features. SpeedLinks creates automatic hyperlinks from entries beginning with www, ftp, http, or mailto and from custom SpeedLinks you specify. Format-As-You-Go automatically corrects certain formatting, such as automatic capitalization of the first letter in a sentence and deletion of an accidental double space between two consecutive words. SmartQuotes lets you customize whether to use double or single quotation marks by default. Explore these tabs to harness full control over the power of QuickCorrect!

- *Prompt-As-You-Go*. Prompt-As-You-Go is the granddaddy of all automated writer's tools because it's a spelling, grammar, and thesaurus tool all rolled into one. As you type, Prompt-As-You-Go automatically catches spelling and grammar errors and displays them in the Prompt-As-You-Go box on the Property Bar. For words that appear to be entered correctly, Prompt-As-You-Go goes into thesaurus mode to display a list of potential synonyms, if any, that you may want to use instead.

To use Prompt-As-You-Go, click a word and check the Prompt-As-You-Go box on the Property Bar. If there are any spelling or grammatical errors, they will appear in red in the Prompt-As-You-Go box. If there are no errors, Prompt-As-You-Go may nevertheless display the word in black, which tells you that Prompt-As-You-Go has at least one suggested synonym for the word. Click the down arrow at the right of the Prompt-As-You-Go box to view all suggested corrections/alternatives. Clicking an item in the Prompt-As-You-Go list automatically inserts it in your document, overriding your original entry.

You can toggle Prompt-As-You-Go on/off by selecting Format, Proofread from the menu bar and checking or unchecking Prompt-As-You-Go.

WordPerfect 9 also allows you to manually check the spelling of a word or all or part of a document with the Spell Checker. Access the Spell Checker by selecting Tools, Spell Checker. By default, Spell Checker checks the spelling in your entire document when launched and lists spelling errors and possible replacements for each misspelled word. As shown in Figure 6.3, the Spell Checker runs in a separate window beneath your document and provides several buttons by which you tell Spell Checker how to handle each misspelled word. For example, you can tell Spell Checker to skip the misspelled word, add it to the Spell Checker dictionary, auto-replace it throughout the document (which also adds it to the QuickCorrect list), or undo a change you've made.

FIGURE 6.3
The Spell Checker window provides many options for accepting or rejecting recommended replacements for potentially misspelled words.

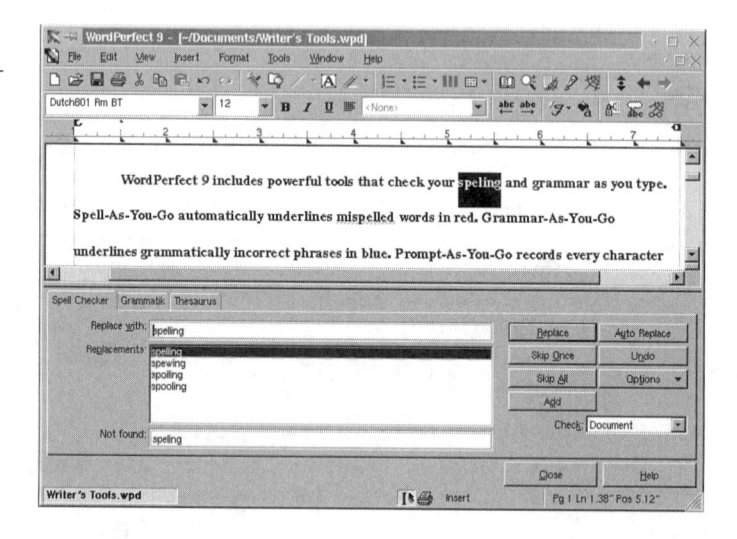

To prevent Spell Checker from automatically spell-checking your document when launched, click the Options button and deselect the Auto Start option. To close Spell Checker and return to your document, click Close.

Grammar Tools

WordPerfect 9 provides three tools that help you proofread your grammar. In WordPerfect jargon, *grammar* is a broad term that includes proper grammar and correct punctuation, usage, style, and even spelling. If you've already mastered WordPerfect 9's spelling tools, you're in luck, because the grammar tools work in much the same way:

- *Grammar-As-You-Go*. Grammar-As-You-Go proofreads your grammar as you type and marks improper usage with a blue underline. Right-click the underlined word for a pop-up list of alternative usage. If you click an alternative from the pop-up list, it's automatically applied to your text. By default, Grammar-As-You-Go is enabled—you can toggle it off by selecting Tools, Proofread, Off from the menu bar.

- *Grammatik*. Grammatik is the grammar equivalent of the Spell Checker, scanning your document for improper grammar, punctuation, usage, and even spelling. To launch Grammatik, press Alt+Shift+F1 or select Tools, Grammatik from the menu bar. As shown in Figure 6.4, Grammatik opens beneath your document to display suggested replacements, a preview of how your sentence will look with Grammatik's replacement, and an explanation of your grammatical *faux pas*. As with Spell Checker, you can choose from several buttons to replace, skip, add, auto-replace, or undo the perceived error. To close Grammatik and return to your document, click Close.

FIGURE 6.4
Grammatik is like Spell Checker plus, proofreading your text for spelling, grammar, punctuation, and usage errors.

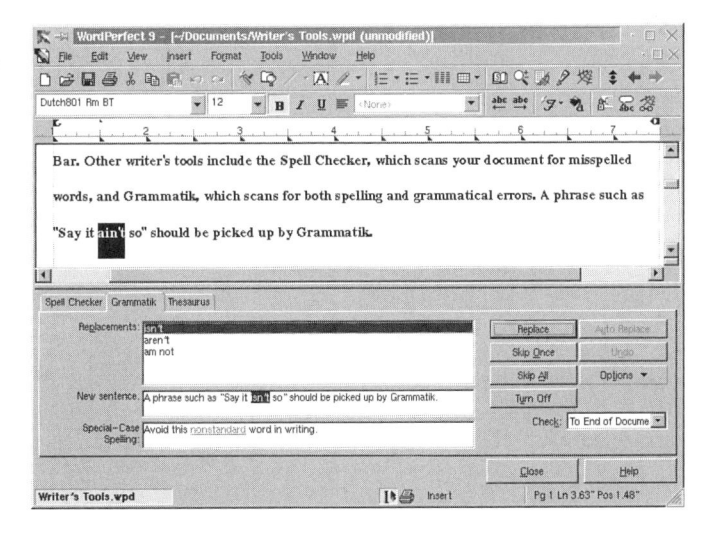

- *Prompt-As-You-Go.* Finally, Prompt-As-You-Go works exactly the same for grammar as it does for spelling.

Finding the Perfect Word with the WordPerfect Thesaurus

You've already seen how Prompt-As-You-Go can work as a thesaurus to suggest synonyms for words as you type. In case you're wondering how Prompt-As-You-Go is so smart, it's got the power of a full thesaurus behind it. To access the WordPerfect Thesaurus, select Tools, Thesaurus from the menu bar.

As shown in Figure 6.5, selecting the word *error* before launching Thesaurus tells Thesaurus to look up the selected word. Thesaurus opens in a window beneath your document, displaying the selected word and, in the left windowpane, a list of definitions. The definitions with plus signs tell you that Thesaurus can suggest synonyms matching the definition. Double-clicking a plus sign opens a list of synonyms. But Thesaurus doesn't stop there—if you double-click a listed synonym, Thesaurus displays definitions and synonyms for the synonym in the right windowpane.

FIGURE 6.5
Thesaurus provides definitions and synonyms of selected words.

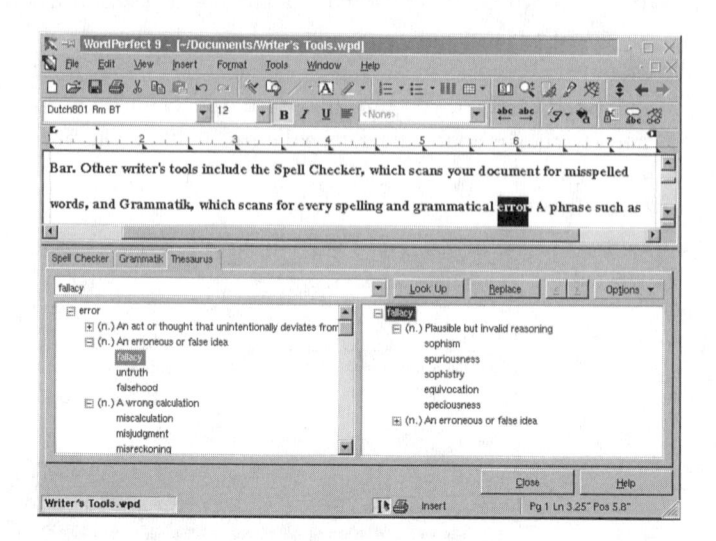

To replace your own word with a synonym suggested by Thesaurus, select any synonym in either windowpane and click Replace. Your chosen synonym automatically replaces your original word. Click Close to exit Thesaurus and return to your document.

> You can also use Thesaurus as a reference to look up words you haven't used in your document. Give it a try by opening a blank document and launching Thesaurus. At the prompt, type in the word *happy* and hit Enter or click Look Up. As you can see, Thesaurus acts like a dictionary, providing several accepted definitions of the word as well as access to many different definition-specific synonyms.

Inserting Special Text

There are times as a writer when you'll need to insert what I call "special text" items that just don't belong in the body of the document. I'm talking about page numbers, headers/footers, and foot- and endnotes, none of which generate much fan mail, but all of which are required elements in many documents.

Here's a quick march through the procedures for working special text into your documents.

To Do: Insert Page Numbers

1. From the menu bar, select Format, Page, Numbering to open the Select Page Numbering Format dialog box shown in Figure 6.6.
2. Although there seem to be many options here, the most important are the Position, Format, Font, and Set Value options.

FIGURE 6.6
The Select Page Numbering Format dialog box lets you easily configure how page numbers are displayed.

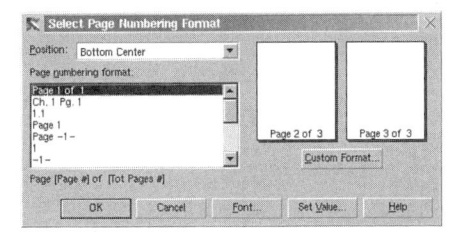

   a. **Position** dictates where your page numbers will appear on the page, such as top right or bottom center. Set Position to Bottom Center.
   b. **Format** lets you choose from a variety of alphanumeric and formatting options. Set your Format to Page 1 of 1.
   c. The **Font** button at the bottom of the dialog box lets you set the font of your page numbers (the default is 12-point Dutch801 Rm Bt). Click the Font button to open the Page Numbering Font dialog box. Set the page number font to Courier 10BT and click OK.

▼   d. The **Set Value** button lets you configure your page numbering to start at a number other than 1. Click the Set Value button to open the Values dialog box. Navigate to the Page tab, set the page number value to 1, and click OK.

3. Click OK to close the Select Page Numbering Format dialog box and return to your document.

To Do: Insert a Header

A header/footer is repeating text that appears, respectively, at the top and bottom of every page in a document. To create a header or footer:

1. Select View, Page from the menu bar to enter Page View mode.
2. Click the page where you want the header/footer to begin and open the Header/Footer dialog box by selecting Insert, Header/Footer from the menu bar.
3. As shown in Figure 6.7, the Headers/Footers dialog box gives you the option of working with two sets of headers and footers: Header and Footer A, and Header and Footer B. You don't need to worry about the "B" set unless you're printing double-sided documents with different headers/footers on odd and even pages.
4. For this exercise, select Header A and click Create. This takes you directly into your new header, where you can add text that will appear on every page.

FIGURE 6.7
The Headers/Footers dialog box.

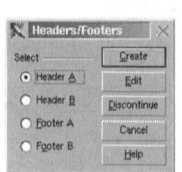

5. In the new header section, type in `My First Header`, then click in the body of the document to exit the header. Your new header will now appear at the top of every page in your document.
6. To edit or discontinue the header/footer, return to the Headers/Footers dialog box, select the header/footer you want to modify, and click either Edit or Discontinue.

   Clicking Edit takes you back into your header/footer, where you can make any changes. Then you can click in the body of your document to exit the header/footer.

   Clicking Discontinue wipes out the header/footer on the current page and every page thereafter.

To Do: Insert a Footnote

1. In Page View, select Insert, Footnote/Endnote from the menu bar to open the Footnote/Endnote dialog box shown in Figure 6.8.
2. Since we'll only be creating a footnote in this exercise, select Footnote, set the number to 1, and click Create. This takes you directly into your footnote, where you can enter all required text.
3. Type in **My First Footnote** and click in the body of your document to exit the footnote/endnote.
4. To edit a footnote/endnote, select Insert, Footnote/Endnote from the menu bar, identify the footnote/endnote you want to edit, and click Edit. This takes you directly into your footnote/endnote to make all necessary changes. Then just click in the body of your document to exit the footnote/endnote.

FIGURE 6.8
The Footnote/Endnote dialog box.

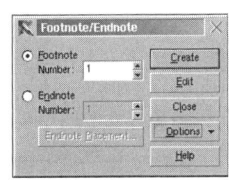

Using Comments for Follow-up and Collaboration

WordPerfect 9's Comments tool is great for jotting down notes, suggestions, or follow-up tasks for any writing project. Whether you're the type of writer who jots down notes to yourself in the margins or you're working with an editor or co-author with whom you need to exchange constant feedback, WordPerfect Comments is the tool for you!

To insert a comment, place your cursor in the exact location in a document where you want a comment to appear. Don't select any text—just click the spot where you want the comment to be viewed. On the menu bar, select Insert, Comment, Create to open the WordPerfect 9 Comment window, shown in Figure 6.9. When the Comment window opens, it may seem as if your original document has disappeared, replaced with a new, blank document. However, several things suggest otherwise: the Title Bar shows that you are in Comment mode, the Property Bar displays the Comment tools shown in Figure 6.9, and your original document is referenced, and can be accessed, on the Application Bar.

FIGURE 6.9
Select Insert, Comment, Create from the menu bar to open the WordPerfect 9 Comment window.

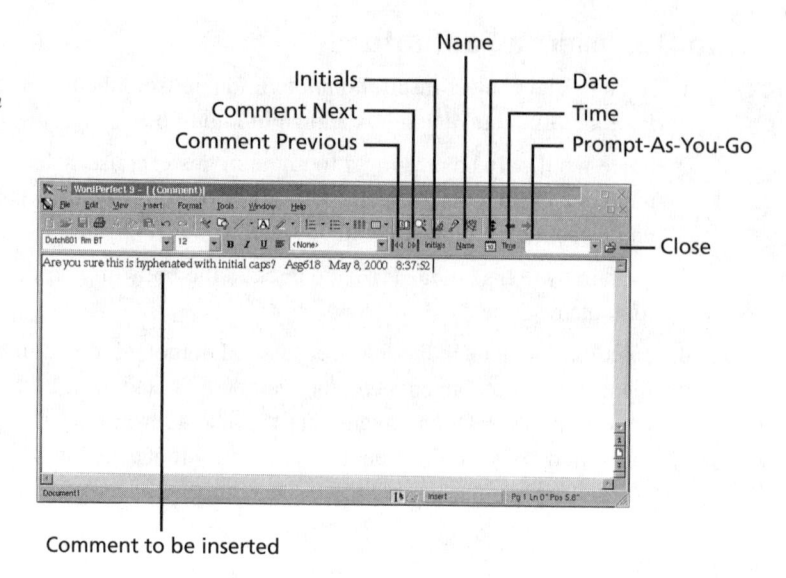

In Figure 6.9, I entered a comment for the author and then clicked the Name, Date, and Time buttons to insert, respectively, my Corel Linux username and the date and time of my comment. To return to your document after entering a comment, close the Comment window by clicking the Close button on the Property Bar or by accessing your document from the Application Bar.

Viewing a comment within your document is easy. In Draft View, each comment is displayed in a gray box, directly at its insertion point. Right-clicking the comment gives you the option to cut, copy, delete, or edit your comment. You can also edit your comment by double-clicking it.

In Page View, comments are not automatically displayed. As shown in Figure 6.10, a balloon in the left margin indicates a comment. Click the comment balloon to view the comment, which appears as a pop-up balloon directly over its insertion point in your text. Right-clicking the comment balloon gives you the option to cut, copy, delete, or edit your comment. Right-clicking the comment itself gives you the Convert to Text, Delete, and Edit options. The Convert to Text option automatically inserts your Comment directly into your document.

FIGURE 6.10
Click the comment icon in the left margin to view a comment.

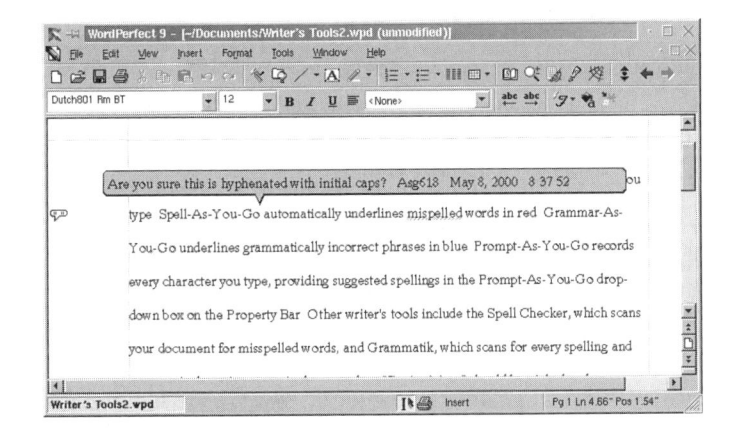

Outlining a Document

WordPerfect 9 provides several tools to help you outline your writing projects. Although you can manually enter numbers and letters to create a basic outline, WordPerfect automatically creates and updates outline headings in sequential order, providing the flexibility to add, delete, or change the order of outline items without interfering with the outline hierarchy.

A WordPerfect outline consists of a series of paragraphs that are each assigned a *level* (typically a number, letter, or symbol) based on a preset hierarchy. For example, level one items in an outline could consist of upper roman numerals (I, II, III, and so on), with level two items represented by capital letters (A, B, C, and so on), and level three items represented by lower roman numerals (i, ii, iii, and so on). The level of an outline item changes as the item is *promoted* or *demoted* within the hierarchy. Thus, outline item I could be demoted two levels to become item i and then promoted one level to become item A.

To grasp the concept of outlining, it's best to view an outline in action. On the toolbar, click the Numbering button shown in Figure 6.11. If you click the down arrow next to the Numbering button, you'll get a choice of outline level hierarchies, but for now just click the button itself. In your document, the default numerical outline is inserted, beginning with 1. The default numerical hierarchy is 1, a, i, and so on. To see how WordPerfect automates much of the outline creation, type some text, hit Enter, and watch as 2 appears directly below 1. Note that 1 and 2 are consecutive outline items in the same *level*.

Hit Enter again to skip a line—because you didn't type any text after 2, WordPerfect skipped a line instead of going on to the next consecutive outline item in the level. Hit Tab to demote 2 to a, the first item in the next level in the default hierarchy. Enter some text and hit Enter again. At b, enter some text and hit Enter. Now press Shift+Tab to promote your active level back up to the first level. If you did all this correctly, your active outline item should be 2, the next consecutive outline item in the first level of the default hierarchy.

In Figure 6.11, I created a meeting agenda using WordPerfect 9's default outline hierarchy. Remember that you can also create an outline using bullet points or other symbols—just click the Bullets button instead of the Numbering button on the toolbar and create your outline using the same procedures.

FIGURE 6.11

A sample outline using WordPerfect 9's automated outlining tools.

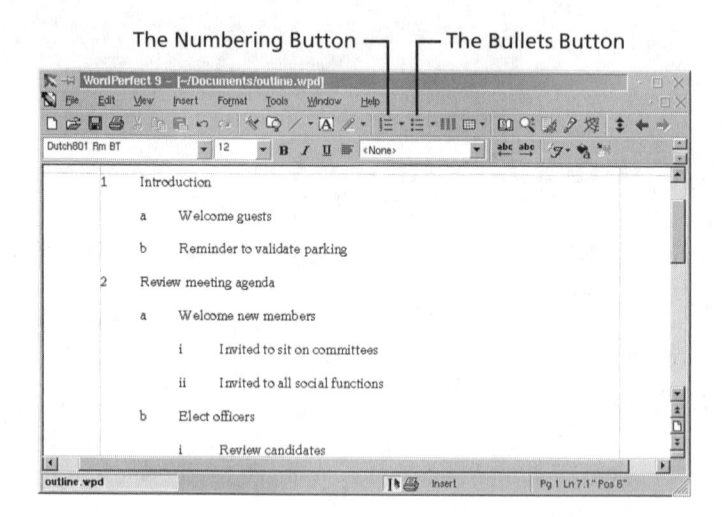

There's a great deal more to WordPerfect's outline tools. Table 6.1 shows all the outline buttons that appear on the Property Bar whenever you begin working in outline mode. Use these buttons in combination with the Tab and Shift+Tab keystrokes to manage your outline items and levels.

TABLE 6.1 The Outline Property Bar

Button	Description
Promote	Promotes the active outline item to the previous level. The left-pointing arrow signifies that the active item will move one level over to the left.
Demote	Demotes the active outline item to the next level. The right-pointing arrow signifies that the active item will move one level to the right. Pressing Tab achieves the same result.
Move Up	Moves the active outline item up one line without changing the level.

Button	Description
Move Down	Moves the active outline item down one line without changing the level.
QuickFind Previous	Jumps to the previous appearance of a selected item in the document. For example, in Figure 6.11, if I click the second instance of the word *Welcome* and click QuickFind Previous, WordPerfect jumps to the previous appearance of *Welcome* in the document.
QuickFind Next	Jumps to the next appearance of a selected item in the document.
Show Family	The outline levels beneath a selected level are members of the selected level's family. Click Show Family to show all members of a selected level's family.
Hide Family	Collapses all levels of a selected level's family.
Show/Hide Body Text	If you have non-outline items within your outline, click Show/Hide Body Text to hide all non-outline elements. Click again to restore non-outline items to view.
Set Paragraph Number	Allow you to manually set the paragraph number for a selected outline item. Note that this will affect all subsequent outline items in the same level.
Modify	Opens the Create Format dialog box to customize the format of your outline level hierarchy.
Show Icons	Toggles on/off outline icons in the left margin that indicate the level of all outline items.
Show Levels	Opens a drop-down menu from which you can select the number of outline levels to display.

Navigating Long Documents

As you continue your mastery of WordPerfect 9, you may find yourself creating long documents that become difficult, or at least time consuming, to navigate as you review, edit, and rewrite the project. That's why WordPerfect comes with several new navigation tools that are particularly suited for long documents—AutoScroll, Browse buttons, and QuickFind. We'll wrap up this hour with a look at these navigation tools.

Cruising with AutoScroll

The new AutoScroll button in WordPerfect 9 works like a scroll mouse, allowing you to glide through your document automatically. As shown in Figure 6.12, clicking the AutoScroll button changes your mouse pointer into the AutoScroll icon and changes the vertical scrollbar button into a floating black box.

When you move your mouse pointer up or down in the document window, the text scrolls in the same direction, and the black box in the scrollbar follows along. The closer you move your mouse pointer to the top of the document window, the faster AutoScroll scrolls toward the beginning of your document. The closer you move the mouse pointer to the bottom of the document window, the faster AutoScroll scrolls toward the end of your document. As you bring your mouse pointer toward the center of the document, AutoScroll slows and will eventually stop.

FIGURE 6.12
Click the AutoScroll button to glide through your document as if using a scroll mouse.

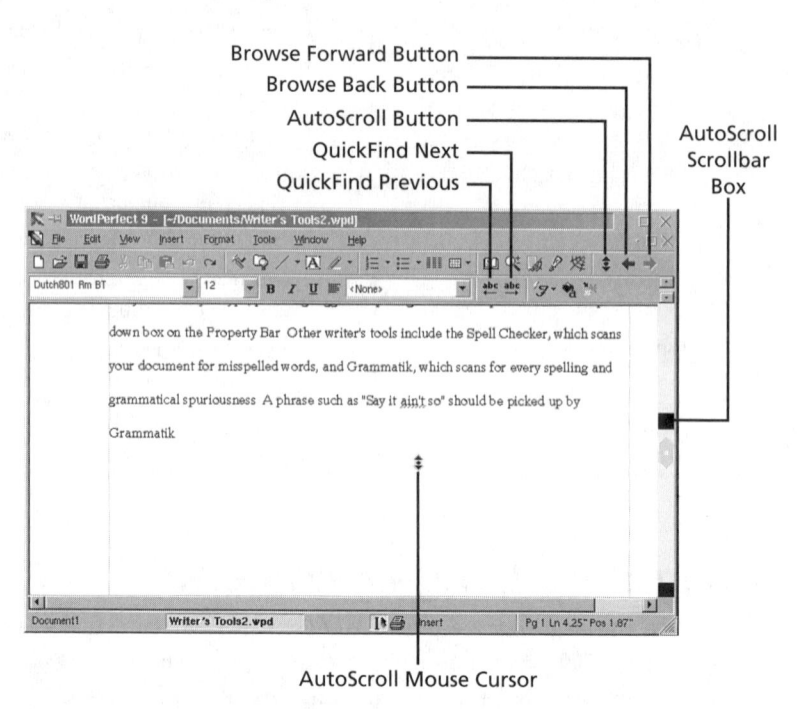

To close out of AutoScroll, click anywhere with the mouse.

The Browse Forward and Back Buttons

The Browse Forward and Back buttons, also shown in Figure 6.12, are another new navigation tool that make it a snap to move around in large documents. Every time you click in a document, you create an insertion point at which WordPerfect is ready to edit or create at your command. The Browse buttons keep track of your insertion point history and allow you to revisit that history by moving backward and forward through your document.

To Do: Navigate with the Browse Forward and Back Buttons

▼ To Do

1. Open a new document and type a full page of text. Navigate to the top of the document and click the first word you typed. Press Page Down and click the last word you typed. Navigate to the middle of the page and click a word that appears in the approximate center of your document.

2. Take a look at the Browse buttons on the toolbar. The Browse Back button should be enabled, whereas the Browse Forward button is dimmed. (The Browse Forward button is only enabled after you use the Browse Back button.) Click the Browse Back button. Is the Browse Forward button now enabled? Click Browse Back again. Now Click Browse Forward. As you can see, the Browse buttons make it simple to jump from one insertion point to another—a neat feat that allows you to leave your current work to go back in your document for editing and then return to your current work with just a few mouse clicks.

▲

The QuickFind Buttons

The QuickFind buttons, also shown in Figure 6.12, work much like the Browse Buttons, except that instead of jumping among insertion points, QuickFind looks for the next occurrence of a selected word.

For example, say you're writing the great American novel. Assume you begin each chapter with a heading consisting of the word *Chapter*, followed by the chapter number, and that you have 10 chapters completed. If you navigate to page 1, click the first appearance of the word *Chapter*, and then click the QuickFind Next button, WordPerfect 9 will automatically jump to the next occurrence of the word *Chapter* (most likely in the heading for Chapter 2). Repeating this operation will take you all the way to the last occurrence of the word *Chapter* (most likely in the heading for Chapter 10).

Naturally, clicking the QuickFind Previous button works the same way, but in reverse.

Summary

In this hour you explored WordPerfect 9's tools for writers. From polishing your prose with the spelling, grammar, and thesaurus tools, to working with special text, comments, outlines, and navigation tools, WordPerfect 9 is a powerhouse application for writers of all levels.

In the next hour you'll learn how to work with tables and columns in WordPerfect 9. From merely organizing your data to performing spreadsheet-like calculations, tables can really spice up boring pages of endless text. Similarly, text formatted in columns is perfect for newsletters and brochures, both of which are a snap to create with WordPerfect. All this and more awaits you in the next hour!

Q&A

Q How do I insert a symbol into my document?

A Position your cursor at the insertion point and select Insert, Symbol from the menu bar (or press Ctrl+W). Navigate through the Symbols dialog box to locate the symbol you need. The Set menu organizes different kinds of symbols into sets that you can also explore. To insert a symbol, double-click it and click Close to return to your document, or you can select the symbol and click Insert and Close.

Q How do I suppress page numbering on the first page of a document?

A Click in the first page of the document and then select Format, Page, Suppress from the menu bar. Check Page Numbering and click OK to suppress page numbering on the current page.

Workshop

The Workshop contains quiz questions and exercises to help reinforce what you've learned in this hour. If you get stuck, the answers can be found in Appendix B, "Answers to Quiz Questions."

Quiz

1. Which writing tool does not check spelling?

    a. QuickCorrect

    b. Spell-As-You-Go

    c. Grammatik

    d. Prompt-As-You-Go

    e. None of the above

2. True or false: You must view a document in Page View in order to see a WordPerfect comment.

3. The Browse Forward button is to insertion point as the QuickFind Next button is to _____.

Exercises

1. Use the WordPerfect 9 Thesaurus to look up the phrase *faux pas*.
2. Create an outline using diamonds.
3. Type the sentence "Every good boy does fine." Insert a comment after the word *boy* that reads, "Shouldn't this be 'Every good person…'?" Return to your document. Go back and edit your comment to put your Linux username at the end of your comment.

HOUR 7

Working with Tables and Columns

Tables and columns can help make certain documents look more professional and elegant. Newsletters, for example, appear more professional when presented in columns of text, typically two columns per page. Other text is best presented in table form, which allows readers to digest a great deal of information with a single glance across the page. Fortunately, WordPerfect 9 provides powerful tools for creating tables and columns.

In this hour you will

- Learn when to use tables or columns to present your data.
- Insert and manipulate a table in a WordPerfect document.
- Use a WordPerfect table to perform spreadsheet-like calculations.
- Lay out a WordPerfect document using columns.

What's the Difference Between a Table and a Column?

A WordPerfect 9 table arranges information into horizontal rows and vertical columns. The area at which a row and a column intersect is called a *cell*, which can contain text, numbers, formulas, or graphics. As shown in Figure 7.1, a table is a "grid" with columns named alphabetically, from left to right, and rows named numerically, from top to bottom. Each cell has a *cell address* that references its column letter and row number. In Figure 7.1, I've typed in the row and column headings, as well as the cell addresses, for each cell in the table. Although these labels don't actually appear in a WordPerfect 9 table, you can always determine your cell address by checking the General Table Status button on the Application Bar.

FIGURE 7.1
You can view a selected cell's cell address on the General Table Status button on the Application Bar.

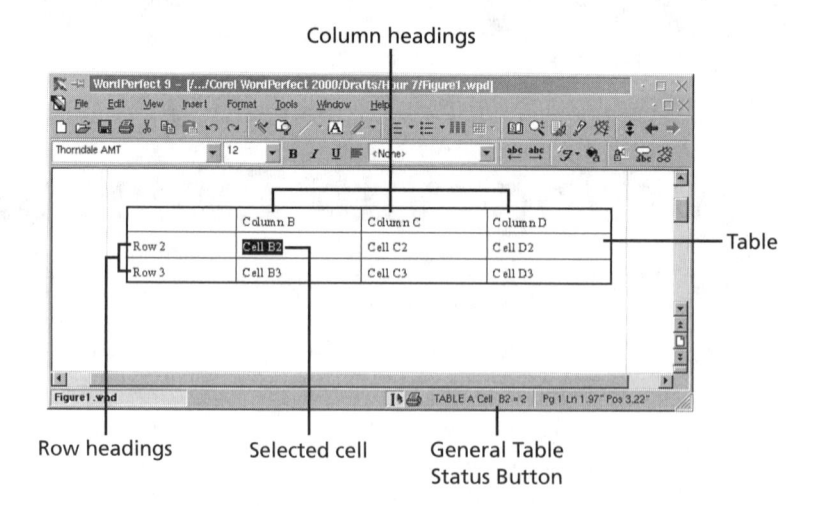

In addition to providing a framework for the neat organization of your data, tables let you insert formulas to perform automatic calculations on data within the table.

Tables are best suited for labeled or multipart lists of information, or for projects that involve some basic number crunching.

In contrast, WordPerfect 9 columns don't include cells or cell addresses, and they cannot perform automatic calculations. As shown in Figure 7.2, columns are primarily used for creating newsletters in which text is continued from the bottom of one column to the top of the next. Columns are also useful for resumes, transcripts, and summaries.

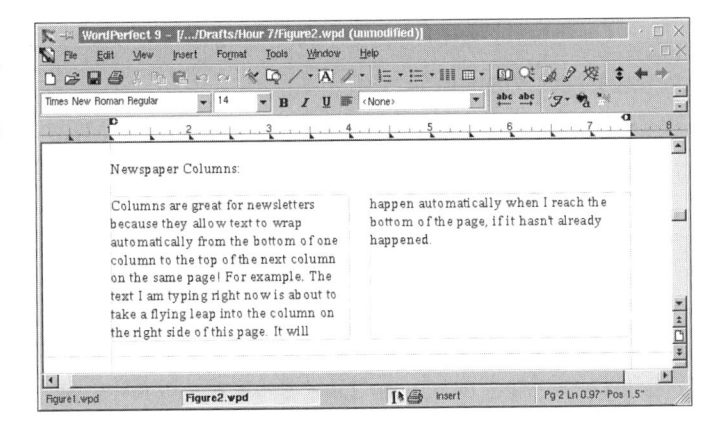

FIGURE 7.2
Text continues from the bottom of one column to the top of the next in newspaper columns.

Creating a Table

Sometimes I think WordPerfect 9 goes overboard in providing several ways to perform the same task. Creating tables is no exception; WordPerfect 9 provides two different ways to create a table—the Table QuickCreate button on the toolbar, and the Create Table dialog box.

The Table QuickCreate Button

The Table QuickCreate button is located on the WordPerfect 9 toolbar between the Column button and the Spell Checker button (see Figure 7.3). Clicking the Table QuickCreate button opens a pop-up mini-grid. As shown in Figure 7.4, you can set the dimensions of a new table by dragging your mouse pointer across the mini-grid.

FIGURE 7.3
The Table QuickCreate button.

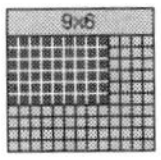

FIGURE 7.4
Creating a 9×6 (nine columns by six rows) table with the Table QuickCreate button.

To Do: Create a Table with Table QuickCreate

1. Open a new document.
2. Click anywhere to mark the insertion point for a new table.
3. Click the Table QuickCreate button and drag your mouse pointer across the mini-grid to create a 5×7 table.
4. Release the mouse button and watch as your new table is automatically inserted in your document.

The Create Table Dialog Box

To create a table using the Create Table dialog box shown in Figure 7.5, select Insert, Table from the menu bar (you can also double-click the Table QuickCreate button or press F12). Enter the number of columns and rows for your table and click Create.

FIGURE 7.5
The Create Table dialog box.

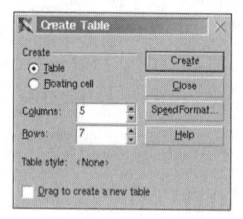

> The Create Table dialog box allows you to apply a predefined format to your table using the Table SpeedFormat feature. After setting your table size in the Create Table dialog box, click the SpeedFormat button to open the Table SpeedFormat dialog box. Select a predefined format, click Apply to return to the Create Table dialog box, and then click Create. A SpeedFormat is automatically applied to the new table inserted in your document.

Mastering Cell Selection

The action in a table takes place in its cells, thus making it crucial to know how to select cells and blocks of cells within a table. What better way to present this information than to place it in a table? Table 7.1 describes the many methods of cell selection in WordPerfect 9 tables.

Working with Tables and Columns

TABLE 7.1 Selecting Cells in WordPerfect 9 Tables

To Select...	Do This...
A single cell	Click the desired cell. To navigate to another cell in the same table, use the Tab or arrow keys or simply click the destination cell.
Two or more adjacent cells at once	Drag your mouse over the desired range of cells. Release the mouse button only after the final cell in the range is highlighted. Alternatively, select the first cell in the desired range, hold down the Shift key, and then click the last cell in the desired range.
One or more columns or rows at once	There are several ways to do this. The easiest way is to place your mouse pointer near the top border of any cell until an upward-pointing selection arrow appears. Double-click and the cell's entire column is selected. Pointing your mouse at a cell's left border will display a left-pointing selection arrow, which you can double-click to select the cell's entire row.
	You can also select rows and columns using row and column indicators, which you can display by clicking in the table, clicking the Table Menu button on the Property Bar, and then selecting Row/Col Indicators. To select a column, click the column's indicator. To select a row, click the row's indicator. To select multiple columns or rows, drag across their respective indicators or hold down the Shift key while selecting multiple indicators.
Select all cells	Click the Select Table button shown in Figure 7.6.

FIGURE 7.6
Selecting rows 1 and 2 using the row and column indicators.

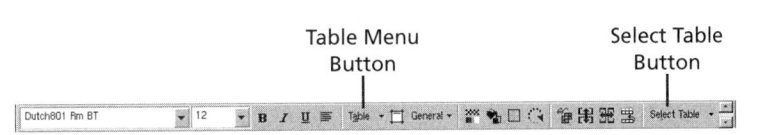

Table Menu Button

Select Table Button

Inputting Table Data

Once you create your table, entering and editing data in each cell works much the same way as entering data in a typical document. The key difference is that you must first select a cell before entering your data. Once you select a cell, all input data is placed in the selected cell until you select another cell or cell block, using one of the methods described in Table 7.1, or click outside of the table to return to your document.

To Do: Insert Data into a Practice Table

1. Open a new document and create a table that's five columns wide by six rows long.
2. Enter the personal expense data shown in Figure 7.7.
3. Name the document Expenses.wpd and save it to a location you'll remember. You'll return to it throughout this hour to build upon your hands-on experience with WordPerfect 9 tables.

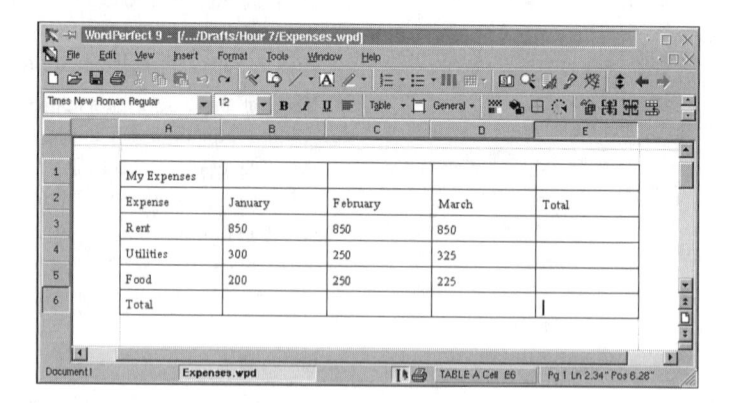

FIGURE 7.7
Entering data into a table.

Performing Calculations in Tables

Although Quattro Pro 9 is the tool of choice for spreadsheets that rely on complex formulas, WordPerfect 9 tables include impressive spreadsheet features that can easily handle simple calculations. In this section, you'll use these features to perform simple addition within a WordPerfect 9 table. Ready? Open the Expenses.wpd file you created earlier in this hour, and let's do it!

QuickSumming Columns and Rows

Using QuickSum is the easiest and fastest way to add numbers in columns and rows. Here's how to do it:

Working with Tables and Columns

1. Click in Expenses.wpd, click the Table Menu button on the Property Bar, and select Row/Col Indicators to turn your table indicators on.
2. Select cell B6, the last cell in column B.
3. Click the Table Menu button and then click QuickSum.
4. Select cell E3 and perform the same procedure to QuickSum the row.

As shown in Figure 7.8, QuickSum added the data in cells B1 through B5 and inserted the sum in cell B6. QuickSum also added the data in cells A3 through D3 and inserted the sum in cell E3. Pretty neat, huh?

FIGURE 7.8
The results of applying QuickSum to cells B6 and E3.

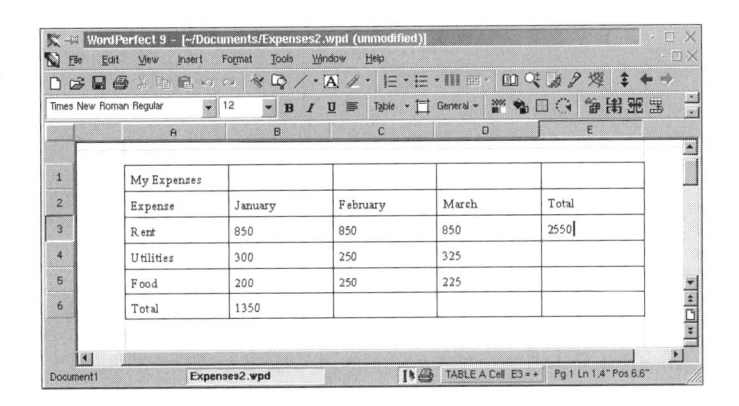

To Do: Apply Other Calculation Techniques

Continue to perform calculations within Expenses.wpd by following these steps:

1. Select cell C6.
2. Click the Table Menu button on the Property Bar and select Formula Toolbar to open the Formula toolbar.
3. In the Formula Edit box, type **SUM(C3:C5)** and press Enter.
4. Select cell E4. Type **SUM(B4:D4)** in the formula box and press Enter.
5. Select cells B5 through E5. Click the QuickSum button on the Formula Bar.
6. Drag the column indicators for columns D and E and then click the QuickSum button.

Congratulations! You've just used three different techniques for applying formulas to data contained in WordPerfect 9 tables. If you've done everything correctly, your table should look like Figure 7.9.

FIGURE 7.9

Your completed Expenses.wpd table after entry of all formulas.

My Expenses				
Expense	January	February	March	Total
Rent	850	850	850	2550
Utilities	300	250	325	875
Food	200	250	225	675
Total	1350	1350	1400	4100

You're not through with this table yet, so be sure to save your work.

> WordPerfect 9 borrows heavily from Quattro Pro 9's spreadsheet features, which are discussed in Hours 10 through 13. This section is intended to give you a very brief introduction to performing simple calculations in WordPerfect tables without bogging you down in spreadsheet concepts. If you're new to spreadsheets, don't sweat it. Work through the hours dedicated to Quattro Pro 9. After that, WordPerfect 9's relatively basic spreadsheet functions will make more sense!

Formatting Tables

You can apply to tables the formatting techniques that were covered in Hour 5, "Formatting WordPerfect 9 Documents." Items such as font face, font style, and QuickFormat all work the same way when applied to the data in your tables. Just select the desired cell or range of cells and format to your heart's content!

> Table formatting follows three rules of priority that you should keep in mind. First, any formatting applied to a cell overrides existing formatting applied to a column, row, table, or to the entire document. Second, column and row formatting overrides existing formatting applied to the table or to the entire document. Third, general table formatting will follow the same formatting of your document unless you change it.
>
> In other words, you should approach table formatting from the top down, establishing formatting settings in the following order: document, table, column, row, and cell.

Working with Tables and Columns 137

> There are some formatting features that are specific to tables. WordPerfect 9 stashes these special tools in the Properties for Table Format dialog box (shown in Figure 7.10), which you can access by selecting Table, Format from the Table Menu button on the Property Bar. You can also access this dialog box by clicking the General Table Status button on the Application Bar (refer to Figure 7.1 for a reminder of where to find this button). The Properties for Table Format dialog box contains several tabs that provide additional formatting controls: Cell, Column, Row, Table, and Skew. Navigate through each tab to explore these additional formatting controls.
>
> **FIGURE 7.10**
> *The Properties for Table Format dialog box.*

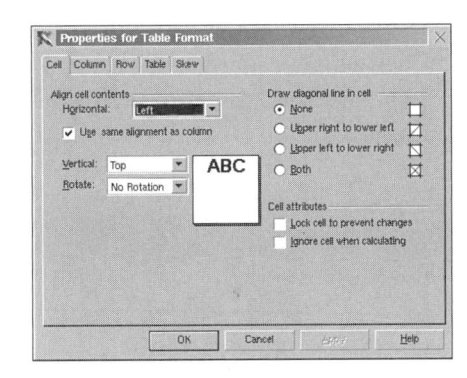

Creating a Table Header

Table headers are column headings that repeat on each page of a multipage table. Follow these steps to create a table header in your `Expenses.wpd` table:

1. Select the top row of the table.
2. Right-click in the selected row and choose Join Cells to merge all cells in row 1 into a single cell.
3. With row 1 still selected, apply center alignment by clicking the Alignment button on the Property Bar and selecting Center. The Alignment button is the next button to the right of the Title Menu button.
4. Click the Table Menu button (or right-click the selected row) and select Format. In the Properties for Table Format dialog box, navigate to the Row tab (if it isn't open by default).
5. Check the Header Row box and click OK.

You can add more header rows by selecting the desired rows and repeating steps 4 and 5.

Inserting Rows and Columns

You'll probably find yourself frequently needing to add rows and columns to your table, especially if it contains a growing list of items such as addresses or, sigh, expenses. The drill is generally the same for columns and rows. Keep in mind that the new insertion will adopt the same formatting attributes of the column or row in which the insertion point is located.

To Do: Insert a Column or a Row

1. Place your mouse pointer to designate the insertion point at the row or column next to which you want the new row or column to be inserted.
2. Click the Table Menu button on the Property Bar (or right-click at the insertion point) and select Insert to open the Insert Columns/Rows dialog box shown in Figure 7.11.

FIGURE 7.11
The Insert Columns/Rows dialog box.

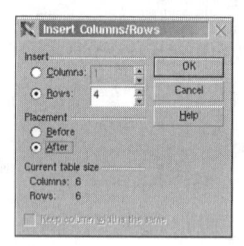

3. Check Column or Row, depending on which you want to insert, and then enter the number of columns or rows you want to insert.
4. Check whether to insert the new columns/rows before or after the current selection.
5. Check Keep Column Widths the Same if you are inserting columns and want all columns to be of equal width.
6. Click OK.

> You can also use keyboard shortcuts to quickly insert a single row. Press Alt+Insert to insert a row above the insertion point, and press Alt+Shift+Insert to insert a row below the insertion point. Note also that when you click within a table to send the Property Bar into table mode, the last button on the Property Bar is the Insert Row button, which inserts a row above the insertion point.

Deleting Rows, Columns, and Cell Contents

You can easily delete whole rows and columns, the contents of selected cells, or just the formulas of selected cells. Here's how these deletion options work:

- Deleting columns and rows wipes out not only cell contents but also the columns and rows that contained the cell contents.
- Deleting cell contents only wipes out the data within the cell, but the actual column, row, and cell remain intact.
- Deleting formulas only wipes out the actual formulas inserted into your spreadsheet—amazingly, the results of the deleted formulas remain intact.

The procedure for performing each of these deletions is essentially the same. Select the cell or any part of the column or row you want to delete. Right-click and select Delete from the pop-up menu to open the Delete Structure/Contents dialog box. Select whether to delete columns or rows, cell contents only, or formulas only. Then click OK.

> You can also press Alt+Delete to delete a selected row.

Deleting Tables

As with columns, rows, and cells, WordPerfect 9 gives you several ways to delete an entire table. Here's what you can delete:

- Everything, including table structure and contents
- Contents only, leaving an empty table structure
- Formulas only, leaving their results and the table structure intact
- Table structure, which leaves the contents of the table as normal tabbed text in your document

To use one of these options, select the entire table and press the Delete key to open the Delete Table dialog box. Select whether to delete the entire table, table contents only, formulas only, or table structure only. Then click OK. There are also options for converting the table data to a merge data file—you'll learn more about merge data files in Hour 9, "Advanced WordPerfect 9 Techniques."

Working with Columns

Columns offer several neat ways to organize and present text, graphics, and other information. WordPerfect 9 lets you place up to 24 columns on a page, and it gives you full control over column width and the spacing between columns. Each column acts almost like a page unto itself, into which you can insert objects and apply formatting.

There are two main types of columns available in WordPerfect 9:

- *Newspaper columns*. These operate just the way they sound, running text and information from top to bottom in one column and then continuing the text at the top of the next column. An example of this type of column was shown earlier in Figure 7.2.
- *Parallel columns*. These are read across the page, grouping related columns into rows. As shown in Figure 7.12, the next row is placed beneath the longest column in the preceding row, and so on.

FIGURE 7.12
Parallel columns appear in rows across the page.

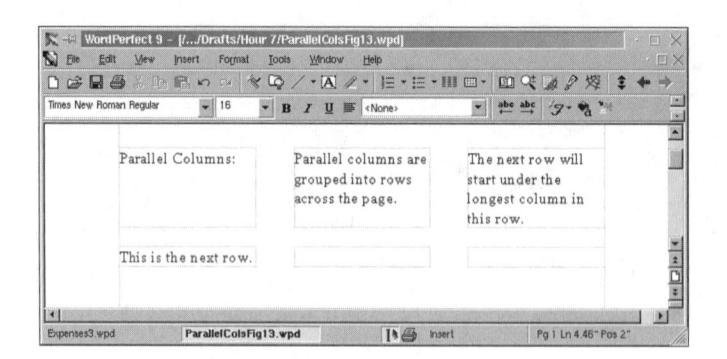

Creating Columns

The quickest way to create equally sized newspaper columns is to position your mouse pointer at an insertion point in your document and press the Columns button on the toolbar. From the pop-up menu, select the number of columns, as shown in Figure 7.13, and your columns are automatically inserted into your document.

FIGURE 7.13
Creating newspaper columns with the Columns button.

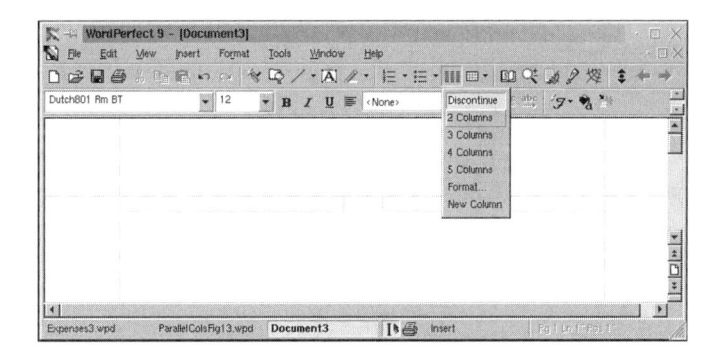

Exploring the Columns Dialog Box

You can exercise greater control over column creation by clicking the Columns button on the toolbar and selecting Format to open the Columns dialog box, shown in Figure 7.14. To create a column from the Columns dialog box, specify the type and number of columns you want, choose spacing and width options, and click OK.

FIGURE 7.14
The Columns dialog box.

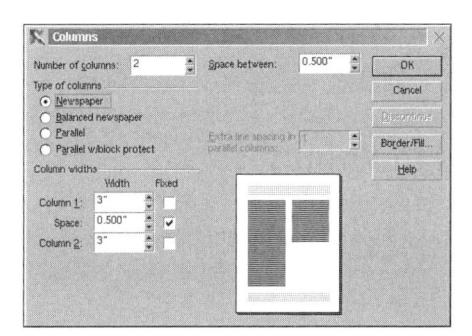

When you first open the Columns dialog box, the default column configuration is two newspaper columns of equal width, with a half-inch space between them. The Columns dialog box provides a preview of the layout, which changes as you customize the settings. Change the number of columns to four and notice the changes in the Preview and in the Column Width sections of the dialog box.

Click the Balanced Newspaper radio button and watch the preview. See how the text in the columns adjusts to equal lengths?

Click the Parallel radio button. In the Extra Line Spacing in Parallel Columns box, gradually increase the line spacing from 1 to 13 and watch the preview. Increasing the line spacing moves the bottom rows down and, ultimately, onto the next page.

Click the Parallel with Block Protect radio button. This option forces all the lines in each row to remain together on the same page. Gradually decrease the extra line spacing to 1. See how entire blocks of rows, instead of just lines, move back onto the page?

Finally, click the Border/Fill button on the right side of the dialog box to open the Column Border/Fill dialog box, shown in Figure 7.15. From here you can apply border, fill, and shadow effects to your columns. Try experimenting with various settings for each type of column.

FIGURE 7.15
The Column Border/Fill dialog box.

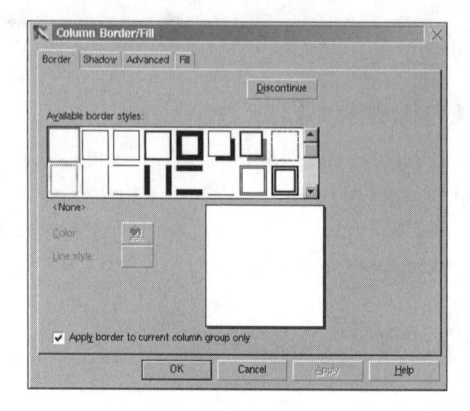

Getting Around in Columns

Once your columns are created, you can go straight to entering and editing text and other objects within them. Just use your mouse and the shadow cursor to move your insertion point anywhere within or between columns, and then type away!

Here are a few general rules to keep in mind as you begin working in columns:

- In newspaper columns, text wraps inside the first column until it hits the bottom margin or a column break; then it jumps over to the top of the next column.
- When you're typing in a balanced newspaper column, your text may shift backward into a preceding column in order to maintain proper balance.
- In parallel columns, text flows down a column until you insert a column break by pressing Ctrl+Enter. This will take you to the top of the next column.
- When you're finished working in your columns, you'll need to discontinue them to get back to the main document. Move your mouse pointer to the insertion point at which to end your columns. Click the Column button and select Discontinue. Alternatively, select Format, Columns from the menu bar and click the Discontinue button.

Formatting Columns

You can format the contents of your columns using the same tools that you use for formatting any other document. Like tables, columns have some special formatting options, such as spacing, width, and vertical lines inserted between columns.

- *Adjusting column spacing.* To increase or decrease the spacing equally between columns, select Format, Columns from the menu bar to open the Columns dialog box and then enter the new spacing value in the Space Between box. If you don't want equal spacing between three or more columns, you can control column spacing from the Column Widths section of the Columns dialog box. First, uncheck the Fixed box in the Space line for each column; then adjust the spacing as desired and click OK.

  Just like with tables, you can also adjust column spacing by dragging the column guidelines across the screen. If column guidelines are not visible, from the menu bar select View, Guidelines to open the Guidelines dialog box. Make sure Display Guidelines for Columns is checked and then click OK.

- *Adjusting column width.* The simplest way to adjust column width and keep the same column spacing is to place your mouse pointer in the space between two columns and drag the space to a new position.

  You can adjust column width without preserving spacing by dragging a column's guideline left or right.

  You can also adjust column width in the Columns dialog box by specifying the width for each column you want to resize.

- *Inserting vertical lines.* To insert vertical lines between columns, open the Columns dialog box, click the Border/Fill button, and navigate to the Border tab. Scroll to the bottom of the Available Border Styles box, select the single vertical line, and click OK. In the Columns dialog box, click OK again to return to your document.

Deleting Columns

To delete a column and all its contents, move your insertion point to the beginning of the column. From the menu bar, select View, Reveal Codes to turn on Reveal Codes. Click the `Col Def` code and drag it out of the Reveal Codes box. When you do this, any column breaks will automatically be converted to hard page breaks, which are coded as `HCol-SPg`. If you drag these from the Reveal Codes box, the text that previously appeared in the columns will all appear on a single page, formatted as a normal paragraph.

Summary

In this hour, you learned how to create and format tables and columns, and you practiced entering and editing data in tables and columns. You also used a WordPerfect table to perform some basic spreadsheet calculations.

In the next hour, you'll learn how to work with graphics and special effects in WordPerfect 9. You'll see how to create, edit, and position professional-looking graphics in your documents with WordPerfect's powerful, yet easy-to-use graphics tools. Get ready to have some fun!

Q&A

Q Why can't I just drag my mouse across a document to define the outer dimensions of a new table?

A You can! Drag your mouse across a document at the insertion point for your table. When you release the mouse button, select Table from the pop-up menu that appears. This opens the Create Table dialog box, where you can configure your table as described in this hour.

Q I've seen tables with headers that appear vertically instead of horizontally on the page. How do I do this for my WordPerfect table headers?

A You can rotate the contents of any cell, not just headers, using the Rotate Cell button on the Property Bar. (The Rotate Cell button contains a dotted circle with an arrow pointing clockwise.) To rotate a cell, select the desired cell and click the Rotate Cell button. Each time you click the button, the cell contents will rotate 90 degrees clockwise until they come full circle.

Workshop

The Workshop contains quiz questions and exercises to help reinforce what you've learned in this hour. If you get stuck, the answers can be found in Appendix B, "Answers to Quiz Questions."

Quiz

1. True or false: Columns are better than tables for creating invoices that calculate the total amount due.
2. How do you put a break in a column?
3. What is the cell address of a table cell that lies at the intersection of row 14 and column F?

Exercises

1. Create a 6×66 table with a header row title that reads "Wish List."
2. Create a 4×4 table and apply the Fancy Label SpeedFormat style to it.
3. Create your resume using columns so that your Objective, Skills, Experience, and Education headings appear on the left side of the page and the details for each heading appear on the right side of the page.

HOUR 8

Creating and Working with Graphics in WordPerfect 9

As noted in Hour 1, "Exploring WordPerfect Office 2000 for Linux," one of the differences between versions 8 and 9 of WordPerfect for Linux is the elimination of WordPerfect Draw from version 9. WordPerfect Draw was a neat little illustration program that has no real counterpart in WordPerfect 9 (although WordPerfect Draw's illustration tools live on in Presentations 9).

This isn't to say that WordPerfect 9 leaves you hanging when it comes to working with graphics. WordPerfect 9 recognizes that graphics play an increasingly important role in the documents we create and includes many tools for editing graphics imported from other sources, such as drawings created in other programs such as Presentations 9 as well as clipart and photographs copied from a CD-ROM or downloaded from the Internet. This hour will open your eyes to the surprisingly sophisticated graphics capabilities of WordPerfect 9, an application predominantly known for processing words.

In this hour you will

- Master two techniques for inserting graphics into your WordPerfect documents.
- Explore the graphics resources included with the office suite, including the Scrapbook and free clipart and photographs on the WordPerfect Office 2000 for Linux CD-ROM.
- Learn how to use WordPerfect 9's editing tools for graphics, including the size, placement, attribute, border, fill, and shadow controls.

Inserting Graphics into a Document

Certain documents cry out for graphics. Newsletters, Web pages, professional announcements, birthday party invitations—all of these documents benefit when you take the time to add pretty pictures. Although WordPerfect isn't the tool of choice for creating images to use in your documents, it includes powerful tools for importing and editing all kinds of graphics from other sources.

In order to take advantage of WordPerfect's graphics-editing tools, you've first got to bring your graphics into a WordPerfect document. There are two ways to do this:

- *Create a graphics box with your mouse.* You can insert a graphic with one hand tied behind your back and one hand glued to your mouse. Find a blank space in an open document and click and drag diagonally with your mouse to create a box that will hold the graphic you'll import from another source. As shown in Figure 8.1, when you release the mouse, a pop-up menu provides several options for the box you've created. Choose one of the first two options, Clipart or Image from File, to add a graphic to your document. I'll cover both of these options later in this hour.

FIGURE 8.1

Click and drag in a blank space to create a graphics box to hold an imported graphic.

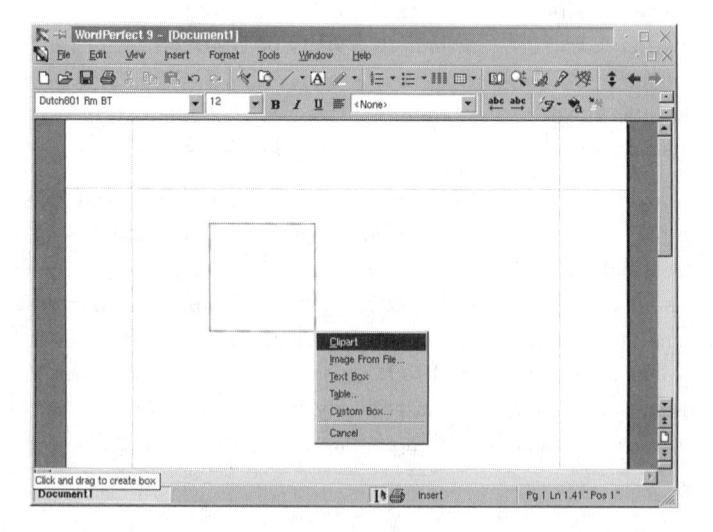

- *Insert a graphic using the Insert command.* Alternatively, you can use the Insert command from the menu bar to insert a graphic. Position your cursor in a blank space in an open document where you want a graphic to appear. The cursor will be the point of insertion for the upper-left corner of the graphic. From the menu bar select Insert, Graphics and choose either Clipart or Image from File to add a graphic to your document.

> Between these two methods, I recommend using a graphics box because it provides some control over the size of an incoming graphic. For example, if you drag out a graphics box that's roughly two inches long and three inches wide, WordPerfect will import the graphic to match these dimensions as closely as possible without distorting the graphic or interfering with your text. In contrast, if you insert the same graphic using the Insert command, WordPerfect will insert the graphic at its full size, potentially displacing existing text on the page.
>
> Although you can always undo or delete a meddlesome graphic or even try resizing the graphic to cure the damage done, your best bet is to control graphic size at the outset by dragging out a graphics box.

Inserting Graphics from the Scrapbook

As shown in Figure 8.2, selecting Clipart as your image source launches the Scrapbook, which contains dozens of graphics you can add to your documents. As far as the Scrapbook is concerned, the term *graphics* covers two types of artwork you can insert into your documents: drawings (technically referred to as *vector-based*, or *object-oriented*, drawings) and photographs (technically referred to as *bitmap images*). The Scrapbook houses each type of graphic separately, with drawings collected under the Clipart tab and photographs collected under the Photos tab.

FIGURE 8.2
The WordPerfect Office 2000 for Linux Scrapbook.

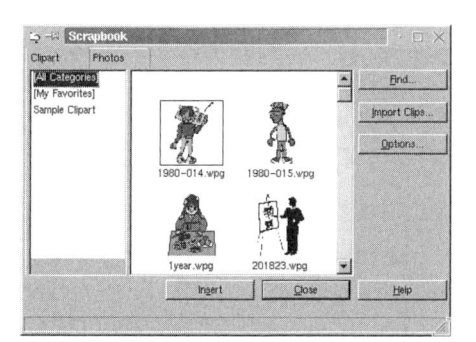

> There's actually a third way to insert a graphic into a WordPerfect document, but it only applies to Scrapbook graphics. It works almost the same way as the Insert command: Position your cursor in a blank space in an open document where you want a graphic to appear. Instead of reaching for the Insert command on the menu bar, click the Clipart button on the toolbar to launch the Scrapbook (see Figure 8.3). Then just use the Scrapbook to insert your image as described later in this section.

FIGURE 8.3
You can also use the Clipart button on the toolbar to insert a Scrapbook graphic into your document.

Although they house different types of graphics, the Clipart and Photos tabs work the same way. The left side of the Scrapbook window contains a list of categories that organize graphics within the Scrapbook. The default categories for the Clipart tab are All Categories, My Favorites, and Sample Clipart. When you select a category, the graphics within that category are displayed on the right side of the screen. Selecting All Categories lets you see all graphics collected under the tab you're working in. For example, selecting All Categories while working under the Clipart tab will display all clipart graphics in every category, but it will not display graphics in categories located under the Photos tab.

To insert a graphic from the Scrapbook, double-click it or select it and click Insert. The graphic is automatically inserted into your document and you can close the Scrapbook unless there are additional graphics you want to add.

> WordPerfect 9 shares the Scrapbook with Presentations 9, and you can access and use the Scrapbook from Presentations 9 using the same methods you learn about in this hour.

To Do: Add Graphics to the Scrapbook

1. Click Import Clips to open the Insert File dialog box. Graphics under the Clipart tab are stored in the directory `/usr/lib/corel/wpo/graphics/ClipArt`.
2. If you use the drop-down menu in the Insert File dialog box to navigate up to the `graphics` folder, you'll find additional resources you can tap to add graphics to your Scrapbook.

▼ 3. You'll find additional folders containing backgrounds, borders, pictures, and textures, all of which you can open to select a graphic to add to your Scrapbook. Double-clicking a graphic in any of these folders automatically adds it to your Scrapbook.

4. You can use the same method to add graphics to your Scrapbook from a CD-ROM. Simply load a CD-ROM containing graphics into your CD-ROM drive and navigate to your CD-ROM drive in the Insert File dialog box.

▲ 5. Find the graphic you want to install from the CD-ROM and double-click on it.

> Both editions of WordPerfect Office 2000 for Linux include royalty-free graphics you can add to your Scrapbook and use in your documents. The Standard edition includes more than 1,200 clipart graphics and more than 20 photographs; the Deluxe edition includes more than 12,000 clipart graphics and more than 200 photographs. To add these graphics to your Scrapbook, insert Disc 2 of your WordPerfect Office 2000 software into your CD-ROM drive. When you get to the Insert File dialog box, navigate to the CD-ROM drive and open the `graphics` folder to find a wealth of additional clipart and photos. Double-click any graphic to add it to your Scrapbook.

Managing Graphics within the Scrapbook

When you double-click a graphic to add it to the Scrapbook, something unusual happens. Instead of immediately returning to the Scrapbook with your new graphic ready to roll, you're asked to define the graphic's properties. This final step in adding to your Scrapbook will help you effectively manage and organize your Scrapbook items:

From the Scrapbook, click Import Clips to open the Insert File dialog box. Use the drop-down menu to navigate to the `/usr/lib/corel/wpo/graphics` directory.

Double-click Textures, Stone, then `blue and gold marble.bmp`. The `.bmp` extension tells you this is a bitmap image, which means it will automatically be filed under the Photos tab of your Scrapbook.

Double-clicking the image launches the Scrapbook Item Properties dialog box shown in Figure 8.4. (For this exercise, I assume you're using the Deluxe edition of WordPerfect Office 2000 for Linux. If you're using the Standard version, which may not include the `blue and gold marble.bmp` image, substitute any `.bmp` image from the graphics folder to complete this exercise.)

Note that most of the information in the Scrapbook Item Properties dialog box is dimmed. The Scrapbook does this automatically to protect against accidental alteration or deletion of the default images installed on your hard drive. There are, however, several things you can do here to catalog the graphics in your Scrapbook.

First, you'll want to add some keywords to describe your graphic. The Scrapbook includes its own Find utility that lets you search the Scrapbook by keyword, filename, and graphic type. Plugging in a few logical keywords now to describe the characteristics of your graphic will enable you to recall it later with a keyword search. In Figure 8.4 I've added several keywords that will call up the blue and gold marble graphic when I perform a keyword search.

As you begin adding graphics to the Scrapbook, you may want to create your own categories to keep your graphics organized. For example, you may have a set of graphics for your business newsletter that you want to keep separate from the graphics you're collecting for the invitations to your daughter's birthday party. The Scrapbook Item Properties dialog box gives you a chance to file your new graphic within an existing category or to create a new category. To file your graphic in one or more existing categories, simply check off the desired categories in the Categories list. To create a new category, click New Category, enter a name at the prompt, and hit Return or click OK.

In Figure 8.4, I've elected to file my blue and green marble graphic in My Favorites and in a new category I created named My Textures. When you're through designating your item properties, click OK to return to the Scrapbook.

FIGURE 8.4
Use the Scrapbook Item Properties dialog box to "catalog" your graphic for future reference.

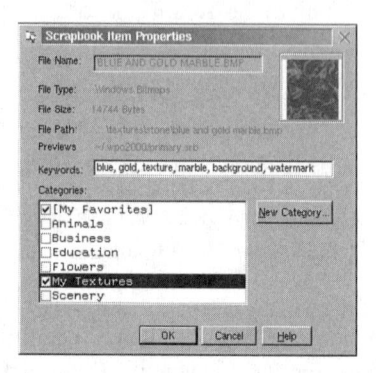

The Scrapbook automatically opens to the Photos tab, with My Favorites selected and the new graphic displayed in the preview window. Navigate down your category list and select My Textures to confirm that the new graphic was also added there. As shown in Figure 8.5, you can edit the graphic's properties and how it is displayed in the Scrapbook by selecting the graphic and clicking the Options button. In Figure 8.5, I've selected

Creating and Working with Graphics in WordPerfect 9

Keywords to display the keywords previously assigned to the graphic in the preview window. To edit the graphic's properties, click Options and select Item Properties to return to the Scrapbook Item Properties dialog box. You can also get there by right-clicking directly on the graphic in the preview window and selecting Item Properties.

FIGURE 8.5
You can use the Options button to control the preview display and to edit categories and item properties.

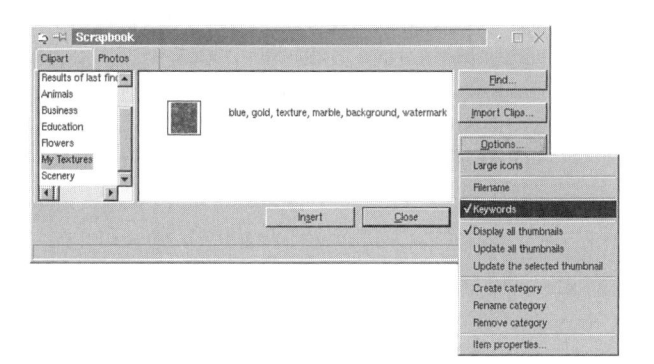

Note that you can also add, remove, or rename a category in your Scrapbook using the Options button. To add a category, click Options, select Create Category, enter the name of your new category at the prompt, and click OK. You can follow the same procedure to rename and remove categories at any time.

More than just a place to store your graphics, the Scrapbook is a sophisticated database you can search to recall all graphics that meet certain criteria specified by you. You can search your Scrapbook to locate graphics by keyword, filename, and graphic type. To do this, open the Scrapbook and click the Find button to open the Find Scrapbook Item dialog box. This dialog box presents all three search criteria at once, but you can search the Scrapbook using one, all, or any combination of the three:

- *Keyword*. Search by keyword to call up all graphics that match the descriptive keyword terms assigned to each graphic in the Scrapbook Item Properties dialog box. A keyword search is particularly helpful if you've consistently designated the same keywords to graphics that have something in common. For example, if you're looking for background images to use as a watermark and you've tagged all potential candidates with *watermark* as a keyword, performing a keyword search for *watermark* will recall every graphic so designated.

- *Filename*. Search by filename when you know all or a portion of the exact name of your graphic. For example, a search for graphics with *Baby* in the filename will call up graphics named *Baby Shower*, *Baby Gifts*, *First Week Baby*, and *Jen's Baby*.

- *Item type*. Search by item type when you need to use a specific graphics format and you want to see what's available in your Scrapbook. For example, if you're using WordPerfect to create a Web page, you may want to check your Scrapbook for all Web-friendly JPEG or bitmap images.

Once you've designated your search criteria, click the Find Now button to launch your search. You'll quickly be returned to the Scrapbook with your search listed and selected in the category window and the results displayed in the preview window.

Inserting Graphics from a File Location

With so much time dedicated to the Scrapbook, don't forget that you can sidestep the Scrapbook entirely and import an image directly from a file.

To do this, follow the steps to insert a graphic by dragging out a graphics box or by using the Insert command on the menu bar. When given the option of selecting Clipart or Image from File, select Image from File to open the Insert Image dialog box. Use the drop-down menu to navigate to the file location where your graphic is stored and double-click the graphic you want to insert.

> What's the advantage of using this method over the Scrapbook? There may be times when you're in a hurry and don't want to waste time adding a graphic to your Scrapbook and designating its item properties. If you know the precise file location of your graphic and don't need to preview it or catalog it for future reference, skipping the Scrapbook and heading straight to the source is a quick and convenient way to get the job done. If you choose, you can always come back and add the graphic to your Scrapbook later.

Editing Graphics in WordPerfect 9

Before you learn how to edit the graphics you insert in a WordPerfect 9 document, you've got to have a graphic to work with. Begin a new document and open the Scrapbook to the Clipart tab. Choose a fun graphic to work with and double-click it in the preview window or select it and click Insert. It doesn't matter which graphic you use; for the following figures, I imported a graphic named `POOCH.wpg` from the WordPerfect Office 2000 for Linux Deluxe CD-ROM. From hereon out, I'll just refer to it as *Pooch*. Close the Scrapbook and take a look at your document, which, except for a different image, should look like Figure 8.6.

Creating and Working with Graphics in WordPerfect 9

FIGURE 8.6
The Pooch graphic inserted in a new WordPerfect 9 document.

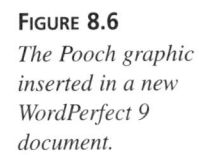

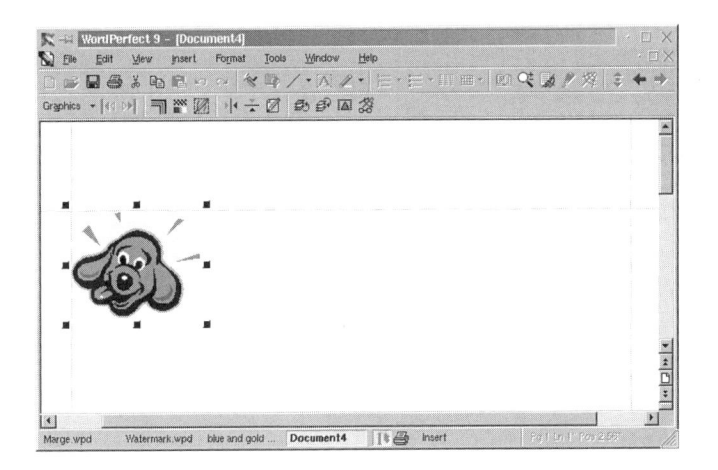

To Do: Resize a Graphic

One of the first things you'll notice about an inserted graphic is that upon insertion, it remains active, or *selected*, and ready for editing.

You can tell that the graphic is selected because eight black squares, called *resizing handles*, appear around the border of the graphic. Not surprisingly, the resizing handles are used to resize a graphic. They also, however, indicate the boundaries of the graphics box that contains your graphic on the page.

Give the resizing handles a try:

1. Position your mouse pointer directly on any of the resizing handles surrounding your graphic.
2. When the pointer turns into a two-way arrow, click and hold while dragging in one of the directions indicated by the arrow to either enlarge or reduce the graphic.
3. When you release the mouse, your graphic will stretch or shrink to the designated size. As shown in Figure 8.7, stretching a graphic all the way to the right margin alters the graphic's proportions, distorting the image.

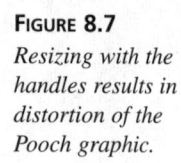

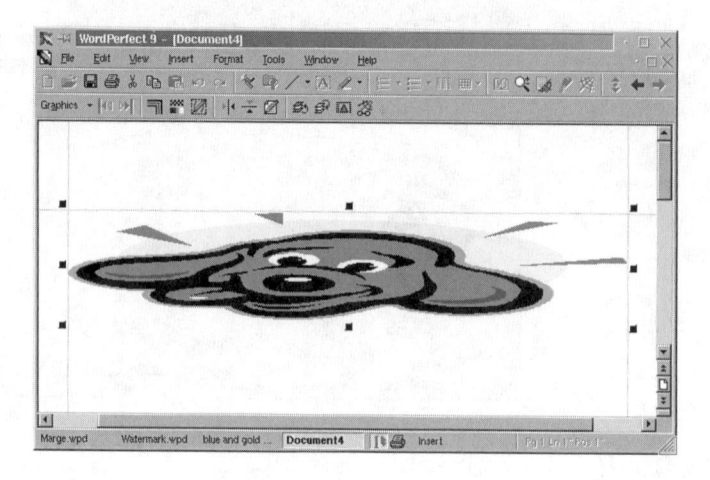

FIGURE 8.7
Resizing with the handles results in distortion of the Pooch graphic.

4. This may not be what you wanted, but note that the Undo button on the toolbar is dimmed and unusable.

5. To undo an edit to a graphic, you'll have to deselect the graphic by clicking in any non-graphic space within the open document.

6. Once the graphic is deselected, you can click the Undo button or press Ctrl+Z to undo the edit.

7. There's a distortion-free way to resize a graphic without messing with its proportions. With the graphic selected, right-click on the graphic and select Size from the pop-up menu to open the Box Size dialog box. Alternatively, you can click the Graphics button on the Property Bar and select Size from the drop-down menu.

8. In the Box Size dialog box, adjust the width to 5.5 inches. For the height, select Maintain Proportions and click OK.

9. As shown in Figure 8.8, the graphic is enlarged to the desired width, and WordPerfect has automatically calculated the appropriate height to maintain the graphic's proportions.

10. You could follow the same procedure to set a precise value for the height and have WordPerfect calculate the proportionate width.

Creating and Working with Graphics in WordPerfect 9

FIGURE 8.8
The Pooch graphic, resized and distortion-free.

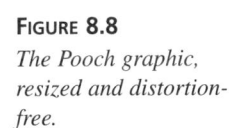

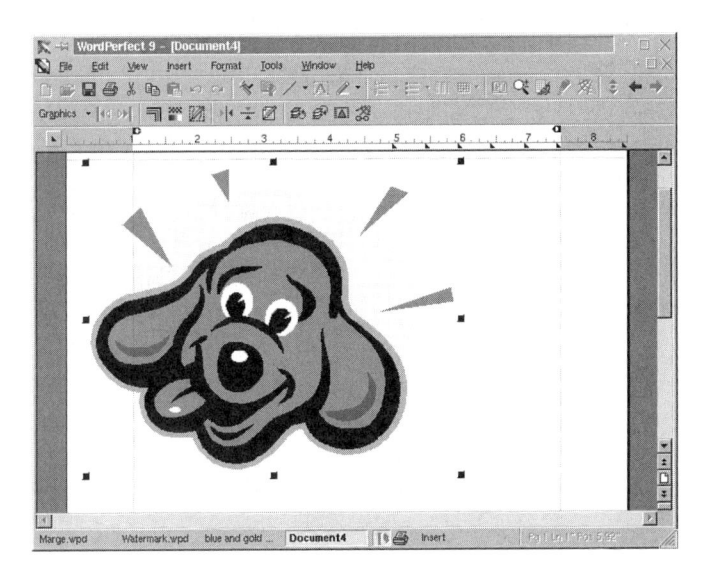

11. For now, click on the page outside the graphic and click the Undo button to restore your graphic to its original size.

Repositioning Graphics

No doubt you'll want to be able to move your graphics around on the page. You can reposition a graphic in two ways: by dragging it with the mouse or by manually entering values to position it more precisely on the page.

To move your graphic with the mouse, position the mouse pointer anywhere on the graphic except on a handle. When the pointer turns into a four-way arrow, click and hold to drag the graphic with your mouse.

The second method of repositioning a graphic requires some thought about the dimensions and margin settings of the underlying page. For example, to position the Pooch graphic in the top center of the page, you may need to be more precise than merely dragging the graphic with your mouse and trying to eyeball it into position.

Instead, right-click the graphic, or click the Graphics button on the Property Bar, and select Position to open the Box Position dialog box. The Horizontal setting 5" from the Right Margin tells you that the far-right border of your graphic sits five inches from the right margin. The Vertical setting 0" from the Top Margin tells you that the upper border of your graphic sits on the top margin. To get your graphic to the center of your page, slightly below the top margin, change the Horizontal setting to 2.5" from the Right

Margin and change the Vertical setting to .2" from the Top Margin. Click OK. As shown in Figure 8.9, this seems to have done the trick.

FIGURE 8.9
The Pooch graphic, perfectly centered with help from the Box Position dialog box.

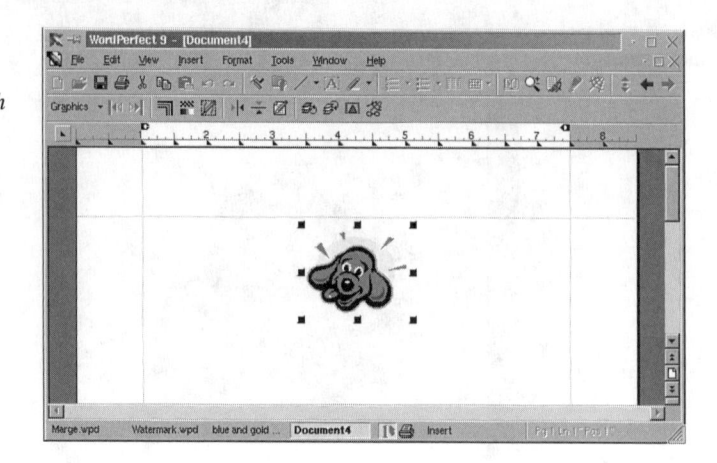

Editing with Image Tools

Until now, your graphics-editing experience has been limited to manipulating (by resizing or repositioning) the graphics box in which your graphic resides. It's time to shift gears and focus on editing the graphic itself with the help of Image Tools, one of WordPerfect 9's most useful graphics utilities.

You can access Image Tools by right-clicking a graphic and selecting Image Tools or by selecting a graphic and clicking the Image Tools button on the Property Bar (it looks like a pencil resting diagonally over a sheet of paper). As shown in Figure 8.10, the Image Tools toolbox is divided into three sections: the top section contains Rotate, Move, Flip, and Zoom controls; the middle section contains color-related controls such as Contrast, Brightness, and Fill; and the bottom section contains controls that let you edit and reset a broad range of attributes for your graphic.

FIGURE 8.10
Image Tools includes powerful controls for editing many different elements of a graphic.

Rotating, Moving, and Flipping Graphics

Let's return to Pooch and get to work with Image Tools. As noted, Image Tools focuses on editing the actual graphic rather than the box in which it sits. This is evident in the series of buttons that appear in the top section of Image Tools:

- *Rotate.* The Rotate button activates a set of four rotate handles around your image that allow you to spin the image clockwise or counterclockwise within the graphics box. It also activates a center point that can be moved anywhere within the graphics box to alter the arc of the rotation. In Figure 8.11, I've altered the brightness of the graphic to make it more transparent (more on this in a few minutes) in order to show you a clear view of the rotate handles and center point. The rotate handles look just like the resizing handles, except they have tiny arrowheads on two corners that point to indicate clockwise and counterclockwise movement. The center point is shown at its default location in the absolute center of the graphic.

  I've also rotated Pooch clockwise just a bit to show you what I mean when I say that Image Tools focuses on editing the graphic within the graphic box. As a result of rotating the graphic, Pooch's left ear has dipped just below the bottom edge of the graphics box and can no longer be seen onscreen. This is similar to photographs in which the subject's head appears "cut off" because it wasn't properly within the camera's view when the picture was taken. If you move your graphic out of the "view" of the graphics box in which it resides, you won't be able to see all or a portion of the graphic.

FIGURE 8.11
The rotate handles and central point allow you to take your graphic for a "spin" within the graphics box.

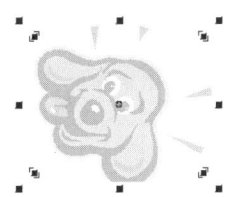

- *Move.* Although clicking the Move button conjures up the same four-way arrow you learned about in connection with repositioning graphics, in the context of Image Tools it allows you to move a graphic only within the boundaries of the graphics box. If you move the graphic beyond the edge of the graphics box, portions of your graphic will be hidden from view.

- *Flip Left to Right/Flip Top to Bottom.* Flipping a graphic means to invert it. Think of your graphic as a pancake with the same image printed on both sides. Flipping your graphic left to right is like using an imaginary spatula to turn the graphic pancake until the left side of the face-up graphic is face down on the right. Because the image is exactly the same on both sides, a left-to-right flip (or a right-to-left flip) displays the equivalent of a mirror image of the original graphic. Figure 8.12 is an example of a left-to-right flip. Of course, flipping top to bottom works in much the same way. Note that when a graphic is selected, flip buttons also appear on the Property Bar and can be used without launching Image Tools.

FIGURE 8.12
Pooch as "flipped" left to right.

Using the Zoom Tools

The Zoom button on the Image Tools palette is different from the normal Zoom button on the toolbar. The Zoom button on the toolbar is used to alter the magnification level of an entire document. The Zoom button on the Image Tools palette is used to alter the magnification level of a graphic within a graphic box—it has no effect on the magnification level of anything outside the box.

As shown in Figure 8.13, clicking the Zoom button in Image Tools opens a flyout bar with three different zoom controls: Magnifier, Zoom Scroll, and 1:1.

FIGURE 8.13
Image Tools provides three different zoom control buttons: Magnifier, Zoom Scroll, and 1:1.

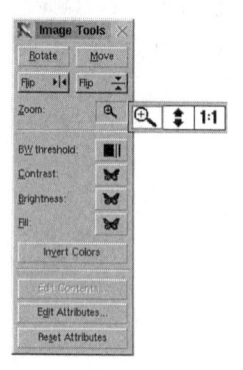

- *The Magnifier button.* Clicking the Magnifier button turns your mouse cursor into a magnifying glass with a crosshair at the center of its lens. You can use the magnifier to zoom in on a portion of your graphic by dragging it over the portion you want to enlarge. When you let go of the mouse button, your graphic box assumes the dimensions of your selection, and the graphic is enlarged to fill the new graphic box.
- *The Zoom Scroll button.* The Zoom Scroll control is a neat gadget that places alongside your graphic a scroll bar that you can use to enlarge and reduce the graphic without changing the size of the graphic box. Slide the scroll button down the scrollbar to enlarge the graphic, and slide it up to reduce the graphic.

Creating and Working with Graphics in WordPerfect 9

- *The 1:1 button.* Like a global "undo" for Image Tools' zoom controls, you can click the 1:1 button to return your graphic to its original size at any time.

Using Image Tools' Color Controls

The middle section of the Image Tools toolbox contains four buttons you can use to edit various color elements in your graphic: BW Threshold, Contrast, Brightness, and Fill. All four buttons work the same way in that you click a button to open a palette containing a range of plates that will affect the use of color in your graphic. Here's a description of what each button and its respective palette does:

- *BW Threshold.* The BW Threshold button allows you to turn your color image into a black-and-white image. The BW Threshold palette contains numerous plates, ranging from dark to light. The darker plates will convert your image using a greater amount of black, and as the plates get lighter, the conversion uses more gray and white to convert your image. Figure 8.14 shows the conversion of the Pooch graphic into a black-and-white image using the BW Threshold palette.

FIGURE 8.14

The raised plate on the BW Threshold palette was selected to convert the colors in the Pooch graphic into black and white.

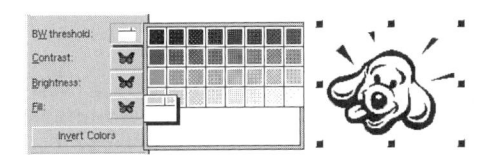

- *Contrast.* The Contrast button allows you to control color shades in your graphic. As shown in Figure 8.15, the Contrast palette provides a range of shades that modify the contrast of your graphic with a single click. Although the Contrast button doesn't allow separate control over the shade of each color, experimenting with different shades may help you achieve a desired result.

FIGURE 8.15

The selected shade from the Contrast palette emphasizes the reds in the Pooch graphic to turn Pooch into a bright red dog.

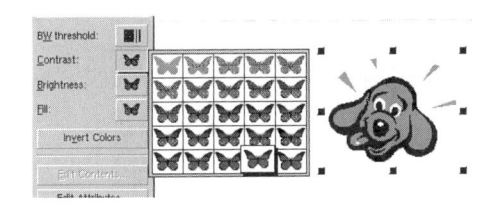

- *Brightness.* As shown in Figure 8.16, the Brightness palette lets you set the intensity of the colors used in your graphic. Lowering the intensity of the colors lightens your graphic to create the illusion of transparency.

FIGURE 8.16
Selecting a lighter plate from the Brightness palette gives Pooch a transparent look.

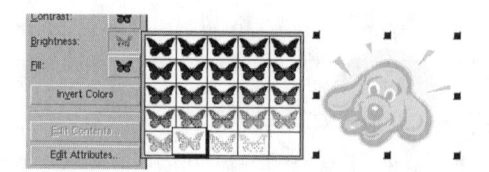

- *Fill.* The Fill palette provides three options to control the fill color in a graphic: Normal, Outline, and Opaque. Normal fill is the default amount of fill color used in the original graphic. Outline fill eliminates all fill color and leaves only an outline of your image. As shown in Figure 8.17, Opaque fill whites out all fill color in the image, leaving only an imprint of the image over any existing background fill.

FIGURE 8.17
Opaque fill whites out Pooch's normal color fill, leaving only an imprint on existing background fill.

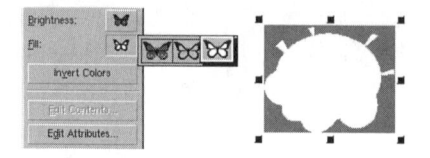

The middle section of the Image Tools toolbox includes a fifth button related to color control. Unlike the other color control buttons, Invert Colors doesn't open a palette of options but instead provides a one-click approach to inverting the color scheme of your image. Invert Colors displays the equivalent of a photographic negative of your graphic.

Editing the Attributes of a Graphic

Finally, the bottom section of Image Tools includes two buttons that allow you to edit the attributes of a graphic. The Edit Attributes button opens the Image Settings dialog box shown in Figure 8.18, which allows you to control many attributes of your graphic from a central location.

FIGURE 8.18
The Image Settings dialog box is command central for controlling many different attributes of your graphic.

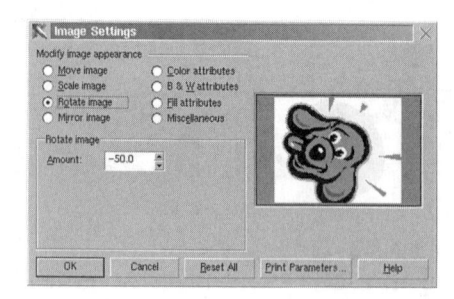

The last Image Tools button may be the most important one. The Reset Attributes button allows you to restore the original attributes of a graphic at any time. No matter how many edits you've made to a graphic, WordPerfect 9 remembers the original settings and will restore them when you click Reset Attributes. The Reset Attributes button also appears as the Reset All button at the bottom of the Image Settings dialog box shown in Figure 8.18.

> You may be wondering why I skipped the Edit Contents button on the Image Tools palette (and, for that matter, why the Edit Contents button is grayed out in Figure 8.10). The Edit Contents button is one of the few glitches Corel missed in porting its office suite to Linux. In the Windows version of WordPerfect 9, clicking the Edit Contents button opened a new WordPerfect 9 window containing the drawing toolbars available in Presentations 9 (sort of like the WordPerfect Draw feature that Corel decided to drop after version 8). Unfortunately, as of this writing, there's nothing you can do to activate the Edit Contents button, and this feature of WordPerfect 9 for Linux is, for now, disabled.

Grouping and Layering Graphics

The concepts of grouping and layering are crucial to working effectively with graphics in any application, including WordPerfect 9. *Grouping* refers to the ability to select several graphics at once, in effect "grouping" them together, in order to treat them as a single item for editing purposes. In order to group two or more graphics, hold down the Shift key as you select each one. With each selection, the selection handles expand to include each graphic added to the group. You can then move, resize, and otherwise edit the entire group the same way you'd edit a single graphic.

Layering refers to the placing of items, including graphics and text, on top of one another on the page. For example, if you insert a graphic in a WordPerfect document and then insert another graphic of the same size directly on top of it, you won't be able to see the first graphic because it rests on the layer behind the second graphic. The ability to control how graphics are layered on the page is a powerful design tool.

The next two figures show WordPerfect 9's layering controls in action. Figure 8.19 shows three versions of Pooch layered on top of one another. I've right-clicked the middle version of Pooch and navigated through the pop-up menu to the Order menu. The Order menu provides you with the option of moving the selected graphic all the way to the front, all the way to the back, forward one layer, or back one layer.

FIGURE 8.19
Three different versions of Pooch layered one on top of the other. Right-click a graphic to access the layer Order controls.

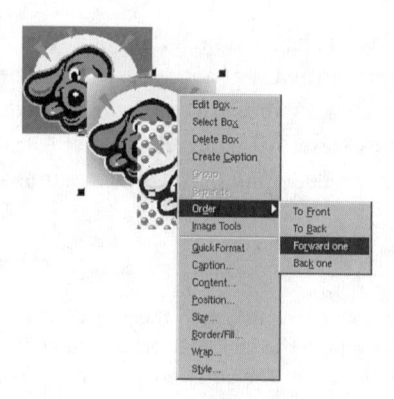

> The Graphics button that appears on the Property Bar when a graphic is selected includes the same layering options listed on the Order menu. The Graphics button includes two additional options that allow you to move your graphic either in front of or behind text.

Figure 8.20 shows the effect of moving the middle version of Pooch forward one layer.

FIGURE 8.20
The middle version of Pooch takes center stage.

Graphics Controls on the Property Bar

Throughout this hour, reference has been made to various controls that appear on the Property Bar when a graphic is selected. Although these controls relate to many of the editing tasks already covered, Figure 8.21 displays each button on the Selected Image Property Bar, and Table 8.1 describes what they do.

Creating and Working with Graphics in WordPerfect 9

FIGURE 8.21
WordPerfect 9's Selected Image Property Bar.

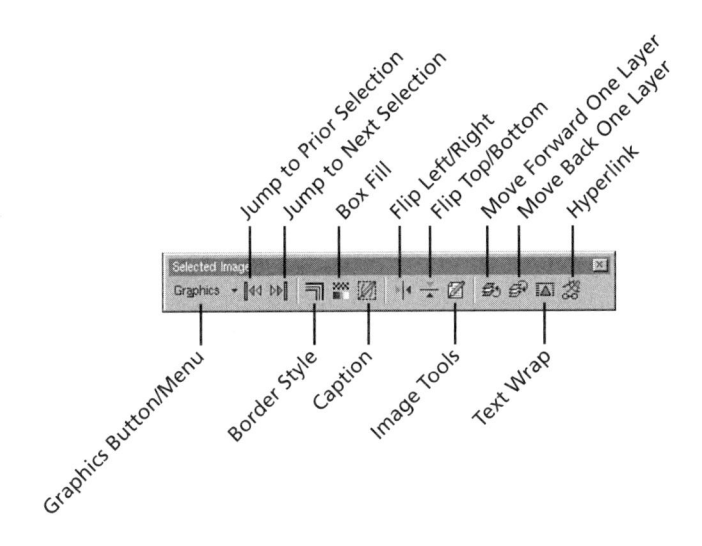

TABLE 8.1 The Selected Image Property Bar

Property Bar Button	Description
Graphics button/menu	Opens a drop-down menu from which you can access many graphic controls, including layering, flipping, sizing, and positioning controls.
Jump to Prior Selection	Jumps to the previously selected graphic when working with multiple graphics.
Jump to Next Selection	Jumps forward to a selected graphic after jumping back to a previously selected graphic.
Border Style	Allows you to insert a border around a selected graphic. Clicking the More button opens the Box Border/Fill dialog box for even greater control.
Box Fill	Allows you to insert color or pattern fills to your graphic. Clicking the More button opens the Box Border/Fill dialog box for even greater control.
Caption	Inserts a caption with the graphic box, just below the graphic.
Flip Left/Right	Flips the image left to right or right to left, as covered in the Image Tools section earlier in this hour.
Flip Top/Bottom	Flips the image top to bottom, as covered in the Image Tools section earlier in this hour.
Image Tools	Opens the Image Tools toolbox.

TABLE 8.1 continued

Property Bar Button	Description
Move Forward One Layer	Moves the selected graphic forward one layer.
Move Back One Layer	Moves the selected graphic back one layer.
Wrap Text	Allows you to control how text will wrap around your graphic.
Hyperlink	Allows you to create a hyperlink from your graphic.

Summary

Despite the integration of its earlier-version drawing tools into Presentations 9, WordPerfect 9 retains many powerful tools for inserting and editing graphics in your documents. In this hour you learned about two of WordPerfect 9's most useful graphics tools: the Scrapbook and the Image Tools toolbox. Although we barely scratched the surface of the many exciting things you can do with graphics in WordPerfect 9, this hour provided the foundation for what is sure to lead to hours of exciting experimentation on your own.

In the next hour, you'll move on to two of WordPerfect 9's most advanced features: macros and the Merge command.

Q&A

Q How do I use a graphic to create a watermark?

A A *watermark* is an image that exists in the background of a document. It is usually faded to better recede into the background in a subtle but visible way. To use a graphic to create a watermark that fills the entire page, right-click it and select Size. In the Box Size dialog box, set Width to Full and set Height to Maintain Proportions. To fade the image so it doesn't compete with other items on the page, open Image Tools and use the Brightness control to lighten the image. To make sure that the image stays put behind text, click the Text Wrap button on the Property Bar and select Behind Text.

Q Does the PerfectExpert provide any help with graphics?

A Yes. Select a graphic and click the PerfectExpert button on the toolbar. The PerfectExpert window contains buttons that provide one-click access to four dialog boxes used to edit your graphics: Box Position, Box Size, Wrap Text, and Box Border/Fill.

Workshop

The Workshop contains quiz questions and exercises to help reinforce what you've learned in this hour. If you get stuck, the answers can be found in Appendix B, "Answers to Quiz Questions."

Quiz

1. Which control cannot be accessed from Image Tools?

    a. Flip Left/Right

    b. Wrap Text

    c. Contrast

    d. Brightness

    e. Zoom

2. The drawing tools previously included in WordPerfect 8 can now be found in which application in WordPerfect Office 2000 for Linux?

    a. Quattro Pro 9

    b. Paradox 9

    c. Presentations 9

    d. WordPerfect 9

    e. CorelCENTRAL Memos

3. Which graphic control can't be accessed from the Selected Image Property Bar?

    a. Move to Back Layer

    b. Wrap Text

    c. Hyperlink

    d. Border

    e. None of the above

Exercises

1. Create a new category called Vacation Pix in the Photos tab of your Scrapbook.
2. Insert a graphic into a WordPerfect document and add a caption that reads, "My First Graphic."
3. Add a drop shadow to an existing graphic.

HOUR 9

Advanced WordPerfect 9 Techniques

If you've completed Hours 4 through 8, you already know more than enough to accomplish just about any task with WordPerfect 9 for Linux. From entering and formatting text and tables, to having fun with graphics, you're no longer a WordPerfect 9 novice. Good thing, too, because we're about to dive into some of the more advanced features of the program.

In this hour you will

- Use macros to complete frequent tasks in less time.
- Create a memo macro that you can customize for your own use.
- Explore the basics of merge documents.
- Use merge documents to create form letters and envelopes.

What Are Macros?

Macros are tiny programs you can use to automate common tasks, keyboard strokes, and commands. Macros can be simple, such as a macro that changes the font size and style of a selected block of text, or complicated, such as a macro that sets up an entire legal pleading. The time you spend learning how to work with macros will spare you countless hours of rote, manual data entry.

As noted, macros are programs that use a programming language called PerfectScript, which allows you to hand-code your WordPerfect macros. Don't go screaming for the door just yet—PerfectScript is a powerful and useful tool, but Corel recognizes that most users don't have the time, interest, or background to master the intricacies of hand-coding their own macros.

Enter WordPerfect's macro tool—a much simpler, graphical means of recording, playing, and editing your WordPerfect macros. In order to get you up and running quickly with WordPerfect macros, this book covers working with macros through the macro tool, without your having to learn a single line of code.

> Although this book's discussion of macros is limited to WordPerfect 9, you can also use the macro basics covered in this hour to create macros in Quattro Pro 9 and Presentations 9.

> If you're truly curious, you can experiment with PerfectScript by clicking Corel Application Starter, Applications, WordPerfect Office 2000, Utilities, PerfectScript 9. For a tutorial on how to use PerfectScript 9, click the question mark button on the PerfectScript 9 toolbar to launch the PerfectScript Help files in Netscape Navigator.
>
> For help with the PerfectScript 9 command language, from the PerfectScript 9 menu bar click Help, Macro Command Browser. The Macro Command Browser lists and describes several thousand PerfectScript commands, all broken down into one of the following four types: PerfectScript, WordPerfect, Quattro Pro, or Presentations.

Macros Provided by Corel

The easiest way to take advantage of the power of WordPerfect 9 macros is to make use of the 23 macros already provided by Corel. From saving an open document to a floppy disk, to closing all open documents, Corel's macros give you a good idea of the types of tasks macros can be used for. You can access the Corel macros from the WordPerfect 9 menu bar by clicking Tools, Macro, Play to open the Play Macro dialog box shown in Figure 9.1.

FIGURE 9.1
The WordPerfect 9 Play Macro dialog box.

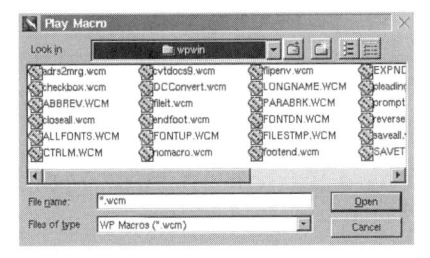

To play a WordPerfect macro, simply select a macro from the Play Macro dialog box and click Open. As a shortcut, you can just double-click the macro. WordPerfect takes it from there, putting the PerfectScript commands contained within the macro into action within your open document.

Give it a try. In the following exercise, we'll play a macro that saves an open document to your floppy drive.

To Do: Play a WordPerfect 9 Macro

1. Get yourself set by inserting a floppy disk into your floppy drive.
2. Open any existing WordPerfect document and select Tools, Macro, Play from the menu. This opens the Play Macro dialog box shown in Figure 9.1.
3. Use the horizontal scroll bar along the bottom of the Play Macro dialog box to find the macro named SAVETOA.WCM. Double-click it, or click it once and then click the Open button.
4. The macro automatically does its thing. WordPerfect tells you that it is saving your document and making a copy on your floppy drive.

That's all there is to it! You've just played your first WordPerfect 9 macro.

> Corel is constantly providing its WordPerfect Office users with free add-ons that can be downloaded from Corel's Web site. You should periodically check to see if there are any new macros you may find useful. To give it a try, in WordPerfect 9, select Tools, Macros Online.

Adding a Macro to the Toolbar

You may be asking, "What's the big deal?" After all, quite a few steps were taken to play the preceding macro, and it didn't seem much faster than manually saving to a floppy, as you learned to do in Hour 3, "Common Tasks in WordPerfect Office 2000 for Linux." But, what if you could do all the above steps with a single click?

Of course, you can, and you already know how to do it. Remember learning way back in Hour 2, "Introducing the WordPerfect Office 2000 for Linux Environment," how to customize the WordPerfect Office 2000 toolbars? You can follow the same basic steps to add a macro as a button on your toolbar.

To Do: Add a Macro as a Button on Your Toolbar

1. Right-click the toolbar and click Edit to open the Toolbar Editor. Select the Macros tab, as shown in Figure 9.2.
2. When you click the Add Macro button, the Select Macro dialog box opens, prompting you to select the macro you want to add as a toolbar button. Except for the title bar, the Select Macro dialog box is identical to the Play Macro dialog box shown in Figure 9.1. Find the SAVETOA.WCM macro, select it, and click Open (or simply double-click the macro).

FIGURE 9.2
You can create a toolbar button for a macro from the Macros tab on the Toolbar Editor.

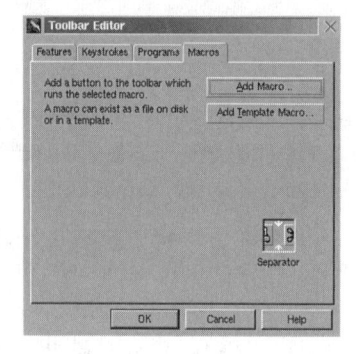

3. As shown in Figure 9.3, a new button bearing an icon that looks like an audiocassette appears at the end of your toolbar. You can click that button at any time to run your macro.

FIGURE 9.3
The new macro button appears at the end of your toolbar.

You now have one-click access to a macro that can save you several steps the next time you need to save a document to a floppy disk.

Advanced WordPerfect 9 Techniques

> There's another way to make a WordPerfect 9 macro easy to use: You can assign it a keyboard shortcut. From the menu bar, select Tools, Settings. In the Settings dialog box, click the Customize button and select the Keyboards tab. To add a macro keyboard shortcut to the WordPerfect 9 default keyboard settings, scroll down the Available Keyboards list, select WPWin 9 Keyboard, and click the Edit button to open the Keyboard Shortcuts dialog box shown in Figure 9.4. Select the Macros tab to display a list of shortcut keys. Scroll down the list to find an available shortcut (or a shortcut you no longer need) and select it. If the selected shortcut is already taken, click the Remove Assignment button to free it up for your macro. Once you have an available keyboard shortcut selected, click the Assign Macro to Key button to open the Select Macro dialog box. Find your macro and double-click it, and the keyboard shortcut of your choice is automatically assigned to your macro.
>
> By the way, if you ever want a refresher on WordPerfect 9's seemingly infinite number of keyboard shortcuts, you now know where to find it!

Figure 9.4
To avoid cluttering up your toolbars, you can easily launch a macro by assigning it a keyboard shortcut.

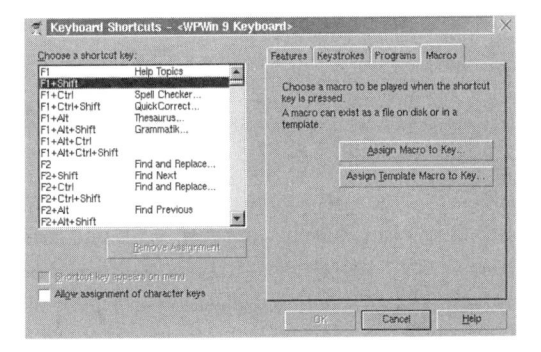

Recording a New Macro

As helpful as they are, you're not limited to the macros provided by Corel—you can create your own macro to perform almost any task in WordPerfect 9.

The best way to show you how to create a macro is to walk you through the process.

To Do: Create a Macro

▼ **To Do**

Follow these steps, and you'll be well on your way to becoming a WordPerfect 9 macro guru:

1. Identify the task you want your macro to perform. For this exercise, you'll create a macro to launch a memo template with a simple keystroke. The easiest approach is to first create the memo template and then program a macro to simply open up the

▼ template. Figure 9.5 provides an idea of what a memo template might look like. Information common to all memos, such as the company name, document heading, and memo author, can all be filled in for inclusion in the template. Name your document something clever, such as `memotemplate`, and save it to the directory of your choice.

FIGURE 9.5
This memo template will serve as the basis for a memo macro. The company name, author, and date are automatically inserted every time the macro is played.

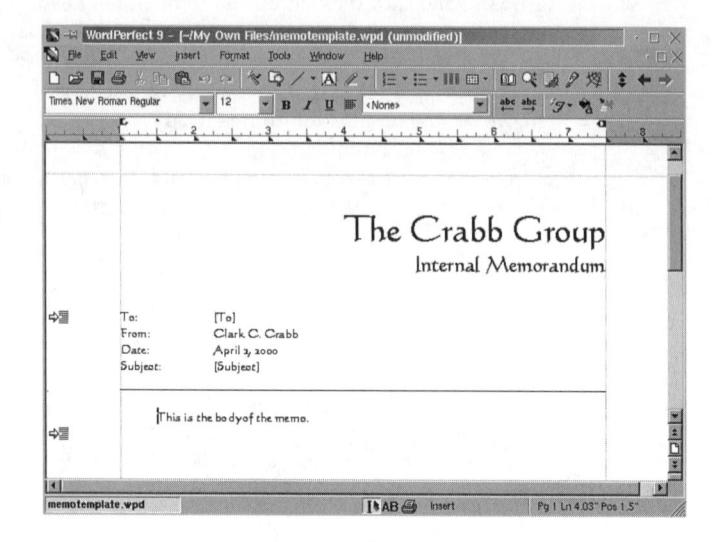

2. Before you start recording, you should do a dry run, in which you rehearse all the keystrokes you'd like to include in your macro. In this case, the memo template has already been created, and the macro's only job will be to open it so you can begin entering data in a new memo. Your dry run is easy—open the memo template you created and make sure everything looks as you planned. Close out of the document, and you're ready to start recording!

3. To start recording your macro, select Tools, Macro, Record to open the Record Macro dialog box. Unlike regular documents in WordPerfect 9, the first thing you need to do is give your macro a name and determine where to file it. By default, WordPerfect 9 files all macros to the `/My Home/Documents/macros/wp` directory. You can change this default by navigating through your file system in the Look In drop-down menu in the Record Macro dialog box shown in Figure 9.6. Note that if you navigate up one folder to the Macros directory, you'll also see the default directories for all Quattro Pro 9 and Presentations 9 macros.

  ▼ As for naming your new macro, select a name that reflects the task performed by the macro, such as `openmemo`.

Advanced WordPerfect 9 Techniques 175

FIGURE 9.6
The Record Macro dialog box prompts you to select a name and location for your new macro, and it automatically assigns all WordPerfect macros a .wcm extension.

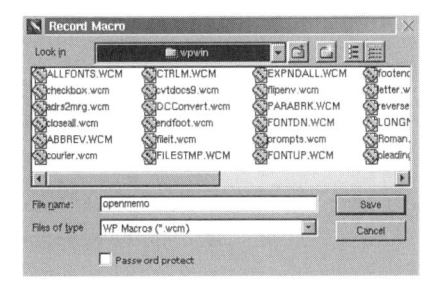

4. When you return to your document after naming and saving your macro, your macro is already being recorded. How do you know? As shown in Figure 9.7, there are two signs that macro recording is on: the Macro Editor Bar at the top of the document and the tiny audiocassette icon with a bright red dot in the bottom right of the KPanel. Because WordPerfect 9 is actively recording your macro, make sure that every keystroke is something you want to include.

FIGURE 9.7
The Macro Editor Bar and the red-lit audiocassette icon in the KPanel indicate that macro recording is turned on.

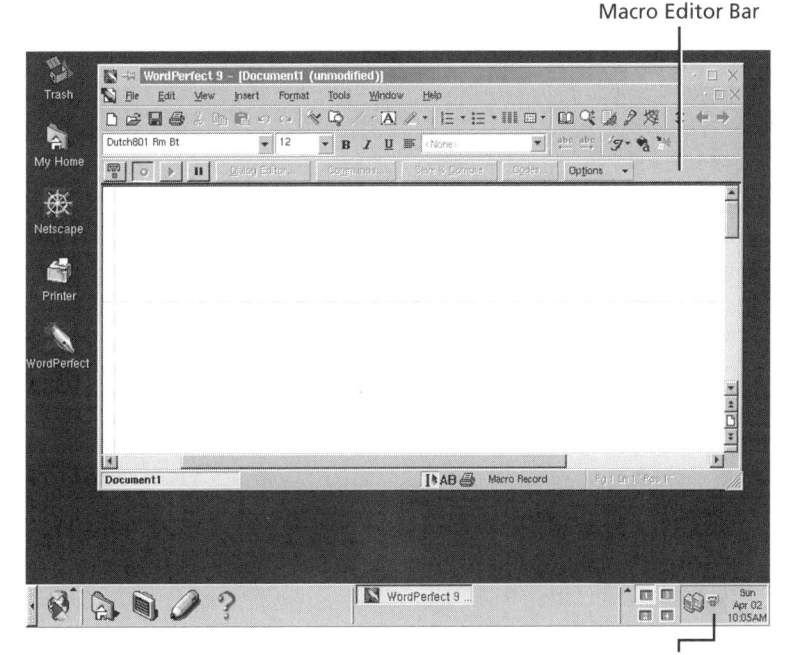

Macro Editor Bar

Record Macro icon

▼ 5. Here's where the real work comes in. Manually enter all the keystrokes you want to include within your macro. For your new memo macro, it's as easy as opening your `memotemplate` document.

  6. Stop recording your macro by clicking Tools, Macro, Record. Close out of your document—you don't need to save it because it's already been recorded and saved
▲   as your `openmemo` macro file.

That's it! You've just created a macro to launch your memo template. You can launch it any time by clicking Tools, Macro, Play and opening the `openmemo` file, or you can make it even easier by creating a toolbar button or keyboard shortcut.

Editing Macros

If you ever need to edit your macro, select Tools, Macro, Edit to open the Edit Macro dialog box. This is identical to the Open, Record, and Play Macro dialogs you've already seen, and it merely prompts you to select the macro you want to edit. As shown in Figure 9.8, double-clicking the appropriate macro icon opens the Macro Editor Bar, under which the actual programming code for your macro appears.

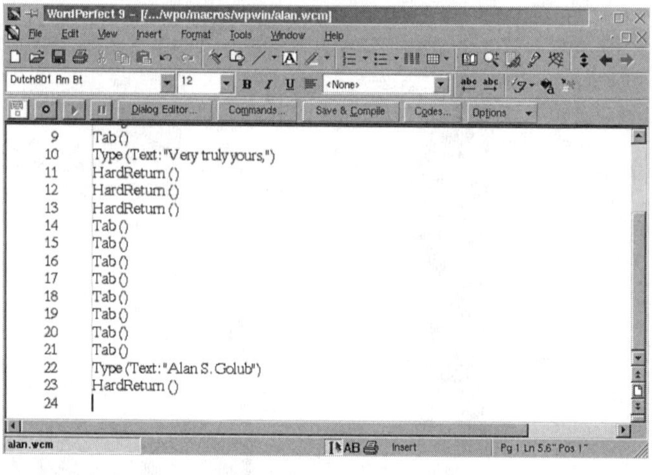

FIGURE 9.8
Advanced macro editing requires some knowledge of the WordPerfect macro programming code, but simple edits to text entry are fair game for all users.

Although this is pretty advanced stuff, don't be afraid to edit simple macros until they perform the way you want them to. For example, Figure 9.8 shows the code for a macro that inserts "Very truly yours, Alan S. Golub" at the end of a letter. If you wanted to change the macro for use by another user, say Roland J. Crabb, you would just manually change the name within the code, click the Save & Compile button on the Macro Editor Bar, and close out of the open window. (Note that if you want to change the name of the macro, select File, Save As and enter the new name before closing out of the open window.)

Try running the same macro after you've entered your changes, and make sure your macro is correctly performing all the changes you made.

What Is a Merge?

When you think of merge, think of mass production. Whenever you have to mass-produce form letters, labels, or envelopes, the merge command is your best friend.

Every merge process has three components: the data source, the form file, and the final document resulting from the merge. In the case of a form letter, the data source is a file listing the names and addresses of the people you want to send the letter to. The form file is the form letter itself, always the same but for the variable information to be inserted from the data source. Performing a merge literally means to merge the data source into the form file to create the third component—a running sheaf of form letters addressed to the individuals included in your data file.

The beauty of the merge operation is that you can use the data source again and again for regular mass mailings to the same individuals. You can also edit your data source to add, delete, or update your contact information. Whether you want to bring all your college buddies up to speed about what's going on in your life or need to send out a mass mailing of your company brochure to potential clients, the merge command is a truly remarkable timesaver you'll be happy to master.

The First Step in Creating Merge Documents: Building the Data Source

Start out by selecting Tools, Merge or pressing Shift+F9 to open the Merge dialog box shown in Figure 9.9. All three components of a merge process—creating data, creating a form, and performing the merge—appear as buttons in the Merge dialog box in the order in which they should be performed.

FIGURE 9.9

Every step in creating merge documents can be performed from the Merge dialog box.

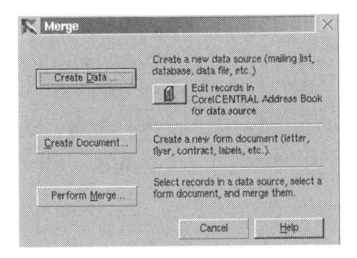

The first step in performing a merge is to build a data source. The data source can be a WordPerfect file, your CorelCENTRAL Address Book, or an existing database or spreadsheet. Most likely you'll be building the data source from scratch as a WordPerfect file or importing contact information from your Address Book. Follow along for the next few minutes and you'll know how to do both.

Take another look at the Merge dialog box in Figure 9.9. The top third of the dialog box is where you create your data source. To create your data source from scratch as a new file, click the Create Data button to open the Create Data File dialog box shown in Figure 9.10.

FIGURE 9.10

Create data fields from scratch in the Create Data File dialog box.

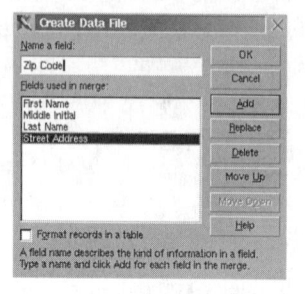

The Create Data File dialog box prompts you to set up field names to be used in the merge. In order to determine appropriate field names, it's important to understand that data files have two components: records and fields. In creating a form letter via a merge, a record will most likely be the full name and address of one of the recipients of your form letter. The information for each recipient would comprise a separate record within your data file.

Fields are a subset of each record. For example, as shown in Figure 9.10, a record used in creating a form letter might consist of the following fields: first name, middle initial, last name, street address, city and state, and ZIP Code. The Create Data File dialog box prompts you to name these fields at the outset.

To create a field name, type the name in the blank white box that appears beneath the Name a Field heading and press Enter or click the Add button. You can create as many field names as you want. To help keep track of them, beneath the Fields Used in Merge heading is a running list of all the field names you've created to use in each record. You can edit, delete, or change the order of any field in the list by selecting a field and clicking the Replace, Delete, Move Up, or Move Down button on the right side of the dialog box.

The last thing to note before leaving the Create Data File dialog box is the checkbox at the bottom, which gives you the option of formatting your records in a table. For now, don't select table formatting—you'll come back to it in a minute.

Click OK to exit the Create Data File dialog box and launch the Quick Data Entry form shown in Figure 9.11. The Quick Data Entry form makes it easy to create data records for your merge based on the fields you created in the Create Data File dialog box. Simply type in the contact information requested in the form. Press Enter or Tab to move from one field to the next; when you get to the last field (Zip Code), pressing Enter or clicking the Add button inputs your record and opens a blank Quick Data Entry form for you to enter the next record.

FIGURE 9.11
Enter records into your data file with the Quick Data Entry form.

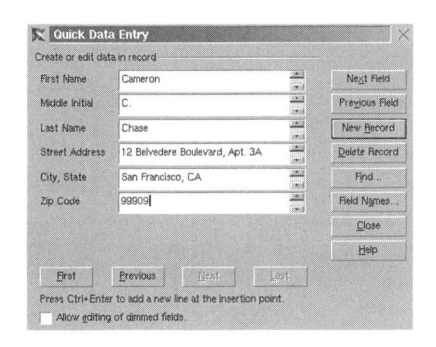

> While entering records in the Quick Data Entry form, you may discover that you need to modify the field names you entered in the Create Data File dialog box. No problem! Click the Field Names button to access the Edit Field Names dialog box, which looks and works almost exactly like the Create Data File dialog box shown in Figure 9.10.

When you are done entering records, click the Close button. When asked whether you want to save your changes to disk, select Yes and name and save your data file to the directory of your choice.

Once you save your data file, you'll see that while you were entering records using Quick Data Entry, WordPerfect was building your data file behind the scenes. Figure 9.12 shows the actual data file created as you input data. WordPerfect assigns a .dat extension to data files and inserts codes that tell the program how to handle the data when a merge is performed. At the top of the data file, the FIELDNAMES code appears before a running list of the field names used in each record. Each record includes ENDFIELD and ENDRECORD codes to signify, respectively, the end of one field or record and the beginning of another. WordPerfect also makes each record easily discernible by separating them with hard page breaks.

FIGURE 9.12

The underlying data file created when you input data in the Quick Data Entry form.

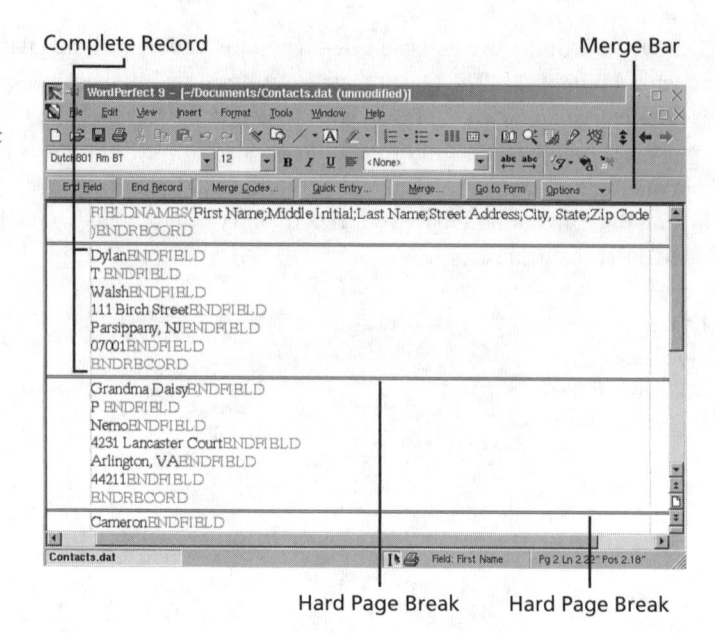

Instead of using the Quick Data Entry form, you can manually enter data directly in your data file the same way you would enter text in any WordPerfect document. The Merge Bar shown in Figure 9.12 provides all the help you need:

- The End Field and End Record buttons enter the most common merge codes you'll need as you input your data. Simply enter the data for a field and click the End Field button to enter the ENDFIELD code directly into your data file. Similarly, when you complete a record, clicking End Record inputs the ENDRECORD code.

- The Merge Codes button gives you access to other merge codes that go far beyond your basic ENDFIELD and ENDRECORD codes. These advanced merge codes are tricky and not for the faint of heart. Fortunately, clicking Merge Codes and then the Help button launches WordPerfect's terrific online help, where you can access a list of all merge codes and how they work.

- The Quick Entry button launches the Quick Data Entry form, the easiest way to add records. Why anyone would do it manually is beyond me.

- The Merge button takes you right into performing a merge, which you'll be doing before this hour is up.

- The Go to Form button takes you to the form file linked with your data file or lets you select or create a form file. You'll learn more about this when you get to the form file section in just a few minutes.
- The Options button is your one-click access to a few different tasks, including the option to sort or print your records and to hide the merge bar or the merge codes in your data file.

Congratulations! You've just created your first data file. Before we move on to the next step in performing a merge, you need to know about two other options you have when creating a data source:

- You can build a data file from scratch in table form.
- You can designate a CorelCENTRAL Address Book as a data source.

Remember the checkbox at the bottom of the Create Data File dialog box that gave you the option of formatting your data file as a table? If you had checked this option, you would have gone through the same exact steps to enter your data using Quick Data Entry, but the resulting data file would be stored in a table, as shown in Figure 9.13.

FIGURE 9.13

A data file in table form is easier to read and edit than a data file in text form.

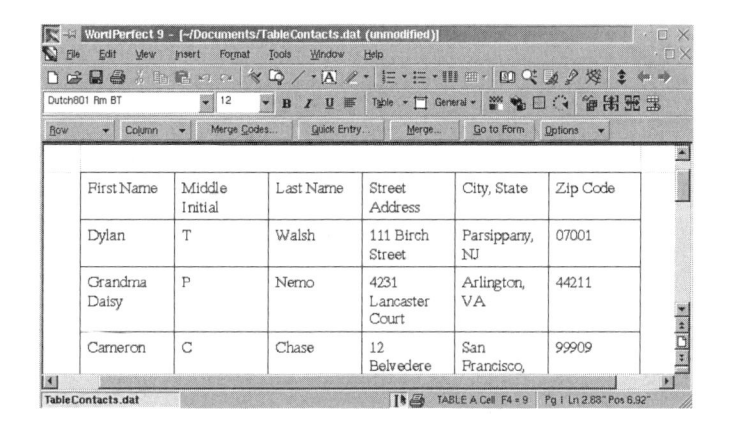

Comparing the text data file in Figure 9.12 with the table data file in Figure 9.13, the table data file is much easier to read. Instead of the merge codes used in text data files, table data files use neat columns and rows to separate fields and records. Table data files have the added advantage of working just like regular tables, making it much easier to modify your data. If you've already mastered Hour 7, "Working with Tables and Columns," you'll no doubt prefer to set up all your data files in table form.

Finally, you can use contact information stored in a CorelCENTRAL Address Book as a data source for a merge document.

To Do: Create a Merge Data File from the CorelCENTRAL Address Book

1. As shown back in Figure 9.9, the Merge dialog box contains a button labeled Edit Records in CorelCENTRAL Address Book for Data Source. Click that button to open your Address Book, from where you can add, delete, or edit addresses to include in your data file.
2. When you are done editing your addresses, select those you want to include in your data file, as shown in Figure 9.14.
3. Click the Insert button at the bottom of the CorelCENTRAL window.

FIGURE 9.14
Inserting CorelCENTRAL addresses into a data file.

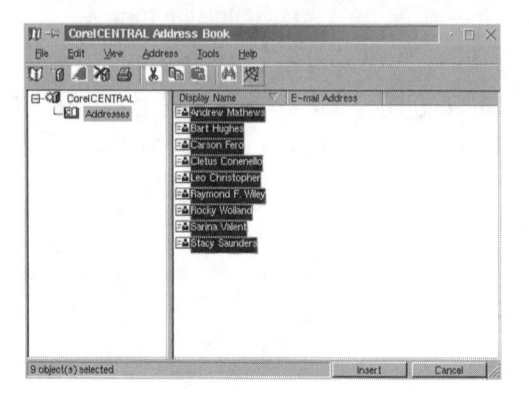

4. This opens the Format Address window shown in Figure 9.15. Select any of the default address formats on the left side of the window or click Custom to create your own format.
5. When you are done, click OK. This takes you back to the Merge dialog box.

FIGURE 9.15
Select a format for your addresses or build your own with the Custom button.

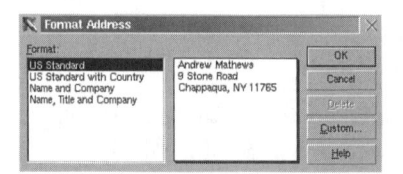

You are now ready to go on to step 2, creating the form file.

The Second Step: Creating the Form File

The form file is the basic template used in creating a merge document. You create a form file just like any other WordPerfect document, except that certain information, such as names and addresses, are replaced by field codes that will be filled in from the data file.

Now that you've already created your data file, you have a few ways to create a form file:

- Select Tools, Merge from the menu bar to open the Merge dialog box shown back in Figure 9.9. The Create Document button gets you on your way to creating a form file.
- Open an existing data file. Click the Go To Form button on the Merge Bar to open the Associate dialog box shown in Figure 9.16. If you don't already have a form file associated with the data file, the Associate dialog box tells you so and gives you the option of creating one by clicking the Create button.

FIGURE 9.16
Click the Create button in the Associate dialog box to create a form file to link to an open data file.

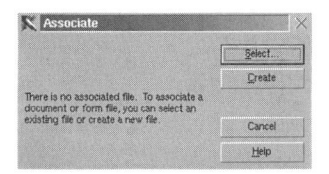

- If you've designated a CorelCENTRAL Address Book as a data source, once you insert selected addresses, as shown in Figure 9.14, you're taken back to the Merge dialog box and the Create Document button.

Give it a try. From the Merge dialog box, click Create Document. When asked whether to use the active file or to open a new document window, select the latter option and click OK to open the Associate Form and Data dialog box shown in Figure 9.17. Unless you really intend to create a form file in an open document, opening a new document is the way to go.

FIGURE 9.17
Associate your new file form with a data file created from scratch or with a CorelCENTRAL Address Book.

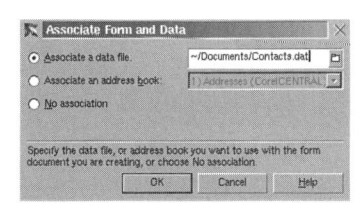

Here's where some of the work you put into building the data file pays off. As you can see in Figure 9.17, the next step is to link, or *associate*, your new file form with a data file. The Associate Form and Data dialog box gives you the option of associating your file form with an existing data file, an existing CorelCENTRAL Address Book, or no data file.

Select the Associate a Data File option and use the little folder icon to navigate to an existing data file. When you click OK, you are taken to a new WordPerfect document window and may begin creating your file form. Note that the Merge Bar is hanging out just under the Property Bar—as you'll soon see, it's there for a reason.

Using Figure 9.18 as your guide, create a heading for a simple form letter. For now, type in only the date and return address and then navigate to the left margin where you'd normally place the name and address of the recipient.

FIGURE 9.18

Start to prepare your form letter by typing in the date and your name and address.

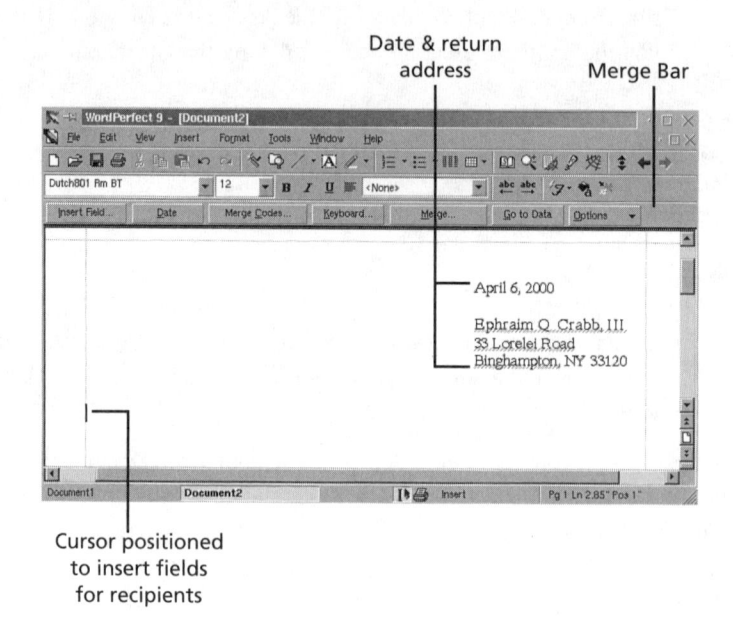

As promised, it's time to put the Merge Bar to good use. With your cursor in position, as shown in Figure 9.18, click the Insert Field button. The Insert Field Name or Number dialog box (see Figure 9.19) opens to show the fields you created in the associated data file.

The idea is to use your fields in place of each element of the name and address that you would normally type in for each recipient. For example, the first element would be your recipient's first name; instead of typing in an actual name, you'll insert the First Name field where the data will be inserted in the body of your form letter. To insert the First Name field, you can either double-click it or select it and click the Insert button in the Insert Field Name dialog box.

FIGURE 9.19
Use the Insert Field Name or Number dialog box to insert the fields from your data file into your form file.

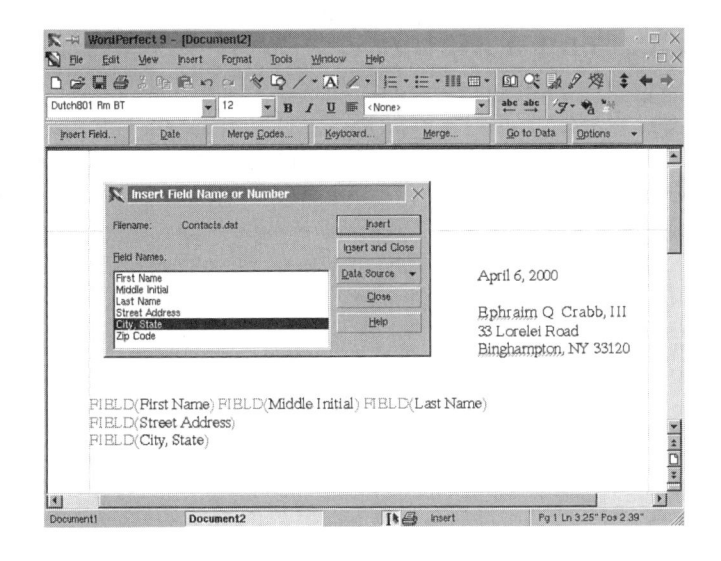

Next, hit the space bar and insert the Middle Initial field, followed by the space bar, Last Name field, and Return. This drops you down to the next line, where you'll insert the Street Address field. Keep on going until you've got all your fields entered into the body of your form letter.

Figure 9.20 shows an enlarged view of how the field codes look inserted in your document. Once they've all been entered, close the Insert Field Name or Number dialog box and type the body of your letter. When you're done, save your document and pat yourself on the back—you've just created a form file, and you're ready to perform your first merge!

FIGURE 9.20
Here's how your fields look when inserted in your form file. Show Paragraph is turned on so you can see where to press the space bar and Enter key as you insert your fields.

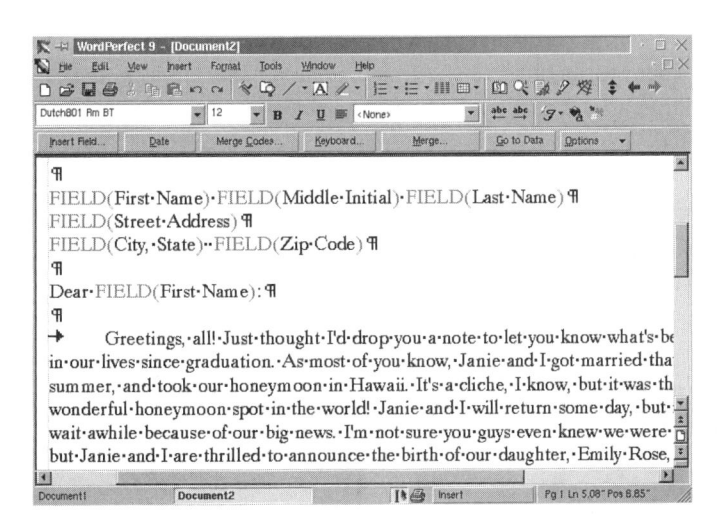

Performing a Merge

At long last, it's time to merge your data file with your form file. From the menu bar, select Tools, Merge and click the Perform Merge button in the Merge dialog box. The Perform Merge dialog box (shown in Figure 9.21) requires you to identify the form file, the data source, and the method of output for your merge document. If you have several form or data files, here's the place where you can mix and match them to create the desired merge document. Simply click the little folder icons to navigate to the form and data files for the merge you want to perform.

The Output button gives you several options as to how to output the final merge document. You can create the merge document as the current document, a new document, a file saved to disk, a print job, or an email. Most of the time it makes sense to output your merge document to a new document, which you can always save, print, email, and so on when you're sure it's working as intended.

FIGURE 9.21
The Perform Merge dialog box with the form file, data source, and output configured and ready to merge.

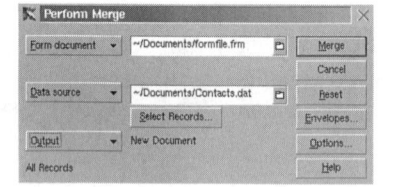

Before you click the Merge button and let 'er rip, take a moment to click the Options button, which gives you control over important elements such as the number of copies of each record to include in the merge and whether to separate each merged document with page breaks.

Once you've configured each element in the Perform Merge dialog box and reviewed and set your options, click the Merge button and sit back to watch WordPerfect do its thing. The end result will be a long document containing multiple copies of your form letter, each addressed to a different recipient, as specified in your data file.

Performing an Envelope Merge

Wouldn't it be neat to be able to use merge to print out all the envelopes you'll need to mail the form letters you've just created? Naturally, WordPerfect 9 for Linux has you covered.

To Do: Perform an Envelope Merge

1. To perform an envelope merge, open a new WordPerfect document. Select Tools, Merge from the menu bar and click the Perform Merge button in the Merge dialog box.
2. Set the Form Document setting to Current Document (it's new, so you won't be writing over anything). For Data Source, select either a name and address data file you've already created or select Address Book.
3. Click the Envelopes button. As shown in Figure 9.22, a new WordPerfect document shaped like an envelope opens, prompting you to enter your return address and the fields for your recipients. Enter your return address in the upper-left corner.
4. Navigate to the center of the envelope where the recipient information goes. Click the Insert Field button on the Merge Bar to open the Insert Field Name dialog box. Just as you did when creating your form file, you can now insert the fields you need to enter addresses on each envelope. When you're done, your envelope form should look similar to the one shown in Figure 9.22.

FIGURE 9.22
In an envelope merge, you create an envelope form with which to merge a data file containing addresses.

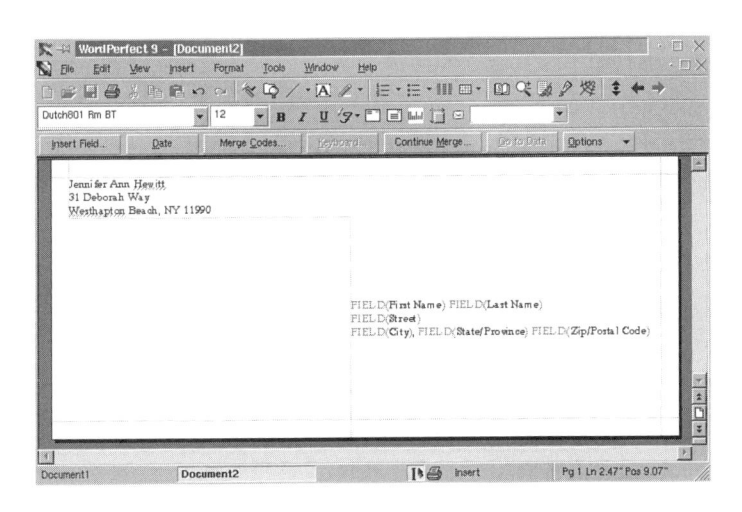

5. Next, click the Continue Merge button on the Merge Bar to take you back to the Merge dialog box. Click the Merge button and, once again, let WordPerfect do its thing. When it's done, as shown in Figure 9.23, you'll have a string of addressed envelopes created as a single WordPerfect document ready for printing.

FIGURE 9.23
The results of your envelope merge, ready for printing.

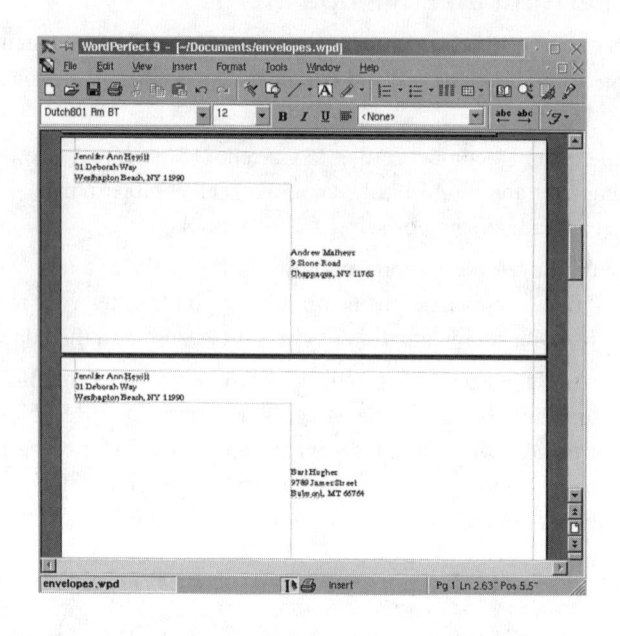

> If you have sheets of adhesive labels that work with your printer, you can also use a merge operation to generate your labels for you. To perform a label merge, click Tools, Merge to open the Merge dialog box and then click the Create Document button. Associate a data file or the Address Book as the data source for your labels and click OK. In the data file, select Format, Labels to open the Labels dialog box. Explore the label setting options until you find the one that matches your labels; click it with your mouse and click Select. Just as with envelopes, this opens a form file that takes the shape of your label. Insert your field codes in the label form, click the Merge button on the Macro Bar, and your label merge will be underway!

That's all there is to it. Although merge documents require a heavy initial investment of time and effort to create the necessary data files, once you have them, they can shave hours off future projects involving form files you create to send to all your contacts.

Summary

In this hour you learned about macros—one of the most advanced features of WordPerfect 9 for Linux. Based on the PerfectScript programming language, macros are tiny programs that automate tasks you perform in WordPerfect 9. You learned how to use the macros provided by Corel and how to create and edit your own macros. You also learned how to make macros even easier to use by placing a macro button on your toolbar or assigning a keyboard shortcut to launch a macro.

This hour also covered merge documents—another sophisticated tool that can save you time when creating form letters or envelopes for a long list of recipients. You learned about the three different components of a merge document and how to create each one of them using data you build from scratch or import from your CorelCENTRAL Address Book. You also learned how to perform an envelope merge to print out envelopes to all your contacts.

This hour brings our study of WordPerfect to a close until we revisit it in Hour 23, "WordPerfect 9 and the Web." The next hour introduces you to another powerful application in WordPerfect Office 2000 for Linux, as you plunge into the wonderful world of spreadsheets with Quattro Pro 9.

Q&A

Q: Can I assign a keyboard shortcut to a macro?

A: Most certainly. Select Tools, Settings from the menu bar and click Customize to open the Customize Settings dialog box. Navigate to the Keyboards tab, select the WPWin 9 keyboard, and click Edit to open the Keyboard Shortcuts dialog box. Choose a shortcut key from the list on the left side of the dialog box. This shortcut key will be the one assigned to the macro, so select a shortcut that isn't already assigned. With your shortcut key highlighted, navigate to the Macros tab on the right side of the dialog box and click Assign Macro to Key. Double-click the macro you want to assign, then click OK. Close out of the Customize Settings boxes to return to your document and give your new keyboard shortcut a try.

Q: Is there a resource that explains all the merge codes and how they work?

A: Of course. From the Merge Bar, click Merge Codes to open the Insert Merge Codes dialog box, which presents a list of merge codes you can double-click to add to your data file. The merge codes have programming-like names such as "IF," "ELSE," and "STEPOFF," which tell you nothing about each code's function. You can obtain more information by clicking the Help button in the Insert Merge Codes dialog box. Navigate through WordPerfect 9's online help in Netscape Navigator to find the help section called, "Overview: Merge programming commands," which is a list of all of merge codes. Click on any code and a pop-up window opens, defining the code and explaining how it works.

Workshop

The Workshop contains quiz questions and exercises to help reinforce what you've learned in this hour. If you get stuck, the answers can be found in Appendix B, "Answers to Quiz Questions."

Quiz

1. What is the name of the programming language used to build WordPerfect 9 macros?
2. Which applications in WordPerfect Office 2000 for Linux are capable of running macros?
3. What are the three components of a merge document?
4. What are the two most common merge codes in a text data file?

Exercises

1. Create a macro to open a personalized form letter.
2. Create a keyboard shortcut for your new letterhead macro.
3. Create a new data file with the following fields: Name, Street Address, City/State, and Zip Code. Set up your data file in table form and input the names and addresses of your three best friends or closest coworkers. Save your data file and use it as the basis for an envelope merge that includes only the first two contacts in your data file. Print out the envelopes.

PART III
Creating Spreadsheets with Quattro Pro 9

Hour

10 Quattro Pro 9 Basics

11 Creating Your First Spreadsheet

12 Updating and Printing Your Spreadsheet

13 Advanced Spreadsheet Design

HOUR 10

Quattro Pro 9 Basics

You have seen how you can use WordPerfect tables to compute totals and formulas and organize almost any kind of information. But for serious number crunching and data reporting, you'll want to take advantage of the power and ease of spreadsheets in Quattro Pro 9.

You can use Quattro Pro 9 spreadsheets to balance your checkbook, create a budget, produce financial statements, and amortize a mortgage or loan. You can analyze your data in countless ways and even highlight certain results, such as when a budget or sales quota is met. You can also effectively present your data in charts, graphs, and even maps, as well as package your results as a single project that you can print or publish to the Web.

Best of all, Quattro Pro is so easy to use, even novices can start ripping through numbers almost immediately! Don't believe it? Then read on.

In this hour, you will

- Understand the basic components of all Quattro Pro spreadsheets, including notebooks, worksheets, cells, values, labels, formulas, and objects.
- Learn how to select and enter data and formulas into the cells of a spreadsheet.
- Navigate through a Quattro Pro spreadsheet using the mouse, arrow keys, keyboard shortcuts, and browsing tools that are unique to Quattro Pro.

What Is a Spreadsheet?

The term *spreadsheet* brings to mind a thick sheaf of ledger paper filled with row upon row and column upon column of handwritten (in pencil, of course) numbers and tabulations. It also induces a nap—the longer, the better.

Electronic spreadsheet applications, however, are much more exciting. Spreadsheet programs were among the very first applications to run successfully on personal computers and for that reason played an important role in launching the PC revolution. Quattro Pro has always been one of the most popular spreadsheet applications, and version 9 for Linux is one of the most powerful and flexible spreadsheet programs on the planet.

When we talk about spreadsheets in this book, we're talking about a task or process created on a Quattro Pro 9 "worksheet" to tabulate, organize, and present data with a specific goal in mind. Far from simple number crunching (although, thank goodness, Quattro Pro can do all your mathematical heavy lifting), Quattro Pro 9 can use your data to generate professional forms, reports, and charts that will dazzle them back at the office.

Before taking a look at the actual program, you have a few new concepts to learn about every Quattro Pro 9 spreadsheet.

The Notebook Concept

A *notebook* is the basic element of a Quattro Pro file, consisting of one or more related spreadsheets, also called *worksheets*, and one special sheet known as the *Objects sheet*. Everything you use or need for a given project can be contained in a notebook.

Each notebook file is given a .QPW file extension identifying the Quattro Pro version 9 format. A new notebook will have the name Notebk#.QPW (where # stands for the incremental order in which you opened new notebooks during a single Quattro Pro session), unless you rename it.

> In earlier versions of Quattro Pro, notebooks were called *workbooks* and were assigned the file extensions .WB1, .WB2, or .WB3, depending on the version. Quattro Pro 9 can open these earlier formats as well as workbooks saved in Excel and other spreadsheet formats.
>
> In fact, if you previously used Microsoft Excel 97, Lotus 1-2-3, or an earlier version of Quattro Pro to create spreadsheets, or need to work on spreadsheets with other folks who still use these applications, don't worry. Not only can you open and save files in each of these formats, you can change Quattro Pro's settings to make it look and work more like Excel or Lotus 1-2-3. These customization features are covered in more detail later in this hour.

Spreadsheets Within a Notebook

Notebooks are comprised of related spreadsheets that organize your data in columns and rows that collectively form "cells" of information. From inputting data and setting formulas, to organizing and formatting that data for maximum impact, worksheets are where the real work of every Quattro Pro spreadsheet actually gets done.

> ### Spreadsheets Versus Worksheets
>
> Is there any difference between a spreadsheet and a worksheet? Technically, *worksheet* refers to the blank sheets that make up a notebook, whereas *spreadsheet* refers to data and formulas applied to one or more worksheets. If you were still creating spreadsheets by hand, a pad of graph paper would be a notebook, each sheet of paper would be a worksheet, and any work product entered on a worksheet would be a spreadsheet.
>
> I find this unnecessarily confusing. To keep it simple, this book eliminates *worksheets* from the Quattro Pro 9 vocabulary. Instead, the hours dedicated to Quattro Pro 9 help you plan, design, and create *spreadsheets* on blank *sheets* within a *notebook*.

An example may help you visualize spreadsheets in action. If you needed to understand your company's gross sales volume and further track the sales record of each of your salespeople, here's one approach you could take using spreadsheets in a Quattro Pro 9 notebook:

- For each salesperson in your company, create a separate spreadsheet that breaks down his or her sales by month and calculates annual gross sales.
- Take each salesperson's annual gross and place it on another spreadsheet in the same notebook that calculates and summarizes annual gross sales for the whole company.

- For maximum impact, depict the results in a full-color pie or bar chart, which you can store on the Objects sheet at the end of your notebook. Objects are briefly discussed in the next section, "Working with Spreadsheet Data," and are covered in more detail in Hour 13, "Advanced Spreadsheet Design."

All these steps represent separate elements of a single notebook comprised of spreadsheets and objects that organize, manage, and analyze your data.

Working with Spreadsheet Data

You can incorporate many types of data into your spreadsheets, including simple data such as text, numbers, formulas, and more complex data, such as charts and slideshows. The former can be broken down into three general categories of data that can be placed directly into your spreadsheets: values, labels, and formulas. The latter is typically categorized under the broad heading of objects that are collected in a special Objects sheet for use in your notebook.

Straightforward data that you plug into your spreadsheets takes the following three forms:

- *Values*. A value is simply a number that's plugged into your spreadsheet. It can be a plain vanilla number, a date, part of a formula, or the result of a formula. The difference between values and labels is that values are always part of a Quattro Pro calculation, and labels are not.

- *Labels*. Labels can consist of numbers, text, or certain symbols. As the name suggests, they are used to label and organize the data in your spreadsheet. Labels can include names, addresses, dates, phone numbers, and any other alphanumeric means of describing or organizing your data. Because they are not incorporated within any calculation performed by Quattro Pro, labels remain constant within a given spreadsheet.

- *Formulas*. Formulas are equations that are the real heart of a Quattro Pro spreadsheet. When you enter a formula, you're identifying values within your spreadsheet and telling Quattro Pro how to handle, crunch, or analyze those values to suit your needs.

> Technically, formulas are values because they obey the same syntax rules as all other values. However, formulas are unique because, unlike all other values, formulas actually *do* something. Conceptually, and for purposes of this book, it's easier to just think of formulas as an entirely separate category.

A couple of syntax rules should be kept in mind when entering data into a spreadsheet. There are two sets of rules—one for labels and one for values and formulas:

- *Label syntax*. Labels can begin with any letter or symbol *except* the following:

=	(
+	$
-	#
.	@

  These symbols can be used anywhere else in a label except as the first character. If you absolutely must begin a label with one of these characters, you'll have to precede the character with an apostrophe ('), a quotation mark ("), or a caret (^) in order to prevent Quattro Pro from reading your label as an error. These special characters will also left align, right align, and center align the label, respectively.

- *Value syntax*. If the value entered is a number, it can be preceded by the minus sign (-) to denote a negative number or a plus sign (+) for a positive number. Decimal points and commas can be used, as can currency symbols and the equal sign (=). Note that you do not need to enter currency symbols, commas, decimals, or spaces for each value you want to enter. You can have Quattro Pro apply them depending on the number format you choose. Numbers align right unless you format them differently.

> Two common typographical errors in spreadsheets are the use of a lowercase letter *l* in place of the number one and an upper- or lowercase letter *o* for the value zero. Be careful with these kinds of typos when entering values in Quattro Pro. If you mistakenly enter a letter in place of a number when inputting a value, Quattro Pro will read the entry as text and interpret it, by default, as a label.

> The Objects sheet is always the last sheet in a notebook and is used to hold special objects, such as animations, charts, and slideshows, that you've incorporated into your notebook. You can insert links to these objects into a particular spreadsheet or display them directly on the spreadsheet.

Introducing the Quattro Pro 9 Workspace

In Hour 2, "Introducing the WordPerfect Office 2000 for Linux Environment," you learned several ways to launch Corel WordPerfect Office 2000 for Linux applications. Now is the time to call upon that knowledge to fire up Quattro Pro 9.

> Sure, you can launch Quattro Pro 9 by clicking Corel Application Starter, Applications, WordPerfect Office 2000 and selecting the icon for Quattro Pro 9. But why not be adventurous? Try launching Quattro Pro 9 by entering the command **quattropro** from the Run command dialog box or from a Console window. If you think you'll make frequent use of Quattro Pro 9, follow the instructions in Hour 2 to create a desktop shortcut.

As you can see in Figure 10.1, the Quattro Pro 9 interface is similar to other WordPerfect Office applications, with a few elements unique to Quattro Pro.

The most significant difference in the Quattro Pro display is the graph- or table-like notebook window that appears as soon the application is launched. Let's explore the notebook window further, as shown in Figure 10.2.

Each notebook contains up to 18,278 separate sheets that are labeled by the tabs at the bottom left of the window, ranging from A all the way through ZZZ. As previously noted, the last sheet is the Objects sheet, in which you can place icons for charts, maps, and slideshows to include in your notebook.

> You can easily change the number of sheets, rows, and columns assigned to each notebook by selecting Tools, Settings from the menu bar and accessing the Compatibility tab shown in Figure 10.3. Here's where you can also change the menus and interface of your spreadsheets to look and work like Microsoft Excel 97, Lotus 1-2-3, or prior versions of Quattro Pro.

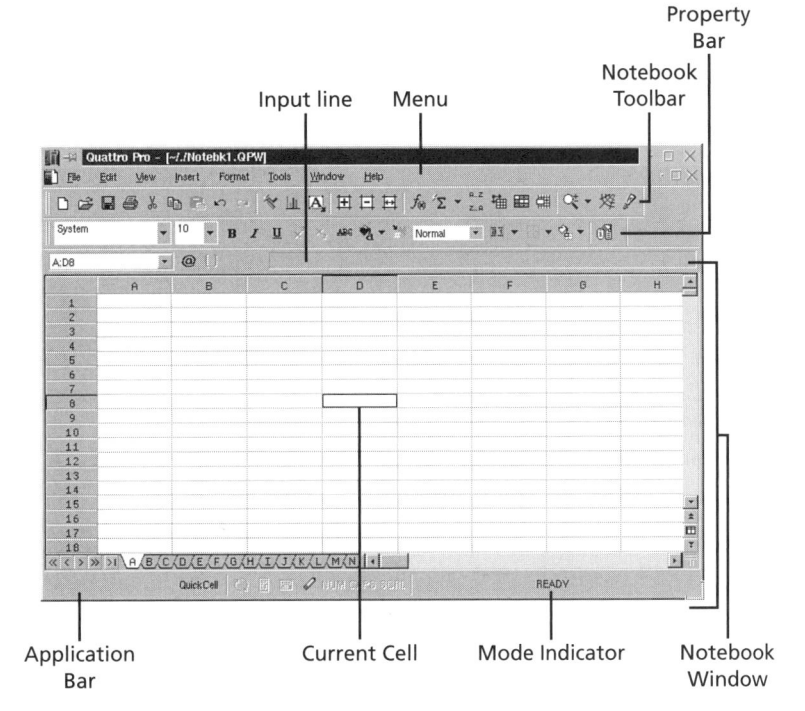

Quattro Pro 9 Basics

FIGURE 10.1
The Quattro Pro 9 for Linux workspace.

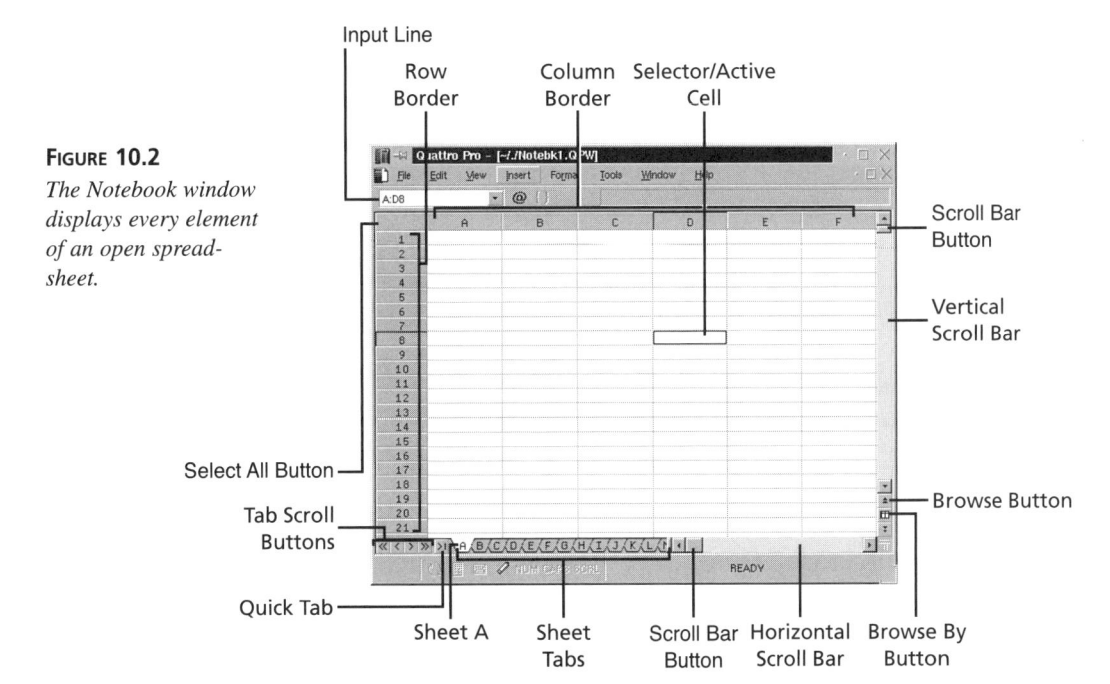

Labels: Input line, Menu, Notebook Toolbar, Property Bar, Application Bar, Current Cell, Mode Indicator, Notebook Window

FIGURE 10.2
The Notebook window displays every element of an open spreadsheet.

Labels: Input Line, Row Border, Column Border, Selector/Active Cell, Scroll Bar Button, Vertical Scroll Bar, Browse Button, Browse By Button, Horizontal Scroll Bar, Scroll Bar Button, Sheet Tabs, Sheet A, Quick Tab, Tab Scroll Buttons, Select All Button

FIGURE 10.3
You can customize your notebook's size and interface from the Compatibility tab.

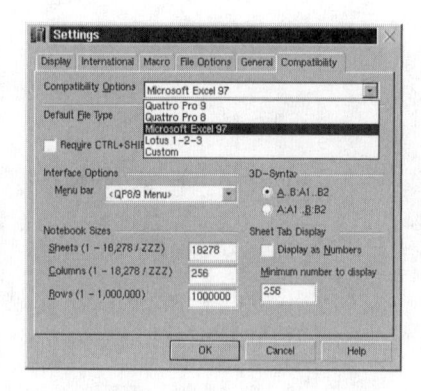

Columns, Rows, and Cell Addresses

Each spreadsheet contains up to 18,278 vertical columns labeled A through ZZZ, and up to 1,000,000 horizontal rows labeled numerically beginning with the number 1, giving you plenty of room to work and probably more than you'll ever need!

At the intersection of each column and row is a cell. Cells are where the action on a spreadsheet takes place—your data, in the form of values, labels, and formulas, are entered into the cells that make up your spreadsheet.

Much of the power and logic of Quattro Pro is based on *cell addressing*. Just like a point on a graph or the intersection of two streets, each cell has a unique address defined by the letter of the column and the number of the row that intersect to form the cell, preceded by a reference to the name of the sheet on which the cell appears. Therefore, in Figure 10.2, the active cell has a cell address of A:D8 because it's located on sheet A, at the point where column D and row 8 meet.

> Cells can be deceiving. A cell may appear to display a simple number when, in reality, that number is the *result* of a formula or function placed within the cell. In such a case, it's the formula, not the resulting value displayed, that constitutes the true contents of the cell. Unlike a simple number value, the displayed numerical result may change.

The Cell Selector

The cell selector tells you which cell is currently active, meaning ready for input, formatting, editing, and so on. As shown in Figure 10.4, the active cell, A:D8, has a bold rectangular border around it. This border is the cell selector, telling you that cell A:D8 is active and ready for action.

Quattro Pro 9 Basics

FIGURE 10.4
The cell selector tells you that the cell located at cell address A:D8 is active.

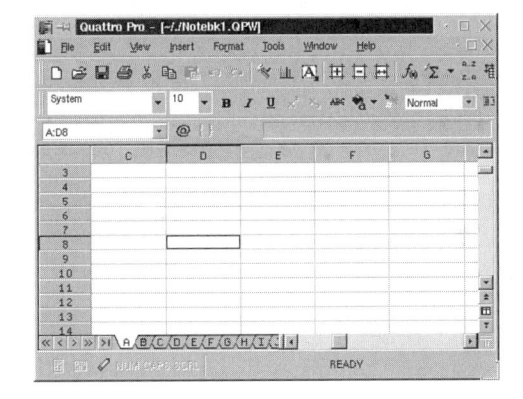

The Sheet Tabs

You can tell which sheet you're in by glancing at the sheet tabs in the lower-left corner of the notebook window. The current, or *active*, sheet tab is always displayed in white. In Figure 10.5, the active sheet is sheet B.

FIGURE 10.5
The white sheet tab in the lower-left corner of the notebook window indicates the active sheet.

> Quattro Pro makes it easy to change the default sheet names. Simply right-click the sheet tab for the sheet you want to rename and select Edit Sheet Tab. The selected sheet tab will expand and the default name will be highlighted, prompting you to type in a new sheet name.
>
> You can achieve the same result from the menu by selecting Format, Sheet and clicking the Name tab, where you'll simply type in the new sheet name in the space provided.

Using the Input Line

Another feature unique to the Quattro Pro 9 interface is the input line, shown in Figure 10.6. The input line displays information about the selected or active cell. It has two components. On the right is a white box that displays the address of a selected cell. The longer, gray box on the right of the input line displays the actual contents of the selected cell. As noted earlier, a cell can contain a value, label, or formula.

FIGURE 10.6
The input line displays the address and contents of the active cell.

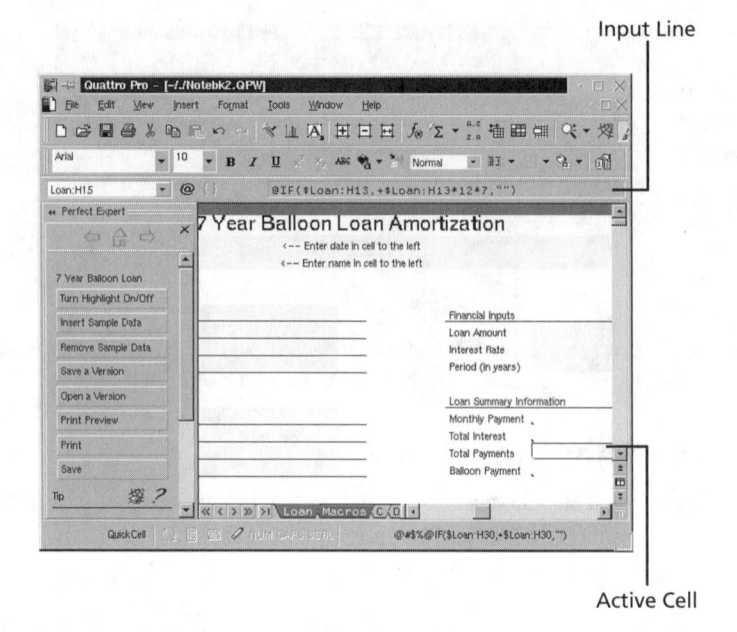

The Quattro Pro Property and Application Bars: What's Different?

Just above the input line is Quattro Pro's default Property Bar, shown in Figure 10.7. Most of the default Property Bar buttons for Quattro Pro 9 are dedicated to formatting the data contained in the active cell, including cell alignment, color, style, and font. We'll cover how to format your cells in Hour 11, "Creating Your First Spreadsheet."

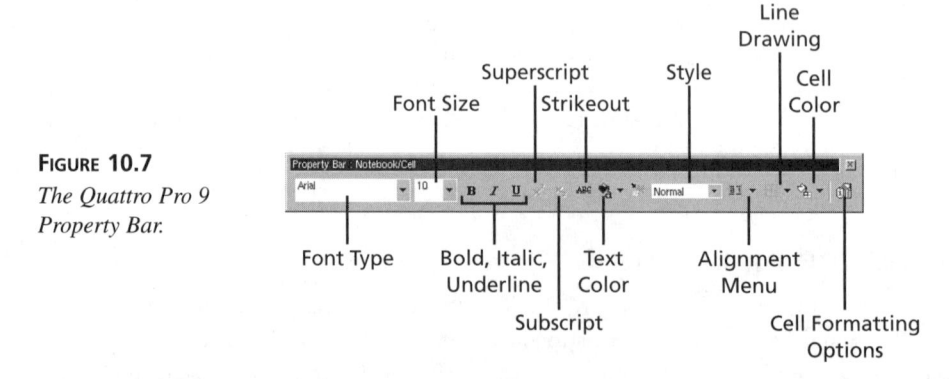

FIGURE 10.7
The Quattro Pro 9 Property Bar.

Across the bottom of the Quattro Pro window is the Application Bar shown in Figure 10.8. The Application Bar is a handy guide to reporting the mode you're working in at any given time. For example, it will display READY when you've selected a cell to enter data, LABEL when you begin to enter text, and EDIT when you make changes to a cell entry. The QuickSum and Calc-As-You-Go features, covered in more detail in Hour 11, are also located on the Application Bar.

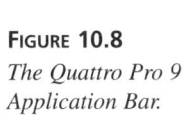

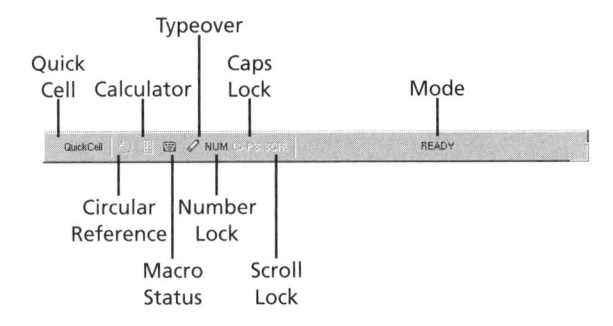

FIGURE 10.8
The Quattro Pro 9 Application Bar.

Customizing Quattro Pro 9

You can customize Quattro Pro to look and work the way you want. As previously noted, general menu and toolbar settings can be customized by selecting Tools, Settings from the menu bar. However, there are many other ways to customize Quattro Pro.

Object View

A quick and easy way to display at any time the objects (charts, maps, graphs, slideshows, and so on) you've included in your notebook is to select View, Objects from the menu bar.

Show/Hide Formulas

Instead of displaying formula results on your spreadsheet, Quattro Pro 9 can display the actual formulas in each cell. Select View, Formulas to toggle this feature on and off.

Changing Display Settings

Using the View menu, you can display your notebook in several different ways:

- Select View, Draft to view sheets without margins, footers, or headers.
- Select View, Page to display your sheets as they will look on the printed page, including all margins, footers, headers, and so on.
- Select View, Page Break to display your sheets with print page breaks.

Understanding Format Options

You can use the Format menu to control how your selections, spreadsheets, and notebooks will look:

- Select Format, Selection to format the contents and appearance—including font type, size, color—of any cell or group of cells you have selected.
- Selecting Format, Sheet lets you set attributes for the active sheet, such as borders, column widths, zoom, sheet name, and the color of a sheet's tab.
- As you might guess, choosing Format, Notebook lets you set various attributes for an entire notebook.

Navigating Through Notebooks and Spreadsheets

To work effectively in Quattro Pro 9, you have to know how to navigate among cells, rows, columns, and sheets. Fortunately, Quattro Pro 9 gives you many powerful tools for getting around easily and quickly. As you'll soon see, the biggest navigation problem in Quattro Pro 9 isn't so much how to get where you're going, but how to get there in the quickest, easiest way!

Activating Cells, Rows, Columns, and Blocks

A cell must be activated before its data can be entered, edited, or formatted. To activate a cell or group of cells, you simply select it in one of the following ways:

- To select a single cell, point your mouse over the cell you want to select and click once. The cell selector immediately appears to let you know the cell has been properly activated.

  Alternatively, you can use the Enter key to move down one cell at a time, the Tab key to move one cell to the right at a time, and your arrow keys (←, →, ↑, and ↓) to move right, left, up, or down one cell at a time. Give it a try, keeping an eye on the cell selector to see how each keyboard entry activates a different cell.

- To select an entire row, guide your mouse over one of the numbered row borders at the far left of the spreadsheet. You'll see a right-pointing white arrow. Click, and the entire row will be selected.

- To select an entire column, guide your mouse over one of the column borders at the top of the spreadsheet and click when you see the white, down-pointing arrow.

- To select a rectangular block of cells, you can save time by entering data or applying an operation to whole blocks of cells rather than repeating the same thing for individual cells. There are two ways to do this:
    - Click and drag your mouse from the upper-left cell to the lower-right cell in the selection.
    - Select the first cell in the block for selection, hold down the Shift key, and click the last cell of your selection. You can also hold the Shift key down and navigate to the last cell in your selection with the arrow keys.

  The first cell of the block will appear white, bordered by the cell selector.
- To select multiple, noncontiguous cells, hold down the Ctrl key as you click the cells you want to select.
- A 3-D block is a block of cells with the same cell address or addresses on two or more consecutive sheets. For example, assume that you have a separate quarterly sales spreadsheet on four consecutive sheets in a notebook, with the quarterly sales totals reported in cell F13 of each spreadsheet. A 3-D block comes in handy if you want to manipulate cell F13 on all four spreadsheets at the same time. For example, a 3-D block would be the quickest way to apply boldface formatting to cell F13 on all four spreadsheets.

  To select a 3-D block of cells, on the sheet where you want to begin the 3-D block, select an individual cell or block of cells as detailed previously. Hold down the Shift key as you click the tab for the last spreadsheet in the series. A black line will appear under all the tabs in the series.
- To select multiple blocks, first select one block of cells and then hold down the Ctrl key as you select the next block of cells. You can repeat this operation for as many block selections as you need.
- To select all cells on a sheet, simply click the Select All button at the upper-left corner of the Notebook window.

> To undo a selection of multiple cells, simply click again on the selection or anywhere on the sheet outside of the selected cells.

> Remember that once you select multiple cells, your immediate next step must be to apply an operation or enter data to the selection. If you left-click your mouse or press any movement key, you'll lose the selection and will have to redo it.

Quattro Pro 9 Keyboard Shortcuts

As helpful and intuitive as they are, point-and-click navigation tools inherently slow you down because they pull one hand away from the keyboard to operate a mouse. To keep things moving, I recommend that you practice using keyboard shortcuts for all Quattro Pro tasks, including all necessary navigation through your spreadsheets. Table 10.1 lists some keyboard shortcuts for navigating through your spreadsheets.

TABLE 10.1 Quattro Pro 9 Keyboard Shortcuts

Keystroke	Action
Ctrl+Pg Dn	Moves to the next spreadsheet (forward)
Ctrl+Pg Up	Moves to the previous sheet (backward)
Pg Up	Moves up one screen
Pg Dn	Moves down one screen
Home	Moves to cell A1 in the active sheet
Ctrl+Home	Moves to cell A1 of the first sheet
End+Home	Moves to lowest-right nonblank cell in the active sheet
End+Ctrl+Home	Moves to lowest-right nonblank cell in the entire notebook
Ctrl+G or F5	Moves to specified cell
Ctrl+Right Arrow	Moves right one screen
Ctrl+Left Arrow	Moves left one screen

Other Quattro Pro 9 Navigation Tools

Figure 10.9 shows the bottom half of an open spreadsheet, where you'll find a bevy of navigation tools that are unique to Quattro Pro.

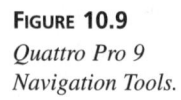

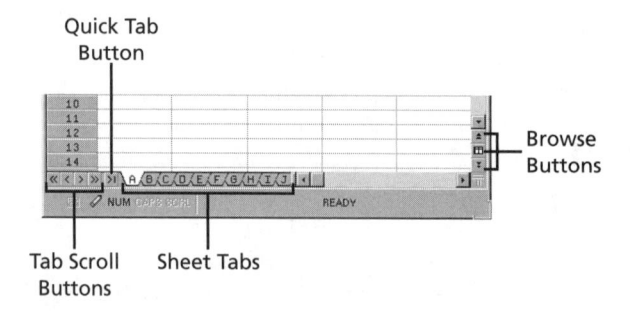

FIGURE 10.9

Quattro Pro 9 Navigation Tools.

Navigating with Sheet Tabs and the Tab Scroll Buttons

We looked at sheet tabs earlier in this hour in the "Introducing the Quattro Pro 9 Workspace" section. As you can probably guess, the easiest way to jump from sheet to sheet is to simply select the sheet tab for the sheet you want to access.

To the left of the sheet tabs are the tab scroll buttons. From left to right, as shown in Figure 10.9, the tab scroll buttons allow you to go back several sheets, go back one sheet, go forward one sheet, and go forward several sheets.

Jumping Around with Quick Tab

The Quick Tab button, located between the tab scroll buttons and the sheet tabs, is your one-click, roundtrip ticket to the Objects sheet that lies at the end of every notebook. Click it once to activate the Objects sheet, and click it again to return to where you started. We'll cover objects in Hour 13.

To Do: Make a Fast Track with the Browse Buttons

The browse buttons on the vertical scroll bar help you navigate through specified cells by type or content.

1. Right-click the center browse button to open a QuickMenu of cell types. By default, the selected cell type is Values.

2. Left-click the center browse button without changing the default cell type, all the cells containing values will be highlighted, and you can use the top and bottom browse buttons, respectively, to navigate forward and backward through the highlighted cells. Note that you can also use the arrow keys to navigate through the highlighted cells.

3. To turn off the Browse feature, simply click once with your mouse anywhere in your open spreadsheet or strike any arrow key.

To Do: Use the "Go To" Command

Once you get comfortable with cell addresses, you may want to use the Go To command to navigate directly to a specific cell address.

1. From the menu bar, select Edit, Go To to open the Go To dialog box. You can also access the Go To dialog box by pressing Ctrl+G or the F5 key.

2. In the box labeled Reference, type in the address of the block or cell to which you want to jump. Remember to use the full *sheet:cell* address if you want to go to a location on another sheet.

3. Click OK or press Enter to jump to your designated cell address.

Summary

In this hour you studied the Quattro Pro environment. You saw that Quattro Pro combines a number of related components into a notebook file to help you organize, manage, and present your data.

You also learned how to navigate through all the notebook components and the various ways to select cells and blocks of cells for the entry, editing, and formatting of your data. Congratulations, you've mastered all the requisite basics of the Quattro Pro interface!

We'll take it a few steps further in the next hour, in which you'll actually enter data and formulas to create your first simple spreadsheet.

Q&A

Q I only need a simple spreadsheet that adds a few rows of data. Can I just use WordPerfect 9 for this?

A Yes. Only you can decide whether to step up to Quattro Pro 9 for more control over how your data is analyzed, organized, and presented. If you only need to add a few rows of data and prefer to keep things simple, WordPerfect 9 may be just the tool you need.

Q Is there a way to increase the size of my spreadsheet, in case I need more room?

A In Quattro Pro 9, Corel increased the size of your notebooks in order to accommodate users switching over from other spreadsheet applications, who found that Quattro Pro could not accommodate their massive spreadsheets. Therefore, by default, each Quattro Pro 9 notebook contains 18,278 sheets, and each sheet contains 18,278 vertical columns and 1,000,000 horizontal rows. This should be more than enough space for any conceivable spreadsheet you would need to work on. Frankly, if you need a bigger spreadsheet, you're not getting out enough.

Workshop

The Workshop contains quiz questions and exercises to help reinforce what you've learned in this hour. If you get stuck, the answers to the quiz questions can be found in Appendix B, "Answers to Quiz Questions."

Quiz

1. Which of the following elements can be included in a Quattro Pro 9 spreadsheet?
    a. Formulas
    b. Slideshows
    c. Charts
    d. Dates
    e. All of the above

2. Which symbols can be used to begin a formula?
    a. Apostrophe (')
    b. Quotation Mark (")
    c. Caret (^)
    d. All of the above
    e. None of the above

3. The cell address LLL:Q46..NNN:Q46 refers to
    a. Three consecutive cells beginning with Q46 on sheet L
    b. A 3-D block consisting of LLL:Q46, MMM:Q46, and NNN:Q46
    c. All the cells in the range between LLL:Q46 and NNN:Q46
    d. Every cell in column Q and every cell in row 46 on sheets LLL through NNN
    e. None of the above

Exercises

1. Change the menus and interface of an open notebook to look and work like Microsoft Excel 97. Ready to switch over to Quattro Pro 9 for good? Restore the default Quattro Pro 9 menus and interface.
2. Locate the following cell addresses: D:B6, XX:Q30, and ZZZ:A100.
3. Use the Quick Tab to jump to the Objects sheet. Now use the Go To command to find cell CCC:Z49.

HOUR 11

Creating Your First Spreadsheet

In the last hour, you became acquainted with the Quattro Pro environment and how to navigate through it and select cells. You also learned about the types of data you can enter in a spreadsheet. It's time to put that knowledge to good use in creating your first spreadsheet in five easy steps. Believe it or not, your first effort will look like the work of a seasoned professional!

In this hour, you will

- Plan and create a basic Quattro Pro spreadsheet from start to finish.
- Learn how to take advantage of Quattro Pro's many shortcuts for entering data.
- Use formulas and functions in Quattro Pro 9 spreadsheets.
- Explore how simple formatting options give your spreadsheets professional polish.

Creating Simple Spreadsheets with Quattro Pro 9

With Quattro Pro, even the simplest spreadsheet can be presented with powerful results. You'll see for yourself as you spend this hour creating a relatively basic spreadsheet designed to present the first quarter sales figures for your new company, Fundamentally Yours, Inc. Along the way, you'll learn the five sure-fire steps to creating a winning spreadsheet with Quattro Pro 9.

Step One: Identifying the Purpose of the Spreadsheet

The first thing to do is identify the purpose of your spreadsheet and its intended audience.

In this example, Fundamentally Yours, Inc. (FYI) is in the business of selling interactive instructional software. FYI employs five sales representatives, who are each responsible for sales in a particular region of the country. The salespeople submit monthly sales reports to the home office. After each quarter, FYI holds a sales meeting to go over performance, identify trends and problems, and make adjustments. The first quarter has just ended, and the quarterly review meeting is scheduled for next week.

You're handed the monthly sales figures shown in Table 11.1 and told that the fate of the company is in your hands.

TABLE 11.1 Monthly Sales Figures for FYI

	January	February	March
Abell	$5,342	$6,262	$10,461
Baker	$8,798	$7,545	$9,425
Doe	$11,450	$8,932	$13,047
Jones	$3,365	$5,477	$4,785
Smith	$7,309	$7,518	$8,650

For the quarterly meeting, you need to prepare a spreadsheet that sets forth the company's first quarter sales and measures the performance of each sales representative. Your audience consists of sales team management and everyone on the sales team. Because you're presenting to a sophisticated audience that will understand and be interested in the information you must convey, the more information you can provide, the better.

> The spreadsheet project you'll work with in this hour will be used and expanded in the next two hours, covering more advanced Quattro Pro 9 spreadsheet techniques. Be sure to save your work at the end of this hour so you can continue to work with it.

Try to envision the structure your spreadsheet should take. At a minimum, you need to display each representative's total sales for the quarter, but you can go further to show performance in each month within the quarter and total quarterly sales volume for the company as a whole.

Congratulations! You have a concept in mind for presenting your data, and you're almost ready to let Quattro Pro do the rest of the work for you.

Step Two: Collecting Your Data

Now that you've determined the purpose of your spreadsheet, you need to identify all the data you'll need. Having your data at the ready will save time when you sit down to build your spreadsheet. For your FYI quarterly sales spreadsheet, you need the names of the salespeople, the months within the quarter, and the monthly sales figure for each representative.

Lucky for you, all the data you need for your first spreadsheet is neatly collected in Table 11.1.

Note that the purpose of your spreadsheet will dictate what data you'll need to collect. For example, FYI management might also want to see how each product is selling, which would require you to obtain more detailed information from the sales department. Similarly, in a household budget spreadsheet, you might want to break down a broad category, such as utilities, into subcategories such as water, electricity, and telephone to better track your expenses.

Step Three: Plugging It In

It's time to enter your data and set up the basic structure of the FYI first quarter sales spreadsheet.

To begin your Quattro Pro spreadsheet, open a new notebook and do the following:

1. Select cell B1, type **Fundamentally Yours, Inc.** and press the up or down arrow key or Enter. All three keys work interchangeably to enter data. You can use whichever you choose, but from hereon, the text refers only to the Enter key.

2. In cell B2 type **First Quarter Sales** and press Enter.
3. In cell C4, type **January** and press Enter. Don't worry about the other two months' names right now—in a page or two, you learn how Quattro Pro can QuickFill those entries.
4. Enter the remaining data from Table 11.1, as shown in Figure 11.1.
5. Save your project as **Quarter1.qpw**.

FIGURE 11.1

Step 3 in creating your FYI quarterly sales spreadsheet is to enter all the data you'll need.

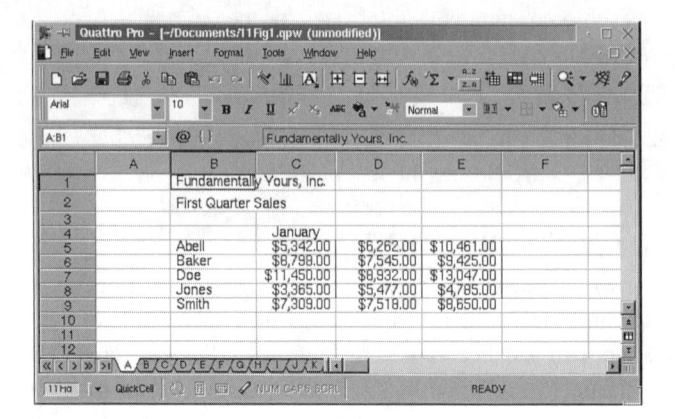

> Select cell B1 and take a look at the input line. As shown in Figure 11.1, even though the text *Fundamentally Yours, Inc.* appears to span across more than one cell on the spreadsheet, it's actually all contained in cell B1. Quattro Pro allows a text entry that's longer than the width of one cell to "carry over" into adjacent cells. This only works for text entries, not for number entries.

Using QuickType to Automate Text Entry

Quattro Pro's QuickType feature lets you speed up the entry of repeated text and names. When enabled, QuickType remembers the patterns of words and names you enter so that when you begin to type the first few letters of a previously entered word, it will automatically complete the new entry for you. Give it a try. After entering the data in Figure 11.1, start retyping the name Baker in a new cell. When QuickType automatically completes the entry for you, press Enter to accept it, or keep typing to reject it and overwrite the QuickType entry.

QuickType is turned on by default. You can toggle it on and off by clicking Tools, Settings and navigating to the General tab. Check or uncheck the Quick Type box to enable/disable the feature and then click OK to activate your selection.

Using QuickFill

Quattro Pro's QuickFill feature can automatically enter labels in a series, such as months of the year, days of the week, or consecutive numbers.

Follow the example shown in Figure 11.2. Select block C4..E4. In this block of three cells, the first one is labeled January, and the adjacent cells are blank. With the block selected, click the QuickFill button on the default toolbar. QuickFill reads the January entry, assumes you want to continue the series, and automatically enters February and March in the blank selected cells.

FIGURE 11.2
QuickFill automatically completes a series in a selected block of cells.

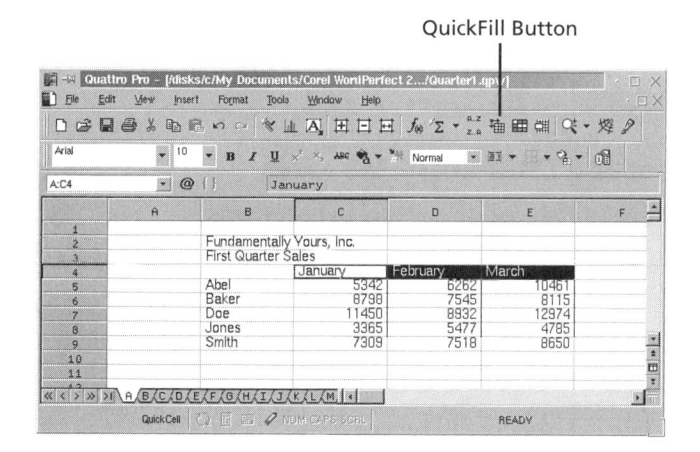

To Do: Use QuickFill

Quattro Pro comes with several default series recognized by QuickFill. To create your own QuickFill series, work through the following steps:

1. Click an empty cell and click the QuickFill button to open the QuickFill dialog box.
2. Click Create to open the Create/Modify Series dialog box shown in Figure 11.3.
3. Give your custom series a name, such as Sales Representatives.
4. Under Series Elements, enter the values you want to include in your series, such as Abell, Baker, Doe, Jones, and Smith.
5. Press Enter or click OK.
6. To use your custom QuickFill series, select a block of cells, click the QuickFill button, and navigate to and select your custom series.
7. Click OK, and your series is automatically added to the range of cells you blocked. You can also type the first value in your series, select a block of cells, and click the QuickFill button.

FIGURE 11.3
The Create/Modify Series dialog box.

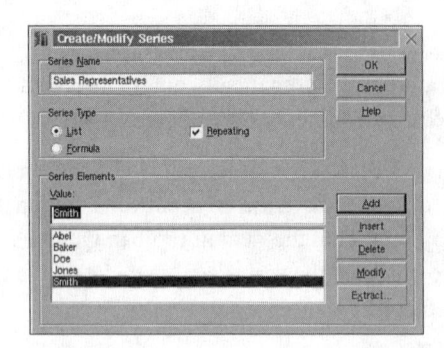

As you'll see later in this hour, you can also use QuickFill to create and enter custom formula series.

Correcting Data Entry Mistakes

You have several ways to correct erroneous data entries:

- Click the cell to highlight its contents and then retype the entry.
- Right-click the cell, select Clear from the pop-up menu, and retype the entry. You can also select the cell and press the Delete key for the same effect.
- Double-click the cell and edit the entry.
- Click the cell to select it and then click the box on the right side of the input line and edit the entry there.

Of course, as covered in Hour 3, "Common Tasks in WordPerfect Office 2000 for Linux," you can always use the Undo/Redo commands to correct errors in entering your data.

Step Four: Working with Formulas

The real power of Quattro Pro is its ability to calculate values from data you enter. In this step, you'll enter a few basic formulas into your FYI quarterly sales spreadsheet. Before you do, let's spend a few minutes getting familiar with how Quattro Pro formulas work and how they're structured.

All calculations in Quattro Pro are based on formulas. Like other data, formulas are placed within cells. In general, formulas are a combination of one or more operators (symbols that represent mathematical operations) that refer to values entered in other cells. The operators act upon these values to produce a result that's displayed in the cell.

Creating Your First Spreadsheet 217

The fastest way to understand how formulas work is to see one in action. Here's how:

1. Open a new notebook.
2. Enter the number 5 in cell A2 and the number 6 in cell B2.
3. In cell D2, enter the formula =A2*B2. In this formula, the asterisk (*) is the multiplication operator, which tells the program what to do with the values contained in cells A2 and B2. Your worksheet should look like the one shown in Figure 11.4.

FIGURE 11.4

The formula in cell D2 tells Quattro Pro to multiply the values of cells A2 and B2 and display the product in cell D2.

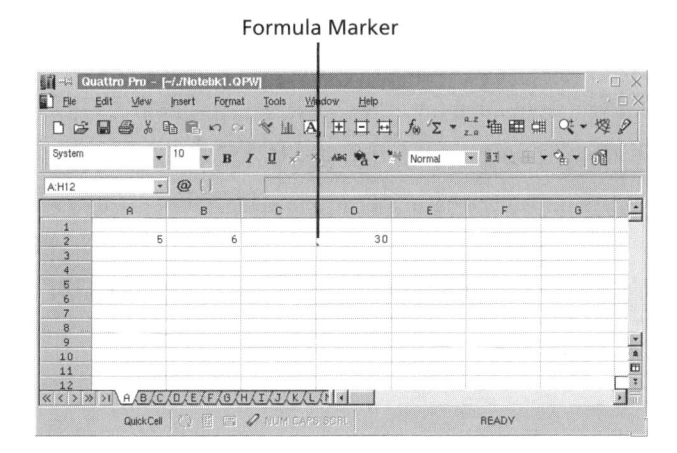

As shown in Figure 11.4, the tiny blue arrowhead in the bottom-left corner of cell D2 is the *Formula Marker*, a new feature of Quattro Pro 9. As the name suggests, Formula Markers tell you which cells in an open sheet contain formulas. You'll come to rely heavily on Formula Markers as a means of distinguishing plain-old value cells, which do nothing but take up space, from dynamic formula cells, which perform mathematical functions on your data and automatically update themselves when your underlying data is modified.

> The Formula Marker also provides a quick way to view formulas directly on the spreadsheet. If you place your mouse pointer on the Formula Marker in cell D2, a text box pops open identifying the simple multiplication formula contained in the cell. Pretty neat!

Structuring Formulas

It's time to spice things up by making the simple multiplication formula shown in Figure 11.4 more complex:

1. Enter the number 7 in cell C2.
2. Right-click cell D2, select Clear, and enter the new formula **(A2*B2)-C2**.

The formula you just entered tells Quattro Pro to perform the following operations in the following order:

- Multiply the values in cells A2 and B2 (5*6=30)
- Subtract from the product the value in cell C2 (30–7=23)
- Display the final result (23) in cell D2

This exercise provides a basic idea of the syntax and structure used by Quattro Pro formulas. When you enter formulas, keep in mind the following guidelines:

- *The first character.* Every formula must begin with one of the following characters in order for Quattro Pro to recognize that you're entering a formula:

    +

    -

    =

    .

    $

    (

    #

    @

- *Common arithmetic operators.* Formulas can include the following common arithmetic operators:

    + (add)

    - (subtract)

    / (divide)

    * (multiply)

    ^ (exponent—to the power of)

- *Order of precedence.* The order in which Quattro Pro performs operations in formulas is determined by each operation's predefined "order of precedence." There are seven orders, or *levels*, of precedence, with level 7 being the highest and level 1 being the lowest. In a formula, operations of the highest order are performed first. Operations of the same order are performed left to right in the order in which they appear. Unless you change the order of precedence (which you'll learn about in a minute), Quattro Pro follows the preset order. Because formula results can vary greatly depending on each operation's order of precedence, you should always keep precedence in mind when creating formulas.

For the common arithmetic operators, the order of precedence is shown in Table 11.2.

TABLE 11.2 Operator Order of Precedence

Operator	Precedence
() (parentheses)	7 (highest)
^ (exponent)	7
+, - (positive, negative)	6
*, / (multiply, divide)	5
+, - (add, subtract)	4

- *Changing the order of precedence.* You can change the order in which operations will be performed by using parentheses, which are given the highest order of precedence. Simply place parentheses around the operation (or operations) you want to be performed first.

For example, the formula (7+4)*6 will produce a result of 66. By adding parentheses to the formula you instruct Quattro Pro to perform the addition operation first (to yield 11), and then multiply the sum by 6 to produce a result of 66.

Taking it one step further, you can also place parentheses within parentheses, which instructs Quattro Pro to perform the operations in the innermost parentheses first and work its way outward. For example, the result for the formula ((7-4)+(3*5))*2 is 36.

Here's how Quattro Pro breaks it down: First, Quattro Pro subtracts 4 from 7 (to yield 3) and multiplies 3 by 5 (to yield 15). Quattro Pro performs these operations first because they're in parentheses within parentheses. Quattro Pro next adds these results (to yield 18) and multiplies the sum by 2 (to yield 36).

Basic Formulas You Can Try

Table 11.3 provides some basic formulas you can create and experiment with in your own Quattro Pro 9 spreadsheets.

TABLE 11.3 Basic Quattro Pro 9 Formulas

Formula	Result
+A2*B2 or =A2*B2	Multiplies the value in cell A2 by the value in cell B2. Note that you can use either + or = to start a formula, but you cannot start a formula with just a cell address.
(A2*B2)+C2	Multiplies the value in cell A2 by the value in cell B2 and then adds the product to the value in cell C2. Note that you could also start the formula with + or =, but it's unnecessary since this formula starts with a parenthesis, which is also permitted.
(A2*B2)/5	Multiplies the value in cell A2 by the value in cell B2 and then divides the product by 5.
+5*(A2/B2)	Divides the value in cell A2 by the value in cell B2 and then multiplies the quotient by 5.
+A2^5/B2	Raises the value in cell A2 to a power of 5 and then divides that result by the value in cell B2.
@SUM(A2..C2)	Adds the values in cells A2, B2, and C2.

To Do: Enter Formulas

Remember, you enter formulas the same way you enter any other kind of data: Just select a cell and begin typing.

Your FYI quarterly sales spreadsheet requires only a basic formula to total a block of cells. The important thing here is for you to get comfortable with combining cell and cell block addresses with operators to create a formula—the most important Quattro Pro skill you'll master.

In your Quarter1.qpw notebook, enter formulas that will give you the quarter totals for each sales representative:

1. Select cell F5.
2. Enter the formula **+C5+D5+E5**.
3. Select cell F6 and enter **+C6+D6+E6**.
4. Follow the same procedures to enter appropriate formulas in cells F7, F8, and F9. If you enter the correct cell addresses in your formulas, your results should look like those in Figure 11.5.

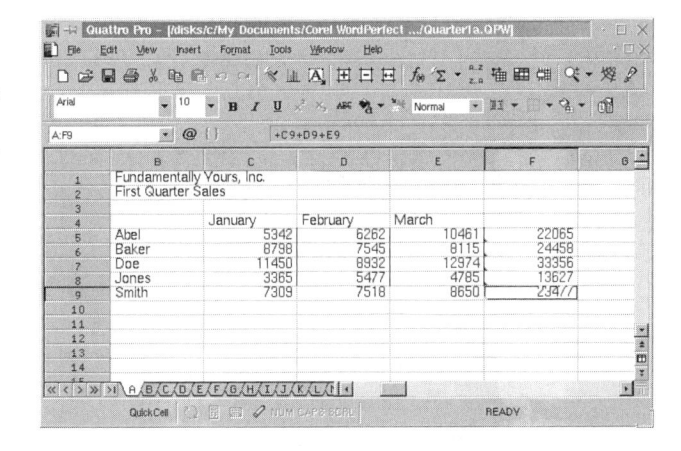

FIGURE 11.5
Cells F5 through F9, all flagged by Formula Markers, display the results of the formulas entered in the cells.

Using Functions

Instead of manually defining formulas, you can take advantage of hundreds of predefined formulas, called *functions*. Every function begins with the @ character. For example, the most common function, @SUM, is used to add the values of cells in a block.

The basic approach is to call up a function and specify the cells or block of cells to which the function should apply. You can enter a function by typing @ followed by the function's name, or you can press the function button (the one labeled "@") on the input line. Give it a try by using @SUM to tally up the quarterly sales of FYI's sales reps:

1. Select cell F10 and click the @ button to open the Functions dialog box (see Figure 11.6).

2. In the Function Category pane on the left, click ALL. In the Function pane on the right, scroll down to find SUM and select it.

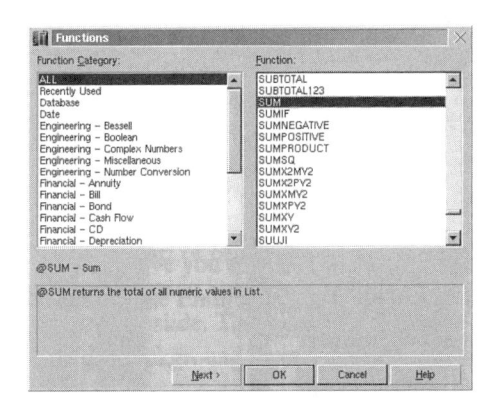

FIGURE 11.6
The Quattro Pro 9 Functions dialog box.

3. Click OK to exit the Functions dialog box.
4. In your spreadsheet, you will see "@SUM" appear in the input line for cell F10. Click the input line and directly after @SUM type in **(F5..F9)**. Press Enter to sum up the range of cells in column F, as shown in Figure 11.7.

FIGURE 11.7
Sum up block F5..F9 with the @SUM function.

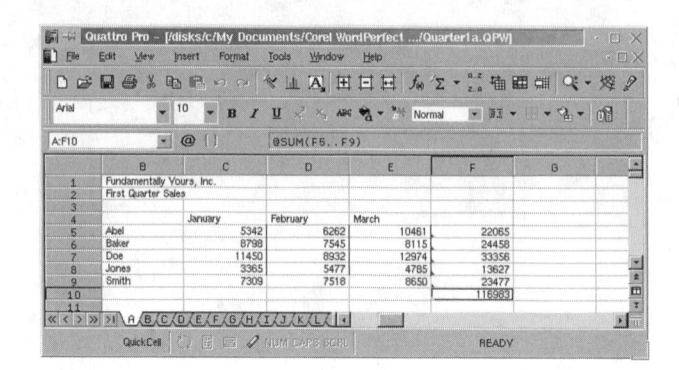

Using Other Tools to Speed Up Spreadsheet Entry

The QuickFunction button (shown in Figure 11.8) on the default toolbar provides one-click access to the most commonly used functions.

FIGURE 11.8
The QuickFunction button applies a function to a cell or block of cells with a single mouse click.

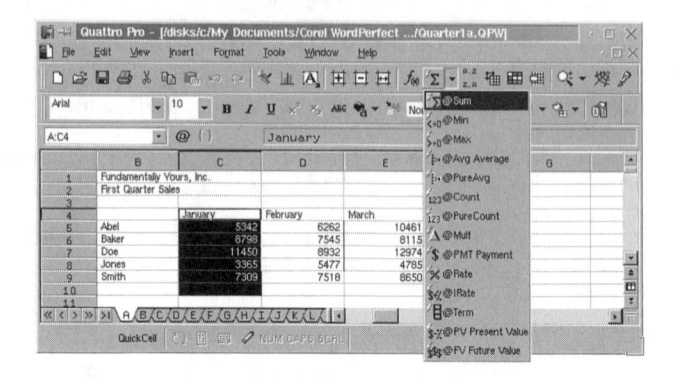

To Do: Use QuickFunction

To give it a try in your FYI spreadsheet, use the QuickFunction button to total up January's sales:

1. Select block C5..C10.
2. Click the down arrow on the right side of the QuickFunction button.
3. In the drop-down QuickFunction menu, click @Sum.

▲ The sum of cells C5..C9 appears in cell C10.

> The QuickFunction button always displays, and will activate, the last function used. This is a real timesaver because it spares you navigating through the drop-down QuickFunction menu when repeating the same function several times over. By default, the QuickFunction button is set to @Sum, which will remain until another function is used. Because @Sum is the default, to sum the block C5..C9 in your FYI quarterly sales spreadsheet, you could have simply clicked the QuickFunction button.

To Do: Automatic Totaling

If you liked QuickFill and QuickFunction, you'll love Quattro Pro 9's new automatic totaling feature. Quattro Pro recognizes special row and column headings, such as Total, and automatically inserts appropriate formulas in the row or column to which the heading applies.

Hold on to your hat and give it a try:

1. Clear block C10..E10 and make sure it stays selected.
2. In cell B10 enter the word **Total**.
3. Formulas will automatically be entered into cells C10, D10, and E10.

Pretty fast, wasn't it? You're almost done entering formulas for your FYI spreadsheet. For your last entry, you need to know about relative and absolute cell addresses.

Using Absolute Cell Addresses

As you've seen, when Quattro Pro copies formulas for you, it converts cell addresses in the formula to reflect the cell to which the formula is copied. For example, if you copy the formula @SUM(F5..F9) from cell F10 to cell E10, the formula automatically changes to @SUM(E5..E9). This is an example of a formula with a *relative* cell address. A formula with a relative cell address is dynamic and changes relative to its current cell address. Quattro Pro assumes all formulas are relative unless you tell it otherwise.

You can tell Quattro Pro otherwise by making a formula *absolute*, also known as *giving it an absolute cell address*. A formula with an absolute cell address is static and will not change even if copied and pasted to another cell address. As always, you'll better understand the concepts of relative and absolute cell addresses by trying them out for yourself.

In your FYI quarterly sales spreadsheet, suppose your boss wants to see the sales total reflected on a separate line for easy viewing. One way to do this would be to enter in another cell (say, D13) the same formula contained in cell F10. To do this, select cell B13 and type **TOTAL ALL SALES:**. Next, select cell F10 and copy and paste this to cell D13. Your spreadsheet should now look like the one shown in Figure 11.9.

FIGURE 11.9

Copy and paste the formula contained in cell F10 to cell D13.

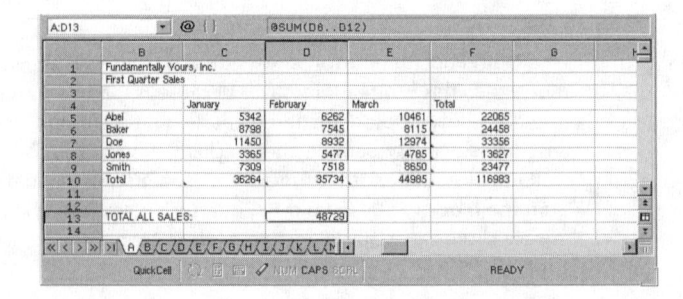

You'll quickly realize that cell D13 does not match cell F10. What happened?

With cell D13 selected, look at the input line to figure it out. Quattro Pro considers the formula copied from F10 to be relative and converts it for application in D13. In other words, the formula in D13 sums the values in the five cells preceding it, D8 through D12, just as the formula in F10 summed the five preceding cells in column F.

To prevent this from happening, you must make the cell references in the formula contained in cell F10 absolute. First, delete the formula from cell D13 and select F10. Click the input line, which will turn white. As shown in Figure 11.10, type a dollar sign ($) before the column and row coordinates of each cell address within the parentheses and press Enter.

FIGURE 11.10

Enter $ before each cell coordinate in a formula to assign the formula an absolute cell address.

The dollar signs before the cell column and row coordinates tell Quattro Pro that they're absolute addresses and are not to be changed when the formula is copied or moved. No matter where you copy or move this formula, it will always sum the block F5..F9.

> To create a formula with an absolute cell address, make sure that both the column and row coordinates of the cell addresses in the formula are preceded by $. If you insert $ before only the column coordinates, Quattro Pro will consider the row coordinates to remain relative and subject to conversion when the formula is copied or moved. If you insert $ before only the row coordinates, the column coordinates will be relative and subject to conversion.

> If you're working with multiple sheets, you can include the sheet reference as part of a formula with an absolute cell address by inserting $ before the sheet reference.

With the absolute cell addresses properly entered, copy and paste the formula from cell F10 to cell D13. Cell D13 displays the same result as cell F10. Save your changes.

Congratulations! You've finished entering all the data and formulas in your spreadsheet.

Step Five: Formatting Your Spreadsheet

With all the data entry and number crunching done, it's time to give your spreadsheet some polish with a little formatting. One of the easiest ways to give your spreadsheet a sophisticated look is to choose different fonts to highlight important information. Aligning your text and ensuring that all figures are properly formatted are also essential to turning the corner from *good* spreadsheet to *great* spreadsheet.

All the font-formatting skills covered in Hour 5, "Formatting WordPerfect 9 Documents," also apply in Quattro Pro 9. Play around with it awhile and see for yourself.

Select cell B2 and click the Bold button on the Property Bar. The entire label is now bold. Click the pull-down font menu on the Property Bar for a list of available fonts. As you navigate the list of available fonts, the Real-Time Preview feature kicks in, giving you an advance peak at how different fonts will display in the selected cell. Quattro Pro 9's implementation of Real-Time Preview is shown in Figure 11.11. Note that you are not limited to formatting your cells one cell at a time—you can make font selection, size, and other formatting changes to a selected range of cells.

FIGURE 11.11
Quattro Pro's Real-Time Preview shows how different fonts will affect the text contained in a cell or block of cells.

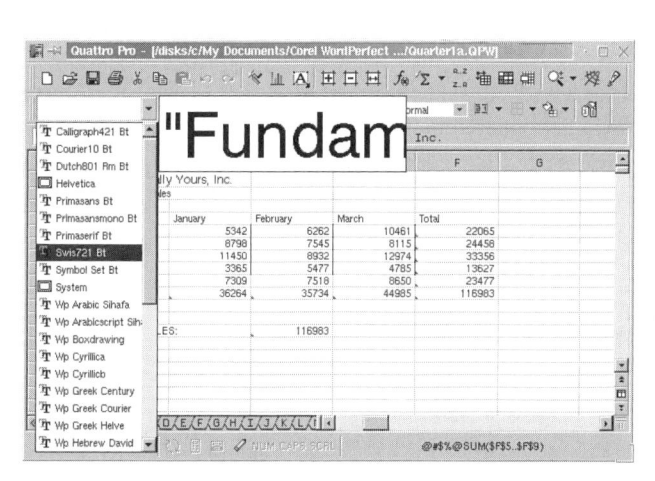

To Do: Align Text

The headings at the top of your FYI spreadsheet can use some work. Centering them across the cells they appear in may help. Follow these steps:

1. Select block B1..F2.
2. Click the Alignment menu on the Property Bar, as shown in Figure 11.12.

FIGURE 11.12
Use the Alignment menu on the Property Bar to align your data within a cell or range of cells.

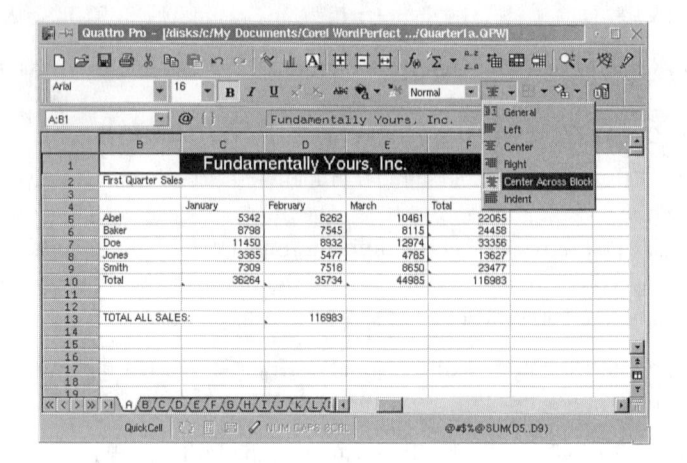

3. Click the Center Across Block option.
4. Click outside the block to deselect it and view your work.

To Do: Format Your Figures

Because you're working with sales totals, your figures should include dollar signs, commas, and decimal points. To add them, follow these steps:

1. Select block C5..F15.
2. From the menu, select Format, Selection to open the Active Cells dialog box. Navigate to the Numeric Format tab shown in Figure 11.13.
3. In the Format options, select Currency. Set the number of decimal places to 2 and click OK to exit back to your spreadsheet. The currency settings you just applied will be reflected in all your numeric data.

Creating Your First Spreadsheet

FIGURE 11.13
The Numeric Format tab within the Active Cells dialog box.

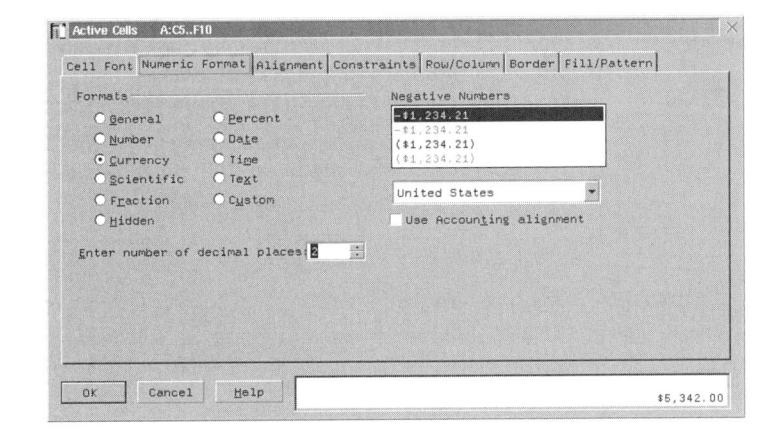

Using QuickFit to Change the Size of Your Cells

If the cells in some of your columns display a series of asterisks, the column is not wide enough to fit your numeric data in one or more cells. The QuickFit feature automatically adjusts the width of each selected column to fit the longest entry in the column.

Give it a try by selecting block C5..F15. Click the QuickFit button on the default toolbar, as shown in Figure 11.14.

FIGURE 11.14
Use QuickFit to adjust selected columns to fit your data.

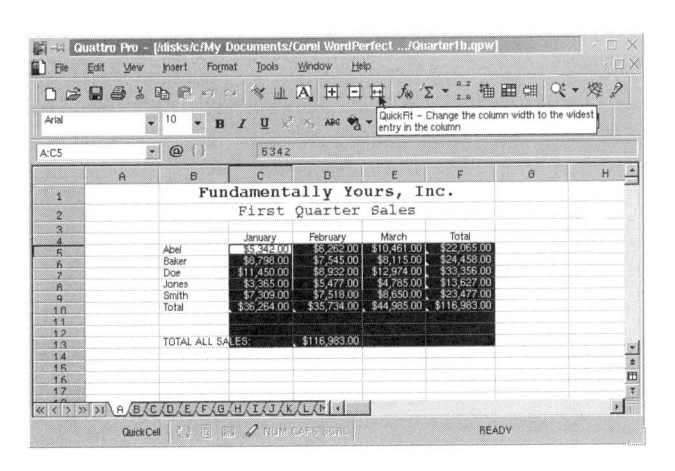

> You can set Quattro Pro to adjust the column width automatically as you work by enabling its Fit-As-You-Go feature. Enable Fit-As-You-Go by selecting Tools, Settings from the menu and navigating to the General tab. Click to activate the Fit-As-You-Go checkbox and then click OK.
>
> As you continue to work after activating Fit-As-You-Go, you'll note that column widths automatically adjust to fit the largest data entry within a column.

That wraps up this hour! Your first spreadsheet is complete, and you learned a great deal about working with formulas and formatting your spreadsheets.

Summary

In this hour, you designed and created a simple yet effective spreadsheet. You mastered manual data entry and formula creation and learned how Quattro Pro formulas and functions are structured. You also became familiar with Quattro Pro's automated data- and formula-entry features and applied some basic formatting techniques to give your spreadsheet a polished look.

In the next hour, you learn how to edit your spreadsheets and manipulate cell contents, columns, rows, and even entire worksheets. You'll also learn how to print spreadsheets, which can often be more involved than printing simpler documents, such as those created in WordPerfect.

Q&A

Q How do I insert a Quattro Pro 9 spreadsheet into a WordPerfect 9 document?

A You can use traditional copy, cut, and paste techniques, but you can also *link* your WordPerfect document to your spreadsheet. The benefit of linking is that if the data in the original spreadsheet (the *source* document) is updated, the data in the linked copy in WordPerfect (the *destination* document) is also updated.

To link a WordPerfect document to a Quattro Pro spreadsheet, make sure that the spreadsheet has been saved on your hard drive. In WordPerfect 9, select Insert, Spreadsheet/Database, Create Link from the menu bar to open the Create Data Link dialog box. For Data Type, select Spreadsheet; for Link As, select Table. Under Filename, click the folder icon and navigate to the spreadsheet you want to link to. Under Range, enter the cell addresses you want to link to. If you want to link to the entire spreadsheet, click once in the Filename box, and then click in the Range or Named Ranges boxes. Quattro Pro automatically inserts the cell addresses for the entire spreadsheet.

Click OK and your spreadsheet appears in WordPerfect as a linked document. If the data in your source document changes, you can update the linked copy as follows. Save the changes to your source document before updating the linked copy. In WordPerfect, click the linked copy and select Insert, Spreadsheet/Database, Update from the menu bar. Click Yes at the Update prompt to update all data links in the linked copy. You can also configure your linked copy to update automatically whenever you open the WordPerfect document by selecting Insert, Spreadsheet/Database, Options from the menu bar and checking the Update When Document Opens box.

Q Can I use QuickFunction to apply a formula to a block of cells?

A An enthusiastic yes! If you have several rows or columns of data to which the same formula will be applied, select the appropriate block of cells. (Make sure that the block ends with a blank cell for each total you want to include.) Press the down arrow next to the QuickFunction button on the toolbar, and select the desired QuickFunction from the drop-down menu. This method enables you to enter all your data and then automatically enter all formulas and totals with just a few mouse clicks.

Workshop

The Workshop contains quiz questions and exercises to help reinforce what you've learned in this hour. If you get stuck, the answers can be found in Appendix B, "Answers to Quiz Questions."

Quiz

1. How do you use formulas created to depict sales totals in a first quarter spreadsheet as the basis for a new spreadsheet for second quarter sales?
2. How do you calculate the average of a row of figures in Quattro Pro?
3. Can relative cell addressing be turned off?
4. Where can you get a list of Quattro Pro's functions?

Exercises

1. Practice applying different fonts and sizes to the Fundamentally Yours, Inc., first quarter sales spreadsheet.
2. Change some of the individual sales figures entered for the five sales people to see how those changes are automatically recalculated.
3. Practice deleting some of the formulas you manually entered and using QuickFill or QuickFunction (@SUM) to obtain the same results.
4. Plan and create a household monthly expense spreadsheet.

HOUR 12

Updating and Printing Your Spreadsheet

In the last hour, you created your first Quattro Pro 9 spreadsheet, and then polished it up with some basic formatting. You now have a strong working knowledge of how millions of people use Quattro Pro 9 every day. But there will come a day when you need to update and print an existing spreadsheet. From correcting values that were improperly entered to entering additional data, understanding how to update and print out existing spreadsheets is crucial to maximizing your use of Quattro Pro 9.

In this hour, you will

- Practice many of the cell, column, and row selection techniques covered in previous hours.
- Get hands-on experience updating a spreadsheet by adding, modifying, and deleting data.
- Learn the ins and outs of printing your Quattro Pro 9 spreadsheets so they look as you designed them on the screen.

Updating Your Spreadsheet

It didn't take long for the executives at Fundamentally Yours, Inc. to find out that you are the company's resident Quattro Pro expert. It's the day before the big sales meeting and you've been hard at work preparing the FYI quarterly sales spreadsheet. All that's left to do is print out your spreadsheet, when you decide to treat yourself to a well-deserved lunch break.

When you return from lunch, there's a memo on your chair from the sales manager requesting that you make sure your spreadsheet includes the following updates:

- Bob Baker and Don Doe were late in submitting their March sales figures, which have to be updated, respectively, to $9,425.00 and $13,047.00.
- Ann Abell's last name is misspelled. In addition, her sales figures for January are mistakenly recorded in her February column, and vice versa. The January and February sales figures need to be transposed.
- Personnel forgot to mention that Julie Jones resigned at the end of February. Sally Smith covered Jones's territory in March and should get credit for Jones's March sales.
- Sales forgot to tell you that they hired a sixth sales representative named Zach Zimmer, whose sales figures need to be included in the quarterly sales spreadsheet.
- The boss has personally demanded that the spreadsheet you're preparing identify the full names of each of the sales representatives so she can remember them at the meeting. She also hates boldface type anywhere on a spreadsheet except for the bottom line and demands that all elements of the spreadsheet appear in the same font size and font type. Finally, the boss wants to see the words "Sales Report: First Quarter, 2000" at the top of the spreadsheet, right under the company name.

Drat! You were so close to finishing your spreadsheet, and it looks like you've got your work cut out for you. Don't worry! With Quattro Pro 9, you'll be able to update your spreadsheet to meet everyone's demands in the time it takes you to work through this hour. Open the FYI quarterly sales spreadsheet you completed in Hour 11, "Creating Your First Spreadsheet," roll up your sleeves, and get ready to crank!

Editing the Cells in a Spreadsheet

In order to update your spreadsheet as requested, you'll have to master eight different Quattro Pro editing techniques. In the following sections, you'll learn how to do these tasks:

- Replace the contents of a cell
- Delete the contents of a cell
- Clear a cell of all formatting
- Clear a cell of all contents and formatting
- Delete a cell
- Insert a cell
- Transpose cell content
- Resize cells

Replacing the Contents of a Cell

To replace a cell's contents, click the cell and type in your new entry, which automatically replaces your original data. Hit Enter to register your change, and that's all there is to it—just point, click, and type.

Give it a try in your FYI quarterly sales spreadsheet. The first task you've been asked to perform is to update Baker's and Doe's sales figures for March. The original data for Baker's March sales appear in column E6, and the original data for Doe's March sales appear in column E7. Use point, click, and type to update Baker's and Doe's March sales: replace the contents of cell E6 with 9425 and the contents of cell E7 with 13047.

As shown in Figure 12.1, Quattro Pro automatically applied the existing numeric format (the dollar sign) when you entered these new figures and updated your totals in cells E10, F10, and D13.

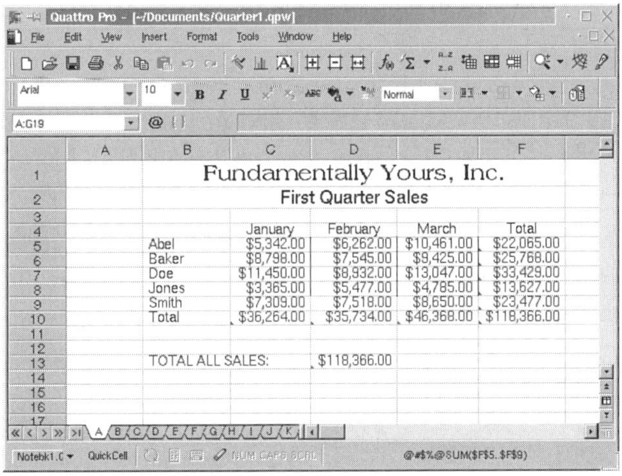

FIGURE 12.1

When you point, click, and type to replace the contents of a cell, Quattro Pro automatically applies existing formatting to your new entry.

To Do: Replace the Contents of a Cell from the Input Line

Although point, click, and type is the easiest way to change the contents of a cell, you can also edit a cell from the Input Line. To see how it works, you'll use the Input Line to correct the spelling of Ann Abell's name:

1. Click to select cell B5, where Abell's name is misspelled as *Abel*.
2. Click anywhere in the Input Line to make it active.
3. To correct the spelling of Ann's last name, you'll need only add an *l* and hit Enter to automatically update the contents of cell B5.

As you can see, the Input Line is best for making small changes because your original entry is preserved, and you can make minor adjustments without retyping the entire entry.

> While you're inputting a change to a cell, you may realize that the Undo command doesn't work. The reason for this is that Quattro Pro's Undo feature only records a change after it has been entered (in other words, after the change is complete and you've hit Enter). Until then, the change isn't recorded, and Undo won't work. If you're in the middle of a change and need to back out of it, hit the Esc key to return to your spreadsheet at the point just before you started making the change.

Deleting the Contents of a Cell

To clear a cell of data without changing the formatting, select the cell and hit the Delete key.

The third task on your list is to give Smith credit for Jones's March sales in recognition of the fact that Jones resigned in February. You could delete the March sales amount for Jones in cell E8. On a scratch pad, you could add Jones's March sales to Smith's to get $13,435. Then you could make the change to cell E9 to update Smith's sales for March.

You're probably asking why you would want to whip out a scratch pad to perform a manual calculation. After all, isn't Quattro Pro 9 supposed to do all the heavy lifting in the math department? The answer is an unequivocal "Yes!"

With Quattro Pro 9's new Paste Special feature, you will cut Jones's March sales figure out of cell E8 and add it directly to Smith's existing sales figure in cell E9.

To Do: Using Paste Special to Perform a Calculation

1. Select cell E8, which contains the sales figures for Jones, and click the Cut button on the toolbar or press Ctrl+X.
2. Select Smith's sales figures in E9.
3. From the menu bar, select Edit, Paste Special to open the Paste Special dialog box, shown in Figure 12.2. At the bottom of the dialog box is the heading Operation. Select Add and click the Paste button.

FIGURE 12.2
The Paste Special dialog box.

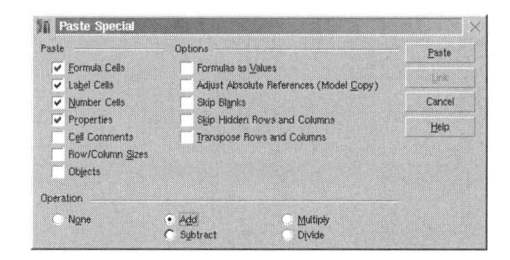

When you return to your spreadsheet, the contents of E8 have been cut from E8 and added to the contents of E9. Not a lick of arithmetic required on your end!

Clearing a Cell of All Formatting

You've been given the heads-up: except for the bottom line, the boss doesn't like to see boldface type in her spreadsheets, and she wants all elements to be the same font size and font type. Fortunately, except for the topmost headings, you've consistently used the same font size and font face for every cell in your FYI quarterly sales spreadsheet.

The headings, however, have several types of formatting applied. As shown in Figure 12.3, the Fundamentally Yours, Inc. banner stretched across the top of the spreadsheet is in boldface, in Americana BT font set at 14-point type. You can tell by selecting cell B1. The Input Line confirms that you're in the cell where the label was originally entered (remember, you aligned your text to center across several columns), and the font type and font size boxes confirm your font settings. The boldface formatting button is depressed, letting you know that your heading is in boldface type.

FIGURE 12.3
You'll need to change the formatting in the headings of your FYI quarterly sales spreadsheet.

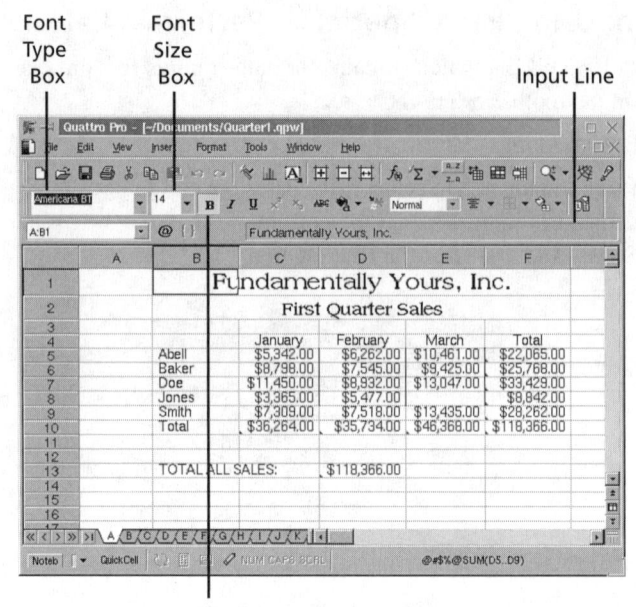

[Figure shows a Quattro Pro spreadsheet with labels: Font Type Box, Font Size Box, Input Line, and Activated Bold Button]

With cell B1 selected, you could manually undo all your formatting in separate steps. Clicking the Bold button on the toolbar, for example, would deactivate the boldface type in your heading. You could also use the drop-down font type and font size boxes to manually conform these settings to the rest of your spreadsheet.

But there's a much faster way to get rid of all the formatting with just a few mouse clicks. With cell B1 selected, click Edit, Clear, Formats from the menu bar. This quick step clears all formatting from the cell, restoring the font type, font size, and cell alignment to the default settings.

Clearing Both Contents and Formatting

You've also got your marching orders for the heading in cell B2. You've got to clear all formatting and edit the text to read "Sales Report: First Quarter, 2000." The easiest way to achieve this is to clear out both the data and all formatting and simply type in the heading the boss prefers.

To zap everything in cell B2, including formatting and content, click B2 and then select Edit, Clear, Cells from the menu bar. All data in the cell is deleted, and the font settings are restored to their defaults. Cell B2 remains active, and you can type in the heading your boss wants to see.

When you're done, your work in progress should look like Figure 12.4.

FIGURE 12.4
So far you've updated Baker's and Doe's March sales figures, corrected Abell's name, given Smith credit for March sales by Jones, and restored your headings to the default format.

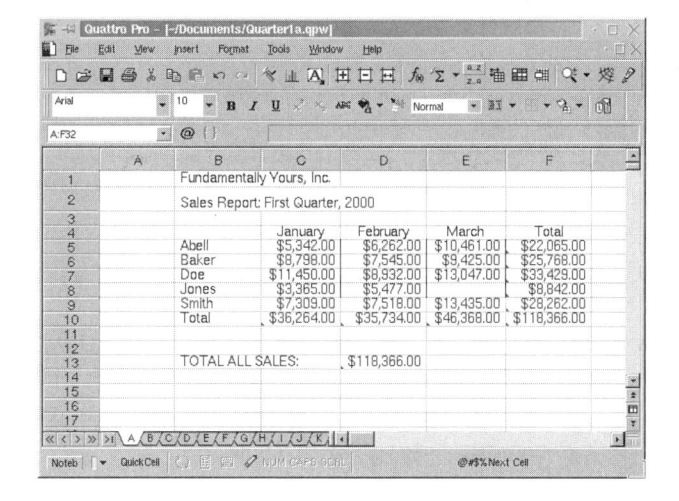

Deleting Cells

Deleting a cell or block is different from clearing a cell's contents and formatting. When you delete a cell, you actually remove the cell from the spreadsheet, causing the cell or cells below, including all formatting, to move up and fill the space.

To delete a cell or block of cells, select the cell or block you want to delete and right-click the selection. In the pop-up menu that opens, select Delete Cells to open the Delete dialog box shown in Figure 12.5. Alternatively, you can open the Delete dialog box by selecting Edit, Delete from the menu.

The Delete dialog box shows the cell or range of cells selected for deletion. Beneath the cells to be deleted are options for adjusting the dimension and span of the deletion. The dimension indicates whether you are deleting a block of cells in a column, row, or sheet, whereas the span indicates whether you are deleting the range of cells selected or every cell within the same dimension.

In Figure 12.5, the selected cells are E:D5..E5. Because these are adjacent cells in the same row, Quattro Pro correctly set the dimension to Rows. The span is set to Partial because Quattro Pro assumes you only want to delete the selected cells, D and E, in row 5. You would set the span to Entire only if you wanted to delete every cell within the same row as your selected cells (in this case, every cell in row 5).

FIGURE 12.5
The Delete dialog box.

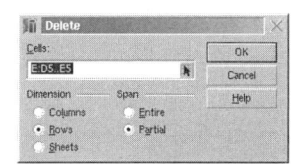

> Be careful using the delete cell feature—you aren't deleting actual cell addresses but merely changing the contents of one or more cell addresses. Remember that Quattro Pro relies on relative cell addresses. As a result, when cells below a deleted selection move up to fill a gap left behind by deleted cells, Quattro Pro formulas that reference the deleted cells may look to these new values, thus affecting your results in ways you may not have intended.

On your FYI quarterly sales spreadsheet, delete block B12..F12. There's no data in these cells, so deleting them won't impact any of your formulas. It will, however, bring the TOTAL ALL SALES cell up to row 12, which may look nicer on the screen and when you print out your spreadsheet later in this hour.

Inserting Cells

You can insert a blank cell or block of cells anywhere in your spreadsheet. When you insert cells into a row, existing cells will move down; when you insert cells into a column, existing cells will move to the right.

You'll need to insert cells into your FYI quarterly sales spreadsheet to achieve two of the additional tasks you've been asked to do: (1) the addition of Zach Zimmer to the roster of sales representatives, and (2) the addition of the first names of all of your sales representatives. Fortunately, the sales department provided you with the data in Tables 12.1 and 12.2.

TABLE 12.1 Supplemental Sales Data, First Quarter, 2000

	January	February	March
Zach Zimmer	$8,690	$12,440	$7,980

TABLE 12.2 FYI Sales Representatives

Sales Representative
Abell, Ann
Baker, Bob
Doe, Don
Jones, Julie
Smith, Sally
Zimmer, Zach

Updating and Printing Your Spreadsheet 239

With this data in hand, it's time to update your FYI quarterly sales spreadsheet to include Zach Zimmer. The best way to do this is to insert a row of cells beneath the sales figures for Smith in row 9. Remember that when you add a row of cells, existing cells drop down from the point of insertion. Therefore, you'll want to insert Zimmer in row 10 and have your totals drop down to row 11.

To Do: Insert a Row of Cells

▼ To Do

1. Select row 10 by placing your cursor over the row 10 heading at the far left of your spreadsheet until you see a right-pointing arrow.
2. Click once to select row 10 in its entirety. Right-click and select Insert from the pop-up menu, as shown in Figure 12.6.
3. You've now got a new, blank row 10 in which to insert Zach Zimmer, and your row of totals has dropped down to row 11. Go ahead and enter Zach Zimmer's sales figures. When you're through, your spreadsheet should look like Figure 12.7.

FIGURE 12.6
To insert a row, right-click a selected row and click Insert from the pop-up menu.

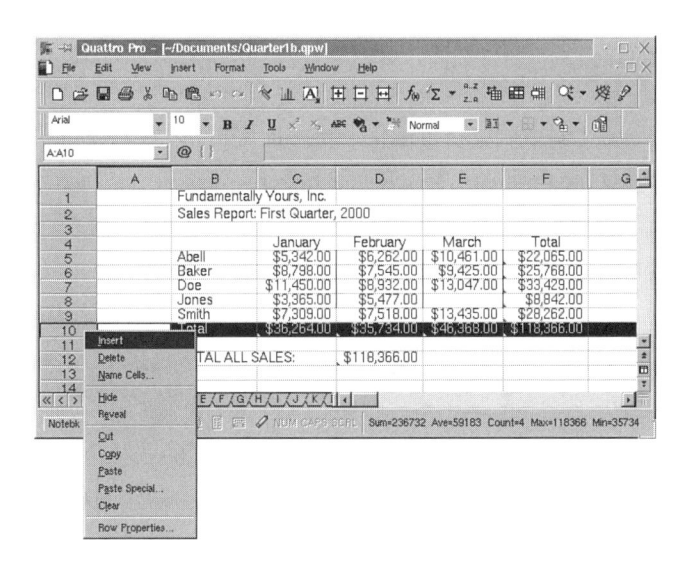

▼

FIGURE 12.7
Zimmer's sales figures assume the proper numeric formatting, but your formulas still need to be updated.

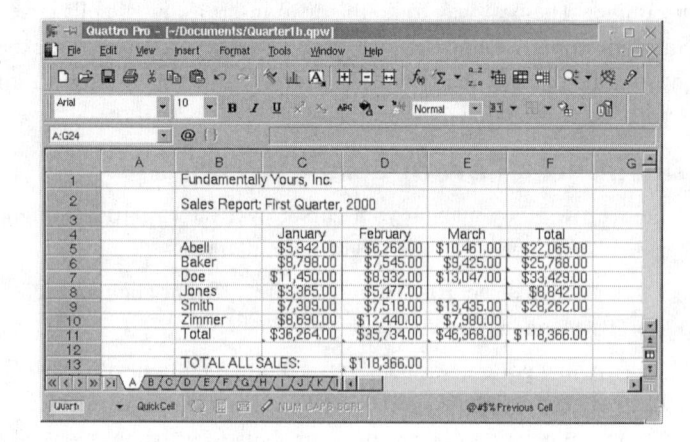

4. Note that you still need to total Zimmer's sales in F10, and the formulas in C11..F11 and D13 need to be updated to reflect Zimmer's sales figures. Go ahead and sum Zimmer's sales figures in F10.
5. Select C11..F11 and clear out the values in the entire cell block.
6. Reset the formulas to include Zimmer's sales figures, and don't forget that F11 needs to be absolute in order for D13 to correctly total all sales figures.

If your spreadsheet looks like Figure 12.8 after adjusting your formulas to reflect Zimmer's sales, you're in excellent shape.

FIGURE 12.8
Your FYI quarterly sales spreadsheet after all formulas have been adjusted for Zimmer.

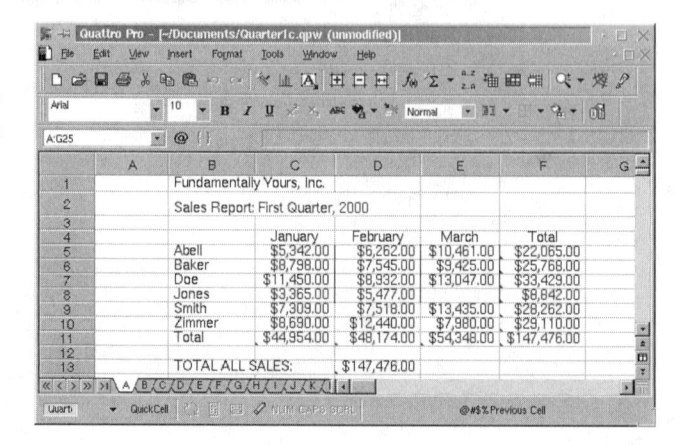

Transposing Cell Contents

Near the end of your task list, you still have to transpose Ann Abell's sales for January and February. Fortunately, Quattro Pro 9 makes this very simple.

Return to your FYI quarterly sales spreadsheet. Ann Abell's January and February sales figures are contained in C5 and D5, respectively. Select C5 and click the Copy button or press Ctrl+C.

Select cell D5 and from the menu bar select Tools, Numeric Tools, Transpose to open the Transpose Cells dialog box. Type **A:D5** in the From line, type **A:C5** in the To line, and click the OK button or hit Enter. When you return to your spreadsheet, C5 now contains the contents of D5, and D5 is still selected. Click the Paste button or hit Ctrl+V to paste the old contents of C5 into D5.

Resizing Columns

The last thing on your to-do list is to add the first names of all the sale representatives so your boss can remember them at tomorrow's meeting. That's easy enough. Use the first names provided in Table 12.2 to update your spreadsheet to your boss's liking.

Chances are, column B is just too narrow to display the full names of your sales representatives onscreen. You need to resize column B to make it just a little wider.

To Do: Resize a Column

1. Place your mouse pointer on the column header at the border between columns B and C until the pointer changes to a black, two-headed arrow.
2. Drag to the right until column B is wide enough and release the mouse. The other columns will retain their sizing and slide to the right to accommodate column B's new size.
3. Alternatively, right-click the column header for column B and select Autowidth from the pop-up menu. Autowidth automatically adjusts the width of a column to accommodate the contents of the cells in the column.

Congratulations! You have completed every additional request and you have no doubt that your spreadsheet will be the talk of the office after tomorrow's big sales meeting. If only you could get the darn thing to print out correctly.

Printing Your Work

You'll wrap up this hour making sure your spreadsheet prints out just the way you've planned. Quattro Pro offers many options for setting up print jobs.

Printing involves two steps:

- *Setting things up*. To produce quality printouts of Quattro Pro 9 spreadsheets, you need to set up your print page, which includes print margins, page breaks, headers and footers, and orientation (portrait or landscape).
- *Previewing your work*. Spreadsheets seem to have a mind of their own when it comes to printouts, but you can take charge by previewing your work before committing it to hard copy. In version 9 of Quattro Pro, the Print Preview feature has been enhanced to include the ability to edit your margin settings directly in Print Preview mode.

The Print Spreadsheet Dialog Box

Open your FYI quarterly sales spreadsheet and try to print it using one of the methods covered in Hour 3, "Common Tasks in WordPerfect Office 2000 for Linux." In case you need a refresher, you can print by selecting File, Print from the menu bar, hitting Ctrl+P, or clicking the Print button on the toolbar.

No matter which method you use, your spreadsheet won't just automatically print. Instead, the Spreadsheet Print dialog box opens, which is unique to Quattro Pro. As shown in Figure 12.9, the Spreadsheet Print dialog box presents several options at the outset, each under its own heading in the dialog box:

- *Current Printer*. This identifies the printer where all your print jobs are headed. If you followed the directions for setting up a printer in Hour 3, the Current Printer should match the default printer you set up in Hour 3. If no printer is listed, review Hour 3 to add and configure a printer.
- *Print*. This gives you control over the scope of the print job, including the number of copies, whether to print the current sheet, the entire notebook, or selected cells, and the range of pages you want to print (from 1 to 999).
- *Copies*. This allows you to set the number of copies to print and whether to collate your print job.
- *Page Setup and Print Preview*. In the bottom-right corner of the Spreadsheet Print dialog box are two buttons that are your gateways to Quattro Pro 9's most powerful print controls: the Page Setup and Print Preview buttons. We'll take a look at each of these tools in the next two sections.

FIGURE 12.9
Quattro Pro 9's unique Spreadsheet Print dialog box.

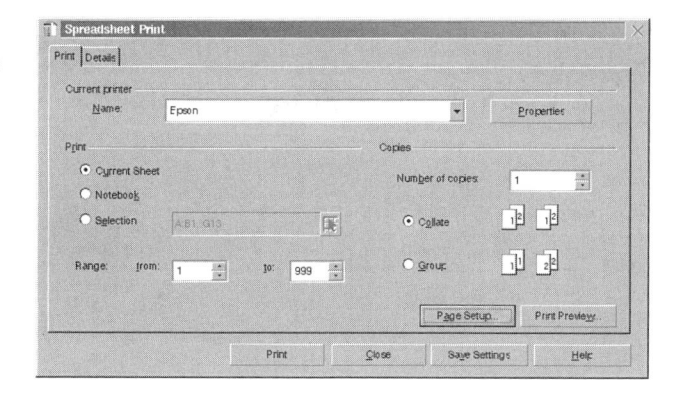

Page Setup

Click the Page Setup button to open the Spreadsheet Page Setup dialog box, which presents six tabs that help you control most aspects of your print job:

- *Paper Type.* As shown in Figure 12.10, the Paper Type tab allows you select the size of the print page and its orientation. The default size is US Letter, and the default orientation is Portrait, which prints your spreadsheet vertically on the page. The Landscape orientation prints your spreadsheet horizontally across the page. For purposes of printing your FYI quarterly sales spreadsheet, the default settings are just fine.

FIGURE 12.10
Setting paper size and orientation on the Paper Type tab.

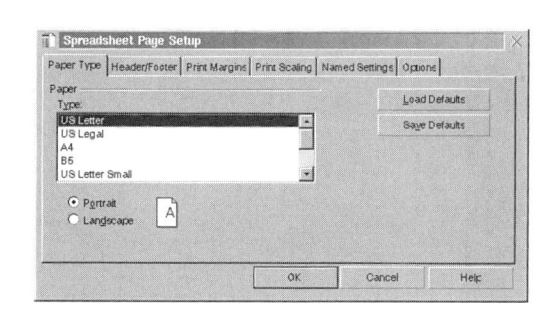

- *Header/Footer.* Headers and footers appear, respectively, at the top and bottom of every page of your spreadsheet, and can be used to place recurring titles, names, comments, or page numbers in a multipage spreadsheet.

    It wouldn't be a bad idea to drop a footer in your FYI quarterly sales spreadsheet to explain why Julie Jones had no sales in March. To do this, in your spreadsheet, insert an asterisk (*) next to Jones's name in cell B8. Hit Ctrl+P to open the Spreadsheet Print dialog box, and click the Page Setup button to open the Spreadsheet Page Setup dialog box.

Select the Header/Footer tab (shown in Figure 12.11). Under Footer, check Create. Click in the box to the right and type **Resigned as of February 28**. Click OK. This takes you back to the Spreadsheet Print dialog box.

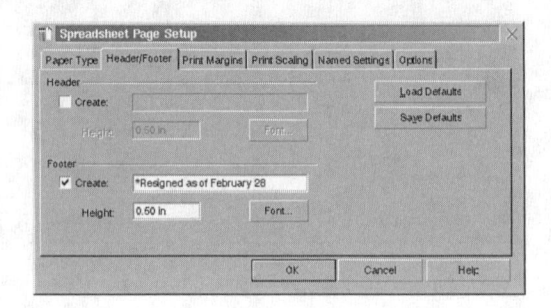

FIGURE 12.11
Adding a footer to your FYI quarterly sales spreadsheet.

To confirm that your footer was properly entered, click the Print Preview button. Your footer appears on the bottom left, barely discernible because of its small size. Double-click the footer to zoom in and confirm that it looks as shown in Figure 12.12. To exit Print Preview, click the button on the far right of the Print Preview toolbar, the one with the printer icon with a blue X running through it. You'll learn more about Print Preview later in this hour.

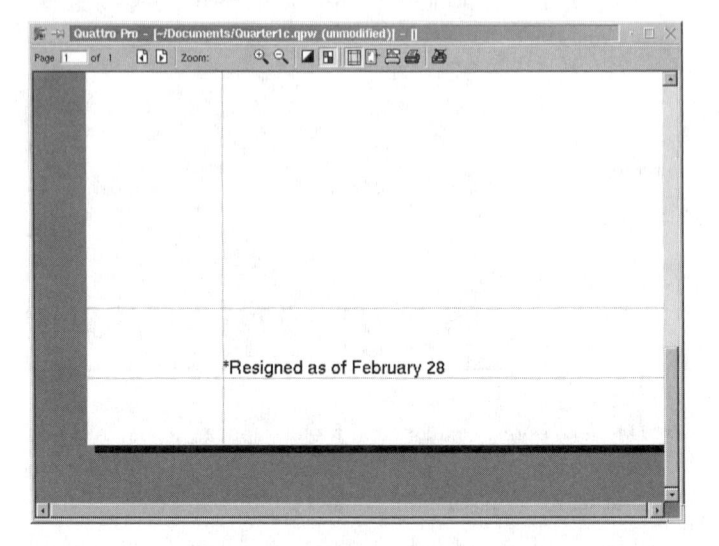

FIGURE 12.12
Zooming in on your footnote in Print Preview mode.

> If you returned to your spreadsheet to check out your new footer, you were probably surprised that it was nowhere to be found. That's because footers, and headers for that matter, aren't entered into the cells of your spreadsheet, the contents of which are the only items viewable onscreen. When in doubt about a header or footer you've entered, the only way to ease your mind is to access it through the Header/Footer tab or to check it out in Print Preview mode.

- *Print Margins.* You control the print area of your spreadsheets from the Print Margins tab. For your FYI quarterly sales spreadsheet, you'll set your margins at one inch all around, meaning that all printing will start one inch from the edge of the page on all four sides. As shown in Figure 12.13, setting your margins at one inch all around is as simple as entering the number 1 in the boxes for top, bottom, left, and right margins.

  The Break Pages check box in the Print Margins tab lets you toggle page breaks on and off for the purposes of printing. By default, Break Pages is on, and your print job will honor all hard page breaks that appear in your spreadsheet. Deactivate Break Pages for printing long spreadsheets on continuous-form paper. Hard page breaks, top and bottom margins, and all headers and footers will be ignored, and your spreadsheet will print out as one continuous document.

FIGURE 12.13
The Print Margins tab set with one-inch margins all around and Break Pages toggled on.

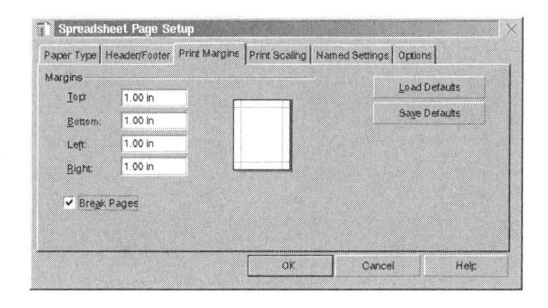

> New in version 9, you can also set your Quattro Pro spreadsheet margins from Print Preview by simply dragging the dotted margin lines across the page.

- *Print Scaling.* Quattro Pro 9 lets you shrink or enlarge your spreadsheet by an exact percentage through the Print Scaling tab. You can also stretch your spreadsheet to print across several pages by specifying the number of pages wide and high on which to print your spreadsheet. Figure 12.14 shows the defaults set to print at 100 percent of normal size, on a single page wide and high.

FIGURE 12.14
The Print Scaling tab with default settings.

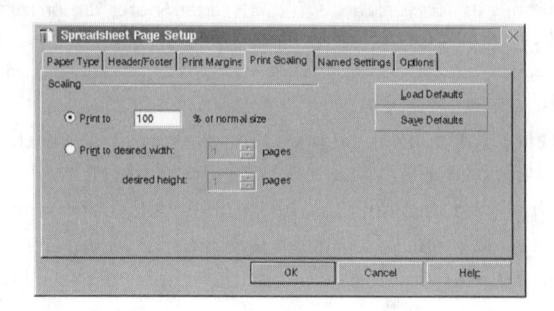

- *Named Settings.* The Named Settings tab allows you to name and save frequently used print settings so that you don't have to reconfigure them when working on a similar print job.

    Give it a try by typing **FYI Quarterly Sales** in the New Set box and clicking the Add button. As shown in Figure 12.15, your new FYI print setting appears in a list below the New Set box. The next time you have to prepare a spreadsheet for an FYI quarterly sales meeting, you can jump to the Named Settings tab, select FYI Quarterly Sales, and click the Use button to use your customized print settings for your new spreadsheet.

FIGURE 12.15
Saving your FYI print settings under the Named Settings tab.

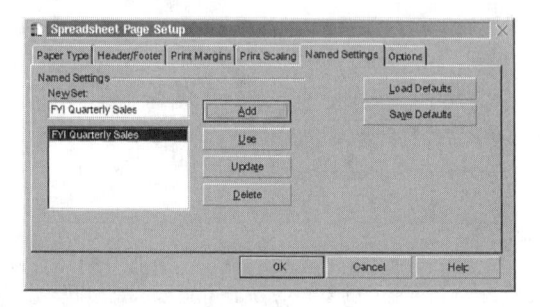

- *Options.* Last but not least is the Options tab, which gives you control over such options as printing gridlines and borders, centering selections on the printed page, and printing cell formulas instead of results.

    One option you might want to try for your FYI quarterly sales spreadsheet is to center your entire spreadsheet on the printed page. As shown in Figure 12.16, this

Updating and Printing Your Spreadsheet 247

is as easy as checking the Center Cells box under Print Options and clicking OK. You can check out the result in Print Preview.

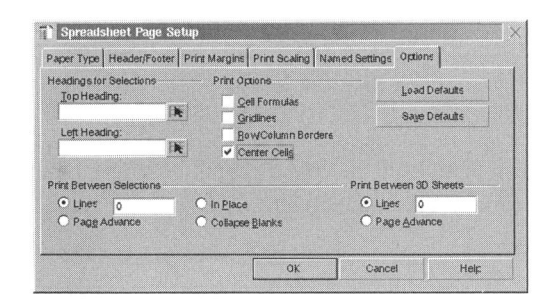

FIGURE 12.16
Printing your spreadsheet in the center of the page is one of many options provided on the Options tab.

Print Preview

Even when you've personally entered all the print settings for a spreadsheet job, it's a good idea to preview your work before sending it to the printer. The Print Preview feature shows you how your spreadsheet will look on the printed page based on the particular printer you are using and the print settings you have selected.

To get into Print Preview mode, select File, Print Preview from the menu bar or click the Print Preview button in the Spreadsheet Print dialog box. Figure 12.17 shows your FYI quarterly sales spreadsheet in Print Preview mode.

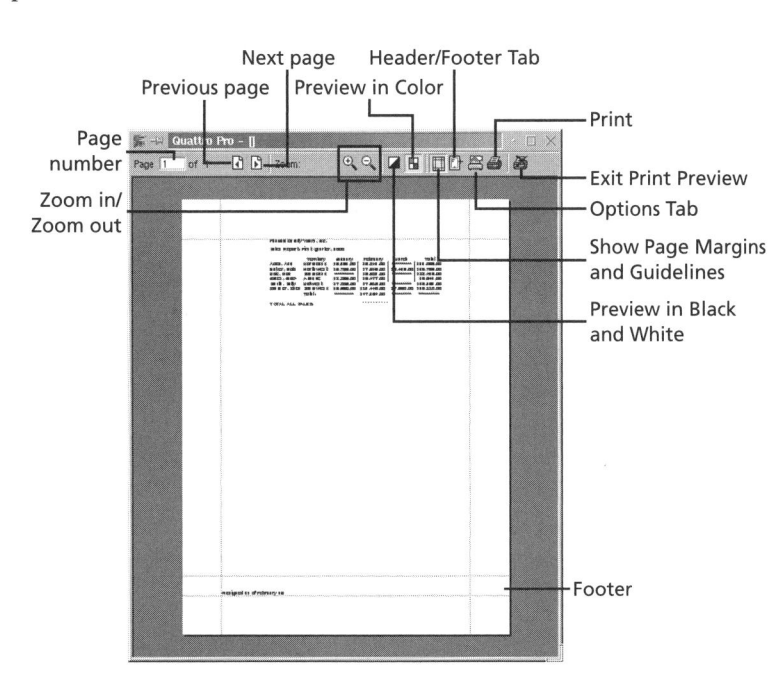

FIGURE 12.17
Your FYI quarterly sales spreadsheet in Print Preview mode.

Aside from giving you a sneak peak at how your spreadsheet will look on the printed page, Print Preview allows you to fine-tune your margin settings by dragging margins across the page until you find the settings that best suit your spreadsheet.

If you think your spreadsheet needs some work, exit Print Preview and make the necessary changes. Otherwise, click the Print button directly from Print Preview to send your work to the printer.

Congratulations! You completed all the last-minute changes that were requested, and you still had plenty of time to print out enough copies of your spreadsheet for tomorrow's big meeting. Well done!

Summary

In this hour you were introduced to many techniques for editing and updating an existing spreadsheet in Quattro Pro. Through a series of hands-on exercises, you actually got to perform many advanced Quattro Pro editing techniques to help you take full advantage of the program's powerful features. You also learned about the many print options involved in getting your spreadsheets to print correctly as well as how to preview your work in Quattro Pro 9's newly enhanced Print Preview mode.

In the next hour, you'll learn some of the advanced spreadsheet design techniques and features available in Quattro Pro 9, such as applying built-in formats and adding borders, text colors, and backgrounds. You'll also see how to enhance your spreadsheets with charts that give your data more of an impact.

Q&A

Q Can I drag and drop a block of cells from one location to another without disturbing my cell formatting?

A Sure. Quattro Pro 9 is smart enough to include all formatting when you move a block of contiguous cells from one location to another. Just select the block of cells you want to move, click it, and hold down your mouse button until a four-way arrow appears. Drag your selection to the desired insertion point—an outline of your selection will appear, moving in synch with your mouse pointer. When you reach the desired location, release the mouse and your data is moved, with the formatting intact. Note that to use drag and drop to copy, instead of move, a block of contiguous cells, use the same procedure but hold down the Ctrl key before releasing the mouse button. When a "plus" sign appears, you'll know you're about to insert a copy of the selected cells.

Q Can I password-protect my Quattro Pro 9 notebooks?

A Of course, although the procedure for assigning a password in Quattro Pro 9 is less than intuitive. To assign a password, select Format, Notebook from the menu bar to open the Active Notebook dialog box. Navigate to the Password Level tab, which presents five security-level options for your password: None, Low, Medium, High, and Edit with Controls Only. Click each option to see a description of the level of security. Select a password option other than None and click OK. At the prompt, enter a password, hit Enter, then retype your password at the Verify Password prompt. The next time you open the notebook, you'll be prompted to verify the password.

Workshop

The Workshop contains quiz questions and exercises to help reinforce what you've learned in this hour. If you get stuck, the answers can be found in Appendix B, "Answers to Quiz Questions."

Quiz

Match the letter of the term to the phrase that describes it:

1. Removes cell formatting.
2. The keyboard shortcut for Print.
3. Allows you to make minor edits to a cell without having to retype the cell contents.
4. Allows you to see how your spreadsheet will print.
5. You can transpose cells with this feature.
6. Removes the contents lof a selected cell without removing formatting.
7. The direction existing columns move when a new column is inserted.

A. Paste Special

B. Edit, Clear, Values

C. Right

D. Double-clicking

E. Input Line

F. Header/Footer

G. Edit, Clear, Formats

8. The direction existing rows move when a new row is inserted.
9. Use this to print page numbers on a multipage spreadsheet.
10. This lets you edit contents directly in a cell.

H. Down

I. Print Preview

J. Ctrl+P

Exercises

1. Right before your big sales meeting, you wake up in the middle of the night uncertain of whether the bottom line total sales figure appears in boldface on your spreadsheet. Make sure that it does.
2. Print out only Ann Abell's sales.
3. Print your FYI quarterly sales spreadsheet so that all formulas are displayed.

HOUR 13

Advanced Spreadsheet Design

You're ready to move on to Quattro Pro 9's advanced tools for designing sophisticated spreadsheets that make a lasting impression. From automated formatting features, to full-color charts, you'll be designing professional-looking spreadsheets in no time!

In this hour you will

- Explore Quattro Pro's automated formatting features.
- Add color, borders, and other formatting to enhance your spreadsheets.
- Create and manipulate a chart from your spreadsheet data.

Overview of Advanced Formatting Techniques

Numbers are a Quattro Pro 9 spreadsheet's stock in trade, but let's face it—there's nothing inherently exciting about numbers presented on a page.

Quattro Pro 9 includes powerful formatting tools that allow you to bring some much-needed creativity to how your spreadsheet data is presented. You've already learned a few basic formatting features available in Quattro Pro 9, such as row and column sizing, cell alignment, and numeric formatting. But these features are only a fraction of what Quattro Pro 9 can do! Table 13.1 summarizes some of the advanced yet easy-to-use formatting tools you'll be working with in this hour.

TABLE 13.1 Advanced Formatting Tools

Feature	What It Does
Project Template	Lets you begin new spreadsheets with predefined formatting
Page View	Displays headers, footers, margins, page breaks, and formatting exactly as they will print
Styles	Allows you to define and apply formatting styles to all or part of a spreadsheet
QuickFormat	Lets you quickly copy formatting from one cell or block to another
SpeedFormat	Automatically applies predefined formatting styles to selected areas
Lines and Borders	Enables you to put lines and borders in and around selected cells
Fill/Text Color	Lets you change the background color of a cell and the color of text within a cell
Header and Footer	Inserts space at the top or bottom of a sheet for recurring information such as page numbers, names, and dates

Working With PerfectExpert Projects

PerfectExpert Projects come in handy for common spreadsheet jobs such as budgets, expense reports, and mortgage amortizations. Quattro Pro 9 comes packaged with many Projects, and more are available from Corel's Web site. You can even customize an existing Project and save it as a new Project, or you can create your own Project from scratch.

To Do: Start a Project

▼ To Do

1. Launch Quattro Pro and select File, New From Project from the menu bar.
2. With the Create New tab selected, as shown in Figure 13.1, the PerfectExpert lists all of Quattro Pro 9's Projects.
3. Let's say you're looking to relocate, and you need to perform a quick analysis of whether to rent or buy a new home. From the Create New tab in the PerfectExpert, scroll down the list of Projects to find the Home Rent or Buy Analysis Project.

Advanced Spreadsheet Design   253

FIGURE 13.1
Use the PerfectExpert to launch Quattro Pro 9's Projects.

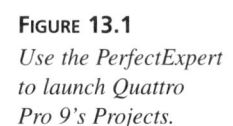

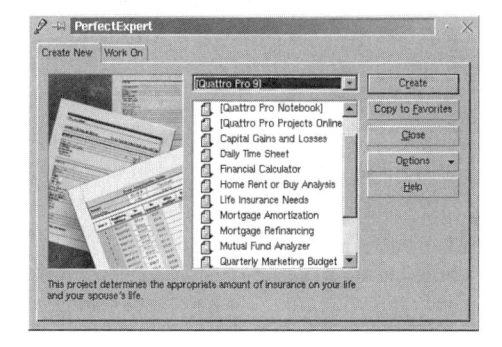

4. Double-click it or select it and click the Create button. The PerfectExpert takes it from there to generate the attractive spreadsheet shown in Figure 13.2.

FIGURE 13.2
The Home Rent or Buy Analysis Project with sample data activated.

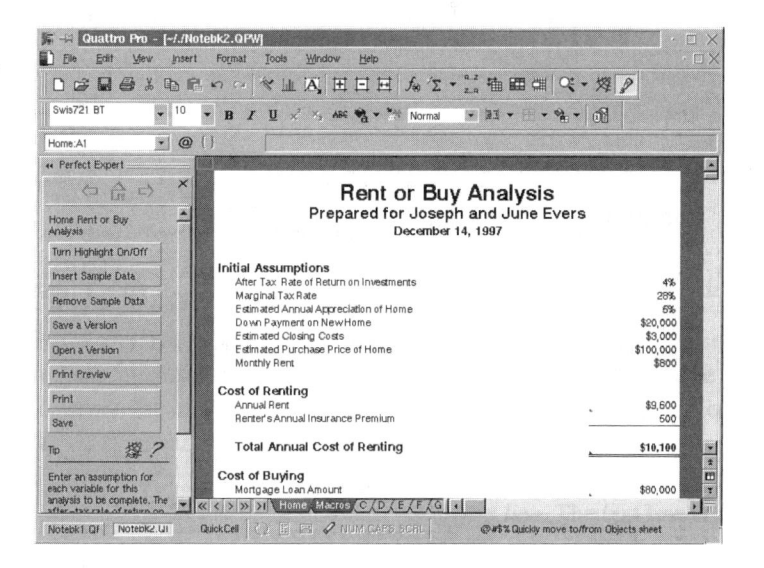

Note that your completed spreadsheet contains all the formatting and formulas you need—all that's left for you to do is enter data. Nevertheless, the PerfectExpert doesn't leave you hanging—the PerfectExpert window stays open on the left side of the screen to assist you in entering data and customizing your new spreadsheet. For example, you can tell the PerfectExpert to give you a quick look at the type of data you'll need for your spreadsheet by clicking the Enter Sample Data button in the PerfectExpert window.

Sometimes PerfectExpert Projects don't quite cut it. Whether you need to add or delete certain information or just tidy up the formatting, it's easy to create your own PerfectExpert Project from an existing Project. To give it a try, from the Corel Application Starter, select Applications, WordPerfect Office 2000, Corel New Project to open the PerfectExpert dialog box. In the top drop-down menu, select Quattro Pro 9 to view all spreadsheet Projects. Select the Statement of Net Worth Project and click Create. When asked whether you want to disable all macros in the document, click No.

> As you learned in Hour 9, "Advanced WordPerfect 9 Techniques," macros are tiny programs you can use to automate common tasks. Macros are also used to create PerfectExpert Projects. Every time you create a document containing macros, you're warned that macros may contain computer viruses, and you're given the option of disabling all macros. If you're uncertain about the origin of a document, click Yes to disable all macros. If you're simply opening a PerfectExpert Project, you're safe in clicking No to keep all macros enabled. If seeing this warning every time you begin a new project really bugs you, you can turn it off by checking the Do Not Show This Message Again box at the bottom-left corner of the warning window.

To Do: Customize Your Template

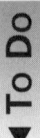

1. When your Net Worth document opens, fill in your name and the date as prompted.
2. To customize it, select cell B5 and increase the font size of the ASSETS label to 16 points. Do the same for the LIABILITIES label in cell F5.
3. Save your new spreadsheet to your Documents directory and name it something fun such as All My Worldly Possessions. Close your spreadsheet without closing Quattro Pro 9.
4. From the menu bar, select New From Project to open the PerfectExpert dialog box. Click the Options button and select Add Project to open the Add Project Wizard. The Add Project Wizard gives you two choices: Add an Existing Project and Add Another Document. To make a new Project out of your All My Worldly Possessions document, select Add Another Document and click Next.
5. At the prompts, type in the name and a description of your new Project. Click Next.
6. The final step is to tell the Add Project Wizard where to find your new Project. Click the Browse button, navigate to /My Home/Documents, and double-click All My Worldly Possessions.
7. Click Finish and the PerfectExpert displays a quick note to confirm that your Project has been added.

Test your new project by opening the PerfectExpert and navigating to the Quattro Pro 9 Projects. Navigate down the list of projects to confirm that `All My Worldly Possessions` has been added. Double-click it to launch your Project and confirm that everything works as planned.

Working in Styles

As you may recall from Hour 5, "Formatting WordPerfect 9 Documents," a *style* is a predefined set of formatting properties that can be applied to selected text. You'll be glad to know that styles aren't limited to WordPerfect—you can use styles to quickly format a cell or block of cells in Quattro Pro 9.

By default, Quattro Pro applies the Normal style to every cell in every spreadsheet. Although you cannot edit the Normal style, you can designate another style as the default or use other formatting or styles to change the look of any cell. Quattro Pro comes with several built-in styles you can customize and use, but you can also create your own styles and obtain additional styles from Corel's Web site.

To create your own style, let's return to your FYI quarterly sales spreadsheet. Assume you want to create a heading style that you can use for the title of your FYI spreadsheet. You've browsed the available fonts and decide you want your FYI heading style to apply the Americana BT font in boldface 14-point type. You'd also like to make the text color stand out in navy blue over a gold background.

To Do: Create a Custom Style

1. To create your custom style, open your FYI quarterly sales spreadsheet.
2. From the menu bar, select Format, Styles to open the Styles dialog box shown in Figure 13.3.
3. In the open box below Define Style For, type **FYI Heading** as the name of your new style.
4. The Included Properties section of the Styles dialog box gives you seven formatting options to customize your style: Alignment, Format, Protection, Line Drawing, Shading, Font, and Text Color. For your FYI Heading style, you want to deselect all but the Shading, Font, and Text Color properties.

FIGURE 13.3
Create a custom style in the Quattro Pro 9 Styles dialog box.

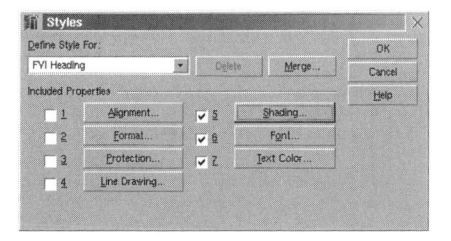

5. Now set your properties one by one. Click the Shading button to open the Shading dialog box shown in Figure 13.4.

6. Quattro Pro's Shading dialog box is a little confusing. It has two color boxes: the Pattern Color box and the Background Color box. These boxes relate to the various pattern boxes shown in Figure 13.4. On your screen these patterns are displayed in two colors: blue and white. When you select a pattern color, the color you select is what is shown in blue in the pattern boxes; when you select a background color, the color you select is what is shown in white in the pattern boxes.

7. Here's the tricky part: To make the background of your cell gold, select the solid blue pattern box. Then click the Pattern Color box, select the gold button on the drop-down color palette, and click OK. It makes no difference what Background Color is set to—your selection of the solid pattern preempts any background color setting.

FIGURE 13.4

You can create styles with custom patterns and colors from the Shading dialog box.

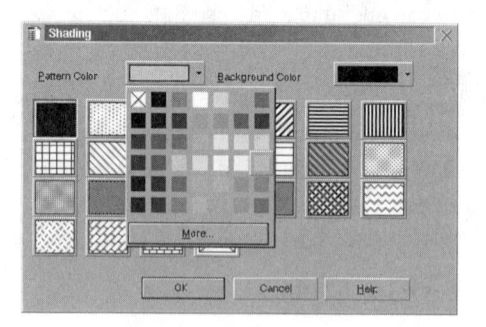

8. In the Styles dialog box, click the Font button to open the Font dialog box shown in Figure 13.5. From this dialog box you can configure three of the desired settings for your font: font face (Americana BT), font size (14 points), and font appearance (bold). Make these selections (note the preview that appears at the bottom of the Font dialog box) and click OK.

FIGURE 13.5

Configure your font face, size, and appearance in the Font dialog box.

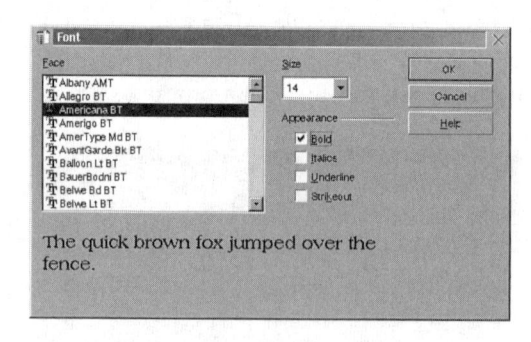

Advanced Spreadsheet Design

9. Click the Text Color button to open the Color Selection dialog box shown in Figure 13.6.
10. Click the Text Color box and select the navy blue square from the drop-down color palette. When the Text Color box changes to navy blue, click OK.
11. Click OK to exit out of the Styles dialog box and return to your FYI spreadsheet.

FIGURE 13.6
You can change the color of your text from the Color Selection dialog box.

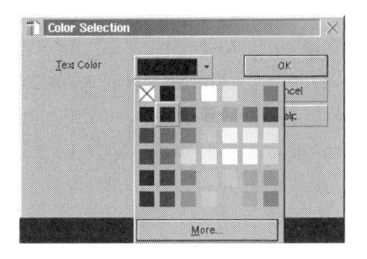

12. To apply your new style, select cell B1, which contains the heading "Fundamentally Yours, Inc." Click the drop-down Style box on the Property Bar and select your FYI Heading style. As shown in Figure 13.7, your new style is automatically applied to the selected cell.

FIGURE 13.7
Your new FYI Heading style is applied to cell B1 in the FYI quarterly sales spreadsheet.

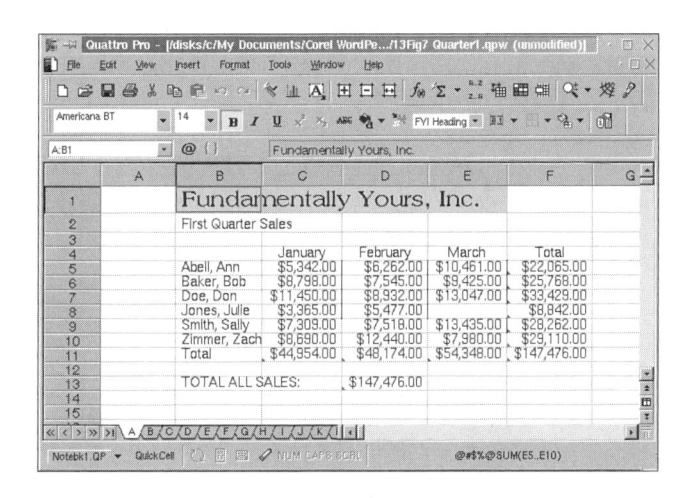

> To edit a style, select Format, Styles from the menu bar to open the Styles dialog box. From the Define Style For drop-down menu, select the style you want to edit. Select the properties you want to include or exclude in the style, edit them as necessary, and click OK. The original style is changed to include your new settings.

Rolling Over with QuickFormat

To apply the same formatting to many cells, you could create a style and manually apply it to as many cells as you like. You could also save yourself a great deal of time by using QuickFormat, which is like "copy and paste" for formatting. QuickFormat allows you to copy the formatting properties of one cell into one or more other cells with just a few mouse clicks.

Using QuickFormat is a snap. Turning back to your FYI quarterly sales spreadsheet, say you're so impressed with your FYI Header style that you want to apply the same formatting to cells B5 through B10, which contain the names of the sales reps, and B11, labeled "Total." Instead of manually applying the FYI Header style to each of these cells, you can you can use QuickFormat.

To Do: Use QuickFormat

1. Your FYI Heading style was applied to cell B1, so that's where you want to start. With B1 selected, click the QuickFormat button on the Notebook toolbar (it's the button that looks just like a paint roller).

2. When you move your mouse pointer back into the spreadsheet window, you'll notice that it has turned into a paint roller. Roll, or drag, your mouse pointer over cells B5 through B11 until they are all selected. Let go of your mouse, and you've "QuickFormatted" cells B5 through B11 with the FYI Header style. When you're done, your FYI quarterly sales spreadsheet should look like Figure 13.8.

FIGURE 13.8

The results of using QuickFormat to copy the format of B1 to cells B5 through B11.

> QuickFormat remains active until you deselect the QuickFormat button on the Notebook toolbar. Although this makes it very easy to apply QuickFormat to many cells or blocks of cells at a time, be careful to avoid unintentionally clicking a cell while QuickFormat is active. Accidentally selecting one or more cells before you realize QuickFormat is on changes the format of more cells than you intended, thus wasting whatever time QuickFormat saved you in the first place.

SpeedFormatting in a Single Bound

With SpeedFormat, you can apply a professional formatting design to an entire spreadsheet in just a few seconds. Quattro Pro 9 includes a number of SpeedFormat designs for you to use.

When you left your FYI quarterly sales spreadsheet in Figure 13.8, the dollar amounts in cells C5..F11 needed some formatting work. You can polish them up with an existing Quattro Pro SpeedFormat design.

Select block C5..F11 and click the SpeedFormat button on the Notebook toolbar (see Figure 13.9) to open the SpeedFormat dialog box in Figure 13.10. The SpeedFormat dialog box has three components: the Formats menu, which lists more than 20 designs, the Include items, by which you control various components of the design, and the Example window, which provides a preview of the design. To see how these three components work together, you're going to use a SpeedFormat design called Yellow3 to touch up your FYI quarterly sales spreadsheet.

Navigate through the Formats menu and select Yellow3. With Yellow3 selected, the Example window shows you a preview of the Yellow3 design as it will appear if you leave checked all the Include items at the bottom of the SpeedFormat dialog box. Keeping in mind the cells selected, recall that you did not select a block of cells with a column or row heading; your block of cells were, however, previously formatted for numeric currency. You should therefore deselect the Numeric, Column Heading, and Row Heading items under Include so that these SpeedFormat items don't override work you've already done. With your selections made, click OK to return to your newly "SpeedFormatted" spreadsheet.

FIGURE 13.9
The SpeedFormat button on the Notebook toolbar.

FIGURE 13.10

Select and configure an existing SpeedFormat design.

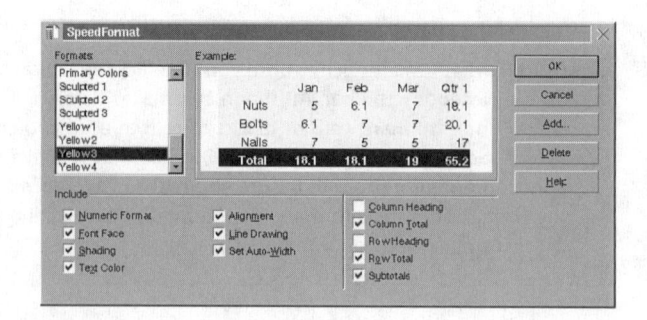

> If you hadn't deselected Numeric under the Include items, SpeedFormat would have replaced your currency formatting with Yellow3's own numeric formatting. When applying SpeedFormat to cells that include previous formatting, be careful to deselect items that you don't want SpeedFormat to override.

You may find yourself repeatedly using your own formatting design in all your spreadsheets. Why not use it to create your own custom SpeedFormat design?

To Do: Create Your Own SpeedFormat Design

1. Open a spreadsheet that includes the formatting you want to use.
2. Open the SpeedFormat dialog box and click the Add button. As shown in Figure 13.11, you'll be prompted to enter a name for your new SpeedFormat and to provide the cell addresses for a block of cells that utilize the desired formatting. In Figure 13.11, I've called my new SpeedFormat True Love, and I've designated cells B4..F11 on sheet A as my "example cells."

FIGURE 13.11

Creating a custom SpeedFormat requires little more than naming your design and providing Quattro Pro 9 with example cells from an existing spreadsheet.

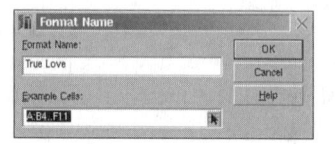

> In order to create a custom SpeedFormat style, your example cells must include a block of cells at least three rows by three columns in size.

Advanced Spreadsheet Design

> Instead of manually entering the cell addresses for the example cells, you can return to your spreadsheet and drag to select the cell block you want to designate. To use this method, click the tiny gray box with the black mouse pointer that sits within the Example Cells window. The Format Name dialog box will minimize to show only its title bar, and you can access your spreadsheet to drag your mouse pointer over the cells you want to use. When your example cells are selected, click once on the minimized Format Name title bar to restore the dialog box with your example cells automatically entered.

3. When you've completed these steps, click OK to return to the SpeedFormat dialog box. As shown in Figure 13.12, your custom SpeedFormat design is automatically added to the Formats menu.

FIGURE 13.12
Your custom SpeedFormat is automatically added to the list of designs. You can use it just like any other SpeedFormat design.

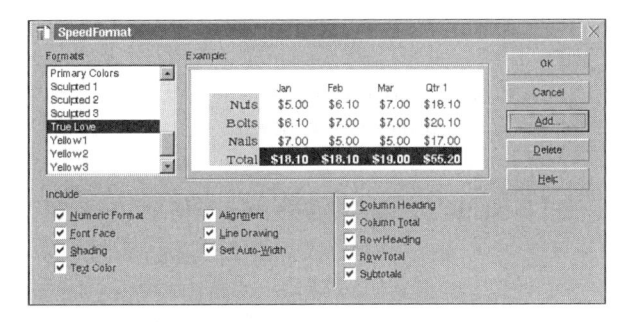

Using Lines and Borders

You can quickly place lines under, above, between, or around cells or blocks of cells by using the line-drawing button on the Property Bar. Returning to your FYI quarterly sales spreadsheet, try using this feature to put a bold border around cells B13..D13 to box the cells together.

To Do: Add a Border

1. Select block B13..D13.
2. Click the down-pointing arrow next to the line drawing button on the Property Bar to drop down the line-drawing palette, shown in Figure 13.13.
3. Select the bold border item at the bottom-right corner of the palette to apply it to cells B13..D13.

FIGURE 13.13
To quickly draw lines around a selected cell or block of cells, use the line-drawing palette, available on the Property Bar.

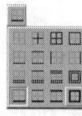

You can exercise greater control over borders applied to active cells by selecting a range of cells and accessing Format, Selection from the menu bar. In the Active Cells dialog box, navigate to the Border tab shown in Figure 13.14.

The Border tab gives you control over three components of a border: Line Segments, Border Type, and Border Color. Line Segments dictates which lines around each cell become part of the viewable border. Selecting All means that every line that comprises each active cell will become part of the applied border. Selecting Outline means that only the outside lines around the active block of cells will become part of the viewable border. Naturally, selecting Inside leaves untouched the outside lines around the active block, and all the interior lines within the cell selection become part of the viewable border.

Border Type and Border Color are easily controlled via drop-down palettes that let you select from a variety of lines for Border Type and colors for Border Color.

FIGURE 13.14
The Border tab in the Active Cells dialog box gives you control over the scope, type, and color of the border to be applied to all active cells.

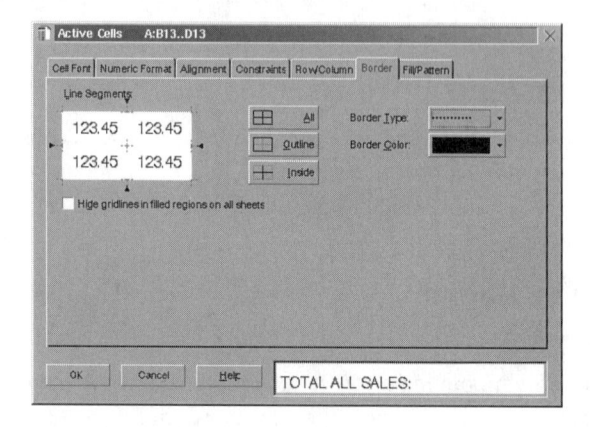

Working in Color

Adding fill and text color is a great way to produce effective and attractive Quattro Pro 9 spreadsheets. Fill color refers to the actual color of a cell—think of it as "filling" your cell with glorious color. Text color refers to the color of your text. Finding the right combinations of fill and text colors can be challenging, but if done well, it can lift your spreadsheets to a whole new level.

If you're tired of looking at the same old black text on white paper spreadsheets, this section is sure to be a blast!

Changing Text Color

Let's return to your FYI quarterly sales spreadsheet to explore how color can be used to jazz things up. You've already placed a bold border around cells B13..D13, but adding a touch of color will really emphasize the total sales results for the quarter.

Let's turn to text color first. Select cells B13..D13 and click the Property Bar's Text Color button, shown in Figure 13.15. This opens the Standard Colors palette, from which you can apply a color to your selected text by simply clicking one of the color buttons on the palette. To see a larger selection of colors, click the More button at the bottom of the Standard Colors palette.

FIGURE 13.15
The Text Color button on the Property Bar.

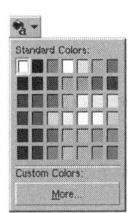

Note that as you move your cursor over the color buttons in the Standard Colors palette, Real-Time Preview actually applies each color to the text selection in your spreadsheet, allowing you to sample several colors until you find one that's just perfect. For this exercise, select a dark green color and apply it to the selected text.

Fill color works much the same way as text color.

To Do: Fill Cells with Color

1. With cells B13..D13 selected, click the Fill Color button on the Property Bar, as shown in Figure 13.16.
2. In order to emphasize cells B13..D13 without clouding the dark green color applied to the text, select a bright color, such as yellow or orange, to fill the selected cells. Try to avoid going too bright, though, as Quattro Pro's flashy neon colors are probably inappropriate for this particular business spreadsheet.

FIGURE 13.16
Use the Fill Color button on the Property Bar to "fill" your cells with color.

Inserting Headers and Footers

Headers and footers allow you to insert repeating information, such as page numbers and dates, on every page of a spreadsheet. The real power of headers and footers lies in the data codes inserted within them. Data codes allow the information in your header/footer to be automatically updated. For example, a "current date" code inserted within a footer automatically displays the current date every time you open the spreadsheet.

Table 13.2 shows a few of the header/footer codes you can insert.

TABLE 13.2 Sample Header/Footer Codes

Code	What It Does
#D	Displays the current date
#p	Displays the current page number
#P	Displays the number of pages in a document
#t	Displays the current time
#n	Moves to a new line
#f	Inserts the notebook's filename
	(vertical bar)	Centers text that follows
|| (two vertical bars)	Right-aligns text that follows

To Do: Insert a Header

For this example, we'll create a header that displays not only the current page but also the total number of pages. Here are the steps to follow:

1. Display your spreadsheet in Page View by selecting View, Page from the menu bar. Remember, only in Page View and Print Preview mode are you able to see headers/footers on the screen.
2. Select File, Page Setup from the menu bar to open the Spreadsheet Page Setup dialog box.
3. Navigate to the Header/Footer tab shown in Figure 13.17.
4. Click the Create box under Header and type **Page #p of #P**, where #p is the code for the current page number and #P is the code for the total number of pages. The rest of the entry is regular text to provide context for what the codes will actually display in your header.

FIGURE 13.17
Creating a header that displays page numbers requires the entry of codes on the Header/Footer tab of the Spreadsheet Page Setup dialog box.

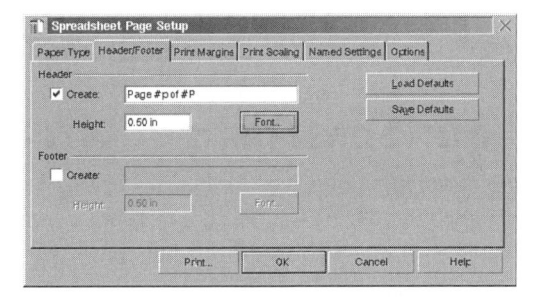

5. As shown in Figure 13.18, the header translates the code to show that you're currently on page 1 of 1 in your FYI quarterly sales spreadsheet. As you add pages to your spreadsheet, your header will automatically change to reflect the current page and the total number of pages.

To edit your header, double-click it in Page View. The display changes to show you the underlying code, and you can edit it directly in the header on your spreadsheet. When you're through making your changes, click anywhere in your spreadsheet to exit the header and view the result of your changes, which automatically take effect.

FIGURE 13.18
In Page View, your header appears as it will look when you print your spreadsheet. Double-click the header to access and edit the underlying data codes.

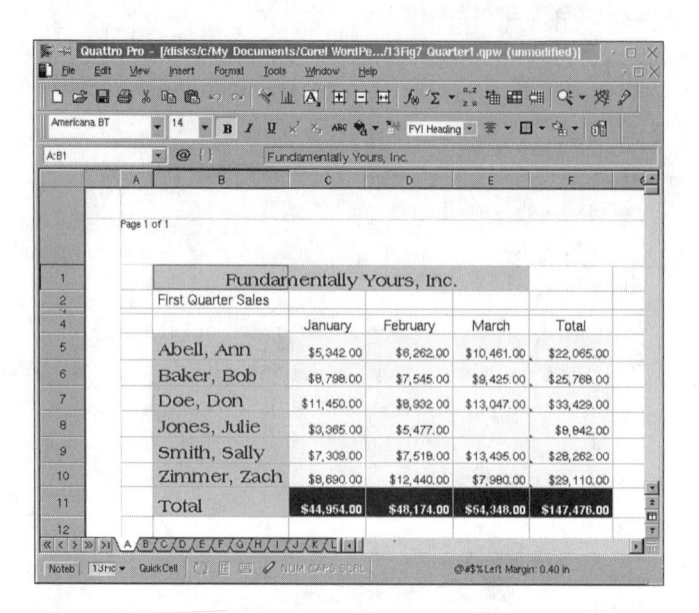

Enhancing Your Spreadsheet with Charts

You can strengthen your presentation even further by creating a chart that graphically depicts the data contained in your FYI quarterly sales spreadsheet. Quattro Pro 9 includes powerful tools to turn your spreadsheets into many types of charts and graphs that update automatically to reflect changes in your spreadsheet data. It's pretty amazing stuff.

Creating a Chart

For the rest of this hour, you'll create and configure a simple bar chart to summarize FYI's first quarter sales in a single, colorful glance. Quattro Pro 9 offers three ways to create a chart:

- You can select Insert, Chart from the menu bar to open the Chart Expert, which will walk you through five simple steps to create a chart.
- You can right-click the cell in which you want to place a chart, select New Custom Chart from the pop-up menu, and build your chart from scratch in the New Custom Chart dialog box.
- Finally, you can select the data to be featured in your chart and click the QuickChart button on the Notebook toolbar. Select a chart style from the drop-down chart palette and then click within your sheet at the location you want the chart inserted.

Advanced Spreadsheet Design

Of the three methods, the first—the Chart Expert—provides the fairest balance between ease of use and flexibility. For this reason, you'll use the Chart Expert to create a "floating" chart—that is, a chart that will float on the same sheet as your FYI quarterly sales spreadsheet.

> In additional to floating charts, Quattro Pro 9 allows you to create free-standing charts. The only difference is that a floating chart resides on the same sheet as an existing spreadsheet, whereas a freestanding chart resides independently on its own sheet.

Let's say you want to create a chart that shows each sales representative's monthly performance relative to cumulative sales for the quarter. The Chart Expert breaks this down into five easy steps: select the data you want to use in your spreadsheet, choose a general chart type, choose a specific chart type, add titles and select a destination, and choose a color scheme for your chart.

Step 1: Select Chart Data

With your FYI quarterly sales spreadsheet open, select Insert, Chart from the menu bar to launch the Chart Expert shown in Figure 13.19. The Chart Expert opens to step 1 of 5, and asks you to identify the data to be used in your chart. Because we'll be incorporating the sales data, sales representatives, and relevant months within the chart, type in **B4..F11** in the Chart Data text box. A preview of your chart appears in the left window pane of the Chart Expert. Click Next.

FIGURE 13.19

In step 1, the Chart Expert asks you to identify by cell address the spreadsheet data to be used in your chart.

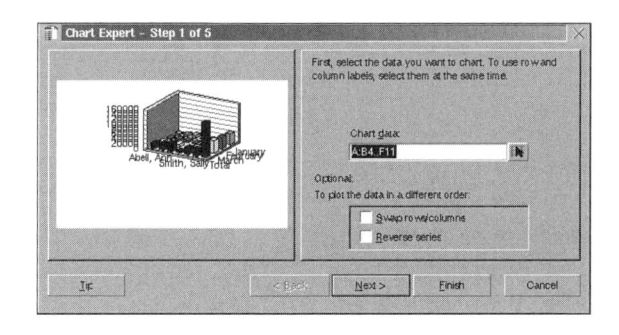

> As you learned earlier in creating your own SpeedFormat design, instead of manually entering the cell addresses for the chart data, you can return to your spreadsheet and drag to select the cell block you want to designate. To use this method, click the tiny gray box with the black mouse pointer that sits within the Chart Data text box. The Chart Expert dialog box minimizes to show only its title bar, so you can access your spreadsheet to drag your mouse pointer over the cells you want to use. When your Chart Data cells are selected, click the minimized Chart Expert title bar to restore the dialog box with your Chart Data cells automatically entered.

Steps 2 and 3: Select a Chart Type

In step 2, the Chart Expert asks you to select a general chart type. As shown in Figure 13.20, you have six chart types to choose from: Bar, Pie, Specialty, Rotated Bar, Line or Area, and Expert's Choice. Try clicking each option for a preview of how each chart type will display your data. The Expert's Choice option is the Chart Expert's suggestion based on the data you've selected for inclusion. For this exercise, select Rotated Bar and click Next.

FIGURE 13.20

In step 2, you select the general type of chart you want to create.

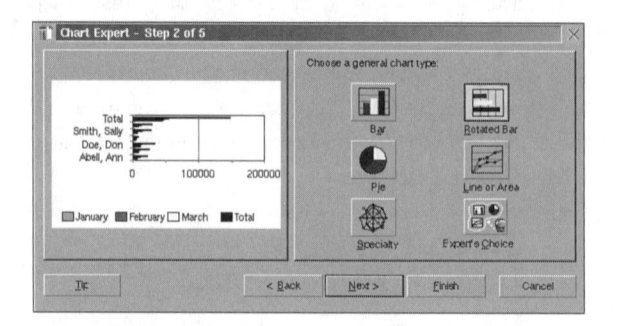

In step 3, you're presented with more specific chart types based on the general chart you selected in step 2. As shown in Figure 13.21, your selection in step 2 results in 9 specific chart types to choose from in step 3. Note that you can continue to click each option for a preview in the left side of the Chart Expert. If you are unhappy with your options, you can also click the Back button to return to any prior step and change your selections. For this exercise, select the very first option presented in step 3 and click Next.

FIGURE 13.21
In step 3, you select a specific chart type.

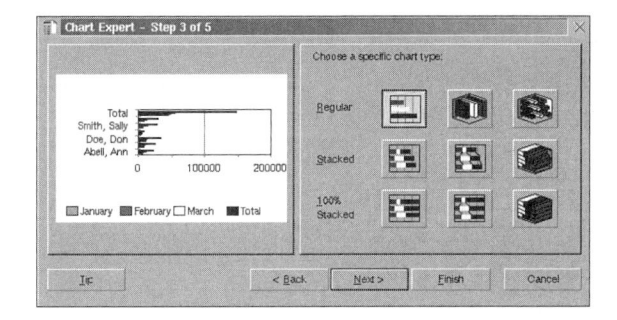

Step 4: Add Titles and Select a Destination

Step 4 requires a little more input. As shown in Figure 13.22, step 4 asks you to specify a title, a subtitle, axes titles, and a destination for your chart.

FIGURE 13.22
In step 4, the Chart Expert asks you to dress up your spreadsheet with a title, subtitle, and axes headings. You also need to specify a destination for your chart.

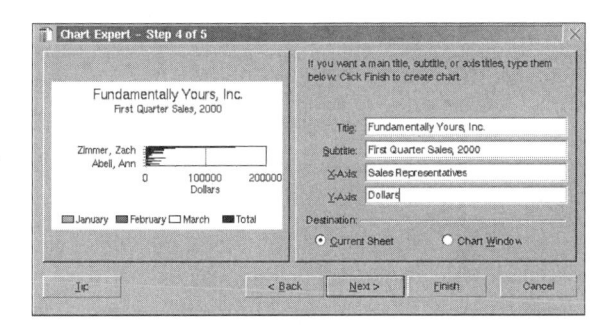

Enter the following data for step 4:

- Type in **Fundamentally Yours, Inc.** in the Title text box. Note how this new entry is automatically added to the preview window.
- In the Subtitle text box, type **First Quarter Sales, 2000**.
- In the X-Axis text box, type **Sales Representatives**. Note how this entry appears in the preview window.
- In the Y-Axis text box, type **Dollars**. Note that this entry may not appear in the preview pane due to a slight quirk—there's simply not enough room for it to be displayed in the preview.
- Because the goal is to create a floating chart that resides on the same sheet as your FYI quarterly sales spreadsheet, select Current Sheet as the destination and click Next to move on to step 5.

Step Five: Select a Color Scheme

In Step 5 the Chart Expert asks you to choose a color scheme to apply to your chart. As shown in Figure 13.23, Quattro Pro 9 includes several different color schemes to tinker with. To preview a color scheme, select it from the Choose a Color Scheme list; the Chart Expert applies this scheme to your chart in the preview window.

You can select any scheme you want. Click Finish and continue to the next section, "Positioning and Sizing Your Chart."

FIGURE 13.23
Finally, step 5 lets you play with various color schemes you can apply to your chart.

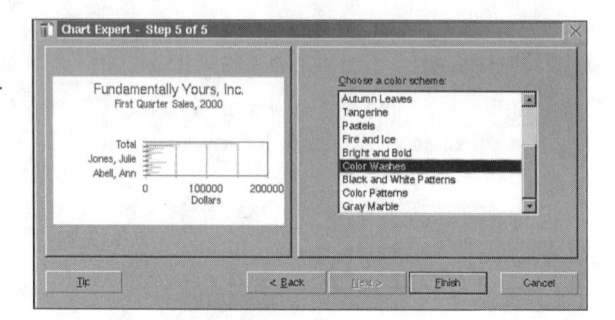

Positioning and Sizing Your Chart

I know, I know. I said there were only five steps to creating a chart with the Chart Expert. Truth is, there's one final step that isn't technically part of the Chart Expert's job—the placement of your chart within your spreadsheet.

When you click Finish to exit the Chart Expert, your mouse pointer changes into a tiny chart icon, indicating that your mouse is "carrying" your chart and will insert it wherever you next click in your spreadsheet. The first cell you click will be where the chart's upper-left corner will be placed, with the rest of the chart draped across adjoining cells. You can also drag across a block of cells to define the chart's size and position.

Try placing your chart in a blank cell beneath your FYI quarterly sales spreadsheet. No need to be too fussy because you're going to resize and reposition the chart in a few seconds. Take a look at your chart. Except for minor inconsistencies due to different color schemes, your chart should look something like the chart in Figure 13.24 (note that the chart in Figure 13.24 is zoomed to 125 percent, and the spreadsheet above the chart is displayed offscreen).

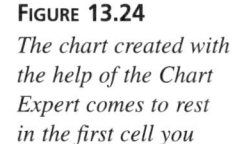

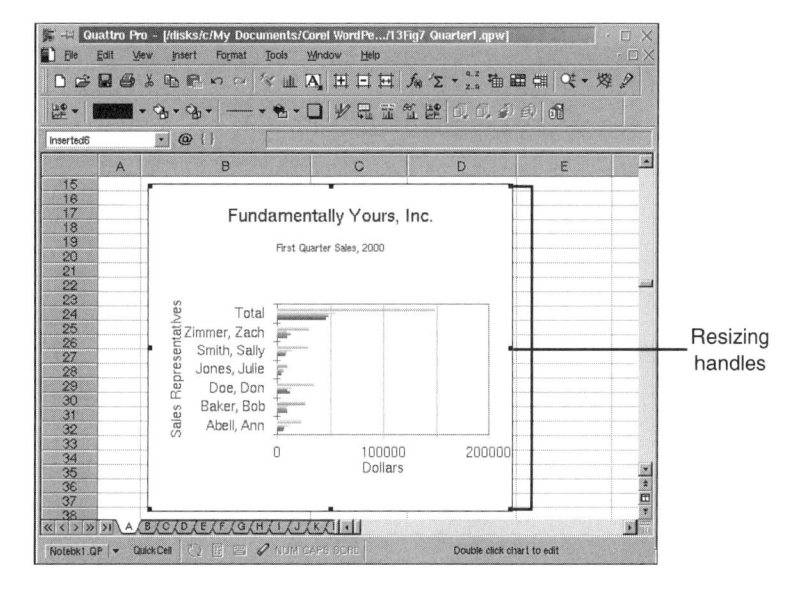

FIGURE 13.24

The chart created with the help of the Chart Expert comes to rest in the first cell you click in your open spreadsheet.

To reposition your chart, move your mouse pointer over any border until it turns into a four-way arrow. When you see the four-way arrow, click and hold to drag the mouse to another location.

You may have noticed that when you click on the chart border, eight tiny black squares appear around the chart border. These are resizing "handles" that let you change the length, width, and diagonal size of your chart. To use a handle, hold your mouse pointer over a handle until it turns into a two-way arrow (if the mouse pointer turns into a four-way arrow, the pointer isn't properly lined up with the handle). When you see the two-way arrow, click and hold to drag that handle's border in one of the directions indicated by the arrow.

Practice repositioning and resizing your chart until it looks just the way you want it.

Editing Charts

Like everything else you create in Quattro Pro, charts are easy to edit. You can change the layout, edit titles, apply colors, and put borders around your charts in no time flat.

To edit your FYI chart, click anywhere inside the chart. As shown in Figure 13.25, two things happen immediately: the chart border changes to a striped-line texture, and the Property Bar morphs to provide chart-editing tools.

FIGURE 13.25
Your FYI chart is ready for editing.

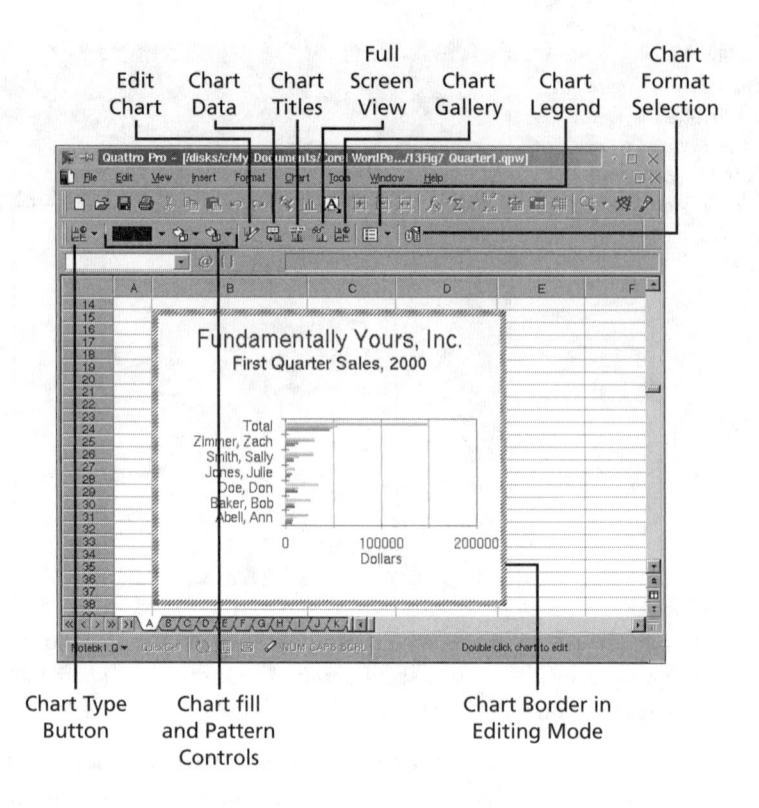

[Screenshot of Quattro Pro with chart in editing mode. Callouts point to: Edit Chart, Chart Data, Chart Titles, Full Screen View, Chart Gallery, Chart Legend, Chart Format Selection, Chart Type Button, Chart fill and Pattern Controls, Chart Border in Editing Mode. Chart shows "Fundamentally Yours, Inc. First Quarter Sales, 2000" with names Total, Zimmer Zach, Smith Sally, Jones Julie, Doe Don, Baker Bob, Abell Ann along axis labeled Dollars (0, 100000, 200000).]

There are four basic methods to edit a chart:

- You can use the various tools provided on the Property Bar.
- You can access additional chart-editing tools by right-clicking anywhere in the chart.
- You can click or double-click certain chart elements, such as titles and subtitles, to edit them directly within the chart.
- You can double-click certain chart elements, such as axes labels and legends, to open dialog boxes that provide additional editing tools.

To give you a sense of how easy it is to edit a chart, click the Chart Type button on the Property Bar and take a look at the drop-down chart palette. Changing your chart layout is as simple as clicking one of the many different chart types in the palette.

Alternatively, right-click within the chart and select Type/Layout to open the Chart Types dialog box, from which you can view available chart types in six categories: Area/Line, Bar, Stacked Bar, Pie, Specialty, and Text.

By now you're intimately familiar with the Quattro Pro 9 interface. You know more than enough to experiment on your own with the various methods of editing your chart to make it look exactly as you want.

Summary

Take a bow! In this hour you learned how to use some of Quattro Pro 9's most advanced features to give your spreadsheets a professional finish. You saw how Quattro Pro gives you a wide variety of design tools, such as SpeedFormat and chart design tools, to quickly and easily design elegant spreadsheets and charts that present your data in a whole new light.

This hour also concludes the lessons dedicated to Quattro Pro 9. In four short hours, you've learned enough to handle any numbers-crunching project that comes your way.

In the next hour, you'll meet yet another heavyweight in the WordPerfect Office 2000 for Linux lineup—get ready to create exciting slide shows with Presentations 9.

Q&A

Q When should I use a style and when should I use QuickFormat?

A This is really a matter of preference. That said, my preference is to use styles for spreadsheet elements that appear regularly but infrequently, such as headings, headers and footers, and certain labels. Because these items appear infrequently, I'd have to hunt and peck for them to apply them to another cell using QuickFormat. As styles, however, I just select the cell and apply my preset style with a couple of mouse clicks. For spreadsheet elements that appear regularly and frequently, particularly on the same sheet, it's easier to use QuickFormat to click on a sample cell and drag with the mouse to apply that cell's formatting to several other cells at once.

Q I've created dozens of Quattro Pro 9 Projects. I love using them, but it's getting difficult to find them in the sea of Projects listed when I launch the PerfectExpert. Is there a way to organize my PerfectExpert Projects?

A Yes. When you select File, New From Project to open the Create New tab in the PerfectExpert, the pull-down menu contains categories into which all PerfectExpert projects are grouped. One category, called Favorites, is the perfect place for you to store your own projects to keep them better organized. To add a project to the Favorites category, select the project and click the Copy to Favorites button within the PerfectExpert Create New tab. To move (instead of copy) the project to the Favorites category, click the Options button and move your mouse pointer over the Move Project menu item. Select (Favorites) from the pop-out menu to move the project.

You can also use the Options button to create, rename, and remove projects and categories from the list. You can thus create your own categories to further organize your projects, within or without the Favorites category.

Workshop

The Workshop contains quiz questions and exercises to help reinforce what you've learned in this hour. If you get stuck, the answers can be found in Appendix B, "Answers to Quiz Questions."

Quiz

1. The color of a cell, block of cells, or chart is also known as its what?
   a. Style
   b. Format
   c. Fill
   d. Value
   e. Property

2. Which of the following would appear as an icon on the Objects sheet?
   a. Chart
   b. PerfectExpert Project
   c. Style
   d. SpeedFormat
   e. Headers and Footers

3. Which of the following can be included within a chart?
   a. Fill pattern
   b. Legend
   c. X-axis
   d. Color scheme
   e. All of the above

Exercises

1. Wondering how that extensive stock portfolio is doing? Try using the PerfectExpert Capital Gains and Losses Project to see if you're in the red or in the black. (Even if you don't have an extensive stock portfolio, use the PerfectExpert's sample data to see how this project works.)

2. Change the text color and fill in the title and subtitle of your FYI first quarter sales chart.

3. Now it's time to make the FYI sales team sweat. The boss has set a minimum monthly sales quota of $7,500 and has asked you to set up your FYI spreadsheet so it will flag each sales representative who fails to meet the quota.

Part IV

Express Yourself with Corel Presentations 9

Hour

- 14 Corel Presentations 9 Basics
- 15 Creating Your First Slideshow
- 16 Advanced Presentations

HOUR 14

Corel Presentations 9 Basics

So far you have learned how to use WordPerfect to present narrative information and Quattro Pro to present numeric information. During the next three hours, you'll learn how to use Presentations when you have information that you want to present in some kind of visually dramatic way.

When many people think of presentations software, they immediately think of slideshows. Although you can make beautiful, professional slides with Presentations, the application is so versatile that there are many more uses that might not be immediately apparent.

In this hour, you will

- Discover the kinds of documents you can create with Presentations 9.
- Understand the difference between slideshows and drawings.
- Explore the Presentations 9 desktop environment.
- Start a Presentations 9 project.

- Learn about slide, layout, and background layers.
- Look at a slideshow through the Slide Editor, Slide Outliner, Slide Sorter, and QuickPlay.

What Is Presentations 9?

Presentations is a graphics-presentation application for creating high-quality, professional drawings and slideshows. Here are some examples of uses for Presentations:

- Project proposals
- Interactive demonstrations
- Multimedia presentations
- Flyers
- Signs
- Banners
- Lecture notes
- Product presentations
- Research summaries
- Invitations

When creating a Presentations file, you can include text, graphics, organization charts, data charts, and drawings and clipart. For slideshows, you can even include sound and animation to create a multimedia show.

When you are ready to display your presentation, you can display it on a computer monitor, project it onto an overhead screen, or publish your presentation as an HTML file on the Internet or your organization's intranet. You can play your presentation on any Windows, Linux, or UNIX computer (running X), even if it doesn't have Presentations installed.

You can create overhead transparencies, projector slides, or black-and-white or color printouts of the presentation.

Starting Presentations

The way you start Presentations varies according to your desktop. Some desktop environments, such as GNOME and KDE, automatically add a WordPerfect Office 2000 submenu to the main menu. You might also have WordPerfect Office 2000 icons automatically created on your desktop. Regardless of your desktop, you can always start Presentations by entering the command `presentations` at a shell prompt in an xterm.

When you start Presentations for the first time, there could be a delay of several seconds to a minute or two while WordPerfect configures the files you need. The first thing you see after Presentations has finished loading is the PerfectExpert dialog box. You will learn more about PerfectExpert later in the hour, but for now, select the Create New tab and click Corel Presentations Slide Show, Create.

Corel Presentations 9 Basics

At first glance, Presentations might seem daunting (see Figure 14.1). The choices are endless; the toolbars are packed with icons, some of which are familiar, but some of which may be strange and new. The great thing about Presentations is that it is as complicated or as simple as you want it to be. You can create a fully functioning, attractive, professional-looking presentation after spending five minutes learning how to use Presentations, or you can design your own, completely customized presentation from the ground up. It's your choice.

FIGURE 14.1

The Presentations desktop looks complicated, but you'll understand everything on it by the end of Hour 16.

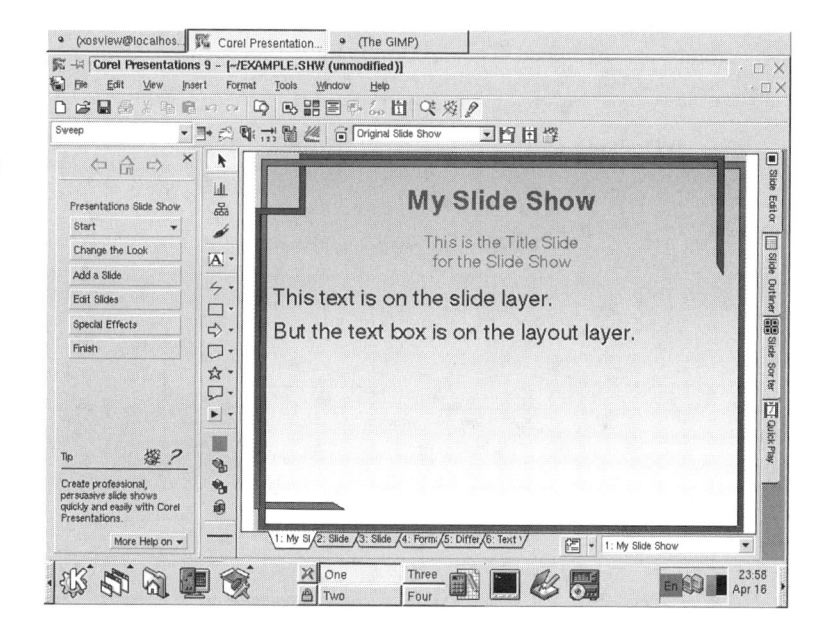

As with the other WordPerfect Office applications, PerfectExpert is there to help you with any task while you are completing it.

Although the uses for Presentations are endless, there are only two basic kinds of Presentations projects: slideshows and drawings.

> A *slideshow* is a series of individual drawings, or *slides*, each of which is a separate, self-contained page. A *drawing* is a single-page item, such as a flyer, poster, or banner. You can include anything in a drawing that you can include in a slide, such as organizational charts, data charts, imported graphic objects, drawn objects, and of course text. You can save Presentations drawings as JPG, BMP, GIF, PNG, and WPG (WordPerfect Graphic) files.

> You can use Presentations as a drawing or paint program as well as a slideshow program. Create a new drawing and then select the Create Bitmap icon on the Tools Palette.

Exploring the Presentations 9 Environment

The Presentations desktop is complex, but it takes only a few minutes to understand how things are organized. The desktop is divided into three major areas:

- Menus, toolbars, and Application Bar
- Drawing window
- PerfectExpert

The parts of the Presentation desktop are shown in Figure 14.2.

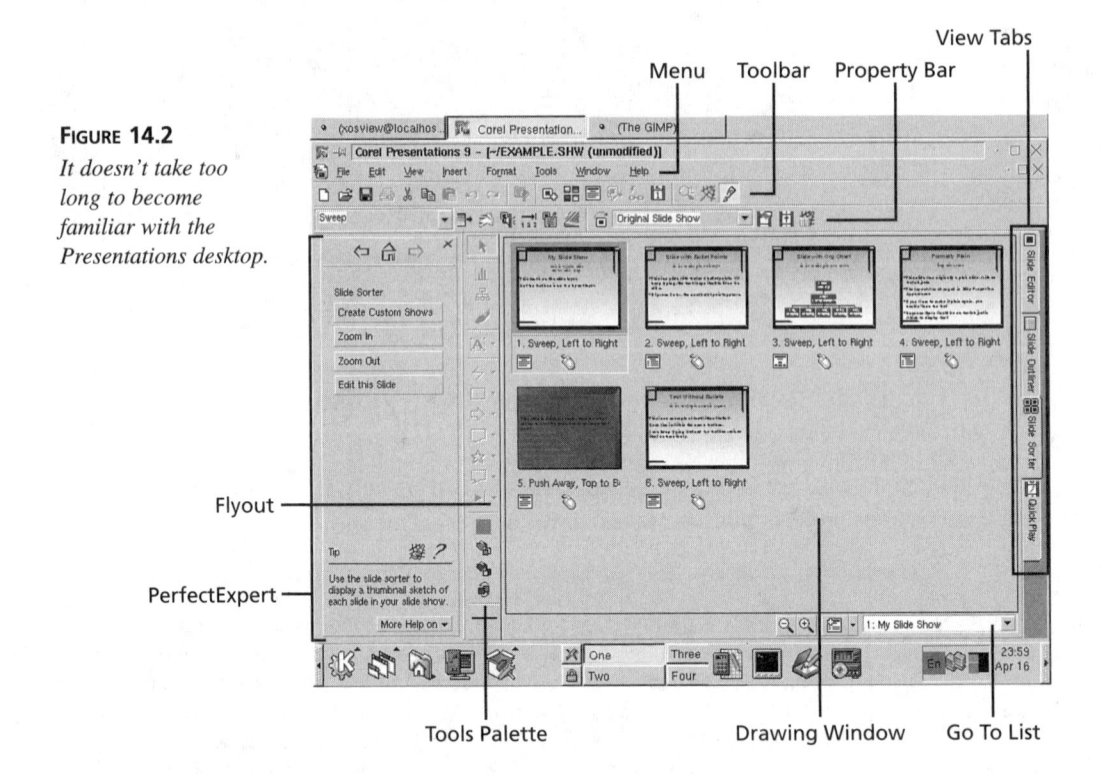

FIGURE 14.2
It doesn't take too long to become familiar with the Presentations desktop.

The Menus and Toolbars

The main menu bar and toolbars are similar to those of most menu-driven office applications. The options available in the menu bar and toolbars vary according to the aspect of Presentations in which you are working. Most of the entries in the menu bar are also available as icons on the toolbar.

The menu bar has entries for most of the commands within Presentations. You can also use the toolbar icons and flyouts. A *flyout* is kind of a subtoolbar, like a submenu on a menu, that contains more tool icons related to the tool on the main toolbar. Flyouts help to organize and save space on the toolbar.

Property Bar

The Property bar contains icons for the available options in Slide Properties. It appears when the slide layer is open.

Tools Palette

The Tools Palette is the vertical toolbar that divides the drawing window and PerfectExpert. Icons for each kind of object and graphic tool that you can add to a slide are available in the Tools Palette.

The Text Object and Shapes icons in the Tools Palette contain flyouts with additional tool icons. Icons in Presentations contain pop-ups with a short description of each icon.

Application Bar

You can have up to nine WordPerfect Office 2000 documents open at the same time. The filename for each document is listed in the Application Bar, located at the bottom of the Presentations desktop.

The Drawing Window

The drawing window is the large window in which the actual work of creating the slide or drawing is done. Slides are displayed in the drawing window in Outliner, Editor, and Sorter views (more about the views later).

In Slide Editor, each slide has a tab at the bottom of the drawing window with its number and title. Click the tab to go to the slide you want. Alternatively, you can click the Go To list on the bottom right of the drawing window. The Go To list is visible in the Slide Editor and Slide Sorter views.

In Slide Editor, clicking the slide in the Go To list opens the slide in the drawing window. In the Slide Sorter view, clicking the slide gives it the focus in the Slide Sorter window.

PerfectExpert

PerfectExpert provides real-time help for whatever task you're doing. With PerfectExpert, you get exactly the kind of help you need at the moment you need it, without having to search through a table of contents or index for the topic. Everything you might want to do with a particular item is presented in PerfectExpert. This is particularly important for an application as complex and powerful as Presentations.

The PerfectExpert menu changes depending on what is in the drawing window. In Slide Outliner, PerfectExpert displays the topics you would want to perform in Outliner: Check Spelling and Import an Outline.

When you click a help topic in PerfectExpert, it actually opens the menu item, tool, dialog box, or window that you need to complete the task. For example, if you click Check Spelling, the Spell Checker opens and checks the spelling of your slideshow automatically.

For a more complicated example, in Slide Editor, if you click Add Graphics and then Add a Bitmap, the bitmap-insertion hand is displayed. Draw the box where you want to insert the bitmap. The bitmap editor automatically opens, and the PerfectExpert displays the help topics that are relevant to editing bitmaps.

> PerfectExpert has two icons that link to more conventional help. The Web icon opens a Web browser to Corel's site *Help on the Web, Tips and Tricks*. The question mark icon opens the WordPerfect Office 2000 online help.
>
> The user's manual that ships with WordPerfect Office 2000 is another excellent source of help. The user's manual is a PDF file that's found on the WordPerfect Office 2000 installation CD-ROM.

Starting a Presentations Project

After you start Presentations, the PerfectExpert dialog box, shown in Figure 14.3, appears.

The first task in PerfectExpert is to decide the kind of Presentations file you want to create: a drawing, slideshow, or master or slide project. To understand the meaning of these choices, it is necessary to understand the ways you can create a new file in Presentations.

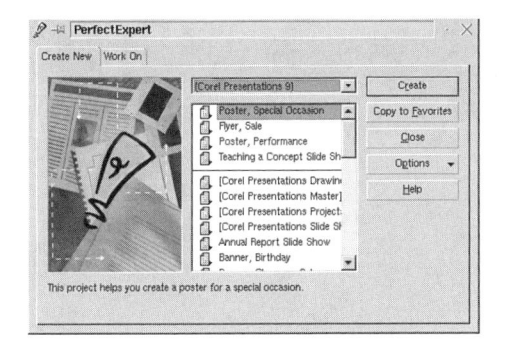

FIGURE 14.3
Create a new file or open an old WordPerfect Office 2000 file from PerfectExpert.

Slide Projects

Slideshows are usually used in some kind of presentation of information, and although they are separate pages, they come together to form a presentation. Slides are connected via *transitions*, which control how the presentation moves from one slide to the next.

You can add sound, animated graphics, and transitions as well as animate the presentation itself in a slideshow

Presentations ships with dozens of predefined slideshows and drawings called *slide projects*. If you look at the Create New tab of the PerfectExpert dialog box, you'll see items such as Flyer, Sale, Interactive Slide Show, Birthday Banner, and Multimedia Slide Show. These slideshows and drawings are already completed and ready for presentation. All you have to do is enter your information onto the slides and play the presentation. If you're in a hurry, are new to Presentations, or just want some ideas, slide projects are a great way to produce professionally designed slideshows, posters, banners, or other presentations in minutes.

To use a slide project, select a slide project from the PerfectExpert dialog box and click Create. The slide project loads into the drawing window. You then enter your presentation information in Slide Outliner, Slide Editor, and Slide Sorter, as you'll learn in this hour and Hour 15, "Creating Your First SlideShow."

After you have loaded a slide project, you can edit and change any aspect of the template the same way you would edit a presentation you design yourself, as shown in Figure 14.4.

FIGURE 14.4
Slide Projects can be modified, or you can just enter your text directly into the ready-made slideshow.

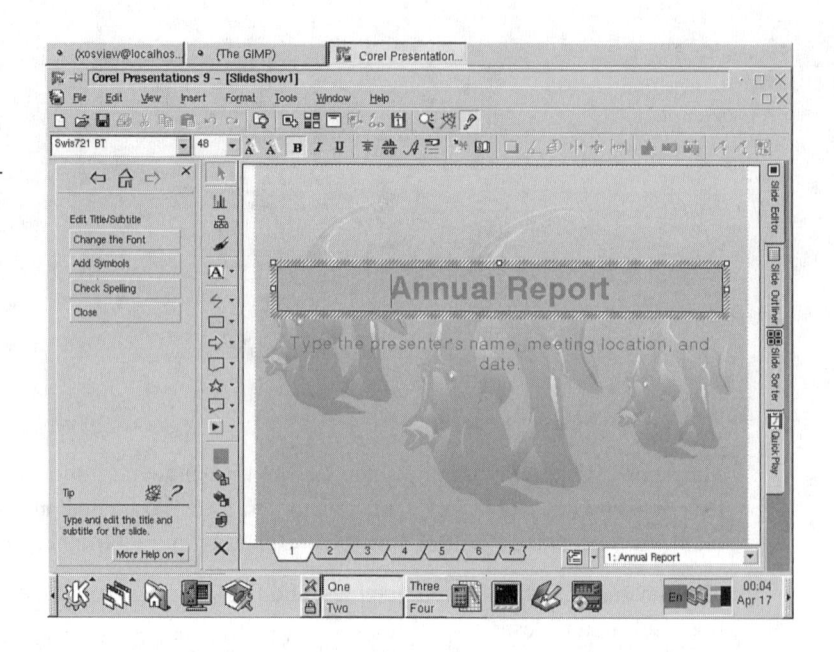

Using the Master Gallery

If you would rather design your own slideshow or drawing, the next step is to select a master template from the Master Gallery. Masters are predefined backgrounds and fonts you can use for your slideshows. A master includes the following items:

- A background for your slideshow
- Default fonts used for text
- Default colors for objects such as organization charts and data charts
- Layout of slides

The Master Gallery is shown in Figure 14.5.

FIGURE 14.5
Use one of the dozens of slide masters that come with Presentations 9, or you can create your own master.

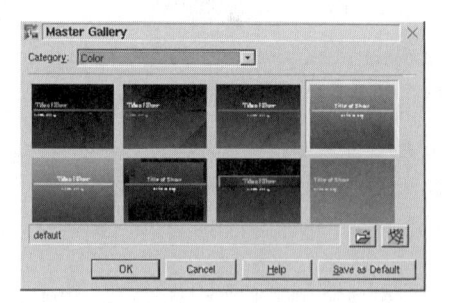

You must use a master to create a new slideshow or drawing, but you aren't limited to the master templates that ship with Presentations 9. If you want to design your own master, select Corel Presentations Master in the PerfectExpert dialog box. You'll learn how to create masters in Hour 16, "Advanced Presentations."

Understanding Slide Layers

When you look at a Presentations slide, everything appears to be arranged on a two-dimensional grid. Actually, slides are composed of three separate layers that lie on top of one another:

- Slide layer
- Layout layer
- Background layer

Each layer contains different parts of your slide, such as text, graphics, and background design. If the concept of layers seems confusing, try reading this section over again after you have read Hour 15, and it will probably make more sense. Understanding layers is fundamental to creating slides in Presentations if you want to prevent hours of frustration.

Slide Layer

The slide layer consists of the actual text, charts, and other objects that make up the presentation. The information on the slide layer usually varies with each slide. The slide layer is the top layer of a slide.

For example, if you open the Annual Report Slide Show project, as shown in Figure 14.6, the title page contains the title *Annual Report*. Below the title are the instructions *Type the presenter's name, meeting location, and date*. The words *Annual Report* and the instructions *Type the presenter's...* are in the slide layer. If you click on Annual Report, a box opens around the words. This box is an object called a *text line*. The text line is a container for the words *Annual Report*. It exists below the slide layer in the layout layer.

Layout Layer

Each item in the slide layer, such as text, bulleted lists, and clipart, must have an object in the layout layer that contains the item on the slide. A layout might consist of a title, text box, and organizational chart or of a title, bulleted list, and graphic. If you don't have an object in the layout layer to hold the text, chart, or other item in the slide layer, the item will not appear on the slide. The layout layer, shown in Figure 14.7, is below the slide layer but on top of the background layer.

FIGURE 14.6
The slide layer contains the text, charts, and graphics for your slide.

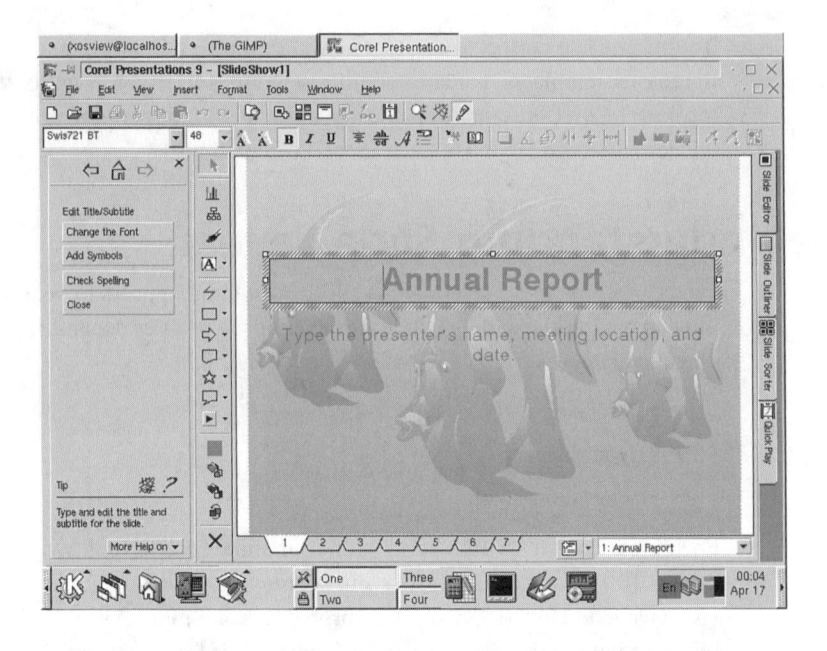

FIGURE 14.7
The layout layer contains the slide objects, such as text boxes, chart objects, and bulleted list objects.

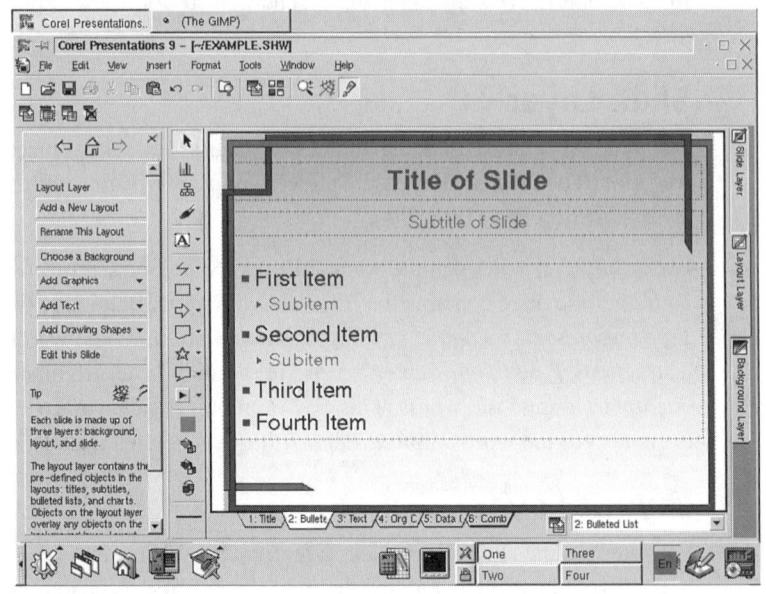

> The layout layer will make more sense after you have studied objects later in this hour.

Background Layer

The background layer contains the background color, pattern, graphics, and page size of the slide. You can place clipart, charts, bitmaps, text, and objects on the background layer, and these objects will appear on the slide behind (or below) the layout and slide layers, on every slide in the slideshow. The background layer is shown in Figure 14.8.

FIGURE 14.8
The background layer contains the background color, text, and images for all the slides in the slideshow.

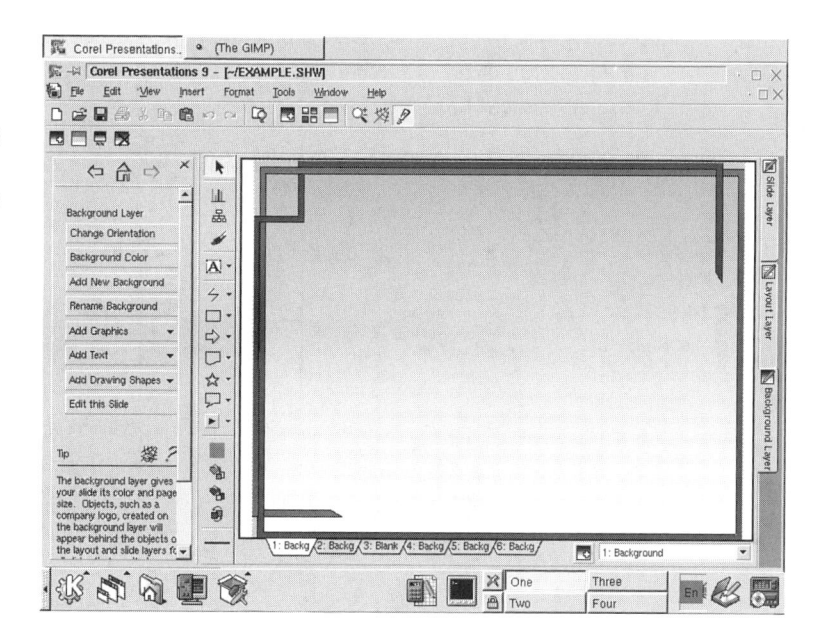

Slide Objects

Slide objects are containers for the text and graphics of your slides. The slide object is the actual "box" that your text and graphics are placed in. Slide objects are in the layout layer of your slide, below the slide layer where the text, graphics, and charts are found.

Text Objects

When you enter text in Slide Outliner or type text directly onto the slide in Slide Editor, you are entering text into a text object. Three kinds of objects hold text in Presentations:

- *Text box*. The text box is an object that can hold many lines of text. The text automatically wraps according to the size of the box. You can resize the text box by dragging it by its sides or corners, and the text will rewrap to accommodate the new size. You can also move the text box, and the text moves with it.

- *Text line.* A text line contains just one line of text. If you type a long string of text on the text line, it will not wrap but will continue off the slide. Text lines can be moved by dragging, but because they consist of only one line, they cannot be resized. It is usually better to use a text box to hold text, unless you want to be able to move lines around individually.

- *Bulleted list.* A bulleted list is similar to a text box, except that each new line is preceded by a bullet. To indicate a new line, press Enter, and a bullet appears. If you decide to get rid of the bullets, you can change the layout object from a bulleted list to a text box.

The three kinds of text objects are shown in Figure 14.9.

FIGURE 14.9
All text must have a text object defined in the layout layer.

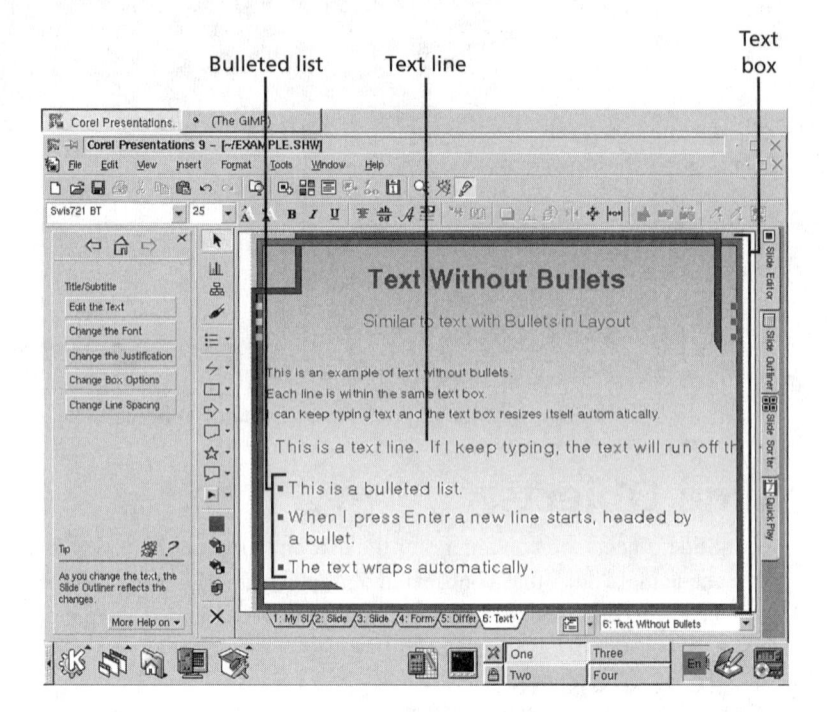

Data Charts

Data charts display numerical information from a datasheet, which is similar to a spreadsheet. Data charts are useful when you have any kind of numerical information you want to display in a format that the audience can quickly grasp and easily understand. You can create data charts from Quattro Pro, Excel, Lotus-1-2-3, PlanPerfect, or ASCII text spreadsheets, or you can enter data manually into the datasheet.

To include a data chart on a slide or drawing, you must have a data chart object defined on the layout of your slide. An example of a data chart is shown in Figure 14.10.

FIGURE 14.10
Data charts show numeric information in an elegant and easy-to-grasp format.

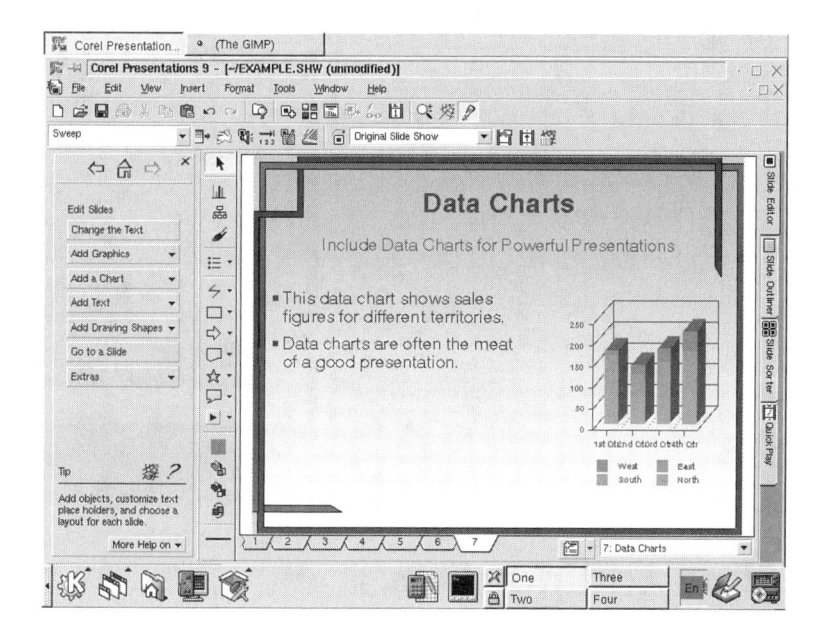

Organizational Charts

Organizational charts are an exceptionally useful feature of Presentations, because you can make them right in the Presentations application. An organizational chart can represent a hierarchical or lateral organization structure, or a combination of the two.

Just like with data charts, you must select a layout with an organizational chart object to display an organizational chart on a slide. An example of an organizational chart is shown in Figure 14.11.

Graphics

Graphic objects hold graphics such as clipart, objects imported from other applications, or drawings. Once you have inserted a graphic into the graphic object, you can edit it in the bitmap editor (if it's a certain file format), or you can resize it right in Slide Editor. You'll learn more about charts and graphics in Hour 16.

FIGURE 14.11
You can create organizational charts right in Presentations 9.

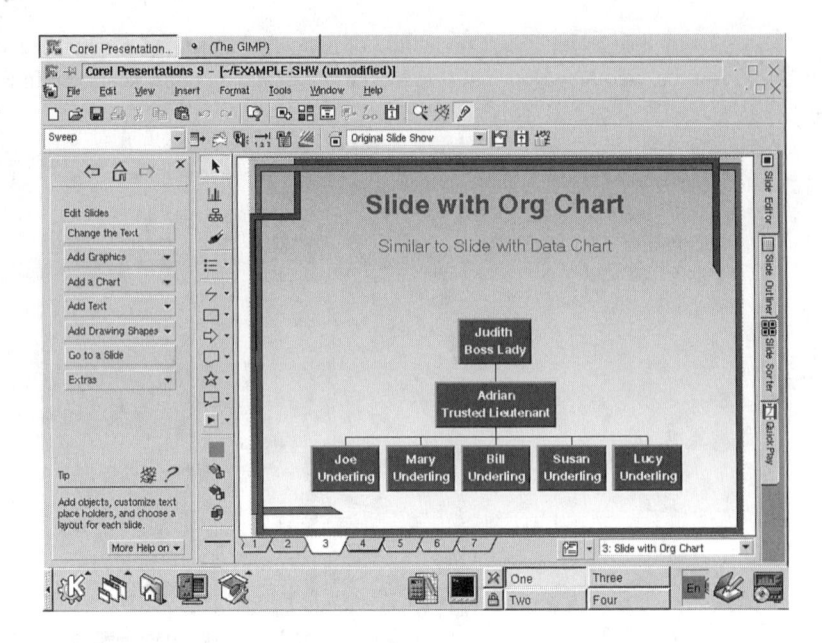

Slide Editing Views

While you are creating your slideshow, it is often useful to be able to look at different aspects of the show. Sometimes you want to look at each slide in detail, to add and delete items and make sure that everything looks exactly as you want it to look. Sometimes you want to look at the entire show all at once, to check the flow of the slides, and to make sure that all the slides look good in procession. It is also useful to be able to look at just the text of the slides, to check grammar, style, and spelling, as well as content.

Presentations has three different views for you to look at your slideshow: Slide Outliner, Slide Editor, and Slide Sorter. Each view shows the slides in different ways so that you can check various aspects of the slideshow. The drawing window on the desktop has tabs on the right side to make it easy to switch between the Slide Editor, the Slide Sorter, and the Slide Outliner.

Slide Outliner

Slide Outliner displays all the text in your slideshow or drawing. Use Outliner to create an outline for the slideshow when you are first starting and then use it to check your spelling and content while you are creating the show. Outliner is also useful for creating speaker notes and for adapting your slideshow text to be used as a handout. You can create the text for the entire presentation in Slide Outliner without opening a single slide. Use Spell Checker to spell check all the slides at once. The Slide Outliner is shown in Figure 14.12.

FIGURE 14.12
Type your slide text right into Slide Outliner or import a WordPerfect document into Outliner.

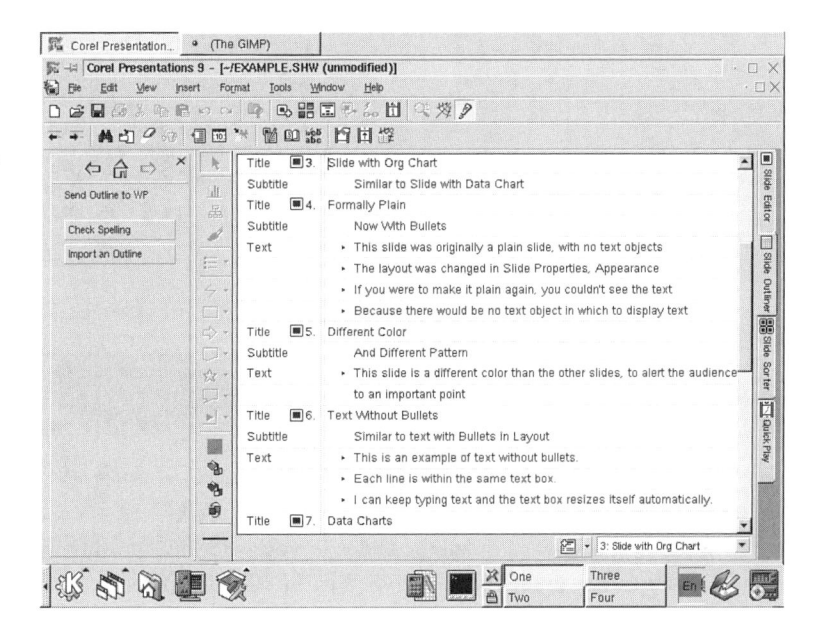

If you prefer to outline your slideshow in WordPerfect, you can insert WordPerfect documents into the Slide Outliner. Each first-level WordPerfect paragraph becomes a slide title. Any second or third-level paragraphs are interpreted as text in Slide Outliner. You can also save the slide outline as a WordPerfect document and then use the slide outline to create audience handouts.

Slide Editor

After you have added all the text for the slideshow in Outliner, open the slide file in Slide Editor to add clipart, data charts, organization charts, and other objects.

Slide Editor displays one slide at a time in the drawing window. Each slide has a tab that displays the slide number and title at the bottom of the drawing window. Move from slide to slide by clicking the Slide tab or by selecting the slide title from the drop-down menu in the drawing window. Slide Editor is shown in Figure 14.13.

FIGURE 14.13
Most of the work of creating a slideshow is done in Slide Editor.

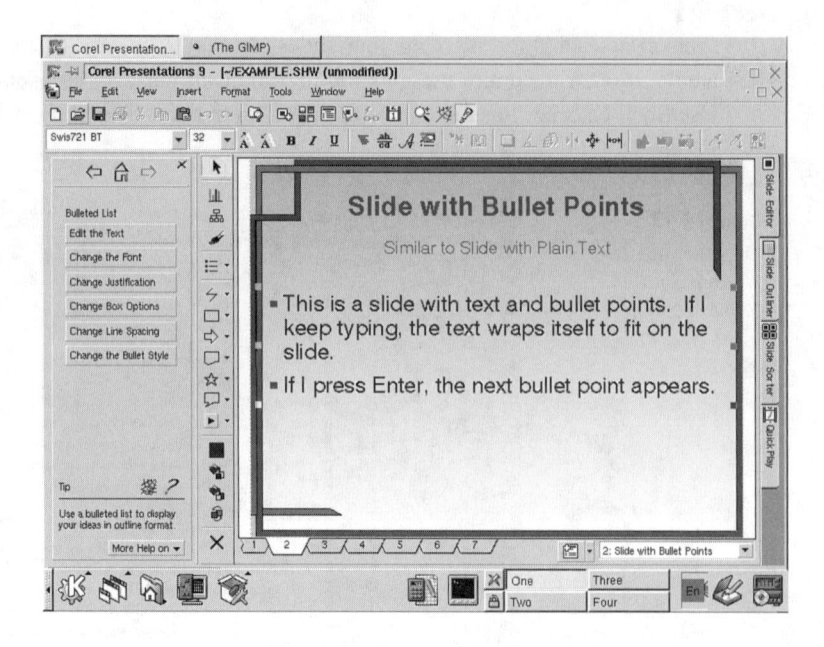

Slide Sorter

Slide Sorter shows you all the slides in your slideshow as thumbnail sketches so that you can sort them in the order you want them. Change the order of slides by dragging and dropping them to the desired location. After you have moved a slide, Presentations reorders and renumbers each slide automatically. Slide Sorter is also the ideal view to add transitions, animations, speaker notes, and sound to your slideshow. Slide Sorter is shown in Figure 14.14.

QuickPlay

QuickPlay is the last tab on the right side of the drawing window. Use QuickPlay at any time while you are creating your slideshow to check your work. QuickPlay plays the slideshow on your computer screen—including sound, transitions, and animations—exactly as it would be played for real. You can use QuickPlay to check different styles and configurations of slides, sounds, and transitions.

FIGURE 14.14
Slide Sorter displays thumbnail sketches of all the slides in your slideshow.

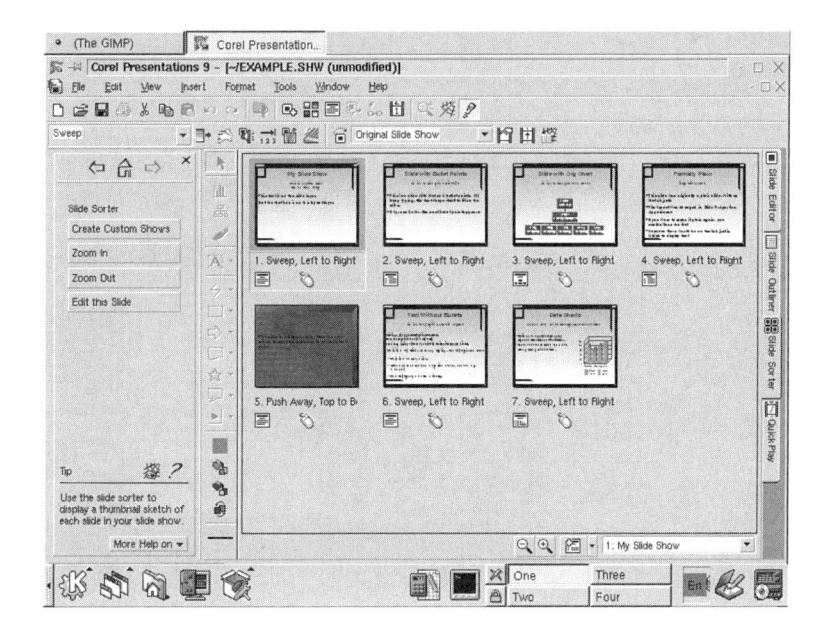

To do a QuickPlay, click the QuickPlay tab. QuickPlay automatically exits and returns you to the Presentations desktop. If you want to stop the slideshow early, press Esc.

Viewing Multiple Slide Shows

You can have up to nine slideshows open at once in Presentations. To switch between slideshows, select Window from the menu bar and click the slideshow you want to look at, or you can click the slideshow title on the Application Bar.

You can have multiple slideshows open at the same time in Slide Editor. they can be viewed in a cascaded, side-by-side, or vertical layout. To view multiple slideshows, as shown in Figure 14.15, first open all the slideshow files you want to display. From the menu bar, click Window and then select Cascade, Tile Top to Bottom, or Tile Side by Side. Double-click in a slideshow to view just that one slideshow in the drawing window.

FIGURE 14.15
You can view up to nine slideshows simultaneously in Slide Editor.

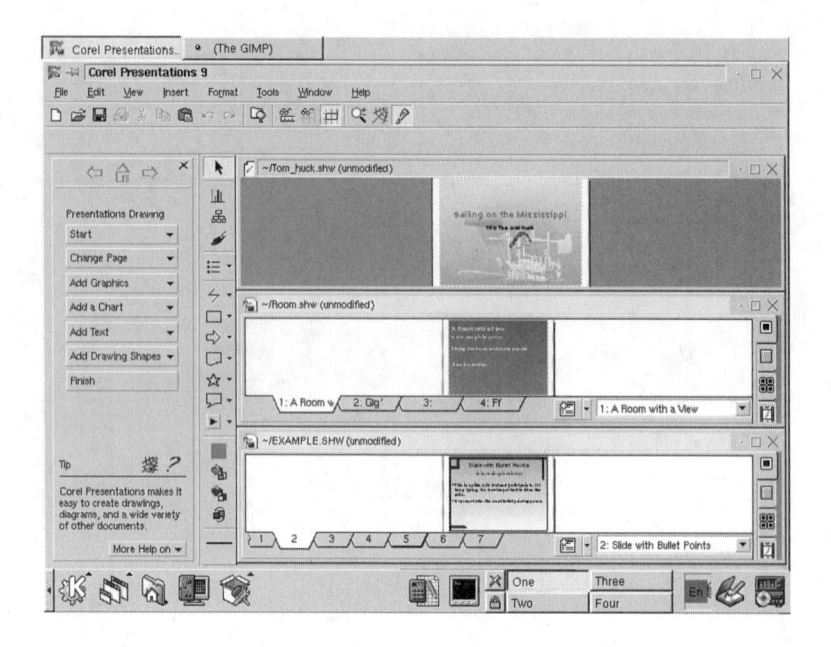

> When you want to combine two slideshows or use elements from one show in another, open both shows and display them both in the drawing window. It makes cutting/copying and pasting much easier.

Summary

In this hour you were introduced to WordPerfect Presentations 9. You learned the difference between slideshows and drawings as well as the kinds of documents you can create in Presentations in the slideshow and drawing file formats. You started a new slideshow using a slideshow project and from scratch by selecting a master from the Master Gallery. You explored the Presentations 9 work environment and learned how to use PerfectExpert to do tasks. You were also introduced to layers and slide objects.

Q&A

Q Can I make a flyer or poster out of a single slide that is already part of a slideshow?

A Yes. To make a poster, banner, or flyer out of a slide in a slideshow, save the single slide as a drawing first.

Q Presentations runs very slowly. What can be done to speed things up?

A Presentations 9 tends to use up a *lot* of system memory. If it runs too slow on your system, check to make sure that you actually need all the processes running in the background. Also, if you log into Linux via a graphical interface (runlevel 5), consider running at runlevel 3 and then starting an X session manually. In a pinch, doing this can free up quite a lot of memory. You might also consider recompiling your kernel so that unnecessary processes are not started.

Workshop

The Workshop contains quiz questions and exercises to help reinforce what you've learned in this hour. If you get stuck, the answers can be found in Appendix B, "Answers to Quiz Questions."

Quiz

1. Name three kinds of documents you can create with Presentations 9.
2. What is the difference between a slideshow and a drawing?
3. In which file formats can Presentations drawings be saved?
4. True or false: The background color for a slideshow can be selected by selecting a master from the Master Gallery.
5. What are the three layers of a slide, and which layer is on the bottom?
6. Which slide layer contains the slide objects?
7. In which text objects does the text wrap automatically?

Exercises

1. Start Presentations. In the PerfectExpert dialog box, select the Teaching a Concept slide project. Save the slideshow as **Teach** and then close the file.
2. Click tab number 6 in Slide Editor view. What is the title of this slide? Click the Go To list. How many slides are there in this project?
3. In PerfectExpert, click the Home icon. What is the title of the menu that appears in PerfectExpert? Click the Select Slides button in PerfectExpert. What happens?
4. Hold the mouse over the last icon in the Tools Palette. What is the name of the icon?

5. Click Edit, Background Layer in the menu bar. What happens? Click the Background tab. What do you see?
6. Click Edit, Slide Layer and then open Slide Outliner. What do you see?
7. Click the QuickPlay tab and then click the left mouse button a few times. When you are ready, press Esc. What happens?

HOUR 15

Creating Your First Slideshow

Last hour, you received a broad introduction to Presentations 9. Now you're ready to create your first Presentations slideshow, from beginning to end. Throughout the chapter you'll learn about the major aspects to creating a slideshow while following the examples in the chapter. The exercises will provide you with the opportunity to use what you've learned and create a slideshow on your own.

In this hour, you will

- Outline your slideshow using Slide Outliner.
- Use PerfectExpert, the toolbars, and the Tools Palette to do tasks.
- Add text, graphics, and audience and speaker notes in Slide Editor and rearrange slides in Slide Sorter.
- Add transitions, animation, SpeedKeys, and sound.
- Customize your slideshow and save it as a QuickShow, Show on the Go, HTML file, and PDF file.

Step One: Outlining Your Slideshow

The first step to creating a slideshow is, of course, to start Presentations. By default, the PerfectExpert dialog box appears when you start Presentations.

> If the PerfectExpert dialog box does not open, click File, New From Project to open the dialog box from within Presentations.

Select the Create New tab, Corel Presentations Slideshow, and click Create. (If you were going to create a drawing, you would click Corel Presentations Drawing). The Corel Presentations desktop appears, but you're not quite ready to work on your slideshow yet. The next step is to choose a master template for your slideshow from the Master Gallery. Browse through the categories and select one you like. The master template is loaded, and you are ready to begin working on your slideshow.

> Don't worry if you're not thrilled with any of the master templates. You can customize any aspect of the master template, including background, font, bullet style, and other formatting, later.

Using the Slide Outliner

In any document, the best way to start out and stay organized is to make an outline first. Working in Presentations is no different, but there is an extra advantage to making an outline here. After you have made the outline, it is automatically inserted into your slideshow, and half the work is done.

To open the Slide Outliner, click View, Slide Outliner. The Outliner is shown in Figure 15.1.

FIGURE 15.1
Enter the slide titles, subtitles, and preliminary text in Slide Outliner.

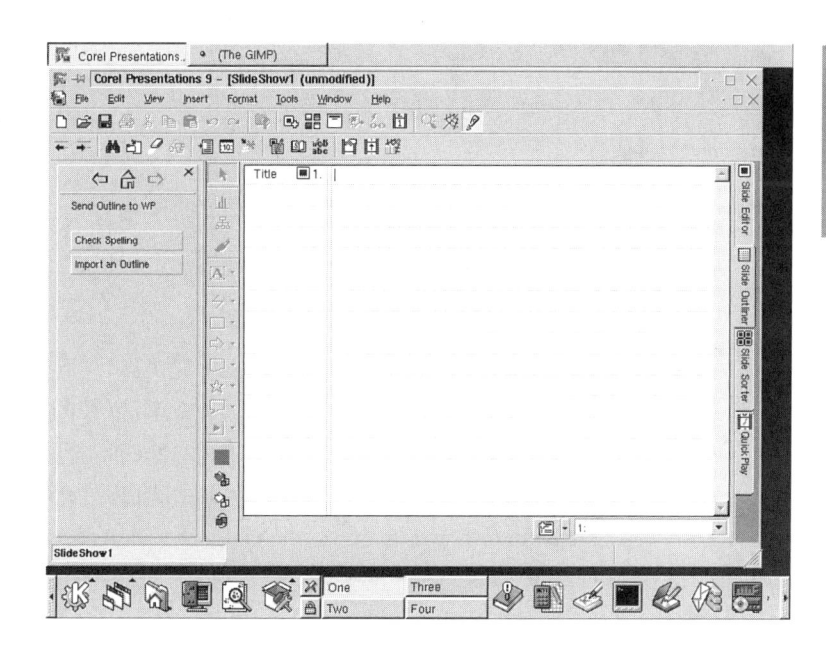

A good method to use when creating a slideshow is to enter into Slide Outliner all the main topics you want to cover first; then add the subtopics and, finally, the text. In Slide Outliner, the main topics are called *titles*. Each title will be the title of one slide.

Choosing Titles, Subtitles, and Text

The first line that appears in the Slide Outliner is the title of the slide. Enter the title and press Enter. The next line is the subtitle, and then come the text lines. If you don't want to include a particular text object in your slide, leave the line blank in Outliner. You can delete the text object later in the Slide Editor.

To add more text lines to the Slide Outliner, press Enter and a new text line appears. We'll add graphics and charts later in Slide Editor.

Adding and Deleting Slides

To insert the next slide into your outline, click Insert, New Slide. Select the layout you want from the New Slide dialog box, shown in Figure 15.2. If none of the layouts match what you want, click the slide that most closely approximates the layout you want. You can add and delete slide objects later. To add more than one new slide, indicate the number of slides you want to add in the Number to Add field in the New Slide dialog box.

FIGURE 15.2
You can create all the slides for your slideshow at once.

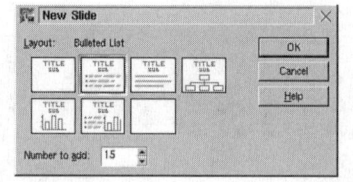

To Do: Delete Slides

1. Select Edit, Delete Slide.
2. The entire slide is deleted.
3. Presentations automatically renumbers the remaining slides.
4. To delete the contents of a slide, while keeping the slide, select Edit, Clear.
5. Select whether to clear the entire slideshow or just the selected slide.
6. The slide or slideshow remains in the Outliner with its text objects intact, but the contents of the slide are erased.

The Context-Sensitive PerfectExpert

When working on your slide, you have three tools you can use to accomplish tasks:

- PerfectExpert
- Tools Palette
- Menus and toolbars

Menus and toolbars are standard in virtually every office application. If you have not used WordPerfect Office Applications, however, you might not be used to a tool like PerfectExpert. PerfectExpert is explained briefly before I continue with the next step in creating our slideshow.

By now, you have most likely noticed the PerfectExpert help topics on the left side of the Drawing Window that seem to change with every click of your mouse. PerfectExpert is ingeniously designed in that every topic you might need help with at a given point in the creation of your slideshow is displayed in PerfectExpert as you need it.

PerfectExpert isn't just a help tool. It actually opens the tools you need to perform the task you select from the menu. If necessary, it also automatically changes your view to the one needed to do the task. You were introduced to PerfectExpert in the last hour, but it is shown here again in Figure 15.3 so that you can refer to the figure during the next section.

FIGURE 15.3
You can do most Presentations tasks via PerfectExpert.

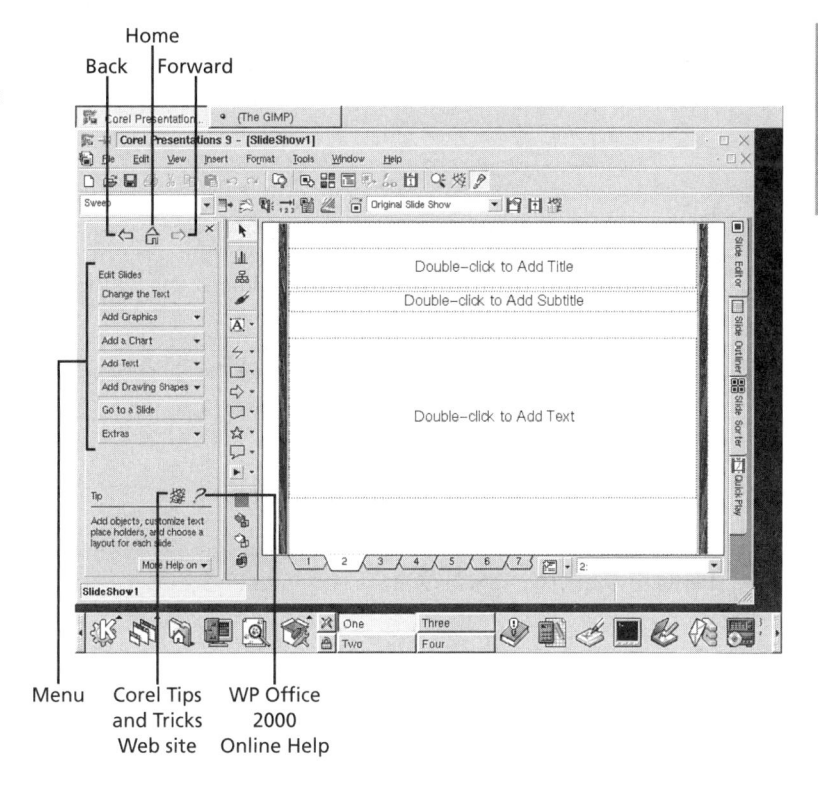

Navigating the PerfectExpert Menus

The PerfectExpert navigation icons are at the top of the PerfectExpert window. Regardless of where you are in Presentations, you can navigate to any topic in PerfectExpert by using the navigation icons. The navigation icons work much like those in a Web browser. The Home icon opens the main topic menu for PerfectExpert. The Back button opens the previous PerfectExpert topic menu, and the Forward button returns to the menu that was open before you clicked Back.

When you open a new Slide View, the relevant PerfectExpert menu opens. For example, if you click the Slide Editor tab, the Edit Slides PerfectExpert menu opens. If you click the Slide Sorter tab, the Slide Sorter PerfectExpert menu opens. To return to the Edit Slides menu, click Back. Click Home to go to the Presentations Slideshow menu, which is the main PerfectExpert menu.

> PerfectExpert is a marvelous tool, but it doesn't explain concepts. Instead, it only helps you complete tasks. For more help on particular subjects, you can go to the help icons.

Working with the Tools Palette

The Tools Palette has icons and flyouts for adding and editing items in a slide. The Tools Palette icons are grouped into four categories:

- Slide objects, such as organizational charts, data charts, and bitmap images
- Text objects, such as text boxes, text lines, and bulleted lists
- Shapes
- Foreground and background colors and patterns

The items in the Tools Palette can also be inserted via the Insert menu or via PerfectExpert. The Tools Palette is shown in Figure 15.4.

FIGURE 15.4
The Tools Palette has icons for inserting most kinds of slide objects.

Step Two: Building Your Slides Using Slide Editor

After you've created the outline for your slideshow and determined the titles and number of slides, it's time to add the main information for each slide. If your slides are mainly or all text, you may find it useful to add all the text in the Outliner. At any point you can switch to the Slide Editor and add more text there.

The Slide Editor is the view where you do most of the nitty-gritty work of creating your slide. You can add graphics, shapes, and charts in Slide Editor as well as change the background and formatting.

The advantage to adding the main body of text in the Editor is that you can see exactly how the text appears on the slide. Even if you add most of the text in Slide Editor, review the text in Outliner to make sure it flows well. You can also spell check all the slides at once in Slide Outliner by clicking Tools, Spell Checker.

Adding and Changing Text

If you find that you must add more lines to the slide, you can either add lines of text in Slide Outliner or alter the layout layer of the slide in Slide Editor.

You must create a text object before you can add text to your slide. If you've already chosen a layout that has a text object, such as a text box, title box, or bulleted list, it's easy. When you enter text into the Slide Outliner, the text object is automatically created for you on the slide.

To Do: Insert Text Objects

To insert a text box, bulleted list, or text line into the slide, follow these steps:

1. In PerfectExpert, click Add Text and choose the text object you want to insert.
2. On the Tools Palette, click the Text Object flyout and select the icon for text box, bulleted list, or text line.

Adding Graphics

Adding graphics is a lot like adding text. First, you insert a graphics object into the slide; then you insert the graphic.

There are endless graphics you can insert into a slideshow. Presentations comes with hundreds of clipart files that are collected in the Scrapbook. You can also create a graphic right in Presentations using the Bitmap Editor, or you can insert a graphic from another file on your computer.

To Do: Insert a Graphic

To insert a premade graphic, follow these steps:

1. From PerfectExpert, on the Edit Slides menu, click Add Graphics. Select Insert a Scrapbook Item or Add a Graphic from File, as appropriate.
2. From the menu bar, click Insert, Graphics and select Clipart or From File.
3. Select the item you want to insert and click Insert.

▼
4. The graphic appears in full size on the slide. Most of the time, you must resize the graphic. Click the graphic to open the graphic object box and click one of the resizing handles.

5. Drag the graphic to the desired size. To move the graphic on the slide, click anywhere inside the graphic object box and drag it to where you want it.
▲

Resized graphics are shown in Figure 15.5.

FIGURE 15.5
You can insert your own graphics file or select an image from the Presentations clipart Scrapbook.

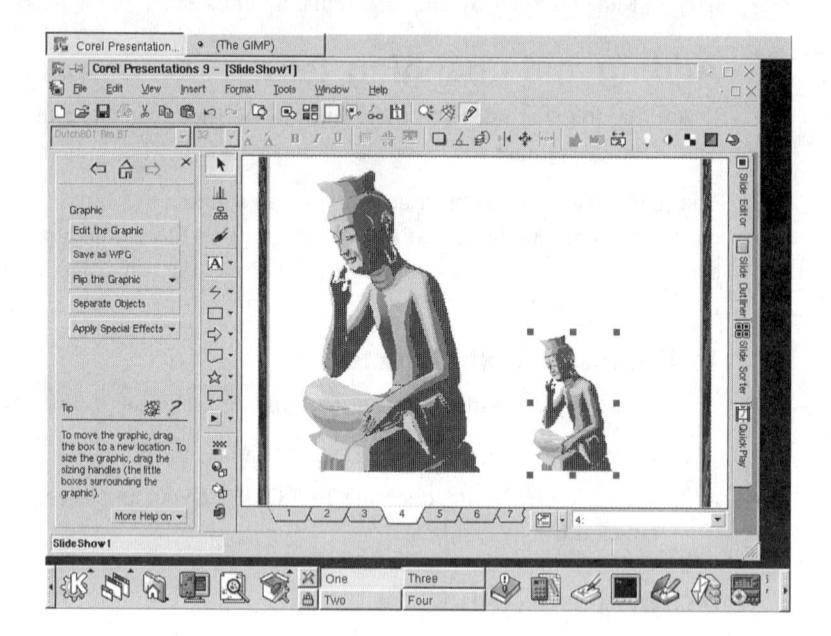

You'll learn how to work with the Bitmap editor in Hour 16, "Advanced Presentations."

Adding Speaker Notes and Audience Notes

You can type extra notes into your slideshow for each slide to use as speaker notes. After you create your speaker notes for each slide, the printout will include a thumbnail sketch of the slide, with your speaker notes below the slide.

Audience notes are somewhat similar to speaker notes, except that instead of notes, blank lines are printed below each slide on which the audience can write notes.

To Do: Create Speaker Notes

To create speaker notes to accompany your slides, follow these steps:

1. From PerfectExpert, in the Edit Slides menu, click Extras, Write Speaker Notes.
2. From the Property Bar, click the Speaker Notes icon.

▼   3. From Slide Sorter, double-click the Slide Properties Bar.

▲   4. From Slide Editor, right-click the slide and select Speaker Notes.

Type your speaker notes in the text box, as shown in Figure 15.6. To include the text from the slide, click Insert Text from Slide.

FIGURE 15.6
Use speaker notes as a tool for your presentation or as handouts for the audience (or both).

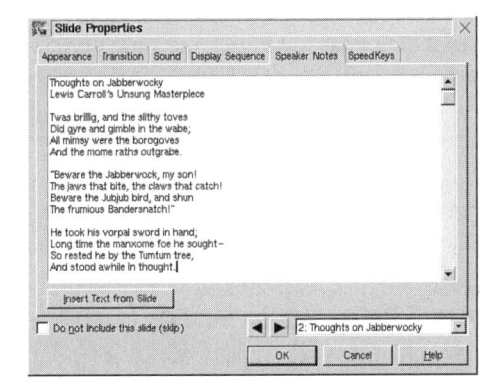

To print your speaker notes, click File, Print and then click the Print tab. Check Speaker Notes to print speaker notes. Check Audience Notes to print audience notes.

Rearranging the Slides in Slide Sorter

When you've finished entering the text for your slides in the Slide Outliner, check their appearance and sequence in the Slide Sorter. You can open the Slide Sorter by either clicking View, Slide Sorter or clicking the Slide Sorter tab on the right of the Drawing Window.

Thumbnail sketches of the slides in your slideshow appear in sequence.

If you want to move a slide in Slide Sorter, click the slide to select it and drag it to the desired location. To move a series of slides, left-click the first slide in the series, hold down the Shift key, click the last slide, and then drag the slides to where you want to insert them. You can also drag more than one slide out of sequence by clicking each slide while holding down the Ctrl key. Drag the slides to their new location, where they will appear in sequence.

You can rearrange as many slides as you like, as many times as you like, until you have them exactly as you want them. Presentations automatically renumbers the slides as you move them.

Step Three: Adding Presentation Effects

After the slideshow is finished, it's time to think about how you want to present it. Presentations has features that enable you to add sound effects, customize how slides will transition from one to the next, and customize and control slide display and animation.

All these items are controlled via the Slide Properties dialog box. In Slide Outliner, to open the Slide Properties dialog box, right-click the slide outline. Alternatively, click Format, Slide Properties and then tab for the property you want to change.

> The Slide Properties dialog box can be opened from the Slide Editor, the Slide Sorter, and the Slide Outliner.

Spicing Up Your Slideshow with Transitions

The Transition tab in the Slide Properties dialog box enables you to control how your slides will transition in the slideshow. There are many effects to choose from, as shown in Figure 15.7.

After you've chosen a transition, select a transition direction. For example, if you choose the Push Away transition, you can choose a direction of Top to Bottom, Bottom to Top, Left to Right, or Right to Left.

FIGURE 15.7
Good transitions make a presentation look more professional.

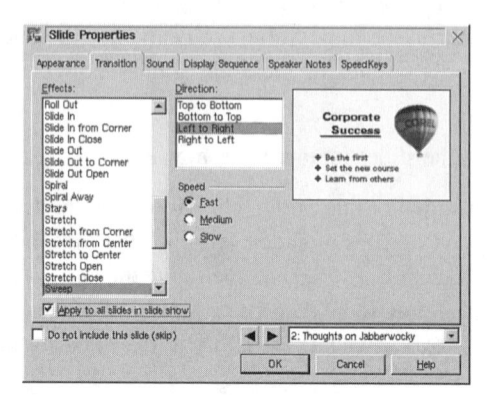

You can also select a transition speed of Fast, Medium, or Slow. Finally, if you want the same transition for every slide, check Apply to All Slides in Slideshow.

Although you can have as many transition types as you have slides, it is best from a design perspective to choose a transition you like and stick with it throughout the show. You don't want your audience concentrating on the transitions and not paying attention to the content of your slideshow. You can use two transitions in the same way you would use two font styles in a document—to emphasize a particular slide.

For example, if you change the transition style right before an important slide, that makes the audience sit up and take notice. They might not know exactly what caught their attention, but it will ensure that you have it (at least for a second). However, do not overuse this technique; otherwise, it will lose its effectiveness.

You can choose the speed of the transition, the type of transition, and (for some transition types) the direction. For a subtle effect, try bringing in most of the slides from the left and then the really important slide from the right.

Controlling How the Slide Is Displayed with Display Sequence

Display Sequence enables you to control how to play the slideshow. You can manually control the display of each slide via a mouse click or keyboard hotkey. You can also make the slideshow play automatically. If you want, the slideshow can even play in a continuous loop. The Display Sequence tab of the Slide Properties dialog box is shown in Figure 15.8.

FIGURE 15.8
Display Sequence enables you to control the timing of your presentation.

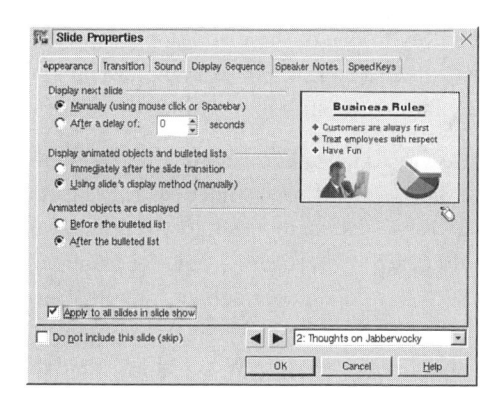

Controlling Animation with SpeedKeys

SpeedKeys are keystrokes that you assign to perform any of the following tasks in a slideshow:

- Advance items in a bulleted list one at a time
- Advance charts, images, or other animated objects
- Start and stop sound clips

- Stop the slideshow
- Launch a Web browser

SpeedKeys are easy to assign. All possible keystrokes are listed in the SpeedKeys tab of the Slide Properties dialog box. To assign a SpeedKey to an action, select the key you want to assign and then assign the key an action, as shown in Figure 15.9.

FIGURE 15.9

Using SpeedKeys, you can control your entire presentation with a few keystrokes.

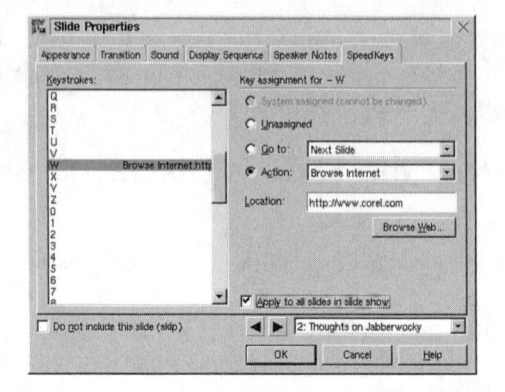

There are two kinds of SpeedKey assignments: Go To and Action. Go To lists the slides. When you assign a SpeedKey to one of these slides, pressing the SpeedKey during the slideshow will cause that slide to appear. For example, if you assign the A key to Next Slide, pressing the A key during the slideshow will advance the show to the next slide.

Action keys are similar to Go To keys. For example, if you want to open a Web page at some point in your slideshow, select Browse Internet from the Action drop-down menu. Assign the action a SpeedKey—for example, *W* for Web. Enter the URL you want to open in the Location field (`http://www.corel.com`, for example). If you don't know the exact URL, click Browse Web to open your default Internet browser. To make the SpeedKey apply to all slides in the slideshow, check Apply to All Slides in the Slideshow. This means that if you press the W key at any time during the slideshow, your default Web browser will open at the Corel Web site.

If you want to change the SpeedKey to I instead of W, select W in the Keystrokes field and check Unassigned. The SpeedKey action is removed from W. Now select I and assign the SpeedKey action to I.

Adding Sound to Your Slideshow

If your sound card is correctly installed and configured in your Linux system, you can add sound to your presentations. Presentations supports WAV, MIDI, and CD sound files. If you include a sound from CD-ROM, you can add an entire track, or you can specify starting and stopping points.

Use sound carefully in your presentations. Music can be an extraordinarily powerful tool, when used wisely. For example, if you want to induce a feeling of excitement and energy into your presentation, you might add some rock music clips. But if you play loud, energetic rock music during the entire presentation, the audience will become desensitized and the music will lose its effectiveness. Rock music of the same kind and intensity, played at the same volume, can actually put your audience to sleep!

The Sound tab of the Slide Properties dialog box is shown in Figure 15.10. You can access it in three ways:

- From the menu bar, click Insert, Sound.
- Right-click the slide and select Sound.
- From the Property Bar, click the Sound icon.

FIGURE 15.10
You can add wave or MIDI files or sounds from a CD to your slideshow.

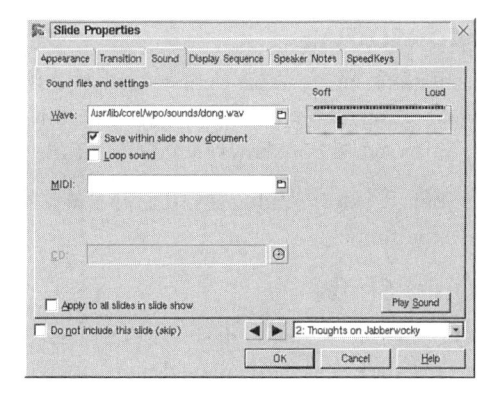

To Do: Play a Wave or MIDI File

To attach a wave or MIDI file, enter the file pathname, then follow these steps:

1. Adjust the play volume with the volume slider.
2. Check Save Within Slideshow Document.
3. If you want the sound to play continuously while the slide is displayed, check Loop Sound.
4. If you want the sound to play when each slide is introduced, check Apply to All Slides in Slideshow.

> If you want to play a sound from CD, insert the CD into your drive and click the Browse button.
>
> Enter the track title and number of the track you want to play in the Side CD-Audio dialog box.

Step Four: Customizing and Playing the Slideshow

You can tailor the same slideshow for different audiences so that you don't have to spend time re-creating the slideshow if you have several audiences. Speaker notes and handouts can also be easily generated from the slideshow.

You can also keep a slide in the file but indicate that it should be skipped in the show. That way, you can create a short and a long version of the slideshow using the same file. To skip a slide, open the Slide Sorter View. Right-click the slide and select Appearance. Check Do Not Include This Slide (Skip). The slide appears paler (or dimmer) than the other slides to indicate that it is a skipped slide.

Customizing Slideshows

If you have several presentations on the same topic to give to different audiences, you can create one master slide presentation and then create your different presentations out of it by skipping slides. Save each set of shows in a different file so that you have the set.

To save a version, click Tools, Custom Audiences. Create a new slideshow, skip the slides you want, and save the show.

To Do: Create a QuickShow

A *QuickShow* is a sped-up version of your slideshow. In a QuickShow, each slide is saved as a bitmap so that the slides can be displayed more quickly. To create a QuickShow, follow these steps:

1. Select View, Play Slideshow and click Create QuickShow.
2. Check Enable Use QuickShow.
3. When you are ready to play the QuickShow, click Play. The QuickShow plays on your screen. The Play Slideshow dialog box is shown in Figure 15.11.

Creating Your First Slideshow   311

FIGURE 15.11
The QuickShow slideshow loads and plays faster than a regular slideshow.

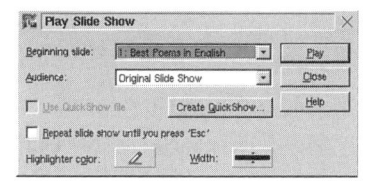

The advantage of QuickShow is, of course, that your slides load faster. The disadvantage is that QuickShow files take up more disk space. Also, every time you make a change to the original slideshow file, you must re-create the QuickShow.

Packing It Up with Show on the Go

When you save your slideshow with Show on the Go, a portable slideshow is created. *Portable* means that the slideshow can be played on any computer that has Windows 3.x, Windows 95/98/NT, or Linux (with X) 2.2x or higher. Note that Corel Presentations need not be installed.

The Show on the Go dialog box, shown in Figure 15.12, guides you through the process. To create a Show on the Go, select File, Show on the Go. Then click Create. A set of defaults is displayed in the Show on the Go dialog box, including the filename, the directory in which to save the file, the system to play the show on, and the display type.

FIGURE 15.12
Show on the Go enables you to play slideshows created in Linux on Windows or Linux machines.

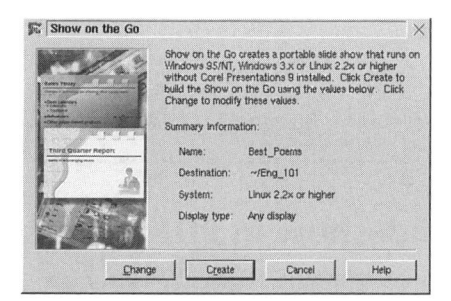

To change any of the summary information defaults, click Change. Next, enter the location on your file system where you want to store the Show on the Go and then check the system type: Windows 95/NT, Windows 3.x/95/NT, or Linux 2.2x running X Windows.

> If you're not sure which format to save your slideshow in, save the show in each format and use a filename that will indicate the system type. For example, you could save the Annual slideshow as `Annual_lx` and `Annual_win95`.

You can also specify any type of display or a display matching the current display. It is prudent to use Any Display to give yourself maximum flexibility.

Click Finish. The values you entered are displayed in Summary Information. If you want the slideshow to loop continuously, check Repeat Slideshow Until You Press Esc.

Click Create and you're done! To play your Show on the Go, just double-click the file.

Publishing the Slideshow As an HTML File

Publishing a slideshow in HTML format converts each slide into a JPEG, GIF, or PNG image, which is then placed into an HTML file. Each HTML file shows up as one Web page. Simply click File, Internet Publisher, and an HTML slideshow is created. The slideshow will not have special effects, animation, transitions or sound, but your audience won't need anything but an ordinary HTML browser to see the slideshow.

To publish the slideshow as an HTML file, click File, Internet Publisher. The Internet Publisher Wizard guides you through the process.

The four choices of graphic format for slideshow images are GIF, JPEG, PNG, and Show It!

Show It! is a Corel browser plug-in (available for Windows Netscape Navigator and Internet Explorer) that will play your animations, transitions, and sound with your HTML slideshow. A person viewing your slideshow must have Show It! installed to use this graphic format.

> Show It! is available for download at www.corel.com.

Publishing the Slideshow in PDF Format

You can also save your slideshow in PDF format. You can then open the slideshow in Adobe Acrobat Reader, which is available for Linux, UNIX, Macintosh, and Windows.

To save the slideshow as a PDF file, click File, Publish to PDF.

Saving Slideshows As Graphics

You can save your slides as graphics so that they can be inserted as graphics into other documents, slideshows, and applications. To save your slideshow as a graphic, click File, Save As and select a file format.

You can save the file in the following formats:

- WordPerfect Graphic
- PostScript
- MS PowerPoint
- Bitmap
- JPEG
- TIFF

If you save the file as a WordPerfect Graphics file, you can continue to edit the file as if it were an ordinary SHW file. If you save the file as a bitmap, JPEG, or other format, it becomes a graphic and you can no longer edit the file as a slideshow. You can, however, edit the graphic in a graphics application such as the GIMP.

Summary

In this hour you created an outline of your slideshow in Slide Outliner, including titles, subtitles, and text. You used PerfectExpert, the menus and toolbars, and the Tools Palette to accomplish tasks in your slideshow. You also added more text and graphics in Slide Editor and created speaker and audience notes for your slideshow presentation. You rearranged your slides in Slide Sorter and added transitions, animation, and sound. You also saved your slideshow as a QuickShow, Show on the Go, HTML file, PDF file, and graphics file.

Q&A

Q Is it possible to import PowerPoint files into Presentations?

A Most definitely. You can import a PowerPoint file, edit it in Presentations, and then save it as a WordPerfect slideshow or as a PowerPoint file.

Workshop

The Workshop contains quiz questions and exercises to help reinforce what you've learned in this hour. If you get stuck, the answers can be found in Appendix B, "Answers to Quiz Questions."

Quiz

1. How do you open the PerfectExpert dialog box from within Presentations?
2. True or false: You can enter charts and graphics in Slide Outliner.
3. What is the difference between deleting and clearing a slide?
4. What does the PerfectExpert Web icon do?

5. What is the difference between speaker notes and audience notes?
6. How would you apply the same transition style to all the slides in the slideshow?
7. Which sound file formats can you attach to your Presentations 9 slideshow?

Exercises

1. Open Presentations 9 and create a new Presentations slideshow.
2. Open Slide Outliner and enter your slide outline. If you don't have a slide outline, try making a presentation out of the chapters of this book.
3. Create a new slide and then delete it.
4. From Slide Outliner, click the Slide Editor tab. In PerfectExpert, click Go to a Slide. What happens?
5. Click OK on the Go To Slide dialog box. Insert a clipart from the Scrapbook into a slide.
6. Make the clipart you inserted in exercise 5 smaller; then move it to the bottom-right corner of the slide.
7. In a new slide, enter "Walrus" in the title box. Add speaker notes to read:

    The sun was shining on the sea,

    Shining with all his might:

    He did his very best to make

    The billows smooth and bright-

    And this was odd, because it was

    The middle of the night.
8. Add a transition to your slideshow.
9. Assign the Q key as a SpeedKey to quit the slideshow.
10. Save your slideshow as a QuickShow, Show on the Go, HTML file, and PDF file.

HOUR 16

Advanced Presentations

You can make slide shows with just text and sound, but adding graphics and charts makes the show more interesting and enhances the audience's understanding of the subject. For some types of presentations, graphics or charts are the central part of the slide show. As you'll see this hour, you can use Presentations for much more than just creating slide shows.

In this hour, you will

- Create data charts using data imported from a spreadsheet and data entered manually into a datasheet.
- Create organization charts to show the structure of an organization or process.
- Add line art and shapes to your slide show or drawing.
- Import bitmap, pixmap, and clipart (vector) graphics into your slide show.
- Edit bitmap and pixmap graphics in the Bitmap Editor.

Working with Data Charts

Data charts make it possible to display numeric information in a way that's visually appealing, simple, and easily grasped by the audience. Using data charts in a slide show is particularly important because your audience often has only a minute or two to digest the information on a slide before the next slide appears. An example of a slide with a data chart is shown in Figure 16.1.

FIGURE 16.1
Data charts present numeric information on a slide or drawing.

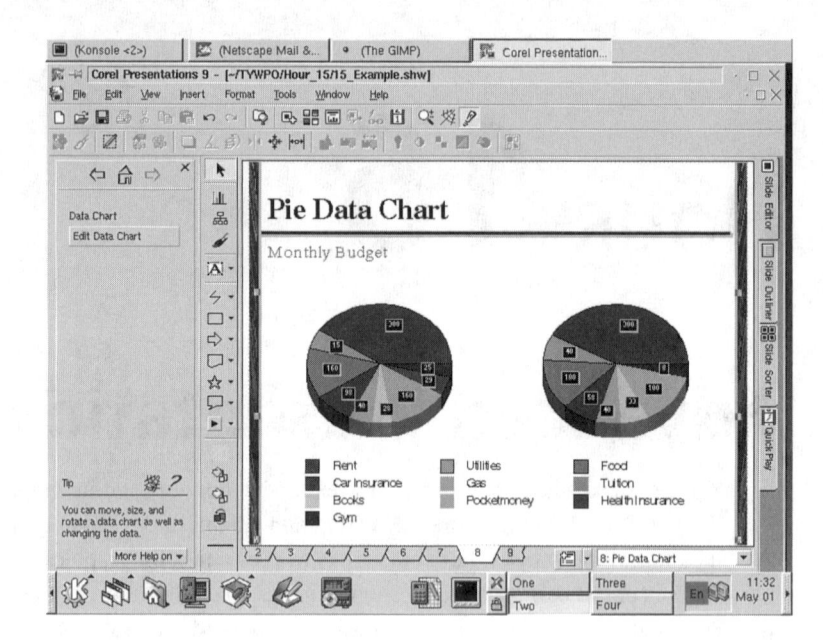

To Do: Create a Data Chart

Define a data chart layout object on the slide, by completing one of the following sets of steps:

1. For a blank slide, select Format, Layout Gallery. Select a layout that includes a data chart object.
2. Double-click the data chart layout object to insert a new data chart.

OR

1. On a slide that already contains information, click Insert, Data Chart.
2. Draw the area where you want the data chart to go. If you need to make room for the data chart, you can resize any other object on the slide by clicking the object and dragging it to its new size. Figure 16.2 shows an example.

FIGURE 16.2
You can insert a data chart after you have added text to a slide.

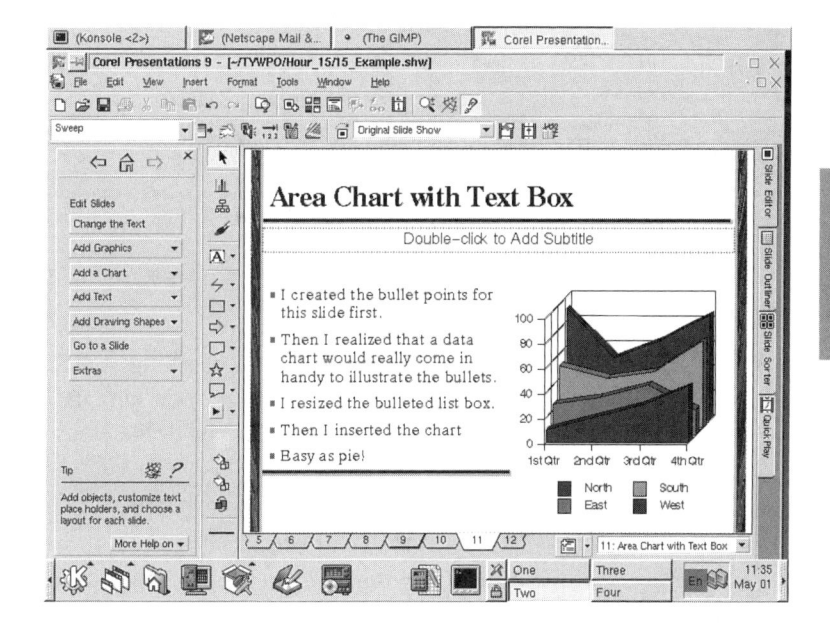

The Data Chart Gallery

After you insert a new data chart object into your slide or drawing, the Data Chart Gallery opens with a list of the available chart styles. The Data Chart Gallery is a collection of predesigned charts that have the design and colors already chosen for you, somewhat like the Master Gallery. All you have to do is select the chart you want and enter your data into the datasheet. The Data Chart Gallery is shown in Figure 16.3.

FIGURE 16.3
The Data Chart Gallery has a chart for every type of data display.

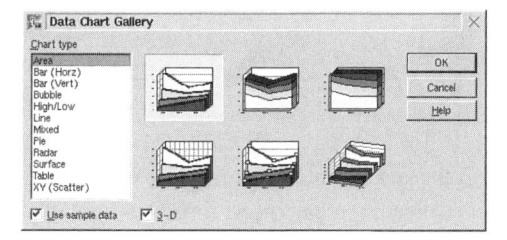

Presentations comes with many different kinds of data charts, including the following:

- Area charts
- Bar charts
- Bubble charts

- High-low charts (show high, low, and close quotes for a stock, index, or other financial item within a specific time period)
- Line charts
- Mixed charts (mix chart types on the same chart)
- Pie charts (good for showing percentages of a whole)
- Radar charts
- Surface charts
- Table charts
- XY scatter charts

To see what the chart style looks like with data, check the Use Sample Data check box to create the chart using sample data. The datasheet opens with the sample data, and the chart is drawn in the chart box on your slide. If you decide to use that chart type, you can replace the sample data with your data.

Entering Data in Your Chart

After you choose a chart style from the Data Chart Gallery, the datasheet appears in the drawing window. The datasheet is used to draw the data chart. Enter your data into the datasheet manually or import it from an existing spreadsheet. A sample datasheet is shown in Figure 16.4.

FIGURE 16.4
The datasheet works like a simple spreadsheet.

	Legend	Labels 1	Pie 1	Labels 2	Pie 2
	MONTHLY BUDGET				
1	Rent	300	300	300	300
2	Utilities	15	40	40	50
3	Food	160	100	100	100
4	Car Insurance	98	63	58	55
5	Gas	40	40	40	40
6	Tuition	0	0	0	0
7	Books	28	33	33	44
8	Pocketmoney	160	100	100	100
9	Health Insurance	29	37	20	0
10	Gym	25	25	0	25

The datasheet works just like a spreadsheet. Each piece of data resides in a cell, which is located via numbered rows and lettered columns. You can add, delete, cut, copy, and paste just like in a spreadsheet. You can insert formulas into a datasheet. You can also transpose the rows and columns of data as well as mark data on the datasheet to be excluded from the chart.

> All data in the datasheet must be numeric, except for cells containing labels and legend information.

> When deleting data from the datasheet, use the Delete key, not the spacebar. If you use the spacebar, the data cell appears empty but still contains a space character. This can alter your data plots.

Importing a Datasheet

You can import data from a spreadsheet using the following file formats:

- Quattro Pro
- Microsoft Excel
- Lotus 1-2-3
- PlanPerfect
- ASCII text
- ANSI text

You can link the datasheet to an existing spreadsheet so that when you make changes to the spreadsheet, the Presentations chart data is automatically updated the next time you open the file containing the chart.

To Do: Import Data from a Spreadsheet

1. Open a datasheet and click it to change the main menu from the text menu to the data chart menu.
2. On the main menu, click Data, Import or from the Datasheet menu in PerfectExpert, click Extras, Import the Data.
3. In the Import Data dialog box (see Figure 16.5), type the path and filename of the file containing the spreadsheet data.

FIGURE 16.5
You can import data into the datasheet from a spreadsheet. Link the datasheet to the spreadsheet if the spreadsheet data will change often.

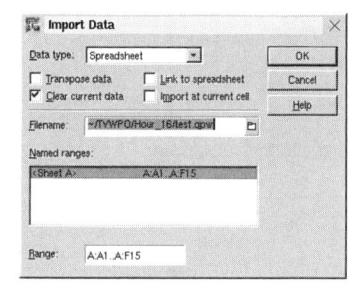

The Import Data dialog box has other options you can use when importing data:

- *Transpose Data*. Switches data from columns to rows and rows to columns.
- *Clear Current Data*. Deletes all the data already in the datasheet.
- *Link to Spreadsheet*. Links the imported data to the data chart.
- *Import at Current Cell*. Imports data at the selected cell.

Entering Data Manually into the Datasheet

To add data manually to the datasheet, click the cell and type in the data. Alternatively, double-click the cell to open the Edit Data Cell dialog box, which contains the cell address. Generally, it's easier just to add data directly to the cell, unless you want to be sure you have the correct cell address.

To insert rows and columns in the datasheet, right-click where you want to insert the row or column and click Insert. A new row or column is inserted. To insert multiple rows or columns, click Edit, Insert or, from PerfectExpert, click Insert Rows or Columns in the Datasheet menu. Check the Rows or Columns box and enter how many rows or columns you want to insert.

Follow the same procedure to delete rows and columns.

Using Formulas

You can apply formulas to data after it has been entered in the datasheet. You can also gather statistics about your data for display in the data chart. For formulas, click a data cell in the datasheet and then click Data, Formulas. For statistics, click Data, Statistics. Some of the formulas available are shown in Figure 16.6.

FIGURE 16.6
Average and Cumulative Total are two of the formulas available for your datasheet.

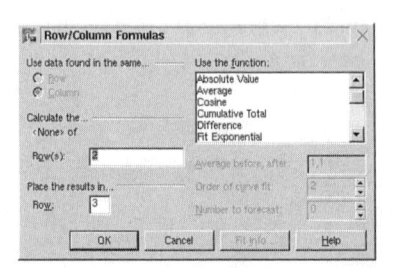

Modifying the Layout

After you have worked on your data chart, you might decide that another chart type would be better. You can easily keep the same datasheet and change the chart type. Click the chart to change the main menu to the data chart menu and then select Chart, Layout/Type. Click the new chart type. Your data is redrawn in the new chart type.

You can change the colors that your chart is drawn in as well as add patterns, textures, and gradients to the chart display. From the main menu, select Chart, Series and then click the Fill tab. The options for colors, patterns, and textures are the same as those for shapes. You'll learn more about coloring shapes in the next section.

Keeping Things Crystal Clear with Titles, Legends, and Labels

The title and subtitle of your chart are different from the title and subtitle of the slide. The chart title and subtitle are created within the chart object rather than on the slide itself.

To Do: Add a Title and Subtitle to Your Data Chart

1. In PerfectExpert, click Edit Data Chart, Change Elements, Change the Title.
2. In the main menu, click Chart, Title and open the Title Options tab. Check the Display Chart Title option and enter the chart title.
3. You can select left, right, or center justification for the title position by checking Position. A sample chart thumbnail demonstrates your choice.
4. The same steps apply for subtitles, except you would choose the Subtitle menu entry. You can change the title font, size, and title/subtitle box type in the Title or Subtitle Properties dialog box. You can also add colors, patterns, outlines, and box fill patterns. The Title Properties dialog box is shown in Figure 16.7.

FIGURE 16.7
Jazz up your data charts by adding colors and patterns to the chart title and subtitle.

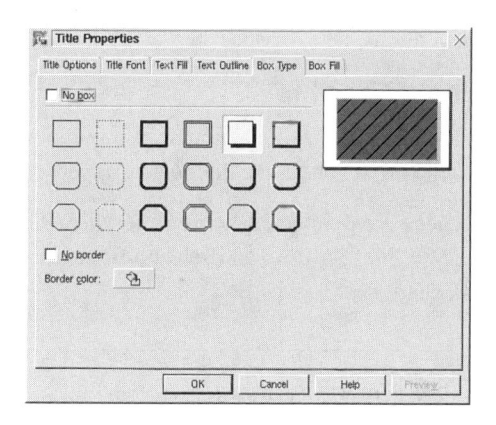

The last thing to do when creating a data chart is to add data labels and a legend. The *legend* is the key to understanding the chart. It lists all the data types on the chart and which colors, patterns, and so on represent which data. If your data in the datasheet was already marked with a legend, it will automatically translate to a legend on the chart.

Labels identify the data on the chart itself and are also automatically created from the datasheet.

You can change the legend and labels right in the datasheet by editing the legend and label cells directly, but the Legend and Label Properties dialog boxes enable you to specify position, font, fill, and box type as well as to change the labels and legend titles themselves. To open the Label Properties dialog box from PerfectExpert, click the data chart to open the Edit Data Chart menu and then click Change Elements, Change the Labels.

To change the legend properties, click in the data chart and from the main menu click Chart, Legend.

Saving the Data Chart

You can save the data chart within your slide show, but you can also save the slide with the chart as a separate drawing. You can save the data chart as a graphic or just export the data itself to a spreadsheet without saving the chart at all.

Exporting Data

If you want to save the data from the chart for use in another data chart, spreadsheet, or drawing, simply export the data. Exporting data to a spreadsheet is almost the same process as importing data. Click the datasheet and then click Data, Export on the main menu. From PerfectExpert, click Export the Data. Enter the file and file format in the Export dialog box. At present, you can only export the datasheet as ASCII or ANSI text, delimited (separated) by commas, tabs, or spaces.

Saving the Slide As a Graphic

You can save a single slide that contains a data chart as a graphic for use elsewhere. Select the data chart by clicking it. The Save dialog box appears.

In the Save dialog box, check Save Selected Items (otherwise, the entire slide show will be saved as a graphic). Click File, Save As and select a filename and graphic file format in which to save the data chart.

> If you save the data chart as a WordPerfect graphic, you'll still be able to edit the datasheet. If you save it as another graphic file format, it will just become like any other graphic, in that you would not be able to edit the data.

Working with Organization Charts

Organization charts have many uses other than as the traditional company hierarchy chart. Use an organization chart whenever you want to show relationships between people, services, processes, or things. Organization charts show the structure of an organization and the relationships of the people in the organization. They can also show the relationship between processes in a workflow or any items in a flowchart.

You can use a Presentations organization chart to show different procedural relationships, such as the reporting structure of an organization versus the working structure. You can create a workflow diagram or other procedural diagram or flowchart. You can also use the organization chart to show the relationship between departments or products.

Organization charts work much like data charts in that there are several predetermined layouts you can use when you first create the chart. You can save an organization chart as graphic or drawing or as part of a slideshow. A sample organization chart is shown in Hour 14, "Corel Presentations 9 Basics," in Figure 14.3.

Creating an Organization Chart

You create an organization chart in a slide by selecting the layout style that contains an organization chart object or by inserting the org chart into the slide using Insert, Organization Chart. Alternatively, click the Org Chart icon on the Tools menu and draw your org chart on the slide. Once your organization chart object is in place, double-click it and a sample org chart is drawn.

You can orient an organization chart top to bottom to create a hierarchy or left to right to create a flow chart. Click Format, Branch Structure to open the Branch Layout dialog box, shown in Figure 16.8.

FIGURE 16.8

Use the Branch Layout dialog box to orient and control the layout structure of your chart.

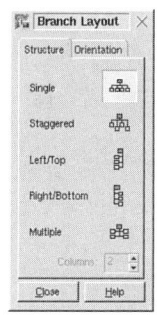

To add text to your organization chart, double-click the chart square and type the text. To add branches to the chart, right-click the chart, select Insert, and then click one of the following options:

- *Subordinates*. Adds a square one value below the current square.
- *Staff*. Adds a square branching off the main subordinate branch.
- *Coworker*. Adds a square to the same branch as the selected square.
- *Manager*. Adds a square directly above the selected square.

If you're creating a flow chart rather than an organization chart, the insertion style names may be off-putting at first, but once you get used to them, you can make flowcharts very quickly, albeit without the flowchart symbols. Figure 16.9 shows how the insertion styles work.

FIGURE 16.9
The insertion styles enable you to quickly expand your org chart.

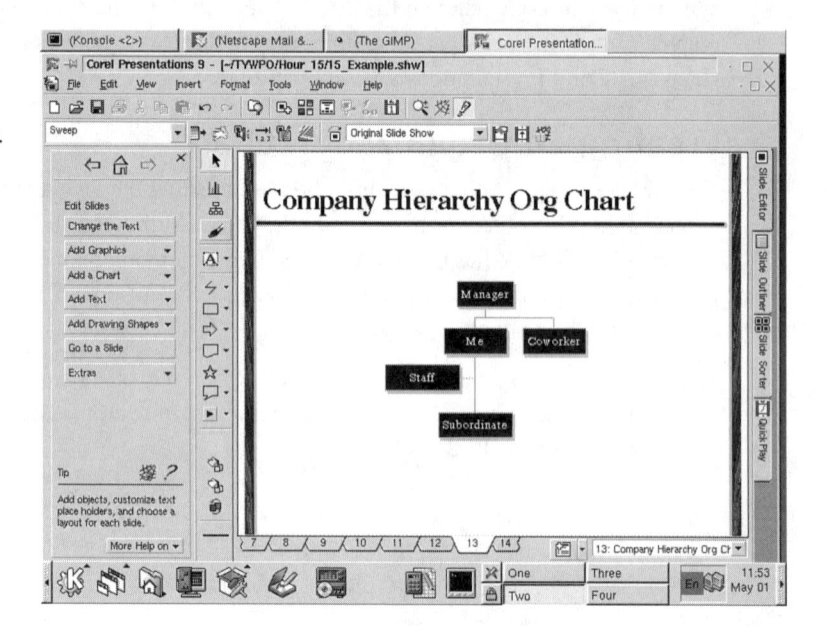

Incorporating Images into Your Presentations

Graphics and other images are great for adding visual interest to a slide show. For some slide shows, such as lectures, sales pitches, or research presentations, they can play an integral role. In Presentations, you can easily import graphics from external sources as well as create your own shapes and line drawings.

There are two main kinds of images in Presentations: graphics and line drawings. Graphics are pictures, patterns, or photographs that you insert from an external file, or from the WordPerfect Clipart Scrapbook. You can edit your graphics within Presentations using the Bitmap Editor. Line art consists of simple shapes and patterns that you can create using the Tools Palette.

Using Lines and Shapes

Line drawings are useful for pointing out relationships among items on a slide, and you can to draw attention to an item by encasing it within a shape. Presentations also includes several kinds of callouts you can use to add interest to your text or to add descriptions to parts of a graphic. You can also combine a graphic with callouts to create a diagram.

You can create more than 100 different shapes with the shape-drawing tools. Here are some examples:

- Line shapes
- Basic shapes
- Arrows
- Callout shapes
- Flowchart elements
- Action shapes
- Star shapes

To Do: Add a Shape to a Slide or Drawing

1. Click the flyout of the shape category and select the shape you want by clicking it.
2. Place the cursor in the drawing window where the shape is to go.
3. Drag the mouse to draw the shape on the slide. Draw diagonally to get a nondistorted shape or vertically to get the height right and then horizontally to get the width. Some sample shapes are shown in Figure 16.10.

FIGURE 16.10
Draw attention to a point on the slide by encasing it in a shape.

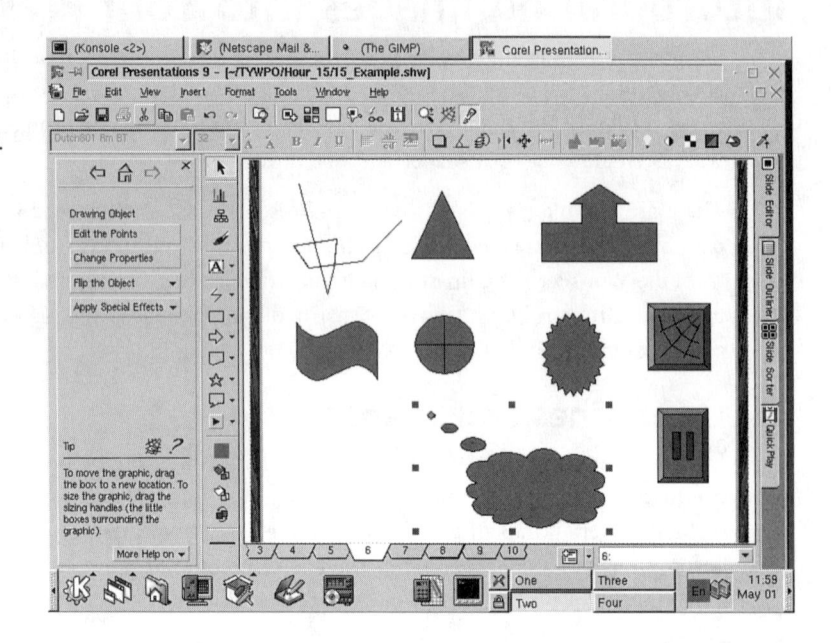

To make a shape thinner, wider, longer, or shorter, click the shape and drag a handle until the shape is the size you want.

To Do: Using Guides and Gridlines

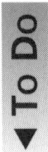

1. To draw a shape with precision, click View, Grid/Guides/Snap and check the options you want from the following list:
   - Display Grid
   - Snap to Grid
   - Display Guides
   - Snap to Guides

2. The Grid/Guide/Snap options enable you to make the guide lines smaller or larger using the Interval option.

3. You can also make the horizontal and vertical spaces between the guides shorter or longer. The interval is counted out on the ruler.

4. Use the Snap Zone option to indicate how close you must drag the shape to the grid before it snaps in place.

Using Colors, Patterns, and Textures

To make your shapes and line drawings more interesting, you can use a fill. The Presentations fills include the following:

- *Solid colors.* These are chosen from a color palette.
- *Bitmaps (textures).* Bitmap graphics that can be inserted into a shape.
- *Color gradients.* These consist of two colors blending into one another.
- *Color patterns.* These include a background color and a pattern color.
- *Bitmap textures.* Usually photos that are applied as patterns.

To apply a fill to the shape, select Format, Object Properties, Fill. Alternatively, from PerfectExpert, select the object to bring up the Drawing Object menu. Clicking Change Properties brings up the Object Properties dialog box, shown in Figure 16.11.

FIGURE 16.11
Colors, patterns, and textures emphasize important points and add life to your slide show.

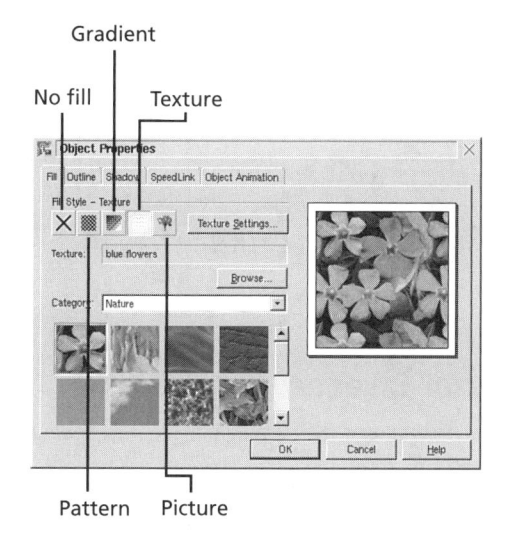

Here are the fill styles from which you can select:

- No fill
- Pattern
- Gradient
- Texture
- Picture

For patterns and gradients, select the pattern you want and then select the foreground color and the background color. Click OK to apply your selection to the shape.

For fill textures, select Texture or Picture. Texture applies a bitmap graphic texture, which acts as a repetitive pattern that fills the shape. A picture is also a bitmap graphic, but a picture consists of an image that's resized automatically to fit into the shape. Figure 16.12 shows the difference between a texture and a picture.

FIGURE 16.12

In a texture, the image bitmap repeats as a pattern to fill the shape. A picture is one image that automatically resizes to center and fill the shape.

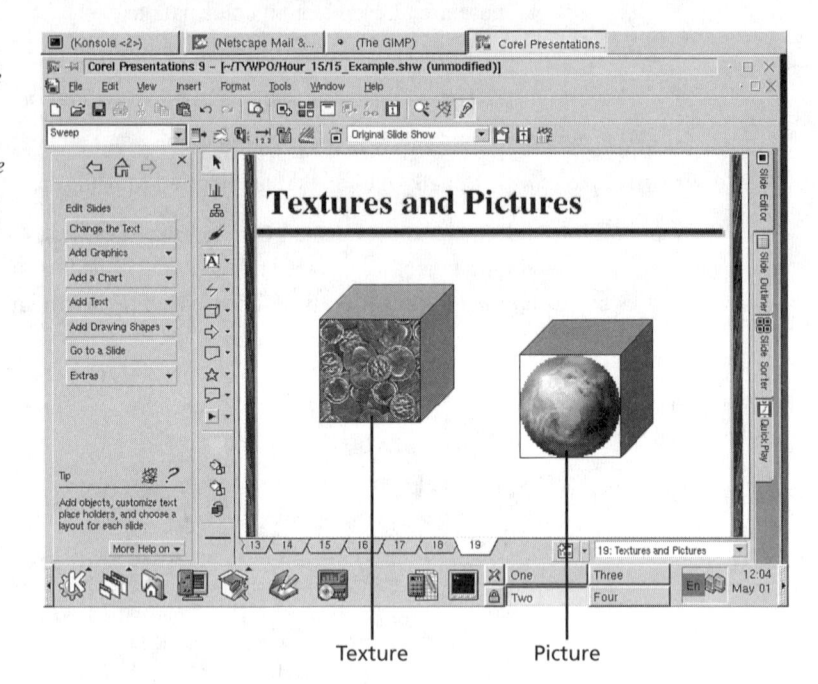

Applying Special Effects

In addition to the color and pattern fills, Presentations has special effects tools you can apply to your shapes and line drawings. The special effects tools include the following:

- *Watermark*. Fades and blurs the image so that when it is applied to the background layer of your slide, the image appears as a watermark.
- *Gray Scale*. Turns color images to corresponding shades of gray. This is useful for making black-and-white presentations or handouts. The Gray Scale tool makes the shades of gray sharper and improves the look of the image, rather than letting the printer driver determine which shade of gray corresponds to the colors in your image.
- *Invert Colors*. Switches the foreground and background colors.
- *Silhouette*. Produces a shadow of the image.

Advanced Presentations

- *Outline*. Displays a line sketch of the main lines of the image (just enough so you can see the image).
- *Coloring Book*. Displays a bold outline of the image.
- *Outline All*. Displays a detailed line drawing of the image.
- *Transparent*. Removes the fill from the object so you can see objects behind it.

Figure 16.13 shows some of the special effects.

FIGURE 16.13
You can apply special effects to any shape or line drawing, but not to bitmaps.

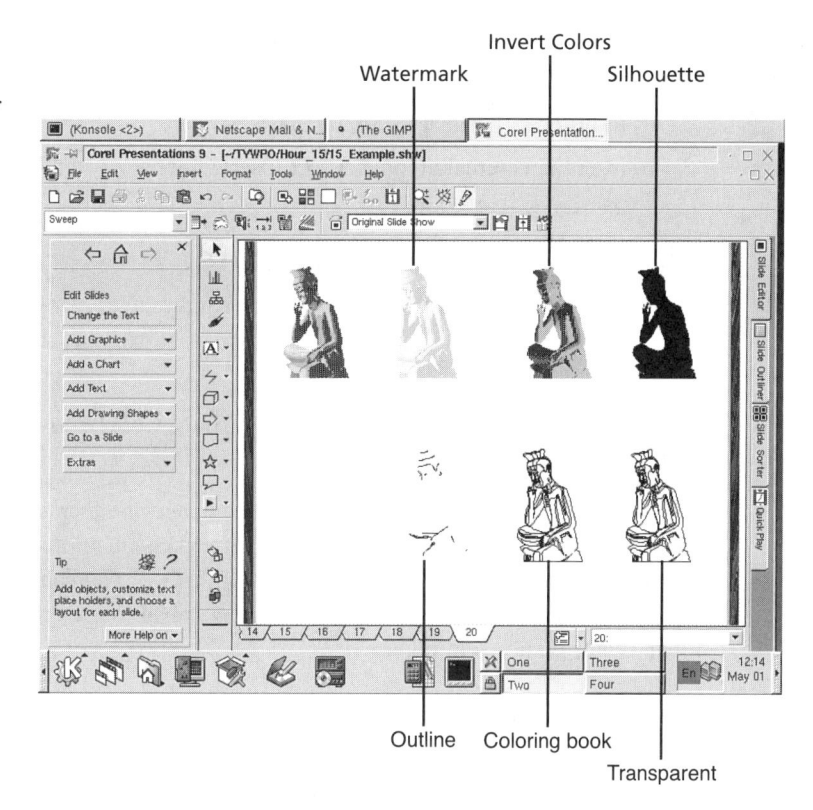

Image tools alter the overall look of a graphic. Play with the following settings until your graphic looks exactly the way you want it:

- Brightness
- Contrast
- Black and White

To Do: Insert Text into a Shape

You can insert text anywhere in your shape by inserting a text box inside the shape.

1. Click the Text flyout on the Tools Palette bar.
2. Click inside the shape and drag the text box to the desired size.
3. Click inside the text box and type your text.

To Do: Insert an Image from an External Source

Presentations comes with a scrapbook of clipart and photographs you can insert into your slides. You can also insert your own graphic from a file.

1. To insert clipart, select Insert, Graphics, Clipart.
2. To insert an external graphic, select Insert Graphics, From File and then browse to the file.

Editing Images in Bitmap Editor

Presentations comes with a Bitmap Editor you can use to edit any bitmap or pixmap graphic. You can also edit a vector graphic (such as clipart) if you first convert the vector graphic to a bitmap file.

To convert a vector graphic to a bitmap, select Tools, Convert to Bitmap. You can then edit the graphic in the Bitmap Editor.

To edit an image in the Bitmap Editor, click the image and then click Edit, Edit Bitmap. The image appears as a collection of pixels that you can manipulate. Click the Edit the Pixels button in PerfectExpert to zoom the image so that you can work with the individual pixels. Click the Full Bitmap area to move the pixel image around in the editor. The Bitmap Editor is shown in Figure 16.14.

Cropping Images

If you want to crop an image, open it in Bitmap Editor. In the Bitmap Editor, the image is contained within a frame. To crop an image, drag the frame around the portion of the bitmap that you want to keep. When you save the image and close the Bitmap Editor, the parts that are not within the frame are not included in the image when it is inserted in the drawing or slide.

FIGURE 16.14
You can edit any image in the Bitmap Editor if you've converted it to a bitmap (pixmap) image.

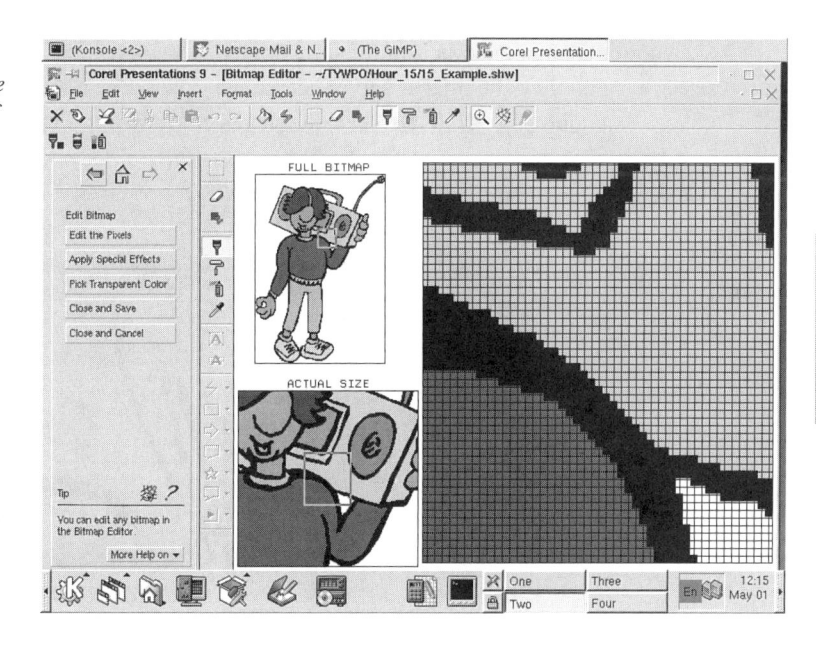

> When you are not in Bitmap Editor, changing the size of the frame resizes the image. In Bitmap Editor, the size of the image does not change when you resize the frame.

Resizing, Rotating, and Skewing an Image

Regardless of whether your image is a bitmap, a vector graphic, or a line drawing or shape, there are some manipulations you can make to the image within the drawing window of the slide editor.

To resize an image, select it and then drag the handles diagonally outward or inward to increase or decrease the size of the image, respectively.

Rotating an object turns it around on the page, either clockwise or counterclockwise. To rotate an image, select it, right-click the image, and click Rotate. Then drag a *corner* handle to rotate the object around an imaginary axis in the center of the image object area.

Skewing the image distorts it in the direction you drag a handle. To skew an image, select it, right-click the image, and select Rotate. Then drag a *side* handle to skew the image. Examples of rotated and skewed images are shown in Figure 16.15.

FIGURE 16.15
Rotating and skewing enable you to add unusual effects to your slides and drawings.

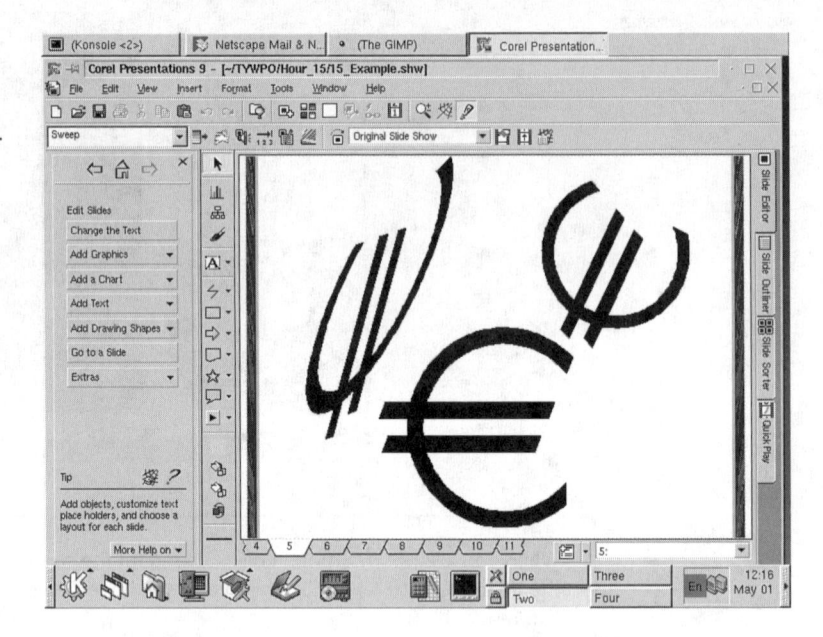

> Notice that the processes to rotate and skew an image are similar, except you drag a corner handle to rotate the image and side handle to skew it.

Summary

In this hour you added data charts to your presentation. You imported data from a spreadsheet for a data chart and you learned how to enter data manually into the datasheet. You learned how to create organization charts to show relationships. You created line drawings and shapes, filled shapes with color, patterns, and text. You also imported graphics into your slide show and learned how to edit graphics in the Bitmap Editor.

Q&A

Q Sometimes when I try to open Presentations, I get a message stating "Presentations has encountered a fatal error. If the error persists, contact Corel Tech Support."

A If Presentations (or any WordPerfect Office 2000 application) exits ungracefully, sometimes the socket file for the wine server will not be deleted. In your home directory, delete `$HOME/wpo2000/wineserver-localhost.localdomain/socket` and start Presentations. (Wine is a free implementation of Windows that enables Windows applications to work in UNIX environments. WordPerfect Office 2000 for Linux is at heart a Windows application running on top of a heavily altered wine program. For more information on wine, see `http://www.winehq.org`.)

Q Does a graphic have to be in BMP format to edit it in the Bitmap Editor?

A No. You can edit any WordPerfect-recognized graphic that uses pixels, such as PNG, in the Bitmap Editor. Vector graphics must first be converted to bitmaps.

Workshop

The Workshop contains quiz questions and exercises to help reinforce what you've learned in this hour. If you get stuck, the answers can be found in Appendix B, "Answers to Quiz Questions."

Quiz

1. Name the two chart types in Presentations and explain the difference between the two.
2. Name five data chart types available in Presentations.
3. Can you have nonnumeric data in the datasheet?
4. How would you create an organization chart on an existing slide?
5. What must you do to edit a non-bitmap graphic in the Bitmap Editor?

Exercises

1. Create a new slide containing an area data chart using the sample data that automatically appears in the datasheet when you open a new data chart.

2. Open the datasheet and add a new category to the legend: Southwest. Enter the following data:

1st Qtr	10
2nd Qtr	25
3rd Qtr	50
4th Qtr	35

3. Change the data chart type of the chart you made in exercise 1 from an area chart to a line chart.

4. Save the chart you made in exercise 3 as a JPEG file.

5. Re-create the organization chart shown in Figure 16.9.

6. Re-create the images in Figure 16.12.

PART V

Managing Your Life with CorelCENTRAL 9

Hour

17 Getting Organized with CorelCENTRAL 9

18 Managing Contacts with CorelCENTRAL 9 Address Book

HOUR 17

Getting Organized with CorelCENTRAL 9

CorelCENTRAL 9 is the Personal Information Manager for WordPerfect Office 2000. Comprised of three productivity tools—a calendar, an address book, and a memo application—CorelCENTRAL is the central place for you to organize your tasks and your time, helping you to be more productive.

In this hour, you will

- Explore the Corel Calendar environment.
- Add and edit events in your calendar, including repeating and all-day events.
- Add and edit tasks in the Task list and divide larger tasks into subtasks.
- Search for strings in the calendar and Task list using Find and apply filters to the task list.
- Create links to memos, applications, files, and URLs from an event or task.

Working with CorelCENTRAL 9 Calendar

The CorelCENTRAL calendar can be the central focus of all your WordPerfect 2000 projects. Small and fast, the calendar incorporates the most important features of planning software, without the many confusing features that slow down other calendar applications. Although you probably didn't buy WordPerfect Office 2000 for CorelCENTRAL, it's the sleeper application of the bunch. It does the job with speed and efficiency, giving you the time to be more productive.

You can start the Calendar in several ways. From the WordPerfect Office 2000 menu bar on your desktop, start CorelCENTRAL 9. The Calendar opens by default. You can also open Utilities, CorelCENTRAL Calendar, or enter `cccalendar` from a shell prompt

What's more, you can start from WordPerfect, Quattro Pro, Presentations, or Address Book by clicking Tools, CorelCENTRAL Calendar.

The Calendar workspace is pretty intuitive. Virtually all the options are available from the menu bar and/or toolbar, but there are also a few right-click menus that come in handy when you have a quick job to do. In the default Day view, the Calendar desktop is divided into four main sections:

- Menu and Toolbars
- Calendar tabs and six-month calendar view
- Events list
- Task list

You can have multiple calendar files for multiple tasks. For example, you can have a calendar for personal appointments and tasks, a calendar for work, a calendar to track time, and a calendar for team events. Each calendar has a tab for easy access. To switch to a new calendar, simply click its tab. Corel Calendar is shown in Figure 17.1.

Getting Organized with CorelCENTRAL 9

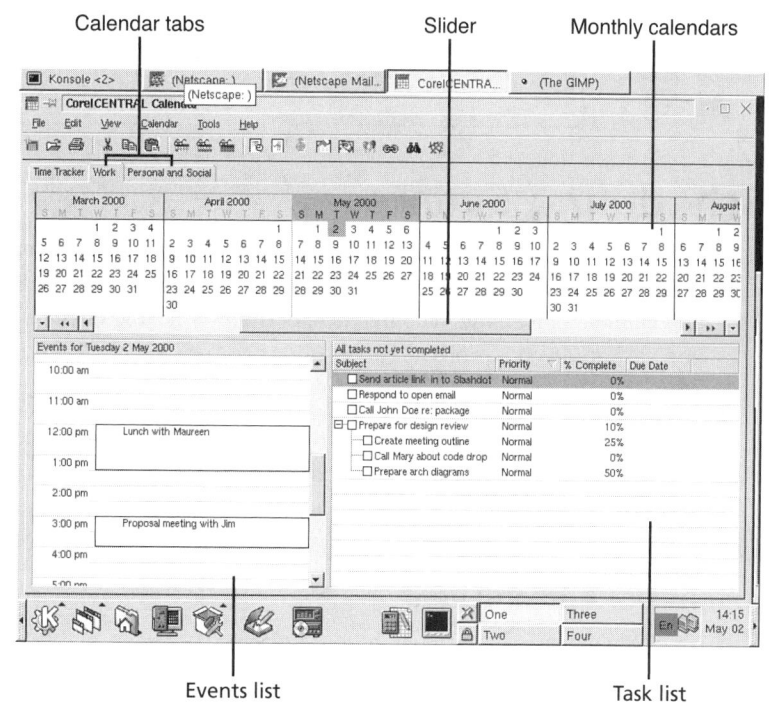

FIGURE 17.1
Corel Calendar has a simple, clean interface.

> You can import calendars from CorelCENTRAL 8 as well as export calendars to other calendar applications in ASCII text format. See the online help for information.

In the Day and Week views, the year's monthly calendars are displayed in six-month increments. A slider below the calendars enables easy access to the entire year.

The Events list in the subwindow on the left shows either the day's or the week's scheduled events (appointments) in the Day or Week view.

The Task list can be both your daily to-do list and your master to-do list. You can specify which tasks to display and their characteristics, such as priority, percentage complete, due date, and so on. You can also divide tasks into subtasks and display them under the main tasks.

> You can view your calendar by the day, week, or month. To change the view, select View, and click Day, Week, or Month.

> To save space, the Task list is displayed only in the Day and Week views, not in the Month view.

Scheduling Events

The term *event* has a special meaning in Corel Calendar. An event is anything you want to enter in your Calendar with a set date and time. For example, an event can be an appointment, a meeting, a conference, or a time-tracking device for logging the hours you've worked on a project.

You can schedule an event by typing directly in the Events list. You can schedule events for the future or take note of events that happened in the past. You can schedule all-day events (such as conferences and holidays) to appear in your calendar but leave the hour blocks open. You can also schedule an event to automatically appear as a repeating event (such as a recurring appointment).

To Do: Add an Event

To create a new event, follow these steps:

1. From the menu bar, click Calendar, New Event. Alternatively, from the toolbar, you can click the New Event icon.
2. Click the name of the event in the Subject field. The subject appears in the Events list.
3. Enter the start date and the amount of time you want to block off for the event. You can also enter a location and notes.

An easier way to add an event is to add it directly to the Events list in Day view. Simply click the time when the event should start, type the event, and press Enter. Drag the bottom of the event box to cover the length of the event. For example, if your event starts at 10 a.m. and ends at 12 p.m., enter the event at 10 a.m. and then drag the event box until it reaches 12 p.m. You can also open the Edit - New Event dialog box from the event list. Double-click an event to open this dialog box. The Edit - New Event dialog box is shown in Figure 17.2.

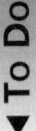

FIGURE 17.2
Adding new events in the Edit - New Event dialog box.

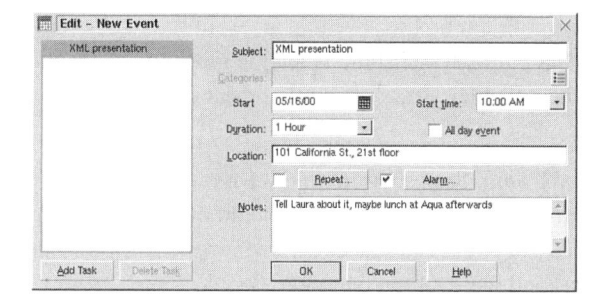

Repeating and All-Day Events

Corel Calendar has two special event categories you can set up in the Edit - New Event dialog box. If an event will last the entire day, check All Day Event. The event will appear at the beginning of your day's event list with the All-Day Event icon. The rest of the day will appear empty, so you can schedule subevents.

For example, if you were to schedule a day at the beach as an all-day event, "Day at the Beach" would appear at the top of your day's events, but the hourly blocks would be empty. You could schedule an early-morning fishing expedition from 4 a.m. to 7 a.m., followed by an hour of surfing, then breakfast on the beach for an hour, then five hours of sun tanning. (Don't forget to set an alarm for your 2 p.m. massage appointment.) A sample all-day event is shown in Figure 17.3.

FIGURE 17.3
You can schedule an all-day event and still enter hourly events for the day.

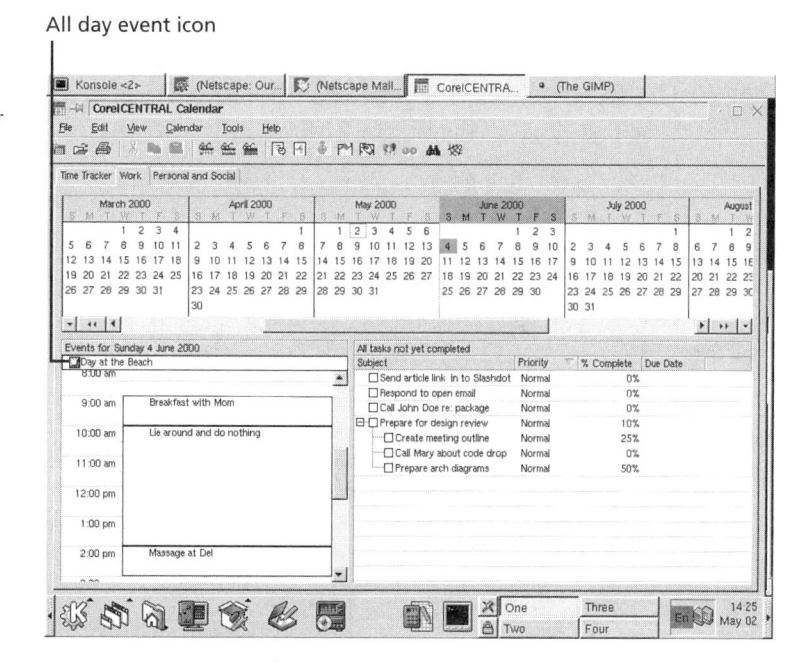

Check the Repeat Event box to schedule an event that will occur at regular intervals. Click the Repeat button to schedule when the repeating event should occur. The Repeat Event dialog box enables you to schedule repeat events with great precision. Here are your options:

- *Weeks of Month.* Repeats from every 1 month to every 12 months. Specify a specific day of the week the event should occur and which week of the month. For example, you could enter a design review to occur every three months on Monday of the second week of the month.

- *Days of Month.* Repeats on a particular day in a interval of 1 to 12 months. For example, you could schedule an inventory audit on the 15th day of the month, every six months.

- *Weeks.* Repeats on a particular day of the week, every week, or a weekly interval of up to every 52 weeks. For example, you could schedule a manicure every other Tuesday.

- *Days.* Sets an interval of a certain amount of days, from every day to up to every 364 days. For example, you could remind yourself to back up your nonessential files every three days, to check your tire pressure every 10 days, or to fast every 60 days.

- *Days of Year.* Schedules an event to occur on a particular day every year or an interval of years, up to 25 years. For example, you could schedule your boss's birthday on April 13, every year, or you could schedule an employee's five-year increment anniversary on March 3, every five years.

- *Weeks of Year.* Schedules an event to occur every year or an interval of years, up to 25 years. For example, you could schedule your family reunion to occur Sunday, the first week of August, every two years.

The Repeat Event dialog box is shown in Figure 17.4.

FIGURE 17.4
A repeating event occurs at regular intervals.

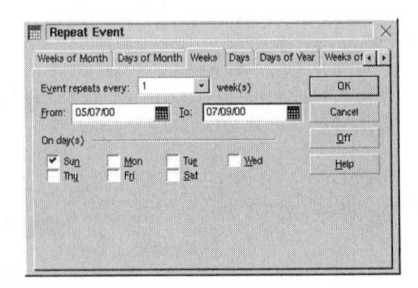

Getting Organized with CorelCENTRAL 9

When you no longer want the event to repeat, open the Repeat Event dialog box for the event and click Off. All future occurrences of the event will be deleted. To delete a repeating event, follow these steps:

- Right-click the event and select Delete.
- In the Delete Repeating Event dialog box, specify whether you want to delete all occurrences of the event or just the one current event.

To Do: Set Up an Alarm for an Event

1. To set an alarm, check the Alarm check box.
2. In the Set Alarm dialog box, you can specify when the system should remind you of the event, from one minute to seven days before the event is scheduled to occur.
3. You can also set a snooze interval. When the alarm sounds, you can click the Snooze button to temporarily turn off the alarm. The alarm will sound again in the time that you set in the snooze interval.
4. Use the default alarm sound or choose another wave file to act as the alarm. The Set Alarm dialog box is shown in Figure 17.5.

FIGURE 17.5
Use alarms to remind yourself of important appointments or due dates.

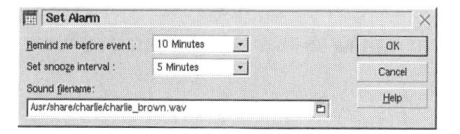

When the alarm goes off, the audio alarm will sound, and the alarm message appears.

> You must have sound configured on your computer for the audio alarm to work. If you don't have sound, the alarm message box will still open when the alarm should go off.

Editing and Deleting an Event

To delete an event, right-click the event and select Delete Event. The event is deleted. If you've enabled the dialog box warnings, you'll get a confirmation message before the event is deleted. Otherwise, the event is simply deleted.

> There is no "undo" option in Calendar, so it's a good idea to keep the dialog box warnings enabled. To re-enable the warnings after they have been turned off, click Tools, Reset Warnings. This option is not always reliable, so be careful.

To edit an event, right-click the event and select Edit Event. The Edit dialog box appears, which is exactly the same as the dialog box that appears when you add a new event.

Using the Task Feature to Create a To-Do List

The event list enables you to keep a running to-do list. You can add as many tasks as you want, and you can also add unlimited subtasks, up to seven levels deep. You can set or change the priority of the task, keep track of completion percentage and make other edits.

To Do: Add a Task

To add a task to the event list, follow these steps:

1. From the menu bar, click Calendar, New Task. Alternatively, you can click the Create New Task icon on the toolbar or right-click an empty line on the event list and select Add Task.
2. The Edit - New Task dialog box appears. It's similar to the Edit - New Event dialog box.
3. Enter a subject, which is the name of the task that appears in the task list.
4. You can select a category for your task. Categories are useful when you want to filter the event list to see only tasks that fit into particular categories. By default, Business and Personal are predefined for you. Adding a new category is simple; just type a category in the Categories field and it's automatically added to your list. To view the Categories list, click the Categories icon at the end of the Categories field. You will see your new category added, and checked as the current category. You can also add new categories in the Categories dialog box. Enter the new category and click Add.
5. The start date is today's date by default, but you can change the start date to any future or past date. Check the Due Date box and enter a due date, if desired.
6. You can add a percentage complete in any whole percentage from 0 to 100 percent. You can also assign one of five priorities for the task, from Highest to Lowest.
7. Repeating tasks work just like repeating events. Click Repeat and check the check box to set up a repeating task.

Getting Organized with CorelCENTRAL 9   345

The Edit - New Task dialog box is shown in Figure 17.6.

FIGURE 17.6
The Edit - New Task dialog box is similar to the Edit - New Event dialog box.

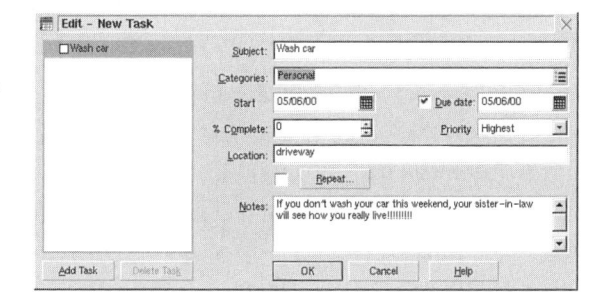

Adding Subtasks

One of the more useful features of Calendar is the use of *subtasks*, which are the smaller tasks (or steps) that must be completed in order to finish a main task. For example, if you have a task to write a report, you could enter the report as a task. Then, you could enter subtasks under the task, such as conduct interviews, do research and take notes, compile notes into an outline, write a rough draft, refine the draft, hold a meeting to discuss the report, write the final draft, and disseminate the report. An example of subtasks is shown in Figure 17.7.

FIGURE 17.7
Subtasks enable you to break up large tasks into small, manageable pieces.

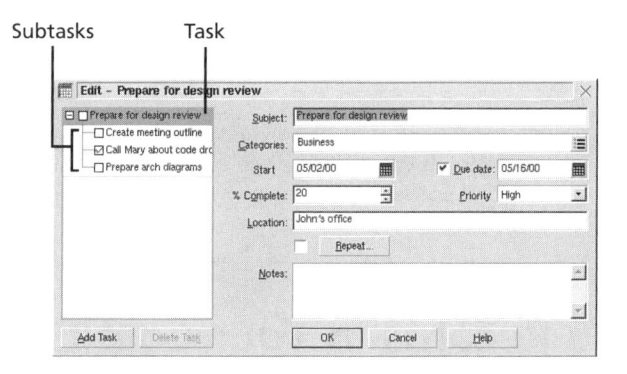

To Do: Enter a Subtask

1. Right-click the task and select Edit Task or simply double-click the task.
2. Click Add Task (in the Edit Task dialog box).
3. Enter the information for the subtask just as you did for the main task.

You can have an unlimited number of subtasks under a task, but only six sublevels of subtasks under the main task. In other words, you can have a sub-sub-sub-sub-sub-subtask.

Editing a Task

After you've created a task, you can open the Edit Task dialog box and change any aspect of the task using the following settings:

- *Subject*. Edit the Subject field to rename the task.
- *Categories*. Edit the Categories field to add or delete the task's categories (a task can belong to more than one category).
- *Start*. If you decide to start and finish the task on different dates, change the Start and/or Due Date fields.
- *% Complete*. Update the % Complete field as often as necessary.
- *Priority*. Be sure to keep the priority of your tasks up to date, if nothing else. The Priority field can be the most important field in your event list.
- *Repeat*. You can make an ordinary task a repeating task, or you can turn off the repeat feature to make a repeating task a one-time task.

Of course, you can always enter new location information and notes at any time.

> The Location field is independent of anything in CorelCENTRAL; it's more of a miscellaneous field. Use it to enter the pathname of a file or the location of a meeting you must attend, for example.

> Calendar has a quick way to update the percentage complete or priority of your tasks if you don't want to bother with opening the editor. Right-click the task and select the new priority or percentage complete (in 25-percent increments).

Locating Records in Your CorelCENTRAL 9 Calendar

With so many different possible views of your calendars, tasks, and subtasks, it can be difficult to remember exactly where you wrote a certain task or whether you created a task or an event. Also, it can be a tedious waste of time to scroll back manually through months of records to find references to a particular client or project. Fortunately, Corel Calendar has three tools—Find, Filter and Sort By—to help you find information quickly and to filter your event list to display only certain kinds of information.

Using Find to Search Your Calendar

The Find tool can be used to list every occurrence of a word or text string across all your calendars. It can also search in events, tasks, and subtasks. However, Find searches only the event, task, or subtask's Subject field, so if the reference is in Notes or Location, but not Subject, Find will not be able to locate it. Find does, however, work across all your calendars.

To find a word or other string of characters, select Edit, Find from the menu bar. Enter the string in the Find dialog box and click Find Now. The search can take many seconds, depending on how large your calendar files are and how many calendars you have.

After Find goes through your calendars looking for the string, it displays every occurrence in the Find dialog box, including the type of item (event, task, or subtask), the subject, and the date/time of the item. To go to the item, double-click it in the Find dialog box. The correct calendar will open to the page that contains the string, and the item will be selected. A sample Find search is shown in Figure 17.8.

FIGURE 17.8
Use Find to search for references to a person or item across all your calendars.

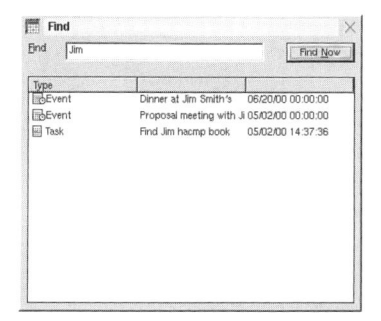

Using Filters to Sort Your Event List

After you've been using Calendar for a while, your event list can get too long to handle. Use the Filter and Sort By features to keep control of your tasks. Filter enables you to filter out tasks based on category, completion status, and time period. Sort By enables you to sort your tasks according to subject, percentage complete, priority, due date, or start date.

To Do: Filter Your Tasks

1. From the menu bar, select View, Filter Event list.
2. Enter a category, status, or time period to display. Note that you can enter only one category at a time. Also, for the status, you can check Complete or Not Complete, or you can check both to display all tasks. For the time period, you have the following options:

▼   All
            Due This Month
            Due This Week
            Due Today
            Not Started
            Past Due
            Started

   3. The filter is applied to your event list. To change the filter back, reopen the Filter
▲   Event list dialog box and change the filter options.

The Filter Task List dialog box is shown in Figure 17.9.

FIGURE 17.9
You can keep your master, weekly, and daily to-do items in the one event list and then apply filters.

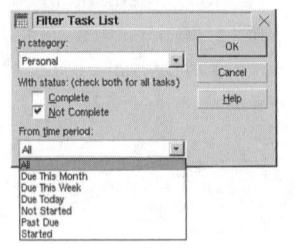

Linking Events and Tasks

Linking is one of the most exciting features of Calendar—it ties all your WordPerfect Office applications together. When you set a link in Calendar for an event or task, you can click the link to directly open the file/document, Web site, or memo that deals with that task or event. You can set a link to the following items:

- A memo
- Any file, including executable files (applications)
- A directory
- A URL for a Web, FTP, or other Internet site

To Do: Set a Link to an Event, Task, or Subtask

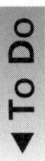

▼ 1. Click an event or task to select it.
   2. From the menu bar, select Tools, Link To and then select the type of link (memo, file/application, folder, or URL).
   3. Enter the name of the link in the Link Text field. The link text appears on the Link button that opens the link.
▲ 4. Enter the filename, directory, or URL or select the memo that you want to link to.

Getting Organized with CorelCENTRAL 9

The Link icon appears next to the task. To open the link, click the Link icon once (be careful not to double-click or else you'll open the event or task editor). The Link button appears with the link text you entered when you created the link. Click the Link button to open the link. Here are some points to keep in mind:

- If the link is a memo, Corel Memo opens to the memo you linked to.
- If the link is a file, the file opens in its native application.
- If the link is an application, the application starts.
- If the link is a URL, your default browser or Internet application opens to the URL.

An example of a link is shown in Figure 17.10.

FIGURE 17.10
Links make it easier to access the items you need for a task quickly and efficiently.

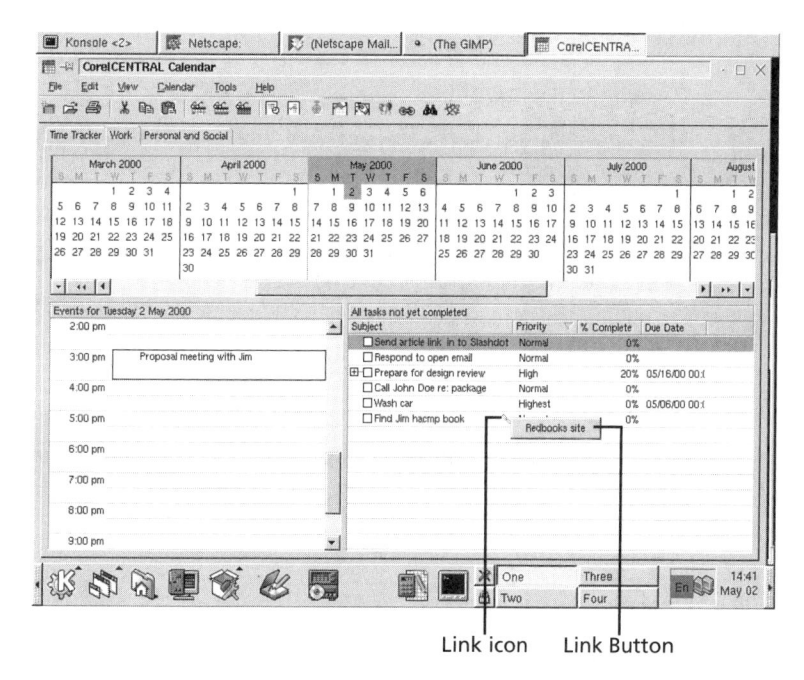

Editing and Deleting Links

To edit a link, right-click the event or task and select Edit Link. The list of links for that task or event opens. Select the link you want to edit, and the proper link editor opens.

To delete a link, right-click the event or task and click Delete Link. Select the link you want to delete, and click OK.

Summary

This hour, you worked with the calendars, events, tasks, and subtasks in Corel Calendar. You created events, repeating events, and all-day events as well as created tasks and subtasks in the Events list. You also learned how to search for a string in all your calendars and in the Events list using Find, you applied filters to your Events list, and you added links to your events, tasks, and subtasks.

Q&A

Q Can I turn events into tasks or do I have to cut and paste?

A If you enter a task and then decide to make it an event, simply click the task and drag it to the events list. You can also convert an event to a task by dragging the event to the event list.

Q I renamed My Calendar as Work, but I can't find the calendar file in my home directory.

A The default calendar that appears when you first start Corel Calendar is called My Calendar, and the calendar file in your home directory is `calendar.ccc`. You can rename the default calendar from My Calendar to another name, but the file containing the default calendar will still be called `calendar.ccc`.

Workshop

The Workshop contains quiz questions and exercises to help reinforce what you've learned in this hour. If you get stuck, the answers can be found in Appendix B, "Answers to Quiz Questions."

Quiz

1. Can you export Corel Calendar files?
2. What is the difference between an event and a task?
3. What is the difference between a task and a subtask?
4. Which tab would you open on the Repeat Event dialog box to schedule your wedding anniversary?
5. How do you get your delete warning boxes back once you've disabled them?
6. How do you enter a subtask below a task?

Exercises

1. Open Corel Calendar from Presentations.
2. Switch your calendar view from Daily to Weekly to Monthly.
3. Schedule "Lunch with Linus and Richard" today, from 1 p.m. to 2 p.m.
4. Schedule yourself an all-day event, such as "Day at the Beach," on the date of your choice.
5. Set an alarm to go off 30 minutes before your lunch with Linus and Richard (from Exercise 3).
6. Create the task "Buy Myself Flowers" with a due date of your next birthday. Put the task in the Personal category.
7. Create the subtasks "Check Bank Account" and "Decide Which Flower Is My Favorite" under the task to buy yourself flowers that you created in Exercise 6.
8. Find all references to "flowers" in your calendar.
9. Link `http://www.flowers.com` to the task to buy yourself flowers.

HOUR 18

Managing Contacts with CorelCENTRAL 9 Address Book

Like Calendar, CorelCENTRAL 9 Address Book is simple and easy to use, yet powerful enough for the longest and most complex contact management needs. Address Book is simple, but it provides you with the tools you need to customize it to suit your requirements.

In this hour you will

- Explore the Corel Address Book environment, including starting Address Book, looking at the different record types, and learning about the Address Book window.
- Create and edit address records.
- Add custom fields to your records and add new address books.
- Import and export address books into and from Corel Address Book.
- Find address records in your address books with the help of the Find feature.
- Filter records in your address books.

Working with the CorelCENTRAL 9 Address Book

By default, Address Book opens with one address book, called *Addresses*. An address book window is split into two parts: the tree pane and the summary pane. You can create an unlimited number of additional address books, for as many kinds of addresses as you want. The Address Book window is shown in Figure 18.1.

FIGURE 18.1
The tree pane displays all the address books, whereas the summary pane displays the records in the active address book.

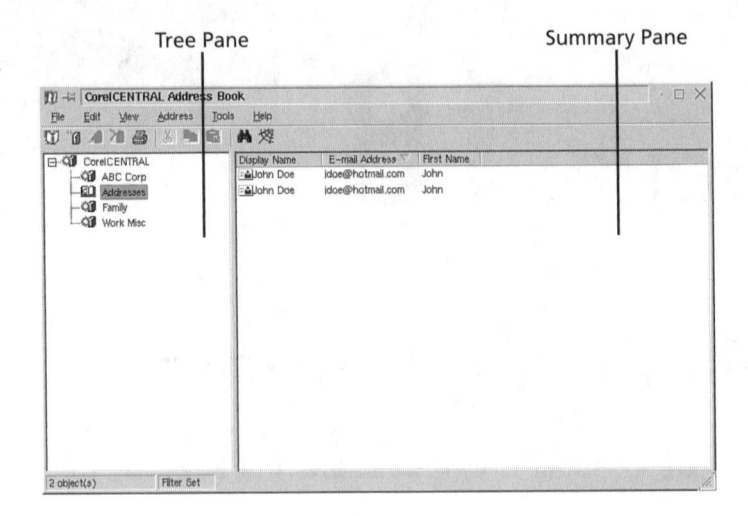

For example, if you want to keep all addresses in one large book, you can organize the addresses into groups. If you would prefer to split the addresses into separate address books, you can create separate books called Business, Family, Personal, Volunteer, School, and so on. All your address books appear in the tree pane of Address Book.

Only one address book can be open at a time. A one-line quick view of each entry in the open address book is displayed in the summary pane.

Starting the CorelCENTRAL 9 Address Book

Starting Corel Address Book is similar to starting Calendar:

- From Corel Applications in your desktop menu, click Utilities, CorelCENTRAL Address Book.
- From another WordPerfect Office 2000 application, click Tools, Address Book.
- From an Xterm shell prompt, enter `ccaddressbook`.

The CorelCENTRAL 9 Address Book Interface

There are four kinds of entries in an address book:

- *Person*. You will probably use this entry type most often. It is also the most detailed. Enter the name, email address, phone, mailing address, personal information, business position, comments, and so on in a person's address book entry. Address Book has default fields for simple name and address entries and for complex contact management entries. An example of a Person entry is shown in Figure 18.2.

FIGURE 18.2

A person's Properties dialog box has the most possible fields of all the record types.

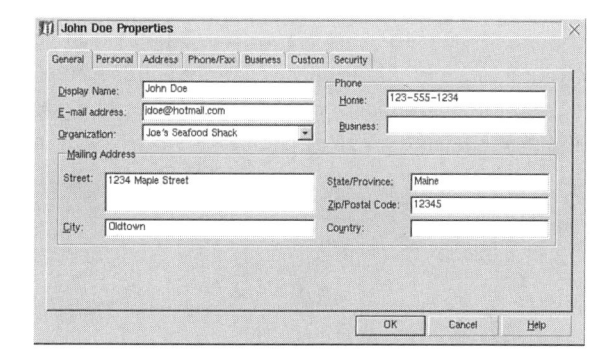

- *Organization*. To make it easier to find contacts, it's useful to have entries for both individual people within an organization and the organization itself. The Organization Properties dialog box, shown in Figure 18.3, contains fields for the organization's name, addresses, and phone numbers.

FIGURE 18.3

The organization entry is useful for listing an organization, rather than a person.

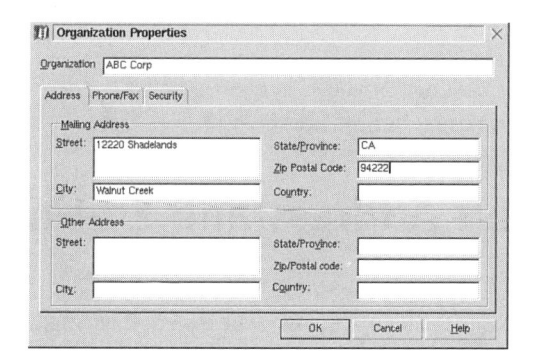

- *Resource*. A *resource* is an item such as a server, shared fax machine or printer, car or truck in a company pool, or any other item you might need to keep contact information for. A resource's Properties dialog box is shown in Figure 18.4.

FIGURE 18.4
The resource entry is useful for equipment that has some kind of address, such as a phone number for a fax or hostname and IP address for a server.

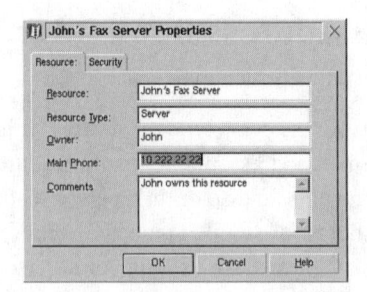

- *Group.* This is a special kind of address book entry in that it enables you to create groups of individual entries in your address book. When you create a group, you choose from a menu of all the entries in your address book and decide which entries to add to the group. Groups are useful for when you want to send an email (or snail mail) to a large group of people, or when you want to create a telephone tree. The Group Properties dialog box is shown in Figure 18.5.

FIGURE 18.5
Create a group record to make it easy to send messages to a group of people.

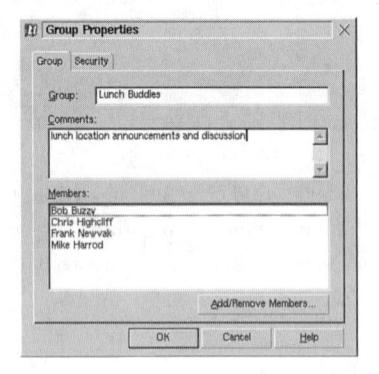

The entry type is the first option you select when creating a new entry, because each entry type contains different information fields.

Adding a New Address and Editing Addresses

You can enter addresses manually into the address book or import a database of addresses from a spreadsheet, word processing document, or other address book application. You'll learn how to import addresses later in this hour.

To Do: Add a New Address to the Address Book

1. From the menu bar, click Addresses, New. Alternatively, you can click the New Address icon on the toolbar or right-click the summary pane and select New.

2. Enter the information about your contact in the appropriate fields. When you click OK, the entry is automatically saved into the open address book.

Editing Address Information

After you have created an entry in an address book, you can always go back and add or change information.

To Do: Edit an Address Book Entry

1. Select the address you want to edit in the summary pane. From the menu bar, click Address, Edit. Alternatively, you can select the address you want to edit and click the Edit Address icon on the toolbar or right-click the address entry in the summary pane and select Edit.

2. Add new information or overwrite old information in the Properties dialog box. When you click OK, the changes are automatically saved.

Customizing Address Fields

If you have information that won't fit into one of address book's fields, you can add your own custom fields. This is a real advantage to using Corel Address Book. The disadvantage to the custom fields feature is that you can't choose which entry type the custom field or fields will appear in. Once you create a custom field, a new tab called *Custom* appears in all address book entries, with all your custom fields displayed.

To Do: Create a Custom Entry

1. Click the address book in the tree pane for which you want to create the custom field. No individual addresses should be selected in summary view.

2. From the menu bar, select Edit, Custom Fields.

3. In the Custom Fields dialog box, click New.

4. Enter the new field name, click OK, and close the Custom Fields dialog box.

Use the Custom Fields dialog box to delete and rename custom fields as well as to create new fields.

Adding a New Address Book

You can have an unlimited number of address books in Address Book. It's often useful to separate your addresses for work into a different book from your personal addresses. You can split addresses for different companies, groups of clients, volunteer projects, family members, and so on.

To Do: Create a New Address Book

1. From the menu bar, select File, New.
2. Select CorelCENTRAL and click OK.
3. Enter the name of your new address book.

The address book appears in the tree pane.

> You can read address books off a directory server by selecting Directory Server instead of CorelCENTRAL when creating a new address book. Creating an address book off a directory server is beyond the scope of this book. Consult the CorelCENTRAL Address Book online help for more information.

Importing and Exporting Addresses

If you already have another address book software program or your current list of addresses is in a document or spreadsheet, you can import the addresses to Corel Address Book. You can also easily export your addresses from Address Book to another address book software application.

Corel Address Book imports files that are in ASCII text format. For you to import a file successfully, the fields and records in your file must be delimited by a comma or tab.

New Term A *delimiter* is a character or string—usually a nonprinting character such as a space or tab or a symbol such as a comma—that separates pieces of data in a file. Delimiters help applications such as spreadsheets and databases to sort the data into the correct places.

When you export an address book file from another application, the fields should appear at the top, delimited by commas or tabs. The records should appear after the fields, also delimited. Note that the delimiter for the records does not have to be the same as for the fields, as long as it's a delimiter that Corel Address Book recognizes.

To Do: Import Your Address Book File into Corel Address Book

▼ To Do

1. From the menu, select File, Import.
2. Browse for the file (or just enter the full pathname) in the Import dialog box, as shown in Figure 18.6, and click Open.
3. Select the correct delimiter used to separate the field names in the Field Delimiter drop-down menu.

FIGURE 18.6
Use the Import dialog box to import an ASCII delimited text file of addresses into Address Book.

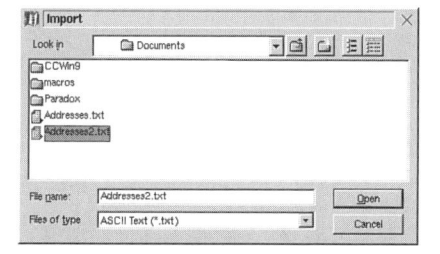

4. Select the correct delimiter used to separate the record entries and click OK to display the Field Mapping dialog box.
5. In the Field Mapping dialog box, the fields for the imported file are mapped to the fields in Corel Address Book. Fields that have the same name in both address books are mapped automatically. Use the Field Mapping dialog box, shown in Figure 18.7, to map the fields from your old address book to the Corel Address Book fields.

FIGURE 18.7
Map the fields in your ASCII text file to Address Book's fields.

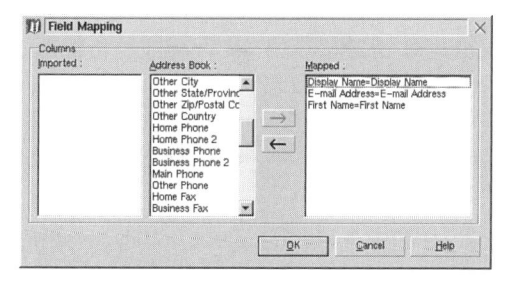

6. After you click OK in the Field Mapping dialog box, you get a message indicating whether the import succeeded or failed. Unfortunately, the "Import Failed" message doesn't tell you anything helpful for troubleshooting.

▲

To Do: Export Your Address Book to an ASCII Delimited Text File

1. Select the address book you want to export in the tree pane.
2. From the menu bar, select File, Export.
3. Enter a directory and a filename for your exported file in the Export dialog box, shown in Figure 18.8, and click Open.
4. Select a field delimiter and a record delimiter from the ASCII Delimiter Setup dialog box.
5. Check the fields you want to export to the ASCII file. Fields that contain information in the records are automatically checked for you.
6. When you click OK, you should get an "Exported Successfully" message.

FIGURE 18.8
Exporting is a little easier than importing because you don't have to map fields.

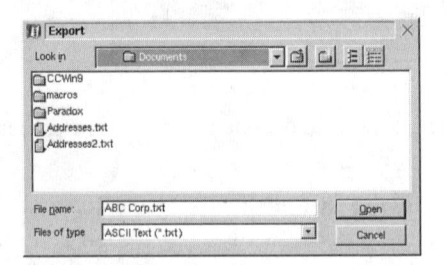

Using the Find Feature to Search Your Contacts

The Find feature is useful when you have more contacts than can be easily searched by scrolling. The Find feature in Corel Address Book is more limited than the Find tool in Calendar. In Address Book, Find searches only one address book at a time. If you're looking for a contact across multiple address books, you must apply Find to each address book individually.

Also, Find searches only the Display Name field, so if your string appears in any other field in a record, Find is not be able to locate it. On a positive note, Find is not case sensitive, and it also displays the search item when it appears as part of a word. For example, if you search for John, Find displays entries for john, John's and johndoe. If you search for John Doe, Find displays entries for John Doe and johndoe.

To Do: Find a Word or Phrase

1. From the menu bar, select Edit, Find.
2. Enter the item you want to find in the Find field. Click Find Now.
3. The results of your search are displayed in the Find dialog box. The results of a Find are shown in Figure 18.9.

FIGURE 18.9
Find is especially useful when you have an address book with hundreds of records.

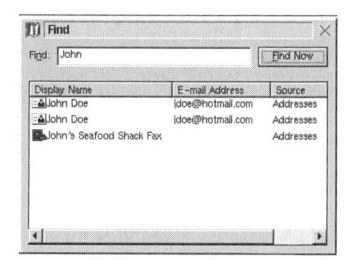

Using Filters to Sort Your Contacts

The Filter feature displays address book records that contain information in certain fields. The records that have no information in the filtered fields are not displayed. For example, if you want to filter your address book for email addresses, only records that contain an email address are displayed. If you have some records that contain a name and phone number but no email address, those records do not appear when the filter is applied.

To Do: Apply a Filter

1. From the menu bar, select View, Filter.
2. Select the field you want to filter from the drop-down menu. Accept the equal sign (=) default and leave the record field blank. The last button should be labeled End.
3. When you click OK, only the records that contain the field you chose are displayed in the summary pane. A simple filter example is shown in Figure 18.10.

FIGURE 18.10
Use filters to make it easier to find groups of records.

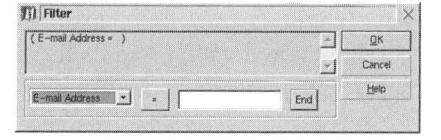

Now that you know how to apply a simple filter, let's complicate things a bit. Most people have address books in which some of the entries contain only names and email addresses, others have email addresses and phone numbers, and still others have email addresses, phone numbers, and street addresses. If you want to see the records that contain both email addresses and phone numbers, you would filter for both fields using the AND operator.

To Do: Apply a Filter for More Than One Field

1. From the menu bar, click View, Filter.
2. Select the first field to filter (in this example, Email Address).
3. Accept the default equal sign (=) button and leave the record field blank.
4. Click the End button and select Insert Row to add another field filter.
5. Notice that the End button changes to the AND operator.
6. Enter the second field filter in the second drop-down menu (in this example, Business Phone).
7. Notice that the last button is now labeled End.
8. When you click OK, all records that have information entered in the Email Address and Business Phone fields are displayed in the summary pane.

If you want to filter for records that contain *either* an email address *or* a phone number, use the OR operator. Follow the previous procedure, except click the AND button to display the operator menu, and select OR. When you apply the filter, all records in your address book that contain either an email address or a phone number, but not necessarily both, are displayed.

> You can apply as many field filters as you want. Just click the End button and select Insert Row to add a new filter option. You can also combine OR and AND operators to different fields to refine your filter.

You can also filter the individual entries themselves to look for records that meet certain criteria. For example, if you want to filter for all records with mailing addresses in the state of Maine, you would apply a record filter.

Table 18.1 lists the operators you can use with record filters to refine your search.

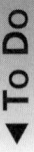

Managing Contacts with CorelCENTRAL 9 Address Book

TABLE 18.1 Filter Operators

Operator	Filter In
=	Equals the string
<	Less than the string
>	Greater than the string
<=	Less than or equal to the string
>=	Greater than or equal to the string
[ ]	Contains the string

Address Book's Filter tool uses the ASCII text values in the less than and greater than operators when applying values to the alphanumeric text you want to filter.

> ASCII text values are lowest for nonalphanumeric characters such as the ampersand, comma, and apostrophe. Numerals come next, followed by capital letters, followed by lowercase letters. Address Book filters are not case sensitive, so a lowercase letter has the same value to the Filter tool as its uppercase counterpart.

For example, if you want to see all entries with display names from A to D, you would apply a filter for entries less than (<) E, assuming you have no display name that begin with a number or special character.

To Do: Apply Filters to Individual Fields in an Address Book

1. Select View, Filter to open the Filter dialog box.
2. Enter the field where you want to apply the filter (in this example, State/Province).
3. Click the operator button and select the operator you want (in this example, either = or []).
4. Enter the string that you want to filter (in this example, Maine). You might have entered *ME* instead of spelling out *Maine*, so insert another row with the = or [ ] operator and enter **ME** into the record string field.

Another example would be to display all records from A to D. You would filter the display name, less than or equal to (<=), and then *D* in the record string field. If you for some reason have display names that begin with numeric or special characters, you would add another filter row to filter records greater than or equal to (>=) A. The record filter is shown in Figure 18.11.

FIGURE 18.11
Use record filters to perform a refined filter of your records.

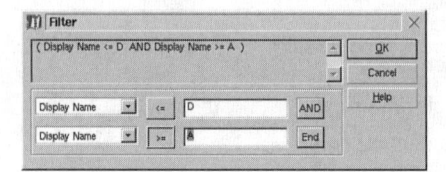

Summary

This hour, you explored the Corel Address Book interface. You added new addresses to the address book, and edited address entries. You created a custom field for your address book records, and you created new address books. You imported an address book from another contact management application, and exported a Corel address book into an ASCII delimited text file. You used the Find and Filter tools with your address book. In the next hour, you will learn about the Corel Paradox 9 database application.

Q&A

Q When applying a filter, is it possible to filter for fields or records that are not there, rather than fields that are?

A No. You can only "filter in" fields; you cannot "filter out" fields. To find records that are missing fields, such as an email address, you could apply the filter to list all records with email addresses and then export the filtered list to Quattro Pro or another spreadsheet. You could then export your entire address book to Quattro Pro and compare the two address books for the missing names. The resulting list would be all records that do not have email addresses. Admittedly, this is a kind of convoluted way of doing things; hopefully future Corel releases will add the option to filter for missing fields.

Q I want to add a custom field to my resource records, but the field appears in all the records. Is there a way to apply a custom field just to certain kinds of records?

A Unfortunately, you cannot apply a custom record field to only certain records or record types. Once you create a custom field, it appears in all the records in your address book.

Workshop

The Workshop contains quiz questions and exercises to help reinforce what you've learned in this hour. If you get stuck, the answers can be found in Appendix B, "Answers to Quiz Questions."

Quiz

1. What is the difference between an organization entry and a group entry?
2. What file format can you import into Address Book?
3. What file format can you export from Address Book?
4. How would you add a hostname field to your records?
5. What record field does the Find feature search?

Exercises

1. Start Corel Address Book from an Xterm shell prompt.
2. Create the person entry Jane Doe, with the email address `jdoe@xyz.com` and the street address 1234 Maple Lane, Jackson, MI 12345.
3. Create an organization entry for XYZ Corporation, with the phone number 123-555-1234 and the street address 12345 Market Street, San Francisco, CA 94111. Use the Toolbar icon.
4. Create a group entry called *Group* that includes Jane Doe and XYZ Corporation.
5. Create a new address book called *Family*.
6. Apply the filter for email addresses to the address book that contains the entries for Jane Doe and XYZ Corp. Which entries appear after you place the filter?
7. Remove the filter by clicking View, Remove Filter. Apply a new filter for all records that begin with X. Which entries appear?

PART VI
Creating Databases with Paradox 9

Hour

19 Paradox 9 Database Basics

20 Creating Your First Database

21 Managing Paradox 9 Data

22 Advanced Paradox 9 Techniques

HOUR 19

Paradox 9 Database Basics

Many users often ignore the database applications in office suites. They can seem so complicated and difficult to use that the initial learning curve seems too high. Make no mistake, Paradox is a complex, powerful relational database that could take months to completely master. Still, you can learn the basics in about 15 minutes, and Paradox comes with so many Experts and Project database templates that even the most casual user can learn to use it and profit by the knowledge.

In this hour, you will

- Explore relational databases.
- Learn about Paradox database objects.
- Explore the Paradox interface, including the Welcome screen, PerfectExpert, and the desktop.
- Use the Project Viewer to open a database, examine the database object files, and set the working directory.
- Set a private directory as well as create and use aliases.

What Is a Database?

A *database* is nothing more than a file that contains information, or *data*. Any kind of file can be a database. Here are some examples:

- The ASCII text file you created in Hour 18, "Managing Contacts with CorelCENTRAL 9 Address Book," to export an address book is a database.
- A WordPerfect document containing a list of your favorite ice cream flavors is a database.
- A Quattro Pro spreadsheet containing your business's expenses, profits, and accounts payable is a database.

An application like Paradox that manipulates data in a database to enable you to track your data, answer questions, and discover trends is called a *database program*. Database programs make it possible to arrange the data in different ways and to make reports of the data so you can put the information in your database to good use.

There are two kinds of databases in the preceding examples: a flat-file database and a relational database.

A *flat-file database* is like a WordPerfect table, Quattro Pro spreadsheet, or CorelCENTRAL address book. Each piece of information (data) is organized into a table consisting of columns and rows (also called fields and records).

New Term   A *field* is a vertical column in a database table that contains a particular kind of data. For example, a table containing employee information would contain fields for the employee number, first name, last name, job title, monthly salary, and so on.

New Term   A *record* is a horizontal row in the table that contains the information for one entry in the table. For example, in the employee table example, one record would contain information in each field pertaining to one employee.

Flat-file databases are great if you have a small amount of information that fits comfortably into a table or spreadsheet of fields and records. When a flat-file database gets very large or when you have several flat-file databases that tend to repeat a lot of the same information, it's time to graduate to a relational database such as Paradox.

Relational databases have multiple tables that are linked together by relationships between data fields. The whole idea of a relational database is that instead of having one large table with many fields, you have several small tables with just a few fields each. Each table contains a certain type of information, such as orders, customers, or prices. An example of a relational database is shown in Figure 19.1.

FIGURE 19.1
Relational databases consist of multiple tables linked together.

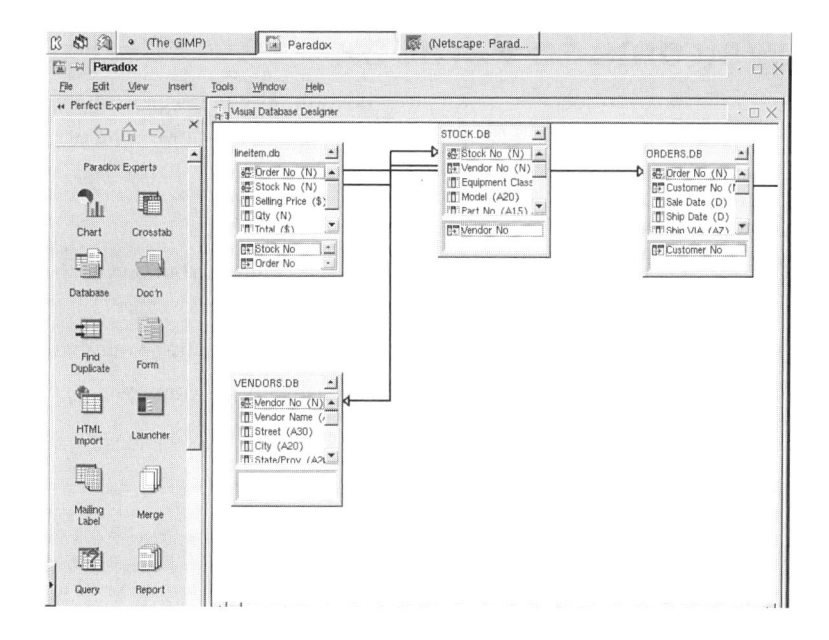

> All the examples in this hour are taken from the sample database that comes with Paradox, found in $HOME/Documents/Paradox/Samples. ($HOME is a prefix that stands for your home directory. For example, for the user mary, $HOME/Documents/Paradox/Samples is the same as /home/mary/Documents/Paradox/Samples.)

You can use a relational database to perform tasks like the following:

- Keep track of clients, work hours, work accomplished.
- Track medical patients' histories and discover trends or compare an entire group and discover trends and commonalities.
- Keep track of all your financial information, including income and expenses, investments, budget/spending plan, checkbook register, and net worth.
- Record all your belongings, including location, value, age, and serial number or identifying mark.
- Track your inventory, orders, customers, and prospects as well as make predictions of future trends based on past data.
- Make sense of huge amounts of data in different ways to help you in your business, home, or project.

Welcome to Paradox

Paradox can seem extraordinarily daunting if you haven't used a relational database before, but once you learn how to use it, Paradox can be one of your most powerful tools.

There are three ways to use Paradox:

- Use a premade relational database template from one of the database Projects to create your database.
- Use the Paradox Experts to guide you in creating your own database.
- Create a database from scratch manually on your own.

Regardless of which way you choose to create your database, you must understand some basic terms in order to use Paradox.

Paradox 9 Database Objects

Central to the concept of a relational database is a *database object*. A database object is a component of the database that somehow manipulates the data but is not data itself. Objects are used to store, organize, display, sort, or input data. Here are the basic Paradox database objects you must understand in order to use Paradox:

- Tables
- Keys
- Indexes
- Forms
- Reports
- Queries

Tables contain the actual data in the database. A database can consist of one or many tables that are linked together via common fields. A table looks much like a spreadsheet because the data is stored in columns of fields and rows of records. An example of a table is shown in Figure 19.2.

FIGURE 19.2

This table from the relational database Paradox looks a lot like a spreadsheet from Quattro Pro.

Species No	Category	Common Name	Species N
1	90,020.00 Triggerfish	Clown Triggerfish	Ballistoides conspicillu
2	90,030.00 Snapper	Red Emperor	Lutjanus sebae
3	90,050.00 Wrasse	Giant Maori Wrasse	Cheilinus undulatus
4	90,070.00 Angelfish	Blue Angelfish	Pomacanthus nauarchus
5	90,080.00 Cod	Lunartail Rockcod	Variola louti
6	90,090.00 Scorpionfish	Firefish	Pterois volitans
7	90,100.00 Butterflyfish	Ornate Butterflyfish	Chaetodon Ornatissimus
8	90,110.00 Shark	Swell Shark	Cephaloscyllium ventrios
9	90,120.00 Ray	Bat Ray	Myliobatis californica
10	90,130.00 Eel	California Moray	Gymnothorax mordax
11	90,140.00 Cod	Lingcod	Ophiodon elongatus
12	90,150.00 Sculpin	Cabezon	Scorpaenichthys marmorat
13	90,160.00 Spadefish	Atlantic Spadefish	Chaetodiperus faber
14	90,170.00 Shark	Nurse Shark	Ginglymostoma cirratum
15	90,180.00 Ray	Spotted Eagle Ray	Aetobatus narinari
16	90,190.00 Snapper	Yellowtail Snapper	Ocyurus chrysurus
17	90,200.00 Parrotfish	Redband Parrotfish	Sparisoma Aurofrenatum
18	90,210.00 Barracuda	Great Barracuda	Sphyraena barracuda
19	90,220.00 Grunt	French Grunt	Haemulon flavolineatum
20	90,230.00 Snapper	Dog Snapper	Lutjanus jocu
21	90,240.00 Grouper	Nassau Grouper	Epinephelus striatus
22	90,250.00 Wrasse	Bluehead Wrasse	Thalassoma bifasciatum

A *key* is a field or group of fields that serves as an identifier for a record. Every key in a table must be unique; no two records can have the same key. Keys prevent duplicate records in the table and comprise the primary index for the table.

An *index* sorts all the records in a table so that Paradox can access the records in order. The primary index uses the key field to sort the records in the table. If you want to sort records another way, you can create a secondary index.

Use a *form* to quickly and easily enter data into the database table. A form looks like an application dialog box. The form contains fields that correspond to the fields in the table. After you type information into each field, a new record is made in the table. If you just want to look at your data, you can use a form to view one record at a time. An example of a form is shown in Figure 19.3.

FIGURE 19.3
Think of a form as just another way of entering and viewing the data in a table, one record at a time.

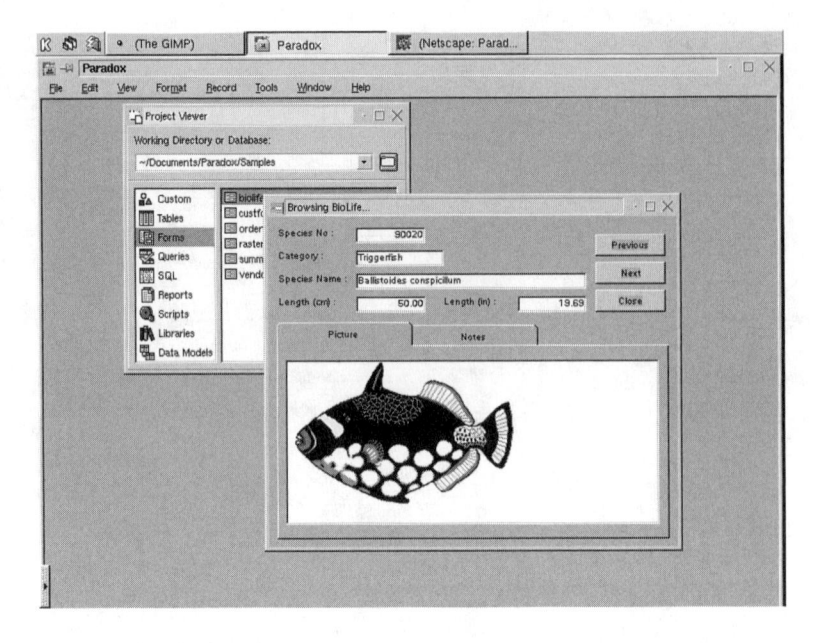

Reports display the data from a table or tables in a way that is visually appealing and easier to grasp than the tabular information. You can also use reports to organize the raw tabular data into formats that are useful, such as building an invoice report out of a table that lists parts and labor costs. An example of a report is shown in Figure 19.4.

FIGURE 19.4
Reports usually include design objects such as charts, borders, boxes, and different fonts.

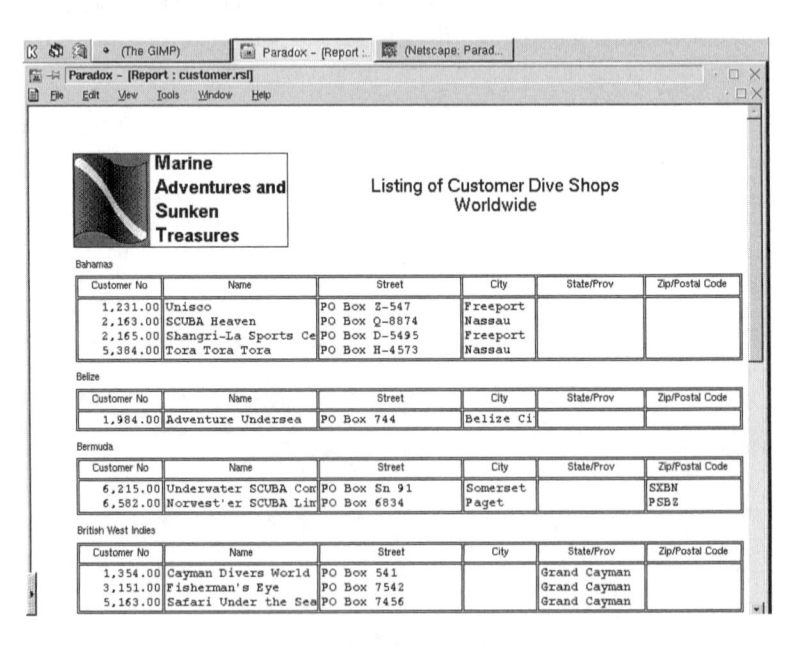

Queries provide a way for you to gather specific data from all the information in a table or tables. For example, if you have a database with tables for your CD, video, and DVD collections, you could run a query to list all the purchases you made in 1989 of all three types of media. You can think of a query as a question that you ask Paradox about your data.

Paradox also has design objects, such as boxes, text, lines, charts, buttons, document pages, and graphics, that you use to design your forms and reports. There are many other objects, such as scripts, libraries, and data models, that you'll learn about later.

Exploring the Paradox 9 Interface

The Paradox interface itself is quite complicated and not always intuitive. Before you begin creating a database, you'll spend some time learning about the Paradox environment, beginning with how to start Paradox.

Starting Paradox is similar to starting any other WordPerfect Office 2000 application:

- To start Paradox from the WordPerfect submenu on your desktop main menu, select Applications, WordPerfect Office 2000, Paradox 9.
- To start Paradox from the command line in an Xterm, enter **paradox**.

Paradox is a complex application, so it may take a minute or two to start the first time.

The Welcome Screen

When Paradox starts, you are greeted with the Welcome screen (see Figure 19.5). Although the welcome screens of some applications provide little more than a tip or two, the Paradox Welcome screen can be an invaluable tool to help you feel your way around the program.

FIGURE 19.5
The Welcome screen has icons to help you find your way around Paradox.

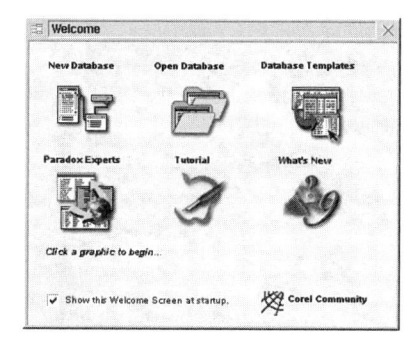

The New Database icon opens the Visual Database Designer, which is the tool you use to create a new database from scratch. When you create a relational database consisting of several different tables that are connected, the Visual Database Designer graphically displays the relationships between the different tables.

The Open Database icon opens an existing database.

The Paradox Experts icon opens the Paradox Experts, which guide you step by step through creating your database objects, including tables, forms, reports, queries, charts, mailing lists, and design objects. You can create all these objects manually, but when you are first learning, the Experts enable you to create your first database in a few minutes.

The Tutorial icon opens a hands-on guide to learning how to create tables, links, data models, forms, reports, and queries manually. The tutorial is well written and full of useful information, but it assumes a bit of background knowledge about Paradox. You might find it more useful to complete the four hours in this book on Paradox and read the online help before doing the tutorial.

> There's also a tutorial on ObjectPAL, which is a scripting language for Paradox, available from the Help menu.

The Database Templates icon opens the database templates, which are fully designed database projects, complete with forms, tables, reports, and other objects. All you need to do is choose a template and begin entering your data. You can use a template just as it is, or you can modify it in any way. The database templates that come with Paradox 9 include the following:

- Home Assets
- Contact Management
- Job Costing (materials, labor, other project costs)
- Expense Report
- Human Resources
- Call Tracking System
- Music Collection

What's New provides a list of the new features and improvements of Paradox 9 over Paradox 8.

The Paradox 9 Desktop

The desktop is your main Paradox workspace and the central area where you control your objects. Objects are displayed in separate windows on the desktop. The desktop contains menus and toolbars like most other windowed applications. You may have noticed that the menus in WordPerfect Office 2000 applications are not static but change depending on the task you are performing. In Paradox, both the menus and the toolbars change according to the windows that are open on the desktop. For example, if you have the Query window open, the Run Query icon appears in the Standard toolbar. At the bottom of the desktop is the Status Bar. The Status Bar displays information about tasks, open files, and objects. The desktop is shown in Figure 19.6.

FIGURE 19.6

All your objects are opened in windows on the Paradox desktop.

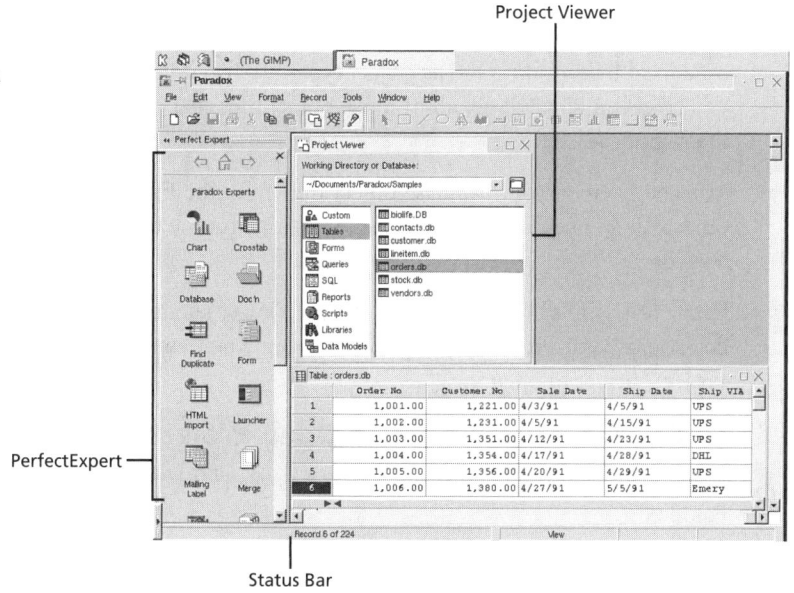

> You can move the Status Bar on the desktop by right-clicking it and selecting a new location from the menu.

PerfectExpert

PerfectExpert is useful in all the WordPerfect Office 2000 applications, but in Paradox it is invaluable when you are first learning.

To Do: Display PerfectExpert

1. Select Help, PerfectExpert to display a window that contains all the Expert icons.
2. The PerfectExpert menus change as you open different objects and perform different tasks on the desktop.

Project Viewer

As you'll see, even the simplest database consists of many different files. Each table, report, form, and query is a separate file, not to mention the files that Paradox generates automatically. If you were to keep those files all together in a folder, it would be confusing and difficult to remember which file represented what. Paradox solves this problem with the Project Viewer.

The Project Viewer enables you to see all your database objects for a particular project, organized by object type. The object types are listed in a column in the left pane. When you select an object type, all of those object files that exist in your project are listed in the right pane.

You can open all your database object files from the Project Viewer. Double-click the object file to open it. To see a menu of actions for the object, right-click it in Project Viewer.

Every time you start Paradox, the Project Viewer should automatically appear on the desktop. If your Project Viewer doesn't open when you open Paradox, select Tools, Project Viewer to open it.

To Do: Set a Preference to Open Project Viewer

These steps will set a preference to open Project Viewer automatically when you start Paradox:

1. From the menu, select Tools, Settings, Preferences.
2. In the General tab, check Open Project Viewer on Startup.

The Project Viewer lists the working directories and private directories.

Setting the Working Directory

The *working directory* is where you store all the files having to do with your current project. If you are working in more than one database project, you'll have a separate working directory for each database and will have to change working directories to change projects.

For example, say you're working on a database for a project to remodel your house in order to keep track of contractors, labor costs, materials, and so on. You're also working on a database of all your personal property, including value, date purchased, serial numbers, and so on. Because these databases are completely separate, they would be kept in two separate working directories. You could only work on one database at a time because there can be only one working directory at a time.

After you set the working directory, all the objects stored in that directory for your database project are displayed in the Project Viewer according to object type.

To Do: Set or Change the Working Directory

1. From the menu bar, select File, Working Directory.
2. Browse to the directory you want to set as the working directory.
3. Enter the full pathname of the directory you want. If an alias is assigned (more on aliases in a minute), you can choose one from the alias drop-down menu instead of entering the full pathname.

> Paradox ships with a complete sample database for a fictitious company called Marine Adventures and Sunken Treasure. By default, the database is located in $HOME/Documents/Paradox/Samples. Set the working directory to the Samples directory so that you have a working database populated with data to use when learning Paradox.

Using the Private Directory

The *private directory* is useful when you're working on a database project with multiple users. You can store database files in the private directory so other users can't overwrite them. Paradox also uses the private directory to store temporary tables, such as query answers. The default private directory for each user is $HOME/.wpo2000/Paradox/Private.

To Do: Change Your Private Directory to a New Directory

1. From the menu bar, select Tools, Settings, Preferences, Database.
2. Enter the full pathname of the directory you want.
3. Paradox automatically assigns the alias PRIV: to the new private directory.

> When you change private directories, Paradox deletes all temporary tables. Be sure to back up your original private directory before changing to a new private directory if you want to save anything in it.

Setting Preferences

Preferences enable you to customize the look and feel of your Paradox desktop as well as set defaults for many of the overall settings and operations. To set preferences, select Tools, Settings, Preferences.

In the Preferences dialog box, you can perform the following tasks:

- Change the default Paradox desktop title from "Paradox" to any title you want.
- Add a bitmap background to the Paradox desktop.
- Set the default to start an Expert when creating a form, report, or table.
- Set query defaults.
- Set the private directory.
- Set a network file system refresh rate.

Those are just a few examples. The Preferences dialog box is shown in Figure 19.7.

FIGURE 19.7
Customize the look and feel of your Paradox desktop by using the Preferences dialog box.

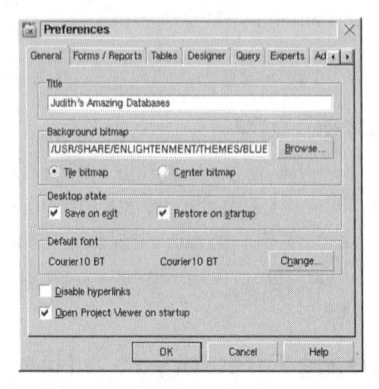

Setting Aliases

You can set an alias for the full pathname of a directory so that you don't have to type in the full name. There are two aliases that are automatically set by default in Paradox:

- Paradox gives your working directory the alias `WORK:`.
- Paradox gives your private directory the alias `PRIV:`.

In addition to the default aliases, there are two kinds of aliases that you can set:

- *Public aliases* are available from all directories, including all working directories.
- *Project aliases* are only available when you're using Paradox in the working directory in which you created the aliases. When you change working directories, the project aliases from the old working directory are cleared, and the aliases from the new working directory are set.

To Do: Create an Alias

1. Create a new directory where you want your alias to point (if the directory doesn't already exist).
2. From the menu bar, select Tools, Alias Manager, New.
3. Check the Public Alias option if you want the alias to be public.
4. Enter the name of the new alias in the Database Alias field.
5. Select the driver type STANDARD. (See the online help for an explanation of the other driver types.)
6. Enter the full pathname that the alias will represent in the Path field.
7. If you have more aliases to create, click New. To save your new aliases and close the Alias Manager, click OK.

The Alias Manager is shown in Figure 19.8.

FIGURE 19.8
Aliases are useful if you have long pathnames.

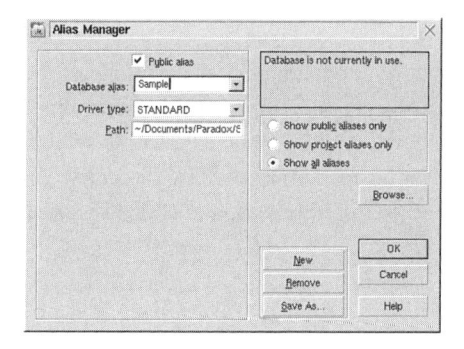

You cannot have a project alias with the same name as a public alias.

To Do: Open a Project Using an Alias

To Do

Here's how to use the Project Viewer to open your project using the alias for your project:

1. In Project Viewer, click the Browse icon in the Working Directory or Database field.
2. Select one of the aliases from the drop-down list.

You can change the definition of an alias at any time, and Paradox objects that use the alias automatically point to the new pathname. Paradox automatically saves alias settings when you create or change the alias.

To change an alias, open it in Alias Manager and overwrite the information you want to change.

To remove an alias, open Alias Manager, select the alias in the Database Alias box, and click Remove.

> Paradox gives you no prompt or warning when you remove an alias; it also gives you no message that the alias has been removed, so be careful. If you delete the wrong alias, click Cancel.

Summary

This hour you learned about relational databases and some of their uses. You were introduced to Paradox database objects, including tables, forms, reports, queries, keys, and indexes. You explored the items on the Paradox Welcome screen and the Paradox desktop. You used Project Viewer to open your working directory. You also set a private directory for temporary files, set preferences, and created aliases for your database project pathnames.

Q&A

Q Can I use databases that were created in Paradox 9 for Windows in Paradox 9 for Linux?

A You should be able to use both versions of Paradox 9 interchangeably, as long as you are not using items that are not supported in Linux, such as OLE (Object Linking and Embedding). Subscribe to the newsgroups `corelsupport.faqs.paradox` and `corelsupport.linux.office2000.paradox` for more information.

Workshop

The Workshop contains quiz questions and exercises to help reinforce what you've learned in this hour. If you get stuck, the answers can be found in Appendix B, "Answers to Quiz Questions."

Quiz

1. What kind of database is a Quattro Pro spreadsheet? What kind of database does Paradox enable you to create?
2. What is another name for a column of values in a database table? A row of values?
3. How are tables linked in relational databases?
4. Is a database object considered data?
5. What is the relationship between a key and the primary index in a table?
6. How are database project files organized in the Project Viewer?

Exercises

1. Display PerfectExpert on the desktop if it's not already displayed.
2. Open Project Viewer if it's not already open on the desktop. Set the Preferences dialog box to open Project Viewer by default.
3. Set the working directory to the sample database that comes with Paradox (most likely in $HOME/Documents/Paradox/Samples; check with your administrator if you can't find it).
4. Click Tables in Project Viewer and open a table; then open a form.
5. Determine the pathname of your private directory by checking the pathname for the :PRIV: alias.

HOUR 20

Creating Your First Database

Now that you know your way around Paradox, you're ready to create your first database tables. Tables are the meat of the database; they're where all your data is stored. First, you'll get your feet wet by creating a table using the Table Expert. You'll then create a table from scratch.

In this hour you will

- Create database tables using Paradox Experts—via a template and by selecting fields individually.
- Create a database table manually using the Field Roster and assign a field code and key field.
- Assign validity checks, including field size, minimum and maximum values, default values, and picture codes.
- Create table lookups for a field and assign passwords to the table.
- Link tables and ensure that all the data in the tables are linked correctly using the Visual Database Designer.

Instant Databases with the Paradox 9 Experts

As you learned in Hour 19, "Paradox 9 Database Basics," you can create a database from scratch by using database templates or by using the Paradox Experts. Using a template is a great way to learn about tables and other database objects; you'll soon be ready to create your own custom database.

Working from Database Templates

Creating a database from a template is as easy as clicking Next. The only decision you have to make is which database template most closely approximates your needs. The best part is that after you create a database from a template, you can customize absolutely everything using the same techniques as if you had created the database from scratch.

To Do: Create a Database from a Template

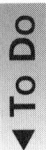

1. From the Welcome screen, click Database Templates. Alternatively, from PerfectExpert, select the Database Expert. You can also create a database from a template in the PerfectExpert dialog box that appears when you click Create From New.

2. Select a database template from the three template types—Personal, Business, or Corporate—as shown in Figure 20.1. Check the View Information About the Selected Database box.

FIGURE 20.1
Different templates are available for personal, small business, and corporate use.

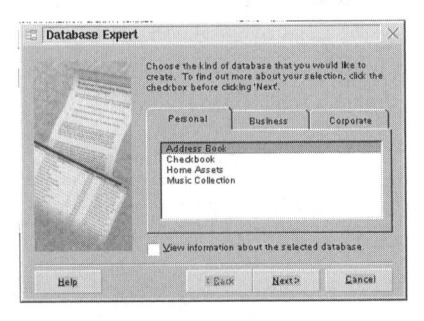

3. Click Next to read the detailed descriptions of the tables, forms, and reports that are created with the template. When deciding which template to use, remember that you can customize every object in the database after you have created it. For example, the database template Video Store Manager could be used as the basis for any database needed to track customers, inventory, sales, and product information.

4. After the database objects' descriptions, a dialog box appears in which you can customize the tables in your database. Each table that will be created is listed in the Table drop-down menu. The template fields for each table are listed in the Fields in the Table drop-down menu, as shown in Figure 20.2.

FIGURE 20.2
You can mix and match fields from different table templates.

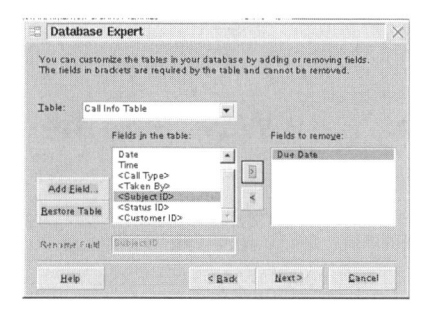

5. If you don't want a particular field, select it and click the arrow to move the field to the Fields to Remove list. Fields with brackets around them represent links to other tables. These fields cannot be removed in the Database Expert, but you can remove them later manually.
6. If you want to add a field that does not appear, click Add Field. All the fields in every database template are listed in the field catalog. Browse through the table template fields and select the field you want to add. When you click OK, the field is added to the table.
7. If you decide that you don't like your changes, click Restore Table to return the table to the original default template state.
8. After you have made your changes, click Next. Enter the pathname for where you want to keep your database project and click Finish.

Using the Paradox Experts

After you have created a database template with PerfectExpert, you can use the Paradox experts to make any changes. You'll learn how to use these experts as each task is described in this and the following two hours.

Building a Database from the Ground Up with Tables

Although useful when you're first learning or in a pinch, database templates will only get you so far in creating databases. Eventually you'll find that creating your own database from scratch is necessary. Because of the nature of relational databases—that is, creating something complex from simple components—it is quite simple to create your own tables and link them manually.

Creating Tables the Easy Way with the Table Expert

Table Expert contains dozens of table types with the fields already defined for both business and personal databases. To create a table with Table Expert, select a table template from the menu, decide which of the ready-made fields to include in your table, and, if necessary, rename the fields to suit your table. Table Expert can create keys for you and has tools to make it easier to create indexes.

To Do: Create a New Table Using the Table Expert

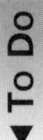

1. From the menu bar, click File, New, Table or right-click the Table object in Project Viewer and select New.
2. Click Table Expert to start the Table Expert.
3. The Table Expert has two separate lists of table templates: Business and Personal. Check the list that you want to display.
4. The Table Templates field displays a list of all the table templates. As you select a table template, the fields that you can select for that table appear in Available Fields.

   Select the table you want to create from the Table Templates list.
5. Select a field to include in the table from the Available Fields list. Click the left arrow to add the field to your table. If you want to include all the available fields, click the double right arrow. To remove a field you have selected, click the left arrow. Click the double left arrow to remove all the fields from the Fields in My Table list.

> You can add fields from different table templates to your table. Just select a new template from the Table Template list and add the fields you want using the right-arrow button.

▼ 6. As you select a field to add to the table, you can edit the field name by overwriting it in the Edit Name field.

7. When you have finished adding and editing fields for your table, click Next. The Table Expert dialog box is shown in Figure 20.3.

FIGURE 20.3
Table Expert is similar to a database template, but you select fields individually instead using a ready-made table.

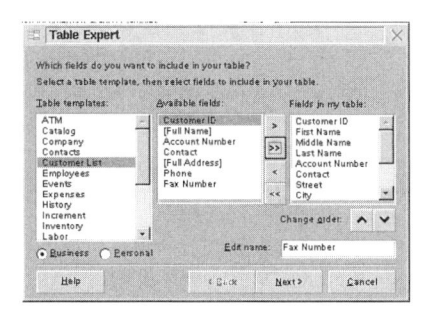

8. Select whether you want to create a key yourself from the fields, have the Table Expert do it, or have no key. If you have the Table Expert create the key, you'll be able to sort the table on the fields you select. If you want to create your own key, you must decide which field (or fields) creates a unique value for each record.

9. Enter the full pathname for the new table. Check the proper box for how you want to add data to the table:

- If you want to add the data directly to the table, the table will open and you can add data directly to the cells in the table. Click the arrow keys or press Enter to move from field to field. Press Tab to create a new record or move among records.

- If you want to add data using a form, Table Expert will create a form for you based on the fields in your table.

▲
- If you want to edit the table, the Restructure Table dialog box will open. You'll learn more about restructuring tables later this hour.

Creating Tables from Scratch with the Field Roster

Instead of using the Table Expert, you can create your tables entirely from scratch using the Field Roster.

To Do: Create a Table from Scratch

1. Select New, Table and click Blank in the New Table dialog box.
2. In most cases, select Paradox 7,8,9 in Table Type.
3. The Field Roster tab in the Create Paradox dialog box enables you to add fields to your table with all the required information (see Figure 20.4).
4. Select a table language from the drop-down menu. For most cases, the default, ASCII ANSI, should be correct.

FIGURE 20.4

When you create a table from scratch, you have complete control over every aspect of the table.

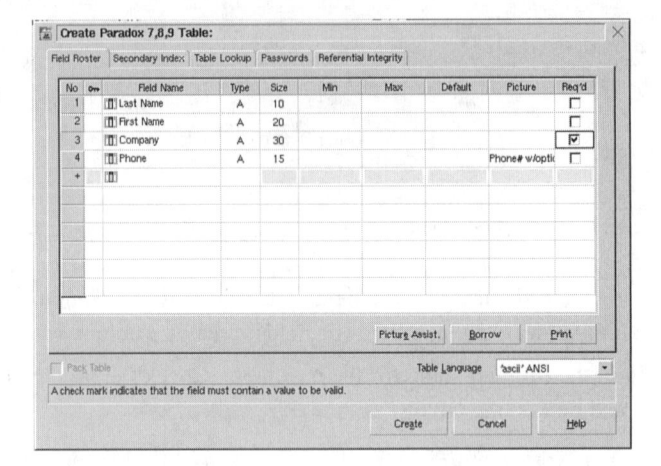

5. Enter the name of the first field you want for your table in the Field Name column.
6. Press Tab or Enter to scroll through the columns in the Field Roster.
7. Click in the Type cell and select a type from the drop-down menu. The different types are explained in the next section.
8. To set validity checks, enter values in the Size, Min, Max or Default, and Picture columns. Validity checks are also explained in the next section.
9. Check Required if the field must be filled in for each record.
10. Press Enter to create a new field.

Field Types

The field type is required for all fields. The type tells Paradox what kind of data is stored in the field. The field types are described in Table 20.1.

TABLE 20.1 Paradox Field Types

Field Type	Description
Alpha	Contains letters, numbers, and symbols (any printable ASCII character). You must specify a field size.
Number	Can contain numbers between 1.2E –38 and 1.2 to 3.4E38, including sign and decimal point.
Money	A number displayed to two decimal places with the currency symbol.
Short integer	An integer (whole number, no decimals) between –32,768 and 32,767.
Long integer	An integer between –2,147,483,648 and 2,147,438,647.
BCD	Binary coded decimal is used when you need a higher level of precision than a number or long integer.
Date	Contains a date between January 1, 9999 BC to December 31, 9999 AD. There are several date formats.
Time	Displays the time in one of several formats.
Timestamp	Displays the date and time.
Memo	Used for text strings that are too large for the Alpha field.
Formatted Memo	Same as Memo fields, except the font, style, color, and font size can be formatted.
Graphic	A picture in BMP, PCX, TIF, GIF, EPS, or JPG format. Converted to BMP when pasted into the Graphic field.
Logical	Contains true/false or other binary values, such as male/female and yes/no.
Autoincrement	A read-only field that Paradox increments. This field has a value of 1 in the first record in the table, and Paradox automatically increments each following record by 1.
Binary	Used with ObjectPAL routines for data that Paradox cannot interpret. For advanced users.
Bytes	Used with ObjectPAL routines for data that Paradox cannot interpret. For advanced users.

Designating a Primary Key Field

The key fields make up the primary index, which is how Paradox primarily sorts the records in the table. You should designate as many fields as necessary to uniquely identify each record.

For example, if you were creating a customer table with information about each customer, a customer name or number might be the only key field. If you were creating a table of customer work orders, the customer number and work order number would be the key fields. You might have work orders with the same number for different customers, but you wouldn't have two work orders with the same number for the same customer.

To make a field a key field, click the Key column. A key icon appears, designating that field as a key field. This means that for each record in the table, Paradox will use this field as the unique identifier. For example, in a table that listed all your customers, you could designate the customer number (if you had one) or customer name as the key field.

> Only certain types of fields can be key fields. Memos, formatted memos, graphics, binary, and byte fields cannot be key fields.

Validity Checks

Validity checks are not required for the fields in a table, but they're indispensable for ensuring that the data entered into your database makes sense, is the kind of data that belongs in the table, and relates to data from other tables in a relational database. It can also make data entry much easier and faster as well as reduce errors.

Set validity checks in the Field Roster when you create the table field. There are four kinds of validity checks:

- Size
- Min/Max
- Default
- Picture

The Size validity check makes sure that a value entered into the field is of the correct size. For example, say you're creating a customer table that will contain all the information about your customers. Each customer has a four-digit number. When creating the Customer Number field, you can enter 4 in the Size column. When you enter the customer numbers into your table, any numbers that are not four digits will not be allowed.

For some field types, Paradox will automatically enter a size, such as 30 characters for an Alpha field type. This means that the field can contain no more than 30 characters.

The Min and Max validity checks enable you to enter a minimum value and/or a maximum value for a field. For example, say you're entering prices into a price list table. The minimum value could be the price of the least expensive item in your inventory (for example, $0.99) and the maximum value could be the most expensive item (for example, $1499.00). If you were to enter a price with an extra digit by mistake, such as $12999.00, Paradox would not allow the value to be entered, thus catching the error.

The Default value is useful when you have a value that is used often. When you enter a string in the Default column, that string appears automatically for every record in that field. You can then overwrite the default for individual records. For example, in the customer table example used earlier, if most of your clients are located in California, you could enter California as the Default value for a State field. You could then overwrite the California default for those few customers in other states.

Creating a Picture

A *picture* is code that represents what's permitted in a particular field. A powerful tool, the picture code restricts data entries to only valid data. You create a picture using the Picture Assistant, shown in Figure 20.5.

FIGURE 20.5
The Picture Assistant enables you to create very specific validity checks.

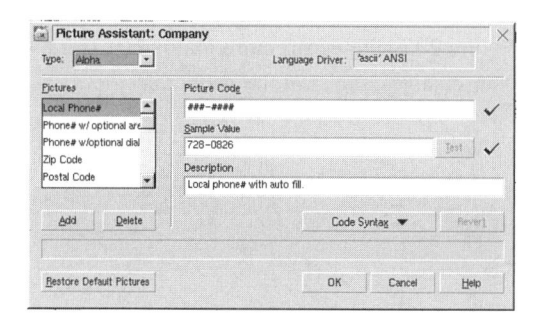

To Do: Create a Picture with Picture Assistant

1. Click Picture Assistant in the Field Roster.
2. Click Code Syntax for a guide on the picture codes.
3. Click Add.
4. Enter a name for your picture, such as *Phone Number*.
5. Enter a code that stands for how the information in the field must look. For example, for a phone number, you could enter (###)###-####. As described in the Code Syntax guide, the # symbol stands for any numeric symbol. If the phone number entered does not match the picture, it will not be allowed in the field.

6. You can enter a sample value to test your picture code. The Picture Assistant will tell you whether the picture code does what you want it to do.

7. You can add a description of the picture to make it easier for others to understand the picture code.

8. Click OK to create the picture.

Editing Your Table

After you have created your table, you can edit it until it is exactly the way you want it. It doesn't matter if you use an Expert or create your table manually—the editing process is the same. You can add and delete fields as long as they are not linked to other tables. You can also create a secondary index, table lookups, and so on.

To Do: Open a Table For Editing

1. Select the table in Project Viewer.

2. Right-click the table and select Restructure. Alternatively, from the menu bar, click Tools, Utilities, Restructure.

3. Select the table in the Select File dialog box and click Open.

As you can see in Figure 20.6, the Restructure dialog box is the same as the Create Table dialog box. Make your changes and save the new table.

FIGURE 20.6

You can restructure tables you created using a database template or PerfectExpert, as well as those created manually.

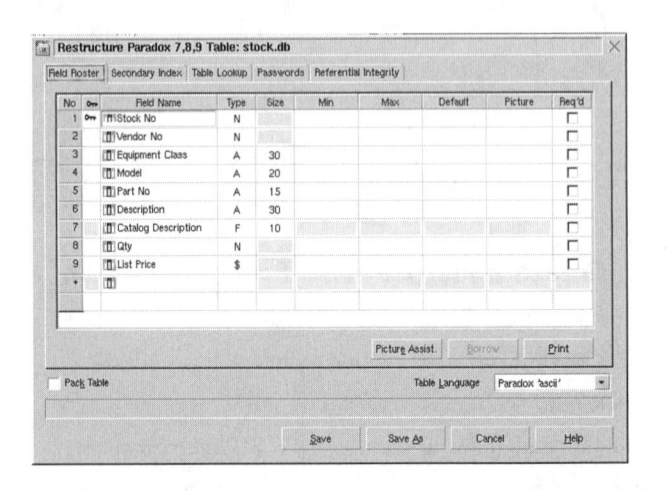

Creating a Secondary Index

Secondary indexes are useful when you regularly sort your records in a way other than by the primary index. For example, if the primary index for a table of customers is the customer number, but you generate sales reports alphabetically by customer name or by sales, you can create a secondary index to speed up the sorting of records and generation of queries and reports.

Paradox also uses secondary indexes when linking tables.

To Do: Create a Secondary Index

1. Open the table in the Restructure dialog box, if it's not already open, and select the Secondary Index tab, shown in Figure 20.7.
2. Click Add and type a name for the secondary index.
3. Click the field on which you want to create the secondary index and click the right arrow to move the field to the Selected Index Fields list.
4. Select a sort order in the Sort column by clicking the column and selecting an option from the drop-down menu.

FIGURE 20.7

A secondary index is useful when you sort the database table in ways other than by the primary index.

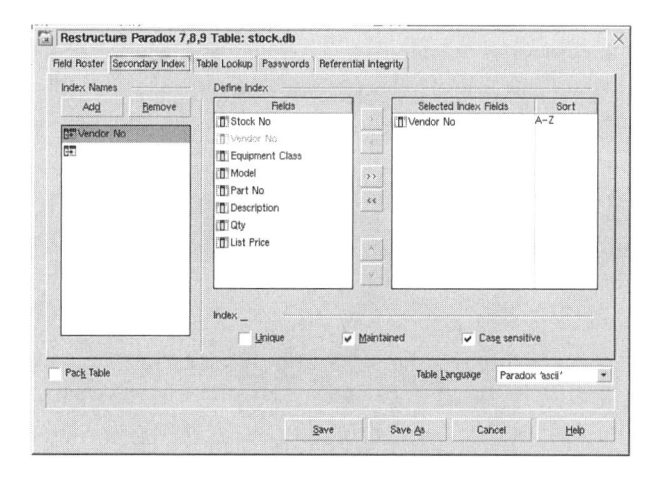

5. You can create a composite secondary index by adding more than one field to the Selected Index Fields list. Click the up and down arrows to indicate the order that fields should be sorted in.
6. Check Case-Sensitive if your secondary index should sort records that begin with uppercase letters before records that begin with lowercase letters.

▼   7. Check Maintained if you want Paradox to automatically update the secondary index whenever the table is updated with new data. You should check this option unless you have a good reason not to.

8. Check Unique if you don't want to allow duplicate values in the secondary index. You must check Maintained in order to check Unique.

9. Click Save to save the secondary index. Click Save As to save the secondary index
▲   as a separate file.

Creating and Using Table Lookups

Table lookups are yet another way to make data entry faster and to ensure that the data entered into your table is valid. In a relational database, tables are related to each other by particular fields. Table lookups restrict the data that can be entered in a field to values that already exist in another table.

For example, say you're creating a database of all your belongings. If you have one table that lists all your possessions and another table for periodic maintenance, you could create a table lookup in the periodic maintenance table using the possessions list table. That way, you could ensure that the maintenance actions all corresponded to an actual possession from the possession table. You'll usually use another table from your database to create a lookup, but you can also create a new table if you want. An example of a table lookup is shown in Figure 20.8.

FIGURE 20.8

Lookup tables restrict field entries to those already part of your database.

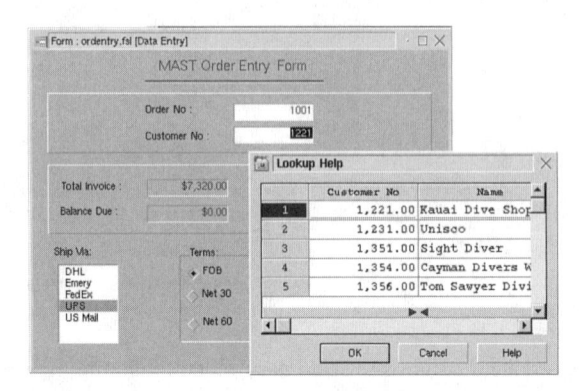

When you create a table lookup, you can specify whether the person entering the data can actually see the lookup table and select a value from it or is only restricted from typing a value that is not in the lookup table.

The field you want to create a lookup table for must have the same field type and size as the lookup table. The field of valid entries must be the first field in the lookup table.

You can specify whether to include all applicable fields in the table lookup or whether only the field for which you created the lookup table is entered. For example, if you create a lookup table for customer name, but you also have fields for the address and phone number, you can have Paradox copy the name, address, and phone number from the lookup table to the table in which you are entering data. Alternatively, you can have only the customer name entered but not the other data.

To Do: Create a Table Lookup

1. Select the Table Lookup tab from the Create Paradox 7,8,9 Table (or Restructure Table) dialog box. The Table Lookup tab is shown in Figure 20.9.
2. Select the field for which you want to create a lookup table from the Fields list. Click the right arrow to move the field to the Lookups Defined Field list.
3. Select from the drop-down menu the alias or pathname that contains the table you want to use as a lookup. The available tables are displayed in the Lookup Tables list. If the table meets the right criteria to be a lookup for the selected field, it appears in black. If it does not meet the criteria, the table appears grayed out. Select the table you want to use as a lookup and click the left arrow to move the table name to the Lookup Table list in the Lookups Defined list.

FIGURE 20.9
You can create a table lookup for a field when creating a table or when restructuring an existing table.

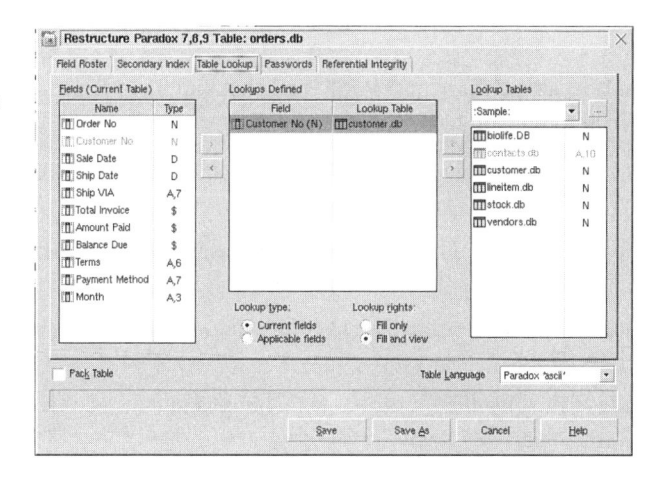

4. Check the Current Fields box to enable the lookup table to only fill in the field for which the lookup is defined.
5. Check the Applicable Fields box for Paradox to fill in all fields that match the current table and the lookup table.

6. Check Fill Only if you don't want the lookup values to be displayed in the field when entering data. (Invalid data will not be entered.) Check Fill and View if you want a drop-down menu with all valid entries from the lookup table to be displayed.

7. Click Save to save the lookup. Click Save As to save the lookup as a new table.

Setting Passwords

Passwords protect your tables from unauthorized access. There are three levels of security you can set on a table:

- Master password
- Auxiliary passwords
- Table rights

The master password prevents unauthorized users from opening a table. The master password must be defined before you can define auxiliary passwords or table rights. To set a master password, select the Passwords tab (shown in Figure 20.10) in the Restructure Table dialog box. Click Define under the Master Password area, enter a password, and then enter the password again to verify it.

After you define a master password, you can define an auxiliary password.

To set an auxiliary password, click Add in the Auxiliary area. Type the auxiliary password.

After you type an auxiliary password, the Table and Field Rights sections are activated. Check which rights you want your password to enable:

- *All*. Provides full access to the table when the auxiliary password is entered, including the ability to change passwords.
- *Insert and Delete*. These rights enable a user to add and delete records but not to change the table itself.
- *Data Entry*. Enables the user to insert and change records but not to delete or clear records.
- *Update*. Enables the user to view the table and edit records but not insert or delete records or edit key fields.
- *Read Only*. Enables the user to only view the table.

You can further define a user's access with an auxiliary password by using field rights. For each field in the table, click the Access column to define one of three levels of access:

- *Full.* This access to the field is defined by the table right.
- *Read Only.* This access to the field means that the user can view the field but not edit it.
- *None.* This means that the field will not appear in the table at all.

FIGURE 20.10
Passwords enable you to control different users' access to tables and table fields.

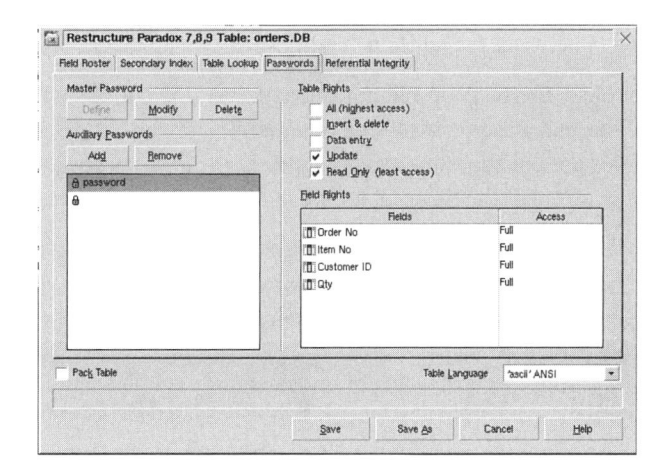

Ensuring Referential Integrity

Referential integrity is a central concept to relational databases. It means that if you change or delete records in one table, links to records in other tables will be maintained. Referential integrity prevents orphan records. This means that a record in a parent table cannot be deleted unless the record is deleted in all the child tables that are linked to the parent first. Also, you cannot add a new record to a child table unless the record is in the parent table.

For example, say you have a database of all your employees' Human Resources information. One of your employees quits and is then rehired with a new employee number. The employee number is the primary key in your employee listing table. If you were to change the employee number in the employee listing table, all the tables that are linked to the employee listing table would also reflect the new employee number.

Referential integrity is automatically maintained when you link tables with the Visual Database Designer. You can also establish referential integrity links manually in the Restructure (or Create) Table dialog box.

The Visual Database Designer

The Visual Database Designer shows you all the relationships among tables in your database at once. It displays your tables graphically, enables you to create links using drag and drop, and then displays the links graphically as arrows. You can use the Visual Database Designer to design a new database, create and edit tables, and establish the relationships between the tables using links.

Links put the "relational" in relational databases. Links provide the relationships between tables in your database by assigning relationships to similar fields in different tables. When tables are linked, referential integrity is ensured, because when a linked field in one table is updated, the other tables are automatically updated as well.

Linking two tables in the Visual Database Designer is as simple as dragging a field from the child table to the parent table. To link two tables, the tables must have a common field, meaning they should be of the same type and size. Also, the linked field on the parent table should be a key field.

To Do: Link Tables with the Visual Database Designer

1. Set the working directory for the database you want to work on in Project Viewer.
2. From the menu bar, select Tools, Visual Database Designer.
3. Right-click the workspace in Visual Database Designer and select Add Table.
4. Select each table you want to include in the linked database and click Add. The tables appear in the workspace.
5. Each field in a table is assigned an icon, depending on the field's purpose. The icons are labeled in Figure 20.11.
6. Select the field on the child table you want to link and drag it to the field on the parent table you want to link. In the parent table, the linked field is the key field, and in the child table, it's just an ordinary field.
7. Enter a name for the link in the Link dialog box (usually the same name as the linked fields).
8. Check Cascade to make the linked field in the child table reflect any changes made to the key field in the parent table.
9. Check Prohibit to make it impossible to change the value of the key field in the parent table if there are records that match the value in the child table.

FIGURE 20.11
The field icons enable you to instantly see your key, linked, and indexed fields.

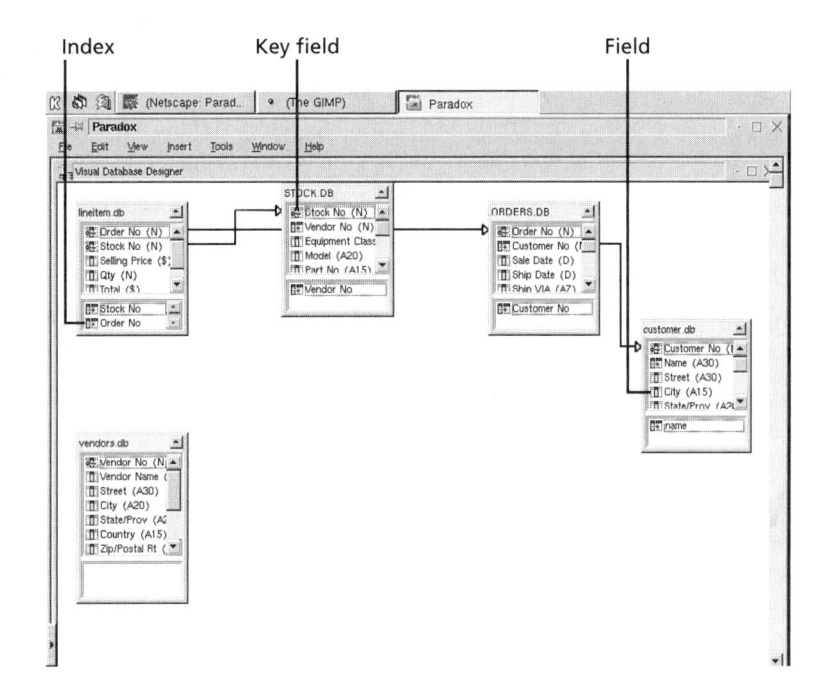

Summary

In this hour, you created a database using a database template, and you created a table using the Table Expert. You created a table from scratch by entering the fields in Field Roster. You also learned how to include key fields, specify a field type, enter validity checks, and create picture codes. You edited an existing table using Restructure Table, created a secondary index on a table, created table lookups on a field, and set passwords for your table. You also ensured referential integrity by linking fields in the Visual Database Designer.

Now that you know how to create tables, you are on your way to creating your database. The first and most important part of creating a database is deciding what kinds of tables you need, what kinds of data should go in them, and how they should be linked. Next hour, you will learn how to add data to your tables.

Q&A

Q When designing my database in Visual Database Designer, I realized I needed a new table. Do I have to exit Visual Database Designer to create a new table?

A No. You can create and restructure tables right in Visual Database Designer. To create a new table, right-click the Visual Database Designer workspace and select Create New Table. To edit an existing table in Visual Database Designer, right-click the table and select Restructure.

Q Can a table be a child and a parent simultaneously?

A Yes. The concept of child and parent tables is specific to each linked field. Depending on the way fields are linked, the same table can be a parent table in one relationship, and a child table in another. Usually, however, tables are linked by only one field.

Workshop

The Workshop contains quiz questions and exercises to help reinforce what you've learned in this hour. If you get stuck, the answers can be found in Appendix B, "Answers to Quiz Questions."

Quiz

1. True or false: You cannot add or remove fields from a database template.
2. What two categories of tables does the Table Expert contain?
3. When creating a table, can you add fields from both the business and personal table templates to the same table, or can you add fields from only one template category?
4. How would you add your own custom field to a table created from the Table Expert?
5. What is the difference between a number and an alpha field type? A time and a timestamp?
6. In Visual Database Designer, which table is the parent and which is the child?

Exercises

1. Create a database from the Job Costing database template. Accept all defaults.
2. Close the Job Costing dialog box. Change the working directory to your job costing database. Restructure the CLIENT.DB table from the database you created in exercise 1.

3. Which field or fields are key fields in the CLIENT table? How do you know?
4. Create a secondary index by company and last name. Call it *Companies*. Make it "maintained."
5. Open the database in the Visual Database Designer. Are there any links?
6. In Visual Database Designer, which table is the parent and which is the child?

HOUR 21

Managing Paradox 9 Data

After you have created and linked the tables of your database, you still have nothing more than a container until you actually put information in the tables. There are two ways to input data into your database: You can type the data directly into the table, or you can create a form and input the data into the form, which creates one record in the table. This hour, you'll input data directly into the tables of your database. Next hour, you'll create forms to enable you to input and view data, one record at a time.

In this hour you will

- Open a Paradox table in table view, memo view, edit mode, and view mode.
- Navigate around the table using horizontal scroll lock and the scroll buttons on the toolbar.
- Add, delete, and edit records in the table, including memos and graphics.
- Locate and sort data in the table.

A Table with a View

Last hour you created and restructured tables using the Table Expert and Field Roster. You can open a table in table view to view all the data in your table at once and to directly input data into the table.

To Do: Open a Table in Table View

1. Set the database directory that contains the table as the working directory.
2. Select the Tables object in Project Viewer.
3. Double-click the table you want to view, or right-click the table and select Open.

Using the Table View

If you've used spreadsheets before, table view will look familiar. Each table field appears as a column, with the field name as the column label. Each table row represents one record. As in a spreadsheet, the records are numbered. These numbers represent the Paradox record number and are independent of the data itself. A table from the Paradox Samples database is shown in Figure 21.1.

> Open the Paradox Samples database (by default, it's in $HOME/Documents/Paradox/Samples) to see examples of tables already populated with data.

FIGURE 21.1
Data is kept in tables of fields and records.

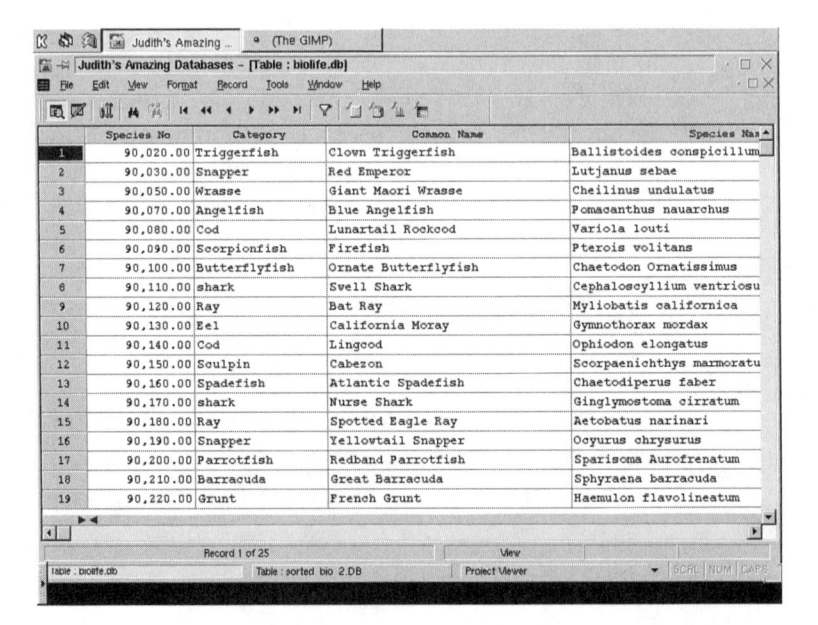

Navigating in Your Table

Paradox has a few navigation features that enable you to move around in your tables without getting lost. One of the more useful features is the horizontal scroll lock. You can set the horizontal scroll lock to lock as many columns as you want in place. When a column is locked in place, it will not move off the screen as you scroll horizontally across your records.

For example, if you are scrolling through the biolife table in the Paradox Samples database, you can lock the Species No., Category, and Common Name columns. As you scroll horizontally across the records, you always know the name of the species whose information you are viewing. To lock a column, drag the scroll lock to the right of the last column you want to lock.

To Do: Navigate Using the Toolbar Navigation Buttons

If you have the Property Bar enabled, you can use the toolbar navigation buttons to move through the records of your table. Follow these steps:

1. Select View, Toolbars and check Property to display the Property Bar.
2. Click the field you want to view. The navigation buttons scroll through each record on the field you select.
3. Click the navigation buttons to move around your records:

    - The first navigation button moves you to the first record in the table.
    - The double left-arrow button moves you up to the first record in the window and scrolls to the next window of records.
    - The single left-arrow button moves you up one record.
    - The single right-arrow button moves you down one record.
    - The double right-arrow button moves you down to the last record in the window and scrolls to the next window of records.
    - The last navigation button moves you to the last record in the table.

The horizontal scroll lock and the navigation buttons are labeled in Figure 21.2.

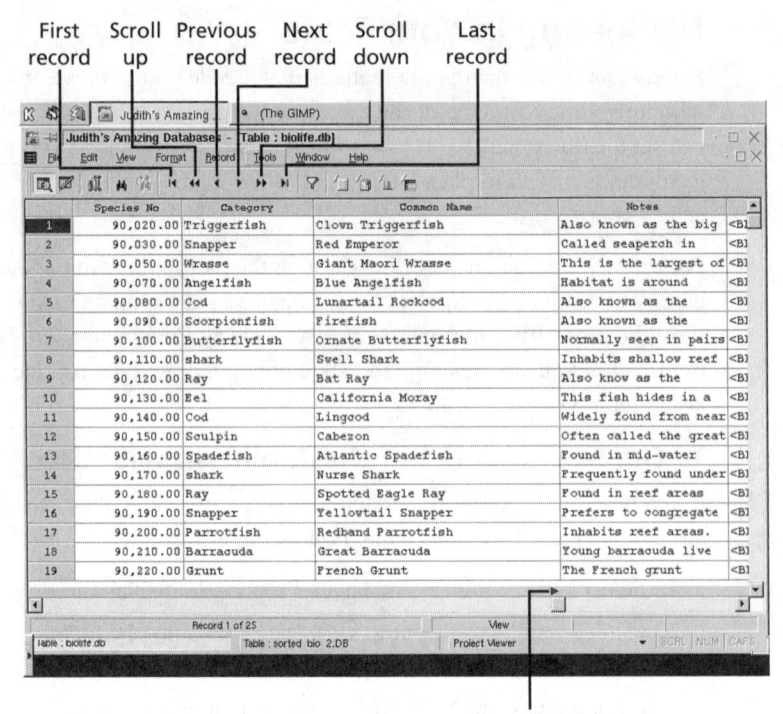

FIGURE 21.2
The horizontal scroll lock is particularly useful when you have tables with many fields.

Adding and Deleting Data

Adding data to the table is somewhat similar to adding data to a spreadsheet in Quattro Pro, except there are a few extra aspects, including modes and the way Paradox saves data.

There are two modes to working with a table: view mode and edit mode. In view mode, you can see all the records in the table, but you cannot make changes. Before you make any edits to a table, including adding and deleting data, you must be in edit mode.

To Do: Switch Between Edit Mode and View Mode

1. Press F9 or click View, Edit Data.
2. The Status Bar displays which mode you are in.
3. When you're ready to return to view mode, press F9 again or click View, View Data.

After you change to edit mode, you are ready to add data to your table.

To Do: Add a New Record to Your Table

1. Press F9 or click View, Edit to go into edit mode.
2. Click Record, Insert. A new record is opened above the insertion point (where your cursor is located).
3. To enter a record at the bottom of the table, place the cursor in the last field in the last record of the table and press Tab or Enter. A new record is created after the last record.
4. After you've created and moved off the record, the new record is posted and moved to its proper place in the table, according to the key field.

> To insert today's date into a date field, press the spacebar three times (for day, month, and year).

To delete a record, click the record to select it and select Record, Delete. The entire record is deleted.

> Once you've deleted a record, you cannot undo the delete. A much safer way to delete a record is to select one field in the record and press the Delete key or click Edit, Delete. Check to ensure that you deleted a field from the correct record; then click Record, Delete. That way, if you find that you deleted the wrong record, you can recover using Edit, Undo or the Esc key.

Editing Data

To edit a field, enter edit mode by pressing F9. Click a field and press Delete or overwrite the data in the field with the new data. If you edited the wrong field, press the Esc key or click Edit, Undo.

> Undo works only if you have not moved the cursor to another record. If you make an edit that you want to change after leaving a record, press Esc to return the data to its original state. Esc only works for the last edit you've made, so be careful. When you exit the table, all the changes you've made are automatically saved.

Using Field View and Persistent Field View

When you edit data in a field, usually the entire field disappears when you begin your edit. This makes simple changes such as correcting a misspelled word or altering one digit in a field difficult, because you have to reenter all the contents of the field. Field view enables you to change one small part of the field, without having to retype everything in the field.

To Do: Enter into Field View

1. Verify that you are in edit mode or press F9 to enter edit mode.
2. From the menu bar, select View, Field View.
3. The field is unselected and the edit cursor appears. You can make changes to individual characters.

Field view lasts for only one cell. As soon as you click another field, field view is turned off and you go back to the default table view. This can be annoying if you have multiple small corrections to make in different fields. In this case, persistent field view is useful.

In persistent field view, the edit cursor remains as you move from field to field. You remain in persistent field view until you uncheck Persistent Field View in the View menu. To open persistent field view, from the menu bar, select View, Persistent Field View. When you are ready to enter table view again, click View, Persistent Field View again to uncheck the menu entry.

Inserting Memos and Graphics

Memo and graphic fields are handled differently from the other fields because the values in these fields usually require much more space. To enter data into a memo or graphic field, double-click the field, or press Shift+F2. The field opens in memo view, in which the field is maximized to the entire workspace area. There is no limit on the amount of data you can enter in the Memo field. To leave memo view and return to table view, press Shift+F2 again.

If the field is a formatted memo, you can apply formats to the text in memo view. Click View, Toolbars and check Text Formatting to display the Formatting toolbar.

> If you forget how to move among the different views, the Status Bar contains hints.

An example of memo view is shown in Figure 21.3.

FIGURE 21.3
Memo view enables you to see the entire contents of your memo field.

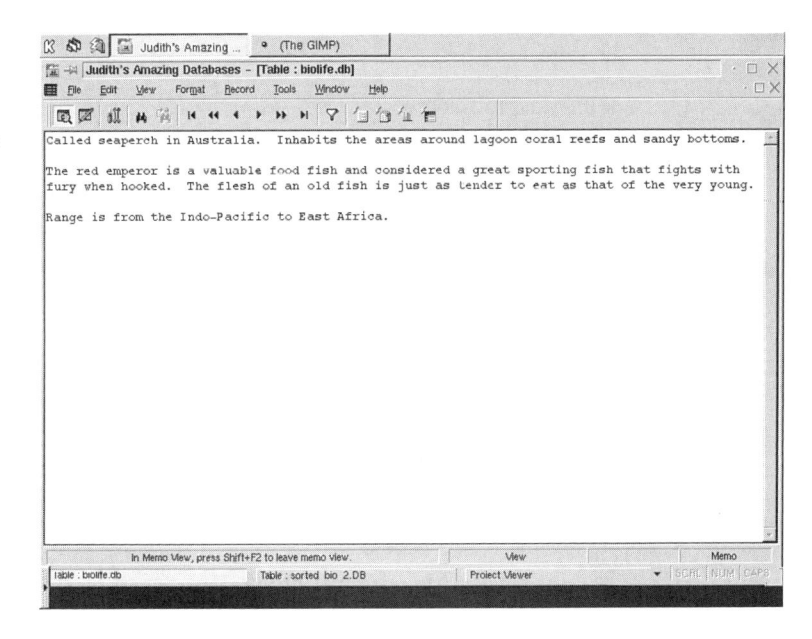

You can view graphics in memo view by double-clicking the graphic field or selecting it and pressing Shift+F2.

To Do: Insert a Graphic

1. Press F9 to change to edit view.
2. From the menu bar, click Edit, Paste From.
3. Browse to the location of the graphic you want to paste and click Open.
4. The graphic is converted to BMP format and pasted into the graphic field.

An example of a graphic field displayed in memo view is shown in Figure 21.4.

FIGURE 21.4
All graphics are stored as BMP files in Paradox.

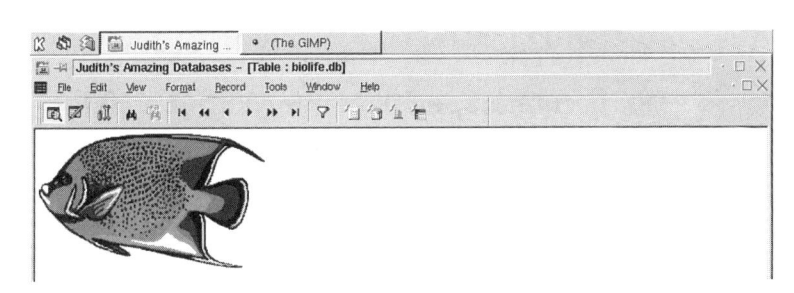

To Do: Copy Your Data to a File

You can copy individual fields, including memo and graphic fields, to an external file. Here are the steps to follow:

1. Click the field to select it.
2. Click Edit, Copy To.
3. Enter the filename for the file you want to copy the field to and click Save.
4. A file containing the field is created. The file is in BMP format for graphics; text format is used for other field types.

Locating Data

In Paradox, you have several ways to locate and edit specific data. You may need to

- Locate a table record according to record number.
- Locate a field in a table that has too many fields to easily scroll through.
- Locate a value within a field.
- Locate and replace values within a field.
- Find and replace strings in a memo.

To Do: Locate a Table Record

1. From the menu bar, select Record, Locate, Record Number.
2. Enter the record number you want to locate.
3. Paradox highlights the record at the field where the cursor was when you began the locate operation.

To Do: Locate a Field

1. From the menu bar, select Record, Locate, Field.
2. Highlight the field you want to locate.
3. Paradox highlights the field at the record where the cursor was when you began the locate operation.

To Do: Locate a Specific Value Within a Field

1. From the menu bar, select Record, Locate, Value.
2. Select the field where you want to locate the value.
3. Enter the value string.
4. Check Case-Sensitive for a case-sensitive search.
5. Check Exact Match if you want Paradox to search for the exact string you entered.

Managing Paradox 9 Data 413

▼ 6. Check @ and .. if you used the @ and .. wildcards in the Value Search field (see Table 21.1 later in this hour).

7. Check Advanced Pattern Match if you used any other wildcards in the Value Search field. Paradox highlights the field at the record where the cursor was when you began the locate operation.

▲ 8. If you want to locate more than one instance of the same value, click Locate Next.

The Locate Value dialog box is shown in Figure 21.5.

FIGURE 21.5
The Locate Value and the Locate and Replace (discussed in the next section) dialog boxes are similar.

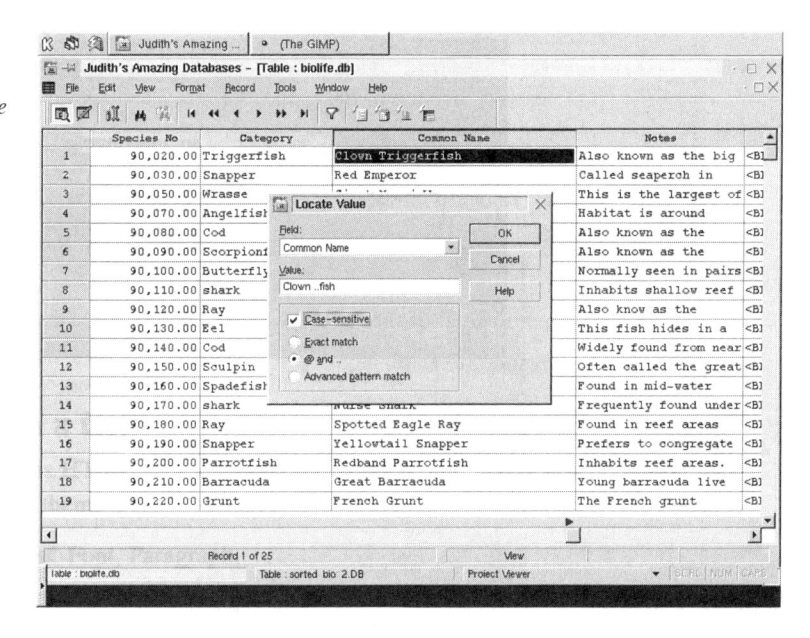

> When using Locate Value, remember that Paradox is looking for values, not for strings. You must enter the entire value or part of the value and a wildcard. For example, if you were searching for the Nurse Shark value in the Common Name field of the biolife table, you would have to enter **Nurse ..** or **Nurse Shark** in the Locate Value dialog box. If you enter just **Nurse**, Paradox would not find the record.

21

To Do: Locate and Replace a Value

1. Press F9 to enter edit mode.
2. Follow the same steps as for locating a value, except enter a value in the Replace With field as well as the Value field in the Locate and Replace dialog box.
3. When Paradox finds a match, the Found a Match dialog box appears, with the following options:

   - *Skip This Occurrence*. Skips the located value without replacing it with the new value.
   - *Change This Occurrence*. Changes the occurrence; then Paradox moves to the next occurrence of the value.
   - *Change All Occurrences*. Changes all occurrences of the value at once.

To Do: Perform a Find-and-Replace Operation in the Text of Memo Fields

1. Press F9 to enter edit mode.
2. Click the memo field of the record where you want to "find and replace" a string.
3. Click Edit, Find and Replace.
4. The memo field opens into memo view.
5. Enter the Search For and Replace With values.

The Find and Replace dialog box is shown in Figure 21.6.

FIGURE 21.6
Find and Replace in Paradox is similar to Find and Replace in other WordPerfect Office 2000 applications, except for the wildcards.

Using Wildcard Symbols

Often, when locating data, you might not know the exact spelling of the string you are looking for, or you may want to locate several versions of a string. For example, you may want to locate all spellings of *Smith*, including Smith, Smithe, and Smythe. Rather than typing each version of Smith in the Locate Value field, you could use a wildcard, such as `Sm@th@`. Wildcards are also useful when you are searching for a very long string because you don't have to type the whole string. For example, if you wanted to locate the record for the Amphistichus rhodoterus, you could type `Amph..rho..` instead of typing out the entire value.

Table 21.1 lists the wildcards used by the Advanced Pattern Match feature in Paradox.

TABLE 21.1 Wildcard Symbols

Wildcard	Description
@	Any one character
..	Any character or characters
^x	String at the beginning of the field
x$	String at the end of the field
x?	One or none of the character before ? (for example, `Peters?` stands for Peter or Peters)
x|y	Either *x* or *y*
[xyz]	X, y, or z
[^xyz]	Any character except *x*, *y*, or *z*
(string)	The exact string within the parentheses
\w	Interprets a character that's normally a wildcard as an actual character (for example, \? searches for "?")

Sorting Data

By default, records in Paradox tables appear in the order of the key field. Sorting enables you to display your records in any order. When you sort a table, a copy of the table is created and the data is sorted in the new table. The original table remains the same.

> The key field determines where records are physically kept in the table file.

To Do: Sort a Table

▼ To Do

1. From the menu bar, select Format, Sort.
2. In the Sort Table dialog box, select the fields you want to sort by selecting a field and clicking the right arrow to move it to the Sort Order list.
3. Use the up- and down-arrow buttons to change the sort order after you have determined which fields to sort.
4. If the table is keyed, a new table must be created to sort the fields. Enter a name for the new table. If the table is unkeyed, you can choose to either sort the table and save it or make a copy of the table and sort the copy.
5. Click a field and then click the Sort Direction button to specify the sort order of each field (+ specifies ascending order and – specifies descending order).
6. Check Sort Just Selected Fields to have Paradox sort only the fields that are listed in the Sorted list.

▲

7. Check Display Sorted Table to have the sorted table displayed.

The Sort Table dialog box is shown in Figure 21.7.

FIGURE 21.7
Sort the table when you want to rearrange your fields.

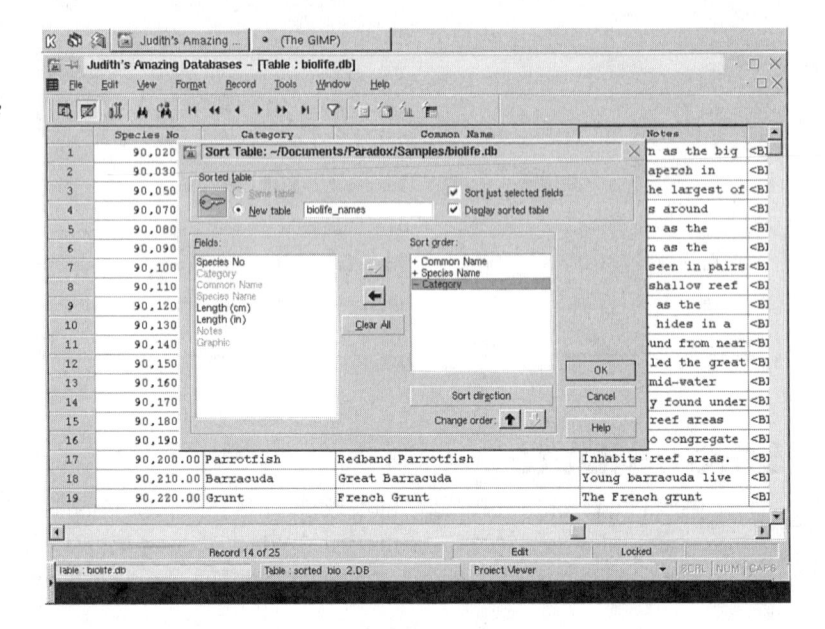

Summary

In this hour, you opened your table in table view and navigated through the table using horizontal scroll lock and the Property Bar's navigation buttons. You added, deleted, and edited records using edit mode. You viewed and edited memos and graphics in memo view, and you also located and sorted records in your table.

Q&A

Q I tried to enter data into a field, but now I can't leave the field. Why not?

A Look at the Status Bar for help on the problem. If you can't leave a field after entering data, you probably entered invalid data.

Q If I'm editing a record in a table, what would happen if another user tries to edit the same record at the same time?

A When you edit a record, Paradox automatically locks it until you move to the next record. A lock prevents other users from editing or deleting the record, although they can view the record. Locks also prevent other users from restructuring the table while you're using it. You can manually lock a record by selecting it in edit mode and clicking Record, Lock.

Workshop

The Workshop contains quiz questions and exercises to help reinforce what you've learned in this hour. If you get stuck, the answers can be found in Appendix B, "Answers to Quiz Questions."

Quiz

1. Name two ways of inputting data into a table.
2. When you first open a table in table view, what step must you always take before you can edit the table?
3. Can you undo an edit if you have not moved off the record where the edit was made? What happens if you try to undo an edit after you have moved to a different field in the same record? What happens if you try to undo the edit after you move to a different record in the same field?
4. What is the difference between field view and persistent field view?
5. What file format are graphics saved in when you use Copy To to copy a graphic field to a file?

6. Which Paradox tool do you use to locate and replace items in a field? In a memo?
7. Which wildcard value would you use to search for either one value or another?
8. Can you sort a keyed table without making a new table?

Exercises

1. Open the customer table in Paradox Samples (by default, it's located in $HOME/Documents/Paradox/Samples) and switch from view mode to edit mode. How do you know which mode you're in?
2. Set the horizontal scroll lock in the customer table to lock the Customer No and Name fields. What date was the first contact for Island Finders?
3. Resize your table so that 15 records are showing. Display the Property Bar. Go to the last record in the table in one click. What is the customer name? Repeat this for record numbers 40, 42, 27, and 1, in that order.
4. Open the Contacts table and add Jimmy Buffett at Sam's Dive Shoppe (123-555-1234) to the table.
5. Change Sam's Dive Shoppe to Sam's Dive Emporium using field view.
6. Open the biolife table. Double-click the Bat Ray Graphic field. What happens? Close memo view. Double-click the Notes field and close it.
7. How many sharks are there in the Common Name field of the biolife table? How would you find them?

HOUR 22

Advanced Paradox 9 Techniques

Forms, reports, and queries are tools for viewing, editing, manipulating, and summarizing the data in your tables. A *form* is primarily for editing data and for viewing records one at a time. A *report* is primarily for printing records and viewing all your records at once. A *query* is a way of questioning your database to get specific information about the data. You can use forms and queries to edit your data, but not reports.

In this hour you will

- Create forms using Quick Form and the Form Expert, and create data models for multitable forms.
- Edit your forms in the Design window, using the design buttons and the Design Layout dialog box.
- Deliver a form to users (so that they can use it to enter data), enter data into the form, and print the form.
- Create reports using Quick Report and the Report Expert.
- Create queries using the Query Expert.

As you create forms and reports this hour, you'll follow a basic design plan:

1. *Create a data model*. Decide which data you want to include on your form or report.
2. *Create a layout*. Organize and arrange the data on the form or report so that it makes sense.
3. *Design the form or report*. Create extra items for your form, such as buttons that perform an action, text boxes and lines, and shading and graphics.

Creating and Using Forms

When you view your data in a form, you are seeing the same data that's in the table, just in a different format. You can design forms to show all the fields in the table, exactly as they appear in the table. You can also rearrange the fields on the form, or you can have only certain fields appear.

You can also create calculated fields that manipulate the data in the tables to show a calculated value, such as two fields added or multiplied, or a summarized field, such as the sum of all the data in a field.

Forms are particularly useful when working with a relational database of linked tables, because you can use one form to add data to different tables.

Forms make it easier to input data compared to just typing it directly into the table. You can design different forms for different views of the same data, to show data from different tables, or to enter data for different tables at the same time. If you have memo fields, graphics, or URLs, it is often more convenient for the reader to use a form, rather than go directly to a table. An example of a form is shown in Figure 22.1.

FIGURE 22.1

Use forms to enter data into your tables as well as to view and print individual records.

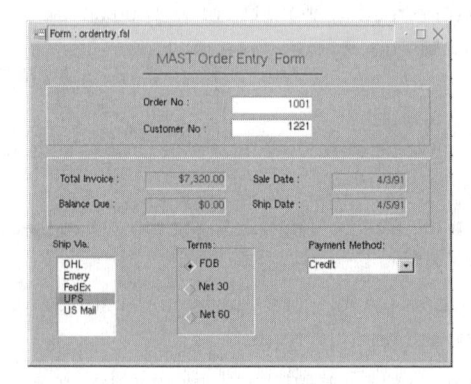

Quick Form

There are three ways to create a new form:

- Using Quick Design, which creates a Quick Form
- Using the Form Expert
- Creating it manually using the Form Design window and the Design Layout dialog box

Using Quick Form is the simplest way to create a form. If you have a single-table form to create, you can create your form using Quick Form and then refine the design in the Design window.

To Do: Create a Form with Quick Form

1. Open a table by double-clicking it in Project Viewer.
2. Select Tools, Quick Design, Quick Form.
3. The form is created and displayed in View Data view. The form is a single-record, column layout of all the fields in the table, in the order they appear in the table.

An example of a quick form is shown in Figure 22.2.

FIGURE 22.2
Quick Form is ideal for creating simple data-entry forms.

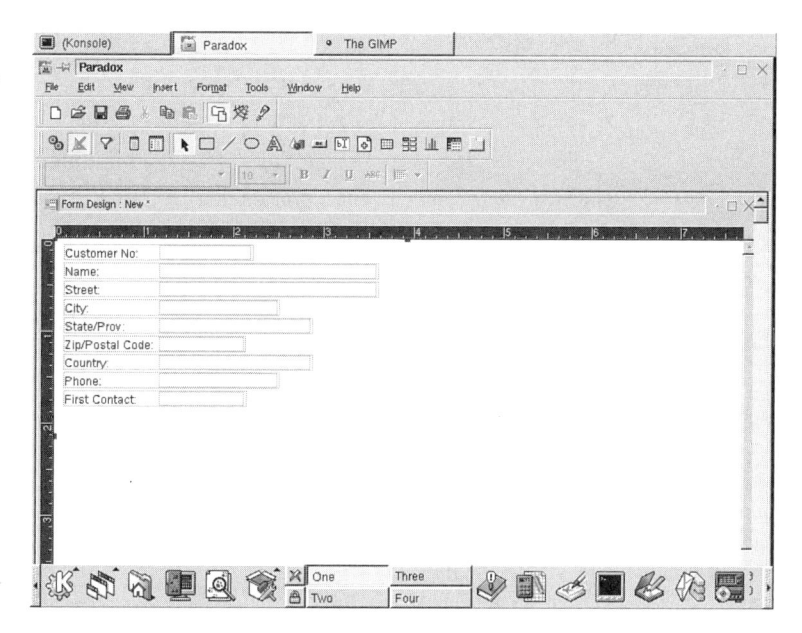

Building Forms with the Form Expert

To create more complex forms, use Form Expert. Although not difficult to use, Form Expert enables you to create forms complex enough for most uses. To start Form Expert, select New, Form, Expert, Run Expert.

> To always use experts to create your forms and reports, set Always Use Expert in Paradox Preferences (Tools, Settings, Preferences).

To Do: Create a One-Table Form Using the Form Expert

1. After you have opened the Form Expert, check Data from One Table and click Next.
2. Use the browse button to select your table and click Open.
3. All the fields from the table appear in the Available Fields list. Click the right-arrow button to move fields to the Display These Fields list. Click the double right-arrow button to display all the fields and click the left-arrow buttons to remove fields from the Display These Fields list. Click Next.
4. Select the layout of your form:
   - *Single-record*. Displays one record at a time.
   - *Tabular*. Displays all your data in columns of fields and rows of records, similar to your table (except you can choose which data to display).
   - *Multi-record*. Displays several records at a time, each repeating the same layout. Data is displayed in columns, and is similar to the form made by Quick Form.
5. Select a style from one of the style sheets. As you highlight a style, a preview is displayed in the dialog box, as shown in Figure 22.3.

FIGURE 22.3
Style sheets are useful for maintaining design standards across all the forms and reports in your database.

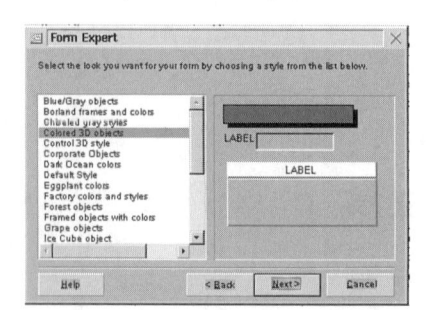

> A *style sheet* is a form design template that includes text fonts, labels, buttons, colors, shading, and a background. Use a style sheet when you want to create several Paradox documents with the same look. You can use one of the style sheets that comes with Paradox, or you can create your own style sheet in the Design window.

6. Give your form a filename. Check View Form in Run Mode to use your form right away to view data. Check View Form in Design Mode to add some finishing design touches.

Two-Table Forms

When you have more than one table in your form, one table is the *master* table and the other tables are *detail* tables. Usually, you have a value in the master table for which you want to use the detail tables to get information. For example, to display all orders for each customer for the year, you could create a form that would use the Customer table as the master table and the Orders table as the detail table. Every order would be displayed on the form for each customer, one page per customer.

The master and detail tables must be linked before you can create a two-table form. When you link two tables, Paradox takes the value in the master table and looks for matching values in the detail tables. That's why you must have an index in the detail table on the value that you want to link. If there were no index, Paradox wouldn't know where to look for values in the detail table. The index can be either a primary index or a maintained secondary index. To link fields, they must be of the same type and size—for example, both fields could be alpha type with a size of 30 characters. An example of a linked master table and detail table is shown in Figure 22.4.

To Do: Create a Two-Table Form

1. Open the Form Expert as described in the last section.
2. Select Data from Two Tables and click Next.
3. Select the master table from the drop-down menu.
4. Select the detail table.
5. Select the fields to be included on the form from the master table and the detail table.
6. Select a layout for your form. For most forms, a column master followed by table details is ideal, but experiment to see which layout works best for your form.
7. Select a style from the style sheet.

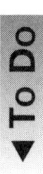

▼ 8. Give your form a filename and check whether to run the form or open it in the Design window.

FIGURE 22.4
A master table and a detail table must be linked on a field to be used to create a form in the Form Expert.

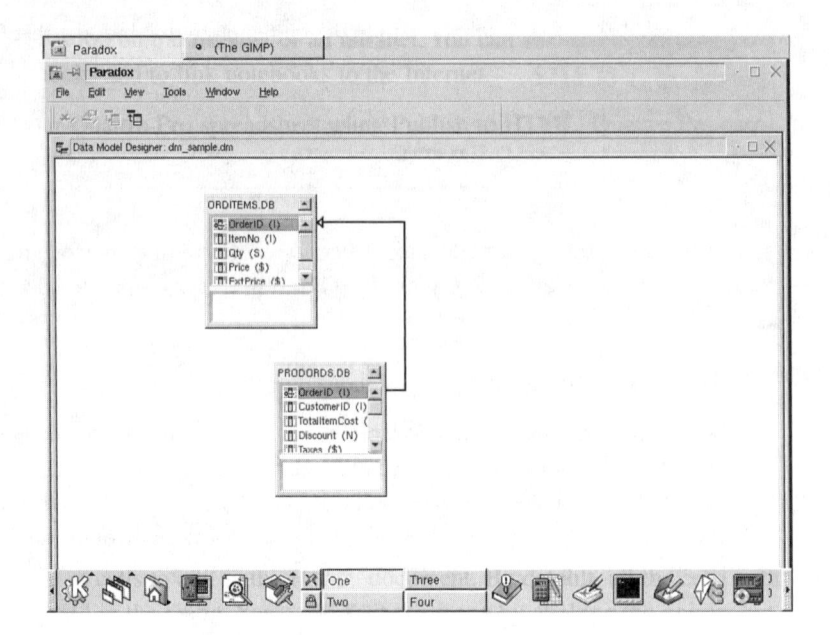

▲

Multitable Forms

When you want to design a form using data from three or more tables, you must create a data model before creating the form. A data model enables you to see the relationships between different pieces of data. You can also see how to organize your form and how to group entry items.

Creating a data model is similar to linking tables in practice. The difference is that the links are actually saved as part of the database files, whereas data models are just a way of looking at the database. You can create as many different data models as you want and save them under different filenames. They don't affect the database tables at all, although they form the basis of multitable forms.

To Do: Create a Data Model

1. Select New, Data Model or select New, Form, Data Model to open the Data Model Designer.
2. Add the tables you want to include in your data model from the Add Object dialog box. When you're finished, click Close.

Advanced Paradox 9 Techniques

> You can add another table at any time by right-clicking the workspace of the Data Model Designer and selecting Add Object.

3. Link the tables in the Data Model Designer by dragging the linked field from the master table to the detail table.
4. When you're done, save the data model design in your working directory.

To Do: View the Data Model of a Form

1. Open the form or report and click View, Design Form.
2. Click Format, Data Model to display the data model used to create the form.
3. If the data model is saved as a separate object, you can also open the data model from Project Viewer.

An example of a multitable data model is shown in Figure 22.5. Now you're ready to create a multitable form.

FIGURE 22.5
Once you understand the concept of master and detail tables, you can create forms using fields from several tables.

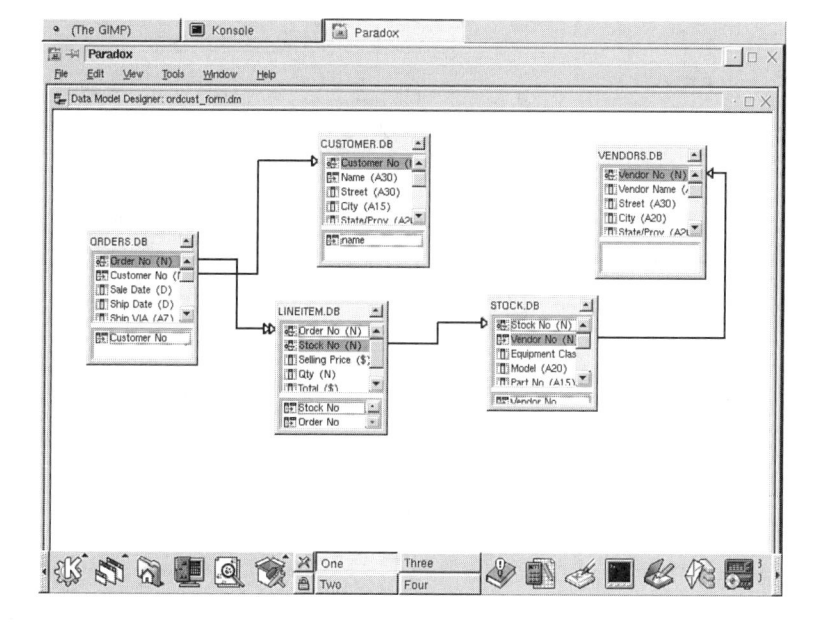

To Do: Create a Multitable Form

1. Open the Form Expert as described earlier.
2. Check Data from Multiple Tables and click Next.

▼ 3. Select the data model to use in creating the form. The Form Expert lists the data models in the working directory in the drop-down menu.
4. Select the fields to include in the form from each table.
5. Select the layout you want for the form.
6. Select a style sheet for your form.
7. Give your form a filename and select whether to view the form in run mode
▲ (to view the data right away) or design mode (opens the Design window).

Fine-Tuning the Design of Your Forms in the Design Window

After you have created a form using Quick Form or the Form Expert, you can change any aspect of your form in the Design window. To open a form in the Design window, open the form and then click View, Design Form. You can add design objects, such as buttons, fields, text, shading, color, graphics, and shapes, in the Design window. You can also use the Design Layout dialog box to change the layout of your form.

> Once you become adept at creating forms, you can use the Design window and the Design Layout dialog box to create forms from scratch.

To open the Design Layout dialog box, select File, New, Form and then click Format, Layout. The Design Layout dialog box is shown in Figure 22.6.

FIGURE 22.6

If you want to change the layout of your form after creating it in the Form Expert, use the Design Layout dialog box.

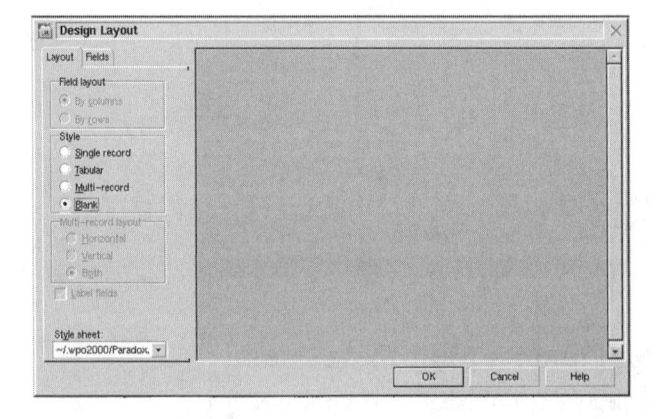

Select a new layout style by checking one of the layout styles listed. The layout styles are the same as in the Form Expert except for the Blank layout. Blank displays nothing. All fields are removed from the design, so you can add each field individually.

Use the Fields tab to add and remove fields from the form. If you have more than one table linked in the data model, the tables are listed in the Table menu. All the fields in the table are listed in the Selected Fields list. Remove a field from the form by selecting the field and clicking Remove. You can also reorder the fields on the form by using the Order buttons. To return the fields to their initial state, click Reset Fields.

In the Field Layout tab, check By Columns to display the fields vertically in columns along the page. Check By Rows to display the fields in rows horizontally across the page. Check Label Fields to have labels for your fields next to the actual fields.

> You can also decide to individually display labels (or not) in the Design window. Simply right-click the fields and select Properties.

Choose a new style sheet in the Layout tab. To select a style sheet, highlight the style sheet filename in the Layout tab of the Design Layout dialog box. A preview of the style sheet is displayed in the Design Layout dialog box.

> You can create your own style sheets in the Design window. Create each of the design objects in the Design window and then click Format, Style Sheet. Click Save As and select a name for your style sheet; then click OK. Style sheets with .FP extensions are designed to be printed, whereas style sheets with .FT extensions are designed to be viewed onscreen.

Adding Design Objects in the Design Window

The Design Object toolbar contains icons for each of the form objects, including buttons, text, fields, graphics, shapes, and lines. To display the Design Object toolbar, click View, Toolbars, and click Design Object. The Design window is shown in Figure 22.7.

FIGURE 22.7

Use the Design window to add new objects, such as text, buttons, addition fields, shading, color, and graphics, to your form.

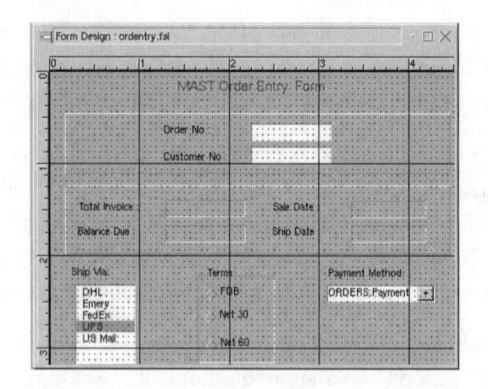

To add an object to the form, click the object icon on the Design window toolbar and then click the form to place the object. For some objects, an expert appears to help you create the object. For example, when you add text, the Text Expert appears. The Text Expert guides you through adding the text you want, choosing a font size and style, and selecting formatting options. When you add a field, the Field Expert appears. You can add individual fields, including fields from unlinked tables, using the Field Expert.

> To add more than one instance of the same object to the form, hold down the Shift key as you add objects to the form. Every time you click the form, a new object is created, until you click the Selection icon or another object icon in the Design window toolbar.

To work on an object, you must first select it by clicking it. You can then move it, resize it, or apply design properties to it. To select multiple objects, hold down Shift or Ctrl while selecting the objects.

The Design window has a ruler you can use to size your objects. To display the ruler, select View, Ruler. You can also display gridlines to enable you to set the size and alignment of your objects with precision. To set the grid, click View, Grid. To have your objects snap to the grid, click Format, Snap to Grid.

Sometimes you'll want to make an object unselectable so that it can't be altered by mistake. To make an object unselectable, right-click the object and select Properties, Design. Uncheck Selectable. The object cannot be selected and therefore cannot be altered. If you want to make the object selectable again, follow the same steps and check the Selectable box.

Once you have a design object exactly the way you want it, you can duplicate it. Duplicating an object is the same as copying and pasting it. For example, you can duplicate a field and change its name to get a completely new field with the same design characteristics as the original. This is useful for creating calculated fields on a form that do not appear in the table. To duplicate a field, select a field and then click Edit, Duplicate. The new field appears next to the old field. You can then move, rename, resize, or make any other edits to the new copy.

> You can only duplicate objects within the same Design window.

Sometimes it's useful to make several objects in the Design window act as one object—for example, if you want to move the objects as a group. To set a group, hold down Shift while clicking each object you want to group. Click Format, Group. To ungroup the objects, select the group and click Format, Ungroup.

You can align objects horizontally or vertically as well as to the left, right, or along a center line. To align objects, select them; click Format, Alignment; and select the alignment you want. Align Left, Center, and Right align vertically. Align Top, Bottom, and Middle align horizontally.

Delivering Your Form to End Users

A *delivered form* is a copy with all the source code removed. When you deliver a form, it can be used to view and edit data, but it cannot be opened in design mode. Therefore, the format and design of the form cannot be changed. To deliver a form, open the form in the Design window and click Format, Deliver. The form file is saved as an FDL file. The original form is saved as an FSL file.

Viewing Data and Entering Data into the Form

To enter data into the form, click View, Edit Data. Click a field and type data into it. To move to the next field, press Tab or click an arrow key. When you're finished entering data, press Enter. The data is added to the table (or tables) as a new record, and a blank form is displayed for you to enter the next record. The data is automatically saved as soon as you press Enter.

To view data in the form, click View, View Data. Depending on whether your form is a single-record or multirecord form, you can view one or several records at a time onscreen. To move to the next record, use the form navigation buttons. Select View, Toolbars, Property to display the toolbar with the navigation buttons. The navigation buttons are just like those for table records, which you learned about in Hour 20, "Creating Your First Database."

> You can also use Page Down to scroll forward and Page Up to scroll backward through your records.

Printing the Form

When you print a form, only the current record is printed. To print the design of a form with no data, click View, Design Window and then click File, Print.

To print a record, open the record on the form in Edit Data or View Data mode. Click File, Print.

> If you want to print multiple records, you should use a report.

Presenting Your Data in Reports

Reports are useful for presenting data, particularly if you need to gather the same kind of data periodically. Reports can create summaries or details for groups of records, whereas forms can only show individual records. For example, you would use a form to print one customer's invoice. You would use a report to print all your accounts payable.

Creating a report is similar to creating a form; in fact, the Design window is the same. There are a few differences that are discussed here, but you have already learned most of the information you need to create a report by learning how to create a form.

Instant Reports with Quick Report

The fastest way to create a report is via the Quick Report tool. Quick Report produces a report in tabular format of all the data from one table, with minimal design formatting. An example of a report created with Quick Report is shown in Figure 22.8.

FIGURE 22.8
Quick Report creates a simple, no-frills report from one table.

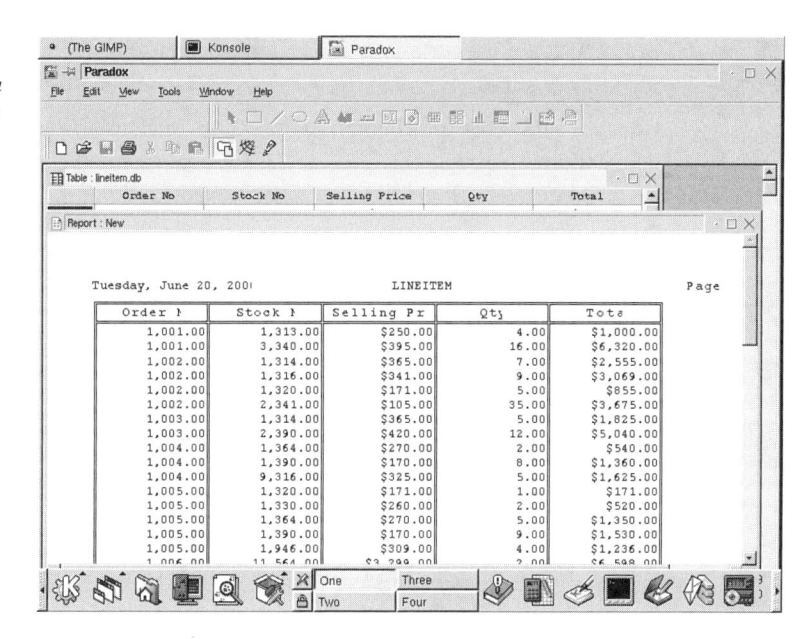

To Do: Create a Quick Report

1. Open the table for the report.
2. Click Tools, Quick Design, Quick Report.
3. The report is displayed in a new window. To save the report, click File, Save As and give the report a name.

To Do: Create a Report with Report Expert

The Report Expert works much like the Form Expert. Follow these steps:

1. To open the Report Expert, select Tools, Experts, Report and click Run Report.
2. Check whether you want to create a report from one table or two tables.
3a. If you checked Data from One Table, select a table for your report and then add the fields that you want to include in the report.
3b. If you checked Data from Two Tables, select a master table, click Next, and then select a detail table. The two tables must be linked.
4. Select groups to organize the report in. For example, using the stock.db table from the Samples database, if you wanted to create a report of all the stock based on equipment class, you would create an equipment class group.
5. If you want to summarize any of the groups, select the group to summarize and select the type of summary from the Summary drop-down menu.

6. Select a style for your report and check whether to print individual or multiple records per page.
7. Check to add other information to the report, such as a title, page numbers, and the date and time.
8. Enter a filename for the report and select whether you want to print it right away.
9. Click Finish. The report is displayed in a new window.

An example of a report is shown in Figure 22.9.

FIGURE 22.9
Reports enable you to analyze and present your data.

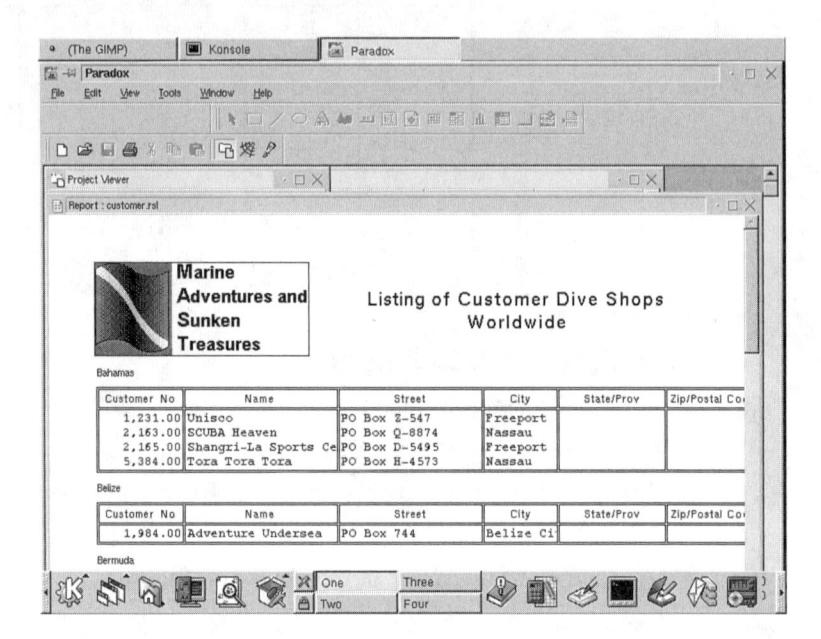

Retrieving Information with Queries

A *query* is a question that you ask of your database to get information from the database. Queries enable you to find particular data in a table, perform calculations on your data, or create a new table from data in other tables, to name just a few things. For example, you could query your database to find out which clients owe you more than $1,000, how many shark species you have in inventory, or which customers bought DVD players from you over the Internet in April.

After you construct your query, Paradox looks through your tables to find the data and presents it in a new, temporary table called the *answer* table.

You can use several methods to create a query:

- Create a simple query with Query Expert.
- Use Query-By-Example to create complex queries without scripts.
- Use the Visual Query Builder for maximum power and flexibility.
- Edit queries directly using the SQL Editor.

Queries are powerful and complex tools that could easily take several chapters to explain thoroughly. Using the Query Expert is the easiest method of creating a simple query, and anyone can use it with no experience. To give you an idea of how to use queries, we cover the Query Expert in this book.

To Do: Create a Quick-and-Dirty Query with the Query Expert

1. Select Tools, Experts, Query, Run Expert.
2. The working directory is loaded by default, but you can also use Browse to locate tables in a different directory (although to keep things simple, it's better to switch the working directory to the database you want to query).
3. Select the fields you want to query from each table. You can query as many fields from as many tables as you want. If the tables are not linked, the Query Expert opens a dialog box for you to create a relationship.
4. Select Detail if you want to query data directly from the tables. Select Summary if you want to use an operator to get a summary of values from your records, including average value, maximum and minimum values, count of the number of values, and sum of all the values.
5. If you selected Detail in the last step, select an operator for comparing the values, such as "is greater than" or "is like." Then select a field or value to compare, such as 10,000 or Shark.
6. Click Preview to get a display of what the query answer table will look like. Use Preview to make sure your query is set up properly.
7. Use the next dialog box in the Query Expert to sort your results.
8. Specify a name and location for the query (this is ideally the working directory).
9. Check the appropriate box to run your query right away, edit it in Virtual Query Builder (beyond the scope of this book), or save the query and exit the expert.

This section was just a quick introduction to queries. There are countless more things you can do with queries, including querying multiple tables at once (called a *relational query*), using operators and wildcards to refine your selection criteria, calculating summary values, changing and deleting data in your tables, and finding duplicate information in your tables. There are even more options if you use Visual Query Builder or SQL Editor to directly edit your query.

Summary

In this hour, you created single-table, dual-table and multitable forms. You learned how to edit the design of your forms in the Design window and how to add objects to the form. You learned how to deliver your form to users, so that the form can be used to enter data. You also used the form to view data one record at a time. You created reports using Quick Report and the Report Expert. You were also introduced to queries and created a simple query using the Query Expert.

Q&A

Q I'm still having a hard time understanding how to put all the Paradox tools together to make a database. How do I make them all work together?

A If you still don't understand the big picture, be sure to read *Case Study: The MAST Company*, in the Paradox Help Topics. It brings all the information you've learned together in a study of how one small business uses Paradox. The case study can help to clarify some of the more esoteric concepts, such as secondary indexes, keys, and referential integrity. You also might be surprised at how a small company can use relational databases.

Workshop

The Workshop contains quiz questions and exercises to help reinforce what you've learned in this hour. If you get stuck, the answers can be found in Appendix B, "Answers to Quiz Questions."

Quiz

1. True or false: You can use one form to enter data into two different tables.
2. Can you create forms or reports from multiple tables using Quick Form or Quick Report?
3. Can you edit your table using a report? What is the best tool to use to enter data into a table, other than directly editing the table itself?

4. Which form layout would you choose to display several records at a time on a form?
5. How do you view the data model of a form?

Exercises

1. Use Quick Form to create a form for the contacts.db table in Paradox Samples ($HOME/Documents/Paradox/Samples).

2. Create a two-table form using the custord.dm data model in the Paradox Samples database. Enter customer.db for the master table. Enter Orders.db for the detail table. Include the Customer No field from the Customer table and all fields from the Orders table. Accept all other defaults.

3. Deliver the form you created in exercise 2.

4. Create a report of the contacts.db table using Quick Report.

5. Use the Query Expert to determine how many snapper species there are in the biolife.db table in the Paradox Samples database ($HOME/Documents/Paradox/Samples).

PART VII

WordPerfect Office 2000 for Linux Web Tools

Hour

23 WordPerfect 9 and the Web

24 Web Integration in Other WordPerfect Office Applications

HOUR 23

WordPerfect 9 and the Web

WordPerfect is not just a word processing application; it also enables you to seamlessly create and publish documents to the World Wide Web in HTML or PDF format. You can format preexisting WordPerfect documents as HTML documents or use the Web Editor to create new HTML documents within WordPerfect.

In this hour you will

- Convert a WordPerfect document to HTML and convert an HTML document to WordPerfect.
- Publish an HTML document to the Internet or an intranet using Internet Publisher.
- Create a Web page using Web Editor and add hyperlinks, tables, lists, and forms to the Web page.
- Add Internet SpeedLinks to your WordPerfect documents.

Introducing the WordPerfect 9 Internet Tools

WordPerfect 9 enables you to perform the following tasks:

- Add Internet links to your documents
- Launch an Internet browser from within WordPerfect
- Convert an HTML file into a WordPerfect document
- Convert a WordPerfect document into an HTML file
- Create new Web documents and Web pages
- Format existing documents for publication to the Web
- Publish HTML documents to an Internet server

> HTML, which stands for *Hypertext Markup Language*, is used to publish documents to the Internet so they can be read and displayed by your Internet browser.

Internet Publisher, shown in Figure 23.1, makes all your WordPerfect Internet tools accessible from one place. To start Internet Publisher, select File, Internet Publisher and then select a publishing option:

- *New Web Document*. Enables you to create or edit Web page templates.
- *Format as Web Document*. Enables you to convert a WordPerfect document into an HTML document. (Any formatting not compatible with HTML will be lost.)
- *Publish to HTML*. Enables you to save an HTML document for publication to an Internet or intranet server.
- *Browse the Web*. Launches your default Web browser.

FIGURE 23.1
Internet Publisher enables you to use WordPerfect as a word processor, HTML editor, and Web publisher.

Formatting Existing Documents for the Web

The Web Editor enables you to convert an existing WordPerfect document to an HTML document for publication to the Web. You can either save the document as an HTML file from within the WordPerfect workspace or open the document in Web Editor.

To Do: Save a WordPerfect Document as an HTML File Using Web Editor

1. Open the document you want to convert.
2. From the menu bar, select File, Internet Publisher, Format as Web Document.
3. The document is converted into HTML.
4. Save the document as an HTML file in the Save As dialog box.
5. Select View, View in Web Browser to open the new HTML document in your default Web browser and check that it appears the way you want, as shown in Figure 23.2.

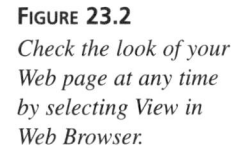

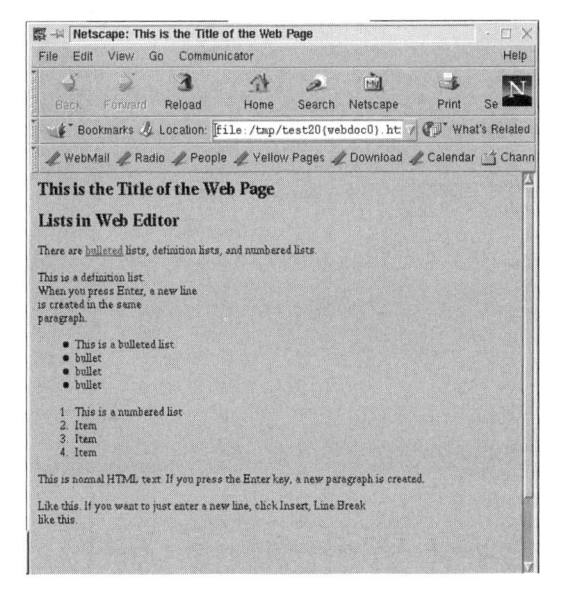

FIGURE 23.2
Check the look of your Web page at any time by selecting View in Web Browser.

> Codes that are used by WordPerfect but not supported by HTML are deleted when you convert a document to HTML. Tabs and indents, for example, are replaced by spaces in the HTML document. Other codes are modified into HTML equivalent codes. Some codes, such as drop caps, are deleted entirely.

Using the Web Editor

The Web Editor is a WYSIWYG (What You See Is What You Get) HTML editor. It is no more difficult to create a Web page in the Web editor than to create an ordinary WordPerfect document. To create an HTML document in the Web Editor, all you have to do is start typing. The content and format of your document are automatically converted to HTML for you, so you don't have to know a single word of HTML code.

If you navigate the WordPerfect menus in Web Editor, you will notice that they are considerably different from those in the word processing mode of WordPerfect. Some of the advanced formatting options available in the normal WordPerfect text editor are not available in Web Editor, because many types of formatting are not possible in HTML. The Web Editor is shown in Figure 23.3

FIGURE 23.3
You can create an entire Web page in the Web Editor without knowing any HTML.

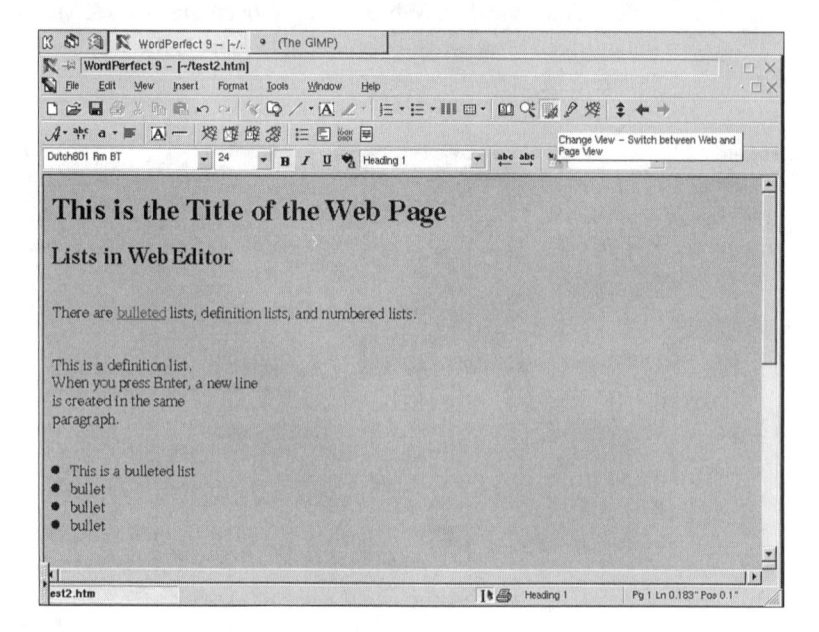

Creating a Basic Web Page with WordPerfect 9

A basic Web page consists of text and images, organized on the page for easy viewing. When you design a Web page, it is a good idea to use lists and tables to make the content easy to read and visually appealing. Use forms when you want to make the Web page interactive. The following sections explain how to use Internet Publisher to build a simple Web page.

Creating a New Web Document

You can create Web documents without knowing a single word of HTML. The Web Editor converts your input to HTML automatically.

> The Web Editor can also convert an HTML document to a WordPerfect document. When you open an HTML document in WordPerfect, the Format as Web Document button in Internet Publisher becomes Format as WP Document. Follow the same steps to format an HTML document as a WordPerfect document as you would to format a WordPerfect document as an HTML document.

To Do: Create a New Web Document

1. From the menu bar, select File, Internet Publisher.
2. Click New Web Document.
3. Highlight Create a Blank Web Document and click Select.
4. The new document opens in Web Editor mode.
5. Type your text into the document. The text is automatically converted to HTML.
6. Just as in the ordinary word processing mode, you can apply styles to your text, such as different font types, sizes and colors, paragraph styles, and lists. The Web Editor converts everything to HTML code.
7. When you are ready to save your file, click Save As and select HTML File in the Files of Type field.

Setting the Properties for Your Web Page

After you have created the text for your Web page, you can make the page more interesting by changing the text fonts and colors and by adding background color or wallpaper. To keep your design clean and uncluttered, you should set your selections as the default for your entire Web page. Finally, you must select a title for your Web page. The title appears in the title bar of the reader's browser.

To Do: Set Text Colors, Fonts, and a Background

Here's how to set the default colors for the main text and hyperlinks in the HTML Document Properties dialog box:

1. Click File, Properties and select Text/Background Colors, as shown in Figure 23.4.
2. Select the color for each kind of text. Remember to test your colors in different browsers because colors appear differently from browser to browser.

3. Set a background color by selecting the desired color from the palette.
4. To set a wallpaper, enter the pathname for the JPG file you want to use.

FIGURE 23.4
Coordinate the colors of your text with the wallpaper/background color for easy reading.

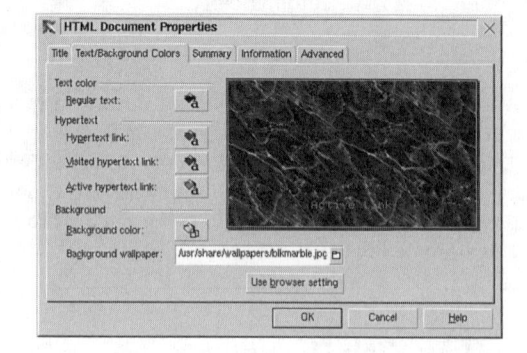

5. To change the fonts, click Format, Font. Select the font and font size for each heading and text style, as shown in Figure 23.5.

FIGURE 23.5
You can change the font style and size for your Web page, but be sure to choose styles that match the overall style of your Web page design.

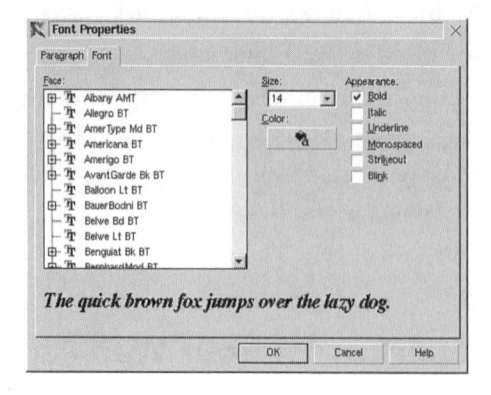

> If you use wallpaper, try to use a style that is not too intrusive and that enables the text to stand out.

To Do: Create a Title for Your Web Page

1. From the menu bar, select File, Properties.
2. Click the Title tab on the HTML Document Properties dialog box, as shown in Figure 23.6.
3. Enter the title in the Custom Title field or check First Heading to make the first heading in your Web page also appear as the title.
4. The title appears in the title bar of the browser when the Web page is opened.

FIGURE 23.6
Set the first heading of the Web page as the title or create your own custom title.

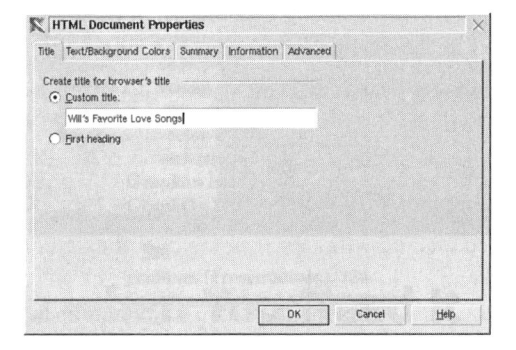

To Do: Create a List

The Web Editor has HTML styles defined for bulleted, numbered, and definition lists. Here's how to use them:

1. Select Format, Font, Paragraph.
2. Highlight the list format you want.

    Bulleted and numbered lists are the same as those in WordPerfect word processing documents. Definition lists are similar to normal text by default, but the Enter key produces a hard line break instead of a new paragraph (see the following tip).

3. Click OK and begin typing.

> You can produce an indented paragraph by selecting Indented Quotation.

> When you press the Enter key in Web Editor, WordPerfect creates a new paragraph in HTML. To create a hard line break within the same paragraph (like pressing Enter in word processing mode) rather than a new paragraph, click Insert, Line Break or press Ctrl+Shift+L.

Working with Hyperlinks

Hyperlinks are special highlighted words in an HTML document that transport your browser to a specific destination on the Web with a click of your mouse.

To Do: Create a Hyperlink

1. Highlight the text you want to use as a link.
2. From the menu bar, click Tools, Hyperlink or click the Hyperlink icon on the Internet Publisher Property Bar.
3. In the Hyperlink Properties dialog box, shown in Figure 23.7, enter the full URL address that will be the destination of your link. Here are two examples:
   - `http://www.company.com`. This opens a new Web page at the URL specified by the hyperlink.
   - `mailto:myname@company.com`. This will open a new email message window in a Web browser with the specified email address in the To: field.
4. The text that you marked will appear in the hyperlink color (blue by default) and underlined to signify a hyperlink. Alternatively, check Make Text Appear as Button to have the selected hyperlink text appear as a button instead of a different color.
5. You can also use images as hyperlinks.

FIGURE 23.7
Hyperlinks distinguish Web pages from ordinary linear text documents.

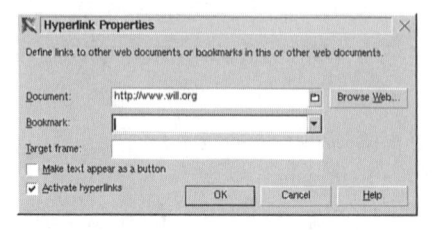

Adding Bookmarks

Bookmarks are similar to hyperlinks, but rather than take you to a different Web page, a bookmark takes you to a different section of the same Web page. Bookmarks enable readers of your Web page to jump from one section of a Web page to another section within the same page. For example, you could create a menu or index with bookmarks at the beginning of your page for readers to jump to corresponding sections further down in the page.

To Do: Create a Bookmark

1. Place the cursor at the point in your document where you want to place a bookmark.
2. Click Tools, Bookmark, Create. Give your bookmark a name.
3. To make the bookmark useful, you must create a link to the bookmark. Highlight the word or phrase that you want the bookmark to link to.
4. Click Tools, Hyperlink. Click Bookmark and select the bookmark to which you want to link.

Inserting Graphics in Your Web Page

It is simple to insert graphics into your Web page right in Web Editor. Graphics must be in JPG (JPEG) or GIF format.

> JPG files are more commonly used for complex images with many colors, such as photographs, whereas GIF files are used for more simple graphics.

To insert a graphic in Web Editor, click Insert, Graphic.

To change the properties of the image, right-click the image and choose HTML Properties to open the HTML Properties dialog box (see Figure 23.8). From here, you can perform the following tasks:

- Enter text to appear in place of the image if it is not loaded on the Web page.
- Resize the image.
- Apply a border to the image.
- Use the image as a hyperlink.

> When you insert a graphic into the Web Editor, it is automatically converted into a GIF or JPG file when you publish to HTML.

FIGURE 23.8

Be careful not to overcrowd your Web page with too many images. The text is what's important.

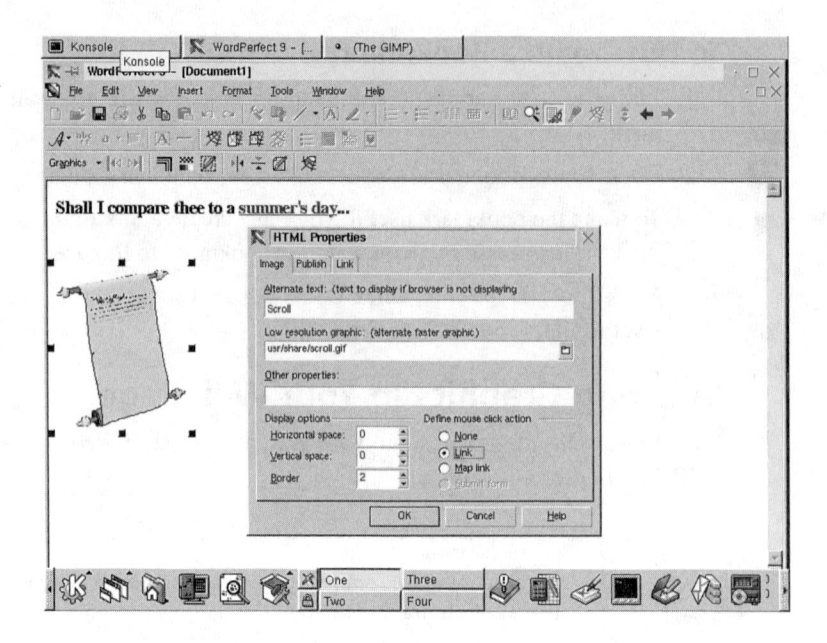

Inserting a Table in Your Web Page

Because the rows and columns of a table can be made invisible, tables are commonly used in Web design to enhance the layout of a Web page.

You can create tables in the Web Editor mode by clicking Insert, Table and specifying the number of columns and rows you would like. If you prefer an invisible table, set the Table Borders value to 0. You can define the cell spacing and inside cell margins (padding). You can also define the dimensions of the table as a percentage or number of pixels. Finally, you can define the background color of your table to contrast with the background color of the page. A sample table is shown in Figure 23.9.

> Because the readers of your Web page may have different screen resolutions, it is a good idea to design a Web page with a table of fixed size to preserve its look across screen resolutions. If you choose a table width of 600 pixels, you ensure that readers with the smallest screen resolution see your page the same way as readers with large screen resolutions. Centering the table on the page will leave an equal amount of white space to the left and right of your page content, depending on the screen resolution of the viewer.

FIGURE 23.9
Tables keep your information neat and easy to read.

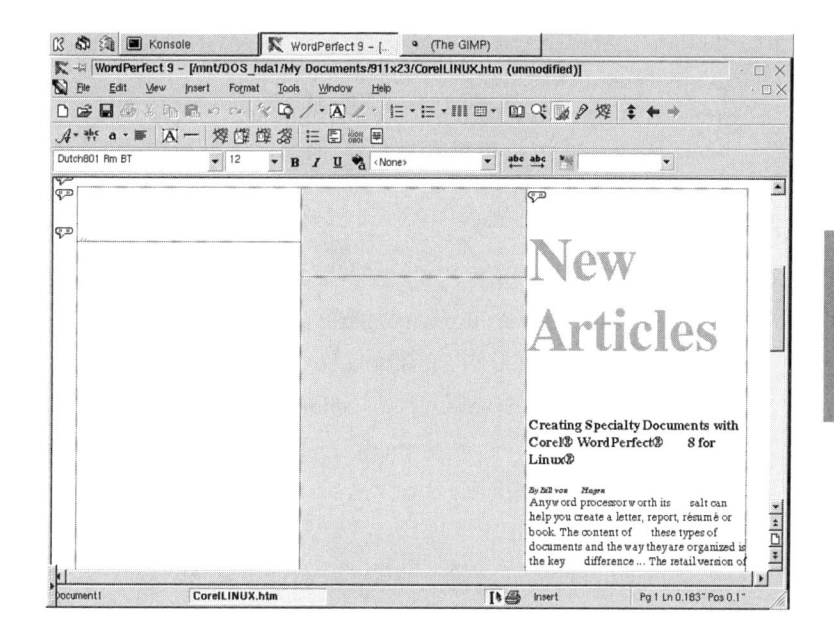

> If you are not sure about the number of columns and rows you'll need for the design of your table, you may want to create a 1×1 table and later split your table into cells by right clicking the table and choosing Split Cells.

> For advanced users: If you want only a certain section of your Web page to appear in a different color, create a table using the different color within a cell of an existing table. It is possible to specify individual cells to contain different colors, but only Microsoft Internet Explorer supports this feature. Therefore, this trick is not recommended.

Creating a Form

You can use forms on your Web page to enable visitors to communicate messages (email, guest book entries, passwords, and so on) or search the content of a Web site. In HTML, form objects are already predefined—all you have to do is specify the order, type, and size of the objects. Form objects include text boxes, selection lists, check boxes, radio buttons, and Submit and Reset buttons.

Because forms work with scripts that actually execute the commands sent by the forms to a Web server, designing a form on a Web page is not enough. You also need a script to perform the action of the form component. Such scripts are beyond the scope of this book, but see Matt's Script Archive at http://www.worldwidemart.com/scripts for some examples of useful CGI (Common Gateway Interface) scripts. Be sure to check the scripts for security leaks before you use them.

Here are definitions of some of the form components you can use:

- *Text box*. Enables users to enter a paragraph of text, such as a comment or question
- *Text line*. Similar to a text box, but it's one line
- *Radio button*. Gives users one choice from a group of items
- *Check box*. Gives users multiple choices from a group of items
- *Selection list*. Enables users to scroll through a group of items and select one or more
- *Submit button*. Enables users to send the information they entered in the form
- *Reset button*. Erases previously entered data in the form fields

Publishing Documents to the Internet or an Intranet

After creating a Web document, you can publish it to a Web site via Internet Publisher. You must have the server mounted in your Virtual Filesystem (VFS) to publish the document using Internet Publisher.

If you just want to create an HTML file in your local filesystem, create a server entry with a local directory in the Publish to HTML dialog box.

To Do: Publish a Web Document to a Web Site

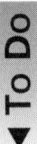

1. If the Web server is remote, mount the server onto your filesystem.
2. From the menu bar, click File, Internet Publisher.
3. Click Publish to HTML to open the Publish to HTML dialog box (see Figure 23.10).
4. Enter the hostname of the server where you want to publish your file.
5. If your server hostname is not in the menu, click Add.
6. Enter the server hostname in the Label field. Enter the full pathname in the Directory field (you can browse through the filesystem by double-clicking each directory icon to drill down to the correct subdirectory).
7. If you have graphics or sound files to go with the HTML file, enter the file type, source pathname, and destination pathname for each sound and graphic file.
8. Click Publish.

FIGURE 23.10
Publishing your documents to the Web is simple if you have all the required information for the Web server.

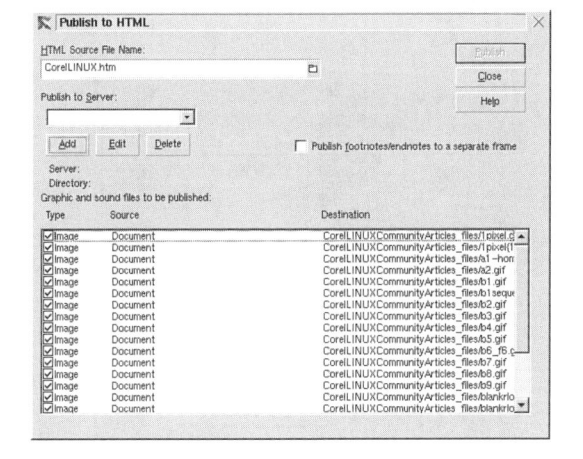

> The Browse the Web button on Internet Publisher simply opens your default Internet browser (such as Netscape Navigator) for quick access.

Bringing the Web into Your WordPerfect Documents with SpeedLinks

Internet hyperlinks are automatically integrated into ordinary WordPerfect documents. When you type text beginning with http, mailto, or ftp in a document, SpeedLinks automatically converts the text into a hyperlink. When you click the text, your browser or email client opens automatically to display the address.

If you have recurring links in your documents, such as your company Web site or personal email address, you can specify a keyword that will automatically create a particular hyperlink.

To Do: Create a SpeedLinks Keyword

1. Click Tools, QuickCorrect to open the QuickCorrect dialog box. Then select the SpeedLinks tab, shown in Figure 23.11.
2. In the Link Word field, enter the word you want to use, such as **web** or **mail**.
3. Enter the URL (for example, www.mycompany.com or mailto:myname@mycompany.com) that the keyword will represent.
4. Click Add Entry.

5. In your document, when you type **@keyword** and press Enter or the spacebar, the hyperlink is created.

FIGURE 23.11
SpeedLinks enable you to quickly reference a common URL throughout your document.

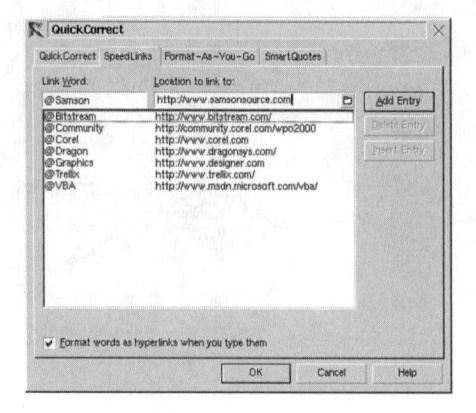

Summary

In this hour you learned how to convert WordPerfect documents from WordPerfect to HTML and how to convert HTML files to WordPerfect documents. You used the Web Editor to create a new Web document in WordPerfect and added text, hyperlinks, bookmarks, graphics, lists, and tables to the document. You also learned how to create forms in Web Editor and how to use SpeedLinks in your WordPerfect documents.

Q&A

Q Is there a way to add code manually to an HTML document in Web Editor?

A As you learned earlier, the Web Editor doesn't support all HTML tags, but you can manually format the HTML code for your document. Click Format, Custom HTML and enter the HTML code directly. When you are finished, click Format, Custom HTML again to return to Web Editor.

Workshop

The Workshop contains quiz questions and exercises to help reinforce what you've learned in this hour. If you get stuck, the answers can be found in Appendix B, "Answers to Quiz Questions."

Quiz

1. What is the difference between Publish to HTML and Format as Web Document in Internet Publisher?
2. How many HTML headings are available in Web Editor?
3. Where does the title of the Web page display in the Web browser?
4. What does pressing Enter in the Web Editor create?
5. What is the difference between a bookmark and a hyperlink?
6. What happens if you place a form object on a Web page without an accompanying CGI script?

Exercises

1. Make a copy of a WordPerfect document. Save it as an HTML file.
2. Save the HTML file back to a WordPerfect document.
3. Create a Web document using Internet Publisher. Enter the text "This is my Web Page" as Heading 1.
4. Make the background light yellow and the text dark blue. Make the hyperlink text purple.
5. Add the text "I like to make HTML files in Web Editor, which is part of Corel WordPerfect 9." Hyperlink the word *Corel* to the Web address http://www.corel.com.
6. Insert a graphic into your Web page.

HOUR 24

Web Integration in Other WordPerfect Office Applications

The entire WordPerfect Office 2000 suite is designed to be used with the Web. Because the formatting is more complex, the Internet publishing tools for Quattro Pro, Presentations, and Paradox are somewhat more complicated than those for WordPerfect. They are also not quite as stable. Still, it's not too difficult to learn how to publish all your documents to the Internet or an intranet for instant dissemination throughout your organization.

In this hour you will

- Convert a Quattro Pro notebook to an HTML file and add hyperlinks to a Quattro Pro spreadsheet.
- Publish a Presentations slideshow to HTML.
- Publish a Corel Calendar events calendar and task list to HTML.
- Convert a Paradox table, report, and form to HTML.
- Insert hyperlinks into a Paradox table and import data from an HTML table into a Paradox table.

Publishing Quattro Pro 9 Notebooks to HTML

The Publish to HTML tool enables you to convert a Quattro Pro notebook to an HTML document for publication on the Internet or an intranet. You can also use hyperlinks to link different notebooks and to link notebooks to the Internet.

When you save your Quattro Pro spreadsheet using Publish to HTML, Quattro Pro automatically converts the contents of the spreadsheet to HTML, which can be included in an existing HTML document or saved as a separate document. For example, if you create a Web page and want to add a chart to demonstrate a fact or trend, you can insert the HTML tag <!- - ## CHART ##- -> into the page. Open Quattro Pro and create the chart, save it as an HTML file, and then publish it to the existing HTML file. Quattro Pro automatically inserts the chart in the chart tag position. If you do not have a chart or spreadsheet meta-tag in your HTML file, the HTML spreadsheet/chart is appended to the end of the HTML file in which you inserted it.

To Do: Save a Spreadsheet As a New HTML Document

1. With the spreadsheet file open, click File, Publish to Internet. The Publish to Internet dialog box is shown in Figure 24.1.

2. Select a range of cells to add to the HTML document. By default, all the cells with data are included in the range. You can adjust the range by clicking the pointer button and selecting your own range. Click the pointer button and then highlight the cells you want to include. Click the Publish to Internet button to return to the Publish to HTML dialog box; then click Add.

FIGURE 24.1

The Publish to Internet tool for Quattro Pro is not quite as well designed as that for Presentations or Paradox.

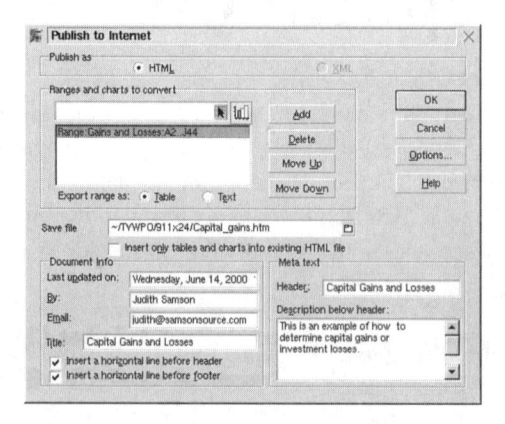

3. Enter any document information and meta-text. Your name and email address appear in a footer. The meta-text appears as a header in the HTML source code but not in the HTML page in the browser.

4. Click Options to specify how the HTML file should look. The Publish to HTML Options dialog box is shown in Figure 24.2. You can specify that the HTML spreadsheet should fit on one page or be spread across multiple pages, depending on its size. Click the Frame-Enhanced Page button to enable frame support for the spreadsheet or chart. In the frame-enhanced page, the tables and charts appear in an index in a separate frame, as does the footer.

5. If you don't like the defaults, specify a color for text, links, and background color or wallpaper in this dialog box.

> When you specify a text color, only the text that is created by the HTML tags responds to your color choice. The actual data from the spreadsheet or chart is the same color as in the Quattro Pro file. Change the text color in Quattro Pro before converting to HTML. Then, your HTML text and spreadsheet text will be the same color.

FIGURE 24.2
Use Publish to HTML Options to determine the layout and colors for your HTML table or chart.

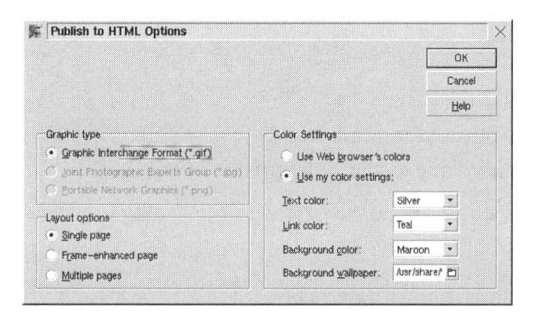

Working with Hyperlinks in Quattro Pro 9 Notebooks

In Quattro Pro, you form a link by entering the link address in a formula. You can link to a file on the Internet or an intranet, another Quattro Pro notebook, or a notebook in a file format supported by Quattro Pro. When you link files, any formula information that changes in one file is automatically updated in the other files.

To Do: Create a Hyperlink

When you type a filename that begins with `html`, `ftp`, `mailto`, or `www`, Quattro Pro automatically converts it to a hyperlink.

You can also create a hyperlink manually:

1. Select the cell where you want to create a hyperlink.
2. Click Tools, Hyperlink. The Edit Hyperlink dialog box is shown in Figure 24.3.

FIGURE 24.3
Use hyperlinks to share data from different notebooks across a network or on the same local system.

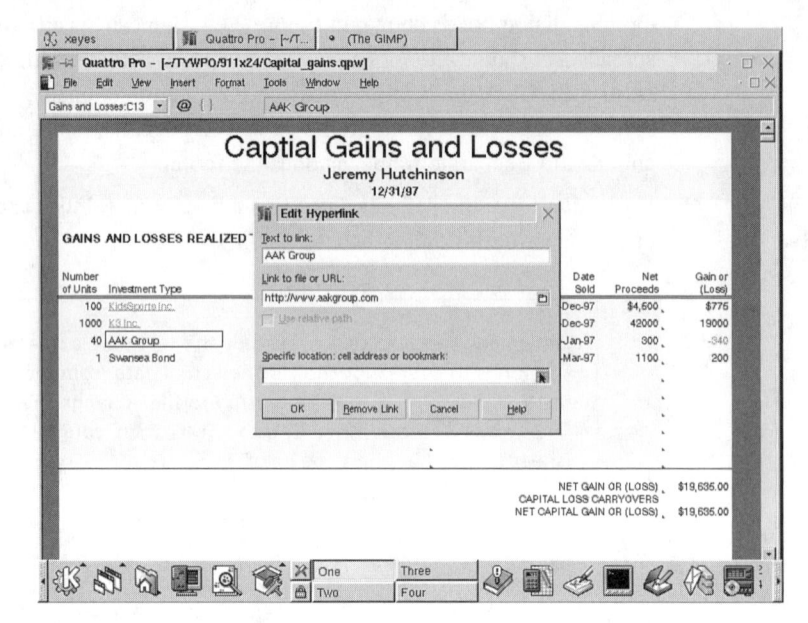

3. Enter a description of the link in the Text to Link box. If you leave the box blank, the URL or pathname to the link appears in the cell.
4. To link to a specific cell or bookmark in the same notebook, enter the cell address or bookmark.

To remove a hyperlink, follow these steps:

1. Select the cell containing the link and then click Tools, Hyperlink.
2. Click the Remove Link button.

Publishing Presentations 9 Slideshows to the Web with Internet Publisher

The Presentations Internet Publisher converts your slideshows and drawings to graphics within an HTML file. Internet Publisher contains a number of layout formatting options. If you don't want to create a custom layout, a few preconfigured layouts are available that you can use to publish a presentation to HTML.

To Do: Publish a Presentation to HTML Using a Preconfigured Layout

1. Open the slideshow file in Presentations.
2. Select File, Internet Publisher to open the Internet Publisher expert.
3. Select Existing Layout to use one of the default Presentations layouts:
   - Frame-Enhanced Page supports frames. The index of the show appears in a frame on the left, and the slide appears in a frame on the right. Navigational buttons appear in a separate frame above the slide.
   - Multiple Pages converts each slide to a separate HTML page.
   - Single Page converts all the slides to one big page.
   - Thumbnail Pages creates thumbnail sketches of each slide that the reader can click to see the full-size slides.
4. Click View Layout to see all the layout details. A sample layout is shown in Figure 24.4.
5. If you are satisfied with the premade layout, click Finish.

> If you choose a premade layout, you can still change any aspect of the layout by clicking Next instead of Finish. This brings you through all the same layout choices as if you had chosen Create New Layout.

FIGURE 24.4
Use a preexisting layout to publish a presentation to HTML with a minimum of effort.

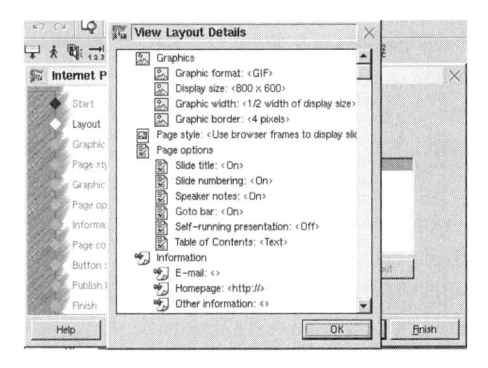

To Do: Create a New Layout

Click Create a New Layout to create your own custom layout for the HTML file; then follow these steps:

1. The first choice is the graphics layout. Choose a format that will enable your readers to see the slides as clearly as possible while keeping in mind the load speed of each slide. As a rule, JPEGs load more slowly than GIFs or PNGs. Here are some other points to keep in mind:
    - GIF files are useful for simple, linear graphics that do not have too many colors.
    - JPEG format should be used for photographs and other complex graphics.
    - PNG format is a graphics file format designed as a free alternative to the GIF format.
    - Show It! is a plug-in you can download from Corel that enables you to save a slideshow to HTML along with all the sound and other effects.

> If you select the Show It! format, you have only two choices of page style: frame enhanced and single page.

> Show It! is not available for Netscape for Linux at the time of writing. If you choose Show It!, only readers with Internet Explorer or Netscape for Windows will be able to view the slideshow.

2. Choose a page style: frame enhanced, single page, multiple pages, or thumbnail sketches.

3. Choose the resolution size for the entire slideshow display. Remember, if you choose a larger display size, readers with small monitor screens might not be able to see the entire slideshow frame. On the other hand, if you choose a large slide graphics size in the next step, the resolution size that you select in this step should also be large.

4. Presentations converts the slides into graphics files when you convert your slide show to HTML. In this step, select the size that the slide graphics should be. If you have lots of speaker notes, you might want your slide to be smaller. If the slide itself contains the important information, select a larger graphics size.

5. If you want a border, select a border style.
6. Select the options to go with the slideshow HTML file:
    - *Title*. Prints the title of the slide above the slide image. This is unnecessary if the slide title in the slide description is the same as that on the slide itself.
    - *Number*. Prints the slide number below the slide image.
    - *Go To Bar*. Displays a drop-down menu with all the slide titles in the slideshow. This is unnecessary if you have a frame-enhanced slideshow. If you have a Go To bar, you don't need the title or slide number as well.
    - *Speaker Notes*. Prints the speaker notes as HTML text below the slide image.
    - *Self-Running Presentation*. If you choose this option, you will be prompted to choose how long each slide should display before the next slide appears. You can also check an option to have the slideshow run continuously.
7. Enter your email address and Web page if you want this information to be displayed on the title page of the HTML slideshow. You can also provide a link for readers to download the original presentation in SHW format. The email address will be used as a link for "Comments and Questions?" and the Web page will be linked to "Home Page."
8. If you don't want to use the default browser text and background colors, select your own custom colors. You can select a background image, but be careful that it doesn't clash with or detract from the slideshow images.
9. Choose a style for the slideshow navigation buttons.
10. Enter the HTML slideshow filename and path.
11. When the layout is exactly as you want it, click Finish. If you want to use the same layout for another presentation conversion, save the layout. It will appear in the list of preconfigured layouts the next time you start Internet Publisher.
12. The slideshow is converted into an HTML file and saved. You can view the show right away in your default browser by clicking Show Me.

An example of a slideshow that has been published to HTML is shown in Figure 24.5.

FIGURE 24.5
This slideshow has been published using the frame-enhanced layout.

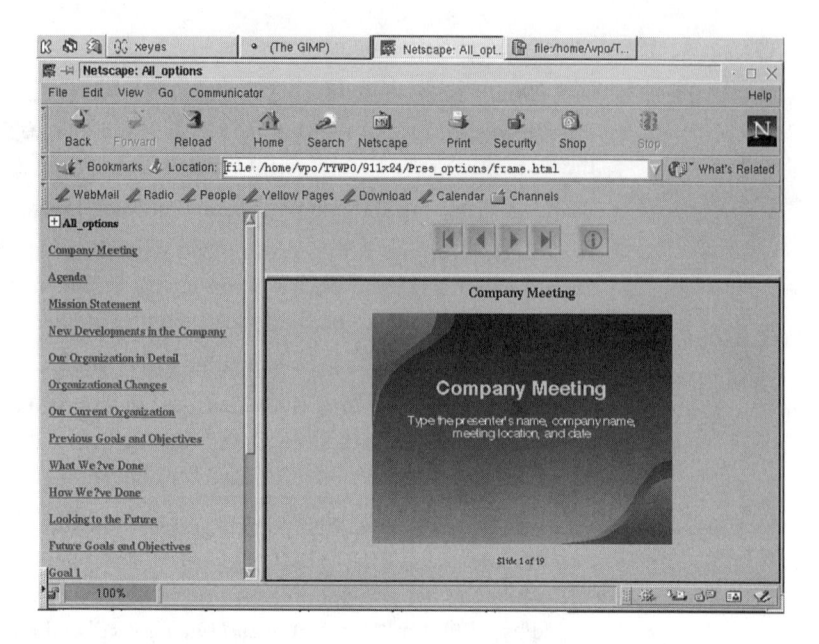

Publishing CorelCENTRAL 9 Calendars to HTML

Publishing your events calendar and task list to the Internet or an intranet is a wonderful way to keep track of schedules, meetings, and task priorities for everyone on a team or for publishing the schedule for a conference. Publishing task lists and events is particularly useful when the members of a project are not physically located in the same place. Examples of an events list and a task list are shown in Figure 24.6.

To Do: Publish an Events Calendar or Task List to HTML

Open Corel Calendar to the calendar to be published and then follow these steps:

1. Select File, Publish to HTML, Events or Tasks.

2. If you are publishing an events list, check which events to publish in the HTML file. For example, you could publish a calendar of company holidays by checking only the Holidays check box. Enter a date range for an HTML events calendar.

3. If you want to include a title for your task list, enter it in the Banner field (note that the Banner field is grayed out for events). Enter any other information you want to include, such as copyright, date, contact name, and email address.

Web Integration in Other WordPerfect Office Applications 463

4. Specify a location to save the HTML file and a prefix to help you identify the file. By default, Corel Calendar names the events file with your prefix, plus the month and year in which the calendar or task list starts. The task list is named with your prefix plus "Task."

> Note that the file pathnames follow Windows conventions, not UNIX conventions. It is a good idea to browse your filesystem for the location where you want to save the file, rather than type in the pathname, to be sure that you don't mix up the slash types and other UNIX/Windows convention differences. The reason for this is that WordPerfect Office 2000 for Linux is not a native Linux application but rather a heavily altered Windows program running on Wine. Wine is a free implementation of Windows for UNIX and Linux. For more information about WINE, see http://www.winehq.org.

5. The HTML file is automatically displayed in your default browser as a monthly calendar or task list. For events, each month is saved as a separate HTML file, and navigation buttons are available for you to navigate from month to month.

FIGURE 24.6
Corel Calendar comes with a well-designed HTML template to publish events and task lists.

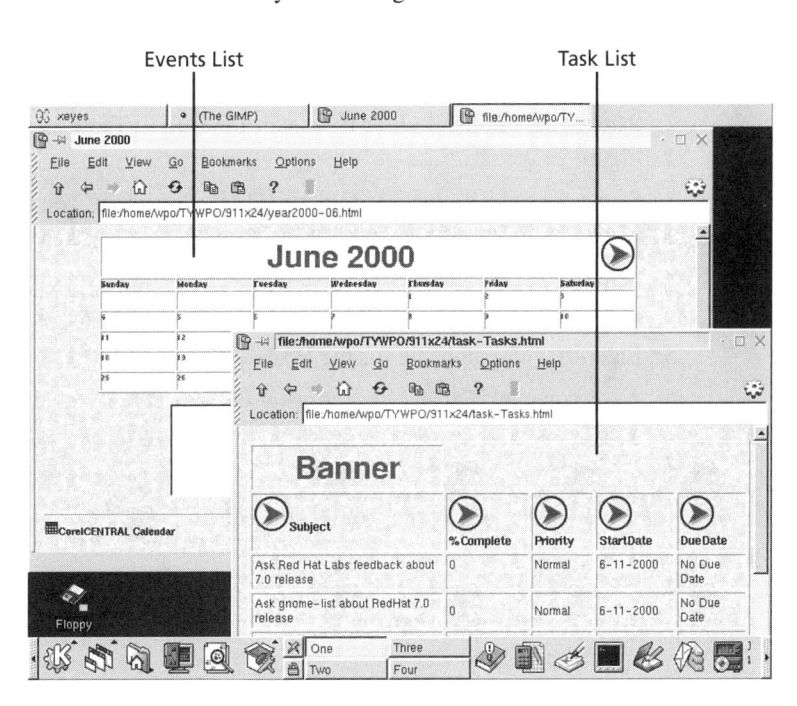

Publishing Paradox 9 Databases to HTML

Paradox comes with two experts that enable you to publish Paradox reports and tables to the Internet in HTML format. You can also publish forms to HTML, import HTML tables into a Paradox database, and add hyperlinks to your database.

> Once you publish a table, form, or report to HTML, the HTML file is not updated dynamically when the database object is updated. If changes are made, you must publish the table, form, or report to HTML again to capture those changes.

The HTML Report Expert and HTML Table Expert

The HTML Report and Table Experts convert a Paradox report or table to HTML automatically. All the elements are converted for you. After the HTML Expert creates an HTML report or table, you can manually edit the file in your favorite editor.

To Do: Publish a Paradox Table to HTML

1. Set the database directory that contains the table as the working directory and open the table.
2. Select File, Publish to HTML to start the HTML Table Expert, shown in Figure 24.7.
3. Select the fields to include in your HTML document. You can alter the order in which the fields are shown by using the Change Display Order arrow buttons.
4. Select a title for the HTML table or accept the default object type and filename. Select text and background colors if you don't want to use the browser defaults.
5. Enter the full pathname for the HTML file.
6. After you click Finish, you can view the new HTML table in your default Web browser.

FIGURE 24.7
The HTML Table and Report Experts have similar interfaces.

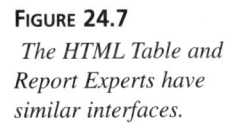

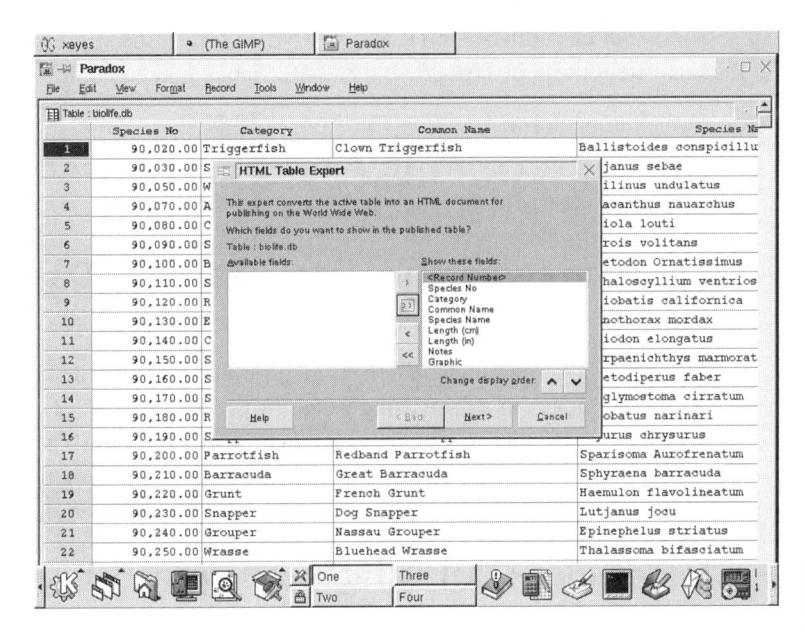

> HTML Table Expert does not automatically include and convert bitmap graphics in the HTML table file. If you want to add graphics to your file, insert the graphics using Web Editor in WordPerfect (a cumbersome workaround, but it works).

To Do: Publish a Paradox Report to HTML

1. Set the working directory. Open the report and click File, Publish as HTML (note that you can also save the report as an RTF, Microsoft Word, or WordPerfect document).
2. Enter a title and set the text and background colors, if desired.
3. If the report has many fields, consider displaying certain band fields as lists that the reader can choose, instead of displaying the report in its entirety. For example, in the Customers report from the Samples database, you could choose to list the customers by country. Each country in the report is listed in the HTML file. When the reader clicks, say, Bermuda, all the customers located in Bermuda are listed. The HTML Report Expert displays the fields that can be used as lists.
4. Select a filename for the new HTML report file. After you click Finish, you can choose to immediately open the HTML file in your browser.

To Do: Publish Forms to HTML

Forms can be published to HTML as well. As a rule, the simpler the form, the more completely it can be converted to HTML. Here's how to publish a form to HTML:

1. Run the form.
2. Select File, Publish to HTML.
3. Save the file as an HTML file.

Inserting Hyperlinks into a Paradox Database

You can insert hyperlinks as data in your forms and tables or as design objects in forms.

To insert a hyperlink in a table or form, type the URL into the field. To insert a hyperlink as a design object in a form, follow the instructions in Hour 22, "Advanced Paradox 9 Techniques," to create a text object on the form. Check the Hyperlink box in Text Expert and enter the URL. Run the form to activate the link. Clicking the hyperlink opens the URL in your default browser.

Importing HTML Tables and Spreadsheets into Paradox 9 Databases

The Paradox *HTML Import Expert* enables you to easily import data from an HTML file into a new or existing Paradox table. This feature makes it easy to import data directly from the Web, saving you the extra step of converting the data into text format.

To Do: Import an HTML Table into a Paradox Table

1. Set the working directory.
2. Click File, Import, HTML Expert.
3. Select the HTML file that contains the data you want to import.
4. If the file contains more than one table, select which table you want to import. If the first row contains the field headings, check Use First Row for Column Headings.
5. If you want to create a new table, check Define Fields from Scratch. For each field, indicate whether it is a key or required field as well as whether or not to import it.
6. If you want to append the data to an existing table, check Match to Fields from Existing Table and enter the table pathname. Map each field from the HTML field to a field in the existing table. Click Remove Target if you don't want to import a field.
7. If the table is new, enter a filename and path. Otherwise, select to append the HTML files to an existing table or to replace the values in an existing table.

Summary

In this hour you converted files from Quattro Pro, Presentations, Corel Calendar, and Paradox into HTML for publication to the Internet or an intranet. You inserted hyperlinks into a Quattro Pro spreadsheet and a Paradox table and form. You also imported data from an HTML table into a Paradox table.

Congratulations! You have completed your day of learning about WordPerfect Office 2000 for Linux. I hope you have enjoyed this book and will use your new knowledge to work more productively and efficiently. I'm sure you will agree that it is a powerful tool for the Linux office.

Q&A

Q Can I publish to XML or SGML in WordPerfect Office 2000?

A At the time of this writing, you can only publish to HTML using the Corel WordPerfect Office 2000 for Linux Internet publishing tools.

Q Can I edit an HTML file manually after the Internet Publisher has created it?

A You can edit any HTML file generated by any of the HTML or Internet publishers. Simply open the file in Web Editor or your favorite text editor.

Workshop

The Workshop contains quiz questions and exercises to help reinforce what you've learned in this hour. If you get stuck, the answers can be found in Appendix B, "Answers to Quiz Questions."

Quiz

1. Which hyperlinks are created automatically when you enter the link data?
2. Which Presentations HTML publisher graphics file format is not available for Linux browsers?
3. When you save a Corel Calendar task list to HTML, where does the banner field appear?
4. Which Paradox database objects can you convert to HTML?

Exercises

1. Open a Quattro Pro project and populate it with sample data. (Click New from Project and pick any Quattro Pro project. In PerfectExpert, click Insert Sample Data.) Publish the spreadsheet to HTML. Include your name and email address. Make the background yellow.

2. Open any Presentations project and publish it to HTML. Create your own layout using the following parameters: PNG format, frame enhanced, 800×600 size, 1/2 width graphics size, no border, title, number, Go To bar, and speaker notes checked. Use the default buttons.

3. Open Corel Calendar. Publish your events calendar to HTML for the current month (it doesn't matter if you have no data in your events calendar). What does the HTML file look like?

4. Set the working directory to the Paradox sample database (usually `$HOME/Documents/Paradox/Samples`). Open the biolife.db table and convert it to HTML with all fields.

Appendixes

Appendix

A Introducing Corel Linux OS

B Answers to Quiz Questions

APPENDIX A

Introducing Corel Linux OS

The Standard and Deluxe editions of WordPerfect Office 2000 for Linux both come with the download version of Corel Linux OS, the latest and greatest distribution of Linux. I therefore thought it worthwhile to provide a brief introduction to this wonderful new operating system. Although it's no substitute for the manual that ships with the Standard and Deluxe editions of Corel Linux OS, this appendix covers enough ground so that you can feel comfortable working in the Corel Linux environment.

Although Linux is an open-source operating system that can be had for free, most Linux users, especially those just starting out, wisely elect to purchase one (or more) of several commercially available "distributions" of Linux. Corel Linux is the newest and finest distribution on the Linux scene, and it has already garnered stellar reviews for its ease of use and installation. Other distributions you may have heard of include Red Hat, Caldera OpenLinux, and SUSE.

As shown in Table A.1, Corel Linux comes in three flavors.

TABLE A.1 The Three Flavors of Linux

Corel Linux Version	Features
Download	Includes Corel Linux OS, Enhanced KDE Desktop, Corel Install Express, and Corel File Manager.
Standard	Includes everything in the Download version plus a user guide, 30-day email installation support, Netscape Communicator, Adobe Acrobat Reader, 20 fonts, and WordPerfect 8 Light.
Deluxe	Includes everything in the Standard version plus 200 fonts, WordPerfect 8 for Linux Deluxe application and user manual, eFax Plus with three free months of service, enhanced sound drivers, BRU Backup software, the *Civilization: Call to Power* game for Linux, and a Penguin mascot toy.

Starting Corel Linux and Logging In

After installing Corel Linux, you'll be greeted by the Corel Linux boot manager every time you boot your machine. If you installed Corel Linux on the same hard drive as Microsoft Windows, the boot manager will present you with the following six options:

- *Corel Linux*. Launches Corel Linux in standard mode for day-to-day use
- *Linux-VGA*. Launches Corel Linux in 16-color VGA mode for troubleshooting when you encounter display configuration problems
- *Linux-Console*. Launches the Corel Linux command-line shell for access to the underlying OS
- *Linux-Debug*. Launches Corel Linux with kernel messages displayed so you can troubleshoot for system features that aren't booting properly
- *Linux-Expert*. Reserved for experienced Linux system administrators
- *MS Windows*. Launches Microsoft Windows

To launch Corel Linux, press 1 or press Enter. To launch any other boot option, press the corresponding number or use the arrow keys to navigate to your selection and press Enter.

When Corel Linux boots, you're presented with a login screen to select a user and enter the user's password. During installation, you're asked to create a new user so when you launch Corel Linux for the first time, you can log in with that username, or as root.

Select the user you want to log in as and press Enter or click the Log In button. You can leave Password blank for now.

When the Corel Desktop appears, you're given the option of changing the password. Create a password for the user you logged in as, retype it for verification, and click OK.

You're now ready to explore the Corel Linux Desktop!

Welcome to the Corel Linux Desktop

As shown in Figure A.1, the Corel Linux Desktop resembles the Microsoft Windows Desktop.

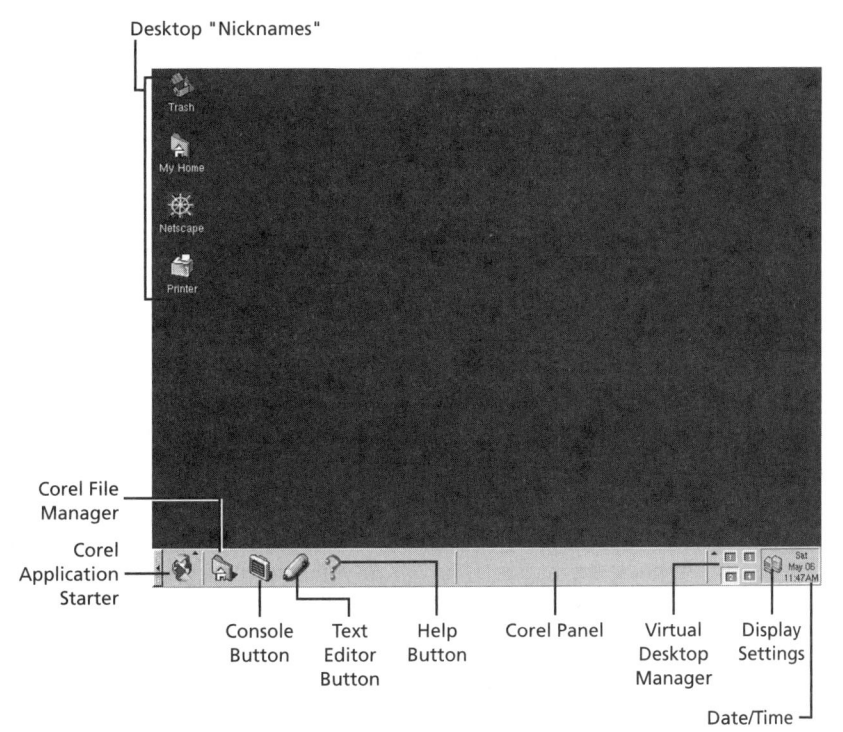

FIGURE A.1
The Corel Linux Desktop.

The Corel Linux Desktop generally works like Windows, with many of the same capabilities, including right-click and drag-and-drop functionality. For example, click the My Home nickname on the Corel Desktop (note that nicknames are the Corel Linux equivalent of desktop shortcuts in Microsoft Windows). You only have to click once—unlike Windows, Corel Linux doesn't require you to double-click a nickname to launch it from the Corel Desktop.

Clicking the My Home nickname opens the Corel File Manager, shown in Figure A.2. The Corel File Manager is the Corel Linux equivalent of Windows Explorer in Microsoft Windows.

FIGURE A.2
The Corel File Manager.

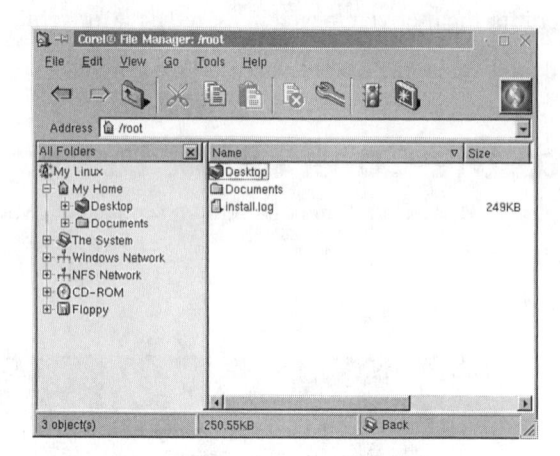

If you're logged in as root, you should have a document called `install.log` displayed in the right window pane of the Corel File Manager. Click and drag `install.log` from the Corel File Manager to the Trash nickname on the Desktop. Works just like Windows, right?

Close the Corel File Manager and right-click the My Home nickname. Just like Windows, you get a pop-up menu with several options, including Properties, which will tell you more about the My Home nickname on your Desktop.

Here's more information about the desktop items shown in Figure A.1:

- *Corel Panel.* The Corel Panel is like the Windows task bar. It contains the Corel Application Starter (from which you launch programs), launch buttons for other applications, the Virtual Desktop Manager, one-click access to display settings, and a Date/Time box. The Corel Panel also displays all open applications.

- *Corel Application Starter.* The Corel Application Starter is like the Start button in Windows. Use it to open applications, launch the Find and Run commands, and access the Corel Control Center, among other things.

- *File Manager button.* This button on the Corel Panel is another way to access the Corel File Manager shown in Figure A.2.

- *Console button.* Provides one-click access to a console window, also known as a *shell* or *command line window*, from which you can enter Linux commands.

- *Text Editor button.* Opens the KWrite text editor, a simple text editor you can use to work in programming languages such as HTML, Java, Perl, C++, and Python.

- *Help button.* Launches Netscape Navigator to open the online Corel Linux Help manual.
- *Virtual Desktop Manager.* The use of virtual desktops is one of the great advantages Linux has over Windows, because it provides four different desktops on which to spread your open applications. Click any of the numbered display boxes in the Virtual Desktop Manager and you'll jump to that desktop. Click the tiny up-arrow icon next to the display boxes and you'll see a pop-up mini preview of the items on each desktop. You can also click a mini preview to jump to that desktop.
- *Display settings.* Click once to jump to the Display Settings dialog box, from which you can configure a host of desktop properties, including the background "wallpaper" for each virtual desktop, plus screensavers, colors, fonts, styles, and video resolution.

Introducing Corel Linux "Windows"

Windows in Corel Linux work almost exactly like they do in Microsoft Windows. As shown in Figure A.3, an open window in Corel Linux has many characteristics that should be familiar to Windows users.

FIGURE A.3
An open WordPerfect 9 window in Corel Linux.

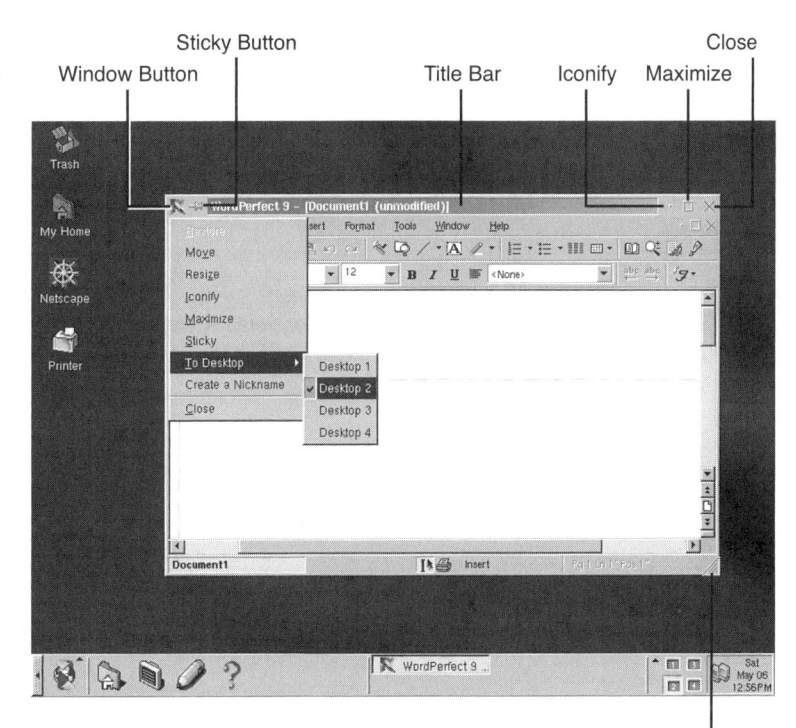

Here's more information about the Corel Linux window features displayed in Figure A.3:

- *Window button.* The Window button has no counterpart in Microsoft Windows. As shown in Figure A.3, it provides several options, including the neat ability to send the window to another virtual desktop.
- *Sticky button.* Another unique Linux feature, the Sticky button allows you to post your open window to all virtual desktops at once. Click Sticky again to limit the open window to your current desktop.
- *Title Bar.* In addition to providing information about the open window, the title bar provides many functions. Click and drag the title bar to move your window across the desktop. Double-click the title bar to "roll" your window up into the title bar like a window shade. Right-click the title bar to access the same options provided by the Window button.
- *Iconify.* This works like the minimize box in Microsoft Windows. Click it once to minimize your window into a box on the Corel Panel.
- *Maximize.* This works similar to the maximize box in Microsoft Windows. Click it once to expand your window to fill the desktop. Click it again to restore the window to its original size.
- *Close.* Click this box once to close an open window.
- *Resize.* Click and drag the bottom right corner of an open window to resize the window. Let go of the mouse when the window reaches the desired size.

Customizing the Desktop from the Control Center

Click the Corel Application Starter and select Control Center to open the Corel Control Center, shown in Figure A.4. The Corel Control Center is like the Settings dialog box in Windows, from which you can control many aspects of your system, including display, printer, network, and sound settings.

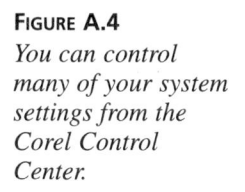

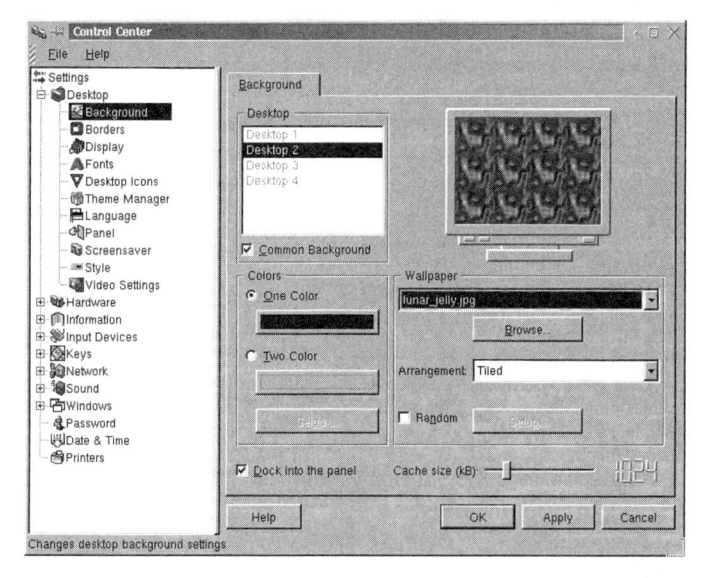

FIGURE A.4
You can control many of your system settings from the Corel Control Center.

Finding Help when You Need It

Although only the Standard and Deluxe editions of Corel Linux include a full user's manual, all three versions include extensive online help you can access by clicking the Help button on the Corel Panel. This opens Netscape Navigator, from which you can browse through the Corel Linux Help manual. This handy guide is in HTML format, and it includes hundreds of hyperlinks to related material within the guide itself as well as on the World Wide Web.

System Updates for Corel Linux

Here's one of the best reasons for choosing Corel Linux OS. Click the Corel Application Starter and select Applications, System, Corel Update. This opens the Corel Update application, shown in Figure A.5. Corel Update provides the easiest way yet to update your Linux system and install, delete, or update third-party software. Corel Update includes a built-in link to Corel's FTP site to check for the latest updates to your system's software. It's also a snap to update software from a CD-ROM without having to enter extensive Linux commands.

FIGURE A.5
Corel Update makes it easier than ever to update your Linux system and all installed software.

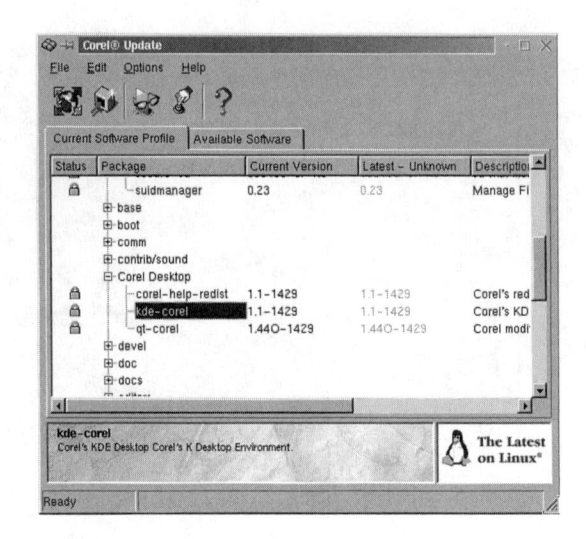

Summary

Naturally, I've only scratched the surface of the wonderful world that awaits you once you install Corel Linux OS. Remember that if you buy either version of WordPerfect Office 2000 for Linux, you also get the download version of Corel Linux on CD-ROM, which provides all the Linux tools most new users will need. Most importantly, don't forget to have fun exploring this exciting operating system!

APPENDIX B

Answers to Quiz Questions

Answers for Hour 2

Quiz

1. The Corel Application Starter
2. **wordperfect**
3. The Property Bar

Exercises

1. Right-click the desktop and select New, Nickname to open the Nickname dialog box. In the Nickname field, replace Untitled App with Paradox 9. In the Target field, enter **/usr/bin/paradox**. Click the Change Icon button. From the pull-down menu, select /usr/X11R6/share/icons. Navigate through the icons and double-click the Paradox 9 icon. Click OK.

2. From the WordPerfect 9 toolbar, click the Web button to access Corel's Office Community Web site for tips, tricks, and free downloads to enhance all your WordPerfect Office 2000 applications.

3. Right-click any toolbar and select Settings from the drop-down menu. In the Toolbar tab, press Create and name your new toolbar. Click OK to launch to Toolbar Editor. All the functions you need are located under File in the Features Categories. Navigate the Features list to find the functions you need. Select each feature and click Add Button to add it to your custom toolbar. Click OK to exit the Toolbar Editor and use your new toolbar.

Answers for Hour 3

Quiz

1. /disks/c/My Documents.
2. Place your cursor at the start of the block you want to select, hold down the Shift key, and then navigate with the arrow keys to the end of the block. Release the keys and then drag the block to the desired location using the mouse.
3. Ctrl+A

    Ctrl+Z

    Ctrl+Shift+Z

    Ctrl+O

    Ctrl+S

    Ctrl+P

Exercises

1. From the Corel Application Starter, select Applications, System and launch the User Manager. In the Users tab, double-click the user who will be granted access to the floppy drive. This opens the Edit User dialog box. Navigate to the Groups tab, find `floppy` in the Available Groups list and double-click it to add it to the Selected Groups for User window. Click OK until you're back in the User Manager. Close out of the User Manager and click Yes when asked if you want to save your changes.

2. Open WordPerfect 9 and enter text into a blank document. Press Ctrl+S or the Save button on the toolbar to open the Save File dialog box. Use the Save In drop-down menu to navigate to the /My Home/Documents directory. In the File Name box, enter `Testing123` and press the Save button. Close WordPerfect 9 and launch the

Corel File Manager from the KPanel or the Desktop. Navigate to your Documents folder and double-click Testing 123 to open it. Make some changes and select File, Save As from the menu bar. Name your new document **321Testing** and click the Save button.

3. Click the printer icon on the desktop to open the Print tab in the Corel Linux Control Center. Click Add to add a new printer (or click Modify and enter the root password if you're not already logged in as root). Follow the prompts to configure your printer. Close out of the Control Center and test your printer by printing out your Testing123 document.

Answers for Hour 4

Quiz

1. Use any keyboard shortcut to access the menu, such as Alt+F (File menu) or Alt+H (Help menu).
2. Alt+F12.
3. Nothing. WordPerfect 9 will read and write to documents created in WordPerfect versions 6 through 8, and vice versa. WordPerfect 9 documents are also 100 percent compatible with documents created in WordPerfect 7 and 8 for Linux.

Exercises

1. Select Tools, Settings to open the Settings dialog box. Click Customize to open the Customize Settings dialog box, which opens at the Toolbars tab. From the list of toolbars, select the Graphics toolbar and click the Options button. In the Toolbar Options dialog box, select Left under Toolbar Location. Click OK and close out of the Customize Settings dialog box. Close out of the Settings dialog box to return to your document.
2. You can open Reveal Codes by using your mouse to drag the Reveal Codes bar up into your document window. Keep on dragging until the Reveal Codes window shares equal space with your document window.
3. Type out the questions and answers. Drag with your mouse to highlight the first answer. Select Format, Font from the menu and check the Hidden box under Appearance. Click OK. Repeat the same procedure for each answer. When you return to your document, deactivate Hidden Text from the View menu to confirm that your Hidden Text works. To delete the Hidden Text code, open the Reveal Codes window and drag all the code buttons for Hidden Text out of the Reveal Codes window.

Answers for Hour 5

Quiz

1. You can open the Font Properties dialog box in any of the following ways:
   - Right-click in a document and select Font from the pop-up menu.
   - Select Format, Font from the menu bar.
   - Use the keyboard shortcut F9.
   - Click the QuickFonts button on the Property Bar and select Font.
2. Alt+F8
3. d

Exercises

1. Close all WordPerfect Office 2000 applications and launch FontTastic from the Corel Application Starter. Uncheck the check box next to Bard font and click Close. Open any WordPerfect Office 2000 application and make sure Bard font no longer appears in the font face drop-down box. Close the application and return to FontTastic. Check the box next to Bard font to turn it back on. Click Close.
2. Right-click the toolbar and select Format. Locate the Double Indent button on the Format toolbar. Every time you click the Double Indent button, your text will move one-half inch away from the left and right margins. Click the Double Indent button four times to set your text two inches in from the left and right margins.
3. Press Alt+F8 to open the Styles dialog box. Click the Create button to open the Styles Editor dialog box. Select the Bard font face, set the font size to 16, and click the Bold and Underline buttons. Under Style Name, enter `Insanely Red`. Under Description, enter a brief description of your new style. Select Format, Font from the menu bar. In the Font Properties dialog box, click the color button and select red from the color palette. Set Shading to 75 percent, set Relative Size to Very Large, and click OK. Click OK in the Styles Editor to return to the Styles dialog box with your new style listed in the Available Styles menu. Click Close to return to your document.

Answers for Hour 6
Quiz
1. e
2. False. You can see comments in Draft and Page View.
3. The next occurrence of a selected word.

Exercises
1. Press Alt+F1 or select Tools, Thesaurus from the menu bar. Type in the word **faux pas** and click Look Up.
2. Position your mouse cursor at the insertion point for your outline. Click the down arrow next to the Bullets button on the toolbar and select Diamonds. The first level of your outline appears in your document, and all outline tools are at your disposal in the Property Bar.
3. Type the required text and click the word *boy*. From the menu bar, select Insert, Comment, Create. Enter the required comment and select your open document from the Application Bar. To edit your comment, select View, Page to enter Page View. Double-click the balloon in the left margin to enter the Comment window. Position your cursor at the end of your comment and click the Name button on the Property Bar to insert your username. Click the Close button on the Property Bar to return to your document.

Answers for Hour 7
Quiz
1. False. Tables are a better choice because you can take advantage their spreadsheet capabilities to automatically perform all your calculations.
2. Ctrl+Enter.
3. F14.

Exercises
1. From the menu bar, select Insert, Table to open the Create Table dialog box. Enter the size of the table and click Create. Select cell A1 and type **Wish List**. Select row 1, right-click it, and select Join Cells. With row 1 still selected, right-click and select Format to open the Properties for Table Format dialog box. Navigate to the Row tab and check Header Row. Click OK.

2. From the menu bar, select Insert, Table to open the Create Table dialog box. Enter the size of the table and click the SpeedFormat button. In the Table SpeedFormat dialog box, scroll down the Available Styles list and select Fancy Labels. Click Apply to return to the Create Table dialog box; then click Create.

3. Create a new document and enter your name, address, and phone number at the top of the page. Position your mouse pointer beneath this information and select Format, Columns from the menu bar. Set the Number of Columns field to 2. For Type of Columns, select Parallel w/Block Protect. Set the width of column 1 to two inches. The width of column 2 will automatically change to four inches. Click OK. Type **Objective** in column 1. Click column 2 and type out your objective. Now press Ctrl+Enter, and a new row will appear. Repeat this for each heading and the details of each heading in your resume. When you complete the last entry, discontinue columns by clicking the Columns button on the toolbar and selecting Discontinue.

Answers for Hour 8

Quiz

1. b
2. c
3. e

Exercises

1. Open the Scrapbook by clicking the Clipart button on the toolbar. Navigate to the Photos tab and select Options, Create Category. Enter **Vacation Pix** at the prompt and click OK.

2. Select the graphic and click the Caption button on the Property Bar. Backspace to delete the default caption that appears below your graphic and type in **My First Graphic**. You can use the normal text-editing tools to change the font and format of your caption. When you're through, click anywhere outside the graphic to exit Caption mode.

3. Select a graphic and click the Border or Fill buttons on the Property Bar. Click the More button to open the Border/Fill dialog box and navigate to the Shadow tab. You can use the controls here to select the direction of the shadow and to set the height, width, and color of the shadow. When you're through, click OK.

Answers for Hour 9

Quiz

1. PerfectScript
2. WordPerfect 9, Quattro Pro 9, and Presentations 9
3. The data source, the form file, and the merge document
4. `ENDFIELD` and `ENDRECORD`

Exercises

1. First, create your personalized letterhead and save it as "letterhead." Close out of the document. Start recording your macro by selecting Tools, Macro, Record to open the Record Macro dialog box. Name your new macro "openletter" and save it. Record your macro keystrokes by simply opening your openletter macro. Stop recording by clicking Tools, Macro, Record. Close out of your document. You can launch your new macro by clicking Tools, Macro, Play and opening the `openletter` file.

2. Right-click the toolbar and click Edit to open the Toolbar Editor. Select the Macros tab and click the Add Macro button. Find the openletter.wcm macro in the Select Macro dialog box, select it, and click Open. A new button for your macro will appear at the end of your toolbar.

3. Press Shift+F9 to open the Merge dialog box. Click the Create Data button. In the Create Data File dialog box, type in the following field names: **Name**, **Street Address**, **City/State**, and **Zip Code**. Check the Format Records in a Table checkbox at the bottom of the dialog box and click OK. Enter all required data in the Quick Data Entry form and click Close. Save your data file to the directory of your choice. To perform an envelope merge that includes only the first two addresses, open a new WordPerfect document. Select Tools, Merge from the menu bar and click the Perform Merge button in the Merge dialog box. Set the Form Document to Current Document. For Data Source, select File On Disk and browse to the data file you created. Click the Select Records button and click the Mark Records radio button. Check the first two records in the Record List and click OK. Click the Envelopes button and enter your return address and the fields for your recipients. Click the Continue Merge button on the Merge Bar to take you back to the Merge dialog box. Click the Merge button to start the merge operation.

Answers for Hour 10

Quiz

1. e
2. d
3. b

Exercises

1. On the menu bar, select Tools, Settings and navigate to the Compatibility tab. In the Compatibility Options drop-down list, select Microsoft Excel 97. Under Interface Options, confirm that Microsoft Excel Menu is selected under the Menu Bar (it should happen automatically). Click OK. To restore the Quattro Pro 9 menu and compatibility options, perform the same steps but select Quattro Pro 9 under Compatibility Options.

2. There are many ways to navigate to the listed cell addresses, but here's one approach for each:

    To locate D:B6, click sheet tab D and use the row and column borders to identify cell D:B6. To access the cell, select it with your mouse.

    To access cell XX:Q30, use the right tab scroll button to get to sheet XX, then use the horizontal and vertical scroll bars to locate cell Q30.

    To access ZZZ:A100, select Edit, Go To in the menu bar, to open the Go To dialog box. Type **ZZZ:A100** in the Reference box and click OK.

    Press Ctrl+Home to get back to cell A1 in sheet A.

3. After using the QuickTab to jump the Objects sheet, press F5 to open the Go To dialog box. Type **CCC:Z49** in the Reference box and press OK.

Answers for Hour 11

Quiz

1. Quattro Pro formulas use cell addresses, not data, to perform calculations. This allows you to enter updated or different numerical data in cells without changing the formula. The same formula used for a spreadsheet showing first quarter sales will work just as well to calculate totals based on sales data for the second quarter.

2. This is very easy. Simply select the block of figures you want to average plus the blank cell directly adjacent to your last figure (if you were calculating the average

of a column, you would also include the blank cell directly below your last figure). Select @Avg from the drop-down QuickFunction menu on the toolbar. The average will be displayed in the last cell of the selected block.

3. Not really. Relative addressing is a very helpful and powerful feature that automatically adjusts formulas when you add or delete columns and rows. It makes sense to have it enabled by default. You can override relative addressing for a particular formula by inserting absolute cell addresses for all the cell references in a formula.

4. The Help section contains descriptions of all the functions available in Quattro Pro, and it gives you the proper syntax to use with each function. In the menu bar, select Help, Help Topics. Type in the word **functions** and scroll down until you see *Types*. Double-clicking Types will bring up a box from which you can search for functions by category.

Exercises

1. Select the cell or block of cells in which Fundamentally Yours, Inc. appears. Change the font type and size in the font face and font size boxes on the Property bar. Press Enter.

2. Select the cell whose value you want to change. Click the Input Line and make your change, or double-click the cell to enter the new value directly in the cell. After changing the value, press Enter to have your change take effect.

3. Here are some things you can try. Select cell F5 and delete the formula. Type **@SUM(C5..E5)** and press Enter. Delete the formula in cell F6. Select block F5..F6 and press the QuickFill button on the Notebook toolbar.

4. Although your monthly expense sheet might vary depending on your financial situation, consider creating a three-column household expense spreadsheet as follows. In cell A1, type **Monthly Expenses**. Beginning in cell A3, enter the following labels and data in the following cells:

Cell	Label	Cell	Data
A3	Mortgage	C3	$1,159.33
A4	Taxes	C4	$457.00
A5	Insurance	C5	$113.12
A6	Electricity	C6	$87.25
A7	Gas -	C7	$101.96
A8	Cable -	C8	$43.50
A9	Auto	C9	$535.83

Cell	Label	Cell	Data
A10	Food	C10	$443.17
A11	Clothing	C11	$123.00
A12	Babysitter	C12	$215.75
A13	Movies	C13	$60.00
A14	Total	C14	@SUM(C3..C14)
A15	blank	C15	blank
A16	Net Income	C16	$3,500.00
A17	Surplus/Short	C17	+C16-C14

Of course, you can change the labels and data (and the formula, as necessary) to reflect your own financial picture, but this example should give you ideas for getting started.

Answers for Hour 12

Quiz

1. G
2. J
3. E
4. I
5. A
6. B
7. C
8. H
9. F
10. D

Exercises

1. Select cell D13 and click the Bold button on the Property Bar.
2. Select block B4..F5. From the menu bar, select File, Print to open the Spreadsheet Print dialog box. Under the Print heading, select Selection and hit Enter or click Print.
3. Select the entire spreadsheet. From the menu bar, select File, Page Setup and navigate to the Options tab. Under Print Options, check Cell Formulas, and hit Enter or click Print.

Answers for Hour 13

Quiz

1. c
2. a
3. e

Exercises

1. Select File, New From Project from the menu bar. Select Quattro Pro 9 from the pull-down menu. Choose Capital Gains and Losses and click Create. Enter your data and check the results, or you can click the Insert Sample Data button to explore how this spreadsheet works.

2. Double-click the title to activate it; then right-click it and select Chart Title Properties. In the Fill Settings tab, select Pattern as the fill style and choose brown for the fill color. In the Text Settings tab, choose the solid fill style and yellow as the text background color. Click OK. Right-click the subtitle and go to Chart Subtitle Properties. In the Subtitle Text Settings tab, select Solid as the fill style and yellow as the color. Click OK.

3. Select Format, Sheet to open the Active Sheet dialog box; then navigate to the Conditional Color tab. In the Smallest Normal Value box, type **7500** and then check the Enable box. In the Options section, check Below Normal Color and select red as the "below normal" color. Click OK.

Answers for Hour 14

Quiz

1. Possible answers include project proposals, interactive demonstrations, multimedia presentations, flyers, signs, banners, lecture notes, product presentations, research summaries, invitations, annual reports, meeting agenda, and outlines. This is by no means an inclusive list. You are encouraged to come up with other uses for Presentations (and email the authors with really good ones)!

2. A *slide show* is a series of slide images presented together. A *drawing* is single image meant to be viewed alone.

3. JPG, BMP, GIF, PNG, and WPD.

4. True.

5. Slide layer, layout layer, and background layer. The background layer is on the bottom.

6. The layout layer.

7. Text boxes and bulleted lists.

Exercises

1. Click the Presentations icon, select Applications, WordPerfect Office 2000, Presentations 9 from the KDE or GNOME menu. Alternatively, you can enter Presentations at a shell prompt in an Xterm.

    When the PerfectExpert dialog box opens, select the Create New tab and choose Teaching a Concept, Create.

2. Click the Slide Editor tab in the drawing window. Click the tab labeled 6 at the bottom of the drawing window. Click the Go To list at the bottom right of the drawing window and scroll down to the last slide, which is slide 32 (a blank slide).

3. The title of the menu is Teaching a Concept Slide Show. The Slide Sorter opens and displays the slide show.

4. When you hold the mouse over an icon, a pop-up appears with the name of the icon. The last icon in the Tools Palette in Slide Sorter view is *Reverse Colors*.

5. When you click Edit, Background Layer, the Slide Editor opens with the slide backgrounds. The Background tab contains an empty blue screen—the background color of the slide show.

6. You can't see Slide Outliner in the background layer, so you must go to the slide layer. Click the Slide Outliner tab in the drawing window or click View, Slide Outliner from the menu bar. All the text from the side show appears in Slide Outliner.

7. The slide show plays on the screen. When you left-click the mouse, text slides into view. When you press Esc, the slide show exits and you are returned to the Presentations desktop.

Answers for Hour 15

Quiz

1. Select File, New From Project.

2. False. You can enter only text in Slide Outliner.

3. Deleting a slide deletes the actual slide; the rest of the slides are reordered and renumbered. Clearing a slide only deletes the information on the slide (in the slide layer); the empty slide remains.

4. Opens the default Internet browser at the Corel Tips and Tricks Web page.

5. Speaker notes include a thumbnail sketch of the slides and notes that you type in. They can also include the slide text. Audience notes include thumbnail sketches of the slides with blank lines beneath the slides for note-taking.
6. Check Apply to All Slides in Slideshow in the Transition tab of the Slide Properties dialog box.
7. Wave (WAV) and MIDI file formats.

Exercises

1. Open Presentations 9, click Create New in the PerfectExpert dialog box, select Corel Presentations Slideshow, and click Create.
2. Click the Slide Outliner tab, click Change the Text in PerfectExpert, or click View, Slide Outliner.
3. To add a new slide, click Insert, New Slide. To delete the slide, click Edit, Delete Slide.
4. The Go to Slide dialog box opens.
5. From PerfectExpert, click Add Graphics, Insert a Scrapbook Item. From the menu, click Insert, Graphics, Clipart. Click a graphic to select it and then click Insert. Click Close to close the Scrapbook.
6. Click the graphic to expose the object handles. Drag a handle inward to make the graphic smaller. Click inside the graphic to move it and then drag it to the corner.
7. Click Insert, New Slide. Click the title object in Slide Editor and add the title, or you can add the title in Slide Outliner.

   To add speaker notes, right-click the slide, click the Speaker Notes icon in Property Bar. Type in the speaker notes.
8. Right-click the slide and select Transition (or click Transition on the Property Bar), select a transition, and click OK.
9. Open the SpeedKeys tab in the Slide Properties dialog box. Click Q in the Keystrokes field and then check Action and click Quit Show. Check Apply to All Slides in Slideshow, if desired, and then click OK.
10. QuickShow: Click View, Play Slideshow, Create QuickShow.

    Show on the Go: Click File, Show on the Go. Change any summary information and click Create.

    HTML file: Click File, Internet Publisher. Follow the Internet Publisher Wizard.

    PDF file: Click File, Publish to PDF. Select a filename and click OK.

Answers for Hour 16

Quiz

1. *Data charts* present numeric information in a visual way. *Organization charts* show relationships between people, processes, or other entities.
2. Possible answers include area chart, bar chart, bubble chart, high-low chart, line chart, mixed chart, pie chart, radar chart, surface chart, table chart, and Xy scatter chart.
3. No. All data in the datasheet must be numeric, except for the legend and labels.
4. Click Insert, Organization Chart and draw the chart object.
5. Convert the graphic to a bitmap using Tools, Convert to Bitmap.

Exercises

1. Open Presentations, click Insert, New Slide. Select a layout that contains a data chart object from the Layout Gallery. Double-click the data chart object and select Area Chart from the Data Chart Gallery.

   Alternatively, create a new slide and then click Insert, Data Chart and draw the data chart on the new slide.

2. The datasheet should open automatically, but if it doesn't, click the data chart and then from the main menu click View, Datasheet. Click the Legend cell under West and enter Southwest. Tab to each cell and enter the information or double-click each cell and enter the information in the Edit Current Cell dialog box.

3. Click Data, Layout/Type to open the Layout/Type Properties dialog box. Select Line from the Chart Type drop-down menu and click OK.

4. Click the data chart. Select File, Save As on the main menu. Check Selected Items in the Save dialog box and click OK. Enter a filename and select Joint Photographic Experts Group in the Files of Type field. Click Save and then OK in the JPEG dialog box.

5. Click Insert, New Slide. Select a layout with an organization chart from the Layout Gallery. Double-click the layout object on the chart. Double-click a square to add the name of the square. To delete an extraneous square, select the square and click Edit, Delete. To add the Staff square, select the Me square, right-click it, select Insert, Staff and click OK in the Insert Staff dialog box.

6. Create a new slide with only the title and subtitle objects from the Layout Gallery. Delete the subtitle object by clicking it and selecting Edit, Delete. Click the cube flyout on the Tools Palette (it might be a rectangle or other parallelogram). Draw

two cubes on the slide or draw one cube and copy and paste the other. Select a cube and click Format, Object Properties, Fill. Click the Texture icon and then select the Objects category and scroll to the coins texture. Click OK. Repeat this for the second cube, except in Object Properties, click the Picture icon and click the World thumbnail from the Business category.

Answers for Hour 17

Quiz

1. Yes, in ASCII text format.
2. An *event* is assigned a particular date and time on the calendar for when the event is to take place. A *task* can have a start date and due date, but it's not scheduled to be completed at a specific time.
3. A *subtask* is part of a task; subtasks are smaller tasks that must be completed in order to complete the larger task.
4. Days of Year.
5. Click Tools, Reset Warnings.
6. Open the Edit Task dialog box by right-clicking the task. Click Add Task in the Edit Task dialog box. Enter the subtask in the new Edit Task dialog box that appears.

Exercises

1. From the Presentations menu bar, click Tools, Corel Calendar.
2. Select View and click Day, Week, or Month.
3. Click Calendar, New Event. Enter **Lunch with Linus and Richard** in the Subject line. Check that the date is for today. Enter **1:00 p.m.** in the Start Time field and **1 Hour** in the Duration field.
4. Click Calendar, New Event. Enter **Day at the Beach** in the Subject line and check All Day Event.
5. Right-click the event "Lunch with Linus and Richard" and select Edit Event. Click Alarm and select 30 Minutes from the Remind Me Before Event drop-down menu. Then click OK. Verify that the Alarm check box is checked.
6. Right-click an empty line in the event listlist and click Add Task or click Calendar, New Task. Enter **Buy Myself Flowers** in the Subject line. Click the Categories icon and check Personal or type **Personal** in the Categories field. Check Due Date and enter your birthday.

7. Right-click the "Buy Myself Flowers" task you created in Exercise 6 and select Add Task. In the dialog box that appears, enter `Check Bank Account` in the Subject field. Click "Buy Myself Flowers" in the task hierarchy list in the Edit Task dialog box. Click Add Task and enter `Decide Which Flower Is My Favorite` in the Subject field. Click OK to save.
8. Click Edit, Find. The Find message box lists all occurrences of "flowers."
9. Right-click the "Buy Myself Flowers" task you created in Exercise 6. Click Tools, Link to, Web Site. Enter `http://www.flowers.com` in the URL field.

Answers for Hour 18

Quiz

1. An *organization* entry includes the contact information for an organization such as main phone number(s), fax number(s), address, and secondary address, if applicable. A *group* entry is a collection of person, organization, and/or resource records that you want to group together for some purpose, such as creating a phone tree.
2. An ASCII delimited text file.
3. An ASCII delimited text file.
4. Create a custom field called Hostname.
5. The Display Name field.

Exercises

1. Start Corel Address Book from an Xterm shell prompt.

   Open an Xterm. At the shell prompt, type

   `ccaddressbook`

2. From the menu bar, click Address, New, Person. Fill in the given information in the proper fields.
3. Click the Create a New Address Entry icon. Select Organization and click OK. Fill in the given information in the proper fields.
4. Click Address, New, Group, OK. Enter `Group` in the Group field. Click Add/Remove Members. Click Jane Doe to select the record and click Add. Select XYZ Corporation and click Add. Click OK to close the Add/Remove Members dialog box and then click OK in the Group Properties dialog box.

5. Click File, New, CorelCENTRAL. Enter the name of the new address book and click OK.
6. Click View, Filter. Select Email Address in the Field drop-down menu and click OK. Jane Doe appears. XYZ Corp. has no email address, so it does not appear.
7. Click View, Filter. Select Display Name in the Field drop-down menu, "=" for the operator button, and enter **x** in the Filter field. Click OK. Only XYZ Corp. should appear.

Answers for Hour 19

Quiz

1. A Quattro Pro spreadsheet (or any other kind of spreadsheet), is an example of a flat-file database. Paradox enables you to create both flat-file (one database.
2. The columns in a table represent fields. The rows represent records.
3. Tables in relational databases are linked by similar data fields in the tables.
4. No. A database object usually contains data but is not data itself, just like a database program enables you to work with a database but the program itself isn't a database.
5. The primary index sorts the table by the key field.
6. By object type.

Exercises

1. From the menu bar, select Help, PerfectExpert.
2. To open Project Viewer, click Tools, Project Viewer. To set the default, click Tools, Settings, Preferences and check Open Project Viewer on Startup.
3. Select File, Working Directory and browse for the directory or enter the pathname for the sample database in Project Viewer.
4. Click Tables and then double-click any listed table. Click Forms and then double-click any listed form.
5. Click the Browse icon in Project viewer and select `:PRIV:` from the drop-down menu. Alternatively, open Alias Manager by clicking Tools, Alias Manager and selecting `:PRIV:` from the drop-down menu. The pathname appears in the Path field.

Answers for Hour 20

Quiz

1. False. You can add and remove fields from all the database template tables. You can also edit every database object that's created from a template as if you had created it from scratch.
2. Business and personal.
3. You can mix and match fields from any of the table templates in Table Expert.
4. To create an entirely new field in an existing table, select the table in Project Viewer and then click Tools, Utilities, Restructure. Add the new field in the Field Roster.
5. Number field types contain only numbers (and signs and decimals points, if needed). Alpha field types contain any ASCII printing symbol, including numbers, letters, and symbols. The time field type contains only the time. The timestamp contains both the time and date.
6. The parent table contains the key field. The child table contains a field that is linked to the key field.

Exercises

1. From the menu bar, select Tools, Experts, Database, Business. Select Job Costing. Follow the expert dialog boxes to create the database.
2. To change the working directory, click File Working Directory. Browse to the job costing directory created in exercise 1. From Project Viewer, select Tables, right-click CLIENT.DB, and select Restructure.
3. Client Rec ID is the key field. The Key column has a key icon in it.
4. From the Restructure Table dialog box, select the Secondary Index tab. Click Add and type **Companies**. Select the Last Name field and click the right arrow; then do the same with the Company field. Check Maintained and click Save.
5. Yes. The Project Rec ID fields of the BILLING, LABOR, and MATERIAL tables are linked to the Project Rec ID field in PROJECT.
6. The PROJECT table is the parent table, and the other three tables are child tables. The arrow originates from BILLING, LABOR, and MATERIAL and points to PROJECT. Also, the Project Rec ID field is a key field in PROJECT.DB.

Answers for Hour 21

Quiz

1. You can input data directly into the table using table view or via a form, one record at a time.
2. Tables open into view mode by default. You must press F9 or click View, Edit Data to switch to edit mode.
3. After you make an edit, once you move the cursor to a new record, the edit is posted and you cannot undo it. You can undo an edit after moving to a different field in the same record, but not after moving to a different record in the same field.
4. In field view, after you move off the field, the entire next record field is highlighted, and you have to click the field to return to field view. In persistent field view, you can move all over the table, using the keyboard, while remaining in field view.
5. BMP format.
6. Locate and Replace. Find and Replace.
7. *value1|value2*.
8. No. Only unkeyed tables can be sorted as the same table.

Exercises

1. From Project Viewer, set the working directory to Paradox Samples (by default, $HOME/Documents/Paradox/Samples). Open the customer.db table. Press F9 or click View, Edit Data to switch to edit mode. Press F9 again or click View, View Data to switch back to view mode.
2. Click the horizontal scroll lock and drag it to the right end of the Name field. Scroll to the First Contact column. You can easily see that the first contact for Island Finders was 6/2/91.
3. Click View, Toolbars and check Property to display the Property Bar. Click the last record button to go to Neptune's Trident Supply. Click the double left-arrow button to go up 15 records to 41. Record 40 is Jamaica Sun, Inc. Click the single right-arrow button to go to 42, Princess Island Scuba. Click the double left-arrow button again to go to record 28. Record 27 is Divers of Blue-Green. Click the first record button to go to record 1, Kauai Dive Shoppe.

4. Press F9 to go into edit mode (if you're not already there) and click Record, Insert to open a new record. Enter the name and phone number.
5. Click View, Field View. Place the cursor at *Shoppe* and change it to *Emporium*.
6. A graphic of the Bat Ray appears in memo view. Use the Close icon or press F2 to close memo view. When you double-click the Bat Ray notes, a note about the Bat Ray appears in memo view. Press F2 to close it.
7. There are two kinds of sharks. Select Locate, Value. Select Common Name for the field and enter `.. shark` in the Value field. Check the @ and .. check box. Click Locate Next to go to the next matching value in the field.

Answers for Hour 22

Quiz

1. True. If your tables are linked, you can use a form to enter data into two or more tables.
2. No. You can only create single-table forms and reports using Quick Form and Quick Report.
3. No. You can only view and print data with a report. Use a form to enter data into a table.
4. Multirecord.
5. Open the form and click View, Design Form. Then click Format, Data Model.

Exercises

1. Set the working directory to Samples. Open the contacts.db table. Click Tools, Quick Design, Quick Form.
2. Click Tools, Expert, Form, Run Expert. Select Data from Two Tables. Follow the expert with the values given.
3. Open the form and click Format, Deliver.
4. Open the contacts.db table. Select Tools, Quick Design, Quick Report.
5. Select Tools, Experts, Query, Run Expert. Select biolife.db as the table. In the Display category, select biolife.Category is equal to Snapper. Run the query. There are three fish in the Snapper category in the biolife table.

Answers for Hour 23

Quiz

1. Publish to HTML enables you to publish your Web document to the Web. Format as Web Document enables you to format a WordPerfect document in HTML.
2. Five.
3. The title displays as the title of the browser window.
4. A new paragraph.
5. A *hyperlink* takes you to a different Internet address. A *bookmark* takes you to a different place on the same page.
6. It doesn't do anything. You must accompany a form object with a CGI script or some other program that activates the form object.

Exercises

1. Open the document in WordPerfect. Click File, Internet Publisher, Format as Web document. Save the document as an HTML file.
2. Open the document in WordPerfect. Click File, Internet Publisher, Format as WP document. Save the document as a WPD file.
3. Click Internet Publisher, Create New Web Document. Type the text and then select Heading 1.
4. Click File, Properties, Text Colors/Wallpaper. Select dark blue from the text palette and purple from the hyperlink palette.
5. Type the text. Highlight *Corel* and click Tools, Hyperlink. Enter `http://www.corel.com` as the link destination.
6. If you don't have a graphic of your own to insert, use an image from Clipart. Place the cursor where you want to put the graphic. Click Insert, Graphics. Select the graphic you want and click Insert.

Answers for Hour 24

Quiz

1. Hyperlinks that begin with `http`, `ftp`, `mailto`, or www.
2. Show Me! is available only for Netscape for Windows and Internet Explorer.

3. The banner field is the title of the list.
4. Tables, reports, and forms.

Exercises

1. Select File, Publish to Internet. Accept the default range. Enter your name and email address under Document Information. Click Options and select yellow under Background Color.
2. Click File, Internet Publisher. Follow the expert's instructions using the assigned parameters.
3. Select File, Publish to HTML, Events. Enter this month for the date range. The HTML file is a calendar for the current month with the events printed on it.
4. Select File, Publish to HTML. Click the double right-pointing arrow to select all fields. Select a pathname and click Finish.

INDEX

Symbols

/ (forward slash), root directories, 50
1:1 button (Image tools), 161
3-D blocks of cells, 205
@SUM function, 221-222

A

absolute cell addresses (formulas), 223-225
accessing
    floppy disk drives, 55-56
    Windows applications on networked computers, 11
    Windows partitions, 57
Action keys (SpeedKeys), 308
activating
    blocks, 204-205
    cells, 204-205
    columns, 204-205
    Objects sheets, 207
    rows, 204-205
active cells, identifying, 200
Active Cells dialog box, 226, 262
active sheets, identifying, 201
adding data to database tables, 408-409
Address Book (CorelCENTRAL), 354
    address fields, customizing, 357, 364
    entries
        adding, 357
        custom entries, creating, 357
        editing, 357
        Group entry type, 356
        Organization entry type, 355
        Person entry type, 355
        Resource entry type, 355
    exporting address books to ASCII delimited text files, 360
    Filter feature, 361-364
    Find feature, 360-361
    importing addresses, 358-359
    interface, 355-356
    merge data files, creating, 182
    new address books, creating, 358
    starting, 354
address fields (Address Book), customizing, 357, 364
addressing cells
    spreadsheets, 200
    tables, 130
administrative users, 50
advanced formatting tools (Quattro Pro), 251-252
alarms (events), setting, 343
aliases (Paradox)
    creating, 381
    deleting, 382
    opening projects, 382
    setting, 380-382
aligning text (spreadsheets), 226
alignment values, 197
all cells, selecting, 205
all-day events (CorelCENTRAL calendar), 341
Application Bar, 41, 202, 281
    customizing, 41
    dragging items between documents, 60
    hiding, 47
Application Bar command (View menu), 79
Application Bar Settings dialog box, 41
application commands, 31
Application Starter, 474
    launching programs, 29-30
applications. *See also* programs
    Corel Update application, 477
    differences in WordPerfect Office 2000 versions, 23
    freezes, troubleshooting, 33
    integration, 16-17
    launching
        desktop shortcuts, 32-33
        from Corel Application Starter, 29-30
        Run command, 30-32

macros, 18
quitting, 33
spreadsheet, 194
Applixware, 10
applying filters (Address Book), 361-364
arithmetic operators, 218
ASCII delimited text files, exporting address books to, 360
Associate dialog box, 183
Associate Form and Data dialog box, 183
associations, 183
audience notes, adding to slides (Slide Editor), 304-305
audio, adding to slideshows, 309
automatic first line indents, 109
automatic totaling feature (Quattro Pro 9), 223
AutoScroll, 21, 124
auxiliary passwords (tables), 398-399

B

Back browse button, 21
background layer (slides), 287
backup settings, customizing, 89
Bitmap Editor (Presentations), 330, 333
bitmap images, 149
BitStream FontTastic Font Installer, 99-100
blocks of cells, 204-205
bookmarks, creating (Internet Publisher), 446-447
Border Style button (Selected Image Property Bar), 165
borders, adding to spreadsheet cells, 261-262
Box Fill button (Selected Image Property Bar), 165
Box Position dialog box, 157
Branch Layout dialog box (Presentations), 323
break pages (printing spreadsheets), 245
Brightness button (Image Tools), 161
browse buttons, 207
Browse Forward and Back buttons, 124-125
Browse the Web button (Internet Publisher), 451
browsers, Show It! plug-in, 312
bulleted list (slide objects), 288
bullets, Reveal Codes, 82
Bullets button (toolbar), 122

buttons
1:1 button (Image Tools), 161
Border Style button (Selected Image Property Bar), 165
Box Fill button (Selected Image Property Bar), 165
Brightness button (Image Tools), 161
browse buttons, 207
Browse Forward and Back buttons, 124-125
Browse the Web button (Internet Publisher), 451
Bullets button (toolbar), 122
BW Threshold button (Image Tools), 161
Caption button (Selected Image Property Bar), 165
Clipart button (toolbar), 150
code buttons, Reveal Codes, 83
Console button, 474
Contrast button (Image Tools), 161
Edit Attributes button (Image Tools), 162
Edit Contents button (Image Tools), 163
File Manager button, 474
Fill button (Image Tools), 162
flip buttons (Image Tools), 159
Flip Left/Right button (Selected Image Property Bar), 165
Flip Top/Bottom button (Selected Image Property Bar), 165
Graphics button, 164-165
Help button, 475-477
Hyperlink button (Selected Image Property Bar), 166
Image Tools button (Selected Image Property Bar), 165
Invert Colors button (Image Tools), 162
Jump to Next Selection button (Selected Image Property Bar), 165
Jump to Prior Selection button (Selected Image Property Bar), 165
Justification button (Property Bar), 106
macro toolbar buttons, creating, 172
Magnifier button (Image Tools), 160

Move Back One Layer button (Selected Image Property Bar), 166
Move button (Image Tools), 159
Move Forward One Layer button (Selected Image Property Bar), 166
Numbering button (toolbar), 121
outline buttons (Property bar), 122-123
Quick Tab button, 207
QuickFind buttons, 125
Reset Attributes button (Image Tools), 163
Rotate button (Image Tools), 159
Rotate Cell button (Property Bar), 144
Select All, 205
Sticky button (windows), 476
tab scroll button, 207
Table QuickCreate button, 131-132
Text Editor button, 474
toolbar buttons, 36-37
Window button, 476
Wrap Text button (Selected Image Property Bar), 166
Zoom button (Image Tools), 160-161
Zoom Scroll button (Image Tools), 160
BW Threshold button (Image Tools), 161

C

calculations (tables), 134-136
formulas, 135-136
QuickSum, 134-135
calendar (CorelCENTRAL), 338-339
default calendar, 350
desktop, 338-339
events
alarms, setting, 343
all-day events, 341
creating, 340
deleting, 343
editing, 344
linking, 348-349
repeating events, 341-343
scheduling, 340-344
turning into tasks, 350
filters, 347-348
Find tool, 347

publishing calendars to the
   Web, 462-463
records, locating, 346-348
starting, 338
tasks
   adding to event list, 344
   creating to-do lists,
      344-346
   editing, 346
   linking, 348-349
   subtasks, adding, 345
   turning into events, 350
Caption button (Selected Image
   Property Bar), 165
cells
   spreadsheet cells, 200
      absolute cell addresses,
         223-225
      activating, 204-205
      active, identifying, 200
      addressing, 200
      blocks, 204-205
      borders, adding, 261-262
      clearing, 235-236
      coloring, 263
      columns, resizing, 241
      data, formatting, 202
      deleting, 237-238
      deleting contents, 234-236
      drag and drop, 248
      formulas, 200
      information, displaying,
         201
      inserting, 238-240
      QuickFormat, 258-259,
         273
      replacing contents,
         233-234
      selecting, 204-205
      selectors, 200
      SpeedFormat, 259-261
      transposing contents, 241
   table cells, 130
      addresses, 130
      contents, deleting, 139
      selecting, 132-133
Chart Expert (Quattro Pro),
   267-270
charts
   data charts (Presentations),
      288, 316-322
      creating, 316
      Data Chart Gallery,
         317-318
      datasheets, 318-320
      entering data, 318-320
      exporting data, 322
      labels, adding, 322
      layout, 320

legends, adding, 321-322
      saving, 322
      titles and subtitles,
         adding, 321
   organization charts
      (Presentations), 289,
      323-324
   spreadsheet charts, 266
      Chart Expert, 267-270
      creating, 266-270
      editing, 271-272
      positioning, 270-271
      sizing, 270-271
child tables, 402
Choose a Directory dialog box, 88
clearing spreadsheet cell
   formatting, 235-236
clipart. *See also* graphics; images
   adding to Scrapbook, 150-151
   inserting into documents,
      149-150
   managing within the
      Scrapbook, 151-154
Clipart button (toolbar), 150
clipboard, cutting and pasting
   items, 61
close box (windows), 476
code buttons, Reveal Codes, 83
color controls (Image Tools),
   161-162
color fills, adding to images
   (Presentations), 327-328
color schemes, applying to charts,
   270
coloring spreadsheet cells, 263
colors
   font colors, 95
   text colors (Web documents),
      443
Column Border/Fill dialog box,
   142
columns, 140-143
   comparing to tables, 130
   creating, 140
      Columns dialog box,
         141-142
   deleting, 143
   formatting, 143
   inserting into tables, 138
   moving around in, 142
   newspaper columns, 140
   parallel columns, 140
   spreadsheet columns
      activating, 204-205
      resizing, 241
      selecting, 204
   table columns, deleting, 139
Columns dialog box, 141-142
command-line interface, 3-4

commands
   application commands, 31
   Edit menu, 207
   Edit Sheet Tab, 201
   Format menu, 201, 204
   Insert command, 149
   killall –9 wine command, 33
   launch commands, 31
   menu commands, 4
   perfectexpert command, 70
   presentations command, 278
   quattropro command, 198
   Run command, launching
      applications, 30-32
   startx command, 29
   Tools menu
      Macros Online, 171
      Settings, 198, 203
   View menu, 203
comments, 119-120
Comments tool, 119-120
configuring printers, 67-68
Console (Corel Linux), 32
Console button, 474
contents of spreadsheet cells
   deleting, 234-236
   replacing, 233-234
   transposing, 241
context-sensitive Property Bar, 40
Contrast button (Image Tools),
   161
Control Center, 476
copy and paste, moving items, 61
copying database table fields to
   files, 412
Corel
   future plans for Linux, 11
   Web site, 312
Corel Application Starter, 474
Corel Control Center, 476
Corel File Manager, 51, 474
Corel Linux, 471-472
   Application Starter, 29-30
   Console, 32
   Control Center, 67-68
   desktop, 473-475
      customizing, 476
   Help manual, 477
   logging in, 472
   starting, 472-473
   system updates, 477
   user passwords, changing, 70
   versions, 472
   windows, 475-476
Corel macros, 170-171
Corel Panel, 474
Corel Update application, 477
Corel Web site submenu
   (Netscape Navigator), 43

504 CorelCENTRAL

CorelCENTRAL, 9, 337
   Address Book. *See* Address
      Book
   calendar, 338-339
      default calendar, 350
      desktop, 338-339
      events, 340-344
      filters, 347-348
      Find tool, 347
      linking events/tasks,
         348-349
      publishing to the Web,
         462-463
      records, locating, 346-348
      starting, 338
      tasks, 344-349
      turning events into tasks,
         350
   overview, 15
correcting erroneous data
   (spreadsheets), 216
Create Data File dialog box, 178
Create Table dialog box, 132
Create/Modify Series dialog box
   (Quattro Pro 9), 215
cropping images (Presentations),
   330
cursors
   red cursor box (Reveal
      Codes), 83
   Shadow Cursor, 79-80
      customizing, 91
custom address fields (Address
   Book), creating, 357, 364
custom entries (Address Book),
   creating, 357
custom SpeedFormat designs,
   creating, 260-261
custom styles (spreadsheets),
   creating, 255-257
Customize Settings dialog box, 89
Customize Settings window, 39
customizing
   Application Bar, 41
   Corel Linux Desktop, 476
   project templates (Quattro
      Pro), 254-255
   Quattro Pro 9, 198, 203-204
   slideshows (Presentations),
      310-311
   toolbars, 38-39
   WordPerfect, 76
      bar views, 78-79
      document views, 78
      file settings, 87-89
      Hidden Text, 84-85
      menu settings, 85, 87
      Reveal Codes, 81-84
      Settings dialog box, 77

      Shadow Cursor, 79-80, 91
      Show Paragraphs view, 80
      toolbars, 89-90
      View menu, 77
cut and paste
   clipboard, 61
   deleting selected items, 60-61
   moving items, 60-61, 70

D

data
   cells, formatting, 202
   entering into documents, 58
   labeling, 196
   organizing, 196
   spreadsheet data
      collecting, 213
      correcting data entry
         mistakes, 216
      entering, 213-216
      formulas, 196
      label syntax, 197
      labels, 196
      manipulating, 196-197
      typos, 197
      value syntax, 197
      values, 196
   transfering between applica-
      tions, 17
data charts (Presentations), 288,
   316-322
   creating, 316
   Data Chart Gallery, 317-318
   datasheets, 318-320
   entering data, 318-320
   exporting data, 322
   labels, adding, 322
   layout, 320
   legends, adding, 321-322
   saving, 322
   titles and subtitles, adding,
      321
data files (merge documents)
   creating, 177-182
      CorelCENTRAL Address
         Book, 182
      entering data manually,
         180-181
      Merge Bar, 180-181
      Quick Data Entry form,
         179
   merge codes, 189
   merging with form files, 186
data models (forms), 424-425
data sources (merge documents)
   building, 177-182
      CorelCENTRAL Address
         Book, 182

      entering data manually,
         180-181
      Merge Bar, 180-181
      Quick Data Entry form, 179
database objects, 372-375
database programs, 370
Database Templates icon
   (Paradox), 376
databases, 370-371
   aliases, setting, 380-382
   creating, 386-387
   database objects, 372-375
   database templates, 376
   desktop, 377
   fields, 370
   flat-file databases, 370
   forms, 373
   indexes, 373
   interface, 375-376
   keys, 373
   Paradox Experts, 376
   PerfectExpert, 377-378
   preferences, setting, 380
   private directory, 379
   Project Viewer, 378
   publishing to the Web,
      464-466
   queries, 375
   records, 370
   relational databases, 370-371
   reports, 374
   sample database, 371
   starting, 375
   support for databases
      created in Windows, 382
   tables, 372, 388
      adding data, 408-409
      child tables, 402
      copying fields to files, 412
      creating with Field Roster,
         389-394
      creating with Table
         Expert, 388-389
      creating with Visual
         Database Designer, 402
      deleting data, 409
      editing, 394
      editing data, 409-410
      entering data, 417
      field types, 390-391
      field view, 410
      graphics, inserting,
         410-411
      horizontal scroll lock, 407
      key fields, designating,
         391-392
      linking with Visual
         Database Designer, 400
      locating data, 412-415

memo view, 410-411
memos, inserting, 410-411
navigating, 407
opening in table view, 406
parent tables, 402
passwords, setting, 398-399
persistent field view, 410
pictures, creating, 393-394
referential integrity, 399
secondary indexes, creating, 395-396
sorting data, 415-416
switching between edit and view modes, 408
table lookups, creating, 396-398
validity checks, 392-393
tutorial, 376
Visual Database Designer, 376
working directory, setting, 378-379
datasheets (data charts), 318-320
default calendar (CorelCENTRAL), 350
default document folder, customizing, 88
default file format, customizing, 88
Default validity check (tables), 393
Delete dialog box, 237
deleting
  aliases in Paradox, 382
  cell contents
    spreadsheets, 234
    tables, 139
  columns, 143
  data from database tables, 409
  desktop shortcuts, 47
  events (CorelCENTRAL calendar), 343
  links (CorelCENTRAL calendar), 349
  selected items, 60-61
  slides from Slide Outliner, 300
  spreadsheet cells, 237-238
    contents, 234-236
    formatting, 235
  tables, 139
delimiters, 358
delivered forms, 429-430
Demote button (Property bar outline mode), 122
Design Layout dialog box (Paradox), 426

Design Object toolbar (Paradox), 427
design objects, adding to forms, 427-429
Design Window (Paradox), 426-429
  Design Object toolbar, 427
desktop shortcuts
  creating, 32-33
  deleting, 47
  editing, 47
desktops
  Corel Linux Desktop, 473-475
    customizing, 476
  CorelCENTRAL calendar desktop, 338-339
  Paradox desktop, 377
  Presentations desktop, 280-282
    drawing window, 281, 292
    menus, 281
    PerfectExpert, 282
    toolbars, 281
  Slide Editor, 281
destinations for charts, specifying, 269
detail tables, 423
dialog boxes
  Active Cells, 226, 262
  Application Bar Settings, 41
  Associate, 183
  Associate Form and Data, 183
  BitStream FontTastic Font Installer, 99
  Box Position, 157
  Branch Layout (Presentations), 323
  Choose a Directory, 88
  Column Border/Fill, 142
  Columns, 141-142
  Create Data File, 178
  Create Table, 132
  Create/Modify Series (Quattro Pro 9), 215
  Customize Settings, 89
  Delete, 237
  Design Layout (Paradox), 426
  Edit – New Event, 340
  Edit – New Task, 344
  Environment Settings, 86
  Export (Address Book), 360
  Field Mapping (Address Book), 359
  File Settings, 87-89
  Filter Event list, 348
  Find, 347, 361
  Find and Replace (Paradox), 414
  Font, 256

Font Properties, 85, 96-98
Footnote/Endnote, 119
Functions (Quattro Pro 9), 221
Go To, 207
Headers/Footers, 118
HTML Document Properties (Internet Publisher), 443-445
Hyperlink Properties (Internet Publisher), 446
Image Settings, 162
Import
  Address Book, 359
  Presentations, 319-320
Insert Columns/Rows, 138
Insert Field Name or Number, 184
Insert Merge Codes, 189
Keyboard Shortcuts, 173
Line Spacing, 100
Locate Value (Paradox), 413
Merge, 177-178
New Slide, 299
Nickname, 32-33
Object Properties (Presentations), 327
Open File, 55
Page Setup, 105-106
Paste Special, 235
PerfectExpert, 44, 282
Perform Merge, 186
Play Macro, 170-171
Preferences (Paradox), 380
Print Spreadsheet, 242-246
Printer Properties, 68-69
Properties for Table Format, 137
Publish to HTML (Internet Publisher), 450
Publish to Internet (Quattro Pro), 456-457
QuickCorrect, 113
Record Macro, 174
Repeat Event, 342
Restructure (Paradox), 394
Run, 31
Run command, 198
Save As, 55
Save File, 53-54
Scrapbook Item Properties, 151
Select Macro, 172-173
Select Page Numbering Format, 117
Settings, 77, 173
  menu settings, customizing, 86

Shading, 256
Show on the Go, 311
Slide Properties
   (Presentations), 306-307
Sort Table (Paradox), 416
Sound, 309
SpeedFormat, 259-260
Spreadsheet Page Setup,
   243-246, 265
Styles, 255
Tab Set, 102
Table Expert (Paradox), 389
Toolbar Options, 89
Undo/Redo History, 62
WordPerfect 9 Print, 66
directories, 50
disk drives, 55-56
display sequence, setting for
   slideshows, 307
Display Settings, 475
displaying
   formulas, 203
   information about cells, 201
   PerfectExpert in Paradox, 378
displays
   notebooks, editing, 203
   Quattro Pro 9, 198
documents. *See also* files
   columns, 140-143
      Columns dialog box,
         141-142
      comparing to tables, 130
      creating, 140
      deleting, 143
      formatting, 143
      moving around in, 142
      newspaper columns, 140
      parallel columns, 140
   comments, 119-120
   creating, 52-54
   data, entering, 58
   footnotes/endnotes, 119
   formatting
      fonts, 94-100
      paragraphs, 100-107
      QuickFormat, 109
      QuickStyle, 108
      styles, 107-108
   graphics
      attributes, 162
      color elements, 161-162
      file locations, 154
      flipping, 159
      graphic boxes, 148-149
      grouping, 163
      Image Tools, 158-163
      Insert command, 149
      inserting, 148-154

layering, 163-164
moving, 159
PerfectExpert dialog
   boxes, 166
repositioning, 157
resizing, 155-157
rotating, 159
Scrapbook, 149-154
Selected Image Property
   Bar, 164-166
watermarks, 166
Zoom tools, 160-161
headers/footers, 118
importing files, 55
install.log, 474
merge documents, 177
   CorelCENTRAL Address
      Book, 182
   data sources, building,
      177-182
   envelope merge, 186-188
   form files, creating,
      182-185
   Merge Bar, 180-181
   merge codes, 189
   merging data files with
      form files, 186
   Quick Data Entry form,
      179
moving items, 59-61
   copy and paste, 61
   cut and paste, 60-61, 70
   drag and drop, 59
navigating long documents,
   123-125
   AutoScroll, 124
   Browse Forward and
      Back buttons, 124-125
   QuickFind buttons, 125
opening, 54-55
outlining, 121-123
page numbers, 117-118
   supressing page number-
      ing on first page, 126
printing, 66-70
   preview, 21
   Print Preview feature, 70
   print settings, 68-69
   printer configuration,
      67-68
proofreading
   grammar tools, 115-116
   spelling tools, 112-115
redo feature, 61-63
saving, 52-54
   to floppy disk drives,
      55-56

as HTML file, 441
naming conventions, 52-53
Save File dialog box, 53-54
scrollbar navigation, 64-66
selecting items, 58-59
Speedlinks, 451-452
symbols, inserting, 126
tables
   calculations, 134-136
   cell contents, deleting, 139
   cell selection, 132-133
   cells, 130
   columns, deleting, 139
   columns, inserting, 138
   comparing to columns,
      130
   configuring outer dimen-
      sions, 144
   creating, 131-132
   deleting, 139
   formatting, 136-137
   headers, creating, 137, 144
   inputting data, 134
   rows, deleting, 139
   rows, inserting, 138
text, entering, 58
translating between plat-
   forms, 10
undo feature, 61-63
Web documents
   bookmarks, creating,
      446-447
   creating, 443
   fonts, changing, 444
   forms, creating, 449-450
   graphics, inserting, 447
   hyperlinks, creating, 446
   lists, creating, 445
   properties, setting,
      443-445
   publishing to Web sites,
      450
   tables, inserting, 448-449
   text colors, setting, 443
   titles, creating, 445
WordPerfect 9 documents,
   inserting Quattro Pro 9
   spreadsheets, 228-229
Zoom feature, 63
Draft command (View menu), 203
Draft view (document views), 78
drag and drop
   moving cells, 248
   moving items, 59
drawing window (Presentations
   desktop), 281
   QuickPlay, 292

files 507

drawings, 149
    Presentations, 279
drives (floppy disk drives), 55-56

E

earlier versions of Quattro Pro, opening, 195
Edit – New Event dialog box, 340
Edit – New Task dialog box, 344
Edit Attributes button (Image Tools), 162
Edit Contents button (Image Tools), 163
Edit menu commands, 207
edit mode (database tables), 408
Edit Sheet Tab command, 201
editing
    Address Book entries, 357
    charts, 271-272
    database table data, 409-410
    desktop shortcuts, 47
    events (CorelCENTRAL calendar), 344
    forms with Design Window, 426-429
    graphics, 154-166
        attributes, 162
        in Bitmap Editor (Presentations), 330, 333
        color elements, 161-162
        flipping, 159
        grouping, 163
        Image Tools, 158-163
        layering, 163-164
        moving, 159
        PerfectExpert, 166
        repositioning, 157
        resizing, 155-157
        rotating, 159
        Selected Image Property Bar, 164-166
        Zoom tools, 160-161
    links (CorelCENTRAL calendar), 349
    macros, 176-177
    notebooks
        displays, 203
        sheet default names, 201
        in Print Preview mode, 21
    records (database tables), 417
    slide views, 290-293
    spreadsheet cells
        clearing all formatting, 235-236
        columns, resizing, 241
        contents, deleting, 234-236
        deleting, 237-238
        drag and drop, 248
        inserting cells, 238-240
        replacing contents, 233-234
        transposing contents, 241
    styles (spreadsheets), 257
    tables (Paradox), 394
    tasks (CorelCENTRAL calendar), 346
    toolbars, 38-39
electronic spreadsheet applications, 194
elements (notebooks), 196
endnotes/footnotes, 119
entering form data, 429
entries (Address Book), 355-357
    adding, 357
    custom entries, creating, 357
    editing, 357
    Group entry type, 356
    Organization entry type, 355
    Person entry type, 355
    Resource entry type, 355
envelope merge, 186-188
Environment Settings dialog box, 86
equal symbol (=), 197
event list (CorelCENTRAL calendar)
    sorting, 347-348
    tasks, adding, 344
events (CorelCENTRAL calendar), 340
    alarms, setting, 343
    all-day events, 341
    creating, 340
    deleting, 343
    editing, 344
    linking, 348-349
    repeating events, 341-343
    scheduling, 340-344
    turning into tasks, 350
events calendars, publishing to the Web, 462-463
Export dialog box (Address Book), 360
exporting
    address books to ASCII delimited text files, 360
    data from data charts (Presentations), 322
Extensible Markup Language (XML), 23

F

Field Mapping dialog box (Address Book), 359
Field Roster (Paradox), creating tables, 389-394
    field types, 390-391
    key fields, designating, 391-392
    pictures, 393-394
    validity checks, 392-393
field view (database tables), 410
fields
    Address Book
        applying filters, 361-364
        customizing, 357, 364
    database tables
        copying to files, 412
        editing data, 409-410
        entering data, 417
        field types, 390-391
        key fields, designating, 391-392
        locating, 412
        memo fields, Find-and-Replace command, 414
        pictures, creating, 393-394
        validity checks, 392-393
        values, 412-414
    databases, 370
file extensions, .QPW, 194
file formats, customizing default file format, 88
file locations, importing graphics from, 154
File Manager, 51, 474
File Manager button, 474
file settings, customizing, 87-89
File Settings dialog box, 87-89
file system (Linux), 50-51
filenames, 52-53
files. *See also* documents
    ASCII delimited text files, exporting address books to, 360
    copying database table fields to, 412
    data files (merge documents)
        CorelCENTRAL Address Book, 182
        creating, 177-182
        entering data manually, 180-181
        Merge Bar, 180-181
        merge codes, 189
        merging with form files, 186
        Quick Data Entry form, 179
    form files (merge documents)
        creating, 182-185
        merging with data files, 186
    graphic files, saving slideshows as, 312-313

files

HTML files
   publishing slideshows as, 312
   saving documents as, 441
importing into documents, 55
install.log, 474
MIDI files, adding to slideshows, 309
moving items, 59-61
   copy and paste, 61
   cut and paste, 60-61, 70
   drag and drop, 59
naming conventions, 52-53
opening, 54-55
PDF files, saving slideshows as, 312
PowerPoint files, importing into Presentations, 313
selecting items, 58-59
WAV files, adding to slideshows, 309
Fill button (Image Tools), 162
fill color (spreadsheets), 263
Fill Color button (Quattro Pro Property Bar), 263
fills, adding to images (Presentations), 327-328
Filter Event list dialog box, 348
Filter feature (Address Book), 361-364
filters
   Address Book
      applying, 361-364
      operators, 362
   CorelCENTRAL calendar, 347-348
Find and Replace dialog box (Paradox), 414
Find dialog box, 347, 361
Find feature (Address Book), 360-361
Find tool (CorelCENTRAL calendar), 347
Flash Player (Macromedia), 11
flat-file databases, 370
flip buttons (Image Tools), 159
Flip Left/Right button (Selected Image Property Bar), 165
Flip Top/Bottom button (Selected Image Property Bar), 165
flipping graphics, 159
floppy disk drives, 55-56
flyouts, 281
folders, 50
   default document folder, customizing, 88
Font dialog box, 256

Font Properties dialog box, 85, 96-98
fonts
   formatting, 94-98
      color, 95
      font face, 94
      Font Properties dialog box, 96-98
      position, 97
      Property Bar, 94-95
      QuickFonts, 96
      Relative Size option, 98
      shading, 97
      size, 95
      styles, 95
      underlining, 98
   installing with BitStream FontTastic Font Installer, 99-100
   Web documents, 444
footers, 118
   inserting into spreadsheets, 264-265
   printing spreadsheets, 243-244
Footnote/Endnote dialog box, 119
footnotes/endnotes, 119
Form Expert (Paradox), 422-423
form files (merge documents)
   creating, 182-185
   merging with data files, 186
Format menu commands, 201, 204
Format toolbar, Page Margins button, 106
formatting
   columns, 143
   fonts, 94-100
      color, 95
      font face, 94
      Font Properties dialog box, 96-98
      installing with BitStream FontTastic Font Installer, 99-100
      position, 97
      Property Bar, 94-95
      QuickFonts, 96
      Relative Size option, 98
      shading, 97
      size, 95
      styles, 95
      underlining, 98
   HMTL code manually (Web Editor), 452
   notebooks, 204
   selections, 204
   cells (spreadsheets)
      clearing, 235-236
      data, 202

QuickFormat, 258-259, 273
SpeedFormat, 259-261
paragraphs, 100-107
   indents, setting, 101, 103-104, 109
   justification, 106-107
   line spacing, 100-101
   page margins, setting, 104-106
   tabs, setting, 101-104
QuickFormat, 109
spreadsheets, 204, 225-228
   aligning text, 226
   numeric formatting, 226
   Quickfit feature, 227-228
   RealTime Preview feature, 225
styles, 107-108
   QuickStyle, 108
tables, 136-137
formatting tools (Quattro Pro), 251-252
forms, 419-426
   creating
      with Form Expert, 422-423
      with Quick Form, 421
      for Web pages (Internet Publisher), 449-450
   data models, creating, 424-425
   database objects, 373-374
   delivered forms, 429-430
   design objects, adding, 427-429
   detail tables, 423
   entering data, 429
   fine-tuning in Design Window, 426-429
   master tables, 423
   multitable forms, creating, 424-426
   one-table forms, creating, 422-423
   printing, 430
   publishing to HTML (Paradox), 466
   records, printing, 430
   style sheets, 423
   two-table forms, creating, 423-424
   viewing data, 429
Formula Marker feature (Quattro Pro 9), 217
formulas, 196, 216-225
   absolute cell addresses, 223-225
   applying to data in datasheets, 320

icons 509

arithmetic operators, 218
automatic totaling feature, 223
basic formulas, 220
cells, 200
displaying, 203
entering, 220
Formula Marker feature, 217
functions, 221-222
hiding, 203
multiplication formulas, 218
order of precedence, 219
QuickFunction button, 222, 229
structuring, 218-219
table calculations, 135-136
versus values, 196
Formulas command (View menu), 203
Forward browse button, 21
forward slash (/), root directories, 50
freezes (applications), troubleshooting, 33
functions, 221-222
Functions dialog box (Quattro Pro 9), 221

G

GIMP, 9
GNOME, Main Menu, 30
Go To command (Edit menu), 207
Go To dialog box, 207
Go To keys (SpeedKeys), 308
gradients, adding to images (Presentations), 327
grammar tools, 115-116
Grammar-As-You-Go, 115
Grammatik, 115
graphical user interface (GUI), 29
graphics. *See also* clipart; images
  adding to Scrapbook, 150-151
  adding to slides (Slide Editor), 303-304
  bitmap images, 149
  editing, 154-166
    attributes, 162
    color elements, 161-162
    flipping, 159
    grouping, 163
    Image Tools, 158-163
    layering, 163-164
    moving, 159
    PerfectExpert, 166
    repositioning, 157
    resizing, 155-157
    rotating, 159

Selected Image Property Bar, 164-166
    Zoom tools, 160-161
  inserting into database tables, 411
  inserting into documents, 148-154
    from file locations, 154
    graphic boxes, 148-149
    Insert command, 149
    from Scrapbook, 149-150
  inserting into Web pages (Internet Publisher), 447
  managing within the Scrapbook, 151-154
  object-oriented drawings, 149
  saving slideshows as, 312-313
  slide objects, 289
  vector-based drawings, 149
  watermarks, 166
Graphics button, 164-165
GraphOn Bridges, 11
Gray Scale tool (Presentations), 328
gridlines (Presentations), 326
Group entry type (Address Book), 356
grouping graphics, 163
  Selected Image Property Bar, 164-166
GUI (graphical user interface), 29
guides (Presentations), 326

H

handles
  resizing handles, 155-157
  rotate handles, 159
hardware requirements (installing WordPerfect Office 2000), 2-3
headers, 118
  inserting into spreadsheets, 264-265
  printing spreadsheets, 243-244
  table headers, creating, 137, 144
Headers/Footers dialog box, 118
Help button, 475-477
Help manual, 477
Help menu, 41
help systems, 41-47
  Netscape Navigator, 41-43
  PerfectExpert, 43-47
    PerfectExpert window, 45-47
  Projects, 44
Help Topics
  Netscape Navigator, 42-43
  Paradox, 434

Hidden Text, 84-85
Hide Bars command (View menu), 79
Hide Family button (Property bar outline mode), 123
hiding
  Application Bar, 47
  formulas, 203
home directories, 50
horizontal scroll lock (database tables), 407
HTML (Hypertext Markup Language), 440
  code, formatting manually (Web Editor), 452
  files
    publishing slideshows as, 312
    saving documents as, 441
  publishing
    CorelCENTRAL Calendars, 462-463
    Paradox databases, 464-466
    Presentations, 458-461
    Quattro Pro, 456-458
  tables, importing into Paradox databases, 466
HTML Document Properties dialog box (Internet Publisher), 443-445
HTML Import Expert (Paradox), 466
HTML Report Expert (Paradox), 464-466
HTML Table Expert (Paradox), 464-466
Hyperlink button (Selected Image Property Bar), 166
Hyperlink Properties dialog box (Internet Publisher), 446
hyperlinks
  creating
    Internet Publisher, 446
    Quattro Pro notebooks, 457-458
  Speedlinks, 451-452

I

iconify box (windows), 476
icons
  Database Templates (Paradox), 376
  Link (CorelCENTRAL calendar), 349
  navigation (PerfectExpert), 301
  New Database (Paradox), 376

Open Database (Paradox), 376
Paradox Experts, 376
Quattro Pro 9, 198
Tutorial (Paradox), 376
identifying
    active cells, 200
    active sheets, 201
Image Settings dialog box, 162
Image Tools, 158-163
Image Tools button (Selected Image Property Bar), 165
images, 325. *See also* clipart; graphics
    cropping, 330
    editing in Bitmap Editor, 330, 333
    inserting into slides, 330
    line drawings
        adding, 325-326
        fills, adding, 327-328
        special effects, adding, 328-330
        text, adding, 330
    resizing, 331
    rotating, 331
    shapes
        adding, 325-326
        fills, adding, 327-328
        special effects, adding, 328-330
        text, adding, 330
    skewing, 332
Import Data dialog box (Presentations), 319-320
Import dialog box (Address Book), 359
importing
    addresses (Address Book), 358-359
    datasheets (Presentations), 319
    files into documents, 55
    graphics, 148-154
        from file locations, 154
        from Scrapbook, 149-154
    HTML tables into Paradox databases, 466
    PowerPoint files into Presentations, 313
    spreadsheet data into datasheets (Presentations), 319-320
indents
    automatic first line indents, 109
    setting, 101-104

indexes
    databases, 373
    tables, creating secondary indexes, 395-396
information about cells, displaying, 201
input line (spreadsheets), 201, 234
inputting table data, 134
Insert Columns/Rows dialog box, 138
Insert command, 149
Insert Field Name or Number dialog box, 184
Insert Merge Codes dialog box, 189
inserting
    columns into tables, 138
    rows into tables, 138
    spreadsheet cells, 238-240
install.log document, 474
installing
    fonts with BitStream FontTastic Font Installer, 99-100
    WordPerfect Office 2000, 28
    hardware requirements, 2-3
interfaces
    Address Book, 355-356
    Paradox interface, 375-376
Internet Publisher, 440-441
    Browse the Web button, 451
    saving documents as HTML files, 441
    Web pages
        bookmarks, creating, 446-447
        creating, 443
        fonts, changing, 444
        forms, creating, 449-450
        graphics, inserting, 447
        hyperlinks, creating, 446
        lists, creating, 445
        properties, setting, 443-445
        publishing to Web sites, 450
        tables, inserting, 448-449
        text colors, setting, 443
        titles, creating, 445
Internet Publisher Wizard, 312
Internet publishing
    CorelCENTRAL Calendars, 462-463
    Paradox databases, 464-466
    Presentations, 458-461
        custom layouts, 460-461
        preconfigured layouts, 459

Quattro Pro
    hyperlinks, creating, 457-458
    Publish to HTML tool, 456-457
Invert Colors button (Image Tools), 162

J-K

Jump to Next Selection button (Selected Image Property Bar), 165
Jump to Prior Selection button (Selected Image Property Bar), 165
justification, 106-107
Justification button (Property Bar), 106

K Menu (KDE), 30
Kcmprint printer configuration utility, 68
KDE User Manager, 56
key fields (database tables), designating, 391-392
keyboard
    selecting items, 58-59
    shortcuts, 4, 36
        assigning to macros, 173, 189
        Hide Bars view, 79
        inserting table rows, 138
        Quattro Pro 9, 206
        Spell Checker, 36
        troubleshooting, 91
Keyboard Shortcuts dialog box, 173
keys (databases), 373
keywords, Speedlinks keywords, 451-452
killall –9 wine command, 33

L

label syntax (spreadsheet data), 197
labels
    adding to data charts, 322
    spreadsheet data, 196
    naming, 197
launch commands, 31
launching
    applications
        from Corel Application Starter, 29-30
        desktop shortcuts, 32-33
        Run command, 30-32

Quattro Pro 9, 198
   X Window System, 29
layering graphics, 163-164
layers (slide layers), 285-287
   background layer, 287
   layout layer, 285
layout layer (slides), 285
legends, adding to data charts, 321-322
line breaks, creating (Web Editor), 445
line drawings
   adding to presentations, 325-326
   fills, adding, 327-328
   special effects, adding, 328-330
   text, adding, 330
line spacing, 100-101
Line Spacing dialog box, 100
line-drawing button (Quattro Pro Property Bar), 261
Link icon (CorelCENTRAL calendar), 349
linking
   events/tasks (CorelCENTRAL calendar), 348-349
   tables with Visual Database Designer, 400
links (CorelCENTRAL calendar), 349
Linux
   command-line interface, 3-4
   Corel future plans, 11
   Corel Linux, 471-472
      desktop, 473-476
      Help manual, 477
      logging in, 472
      starting, 472-473
      system updates, 477
      versions, 472
      windows, 475-476
   file system, 50-51
   office suites, 10
   software, 9
   WordPerfect Office 2000, evolution, 18
lists, creating for Web pages, 445
Locate Value dialog box (Paradox), 413
locating
   data (database tables), 412-415
      fields, 412
      records, 412
      values in fields, 412-414
      wildcard symbols, 415
   records (CorelCENTRAL calendar), 346-348

logging in to Corel Linux, 472
long documents, navigating, 123-125
lookups (table lookups), creating, 396-398

M

Macro Editor Bar, 175
Macromedia Flash Player, 11
macros, 18, 169-177
   adding to toolbar, 171-172
   Corel macros, 170-171
   creating, 173-176
   editing, 176-177
   keyboard shortcuts, assigning, 173, 189
   macro tool, 170
   PerfectScript, 170
   playing, 171
   recording, 173-176
Macros Online command (Tools menu), 171
Magnifier button (Image Tools), 160
Main Menu (GNOME), 30
man (manual) pages, 50
manipulating data (spreadsheets), 196-197
manually formatting HTML code (Web Editor), 452
margins
   printing spreadsheets, 245
   setting, 104-106
Master Gallery (Presentations), 284-285
master passwords (tables), 398
master tables, 423
master templates (Presentations), 298
Matt's Script Archive Web site, 450
Max validity check (tables), 393
maximize box (windows), 476
memo fields (database tables), 414
memo view (database tables), 410-411
memory (system memory), freeing up, 295
memos, inserting into database tables, 410-411
menu commands, 4
menus, 34-36
   Help menu, 41
   keyboard shortcuts, 36
   PerfectExpert menus, 301
   Presentations menus, 281
   settings, customizing, 85, 87
   Tools menu, 35

View menu, 77
   Application Bar command, 79
   bar views, 78-79
   document views, 78
   Hidden Text command, 84-85
   Hide Bars command, 79
   Reveal Codes command, 81-84
   Ruler command, 79
   Shadow Cursor command, 79-80, 91
   Show Paragraphs View command, 80
   Toolbar command, 78
Merge Bar, entering data into data files, 180-181
merge codes, 189
Merge dialog box, 177-178
merge documents, 177
   data files
      merge codes, 189
      merging with form files, 186
   data sources
      building, 177-182
      CorelCENTRAL Address Book, 182
      entering data manually, 180-181
      Merge Bar, 180-181
      Quick Data Entry form, 179
   envelope merge, 186-188
   form files
      creating, 182-185
      merging with data files, 186
Microsoft Office 97, migrating to WordPerfect Office 2000, 20
MIDI files, adding to slideshows, 309
Min validity check (tables), 393
minus symbol (-), 197
modes (Quattro Pro 9), identifying, 202
Modify button (Property bar outline mode), 123
mouse
   drag and drop, moving items, 59
   selecting items, 58-59
   Shadow Cursor, 79-80
      customizing, 91
Move Back One Layer button (Selected Image Property Bar), 166
Move button (Image Tools), 159

Move Down button (Property bar outline mode), 123
Move Forward One Layer button (Selected Image Property Bar), 166
Move Up button (Property bar outline mode), 122
moving
   in columns, 142
   graphics, 159
   items, 59-61
      copy and paste, 61
      cut and paste, 60-61, 70
      drag and drop, 59
multiple cells, selecting, 205
multiple slide shows, viewing (Presentations), 293
multiplication formulas, 218
multitable forms, creating, 424-426
My Home nickname, 473

N

named settings, printing spreadsheets, 246
names
   labels, 197
   sheets, editing defaults, 201
naming conventions (documents), 52-53
navigating
   database tables, 407
   long documents, 123-124
      AutoScroll, 124
      Browse Forward and Back buttons, 124-125
      QuickFind buttons, 125
   notebooks, 204-207
      between sheets (Quattro Pro 9), 207
   spreadsheets, 204-207
navigation icons (PerfectExpert), 301
negative numbers, 197
Netscape Navigator, 41-43
   Corel Web site submenu, 43
   Help Topics, 42-43
New Database icon (Paradox), 376
New Slide dialog box, 299
newspaper columns, 140
Nickname dialog box, 32-33
nicknames, 473
Notebook command (Format menu), 204
Notebook toolbar (Quattro Pro), SpeedFormat button, 259

notebooks, 194-196
   displays, editing, 203
   elements, 196
   formatting, 204
   hyperlinks, creating, 457-458
   navigating, 204-207
   Publish to HTML tool, 456-457
Numbering button (toolbar), 121
numbering pages, 117-118
   suppressing page on first page, 126
numbers, 197
numeric formatting (spreadsheets), 226

O

Object Properties dialog box (Presentations), 327
object-oriented drawings, 149
objects
   database objects, 372-375
   design objects, adding to forms, 427-429
   slide objects (Presentations), 287-289
      data charts, 288
      graphics, 289
      organizational charts, 289
      text objects, 287-288
   spreadsheets, viewing, 203
Objects command (View menu), 203
Objects sheets, 194, 197
   activating, 207
office suites, 10
one-table forms, creating, 422-423
online help, 477
Open Database icon (Paradox), 376
Open File dialog box, 55
opening
   documents, 54-55
   earlier versions of Quattro Pro, 195
   Project Viewer (Paradox), 378
   projects with aliases (Paradox), 382
   tables in table view (Paradox), 406
operating systems (Corel Linux), 471-472
   desktop, 473-476
   Help manual, 477
   logging in, 472
   starting, 472-473
   system updates, 477

   versions, 472
   windows, 475-476
operators
   arithmetic operators, 218
   filter operators, 362
   order of precedence, 219
order of precedence (formulas), 219
organization charts (Presentations), 323-324
Organization entry type (Address Book), 355
organizational charts (slide objects), 289
organizing data, 196
outline buttons (Property bar), 122-123
outlining documents, 121-123
outlining slideshows (Presentations), 298-302
   PerfectExpert, 300-302
   Slide Outliner, 298-300

P

Page Break command (View menu), 203
Page command (View menu), 203
Page Margins button (Format toolbar), 106
page margins, setting, 104-106
page numbers, 117-118
   suppressing page numbering on first page, 126
Page Setup (printing spreadsheets), 243-246
Page Setup dialog box, 105-106
Page view (document views), 78
paint programs, Presentations, 280
palettes, 161-162
Panel, 474
paper orientation (printing spreadsheets), 243
paper size (printing spreadsheets), 243
Paradox, 372-375
   aliases
      creating, 381
      deleting, 382
      opening projects, 382
      setting, 380-382
   database objects, 372-375
   database templates, 376
   databases. *See* databases
   desktop, 377
   forms, 373, 420-426
      data models, creating, 424-425

Presentations 513

delivered forms, 429-430
design objects, adding, 427-429
detail tables, 423
entering data, 429
fine-tuning in Design Window, 426-429
Form Expert, 422-423
master tables, 423
multitable forms, creating, 424-426
one-table forms, creating, 422-423
printing, 430
Quick Form, 421
records, printing, 430
style sheets, 423
two-table forms, creating, 423-424
viewing data, 429
Help Topics, 434
HTML Import Expert, 466
indexes, 373
interface, 375-376
keys, 373
overview, 16
Paradox Experts, 376
PerfectExpert, 377-378
Picture Assistant, 393-394
preferences, setting, 380
private directory, 379
Project Viewer, 378
publishing to the Web, 464-466
queries, 375, 432-434
    Query Expert, 433-434
    relational queries, 434
reports, 374, 430-432
    Quick Report tool, 430-431
    Report Expert, 431-432
sample database, 371
starting, 375
support for databases created in Windows, 382
tables, 372
tutorial, 376
Visual Database Designer, 376
Welcome Expert, 22
working directory, setting, 378-379
Paradox Experts icon, 376
paragraphs, formatting, 100-107
    indents, setting, 101-104, 109
    justification, 106-107
    line spacing, 100-101
    page margins, setting, 104-106
    tabs, setting, 101-104
parallel columns, 140

parent tables, 402
partitions (Windows partitions), accessing, 57
passwords
    Corel Linux user passwords, changing, 70
    Quattro Pro, 249
    setting for tables, 398-399
Paste Special dialog box, 235
Paste Special feature (Quattro Pro), 234-235
patterns, adding to images (Presentations), 327
PDF files, saving slideshows as, 312
PerfectExpert, 43-47, 282, 300-302, 377-378
    accessing, 70
    displaying in Paradox, 378
    editing graphics, 166
    menus, 301
    navigation icons, 301
    new files, creating, 282
    PerfectExpert window, 45-47
    Projects, 44, 252-255, 273
    projects
        starting, 252-254
        templates, customizing, 254-255
    Tools Palette, 302
perfectexpert command, 70
PerfectExpert dialog box, 44, 282
PerfectScript, 170
Perform Merge dialog box, 186
persistent field view (database tables), 410
Person entry type (Address Book), 355
photographs, 149
photos, inserting into documents, 149-150
Picture Assistant (Paradox), 393-394
pictures (table fields), creating, 393-394
PIMs (Personal Information Managers), 15
    failure of CorelCENTRAL 8, 17
Play Macro dialog box, 170-171
playing macros, 171
plug-ins, Show It!, 312
plus symbol (+), 197
portable slideshows (Show on the Go), 311-312
positioning charts, 270-271
positioning text, 97
positive numbers, 197

PowerPoint files, importing into Presentations, 313
preferences (Paradox), setting, 380
Preferences dialog box (Paradox), 380
Presentations, 278-293
    Bitmap Editor, 330, 333
    data charts, 316-322
        creating, 316
        Data Chart Gallery, 317-318
        datasheets, 318-320
        entering data, 318-320
        exporting data, 322
        labels, adding, 322
        layout, 320
        legends, adding, 321-322
        saving, 322
        titles and subtitles, adding, 321
    desktop, 280-282
        drawing window, 281, 292
        menus, 281
        toolbars, 281
    drawings, 279
    gridlines, 326
    guides, 326
    images, 325
        cropping, 330
        editing in Bitmap Editor, 330, 333
        inserting from external sources, 330
        resizing, 331
        rotating, 331
        skewing, 332
    importing PowerPoint files, 313
    line drawings
        adding, 325-326
        fills, adding, 327-328
        special effects, adding, 328-330
        text, adding, 330
    organization charts, 323-324
    overview, 14
    as a paint program, 280
    PerfectExpert, 282, 300-302
        menus, 301
        navigation icons, 301
        new files, creating, 282
        Tools Palette, 302
    QuickPlay, 292
    saving slides as graphics, 322
    shapes
        adding, 325-326
        fills, adding, 327-328

514 Presentations

special effects, adding, 328-330
text, adding, 330
slide editing views, 290-293
   Slide Editor, 291-293
   Slide Outliner, 290-291
   Slide Sorter, 292
Slide Editor, 281, 302-305
   graphics, adding, 303-304
   speaker notes, adding, 304-305
   text objects, adding, 303
slide layers, 285-287
   background layer, 287
   layout layer, 285
slide objects, 287-289
   data charts, 288
   graphics, 289
   organizational charts, 289
   text, 287-288
Slide Outliner, 298-300
slide projects, 283-285
   Master Gallery, 284-285
   transitions, 283
Slide Properties dialog box, 306-307
   Display Sequence tab, 307
   Transitions tab, 306-307
Slide Sorter, 305
slideshows, 279
   building slides with Slide Editor, 302-305
   customizing, 310-311
   master templates, 298
   outlining, 298-302
   presentation effects, adding, 306-309
   publishing as HTML files, 312
   publishing to the Web, 458-461
   QuickShows, creating, 310-311
   rearranging slides in Slide Sorter, 305
   saving as graphics, 312-313
   saving in PDF format, 312
   Show on the Go (portable slideshows), 311-312
   Slide Outliner, 298-300
   speeding up, 295
   starting, 278-279
   troubleshooting, 333
presentations command, 278
previewing documents, 21
print margins (spreadsheets), 245
Print Preview feature, 70
Print Preview mode, 244, 247-248

print scaling (spreadsheets), 246
Print Spreadsheet dialog box, 242-246
Printer Properties dialog box, 68-69
printers, configuring, 67-68
printing
   documents, 66-70
      Print Preview feature, 70
      print settings, 68-69
      printer configuration, 67-68
   forms, 430
   previewing, 70, 244, 247-248
   records (forms), 430
   spreadsheets, 242-248
      headers and footers, 243-244
      named settings, 246
      options, 246
      page breaks, 245
      Page Setup, 243-246
      paper orientation, 243
      paper size, 243
      print margins, 245
      Print Preview mode, 244, 247-248
      print scaling, 246
      Print Spreadsheet dialog box, 242-246
private directory (Paradox), 379
Program Manager, 18
program window, 76
programs. *See also* applications
   database programs, 370
   freezes, troubleshooting, 33
   launching
      from Corel Application Starter, 29-30
      desktop shortcuts, 32-33
      Run command, 30-32
   quitting, 33
project aliases (Paradox), 381
Project Viewer (Paradox), 378
projects
   opening with aliases (Paradox), 382
   Quattro Pro projects, 252-255, 273
      starting, 252-254
      templates, customizing, 254-255
Promote button (Property bar outline mode), 122
Prompt-As-You-Go, 112-114
proofreading documents
   grammar tools, 115-116
   spelling tools, 112-115
properties (Web pages), 443-445

Properties for Table Format dialog box, 137
Property Bar, 40, 202, 281
   Fill Color button, 263
   font controls, 94-95
   Graphics button, 164
   Justification button, 106
   line-drawing button, 261
   outline buttons, 122-123
   Rotate Cell button, 144
   Style drop-down box, 108
   Text Color button, 263
public aliases (Paradox), 381
Publish to HTML dialog box (Internet Publisher), 450
Publish to Internet dialog box (Quattro Pro), 456-457
publishing slideshows as HTML files, 312
publishing to the Web
   CorelCENTRAL Calendars, 462-463
   Paradox databases, 464-466
   Presentations, 458-461
   Quattro Pro, 456-458
   Web pages, 450

Q

.QPW file extension, 194
Quattro Pro, 194
   customizing, 198, 203-204
   display, 198
   icon, 198
   keyboard shortcuts, 206
   launching, 198
   modes, identifying, 202
   notebooks
      hyperlinks, creating, 457-458
      Publish to HTML tool, 456-457
   overview, 13
   sheets, navigating between, 207
   SpeedFunctions, 21
   spreadsheets. *See* spreadsheets
quattropro command, 198
queries, 375, 419, 432-434
   creating with Query Expert, 433-434
   relational queries, 434
Query Expert (Paradox), 433-434
Quick Data Entry form, 179
Quick Form (Paradox), 421
Quick Report tool (Paradox), 430-431
Quick Tab button, 207

QuickCorrect, 113
QuickFill feature (Quattro Pro 9), 215-216
QuickFind buttons, 123-125
Quickfit feature (Quattro Pro 9), 227-228
QuickFonts, 96
QuickFormat, 109, 258-259, 273
QuickFunction button (Quattro Pro 9), 222, 229
QuickPlay (Presentations), 292
QuickShow slideshows, 310-311
QuickStyle, 108
QuickSum, 134-135
QuickTips, 87
QuickType feature (Quattro Pro 9), 214
quitting applications, 33

R

Real-Time Preview, 21, 94-95, 225
Record Macro dialog box, 174
recording macros, 173-176
records
    CorelCENTRAL calendar records, locating, 346-348
    database records, 370
        adding, 409
        deleting, 409
        editing, 417
        locating, 412
    form records, printing, 430
rectangular blocks of cells, selecting, 205
red cursor box (Reveal Codes), 83
redo feature, 61-63
referential integrity (databases), 399
relational databases, 370-371
relational queries, 434
Relative Size option (fonts), 98
Repeat Event dialog box, 342
repeating events (CorelCENTRAL calendar), 341-343
replacing
    spreadsheet cell contents, 233-234
    values in table fields, 414
Report Expert (Paradox), 431-432
reports, 374, 419, 430-432
    creating
        with Quick Report tool, 430-431
        with Report Expert, 431-432
    publishing to HTML, 465

repositioning
    charts, 270-271
    graphics, 157
Reset Attributes button (Image Tools), 163
resizing
    charts, 270-271
    columns (spreadsheets), 241
    graphics, 155-157
    handles, 155-157
    images (Presentations), 331
    windows, 476
Resource entry type (Address Book), 355
Restructure dialog box (Paradox), 394
Reveal Codes, 81-84
    bullets, 82
    code buttons, 83
    customizing, 84
    red cursor box, 83
root directories, 50
Rotate button (Image Tools), 159
Rotate Cell button (Property Bar), 144
rotate handles, 159
rotating graphics, 159
    in Presentations, 331
rows
    activating, 204-205
    cell rows, inserting into spreadsheets, 239-240
    inserting into tables, 138
    selecting, 204
    table rows, deleting, 139
Ruler, tab settings, 101-102
Ruler command (View menu), 79
rules (syntax), 197
Run command dialog box, 198
Run commands, launching programs, 30-32
Run dialog box, 31

S

Save As dialog box, 55
Save File dialog box, 53-54
saving
    data charts (Presentations), 322
    documents, 52-54
        to floppy disk drives, 55-56
        as HTML files, 441
        naming conventions, 52-53
        Save File dialog box, 53-54
    slides as graphics, 322

slideshows
    as graphics, 312-313
    as HTML files, 312
    as PDF files, 312
    spreadsheets as HTML documents, 456-457
scheduling events (CorelCENTRAL calendar), 340-344
    all-day events, 341
    creating new events, 340
    deleting events, 343
    editing events, 344
    event alarms, setting, 343
    repeating events, 341-343
Scrapbook
    adding graphics to, 150-151
    categories, creating, 152-153
    inserting graphics into documents, 149-150
    keywords, entering, 152
    managing graphics, 151-154
    searching graphics, 153-154
Scrapbook Item Properties dialog box, 151
scroll buttons, 207
scrollbars, 64-66
searching
    Address Book (Find feature), 360-361
    CorelCENTRAL calendar
        filters, 347-348
        Find tool, 347
    data in database tables, 412-415
        fields, 412
        records, 412
        values in fields, 412-414
        wildcard symbols, 415
secondary indexes (tables), creating, 395-396
security, table passwords, 398-399
Select All button, 205
Select Macro dialog box, 172-173
Select Page Numbering Format dialog box, 117
Selected Image Property Bar, 164-166
selecting
    cells, 132-133, 204-205
    columns, 204
    items with keyboard/mouse, 58-59
    rows, 204
    toolbars, 37
Selection command (Format menu), 204

selections

selections
  formatting, 204
  undoing, 205
selectors (cells), 200
Set Paragraph Number button
  (Property bar outline mode),
  123
Settings command (Tools menu),
  198, 203
Settings dialog box, 19, 77, 173
  menu settings, customizing, 86
shading (fonts), 97
Shading dialog box, 256
Shadow Cursor, 79-80
  customizing, 91
shapes
  adding to presentations,
    325-326
  fills, adding, 327-328
  special effects, adding,
    328-330
  text, adding, 330
sharing spreadsheets, 195
Sheet command (Format menu),
  201, 204
sheet tabs, 201
sheets
  active, identifying, 201
  default names, editing, 201
  navigating between, 207
shortcut keys, 4
shortcuts
  desktop shortcuts
    creating, 32-33
    deleting, 47
    editing, 47
  keyboard shortcuts, 36
    assigning to macros, 173,
      189
    Hide Bars view, 79
    inserting table rows, 138
    Quattro Pro 9, 206
    Spell Checker, 36
    troubleshooting, 91
Show Family button (Property
  bar outline mode), 123
Show Icons button (Property bar
  outline mode), 123
Show It! plug-in, 312
Show Levels button (Property bar
  outline mode), 123
Show on the Go (portable
  slideshows), 311-312
Show on the Go dialog box, 311
Show Paragraphs View command
  (View menu), 80
Show/Hide Body Text button
  (Property bar outline mode),
  123

single cells, selecting, 204
Size validity check (tables), 392
sizing
  charts, 270-271
  graphics, 155-157
skewing images (Presentations),
  332
Slide Editor (Presentations), 281,
  291, 302-305
  graphics, adding, 303-304
  speaker notes, adding,
    304-305
  text objects, adding, 303
  viewing multiple slideshows,
    293
Slide Outliner (Presentations),
  290-291, 298-300
  adding slides, 299
  deleting slides, 300
  text, adding, 299
  titles, 299
Slide Properties dialog box
  (Presentations), 306-307
Slide Sorter (Presentations), 292,
  305
slides (Presentations)
  adding to Slide Outliner, 299
  creating with Slide Editor,
    302-305
    graphics, adding, 303-304
    speaker notes, adding,
      304-305
    text objects, adding, 303
  data charts, 316-322
    creating, 316
    Data Chart Gallery,
      317-318
    datasheets, 318-320
    entering data, 318-320
    exporting data, 322
    labels, adding, 322
    layout, 320
    legends, adding, 321-322
    saving, 322
    titles and subtitles,
      adding, 321
  deleting from Slide Outliner,
    300
  editing views, 290-293
  images, 325
    cropping, 330
    editing in Bitmap Editor,
      330, 333
    inserting from external
      sources, 330
    resizing, 331
    rotating, 331
    skewing, 332

  layers, 285-287
    background layer, 287
    layout layer, 285
  line drawings
    adding, 325-326
    fills, adding, 327-328
    special effects, adding,
      328-330
    text, adding, 330
  objects, 287-289
    data charts, 288
    graphics, 289
    organizational charts, 289
    text objects, 287-288
  organization charts, 323-324
  presentation effects
    adding, 306-309
    display sequence, 307
    sound, adding, 309
    SpeedKeys, assigning,
      307-308
    transitions, 306-307
  projects, 283-285
    transitions, 283
  rearranging slides in Slide
    Sorter, 305
  saving as a graphic, 322
  shapes
    adding, 325-326
    fills, adding, 327-328
    special effects, adding,
      328-330
    text, adding, 330
slideshows (Presentations), 279
  building slides with Slide
    Editor, 302-305
    graphics, adding, 303-304
    speaker notes, adding,
      304-305
    text objects, adding, 303
  customizing, 310-311
  master templates, 298
  outlining, 298-302
    PerfectExpert, 300-302
    Slide Outliner, 298-300
  presentation effects, 306-309
    display sequence, 307
    sound, adding, 309
    SpeedKeys, assigning,
      307-308
    transitions, 306-307
  publishing as HTML files, 312
  publishing to the Web,
    458-461
    custom layouts, 460-461
    preconfigured layouts, 459
  Quickshows, creating, 310-311
  rearranging slides in Slide
    Sorter, 305

saving as graphics, 312-313
saving in PDF format, 312
Show on the Go (portable slideshows), 311-312
software, Linux support, 9
Sort Table dialog box (Paradox), 416
sorting
   Address Book contacts (Filter feature), 361-364
   data in database tables, 415-416
   event list (CorelCENTRAL), 347-348
sound, adding to slideshows, 309
Sound dialog box, 309
space diamonds (Reveal Codes), 82
speaker notes, adding to slides (Slide Editor), 304-305
special effects, adding to images (Presentations), 328-330
SpeedFormat, 132, 259-261
SpeedFormat dialog box, 259-260
SpeedFunctions, 21
speeding up Presentations, 295
SpeedKeys, assigning to slideshows, 307-308
SpeedLinks, 22, 451-452
Spell Checker, 114-115
   keyboard shortcut, 36
Spell-As-You-Go, 112
spelling tools, 112-115
Spreadsheet Page Setup dialog box, 243-246, 265
spreadsheets, 194-200, 203, 212-228
   advanced formatting tools, 251-252
   applications, 194
   cells, 200
      borders, adding, 261-262
      cell addressing, 200
      clearing all formatting, 235-236
      coloring, 263
      columns, resizing, 241
      deleting, 237-238
      deleting contents, 234-236
      drag and drop, 248
      inserting, 238-240
      replacing contents, 233-234
      selectors, 200
      transposing contents, 241
   charts, 266
      Chart Expert, 267-270
      color schemes, applying, 270
      creating, 266-270
      data, selecting, 267
      destination, specifying, 269
      editing, 271-272
      positioning, 270-271
      sizing, 270-271
      titles, adding, 269
      type, selecting, 268
   data
      data collection, 213
      entering, 213-216
      label syntax, 197
      labels, 196
      manipulating, 196-197
      typos, 197
      value syntax, 197
      values, 196
   formatting, 204, 225-228
      aligning text, 226
      numeric formatting, 226
      Quickfit feature, 227-228
      Real-Time Preview feature, 225
   formulas, 196, 216-225
      absolute cell addresses, 223-225
      arithmetic operators, 218
      automatic totaling feature, 223
      basic formulas, 220
      displaying, 203
      entering, 220
      Formula Marker feature, 217
      functions, 221-222
      hiding, 203
      multiplication formulas, 218
      order of precedence, 219
      QuickFunction button, 222, 229
      structuring, 218-219
      versus values, 196
   headers and footers, inserting, 264-265
   identifying purpose, 212-213
   importing HTML spreadsheets into Paradox databases, 466
   input line, 201
      editing cells, 234
   inserting into WordPerfect 9 documents, 228-229
   navigating, 204-207
   notebooks, 194-196
   objects, viewing, 203
   Objects sheets, 194, 197
   password protection, 249
   Paste Special feature, 234-235
   printing, 242-248
      break pages, 245
      headers and footers, 243-244
      named settings, 246
      options, 246
      Page Setup, 243-246
      paper orientation, 243
      paper size, 243
      print margins, 245
      Print Preview mode, 244, 247-248
      print scaling, 246
      Print Spreadsheet dialog box, 242-246
   projects, 252-255, 273
      starting, 252-254
      templates, customizing, 254-255
   Property Bar
      Fill Color button, 263
      line-drawing button, 261
      Text Color button, 263
   Publish to HTML tool, 457
   QuickFill feature, 215-216
   QuickFormat, 258-259, 273
   QuickType feature, 214
   sharing, 195
   SpeedFormat, 259-261
   styles, 255-257, 273
      creating, 255-257
      editing, 257
   Undo feature, 234
   updating, 232
StarOffice, 10
starting
   Address Book, 354
   Corel Linux, 472-473
   CorelCENTRAL calendar, 338
   Paradox, 375
   Presentations, 278-279
      troubleshooting, 333
   programs
      from Corel Application Starter, 29-30
      desktop shortcuts, 32-33
      Run command, 30-32
   Quattro Pro projects, 252-254
startx command, 29
Sticky button (windows), 476
Style drop-down box (Property Bar), 108
style sheets (forms), 423
styles, 107-108
   QuickStyle, 108

spreadsheets, 255-257, 273
    creating, 255-257
    editing, 257
Styles dialog box, 255
subscript, 97
subtasks (CorelCENTRAL
    calendar), 345
subtitles
    adding to data charts
        (Presentations), 321
    adding to Slide Outliner, 299
@SUM function, 221-222
superscript, 97
symbols, 197
    inserting into documents, 126
synonyms (Thesaurus), 116
syntax rules, 197
system administrator, providing
    users access to floppy drives, 56
System directory, 50
system memory, freeing up, 295
system updates for Corel Linux,
    477

T

tab scroll buttons, 207
Tab Set dialog box, 102
Table Expert (Paradox), creating
    tables, 389
Table Expert dialog box
    (Paradox), 389
table lookups, creating, 396-398
Table QuickCreate button,
    131-132
Table SpeedFormat feature, 132
table view (Paradox), opening
    tables, 406
tables
    calculations, 134-136
    cells, 130
        contents, deleting, 139
        selecting, 132-133
    columns
        deleting, 139
        inserting, 138
        comparing to document
            columns, 130
    configuring outer dimensions,
        144
    creating, 131-132
    deleting, 139
    detail tables, 423
    formatting, 136-137
    forms. See forms
    headers, creating, 137, 144
    HTML tables, importing into
        Paradox databases, 466

inputting data, 134
inserting into Web pages
    (Internet Publisher),
    448-449
master tables, 423
rows
    deleting, 139
    inserting, 138
tables (databases), 372
    adding data, 408-409
    child tables, 402
    creating, 388
        with Field Roster, 389-394
        with Table Expert, 389
        with Visual Database
            Designer, 402
    deleting data, 409
    editing, 394
    editing data, 409-410
    field view, 410
    fields
        copying to files, 412
        entering data, 417
        field types, 390-391
        key fields, designating,
            391-392
        locating, 412
        pictures, creating, 393-394
        validity checks, 392-393
        values, locating, 412-413
        values, replacing, 414
    graphics, inserting, 411
    horizontal scroll lock, 407
    linking with Visual Database
        Designer, 400
    locating data, 412-415
        wildcard symbols, 415
    memo view, 410-411
    memos, inserting, 410-411
    navigating, 407
    opening in table view, 406
    parent tables, 402
    passwords, setting, 398-399
    persistent field view, 410
    publishing to HTML, 464
    referential integrity, 399
    secondary indexes, creating,
        395-396
    sorting data, 415-416
    switching between edit and
        view modes, 408
    table lookups, creating,
        396-398
tabs
    setting, 101-104
    sheets, 201
task lists, publishing to the Web,
    462-463

tasks (CorelCENTRAL calendar)
    adding to event list, 344
    editing, 346
    linking, 348-349
    subtasks, adding, 345
    to-do lists, creating, 344-346
    turning tasks into events, 350
templates
    database templates, 376,
        386-387
    master templates
        (Presentations), 298
    project templates (Quattro
        Pro), customizing, 254-255
text
    adding to images
        (Presentations), 330
    adding to Slide Outliner, 299
    aligning (spreadsheets), 226
    colors
        spreadsheets, 263
        Web documents, 443
    deleting selected text, 60-61
    entering into documents, 58
    fonts. See fonts
    Hidden Text, 84-85
    moving, 59-61
        copy and paste, 61
        cut and paste, 60-61, 70
        drag and drop, 59
    paragraphs, formatting,
        100-107
        indents, setting, 101-104,
            109
        justification, 106-107
        line spacing, 100-101
        page margins, setting,
            104-106
        tabs, setting, 101-104
    positioning, 97
    selecting with
        keyboard/mouse, 58-59
    subscript, 97
    superscript, 97
    underlining, 98
text box (slide objects), 287
Text Color button (Quattro Pro
    Property Bar), 263
Text Editor button, 474
text line (slide objects), 288
text objects (slides), 287-288
    adding (Slide Editor), 303
textures, adding to images
    (Presentations), 327
Thesaurus, 116
title bars (windows), 476

titles
    adding to charts, 269
    adding to data charts (Presentations), 321
    Slide Outliner, 299
    Web page titles, creating, 445
to-do lists, creating (CorelCENTRAL calendar), 344-346
Toolbar command (View menu), 78
Toolbar Editor, 38-39
    macro toolbar buttons, creating, 172
toolbar navigation buttons (Paradox), 407
Toolbar Options dialog box, 89
toolbars, 36-40
    buttons, 36-37
        Bullets button, 122
        Clipart button, 150
        Numbering button, 121
    creating, 39-40
    customizing, 38-39, 89-90
    Design Object toolbar (Paradox), 427
    editing, 38-39
    flyouts, 281
    Format toolbar, Page Margins button, 106
    macros, adding, 171-172
    Notebook toolbar (Quattro Pro), SpeedFormat button, 259
    Presentations toolbars, 281
    selecting, 37
Tools menu, 35
    Macros Online command, 171
    Settings command, 198, 203
Tools Palette
    PerfectExpert, 302
    Presentations desktop, 281
transitions (slides), 283
    selecting for slideshows, 306-307
transposing spreadsheet cell contents, 241
troubleshooting
    application freezes, 33
    keyboard shortcuts, 91
    Presentations
        speeding up, 295
        starting, 333
Tutorial icon (Paradox), 376
Two Pages view (document views), 78
two-table forms, creating, 423-424
typos (spreadsheet data), 197

U

underlining text, 98
undo feature, 61-63
    Quattro Pro, 234
Undo/Redo History dialog box, 62
undoing selections, 205
Update application, 477
updating spreadsheets, 232
user passwords (Corel Linux), changing, 70
usernames, 51
users, administrative users, 50

V

validity checks (tables), 392-393
value syntax (spreadsheet data), 197
values, 196
    alignment, 197
    locating in table fields, 412-414
    replacing in table fields, 414
    versus formulas and labels, 196
vector-based drawings, 149
View menu, 77
    Application Bar command, 79
    bar views, 78-79
    document views, 78
    Draft command, 203
    Formulas command, 203
    Hidden Text command, 84-85
    Hide Bars command, 79
    Objects command, 203
    Page Break command, 203
    Page command, 203
    Reveal Codes command, 81-84
    Ruler command, 79
    Shadow Cursor command, 79-80, 91
    Show Paragraphs View command, 80
    Toolbar command, 78
view mode (database tables), 408
viewing
    form data, 429
    spreadsheet objects, 203
views
    bar views, 78-79
    document views, 78
    slide editing views (Presentations), 290-293
    table view (Paradox), 406
Virtual Desktop Manager, 475

Visual Database Designer (Paradox), 376
    creating tables, 402
    linking tables, 400

W

wallpaper (Web documents), 444
watermarks, 166, 328
WAV files, adding to slideshows, 309
Web Editor, 441-442
    formatting HTML code manually, 452
    graphics, inserting into Web pages, 447
    line breaks, creating, 445
    lists, creating, 445
    saving documents as HTML files, 441
    tables, inserting into Web pages, 448-449
    Web pages, creating, 443
Web Page view (document views), 78
Web pages
    bookmarks, creating, 446-447
    creating, 443
    fonts, changing, 444
    forms, creating, 449-450
    graphics, inserting, 447
    hyperlinks, creating, 446
    lists, creating, 445
    properties, setting, 443-445
    publishing to Web sites, 450
    tables, inserting, 448-449
    text colors, setting, 443
    titles, creating, 445
Web publishing
    CorelCENTRAL Calendars, 462-463
    Paradox databases, 464-466
    Presentations, 458-461
    Quattro Pro, 456-458
Web sites
    Corel, 312
    Matt's Script Archive, 450
    publishing Web pages to, 450
    Wine Development HQ, 333
Welcome Expert (Paradox), 22
Welcome screen (Paradox), 375-376
wildcard symbols, locating database table data, 415
Window button, 476
windows, 475-476
    Address Book window, 354
    Comment window, 119

Customize Settings window, 39
PerfectExpert window, 45-47
Reveal Codes window, 82
scrollbar navigation, 64-66
Windows
    Paradox for Windows, 382
    WordPerfect Office 2000 for Windows, 22
Windows partitions, accessing, 57
Wine, 333, 463
Wine Development HQ Web site, 333
wizards, Internet Publisher Wizard, 312
WordPerfect, 12
    customizing, 76
        bar views, 78-79
        document views, 78
        file settings, 87-89
        Hidden Text, 84-85
        menu settings, 85, 87
        Reveal Codes, 81-84
        Settings dialog box, 77
        Shadow Cursor, 79-80, 91
        Show Paragraphs view, 80
        toolbars, 89-90
        View menu, 77
    evolution, 18
    overview, 12
    program window, 76
    Settings dialog box, 19
    workspace, 76
WordPerfect 9 Print dialog box, 66
WordPerfect Draw, 19
WordPerfect Office 2000
    applications, integration, 16-17
    AutoScroll feature, 21
    CorelCENTRAL 9, 15
    features different from Windows version, 22-23
    help systems, 41-47
        Netscape Navigator, 41-43
        PerfectExpert, 43-47
    history/evolution, 11, 18-20
    installing, 28
        hardware requirements, 2-3
    migrating from Microsoft Office 97, 20
    new features, 20-21
    overview, 10-11
    Real-Time Preview, 21
    SpeedLinks feature, 22
    versions, 12
    Windows version, 22
    workspace, 34-41
        Application Bar, 41, 47
        context-sensitive Property Bar, 40
        menus, 34-36
        toolbars, 36-40
working directory, setting (Paradox), 378-379
worksheets. *See* spreadsheets
Wrap Text button (Selected Image Property Bar), 166

X-Y-Z

X Window System, 29
XML (Extensible Markup Language), 23

Zoom button (Image Tools), 160-161
Zoom feature, 63
Zoom Scroll button (Image Tools), 160
Zoom tools, 160-161

SAMS Teach Yourself in 24 Hours

When you only have time for the answers™

Sams Teach Yourself in 24 Hours *gets you the results you want—fast! Work through 24 proven one-hour lessons and learn everything you need to know to get up to speed quickly. It has the answers you need at a price you can afford.*

Sams Teach Yourself Linux in 24 Hours, Third Edition

Craig and Coletta Witherspoon
0-672-31993-4
$24.99 USA/$37.95 CAN

Other Sams Teach Yourself in 24 Hours Titles

Red Hat Linux
Judith Samson
0-672-31845-8
$24.99 US/$37.95 CAN

Linux Mandrake
Coletta and Craig Witherspoon
0-672-31877-6
$24.99 US/$37.95 CAN

SuSe Linux
William Ball
0-672-31843-1
$24.99 US/$37.95 CAN

GNOME
Judith Samson
0-672-31714-1
$24.99 US/$37.95 CAN

GIMP
Joshua Pruitt and Ramona Pruitt
0-672-31509-2
$24.99 US/$37.95 CAN

KDE
Nicholas Wells
0-672-31608-0
$24.99 US/$37.95 CAN

Internet, 2001 Edition
Ned Snell
0-672-31966-7
$19.99 US/$29.95 CAN

All prices are subject to change.

SAMS
www.samspublishing.com

WELCOME TO THE REVOLUTION

LINUX MAGAZINE
THE CHRONICLE OF THE REVOLUTION

I DON'T WANT TO MISS THE REVOLUTION!

WWW.LINUX-MAG.COM

PLEASE SIGN ME UP FOR:

☐ 1 year (12 issues) **$34.95**   ☐ 2 years (24 issues) **$64.95**

Name

Company

Address

City/State/Zip

Country

Phone   Fax

E-mail

☐ Check Enclosed   ☐ Bill Me

LINUX MAGAZINE
THE CHRONICLE OF THE REVOLUTION

International Rates:
Canada/Mexico Rates: ☐ 1 year (12 issues) $59.95   All other countries: ☐ 1 year (12 issues) $69.95
All non-U.S. orders must be pre-paid in U.S. funds drawn on a U.S. bank. Please allow 6-8 weeks for processing.

9MCB6

DON'T MISS AN ISSUE!

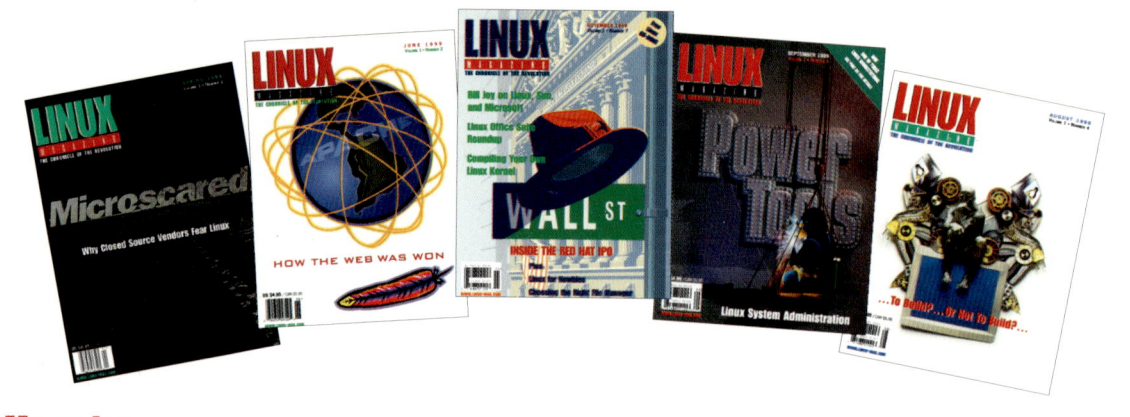

Linux Magazine is the monthly information source for the whole Linux community. Whether you are a system administra developer, or simply a Linux enthusiast, *Linux Magazine* delivers the information and insight you need month after month.

Our feature stories, in-depth interviews, and reviews will help you navigate and thrive in the ever-changing world of Linux a Open Source Software. What does Microsoft really think of Linux? What's the best way to build a Linux machine from scratch? H can you integrate Linux into a Windows-based network? Whatever you are looking for, *Linux Magazine* is where you will find

With regular columns from such Open Source luminaries as Alan Cox, Paul 'Rusty' Russell, Randal Schwartz, and Larry Augus you know you can't go wrong...

So don't miss an issue — Subscribe today to *Linux Magazine*, "The Chronicle of the Revolution."

Check out our website at www.linux-mag.com

BUSINESS REPLY MAIL
FIRST-CLASS MAIL   PERMIT NO. 1384   BOULDER CO

POSTAGE WILL BE PAID BY ADDRESSEE

NO POSTAGE
NECESSARY
IF MAILED
IN THE
UNITED STATES

INFOSTRADA COMM
PO BOX 55731
BOULDER CO 80323-5731